UNDER COVER OF NIGHT:

The United States Air Force
and the
Assassination of John F. Kennedy

SEAN FETTER

American Historian & Investigative Journalist

Volume II of II

(Continued from Volume I)

Arlington Press LLC

UNDER COVER OF NIGHT:
The United States Air Force and the Assassination of John F. Kennedy
By Sean Fetter

Published by:
Arlington Press LLC
1309 Coffeen Avenue, Suite 1200
Sheridan, Wyoming 82801

ISBN: 979-8-218-30640-3

General Curtis Emerson LeMay
was USAF Chief of Staff in 1963.

He was the *only* member of the Joint Chiefs
who absented himself from
Washington D.C. – *and the country!* –
on November 22nd, 1963.

Chapter Twenty-Five:
Seven Days in LeMay

(Continued)

"There are no innocent civilians."

– General Curtis Emerson LeMay
USAF Chief of Staff

"We were planning on a nuclear war."

– General Curtis Emerson LeMay
USAF Chief of Staff

"These things do not just 'happen.'
*They are **made** to happen."*

– John Fitzgerald Kennedy

After ensuring that the smiling killer named Thomas Sarsfield Power had ***not*** eagerly unleashed a nuclear holocaust – and after learning with certainty that John Fitzgerald Kennedy had indeed been slain in Dallas – General Curtis LeMay emerged from the 600-foot-deep subterranean bowels of the Underground Complex and traversed the mile-and-a quarter-long North Tunnel to the exit on the RCAF Station North Bay side of the facility.[1]

Then he boarded an aircraft which took off from the RCAF Station North Bay airfield and delivered LeMay discreetly to the tiny little Wiarton airfield, which borders the eastern shore of Lake Huron in Canada.[2]

To help cover his tracks and effectively obscure his *actual* location and the *true* purpose of his trip to Canada that day, LeMay initially radioed an order to

---

[1] Author's exclusive original discovery.

[2] Author's exclusive original discovery.

Andrews Air Force Base for a USAF plane to come pick him up in the major Canadian city of *Toronto.*

Only ***after** the JetStar was already airborne* did General LeMay call back and divert the trim little four-engine Air Force jet to his *actual* location – the Wiarton airfield – to pick him up.

For decades, *no one was the wiser* until I correctly analyzed the JFK assassination, and – alone – discovered what had really happened.[3]

* * *

LeMay boarded the small blue-and-white USAF JetStar there at Wiarton, Ontario, *still on Canadian soil,* and departed America's northern neighbor at 4:04 p.m. Eastern time to return to the U. S. capital.[4]

Note the time:

4:04 p.m. EST.

After President Kennedy had "officially" been declared dead by doctors.

After Kennedy's death had been announced officially to the media in Dallas by Malcolm Kilduff.

After CBS anchor Walter Cronkite had broadcast the news of JFK's death on network television to a stunned nation.

After Lyndon Johnson had been sworn in at Love Field, aboard Air Force One.

After Air Force One was already taken off and was *en route* back to the capital.

4:04 p.m. EST.

Only then did Curtis LeMay *finally* deign to fly back across the U.S. border and head southeast toward Washington, D.C.

It was a very clever move on the general's part.

By that hour – 3:04 p.m. Central time, which is 4:04 p.m. Eastern time – the scornful USAF general who had regarded President Kennedy with such visceral hatred knew that his former commander-in-chief was definitely dead. LeMay also knew that Lyndon Johnson had officially taken the oath of office as the 36th president, and he knew that the bloody LBJ coup (despite its *nearly disastrous* executional failures down in Dallas) was indeed still "on."[5]

Strangely, on that belated flight back to the capital, General LeMay disobeyed a direct order from his civilian superior, Air Force Secretary Eugene Zuckert, and

---

[3] Author's exclusive original discovery.

[4] Chuck Holmes logbook, p. 3.

[5] Author's exclusive original discovery.

defiantly landed at Washington's downtown National Airport *instead of* at Andrews Air Force Base in suburban Maryland.[6]

After landing at Washington D.C.'s National Airport at 5:12 p.m. Eastern time that afternoon, LeMay's *actual* whereabouts and activities over the next several hours remain (officially) unknown to this day.[7]

* * *

Curtis LeMay co-authored two principal books during his lifetime: *Mission with LeMay: My Story* (1965) and *America is in Danger* (1968).[8] While he was careful to include a few pious phrases falsely declaring his alleged "acceptance" of the fundamental American concept of civilian control of the military, his *actual* words and deeds – on multiple occasions, over a period of *decades* – belied those soothing and false assurances.

LeMay's true beliefs were no secret; he was totally incapable of suppressing them adequately or completely.

In a chilling phrase *reeking* of relevance to the JFK assassination, LeMay declared that men killing other men was necessary "in order to avoid having their loved nation *stricken or emasculated*."[9]

He also dramatically declared that *"no life"* is "too dear" [to destroy in order] "to defend this America . . ."[10]

Certainly not John Kennedy's life.

And strangely enough, there was a chilling echo of the general's bloody thinking in a book published a full four decades *after* JFK's assassination – words

---

[6] So much for LeMay's pious claims of respect for the fundamental American concept of "civilian control of the military." His open defiance is noted *with emphasis* in the Chuck Holmes logbook, p. 3.

[7] Navy autopsy technician Paul O'Connor stated to some interviewers that General Curtis LeMay personally visited the morgue at Bethesda Naval Hospital on the night of November 22nd in order to view (and silently gloat over) President Kennedy's ravaged, mutilated corpse.

The name of the USAF Chief of Staff does *not* appear on *any* of the various "official" documents listing those who were present at the JFK autopsy, but as William Wright and William Housman and Dugald Bell would all point out, "absence of evidence is not evidence of absence." Regardless, one thing is clear: if he did not in fact actually make it into the Bethesda morgue *in person,* Curtis Emerson LeMay was undoubtedly there *in spirit.*

[8] LeMay also co-authored a third book, about the B-29 bomber used by the U. S. in World War II and the Korean War.

[9] Curtis LeMay with MacKinlay Kantor, *Mission with LeMay,* p. 570.

[10] Curtis LeMay with Dale O. Smith, *America is in Danger,* p. 333.

which captured Curtis LeMay's mindset *completely and explicitly,* and which retroactively illuminate the dire threats facing President Kennedy in the 1960s.

* * *

In 2003, a former U.S. Air Force military aide to President Bill Clinton wrote a book called *Dereliction of Duty* (which is **not** to be confused with a totally unrelated and totally *different* 1997 work, with the very same title, by Army officer H. R. McMasters – a book which concerns Lyndon Johnson, Robert McNamara, the Joint Chiefs of Staff and Vietnam).

In that 2003 book, retired USAF Lt. Col. Robert "Buzz" Patterson, who worked in the White House, offered striking criticism of his former Commander in Chief – criticism unprecedented in its boldness and tone. Patterson's charges were all the more impressive because they were made publicly – something which General LeMay had *not* done so openly in the early Sixties, when JFK was still alive and the United States was facing far more direct and immediate risks.[11]

But in a fascinating development, *the words themselves could clearly have come from either man.* They could as easily have been written in 1963 as in 2003. The parallels – and the echoes – are frankly astonishing.[12]

Patterson described his 2003 book as a candid *indictment* of Clinton's self-evident *failure* to lead America with integrity.[13]

Indeed, wrote Patterson scathingly, the President from Arkansas operated *in a manner which harmed America's national security.* The former White House military aide also declared bluntly that Clinton selfishly placed his own base desires above America's necessities.[14]

Patterson was shocked to discover that, in his eyes, Clinton looked at the American military with "contempt," treated the presidency as a "playground," and

---

[11] JFK fired U. S. Army General Edwin Walker, another right-wing extremist in the ranks who had been clumsily and overtly indoctrinating his troops with John Birch Society literature and right-wing harangues. Curtis LeMay, though brash and blunt, was a much cleverer individual who strode right up to the line but never quite crossed it – at least, *not in public.*

However, in meetings at the White House with President Kennedy – and in military privacy at the Pentagon – General LeMay was astonishingly insubordinate. JFK had foolishly and unwittingly *invited* such gross insubordination by personally ordering the JCS to be much more active advisers to him on a wide range of issues following the 1961 Bay of Pigs debacle – so LeMay had "air cover" for his remarks based on Kennedy's own National Security Action Memoranda.

[12] Author's exclusive original discovery.

[13] Robert Patterson, *Dereliction of Duty,* p. 20.

[14] Robert Patterson, *Dereliction of Duty,* p. 20.

bamboozled the United States instead of defending it. Patterson was flabbergasted by Clinton's words, actions and inaction.[15]

In fact, Patterson believed that Clinton exhibited grotesque disregard for America's security and the formation of proper global policies.[16]

The echoes of John F. Kennedy's military critics back in the 1960s are legion. Patterson acidly remarked upon Slick Willie's numerous personal scandals.[17]

He even declared flatly that Clinton himself was *the single largest risk to American security.*[18]

Finally, Patterson wrote that William Jefferson Clinton had caused a tornado of corruption, had put American security in danger, and had severely damaged the armed forces.[19]

Patterson's words sound like a senior prosecutor's summation – *or like a high-minded "justification" for an overthrow of the U. S. government.*[20]

In fact, Patterson made a deliberate point of very ostentatiously quoting, in full, the uniformed officer's oath – required by federal law of all those individuals, except the President, who are "elected or appointed to an office of honor or profit in the civil service or uniformed services":

> *I, [Name], do solemnly swear (or affirm) that I will support and defend the Constitution of the United States against **all enemies, foreign and***

---

[15] Robert Patterson, *Dereliction of Duty,* p. 21.

[16] Robert Patterson, *Dereliction of Duty,* p. 21.

[17] Robert Patterson, *Dereliction of Duty,* p. 22.

[18] Robert Patterson, *Dereliction of Duty,* p. 56.

[19] Robert Patterson, *Dereliction of Duty,* p. 147.

[20] While no one is accusing "Buzz" Patterson of ever having plotted to incite or commit sedition (or assassination, for that matter), I **am** correctly and accurately pointing out the stark and troubling nature of his published words, as well as those words' deeply disturbing and truly startling similarity to the ugly views held by far more powerful, far higher-ranking USAF officers in the early 1960s – *senior* uniformed men of extraordinary power and high-level authority (*unlike* Lt. Col. Patterson).

Those USAF officers unquestionably **did** have seditious views; unquestionably **did** have massive, lethal resources at their disposal; unquestionably **did** act on their own sinister political impulses; and unquestionably **did** knowingly, willingly and actively participate in the bloody coup of November 1963.

The contrast is clear:

William Jefferson Clinton *survived* his presidency in the 1990s **despite** the American military's raging fury and cold contempt.

John Fitzgerald Kennedy did **not.**

domestic; that I will bear true faith and allegiance to the same; that I take this obligation freely, without any mental reservation or purpose of evasion; and that I will well and faithfully discharge the duties of the office on which I am about to enter. So help me God.

Tellingly, Curtis LeMay himself *also* specifically mentioned that very same soldier's oath on the final page of his own co-authored 1965 autobiography.[21]

All enemies.

All enemies, foreign *and domestic.*

In those supposedly "noble" words lie the recipe for – and the *"justification"* for – a military-backed coup in this country.

Patterson described his 2003 book as an urgent advisory to the U. S. populace, and he concluded one section with a clarion call strikingly reminiscent of the language used by General Power and General LeMay in the 1960s – stridently declaring that "we" should never *permit* such "dangerous" and "irresponsible" leaders as William Clinton to ever occupy the Oval Office again.[22]

Strong words indeed.

These were not minor quibbles over arcane issues. Rightly or wrongly, Lt. Col. Robert "Buzz" Patterson clearly regarded President Clinton as *a genuine menace to America* – and to the safety of Americans.

Merely substitute the name *Kennedy* for "Clinton" in *any* of those latter-day 2003 passages, and you will *immediately* be transported back in time to the ugly political zeitgeist of 1963.[23]

And bear in mind that General Curtis Emerson LeMay, *the Air Force Chief of Staff,* had far more power than Robert Patterson ever did.

* * *

Even *years after* the JFK assassination, a still-angry LeMay referred to the "Kennedy crowd" as "cockroaches" – and he bluntly described them as "ruthless" and "vindictive" types, clearly lacking "moral standards."[24]

So the question remains: what happens when a supremely powerful four-star general like Curtis LeMay – the Air Force Chief of Staff, *not* just a mere lieutenant colonel like Robert Patterson – feels this way about a sitting President?

---

[21] Curtis LeMay with MacKinlay Kantor, *Mission with LeMay,* p. 572.

[22] Robert Patterson, *Dereliction of Duty,* p. 22.

[23] Author's exclusive original discovery.

[24] Curtis LeMay oral history for the LBJ Library, 1971.

What happens when a vocal advocate of *preemptive, unprovoked nuclear war* – a man who considers *the incineration of all major American cities as a direct result of his preferred course of action* to be an acceptable topic of casual dinner conversation at a Georgetown soirée – thinks that *the President of the United States is a genuine menace to national security?*

My fellow citizens, *what happens **then?***

How does a man reconcile his officer's oath with his equally firm conviction that the man he is duty-bound to serve is in fact a true "domestic enemy" of both the Constitution and the country itself?

What if the nation's chief executive and Commander-in-Chief is – or *appears* to be, in the dubious judgment of an extreme right-wing clique of senior military officers – a serious threat to the country's existence and its very survival?

What then?

* * *

Serious outrage is felt by the American military *in any era* toward American commanders-in-chief who behave in ways that – in the eyes of the military, at least – put (or *seem* to put) America's national honor, national prestige, and/or national security at risk.

The reaction is furious and visceral.

And without question, William J. Clinton at his worst – just like John F. Kennedy at *his* worst – certainly gave military leaders, political leaders and Secret Service agents alike the legitimate *grounds* (plus the convenient *pretext*) for very grave "concerns" indeed.

Such an extreme level of concern, fear and outrage on the part of high-level military men and government security personnel generates far more than silent (and trivial) "resentment" and "irritation." It provides very fertile ground for *recruitment* – and in the early 1960s, it provided grounds for thinking, and for actually *doing,* the supposedly "unthinkable."

Not that doing the unthinkable was anything new to Curtis LeMay.

He had *already tried it* – multiple times.

* * *

By the time that 1963 rolled around, both USAF Chief of Staff Curtis LeMay *and* his longtime protégé, General Thomas Power of SAC, had each *personally* confronted President Kennedy, *in the White House itself,* and urged him to take extreme courses of action which would have led inexorably to all-out nuclear war – with devastating consequences for America and the entire world.

In face-to-face encounters, General LeMay had accused Kennedy of being guilty of "appeasement" of the Communists, and at least twice had strongly urged Kennedy to launch an unprovoked all-out assault.

Traces of LeMay's and Power's specific contributions to the events of November 22nd would come to light only gradually, over several decades of work by me. Too many otherwise well-intentioned people were looking elsewhere, chasing endless red herrings and trivial data points and false leads.[25]

But one intelligent investigator decided early on that the JFK assassination was not nearly as complex and arcane and obscure a mystery as many others professed to believe. John Judge had begun speaking to Pentagon employees and to members of SAC, and he soon arrived at a blunt conclusion about the slaying of JFK in Dallas:

"We *know* where the bullets came from," Judge would often say in his deep, rich, resonant baritone voice.

"They came from the Pentagon."[26]

* * *

General Curtis LeMay's assistance to LBJ in the assassination of John F. Kennedy did not begin – or end – on November 22nd, 1963.

Hardly.

The top USAF general had all sorts of useful powers, resources and connections that were extremely useful.

For one thing, Curtis LeMay was a friend of a certain Texas oil magnate named David Harold Byrd.

"Dry Hole" Byrd was notable for two things in particular:

First, D. H. Byrd was a co-founder of the Civil Air Patrol, a national civilian auxiliary ("junior Air Force") organization[27] whose members, in the 1950s, included a bright, skinny teenager named *Lee Harvey Oswald.*

---

[25] Many a well-intentioned but naïve JFK assassination researcher has squandered his or her intellectual energies (and, metaphorically, *drowned*) in the empty bayous of Louisiana and the equally vacant swamps of Florida. But the true answers to the JFK case do not reside in New Orleans or Miami. ***And they never did.*** The murder of the president in 1963 was *not* a Clay Shaw/David Ferrie production launched from Louisiana, nor was it a mere "rogue" operation undertaken by "a few bad apples" from the JM/WAVE CIA station in the Sunshine State. For the love of truth, *Wake up, people . . .*

[26] Author interview with John Judge, 2013. John was correct in the *metaphorical* sense, but not in the *literal* sense. I will explain the chilling reason why in a subsequent major book, already underway.

[27] The Texas oil man was even granted the dubious title "Colonel" Byrd thanks to his major financial support of the Civil Air Patrol. (Eddie Barker and John Mark Dempsey, *Eddie Barker's Notebook,* p. 120.)

Second, Byrd was the longtime owner of a multi-story red brick building located at 411 Elm Street in the city of Dallas – a building which overlooks a grassy triangular park area.

The building was called the Texas School Book Depository.

The grassy triangular park area is called Dealey Plaza.

In the autumn of 1963, one of the stock clerks who labored in the TSBD – filling book orders all day – was the now 24-year-old Lee Harvey Oswald.

*And Oswald wasn't the **only** individual working at the Book Depository who was available for use as a designated patsy by Vice President Lyndon Baines Johnson and Air Force Chief of Staff General Curtis Emerson LeMay on the day of the JFK assassination.*

In fact, the United States Air Force actually had *two* (2) *alternate patsies* available in Texas in November 1963 to falsely blame for the JFK assassination in the event that Lee Oswald was absent or somehow incapacitated on the day of the fatal presidential motorcade through Dallas.[28]

* * *

A colleague of Oswald's in 1963 was Billy Nolan Lovelady, age 26. Lovelady had worked at the TSBD since late 1961 – first as a truck driver, then as a stockman (inside the building itself).

Lovelady was a USAF veteran with an extremely checkered recent past – which made him extremely vulnerable to *coercion, blackmail and control.*

A Texan from the town of Myrtle Springs, Lovelady had joined the military in the late 1950s and ended up stationed at *Andrews Air Force Base* in Maryland. There, Airman Second Class Lovelady was part of the 1001st Base Supply Squadron. In late 1960, he made the fateful and unwise decision to join several other USAF airmen in stealing, and then "fencing," some government-owned weapons – namely, a number of .38-caliber revolvers.

The criminal operation did not go unnoticed, and the FBI arrested the military thieves. Lovelady pled guilty in federal court in April 1961 to two counts of violating 18 USC 641; was discharged from the Air Force; and was fined the sum of $200 (equal to approximately $1,400 in today's money). Although he paid more than half of the fine, Lovelady then defaulted, bolted and secretly returned to Texas. In December 1961 – now a federal fugitive – he found work at the TSBD in Dallas.

Lovelady was finally tracked down – and arrested again by the FBI – in early January 1963, *while working at the Texas School Book Depository!*

Most people in such a situation would have been summarily fired, of course.

---

[28] Author's exclusive original discovery.

Instantly.

No question about it.

But incredibly, despite having been *apprehended at his job by two federal agents and carted off to jail,* Billy Nolan Lovelady did not stay behind bars for long; he was released on his own recognizance. In an extremely odd move, Book Depository Vice President Ochus Campbell not only *didn't* fire the man; Campbell actually provided the funds for Lovelady to promptly pay off the remaining $75.00 balance due on his federal fine![29]

And that was it.

The federal government dropped its bench warrant for Lovelady's arrest.

Lovelady – who had a wife and four young children – was able to go back to work at the TSBD *as if nothing had happened.*

But he fully realized that both the federal government *and* his employer knew where he was, knew what he had done, knew where he worked, knew where he lived, and were "responsible" for his (ahem) "freedom."

*They now **owned** him.*

And that made USAF veteran Billy Nolan Lovelady – *a military veteran with a bad discharge and an FBI file* – a very useful fellow indeed to the men plotting John Kennedy's upcoming assassination.

Be advised:

Lyndon Johnson always had back-up plans.[30]

If the ***prime*** patsy candidate, Lee Oswald – another *military veteran with a bad discharge and an FBI file* – were unexpectedly hit by a truck, or laid up in the hospital with severe kidney stones, or struck by lightning, or laid low by food poisoning, or otherwise rendered dead or unfit or simply *unavailable* to be present at work on the day of the deadly presidential motorcade through Dallas, then former USAF airman Billy Nolan Lovelady would be available at the TSBD as a ***substitute*** patsy.

And Billy Lovelady – quickly shot down inside the Texas School Book Depository by a "responding Dallas policeman" in the immediate aftermath of President Kennedy's murder – would have been extremely easy to falsely smear as the supposed "assassin" of JFK.

* * *

[29] FBI documents record the entire Lovelady saga in great depth; see various memos bearing Bureau file number 52-75836. Significantly, many of the Lovelady memos were sent by field agents directly to FBI Director J. Edgar Hoover himself. Hoover had been an LBJ friend, ally and Washington neighbor for decades – and he supplied Johnson with the deeply derogatory information on JFK which played a decisive role in the summer of 1960, as the reader will soon learn.

[30] Author's exclusive original discovery.

But there was yet ***another*** young man available in Texas who could easily be falsely accused (if necessary) of assassinating President Kennedy – an Air Force airman who was *still on active duty,* in uniform![31]

His presence was impossible to explain away innocently, given the shocking circumstances – and the timing – of his entry into the military.[32]

The man's name was Lloyd John Wilson (*alias* Dwight Allen Wilson, *alias* John Allen Wilson, *alias* Lloyd Long).[33]

Like Lee Oswald, he had lost his father at a very early age.

Like Lee Oswald, he was a high-school dropout.

Like Lee Oswald, he was a laborer with a spotty work record.

Wilson was just eighteen years old in the late summer of 1963,[34] and he first came to the federal government's attention when a caller in the northern California area reported him to authorities for violent verbal and written statements made at work and at his living quarters.

The FBI contacted the Secret Service about Wilson on September 9th, 1963.[35]

The head of the SS White House Detail, Gerald Behn, indisputably knew of Wilson by the very next day – September 10th, 1963.[36]

Lloyd John Wilson quit his job at a Santa Clara company and left California on September 14th, 1963. The SS supposedly "couldn't find him" under his alias. Federal Bureau of Investigation agents ultimately located and interviewed Lloyd Wilson up in Washington state, where he had gone to try to join the Air Force in late October 1963.

The SS eventually interviewed Wilson on October 28th and 29th, 1963; *obtained deeply incriminating sworn written statements from him;* and bluntly concluded that he was "a threatening Subject."[37]

Yet here's what happened, America:

Wilson was nevertheless "accepted for enlistment in the U. S. Air Force" on October 31st, 1963.

---

[31] Author's exclusive original discovery.

[32] Author's exclusive original discovery.

[33] SS Cross Reference Sheet, November 22nd, 1963.

[34] SS memo by SA Joseph E. Noonan, Jr., December 23rd, 1963.

[35] SS memo by SA James H. Giovanetti, September 23rd, 1963.

[36] SS memo by WHD agent Anthony Sherman Jr. to Chief Rowley, approved by Gerald Behn, September 10th, 1963.

[37] SS memo by Special Agent W. C. Pine, December 19th, 1963, reflecting earlier SS assessments of Lloyd Wilson.

And two days later – on November 2nd, 1963 – he was transferred to Texas.[38]

The U. S. Secret Service – including SS Chief James Rowley and the Protective Research Section, which was specifically in charge of identifying threats to the president – knew Wilson's real name; knew Wilson's Air Force serial number (AF19777251); and knew Wilson's specific location (Lackland Air Force Base near San Antonio).[39]

Yet in November 1963, *before* the assassination, *the SS closed the case.*[40]

Yes, you read that correctly:

The SS closed the case.

And equally incredibly, the U. S. Air Force welcomed Wilson with open arms.

In fact, the Air Force strangely *paid for Wilson's hotel room* in Spokane![41]

And according to the SS, an Air Force recruiter named Lloyd E. Brown, Jr. actually stated that as soon as the Secret Service "investigation" was concluded, Lloyd John Wilson would be "given further consideration for [USAF] recruitment provided he [Wilson] was not arrested."

Provided he was not arrested.

Huh?!

Incredibly, despite having *threatened the commander-in-chief;* despite having *admitted* to federal agents *in writing* that he had done so; and despite having been labeled as "dangerous" and "threatening" by the FBI and the SS, *Lloyd John Wilson was permitted to enlist in the United States Air Force!*[42]

Moreover, he was then sent to Lackland Air Force Base near San Antonio – *the very first city that President John Fitzgerald Kennedy was scheduled to visit on his upcoming Texas trip!*

The truth is that Lloyd John Wilson was an assassination plotter's dream: an absolutely *perfect* patsy candidate.[43]

And despite (more accurately, *because of*) his very recent threats against the president; despite (more accurately, *because of*) several interviews of him by the FBI and the Secret Service; and despite (more accurately, *because of*) his physical presence in one of the cities that President Kennedy would visit on the fatal Texas trip, Wilson

---

[38] SS memo by San Francisco SAIC Tom H. Hanson, November 27th, 1963.

[39] SS memo by Spokane SAIC Norman Sheridan, November 7th, 1963.

[40] SS memo by Spokane SAIC Norman Sheridan, December 19th, 1963.

[41] SS memo by Spokane SAIC Norman Sheridan, November 7th, 1963.

[42] I've heard of "trying to comply with harsh recruiting quotas," but this was obscene.

[43] Author's exclusive original discovery.

was ***not*** discharged from the Air Force until December 17th or 18th, 1963 [44] – several weeks *after* the JFK assassination![45]

Wilson was "kept around" until he was definitely no longer needed.[46]

After training in Texas, Wilson was sent to Chanute Air Force Base in Rantoul, Illinois.[47] Upon being booted out of the military there, Wilson quickly traveled north to Chicago – where on December 19th, 1963, he contacted the media by phone and then personally showed up at FBI offices in the federal building in order to (supposedly) "confess" that he had (supposedly) been in cahoots with Lee Oswald [*sic*], and to falsely claim that he, Lloyd Wilson, had (supposedly) "paid" Lee Oswald [*sic*] to (supposedly) kill the president.

What happened next was quite sudden – and quite revealing.

After John Kennedy had been assassinated, and *after* Lee Oswald had been murdered and silenced forever, and *after* it was clear that the government's utterly false "lone gunman theory" would be swallowed whole and accepted uncritically by the inept and cowardly American corporate media and the endlessly gullible American public, federal authorities *finally* acted (in late December 1963) as they would have done (and should have done) back in *September* 1963 if they had truly been serious about "protecting" the president of the United States.

Briskly.

Efficiently.

With alacrity.

On December 19th, 1963, they predictably had Lloyd John Wilson arrested by Chicago police;[48]

On December 20th, 1963, they predictably had Wilson examined at the Psychiatric Institute of the Municipal Court of Chicago;[49]

---

[44] SS records on the matter provide two conflicting dates for Lloyd John Wilson's USAF discharge, and two conflicting "reasons" for it. On December 19th, 1963, SS agent Pine wrote that Wilson was discharged on December 17th "as a schizo paranoid"; but on December 23rd, 1963, SS agent Joseph Noonan wrote that, based on a belated SS report to the Air Force, USAF had deemed Wilson a "security risk" and had discharged him on December 18th on *that* basis.

Strangely, Noonan wrote that Lloyd John Wilson's USAF discharge was "termed honorable." According to Noonan, the SS report to the Air Force led to a pre-discharge examination of Lloyd John Wilson by USAF psychiatrists – who reportedly called the eighteen-year-old "a schizophrenic person with strong paranoid tendencies" [an assessment which may or may not have been true].

[45] Author's exclusive original discovery.

[46] Author's exclusive original discovery.

[47] SS memo by Spokane SAIC Norman Sheridan, December 19th, 1963.

[48] SS memo from Chicago ASAIC Maurice Martineau to Chief Rowley, December 19th, 1963.

[49] SS memo by SS agent Joseph E. Noonan Jr., January 30th, 1964.

On December 20th, 1963, they predictably had Wilson quickly transferred to *federal* custody;[50]

On January 16th, 1964, they predictably had Wilson labeled mentally ill at a *federal* hearing;[51]

And on January 24th, 1964, they predictably had Wilson promptly dispatched to a notorious federal prison in Missouri by the order of a newly confirmed federal judge named Abraham Lincoln Marovitz.[52]

Just like that.

But here's the key:

None of those actions occurred until long *after* Dallas.[53]

Nothing at all was done about this allegedly dangerous, allegedly violent, allegedly mentally ill figure until **after** federal authorities were absolutely certain that they would **not** need to blame the JFK assassination on Lloyd John Wilson – who would have been an *extremely* convenient scapegoat in the form of "a highly disturbed young USAF airman with violent tendencies" who had somehow "slipped through the cracks in the system" and "unfortunately" murdered America's head of state.[54]

Remember:

Lyndon Baines Johnson always had contingency plans.[55]

And the U. S. Air Force under General Curtis LeMay provided LBJ with a pair of excellent "back-up patsies" – *Billy Nolan Lovelady and Lloyd John Wilson*[56] – so that Lyndon Johnson's murderous assassination plot would definitely have an extremely well-cast and very believable "scapegoat" even if primary patsy Lee Oswald were caught in an unexpected tornado, or felled by a falling oak tree, or otherwise rendered "unavailable" for framing by LBJ and his accomplices on November 22nd as the president motored slowly through downtown Dallas in that long, dark blue limousine toward his bloody fate.[57]

---

[50] SS memo by SS agent Joseph E. Noonan Jr., January 10th, 1964.

[51] SS memo by SS agent Joseph E. Noonan Jr., January 30th, 1964.

[52] SS memo by SS agent Joseph E. Noonan Jr., January 30th, 1964. (Judge Marovitz was very new to the federal bench; he only received his judicial commission on October 2nd, 1963. Marovitz had been nominated to the post by an obscure politician named John Fitzgerald Kennedy.)

[53] Author's exclusive original discovery.

[54] Author's exclusive original discovery.

[55] Author's exclusive original discovery.

[56] Author's exclusive original discovery.

[57] Had Lee Oswald been ill, injured, absent or otherwise "out of action" on November 22nd, then USAF veteran Billy Nolan Lovelady was right there in the TSBD to be slaughtered in Oswald's place.

* * *

But despite all the assassination help rendered to Lyndon Baines Johnson by America's military brass – and by the head of the U. S. Air Force, in particular – the deceitful Texan from Stonewall made a characteristically devious decision:

LBJ reneged on his deal with LeMay.[58]

The wily and ruthless Texas politician screwed the gruff USAF general out of his promised reward.

LBJ reneged on his deal with LeMay!

In December 1963, Johnson personally and explicitly informed the Joint Chiefs of Staff that he would *not* actually unleash them – to violently expand the American war in Vietnam – until *after* the 1964 presidential election.[59]

That was only the first of *several* betrayals that LBJ would engage in against the uniformed men who had ensured that he became "president" via the bloody assassination of JFK – an actual coup.

Johnson would *not* escalate in Vietnam immediately.

Nor would he invade Cuba *at all.*

Nor would he elevate Curtis LeMay to the top post in the American military.

In April 1964, Lyndon Johnson reappointed General LeMay to his current role as Air Force Chief of Staff – but *only for a period of several months.*

Until after the election.

And it got even worse for old "Iron Ass."

When Johnson made JCS Chairman Maxwell Taylor the new U. S. Ambassador to South Vietnam in 1964, he did **not** make Curtis LeMay the new chairman of the Joint Chiefs in Taylor's place. Instead, Johnson elevated Army Chief of Staff Earle "Bus" Wheeler to the top post – even though by normal rotation, the role *should* have gone to a member of another branch of the military.

LBJ gave LeMay no hope for subsequent elevation, either. Johnson refused to grant LeMay a waiver to permit him to remain in the military past his normally mandated retirement date as a means of making him Chairman at some future date.

Johnson also rejected LeMay's military advice about bombing Vietnam.

And in the unlikely event that Billy Lovelady was *also* unavailable, then Lloyd John Wilson would indubitably have been quickly transported from Lackland AFB (near San Antonio) up to Dallas on some pretext in order to be promptly killed – and framed – in their stead. (Author's exclusive original discovery.)

[58] Author's exclusive original discovery.

[59] LBJ did make one minor concession to the military brass; on the final day of 1963, he authorized the commencement of U-2 overflights of Vietnam for mapping purposes in preparation for (much later) American bombing raids.

Lyndon Johnson had made many promises to his sinister uniformed accomplices, but he fulfilled very few of those pledges *to the degree that they desired.*

Least of all to Curtis LeMay, who had been his most important military ally in terms of the JFK assassination.[60]

LBJ simply *used* LeMay – as he had used virtually *everyone else* in his life (friends, women, politicians) in order to obtain what he wanted from them.

The calculating politician from Texas totally outfoxed and successfully double-crossed the calculating Air Force general from Ohio.[61]

* * *

Those on the inside – the callous "national security" officials in the top echelons of the federal government – knew full well that despite his sickeningly cynical pose as the "peace" candidate in the 1964 election, Lyndon Johnson was clearly going to violently escalate the war in Vietnam just as soon as he finished conning the gullible American electorate.

Most of those officials did *not* know the real reason *why,* however.

Most of them never had a clue.

They weren't smart enough – or bold enough – to figure it out.

* * *

But despite his huge personal debt to the American military for their support on November 22nd, LBJ was (initially) unwilling to go the *nuclear* route in Southeast Asia due to his fears of possible Soviet retaliation. Of course, *any* level of violence *short of* the use of atomic weapons in Vietnam was clearly acceptable to the new President, no matter how vicious or bloody or lethal; however, Johnson did not want his own White House or his own ranch to end up vaporized, glowing in the dark as a result of incoming Soviet missiles.[62]

The unwitting and badly deceived American electorate might go "all the way with LBJ" in 1964, but the cold reality was that *Johnson* would simply not go all the way with *LeMay.*

Johnson kept LeMay on board as a lame duck for *a short period only, through the 1964 election and Johnson's own 1965 inauguration,* in order to prevent LeMay

---

[60] Author's exclusive original discovery.

[61] Author's exclusive original discovery.

[62] Eventually, under severe pressure from the American military, LBJ would modify his initial flat prohibition on nuclear weapons and would *actively* consider the use of nukes against Egypt (in 1967) and Vietnam (in 1968) and North Korea (in 1968). That was no accident, as my own original analysis reveals.

from joining the conservative Barry Goldwater on the GOP ticket – and to avoid suffering the cigar-chomping general's trenchant criticisms or revelations prior to completing the upcoming presidential campaign and commencing a massive *conventional* war in Vietnam.[63]

Both General LeMay and General Power saw the frustrating writing on the wall ("LBJ won't go 'all the way'!") and knew it was all over. Enormously frustrated, they realized that their dreams of apocalyptic nuclear bliss would never be consummated. Lyndon Baines Johnson shared much of their *politics,* but he did not share their warfighting strategy.[64]

* * *

LeMay would be out of the military by early February 1965, just before the enormous and brutal *conventional* escalation of the Vietnam War would fully commence. The exit of General Power of SAC preceded LeMay's own by a few months; Power retired in November 1964 – a year after Dallas.

LeMay's farewell soirée was held not in a downtown Washington hotel but in a special hangar at Andrews Air Force Base, and incredibly enough Air Force One – *the President's own airplane* – had been *moved elsewhere* to accommodate the crowd for this special event.[65] That simple fact perfectly epitomized LeMay's thorough contempt for civilian authority. Despite their shared right-wing views and their mutual hatred of John F. Kennedy, Curtis LeMay and Lyndon Johnson could not manage to march forward in perfect lockstep. LBJ was a president whom LeMay had aided mightily, yet the Texan couldn't bring himself to step over the line with the general

---

[63] Ironically, LeMay's views on nuclear warfare were actually far closer to those of Johnson's 1964 *opponent* – crusty GOP Senator Barry Goldwater, of Arizona – who spoke early, often, casually and enthusiastically about using "nukes." Had Goldwater won the election, LeMay's and Power's dream of actually *employing* their beloved bombs – at least in Asia – would have been virtually assured.

Unfortunately for the two Air Force generals, Goldwater was *not* the President – and, according to all the pre-election polls in 1964, he was not going to *be* the President. Indeed, Johnson crushed Goldwater in November in what was then the biggest electoral landslide in American history. So the only president whom the two senior USAF officers actually *had* was a man who, for all his murderous tendencies, did not possess Barry Goldwater's obvious fondness for (and comfort level with) nuclear weapons.

Thus the Thermonuclear Twins were stymied, their daring dreams dashed. Had the Richard Nixon presidency begun in 1961, or even 1965, then the two most extreme Air Force men who ever lived would have had a shot at getting the occupant of the Oval Office to actually pull the nuclear trigger. Alas for LeMay and Power, it was not to be.

[64] LBJ, a peripatetic and perpetually busy politician, did not propose to pass even a portion of his presidency picking pieces of plutonium out of his picnic plate down on the pastoral banks of the Pedernales. (Alliteration lives . . .)

[65] Curtis LeMay with MacKinlay Kantor, *Mission with LeMay,* pp. 567-568.

into the blinding glow of ballistic bliss. Thermonuclear paradise remained tantalizingly just out of reach.

Bidding LeMay adieu at Andrews AFB that day in February 1965 were a number of notable figures: recently defeated GOP presidential candidate Senator Barry Goldwater (who was a brigadier general in the Air Force Reserves); famed actor Jimmy Stewart (*also* a brigadier general in the Air Force Reserves); and . . . *Stu Symington.*

Yes, *that* Stuart Symington.

Stu Symington: father of the "bomber gap;" father of the "missile gap;" former Air Force Secretary; JFK's *true* choice for Vice President in 1960; and an unbridled proponent of American nuclear superiority.[66]

Absent from the festivities was LeMay's war-crimes accomplice from twenty years earlier, Robert Strange McNamara. Two decades after the deliberate incineration of Tokyo, the Secretary of Defense was busily engaged in new aerial savagery. He was now overseeing the opening stages of a massive but "conventional" bombing assault of Vietnam, using the B-52 fleet that LeMay had originally assembled for incinerating the Soviet Union with hydrogen bombs.[67]

The retired general was now a civilian, for the first time in decades – but the world had not heard the last of Curtis Emerson LeMay.

Not hardly.

* * *

Two years after Dallas, in 1965, LeMay and co-author MacKinlay Kantor released a book called *Mission with LeMay.* Largely based on dictation from the aging general, it was polished and refined (and somewhat restrained) by Kantor into a surprisingly mellow tome, considering its source.

But even a skilled co-author could not hide *all* of LeMay's revelations and inadvertent disclosures. Key facets of his thinking seeped through Kantor's yeoman efforts to re-package LeMay as a wise, thoughtful elder statesman.

Elements of the book displayed the thinking behind LeMay's knowing participation in the 1963 murder of John F. Kennedy. No one recognized it at the time. But in *Mission with LeMay,* the general who had inspired the chilling novel *Seven Days in May* had wittingly and unwittingly left clues to his involvement in the assassination of the president.[68]

---

[66] James Carroll, *House of War,* pp. 298-299. Given Symington's own extremely hawkish views, one *almost* wonders whether President Kennedy would have truly been any safer with *him* as Vice President (instead of the murderous LBJ).

[67] James Carroll, *House of War,* pp. 299-300.

[68] Author's exclusive original discovery.

And *still,* the world had not heard the last of Curtis Emerson LeMay.

* * *

Five years after Dallas, in 1968, Curtis Emerson LeMay was suddenly and unexpectedly back in the public spotlight – for two reasons.

The first was a much more candid bit of writing.

On June 5th, 1968 – the very day that Robert Kennedy was shot at the Ambassador Hotel in Los Angeles – a New York publishing company released a book co-authored by LeMay and a fellow conservative military man, Major General Dale O. Smith, called *America is in Danger.*

It was not what you would describe as a rhetorically "mild" book.

In it, the two generals – speaking in LeMay's single authorial voice – enabled the gruff former Chief of Staff to (verbally) settle some scores in a much more open and direct way than he had dared to do in the far more restrained volume *Mission with LeMay,* his 1965 memoir (which was openly co-authored by MacKinlay Kantor).

Revealingly and significantly, in the much more candid 1968 book *America is in Danger,* Curtis LeMay took great pains to savage *both* JFK *and* LBJ in no uncertain terms. In so doing, the general bared his motivations for actively participating in the 1963 assassination of President Kennedy – and he *also* bared the reasons for his subsequent fury at Lyndon Baines Johnson.[69]

In 333 pages of blunt prose, LeMay excoriated the slain JFK for pursuing peace and détente; for creating the Arms Control and Disarmament Agency; for attempting to limit nuclear proliferation; for preferring limited war over nuclear war; for muzzling the military; for blocking space weapons systems; for military inaction during both the Bay of Pigs invasion and the Cuban Missile Crisis; for canceling the Skybolt air-to-ground nuclear missile; for removing American nuclear intermediate-range ballistic missiles (IRBMs) in Europe after the Cuban Missile Crisis; for negotiating a peaceful end to the Cuban crisis with Nikita Khrushchev; for failing to develop the B-70 manned bomber as a replacement for aging B-47s and B-52s; for introducing permissive action links to limit the unauthorized arming and use of American nuclear weapons by the military; and related sins.

LeMay then blasted the still-very-much-alive LBJ for failing to declare war against Vietnam; for using ground troops instead of massive aerial and naval bombardment against Vietnam; for occasional bombing pauses in Vietnam; for declining to use *nuclear weapons* against Vietnam; for choosing to fight the Vietnamese on their terms; for having excessive regard for other nations' views; for making "puzzling" choices on military policy; for "abetting" NATO's collapse; for

---

[69] Author's exclusive original discovery.

opposing an anti-ballistic missile (ABM) system; and for thereby leaving the U. S. open to the risk of the final collapse of the united States.[70]

LeMay openly and energetically and caustically called for "sensible" people at the very highest levels of American politics.[71]

Five months later, oddly, Curtis LeMay went out and joined the strangest candidate (by far) in the 1968 presidential race.

* * *

The retired USAF general needed an avenue for his rage, and the 1968 book provided one such avenue. But simply having *America is in Danger* published – pillorying LBJ directly in print – was not enough satisfaction for Curtis LeMay.

The general felt that he deserved much more for what he had done on behalf of the devious Texan in 1963 and 1964 – and, in an extremely complex subterranean maneuver, he managed to *get* it.

The actual mechanism of the payoff was decidedly convoluted and bizarre.

In short – and in short order – LeMay *quit, ran* and *received.*

LeMay was chosen – at the very last possible moment, in early *October* 1968, just one month before the presidential election itself! – as the vice-presidential running mate for third-party ultra-conservative politician George Wallace of Alabama. At the time of his belated selection on October 3rd by the infamous southern racist, LeMay was finally earning a comfortable living, serving as chairman of the board of a California company called Networks Electronic Corporation.[72]

The company, like most businesses, did not want itself or its top officer embroiled in partisan politics. So, in order to actually run with George Wallace, LeMay had to give up his highly lucrative $50,000-a-year (roughly $499,000 annually, in 2023 dollars) post.

The nomination of LeMay by Wallace just *weeks* before the 1968 presidential election was a preposterously strange and suspicious move that stunk to high heaven – and which thoroughly perplexed LeMay's naïve and ignorant biographers, even many years later.[73]

On the surface, it made no sense whatsoever.

---

[70] Curtis LeMay and Dale O. Smith, *America is in Danger,* p. 106.

[71] Curtis LeMay and Dale O. Smith, *America is in Danger,* p. 106.

[72] *Not* to be confused with Network Electronics Corporation, a *very* similarly named but *different* entity.

[73] One baffled conventional biographer called it "difficult to swallow" and "not easy to understand." (Thomas M. Coffey, *Iron Eagle: The Turbulent Life of General Curtis LeMay,* p. 445.)

The truth, however, lay far *beneath* the surface – and far beneath the laughably weak excuses, clumsy rationales and obtuse "explanations" proffered by both George Wallace *and* Curtis LeMay.

Strangely, both Wallace and LeMay would later claim that *neither* man wanted LeMay to run.

The asinine Alabama racist who had once shouted "Segregation forever!" complained that his "money men" had insisted on LeMay for VP in 1968. LeMay himself later declared that he hadn't even *wanted* to run; that he *knew* there was no chance of the Wallace-LeMay ticket winning the election; that he had actually supported *Richard Nixon* for president in 1968; and that he, LeMay, had just wanted to somehow steer the country – or at least, its undecided voters – rightward.

All of which was pure unadulterated *poppycock,* of course.

In reality, the relative success of the Wallace-LeMay third-party ticket cost ambitious GOP candidate Richard Nixon five Southern states; ten million popular votes; and 46 votes in the Electoral College.[74] An incensed and resentful Nixon immediately attacked Curtis LeMay and, upon taking office as president, promptly instigated a vengeful IRS audit of LeMay's son-in-law, plus a deeply insulting visit by IRS agents to LeMay's own home.[75]

So much for the myth of "trying to help Nixon."

But it *is* true that LeMay stated that he felt betrayed by Lyndon Johnson.

After all that general had done on behalf of the JFK plot – including identifying an alternate patsy in Dallas; monitoring SAC and preventing nuclear war on November 22nd; flying altered "evidence" to Washington; making a USAF lab available for alteration of the Zapruder and other films; having USAF personnel at Tinker Air Force Base examine all the Dallas media reports from the assassination weekend; providing a USAF "historian" to outline *and write* the fictitious "Warren" Report – LeMay plainly and rightfully felt that he had been very poorly repaid by LBJ.

Johnson had only renewed LeMay's tenure as USAF Chief of Staff for a few months, in a transparently obvious ploy to keep the general aboard (and quiet) through the 1964 election – but unceremoniously eased him out in early 1965 *before* the massive (but to LeMay, frustratingly and unacceptably *conventional*) escalation of the Vietnam War began.

LBJ had ignored LeMay's grand 1964 recommendation for a massive bombing campaign against North Vietnam.

Worst of all, LBJ had – in LeMay's eyes – reneged on his fundamental face-to-face promise to the Joint Chiefs (including LeMay himself) in December 1963, at

---

[74] Warren Kozak, *LEMAY: The Life and Wars of General Curtis LeMay,* p. 381.

[75] Warren Kozak, *LEMAY: The Life and Wars of General Curtis LeMay,* p. 381.

the White House, only a month after Dallas: "You just let me get elected, and then you can have your war."

The JCS were not getting the *totally* unrestrained war that they wanted in Southeast Asia. For all the insane, horrific tonnage of bombs and napalm and chemical poisons being dropped on South Vietnam and its neighbors (exceeding the total explosive power of all such weapons used in World War II), LBJ was clearly *not* following the LeMay desire for *completely* uninhibited aerial destruction of North Vietnam as well.

Now, in late 1968, LeMay's supposed vice-presidential "candidacy" – whatever its other motivations – represented something of a thumb in the eye to his former boss, Lyndon Johnson. LeMay was certainly not going to support LBJ's erstwhile vice president and designated successor, the extraordinarily weak and pathetic Hubert Humphrey, who was now the Democratic nominee.

But there was something else underneath it all – something much more important and revealing than a mere case of "sour grapes" over "differing views on military strategy."

LeMay's employer in 1968, Networks Electronic Corporation, threatened to fire the retired general if he put his hat into the political ring by joining the Wallace ticket. This firing would of course cost LeMay his $50,000 annual salary as chairman of the board for the company (an amount equal to some $499,000 annually in 2023 dollars). Indeed, a lawsuit eventually occurred.

But a savior suddenly appeared in order to cushion the financial blow.

A representative of the George Wallace presidential campaign flew to Dallas, Texas, where he spoke privately to a wealthy Texas oil man. That oil man, the son of America's wealthiest individual, instantly created *a one-million-dollar trust fund* (equal to almost *ten million dollars* in 2023 money) for poor Curtis Emerson LeMay. The former USAF general then promptly abandoned his corporate post and belatedly joined the Wallace campaign in October 1968 for a mere *one-month stint* as its vice-presidential candidate.

On the surface, it might appear to have been simply a magnanimous financial gesture by a LeMay admirer and political junkie with very deep pockets.

Until you understand who the oil man was – and who his father was.

LeMay received his one-million-dollar trust from *Nelson Bunker Hunt.*

Nelson Bunker Hunt had *also* put up money to run the ugly, insulting, ominous, threatening, viciously anti-JFK, black-bordered ad which appeared in Dallas newspapers on the morning of President Kennedy's fatal visit to the city on Friday, November 22nd, 1963.

And Nelson Bunker Hunt's supremely wealthy *father* was none other than H. L. Hunt – the richest man in America at the time, an extreme right-wing billionaire who had long been a supporter and confidante of a certain ambitious Texas politician named . . . Lyndon Baines Johnson.

As far as LBJ was concerned, *the million-dollar payoff to LeMay in 1968 concluded his business with the USAF general once and for all.*

No further dealings would be had.

No further demands would be met.

No further transactions would occur.

Problem solved.

Threat eliminated.

Danger averted.

Curtis LeMay had – *finally* – been paid off (rather handsomely, too)[76] for his vital work in connection with the JFK assassination.[77]

Nevertheless, *it still wasn't enough.*

LeMay was still furious.

He still hated the living Lyndon Johnson.

And he still hated the dead John Kennedy.

* * *

---

[76] In 1964, LBJ verbally offered to arrange a million-dollar payoff to former Senate aide Bobby Baker, Johnson's longtime fixer and accomplice on Capitol Hill, in exchange for his silence. (Lobbyist Robert N. Winter-Berger witnessed the episode and recounted it in *The Washington Payoff: An Insider's View of Corruption in Government.*) Back then "a million dollars" was real money – and apparently it was "the going rate" for keeping the most dangerous witnesses (knowledgeable men like Curtis LeMay and Bobby Baker) from spilling all they knew about LBJ.

[77] Though he initially screamed and wept in the moments after the shooting of the president in Dealey Plaza, Abraham Zapruder was a repulsively greedy individual who, *on the very afternoon of the JFK assassination,* openly declared his determined intention to make a **fortune** off his film of President Kennedy's murder. (Zapruder's ugly avarice was documented in notes made that same day by Dallas SS agent Forrest Sorrels.) Zapruder was paid some $150,000 over the course of several years by CIA conduit TIME/LIFE, whose executives included Agency asset C. D. Jackson.

Decades later, Zapruder's like-minded family made *another* gargantuan financial killing on the imagery by selling the extant *physical strip of film* to the U. S. government for some $16 million – yet the Zapruders separately "donated" the *copyright* of that film to the Sixth Floor Museum in Dallas, which charges large sums for its reproduction.

One of the most bizarre aspects of all this is that the *extant* "Zapruder film" [*sic*], which everyone has seen numerous times, is **not** the camera original shot on November 22nd, 1963. I prove that conclusively in my next major book on the subject, which is already well underway.

Rather, the extant "Zapruder" film [*sic*] is merely a *copy* of an extremely altered film – a dramatically censored, drastically bowdlerized and extensively "sanitized" *version* of the true original. The avaricious Zapruders made a vast fortune over the years from what is, in reality, **a visual fraud perpetrated by personnel working under federal authority;** and the U. S. government paid out some $16 million of your tax money for . . . a very poor copy of *its very own criminal handiwork.*

Only in America . . .

Take Lt. Col. Patterson's (totally understandable) feelings about President Clinton and *magnify them a thousand-fold,* and you will have *some* idea of the kind of enmity which Curtis LeMay (and many other extremely powerful senior American military officers of the 1960s) harbored toward President Kennedy.

A thousand-fold . . .

Of course, Buzz Patterson was simply a Lieutenant Colonel.

Curtis LeMay was a four-star general and also *the Air Force Chief of Staff.* He had massive power and impressive authority. Unlike Buzz Patterson, Curtis LeMay was in a position to actually *get things done* – and the evidence is that when it came to the JFK assassination, *he did so.*

The United States Air Force, through the malevolent authority of Curtis LeMay, performed **at least eighteen (18)** vital tasks of absolutely paramount importance to facilitate, enable, execute and cover up the assassination of President John Fitzgerald Kennedy:

1. The Air Force maintained *full secrecy* regarding LBJ's criminal plot to assassinate the president.

2. The Air Force provided Lyndon Johnson's *secret backchannel* to the Joint Chiefs of Staff in the form of USAF Colonel Howard Burris.

3. The Air Force provided *two alternate patsies* in Texas should one be required.

4. The Air Force provided a *supervising officer* on the ground in Dallas for the JFK assassination.

5. Former Air Force personnel provided *real-time photography* in Dealey Plaza.

6. The Air Force *restrained SAC* on November 22nd.

7. The Air Force flew *combat air patrols* to protect Lyndon Johnson in Dallas following the murder of JFK.

8. The Air Force helped *fly an important Parkland Hospital surgeon back to Dallas* to operate on Governor John Connally.

9. The Air Force *enabled LBJ to flee the country,* if it came to that.

10. The Air Force arranged to *independently retrieve President Kennedy's corpse* from Dallas, if necessary.

11. The Air Force transported President Kennedy's corpse back to Washington.

12. The Air Force provided a secure facility for additional pre-autopsy mutilation of, bullet extraction from, and photography of President Kennedy's corpse.

13. The Air Force provided a *specialized laboratory* capable of ultra-sophisticated film alteration and photo alteration work to censor and "clean up" the damning visual evidence of the utter fiasco in Dealey Plaza.

14. The Air Force physically flew falsified "evidence" to Washington D. C. soon after the assassination.

15. The Air Force assisted with *the censoring of incriminating transmissions* which occurred on November 22nd between Air Force One and Curtis LeMay and other federal government resources.

16. The Air Force literally *wrote the outline* which largely guided the federal government's criminal creation of the fictitious "Warren" Report.

17. The Air Force *helped comb through Dallas media tapes* from November 22nd in search of dangerously incriminating evidence that would have exposed the JFK assassination plot.[78]

18. Finally, the Air Force outlined and actually *wrote* much of the *final text* of the fictitious "Warren" Report itself!

Without the direct, hands-on assistance of the United States Air Force, the JFK assassination plot *would have collapsed and been exposed* – leading to criminal prosecution and punishment for its perpetrators.[79]

In 1963, the *chief* conspirator was Texas native Lyndon Baines Johnson.

A key *accomplice* of LBJ's was Ohio native Curtis Emerson LeMay.

The general's own actions proved it.

So did his own words.[80]

The United States Air Force was a ***major*** accomplice to Lyndon Johnson in the JFK assassination[81] – performing no fewer ***seventeen*** vital services before, during and after Dallas.[82]

In truth, the U. S. Air Force played a much larger and more extensive role in the JFK assassination *than any other branch of the armed forces of the United States.*[83]

* * *

---

[78] Bizarrely, airmen at Tinker Air Force Base in Oklahoma were given this task.

[79] Author's exclusive original discovery.

[80] Author's exclusive original discovery.

[81] Author's exclusive original discovery.

[82] Author's exclusive original discovery.

[83] And a *far* bigger role than the much-touted CIA. (Author's exclusive original discovery.)

Understand this:

The 1968 book which he co-authored with Dale O. Smith served as Curtis LeMay's smug and chilling personal *confession* of – and *justification* for – his own knowing participation in the JFK assassination.[84]

In *America is in Danger,* LeMay repeatedly mocked and derided President Kennedy; openly praised military insubordination;[85] and also revealed his own culpability.[86] Never a subtle or discreet individual, LeMay had always had great trouble controlling his own utterances.

His final book was no exception.

The general's acknowledgment of guilt began in the introduction of his book, where he curiously specifies that he has been "*intimately* associated with matters of foreign, as well as *domestic,* policy" during senior command portions of his military career, *including* his tenure on the Joint Chiefs of Staff from 1961 to 1965.[87]

What?

"Domestic" policy?

A military man?

Domestic policy?

LeMay then launched the main text of *America is in Danger* with a curiously lengthy, unprovoked, extremely bitter and suspiciously defensive ***rant*** about military dictatorship; civilian control of the American military; *military cabals;* and *military coups.* The startling and revelatory passage – which covers nine pages, and constitutes the *entire initial chapter* of the book – amounts to the general's personal confession.[88]

Significantly, LeMay also made very sure to ***mention by name*** *two of his principal American military co-conspirators in the JFK assassination:* USAF General Thomas Power, and U. S. Army General Earle Wheeler.[89]

---

[84] Author's exclusive original discovery.

[85] Curtis LeMay and Dale O. Smith, *America is in Danger,* p. 14.

[86] Author's exclusive original discovery.

[87] Curtis LeMay and Dale O. Smith, *America is in Danger,* p. xi.

[88] Author's exclusive original discovery. To paraphrase an English playwright, "Methinks he doth protest too much." General LeMay's shocking and guilt-ridden diatribe is disturbingly reminiscent of a certain Secret Service agent's similar admission of his own personal involvement in the JFK slaying. (Much more on that in my next major book, which is already well underway and already scheduled for publication.)

[89] Author's exclusive original discovery.

All three officers – LeMay, Power and Wheeler – knowingly aided and abetted LBJ in the 1963 murder of JFK.[90]

The book *America is in Danger* came out in June 1968, five months *before* LeMay joined the George Wallace third-party presidential run in October. It was not a hastily cobbled-together, poorly produced political campaign document dashed off casually at the last minute; it was a book long in the making, like a grenade or a bomb timed to go off for maximum effect.

Apart from LeMay's damning, jaw-dropping, devastatingly self-conscious screed about "demons" wearing U. S. uniforms[91] which opens the book – plus the ostentatiously defensive (and false) avowal of his fealty and commitment to the Constitution (which he had knowingly stained with JFK's blood[92]) – it is the final two pages of *America is in Danger* which are the most explicitly revealing in terms of the former USAF Chief of Staff's 1963 fundamental motivation for joining and supporting Lyndon Johnson's murderous coup against John Kennedy.

The assassination of JFK was a sacred duty, according to LeMay. In chilling prose, he declared that America must *rid itself* of the figures who had "deceived" the country and led it into serious danger.[93]

The general added that such heinous figures were guilty of putting the U.S. at mortal risk, and were responsible for inviting national "oblivion."[94]

For the fanatical Curtis Emerson LeMay, the bloody murder of John Kennedy in 1963 was an act of patriotism and existential self-defense – a necessary step to literally *save the country*.[95] As the general himself put it, as explicitly as he dared, at times extreme "surgery" – *surgery!* – is required in order to remove a deadly "cancer" from a nation.[96]

LeMay was clearly alluding to the deliberate and drastic removal of **JFK** (the putative "cancer") in order to ensure the survival of **America** (the supposed "victim").

---

[90] Author's exclusive original discovery.

[91] Curtis LeMay and Dale O. Smith, *America is in Danger,* p. 8.

[92] Curtis LeMay and Dale O. Smith, *America is in Danger,* pp. 293-294.

[93] Curtis LeMay and Dale O. Smith, *America is in Danger,* pp. 332-333.

[94] Curtis LeMay and Dale O. Smith, *America is in Danger,* p. 333.

[95] In unintentionally revealing statements, Robert McNamara later said that LeMay was indeed operating to preserve America. McNamara stated that Curtis LeMay was ready, willing and able to perform *any necessary killing* to achieve that goal. (McNamara's remarks appear in the 2003 Errol Morris film *The Fog of War*.)

[96] Curtis LeMay and Dale O. Smith, *America is in Danger,* p. 308. (Navy doctor James Humes alerted two FBI agents observing the JFK autopsy to the fact of *criminal "surgery" prior to the official postmortem procedure* at Bethesda.)

But the general was *also* referring to the criminal postmortem mutilation of President Kennedy's corpse.[97]

*Anything – **anything at all** – was deemed "permissible" in order to ensure the survival of the United States of America.*

The U. S. military oath not only permits but *mandates* this, of course.

Remember the words:

All enemies.

Foreign *and domestic.*

* * *

So the mystery of LeMay's bizarre absence, curious unreachability and strange reappearance on the day of Kennedy's assassination now has a solution.[98] No other investigator has ever attempted or achieved such an in-depth analysis. On November 22nd, 1963, Curtis LeMay himself was clearly tapped to undertake the task that he most abhorred, a duty that went against every fiber of his being: *he would serve as Lyndon Johnson's personal "fail-safe" device.*[99]

General LeMay, the man who for several years had advocated – and *personally* tried to *provoke* – nuclear war with the USSR, would (albeit very reluctantly) act as a brake on any nuclear launch by the United States military in the immediate wake of the JFK assassination.[100]

LeMay would not unduly irritate (or needlessly insult, or accidentally provoke) the rabid commander of SAC by traveling directly to Offutt AFB in Nebraska and personally standing over General Power's shoulder all day on November 22nd, but LeMay *would* closely monitor the situation from one of the most secret and sensitive military sites in all of North America, the Underground Complex located at RCAF Station North Bay in Canada for any signs of launch *by the United States* – standing ready to issue any orders necessary to try to shut down General Power and SAC's armada *on the ground* in order to personally forestall global disaster while Lyndon Johnson became president in Texas through the bloody shooting (and the subsequent vicious mutilation) of LeMay's hated commander-in-chief.[101]

---

[97] Author's exclusive original discovery.

[98] Author's exclusive original discovery.

[99] Author's exclusive original discovery.

[100] Author's exclusive original discovery.

[101] Author's exclusive original discovery.

The man who dearly wanted total war against the Communists (*all* Communists, everywhere) was assigned to monitor and *prevent* that war *on this one day* – on *this* day, of all days.[102]

Thus on November 22nd, 1963, Curtis Emerson LeMay gamely carried out a policy – *restraining SAC* – which he totally opposed.[103]

* * *

It is clear that Curtis LeMay was promised something of great value in return for this almost-unthinkable assignment.[104] And it is equally clear that Lyndon Johnson – a man who, in the Kennedy brothers' painfully accurate assessment, *never told the truth if a lie would suffice* – brazenly *reneged* on the deal subsequently.[105]

Whether the quid pro quo that Johnson secretly reached with LeMay was an American military assault on Castro's Cuba in the wake of JFK's murder; or future permission to engage in unrestricted bombing in Vietnam; or LeMay's promotion to Chairman of the Joint Chiefs of Staff in 1964 (or thereafter) scarcely matters.

The fact is that, in whole or in part, in some manner, on some level, to some degree, *Lyndon Johnson failed to honor his part of the deal.*[106]

Hence LeMay's later, bitter characterization of Johnson as a "traitor."[107]

---

[102] Author's exclusive original discovery.

[103] LBJ remarked, as a general principle, "I never trust a man until I've got his pecker in my pocket." That type of "acquisition" was never going to happen with the tough and formidable LeMay, of course – so therefore, by his own definition, Johnson would never fully trust LeMay. Their uneasy arrangement in November 1963 therefore involved *negotiation,* rather than consisting exclusively of the type of crude political castration described above. Of course, Johnson held the ultimate trump card – since once JFK was murdered, LBJ would become Commander-in-Chief, with ultimate power over both LeMay himself and over LeMay's remaining career. Lyndon Johnson did not want to deal with equals; thus he waited until LeMay had been *gone* for a full nine months before loudly and profanely berating the remaining Joint Chiefs of Staff at a White House meeting on Vietnam military policy in November 1965.

Nor did LBJ, a thorough-going coward, want such a forceful personality as LeMay present in upcoming councils of war regarding Vietnam. In early 1965, upon LeMay's retirement, LBJ replaced him as Air Force Chief of Staff with the much weaker, more diplomatic and far more compliant General John P. Connell, the "anti-LeMay" – a polished USAF officer who was far more amenable to Johnson's policies and decisions. LBJ wanted to keep any potential rivals or critics "inside the tent pissing out" rather than "outside the tent pissing in."

[104] Author's exclusive original discovery.

[105] Author's exclusive original discovery.

[106] Author's exclusive original discovery.

[107] In a 1965 book released soon after his ouster, General LeMay went well out of his way to mock LBJ personally and directly by *specifically deriding* people who say, "Come now, let us reason together" – a

Actively or passively, Curtis LeMay – the only man in America who could reliably control the even more rabid General Power of SAC – kept the deadly "birds" from launching on November 22nd, 1963.[108] But this enormous favor to Lyndon Johnson was *not* repaid as the Texan had promised.[109] LeMay's continuing calls for the use of nuclear weapons in Vietnam, and for "early" massive expansion of the war in 1964, went coldly unheeded by the new president from Texas.

Within just five months after the assassination, Curtis LeMay knew beyond any doubt that, incredibly, *he had no future whatsoever in Johnson's administration.* The general was formally "severed" from the military only three months after LBJ's November 1964 election.[110]

When LeMay formally left the military on February 1st, 1965, his farewell soiree took place at Andrews Air Force Base in an aircraft hangar. Tellingly, after an earlier obligatory East Room ceremony for the general, President Johnson did not even travel the ten miles from the White House to Andrews to put in a token appearance at the airfield event.[111] Plainly, Curtis LeMay had simply been *used* – enlisted by Johnson at a critical juncture to handle an essential task of overwhelming importance,[112] and then coldly abandoned – a practice which LBJ had perfected over the years with many subordinates (particularly women), in many different contexts.

The only comfort General LeMay could draw from his understated goodbye party at Andrews AFB was that, in order to make room for the attendees, Air Force One – SAM 26000, the beautiful 707 which was now Lyndon Johnson's aircraft

---

biblical phrase which was one of Lyndon Johnson's favorite speech lines. (Curtis LeMay and MacKinlay Kantor, *Mission with LeMay,* p. 560.)

[108] Author's exclusive original discovery.

[109] Author's exclusive original discovery. As LeMay noted revealingly in 1965, *a man wrongly precluded from reaching the top of his profession* is "robbed" of all incentive to excel. (Curtis LeMay with MacKinlay Kantor, *Mission with LeMay,* p. 531.)

[110] Unsurprisingly, General Thomas Power of SAC exited the military in late 1964 – even before LeMay did. Thomas Power could read the writing on the wall, too. Though a right-winger in many respects, Lyndon Johnson's *actual* loyalty lay with *himself* far more than with any political party or ideology. Johnson the hedonist was ultimately a selfish man, who attended primarily to his own more carnal appetites. As such, LBJ naturally felt no drive to pursue the dubious and purely *theoretical* joys of all-out nuclear combat. Better to enjoy women and booze and food in comfortable surroundings than to worship at the uncertain altar of Armageddon.

Lyndon Johnson loved pleasure; he also loved power. He did *not* love Power.

[111] Neither did Defense Secretary Robert McNamara, who had also deliberately skipped LeMay's swearing-in as USAF Chief of Staff back in mid-1961.

[112] Author's exclusive original discovery.

(thanks in no small measure to LeMay's efforts) – had been moved from its hangar to another location.[113]

For a brief moment at least, the outcast extremist Curtis LeMay had managed to displace the greatest public symbol of the frustratingly devious Texan who now occupied the Oval Office.

It was not enough, of course.

Not nearly enough.

Nothing was enough.

Curtis Emerson LeMay had been *had*.

The toughest individual the Air Force ever produced had been hornswoggled.

LeMay was furious with Lyndon Johnson for the rest of his life.

The general was not mollified even by his enormous million-dollar payoff (equaling some seven million dollars in today's money), delivered to LeMay by the Kennedy-hating Johnson ally, billionaire Nelson Bunker Hunt, in the autumn of 1968. Years later, the cigar-chomping USAF general would specifically and unhesitatingly brand Lyndon Baines Johnson a liar and a traitor.[114]

Until my work, no one had ever performed sufficient analysis on – nor properly understood the meaning of – LeMay's pregnant comments about Lyndon Johnson.

Traitor.

There was only one thing that could generate that type of language (the very type of language that LeMay and others had previously used to describe the hated John Fitzgerald Kennedy).

Traitor.

To a military man, it is the ultimate insult – and not something tossed about casually or lightly.

Traitor.

To be called a traitor by Curtis LeMay, of all people, Lyndon Johnson had to have reneged on something absolutely fundamental to the top USAF general.[115] After all, on November 22nd, 1963, LeMay had certainly violated everything *he* believed in by acting to *prevent* nuclear war – and thereby to forsake certain "victory" over the hated Communists worldwide.

Something *huge* was required in return for such an unpleasant and distasteful sacrifice. This was no mere quibble over, say, *radar* budgets for the Air Force; or increased funding for the frozen base at Thule; or the future adoption of certain *tactical*

---

[113] James Carroll noted this telling detail in *House of War.*

[114] LeMay would also complain bitterly in later years that had *he* (rather than Robert McNamara) been running the air war against Vietnam, the United States would have prevailed. Of such rampant delusions are further catastrophic disasters made.

[115] Author's exclusive original discovery.

weapons systems. Such routine and minor squabbles do not lead to epithets like "traitor."

Rather, there was a major debt on the table – and incredibly, *Lyndon Johnson had not paid up.* Not fully, or adequately, or on time.

Johnson reneged.

Johnson cheated – and *used* – Curtis LeMay.

LBJ would not authorize an immediate assault on Havana. Nor would he follow LeMay's aggressive counsel during 1964 regarding how best to annihilate the Vietnamese. Nor would he free the Air Force's cherished "nukes" for indiscriminate use on a later day. Nor would he elevate LeMay to the post of Chairman of the Joint Chiefs of Staff.[116]

Lyndon Johnson accepted *war* as the price of the Pentagon's key support for his 1963 coup, but not **total** war.[117]

Not unrestrained *nuclear* war.

And certainly not *war right away.*[118]

The Johnson Commission – nominally headed by Earl Warren, but created, funded and selected by LBJ – first had to be goaded into finishing its work *before the 1964 presidential election,* so that Johnson could falsely claim that he had been officially "cleared" of suspicion in his predecessor's murder. And then, of course, there was the pesky election itself to manage.

War, of any kind, could *wait.*

War, of any kind, *must* wait.

Cuba could wait.

Vietnam could wait.

Armageddon itself could wait.

Lyndon Johnson was busy selling himself as a "peace" candidate to the endlessly gullible American electorate.

Everything else – and everyone else – could wait.

Except Curtis LeMay.

He couldn't wait.

---

[116] "By rights, LeMay should have become chairman instead of Wheeler in July 1964," wrote biographer Barrett Tillman (*LEMAY,* p. 165). Tillman was correct on that point. Earle Wheeler was *the third Army general in a row* to be named to the top spot in the American military hierarchy. Previously, the JCS chairmanship had rotated among the Army, Navy and Air Force.

[117] Author's exclusive original discovery.

[118] Author's exclusive original discovery.

For Lyndon Johnson, the JFK assassination was about *seizing the presidency for himself.*[119] For Curtis LeMay, the JFK assassination was about excising a dangerous cancer from the body politic, about "saving" America, and about obtaining something of extreme value in return for *his* role, and the Air Force's role – and the Pentagon's role – as the armed and willing guarantors of the LBJ coup.[120]

And as is now clear, Curtis LeMay had certainly done his part.[121]

Lyndon Johnson, by contrast, *had not.*

There could be no greater betrayal, of course.

Traitor.

John Kennedy himself had certainly been an utter traitor in LeMay's eyes. Lyndon Johnson had now gotten rid of JFK violently – with LeMay's enthusiastic and vital concurrence and support. So LBJ *should* have been a complete *hero* in LeMay's grateful eyes.

Yet Johnson was somehow reneging on their deal![122]

That was completely unacceptable and totally unconscionable. Not even the belated *million dollars* given to him in 1968 (almost *ten* million dollars in 2023 currency) could soothe General LeMay's white-hot wrath and indignation.

Traitor.

LeMay once confided to a friend, fellow World War II USAAF veteran Ralph Nutter, that LBJ had lied to him "so God-damn many times . . ."[123]

Traitor.

Traitor.

Traitor.

---

[119] Author's exclusive original discovery. That is the crux of the JFK assassination – the true reason why. The crime was **not** the ideological initiative or work of "rogue" CIA operatives; nor right-wing Cuban exiles; nor annoyed Mafiosi; nor fanatically extremist, hysterical cliques of right-wing New Orleans homosexuals; nor the Federal Reserve; nor the Bilderberg Group; nor the Freeport Sulphur Company; nor the Shickshinny Knights of Malta.

*LBJ wanted to be president – and **that** is why John Kennedy was murdered. Period.*

The sooner that weak-minded JFK assassination researchers (and utterly gutless corporate media hacks, and cowardly academics, and the rest of America) finally come to grips with that central fact, the better.

[120] Author's exclusive original discovery.

[121] Author's exclusive original discovery.

[122] Author's exclusive original discovery.

[123] Warren Kozak, *LEMAY: The Life and Wars of General Curtis LeMay,* p. 382.

Curtis Emerson LeMay outlived Lyndon Baines Johnson by a full seventeen years. But the general's anger and contempt for the devious Texan who betrayed and discarded him after Dallas never diminished, never evaporated, never subsided.

Never.

* * *

General LeMay's significant role in the JFK assassination reflected his own vast and unquestioned command authority – which, at that time in the Sixties, included *all* Air Force bases and *all* USAF personnel.[124]

Including the Strategic Air Command (SAC).

Including the Tactical Air Command (TAC).

Including Tinker Air Force Base in Oklahoma.

Including Andrews Air Force Base itself, in Maryland.

And including a small but extremely important USAF unit located at a very unusual post out on the West Coast – not far from the glimmering waters of the Pacific.

---

[124] Many long years *later,* both the authority and the role of the Joint Chiefs of Staff were drastically curtailed by congressional legislation; thus, since 1986, the Chiefs have no longer had any operational command of troop units.

But back in 1963, their powers were truly immense and they "ruled the roost" as the top men in uniform for their respective branches of the military. At that time, the JCS could *and did* issue orders – including *combat* orders – to a variety of regional and "theater" military commanders. And the Joint Chiefs also gave orders directly to SAC, which was a special "specified command" reporting directly to them.

USAF personnel at Lookout Mountain Air Force Station
(in California) filmed, produced, edited, revised and distributed
highly classified films of classified events
for extremely select audiences of
high-level United States government officials.

Some film projects – like that pictured above, from 1951 –
were later "sanitized" for public viewing.
The vast majority of the unit's secret work
has never been seen by anyone outside the federal government.

The men of the USAF 1352nd Photographic Group
also called on top Hollywood *civilian* talent
for technical assistance in producing the ultra-classified films.

Chapter Twenty-Six:
Lookout Mountain

"You can't depend on your eyes
when your imagination is out of focus."

– Samuel Langhorne Clemens

"These things do not just 'happen.'
*They are **made** to happen."*

– John Fitzgerald Kennedy

You've seen it a million times.

It's called "the Zapruder film," named for the man who reportedly shot it.

The silent, 8mm amateur film shows President Kennedy's motorcade coming down Elm Street in Dallas, moving from the viewer's left to the viewer's right.

Midway through the brief film, there *appears to be* a massive "explosion" [*sic*] – a nasty pink cloud *apparently* emanating from the top and front of the president's head. Then JFK suddenly flies violently backward and to his left. Large white irregular shapes then "appear" on the right side of John Kennedy's head.

But here's the thing:

*The extant Zapruder film does **not** depict the actual assassination of President John Fitzgerald Kennedy.*[125]

This is a startling and vitally important concept, so I'll say it again:

The extant Zapruder film does not depict the actual assassination of President John Fitzgerald Kennedy.

Notice that I said "extant."

You have *often* seen the *extant* Zapruder film.

---

[125] Author's exclusive original discovery.

N. B.: This is a distinct and completely separate discovery from the simple fact that the extant Zapruder film has been *altered,* which was previously known and has been correctly recognized by many other observers in the past.

My point here is that the extant Zapruder film *does not even capture the actual JFK assassination itself –* as I will explain in stunning detail in my second major book about the JFK case. (Author's exclusive original discovery.)

Thousands of times.

*But you have **never** seen the true **camera-original** Zapruder film.*

Never.

Not once!

Anywhere.

Everything you "see" in the existing remnant of the ***extant*** "Zapruder" film – the dramatic pink "explosion" [*sic*]; the so-called white "flaps" [*sic*] on the skull; even (unavoidably) *the violent rearward "head snap" itself* – are the result of special effects artwork; the elimination of ***hundreds*** *of frames of original film*;[126] and extensive film editing carried out by talented but horribly rushed military and civilian experts working under the direct supervision of military men at a U. S. military facility located in southern California.

There is a reason for that, of course.

And there was a *mechanism* behind that reason.

And there was a man whose rank made him *responsible* for that mechanism.

* * *

The most important things which happened in Dealey Plaza – including the moments of the actual JFK assassination itself – were left on the cutting-room floor.[127]

Literally.

Thirty seconds[128] that tore the heart out of this nation and paved the way for the escalated inferno of Vietnam were patiently snipped from the Zapruder film by experts – *under U. S. Air Force supervision* – and deliberately excised from history in the unholy name of "national security."

Before the nation could see it.

Before even the "Warren" Commission could see it.

Before American citizens could see and understand what a genuine *coup* really looks like.

* * *

Located at 8935 Wonderland Avenue in the Laurel Canyon area of Los Angeles, a USAF facility called Lookout Mountain Air Force Station was, in November 1963, a filmmaker's *dream* – roomy, secure, and very well-equipped.

---

[126] Author's exclusive original discovery.

[127] Author's exclusive original discovery.

[128] Author's exclusive original discovery.

The spacious military building resembled a somewhat utilitarian Hollywood mansion, and it featured everything from screening rooms and numerous film vaults to an actual sound stage. It also had equipment for creating animations and for processing film.[129] The walls were thick concrete; electric fences surrounded the site; and, in an ironic twist, a bomb shelter was provided for the men who often filmed nuclear bomb blasts at test sites in the U. S. and in the Pacific.

Lookout Mountain Air Force Station (LMAFS) was not an airfield or a "base" but a *site*. It was initially constructed in the 1940s and was intended to help direct coastal radar defenses against potential enemy attack during World War II, but soon after the war it became the home of one of the most important military *photographic* units ever created.

And that unit soon functioned as a high-end visual factory for both the U. S. Air Force and the top *civilian* echelons of America's federal government.

* * *

As 1947 turned to 1948, a photographic and movie unit called the Lookout Mountain Laboratory was created by U. S. military officers including a man named Alterio Gallerani.[130] After some five years with the unit, Gallerani was reassigned elsewhere – a typical occurrence in the military – *but he would return in the future at a very crucial juncture.*[131]

The 1352nd Motion Picture Squadron of the U. S. Air Force officially came into existence in May 1952 via General Order Number 56 – issued by Headquarters, Military Air Transport Service (MATS).[132]

The squadron's *official* purpose was to produce classified photos and films of hundreds of American atomic test explosions – but significantly, it was *also* tasked with providing "such *additional* production of motion picture production and still photographs *as directed* by the Commanding General, Air Pictorial Service."[133]

---

[129] William J. Broad, "The Bomb Chroniclers," *The New York Times,* September 13, 2010.

[130] History of the 1352nd Photographic Group, July-December 1963. This roster information comes directly from declassified official Air Force records, made available through a project undertaken by Ned O'Gorman and Kevin Hamilton with support from The University of Illinois at Urbana-Champaign.

[131] Author's exclusive original discovery.

[132] **N.B.:** MATS was *also* the parent unit of the 1254th Air Transport Wing – which provided the air crews, stewards, security police and maintenance personnel for Air Force One and other elite VIP aircraft at Andrews Air Force Base.

[133] Air Force History Index. I need hardly remind the reader that the Commanding General (whomever he might be at any given time) of the Air Pictorial Service (which later became the Air Pictorial and Charting Service) was of course fully subordinate to the Air Force Chief of Staff – and when President

Clearly, that's a mission statement large enough to drive *a presidential motorcade* through.[134]

The 1352nd (which was later upgraded from a Squadron to a Group) did indeed film a number of American nuclear detonations – more than 300 of them.[135]

But the unit actually produced *at least* **6,500** classified films,[136] and as many as **19,000** classified films in all.[137]

The vast disparity between the very *limited* number of *nuclear* "events" shot by the 1352nd and the truly *colossal* number of actual "films" which the unit ultimately produced is astonishing – and the reader is reminded that only an infinitesimal *fraction* of that total work output has ever been declassified.[138]

Clearly, the 1352nd Photographic Group (its eventual designation) was involved in ***much more*** than just documenting periodic nuclear blasts.[139]

Moreover, in the wake of President Kennedy's surprising success in securing rapid passage of the limited nuclear test ban treaty[140] which banned *atmospheric* nuclear tests, the biggest ostensible reason for the 1352nd's very existence largely *evaporated* in 1963 – and it evaporated *prior to* Dallas![141]

Kennedy was assassinated in 1963, the Air Force Chief of Staff was none other than ***General Curtis Emerson LeMay.***

[134] Author's exclusive original insight.

[135] It is notable that President Kennedy actually *did **not** desire that any such films be made* when he (very reluctantly!) resumed atmospheric nuclear testing (under severe pressure from the U. S. military) in 1962.

[136] William J. Broad, "The Bomb Chroniclers," *New York Times,* September 13, 2010.

[137] Atlas Obscura, "Lookout Mountain Airforce [*sic*] Station."

[138] One 1963 film produced by the Air Force at Lookout Mountain was called "Disaster Control Indoctrination" – and featured ominous, threatening music over the Department of the Air Force logo in its opening titles.

[139] Author's exclusive original discovery.

[140] Officially, the name was "Treaty Banning Nuclear Weapon Tests in the Atmosphere, in Outer Space and Under Water."

[141] Author's exclusive original discovery. (The speed of the treaty's passage was truly astonishing. President Kennedy made his famous Peace Speech on June 10th, 1963; secured agreement from the Soviets on July 25th, 1963; got the agreement signed by US, Soviet and British envoys on August 5th, 1963; obtained overwhelming ratification of the treaty by the U. S. Senate on September 24th, 1963; and signed it himself on October 7th, 1963. The treaty formally took effect on October 10th, 1963 – just **four months to the day** after JFK's Peace Speech at American University, and just six weeks before the assassination.)

Yet, strangely, the USAF Lookout Mountain facility remained in operation[142] until the late 1960s – while *Lyndon Baines Johnson* still criminally and illegitimately occupied the Oval Office.[143]

* * *

Back in Washington, D. C., the senior Congressional leaders in charge of appropriations for America's nuclear programs during the 1950s and 1960s received exclusive private showings of the 1352nd's film work.[144] This meant that *a few highly intelligent, highly calculating, very high-level politicians on Capitol Hill* were personally aware that somewhere in America, there was a special military photographic unit of truly exceptional capabilities.

For the record, those highly intelligent, highly calculating, high-level politicians on Capitol Hill included famed Senate Majority Leader *Lyndon Baines Johnson* – who as Vice President under JFK was also (officially and constitutionally) the presiding officer of the Senate.

LBJ ***knew*** about the 1352nd.[145]

And he knew *long before Dallas.*

He had seen their work!

A military photographic unit of truly exceptional capabilities.

That's the kind of inside knowledge that is extraordinarily valuable and useful when you are planning a brazen daylight assassination in a sunlit plaza – an assassination which will inevitably occur in front of civilian witnesses, some of whom will certainly have cameras of their own.

People who might later be tempted to challenge the official story of the crime.

*An advanced government film laboratory **under full U. S. military control.***

It was a coup planner's dream.

* * *

So: who led this extraordinary Air Force outfit in the California hills?

---

[142] Atlas Obscura, "Lookout Mountain Airforce [*sic*] Station."

[143] Author's exclusive original discovery. (Records show that one of the men who worked at Lookout Mountain in the period from late 1966 to early 1968, a few years *after* the JFK assassination, was USAF 2nd Lieutenant Dennis S. Johnson of the 1352nd Photographic Group. No one is accusing him of involvement with the criminal alteration of the Zapruder film in 1963.)

[144] William J. Broad, "The Bomb Chroniclers," *New York Times,* September 13, 2010.

[145] Author's exclusive original discovery.

581

The commander of the 1352nd Photographic Group at Lookout Mountain Air Force Station (LMAFS) in November 1963 was none other than USAF Lieutenant Colonel Alterio Gallerani, who took command of the unit on July 1st, 1963 – *less than five months before the assassination of President Kennedy*.[146]

Lt. Col. Gallerani's "Special Staff" at LMAFS included Executive Officer, Major Kenneth K. Killgore; Operations Officer, Major Robert L. MacKinnon; Materiel Officer, Major Francis J. Brick; Base Procurement Officer, Captain Willliam R. Baldwin; and Chief of Administrative Services Lieutenant Alfred R. Melanson.[147]

And note this: in September 1963 – *just two months before Dallas* – the USAF 1352nd Photographic Group created a special sub-unit called "Motion Picture Services," whose mission included "documenting Air Force events" and "producing motion picture films for the Air Force *and other* Government agencies."[148]

The 1352nd was, by definition, *already doing those things* – so the creation of a special internal unit with ludicrously redundant "responsibilities," *mere weeks before the JFK assassination,* merits piercing scrutiny.[149]

* * *

And, as always, there is more.

In late 1963, the 1352nd Photographic Group *also* worked on a major project labeled "SFP 1250," titled "Command and Control."

One would think that this project had something to do with a documentary feature on the Strategic Air Command, based in Nebraska – but it was not.

Instead, men from the 1352nd conducted "script research" at *Air Force headquarters in Washington* (and at Electronic Systems Division at Hanscom Field in Massachusetts) from November 12th to November 22nd, 1963 – *the very day of the JFK assassination*.[150]

A "concerted effort" was involved in making this project happen; the end product was "required for high-level briefing during the week of 27 Jan 1964."[151]

---

[146] History of the 1352nd Photographic Group, July-December 1963. As noted above, Gallerani had been one of the men who first formed the "Lookout Mountain Laboratory" at this site in the late 1940s.

[147] History of the 1352nd Photographic Group, July-December 1963.

[148] History of the 1352nd Photographic Group, July-December 1963.

[149] Author's exclusive original discovery.

[150] History of the 1352nd Photographic Group, July-December 1963.

[151] History of the 1352nd Photographic Group, July-December 1963.

Strangely, *nowhere* in the unit's official written history for July to December 1963 did I come across *any mention whatsoever* of the bloody daylight assassination of the United States military's Commander-in-Chief, John Fitzgerald Kennedy.

* * *

The Lookout Mountain facility's strategic location in the heart of America's film industry capital was a major benefit to the special Air Force unit, of course.

Although they were members of a military organization, the personnel of USAF's 1352nd Photographic Group had *access* to – and actually *used* – top civilian Hollywood filmmakers and special-effects artists to assist them in their largely classified work at Lookout Mountain Air Force Station.

In other words, the United States Air Force **could** and **did** obtain "technical assistance" from the very best commercial movie talent in the world.[152] One of the men who contributed his deep expertise to the 1352nd was W. Donn Hayes – an experienced, Emmy-winning supervising editor and director who worked as a "motion picture production specialist" with the USAF military unit from 1954 until 1968 [153] – *a period which obviously spans the JFK assassination.*[154]

But make no mistake: the airmen and officers of Lookout Mountain were not merely uniformed "interns" running errands for Tinseltown titans; to the contrary.

At the secret Air Force facility, important cinematic techniques and intricate new gear and various technical advances which later became commonplace in the *commercial* film industry were first explored, tested and perfected by military and civilian workers – *all functioning under USAF control.*[155]

Plainly, Lookout Mountain was a truly cutting-edge facility.

Moreover, *as their own images prove,* the dedicated USAF men of the 1352nd were more than willing to do *multiple versions* – meaning, separate and successive "drafts" – of their highly important, highly classified film work.[156]

And they were doing this – *indisputably* – starting *well before Dallas.*[157]

---

[152] "The lab drew on Hollywood talent and technology to pursue its clandestine ends," according to a later news report. (William J. Broad, "The Bomb Chroniclers," *New York Times,* September 13, 2010.)

[153] Biographical information provided by Michael D. Hayes at IMDb online.

[154] Author's exclusive original discovery.

[155] William J. Broad, "The Bomb Chroniclers," *New York Times,* September 13, 2010.

[156] Author's exclusive original discovery. (While the 1352nd also produced routine training films and other laughably innocuous features, their true "bread and butter" was ultra-classified work on ultra-classified matters.)

[157] Author's exclusive original discovery.

Years before Dallas.

A photo from 1951 (seen at the beginning of this chapter) captures several members of the Lookout Mountain team of that era (several of whom are clearly wearing Air Force uniforms, with winged USAF patches on their sleeves) – and one of them is holding a document whose cover is plainly stamped, in large capital letters:

SECOND DRAFT SCRIPT FOR OPERATION GREENHOUSE.[158]

You read that correctly, America.

Second draft script.

In other words, when the initial "rough cut" of a particular film "project" was deemed somehow "unsatisfactory," the USAF men of the 1352nd *fixed* it.

They *changed* it.

They *altered* it.

They *edited* it.

They *re-edited* it.

They . . . *improved* it.

They created *new versions* of the film.[159]

Then – and **only** then – did they actually distribute a film to their extremely select audiences of high-level military and U. S. government officials back in Washington, D. C.[160]

It had to be, you know, *presentable.*

It had to have *the, um,* ***desired depiction of events.***

It had to be, uh, "right."

The finished product ultimately had to be – there simply is no other possible phrase for it! – *"Good enough for government work."*

And in late 1963, it ***was.***

* * *

John Kennedy did not know that his presidency – and his very life – would end in a hail of gunfire in a pleasant green plaza on a sunny day in November.

John Kennedy did not know that his murder would be caught on film.

And John Kennedy did not know that both his corpse itself, *and the visual record of his own assassination*, would be viciously and deliberately butchered and mutilated beyond recognition.

---

[158] "Operation Greenhouse" was one of a series of American nuclear test explosions in the Pacific Ocean.

[159] Author's exclusive original discovery.

[160] Sanitized, *censored* versions of certain classified films were ultimately made available for wide public release in newsreels, commercial movies and other forums.

Least of all did John Kennedy realize that much of the drastic censorship of the principal film of his own assassination would be perpetrated by USAF men from the 1352nd Photographic Group – men who, until the instant of JFK's violent death in Dealey Plaza, had been military subordinates under his authority as America's constitutional commander-in-chief.

* * *

Cue the carping chorus of crazed choleric critics.

Many deeply ignorant people – including some extremely immature and stubborn narrow-minded JFK researchers – will immediately make angry pompous pronouncements about the supposed "lack of necessity" [*sic*] of editing the true camera-original Zapruder film.

After all, they will fulminate furiously, the ***extant*** Zapruder film still shows "indications of conspiracy" in the form of an apparent "impact" [*sic*] of a shot from the front, and therefore the ***extant*** Zapruder film "must" be "authentic" [*sic*].

It must be!

Gotta be!

It stands to reason, Martha!

It just has to be, goldang it!

They will also simultaneously commence a great deal of noisy whining about the supposed "impossibility" [*sic*] of federal authorities quickly obtaining, transporting and rapidly editing the true camera-original Zapruder film on the weekend of the JFK assassination in order to create the fraudulent ***extant*** clip which is so familiar to millions of extremely gullible people.

It just couldn't have been done, Luther! I can't imagine it!

No how! No way!

There wasn't enough time! Couldn't have been done!

Impossible!

Apparently, those wailing denialists from the AAAAA (Angry Armchair Analysts' Association of America™) have never heard of the United States Air Force – or of the many supersonic jets in its aerial armada in 1963 – or of the astounding abilities and attributes and resources of the 1352nd Photographic Group based at Lookout Mountain Air Force Station in California.[161]

---

[161] Firsthand CIA eyewitnesses stated to the ARRB in the 1990s that separate federal couriers showed up at NPIC and personally delivered **two (2)** different "drafts" of **two (2)** different versions of the already-censored "Zapruder" film to **two (2)** separate teams of CIA analysts on **two (2)** different dates on the very weekend of the JFK assassination in November 1963.

Couriers who delivered these 2 different versions of the film to NPIC *claimed* verbally (**without** producing any evidence or proof or documentation whatsoever) that they had supposedly brought the films (via

* * *

The deed was done largely at a government enclave.

A USAF studio that resembled a wealthy movie director's home.

Key edits and revisions and additions were made repeatedly *during the first 48 hours after the JFK assassination* in a comfortable, attractive, hillside facility not far from where the warm Pacific Ocean gently laps against California's shores.

The savage changes absolutely *had* to be made – because as I pointed out much earlier in this book, the actual "execution" of the JFK assassination plot in Dealey Plaza was **FUBAR.**

A disastrous failure of immense proportions.

It didn't go as planned.

Therefore, the true camera-original "Zapruder" film was flown *west* from Texas to California by a U. S. Air Force jet on Friday, November 22nd, 1963, for extensive, drastic and rapid editing by the 1352nd Photographic Group at Lookout Mountain Air Force Station.[162]

A hastily censored "*first* edited cut"[163] of the film was then flown *east* via U. S. Air Force jet less than 24 hours later.[164] This "*first* edited cut" was ultimately

---

aircraft) from the "Hawkeye Plant," a secret CIA photographic laboratory located up in Rochester, New York. (See Volume IV of Doug Horne's five-volume book, *Inside the ARRB*.)

There was, of course, no way for anyone to actually *verify* that claim (let alone to prove that the deliberate and criminal editing and censorship of the original Zapruder film actually occurred in Rochester); it simply *sounded* logical enough to the NPIC analysts who heard it.

The Lookout Mountain USAF facility in California indisputably possessed extraordinary film and still-photo processing, editing and animation capabilities; the "Hawkeye Plant" CIA photo lab in Rochester, New York reportedly had impressive technical capabilities too.

Obviously, John Kennedy's killers – members of the U. S. federal government, led by *Lyndon Baines Johnson himself* – were perfectly positioned to employ **both** facilities, as needed: Lookout Mountain to perform principal censorship, editing and revision of the camera-original Zapruder film, and "Hawkeye Plant" to perform any specialized post-production *duplication* work required.

Supersonic USAF jets including the T-38, the F-100, the F-101, the F-102, the F-104, the F-105 and the F-106 all made high-speed transcontinental transportation and delivery of small items like film reels *eminently practical* in 1963 – and given all that went wrong down in Dallas, nearly dooming LBJ's murderous plan to failure, the dicey conditions facing Kennedy's killers plainly demanded an all-out effort by all those involved in the JFK plot – including Lyndon Johnson's vitally important subordinates and confederates and accomplices in the United States Air Force.

[162] Author's exclusive original discovery.

[163] Author's exclusive original discovery.

[164] Author's exclusive original discovery.

delivered to the CIA's National Photo Interpretation Center (NPIC) in Washington on Saturday night, November 23rd, 1963.[165]

However, this desperately hurried and hastily assembled *"first* edited cut"[166] was clearly unsatisfactory.

Something wasn't good enough.

Too much damning truth remained.

Frantic late-night telephone calls obviously ensued.

---

[165] As noted in Douglas P. Horne, *Inside the ARRB,* Volume IV.

N.B.: The sheer speed of supersonic USAF military jets flying across the country from California to Washington D. C. (just 3-4 hours, *at most,* to traverse the entire continental United States!) also made the option of an "intermediate" stop up in Rochester, New York easily achievable (if such a stop were necessary or desired for special printing purposes, or other required reasons, at the CIA's special "Hawkeye Plant" photographic facility in that city).

And note this very carefully: Even advanced, top-secret U. S. government labs of the era were *not* all-powerful or all-prepared!

Even the CIA's advanced "Hawkeye Plant" facility up in Rochester, New York, did *not* possess certain enlarging capabilities, according to a federal courier who spoke to NPIC employees in Washington D. C. (Homer McMahon, cited in Douglas P. Horne, *Inside the ARRB,* Volume IV, p. 1224.)

And . . .

The CIA's advanced NPIC photo-analysis facility down in Washington D.C. did *not* even possess something as basic as an 8mm film projector (!) on Saturday night, November 23rd, 1963 – and therefore the CIA had to *acquire one in the middle of the night from a closed commercial store* just to be able to watch the *first* edited version of the Zapruder film. (See the account of NPIC employee Dino Brugioni in Douglas P. Horne, *Inside the ARRB,* Volume IV, p. 1232.)

And . . .

Moreover, the vaunted NPIC facility in Washington D.C. did *not* possess the equipment to *copy* or *reproduce* the (already-altered) Zapruder film as a motion picture. (NPIC employees Morgan "Ben" Hunter and Homer McMahon, cited in Douglas P. Horne, *Inside the ARRB,* Volume IV, p. 1224.)

So much for childish notions of James Bondian omnipotence on the part of the federal government.

The fact is that *no* single USG facility was entirely prepared to totally handle *every single aspect* of the extraordinarily rapid and drastic film censorship and alteration and recreation and duplication required in the wake of the JFK assassination plot's massive failures in Dallas. When a murder itself is **FUBAR,** everything else is rushed and imperfect and is performed under enormous time pressures and extreme stress and daunting logistical challenges – hardly a recipe for perfect work. (Author's exclusive original discovery.)

[166] Author's exclusive original discovery.

N.B.: Even this early "first cut" edited version seen on Saturday, November 23rd was *not* the true camera-original Zapruder film; I determined this exclusively and conclusively by the fact that none of the innocent and unwitting CIA analysts at NPIC on Saturday night saw or reported *any of the actual key events which actually transpired in Dealey Plaza* – events which certainly *were* present on the true authentic camera-original film taken in Dealey Plaza at 12:30 p.m. on November 22nd, 1963.

It was time for a "second draft" – right away.

A *second edited cut* of the "Zapruder" film was therefore hurriedly produced *in less than twenty-four hours*[167] at Lookout Mountain and was *also* flown east by the U. S. Air Force in a supersonic jet – ultimately arriving at NPIC in Washington on Sunday night, November 24th, 1963.[168]

A *second* innocent group of CIA photo analysts (totally unaware of the existence of the *first* group and the *first* edited draft of the film on Saturday night) then examined this *second* version of the Zapruder film on Sunday night, November 24th,[169] while President Kennedy's shattered body lay in a mahogany coffin in the Rotunda of the U. S. Capitol.

One of the CIA men who personally examined the "*second* edited version" of the Zapruder film on Sunday night, November 24th, 1963, in Washington was Morgan Bennett "Ben" Hunter – *a former USAF enlisted man who had previously been stationed at SAC headquarters in Nebraska under the command of General Thomas Power.*[170] Hunter had then joined the Central Intelligence Agency in 1962, just a year before the JFK assassination.[171]

Chillingly, at least one of the men in the tiny group of CIA analysts who examined the "*second* edited version" of the Zapruder film at NPIC on Sunday night, November 24th, 1963, was still able to detect evidence of *as many as eight (8) gunshots fired in Dealey Plaza during President Kennedy's assassination.*[172]

There simply hadn't been enough time to adequately, thoroughly, completely censor and alter and black out *all* of the damning, tell-tale information in the remaining frames – not even by Sunday night![173]

So even the "*second* edited version" clearly wouldn't suffice either; the "official" story *already being promulgated* by the Secret Service and other so-called "authorities" [*sic*] falsely asserted that "just three" [*sic*] shots had been fired in Dealey Plaza, supposedly by just one man [*sic*].

---

[167] Author's exclusive original discovery.

[168] Douglas P. Horne, *Inside the ARRB,* Volume IV, pp. 1221-1228.

[169] Douglas P. Horne, *Inside the ARRB,* Volume IV, p. 1221-1228.

[170] Douglas Horne, *Inside the ARRB,* Volume IV, p. 1222.

[171] Douglas Horne, *Inside the ARRB,* Volume IV, p. 1222.

[172] NPIC photo expert Homer McMahon made this brilliant and startling assessment on the night of Sunday, November 24th, 1963. (Douglas P. Horne, *Inside the ARRB,* Volume IV, p. 1224.) So much for the obscene official lie about "only three shots" [*sic*], which had supposedly been fired only by "Lee Harvey Oswald" [*sic*].

[173] Author's exclusive original discovery. (Remember what I pointed out earlier in this book: *time* is the key to correctly analyzing and understanding the JFK assassination. Not "money," but *time.*)

Obviously, evidence of 6 to 8 shots was totally anathema to JFK's killers.

More work had to be done, and all earlier copies of the film had to be retrieved, replaced or suppressed – immediately.

Meanwhile, blurry, poor-quality, severely censored copies would suffice to generate equally blurry still prints for the CIA-allied TIME/LIFE empire, which had "purchased" commercial rights to the Zapruder film, and would publish poor-quality still images within days of President Kennedy's murder.

* * *

On the government side of things, *only a very few frames* from the **already-altered** Zapruder film – frames carefully selected by the Secret Service, which was up to its murderous eyeballs in the JFK assassination – were used to generate photo enlargements placed on "briefing boards" that weekend to show to high-level federal officials, including CIA Director John McCone. [174]

The bowdlerized, truncated, amputated and savagely censored **extant** "Zapruder film" was subsequently used to falsely accuse (and destroy the reputation of) an innocent USMC veteran named Lee Oswald – and, ultimately, to blind the entire nation (including many well-meaning but weak-thinking JFK researchers) to the ugly reality of what had *actually* happened down in Dealey Plaza.[175]

Be very clear about something:

The **extant** "Zapruder film" *looks* awful – but it isn't *real.*

What *really* happened at 12:30 p.m. on November 22nd, 1963, was *far* more shocking and disturbing – and it lasted far **longer**.[176]

Thirty seconds longer.[177]

Thirty seconds that no one could be permitted to see.[178]

Thirty seconds literally omitted from the "final" film.

Thirty seconds that would have utterly and catastrophically destroyed a certain federal agency forever.[179]

---

[174] Douglas P. Horne, *Inside the ARRB,* Volume IV.

[175] You have *no idea* what actually occurred – but you will learn. From me. Exclusively.

[176] Author's exclusive original discovery. (I repeatedly timed the events which **were** captured in the *true* camera-original Zapruder film.)

[177] Author's exclusive original discovery. (I repeatedly timed the events which **were** captured in the *true* camera-original Zapruder film.)

[178] Author's exclusive original discovery.

[179] Author's exclusive original discovery.

Thirty seconds whose censorship was used to mock and dismiss the accuracy and reliability of the closest eyewitnesses to the actual crime in Dealey Plaza.

Thirty seconds that belong to all of us, as Americans.

Those thirty seconds of censored footage are as precious and essential and important to America as the Declaration of Independence – and the Constitution itself.

Those thirty seconds showed the full horror of Dealey Plaza – a horror quickly obscured by razor knives, and special brushes, and dyes, and special paint, and in-lab "aerial imaging," and optical printers.

The reality of what actually happened during those censored thirty seconds is *far worse* than the gory cinematic *fraud* – little more than a grisly *cartoon* – which remains, and which has been falsely bandied about as "***the*** [sic] Zapruder film."

The missing thirty seconds of the *true camera-original Zapruder film* show treason in broad daylight, and the chilling mechanics of a real-life domestic *coup*.

But those thirty seconds have never been seen publicly.[180]

Remember:

The personnel of the state-of-the-art USAF Lookout Mountain Air Force Station facility on Wonderland Avenue filmed, processed, edited and re-edited *images of top-secret national security events* for the government of the United States.

The men who worked in the 1352nd Photographic Group at LMAFS reported to their superiors in the USAF chain of command.

And in November 1963, the very *top* of that USAF chain of command was an experienced bomber pilot, veteran commander and famous four-star general named Curtis Emerson LeMay.[181]

USAF *Chief of Staff* Curtis Emerson LeMay.

The very same Curtis LeMay who later received a million-dollar trust fund in October 1968 – *for the vital services he rendered to LBJ in November 1963.*[182]

Nice work, if you can get it.

Curtis LeMay.

---

[180] Nor have those full 30 seconds ever been seen by the tiny smattering of JFK assassination researchers who claim – erroneously and ignorantly – to have been "secretly" *shown* the "real" Zapruder film [sic], or an "alternative" similar film [sic], by mysterious, always-anonymous, never-identified "sources."

The truth is that none of The Anointed Ones™ have *ever* seen, or described, or become aware of, or even *imagined,* the worst of *what the actual camera-original Zapruder film shows.*

For the record, I *do* know what it shows – and I will document those chilling events in shocking, incontrovertible detail in my second major book on the JFK assassination, which is already well underway and already scheduled for publication.

[181] Author's exclusive original discovery.

[182] Author's exclusive original discovery.

The very same Curtis LeMay who ultimately would have been buried in *Texas* – instead of Colorado! – had a certain quite diminutive but extremely dangerous and powerful man gotten his way some years earlier on a project of major importance to both the United States Air Force and the nation.

Sam Rayburn was the aging but powerful
(and decidedly lethal) Speaker of the House.

Frustrated and embittered but whip smart,
*Rayburn was the intellectual author of
the murderous plot which killed JFK.*

Author's exclusive original discovery.

Chapter Twenty-Seven:
The Baron of Bonham

*"You don't become president
without going through Sam Rayburn."*

– Lyndon Baines Johnson

*"I know how to
cause trouble if I want to . . ."*

– Samuel Taliaferro Rayburn

"Hale [Boggs] said Rayburn engineered it."

– Gerald R. Ford

"Evil stalks the hills."

– Samuel Taliaferro Rayburn

*"These things do not just 'happen.'
They are **made** to happen."*

– John Fitzgerald Kennedy

The Chief of Staff of the United States Air Force played a major role in the criminal events of November 1963 – but the JFK assassination did not begin, *or end,* with even so fearsome and formidable and ugly a character as General Curtis LeMay.

And the JFK assassination plot did ***not*** occur because of fierce intra-governmental disputes over Vietnam, or Communism in general, or nuclear war, or Cuba, or Berlin, or civil rights, or the Federal Reserve, or the CIA – nor because of President Kennedy's words, policies, actions or inaction on *any* subject.[183]

Period.

---

[183] Author's exclusive original discovery. (Anyone who believes otherwise simply hasn't done their homework; lacks sufficient analytical skill; or has *extremely limited contact with reality.* Some people, of course, plainly suffer from *all three* maladies.)

Moreover, none of the pathetically pseudo-psychological claptrap spewed by Establishment eunuchs over the past several decades in a failed attempt to invent a "motive" for the falsely accused Lee Oswald are accurate in the slightest.

And *none* of the so-called "motives" for Dallas which have been offered by independent JFK researchers over the past several decades are accurate, either.

This is in large part because those researchers (let alone the narcoleptic and lazy corporate media) do not understand the true *purpose* or the true *chronology* of the plot which ultimately took JFK's life.

By fixating on superficial "apparent" motives stemming from simplistic analysis of the many antagonists who made JFK's presidency so volatile, researchers have entirely missed *the reality of the event*.

And that starts with the true ***chronology*** of the event.

You will want to sit down before continuing:

The plot to murder President Kennedy was not initiated in 1963.

Nor in 1962.

Nor in 1961.

The reality is this:

The JFK assassination did not even begin during "Camelot" itself!

Yes, you read that correctly.

The JFK *assassination* pre-dated the JFK *administration*.

The plot actually began in 1956.[184]

The true *origins,* the true *purpose,* the true *chronology,* and the true *intellectual authors* of the 1963 assassination of President Kennedy were a mystery until 2010, when I alone exclusively discovered the answer.[185]

* * *

USAF General Curtis Emerson LeMay died in 1990 – still hating John Kennedy for what LeMay regarded as JFK's betrayal of *America,* and still furious with Lyndon Johnson for what LeMay regarded as LBJ's betrayal of *Curtis LeMay.* The Air Force general died at his California home – but he was *not* buried on the West Coast.

Instead, LeMay's body was transported several hundred miles east for interment on the grounds of the United States Air Force Academy in Colorado.

---

[184] Author's exclusive original discovery.

[185] Author's exclusive original discovery. (In typically blinkered and erroneous fashion, Lifton foolishly and stubbornly and repeatedly insisted to me that the JFK assassination plot supposedly began in **1959,** based on the absurd "reasoning" [sic] that that is when John Kennedy obtained a private campaign airplane. As usual, Lifton could not *possibly* have been more mistaken.)

Located in Colorado Springs, the academy is the Air Force equivalent of the U. S. Military Academy at West Point. Indeed, Colorado Springs ("the Springs," to locals) is so closely identified with the academy that to most people, the name of the town and the name of the institution are synonymous and completely interchangeable (much like Annapolis and the Naval Academy – or, for that matter, Washington D. C. and the White House).

But it wasn't always that way.

* * *

Most people are completely unaware that initially, there were *several* sites around the country which were vying to host the Air Force Academy.

And one of those sites was far to the *southeast* of Colorado Springs, in a place called the Lone Star State.

If a certain locale in Texas had won the competition for the Air Force Academy, then General Curtis LeMay – a major participant in the JFK assassination – would have been interred not far from the grave of *the true intellectual author of the JFK assassination.*[186]

Despite Texas's history of severe thunderstorms and violent tornadoes and even hurricanes, a particular piece of Lone Star land was actually a finalist in the competition to serve as the site of the Air Force Academy![187] Located in the northeastern portion of the state near the Oklahoma line, the proposed site (the city of Sherman, located in Grayson County) was part of the Fourth Congressional District.

Grayson County is immediately adjacent to *another* Texas county known for the presence and influence of one man, who represented the entire Fourth District for almost 50 years – a man quite short in stature, but possessing enormous power and extraordinary political influence.

The county was Fannin.

The town was Bonham.

The man was *Samuel Taliaferro Rayburn.*[188]

* * *

Born in 1882, Sam Rayburn grew up extremely poor – and he worked extremely hard as part of a farming family which had moved from Tennessee to Texas

---

[186] Author's exclusive original discovery.

[187] Anthony Champagne, *Congressman Sam Rayburn,* p. 73. (See also Anthony Champagne, *Sam Rayburn: A Bio-Bibliography,* pp. 25, 82.)

[188] Author's exclusive original discovery.

when Sam was only five years old. He eventually attended college; taught school; successfully passed the Texas state bar exam (without going to law school); and ran successfully for the Texas state legislature. There, Rayburn worked closely with *Lyndon Johnson's father.*[189]

Rayburn's personal ambitions were sky-high, and he lived long enough to achieve most of them. Those ambitions were not limited to the Lone Star State, either. "From his earliest years Mr. Rayburn dreamed of climbing to the top in national politics," wrote Congressman Carl Albert.[190]

The top is, of course, the presidency.

"He wanted to be President – or Vice President," said a later writer flatly.[191]

But a damnable, cursed force[192] coldly obstructed that ultimate dream.

Yes, Rayburn had a successful political career. In 1912 Rayburn ran for Congress and won – the first of an astonishing *twenty-five* consecutive electoral victories in the Fourth Congressional District. In Washington D. C., he ultimately became Speaker of the House, and he held that title longer than any other person in American history.

All well and good – but *not good enough* for the man known as "Mr. Sam."

In 1922, at age forty, Rayburn wrote to a relative: "I would rather link my name indelibly with the living pulsing history of my country and not be forgotten entirely after a while than to have anything else on earth."[193]

He *meant it,* too.

Sam Rayburn would go to **any lengths** to make that happen.

That damnable, cursed obstructive force be damned.

He – or his designated ally – would reach the White House.

Sam Rayburn would figure things out.

And he would indeed go to **any lengths** to make his dream happen.

Any lengths necessary.

Even blackmail.

Even criminal conspiracy.[194]

Even sedition.[195]

---

[189] LBJ made personal reference to this in a later speech. (C. Dwight Dorough, *Mr. Sam,* p. 512.)

[190] Carl Albert's foreword to Anthony Champagne, *Congressman Sam Rayburn,* p. x.

[191] Richard R. Lingeman, *The New York Times,* July 29, 1975.

[192] Keep reading.

[193] Rayburn letter of February 19th, 1922 (quoted in C. Dwight Dorough, *Mr. Sam,* p. 170).

[194] Author's exclusive original discovery.

[195] Author's exclusive original discovery.

Even assassination.[196]

* * *

Rayburn was extremely ambitious and determined – but the energetic and industrious "Baron of Bonham"[197] did not emerge politically out of whole cloth, nor did he succeed completely on his own.

Starting in 1913, Rayburn had an older, very powerful and important political mentor in Washington, D.C. – a fellow Texan who eventually went as high as any Texan could go in that era. That mentor's name was John Nance Garner – but everyone knew him as "Cactus Jack." Garner's story, and his *direct personal influence* on Rayburn, ultimately led to the assassination of *another* Jack: a politician from Massachusetts named John Fitzgerald Kennedy.[198]

* * *

If you were an ordinary person possessed of only an ordinary intellect, then you would think that an obscure former politician couldn't *possibly* have been involved in anything nefarious at the ripe old age of 91.

But you would in fact be *dead wrong.*

Like so many other participants and accomplices and enthusiastic backers of the JFK assassination, an extremely elderly politician from Texas insisted on the veracity of an event *which never happened* – and he attested to the allegedly "innocent" nature of an act which was indisputably criminal.[199]

And that is part of why the history of Cactus Jack – a man who was forced out of politics *more than twenty years before Dallas* – is actually so chillingly pertinent to a full, accurate understanding of the true story of the JFK assassination. The elderly Garner's triumphs – and his bitter failures – illuminate and identify a previously unknown and fundamental player in the case, and they shed stark and direct light on the *true* cause of the murderous volley of gunfire which killed President Kennedy in Dallas, Texas in 1963.

* * *

---

[196] Author's exclusive original discovery.

[197] The author's own original term for Rayburn.

[198] Author's exclusive original discovery. No other historian or journalist has *ever* correctly linked Cactus Jack to the JFK assassination.

[199] Author's exclusive original discovery.

John Nance Garner – a Texas congressman, then Speaker of the House of Representatives, and finally Vice President of the United States – was known to all as "Cactus Jack." It was a colorful, perfect nickname for a man who could indeed at times be as prickly as the desert plant itself. Yet the euphonious moniker actually derived not from Garner's personality, but rather from his failed early effort (in 1901) to persuade Texans to adopt the *cactus* as their state *flower*.

The *cactus*.

Yes, cacti have blooms, and some are indeed quite lovely – but from the start, the idea was doomed to ridicule.

On that particular issue, Cactus Jack was (there is no other way to say it) as dumb as a fence post. Texans rejected his sincere but peculiar proposition and overwhelmingly voted to designate their beloved *bluebonnet* as the official state flower instead.[200]

It was not a difficult decision. Nor was the decision even close.

The bluebonnet had the distinct advantage of actually *being* a flower, and of being a very *attractive* flower as well.

A cactus is – well, a cactus. It does sport flowers, which are sometimes quite lovely, but it also has *spines*. It is, at best, the porcupine of plants. So in this case, Garner was a fool.

But although he was obviously neither a brilliant botanist nor a horticultural hero, Garner was otherwise a very skilled politician – and he got himself elected to the U. S. Congress. Racist, greedy, and parsimonious to a fault, but gregarious and likable to many white political colleagues with whom he drank and played poker,[201] Cactus Jack soon rose to the rarefied height of Speaker of the House.

---

[200] Although bluebonnets actually come in several distinct varieties (thus complicating the issue somewhat), the blue flower – in all its incarnations – beats many cacti by a country mile. Or two. Or three.

[201] Garner, a native of *northeastern* Texas, ruthlessly exploited and threatened poor Mexican and Mexican-American laborers on his vast 23,000-acre property located in the *southwestern* Texas town of Uvalde. (Alfred Steinberg, *Sam Rayburn,* pp. 85, 149.) The tight-fisted and wealthy Cactus Jack owned orchards, ranches, farms and the world's biggest herd of goats. Garner also – rather chillingly – was a major investor in a company which manufactured **coffins.** (James Riddlesperger Jr. and Anthony Champagne, *Lone Star Leaders,* p. 26.)

In May 2022, Uvalde was the site of a vicious, horrifying, brutal and grotesque massacre in which a heavily armed 18-year-old gunman deliberately slaughtered 19 young children and two adult teachers (and wounded many other victims) inside a local elementary school while police authorities outside failed to intervene for more than an hour. The wanton mass murder of helpless innocents – and the cowardly, despicable, inhuman refusal of numerous well-armed authorities to promptly storm the classrooms and neutralize the gunman – stunned, devastated, traumatized and outraged the entire nation.

And on Capitol Hill, John Nance Garner was a longtime mentor to a younger congressman and fellow Texan named Sam Rayburn. As a Capitol Hill colleague correctly observed, Garner actually "*taught* politics to Sam Rayburn."[202]

Cactus Jack and the Baron of Bonham worked very closely together for years. Their Texas pride, their mentor-protégé political relationship – and *the repeated frustration of their national political ambitions* – planted the seeds which culminated decades later in the murder of a president.[203]

*   *   *

Garner substantially toughened Rayburn both by personal example and through bullying and abusive behavior.[204] "Sam, you've got to get your knuckles bloody once in a while," said Cactus Jack sternly to his protégé.[205]

You've got to get your knuckles bloody.

Even more importantly, he introduced Congressman Rayburn to the challenges and intricacies of *running for a spot on a national ticket* by making Sam his campaign manager in 1931 as he (Speaker of the House Garner) sought to win the Democratic Party's presidential nomination in the upcoming presidential race of 1932.

Rayburn was a loyal lieutenant.

Garner also placed Rayburn close to the pinnacle of ultimate power by making Sam his campaign manager *again* in late 1939 for another doomed bid for the top spot on the 1940 Democratic ticket, as well.

Cactus Jack himself – through his victories, and through his even greater *defeats* – taught Sam Rayburn some very valuable but extremely hard lessons which Rayburn absorbed and eventually applied *directly* to the JFK assassination.[206]

*   *   *

Those lessons began *decades* before Dallas.

In 1932, for example, it turned out that even the solid backing of the infamous (and fabulously wealthy) media tycoon William Randolph Hearst – whose gargantuan

---

[202] Cong. Martin Dies, interviewed in 1966 – quoted in Anthony Champagne's book, *Congressman Sam Rayburn,* p. 216.

[203] Author's exclusive original discovery.

[204] Congressman Martin Dies described Garner's abusive verbal treatment of Rayburn in a 1966 interview. (Anthony Champagne, *Congressman Sam Rayburn,* p. 216.)

[205] C. Dwight Dorough, *MR. SAM,* pp. 284-285; Alfred Steinberg, *Sam Rayburn,* p. 93.

[206] Author's exclusive original discovery.

piles of cash, and endless barrels of ink, constituted truly stellar resources for *any* would-be national candidate – could not secure the Democratic presidential nomination for a Texan.[207]

It was a sobering – and understandably embittering – experience.

After all, Hearst owned a supremely powerful media empire – yet he proved unable to achieve the (presumably) relatively simple task of putting a *Texan* into the top spot of a major American political party's ticket.

As it turned out, said task wasn't easy or simple at all.

Even William Randolph Hearst – *Hearst himself!* – couldn't make it happen.

And if a man of Hearst's massive wealth and unbridled power couldn't do it, then who else possibly could?

And *how?*

The answer came in a burst of shots fired in public at an open car in an outdoor park located in a southern American city.

That was the key:

A burst of shots fired in public at an open car in an outdoor park located in a southern American city.[208]

* * *

At the 1932 party convention, Cactus Jack settled for second place on the Democratic ticket as the running mate of northern liberal Franklin Delano Roosevelt (FDR). The two were duly elected that November, and were slated to take office on March 4th, 1933.

Meanwhile, on January 23rd, 1933, the 20th Amendment to the U. S. Constitution was adopted. The portion of the amendment which took effect in October 1933 changed all *future* presidential inauguration dates to January 20th.

But the portion of the 20th Amendment which took effect *immediately, in January 1933,* dictated that in the event the president-elect died prior to inauguration day, *the vice president would take office as president.*

This very nearly occurred before the ink had even dried on the document!

Just weeks prior to inauguration, on February 15th, 1933, FDR went fishing on a boat off the coast of Florida. Upon returning to shore, he rode in an open car to a Miami site called Bayfront Park. There, as Roosevelt sat in his stationary automobile, a diminutive man named Giuseppe Zangara stepped up onto a chair and began firing a pistol toward the president-elect.

FDR wasn't hit, but Chicago Mayor Anton Cermak was mortally wounded.

---

[207] Alfred Steinberg, *Sam Rayburn,* p. 96.

[208] Author's exclusive original discovery.

Has Franklin Roosevelt been killed on that February day by Zangara's bullets, then John Nance Garner – yes, *Cactus Jack himself* – would have been sworn in as president of the United States on March 4ᵗʰ, 1933.

A Texan – *a genuine Texan* – would have become the nation's chief executive.

Cactus Jack would have governed from the Oval Office.

Just like that!

It was enough to make a man (and his loyal lieutenant) think long and hard.

A burst of shots fired in public at an open car in an outdoor park located in a southern American city.

In 1933, it *almost* made a Texan the president of the United States.

In 1963, it ***did.***

* * *

Cactus Jack was Franklin Delano Roosevelt's Democratic running mate in both 1932 and 1936. But especially during FDR's second term in office, the far more conservative Garner came to despise major elements of the ambitious and aggressive New Deal program, and as vice president he fell into open and increasing conflict with the much more liberal president from New York.

As 1940 approached, few observers believed at first that Franklin Roosevelt would seek an unprecedented third term as president. Long American tradition weighed against it. Indeed, the "two-terms-maximum" tradition was so strong that, on the quite natural assumption that FDR wouldn't *dare* violate it, in 1939 Cactus Jack of Texas readied his *own* run for the 1940 Democratic presidential nomination – and he again named his loyal political lieutenant, Congressman Sam Rayburn, to run it.

But FDR cleverly avoided the perception of unwarranted greed and overweening, unseemly personal ambition by piously and falsely declaring that while he longed to conclude his eight-year presidency and retire to New York – and therefore would not *actively seek* the nomination for a third time – he would nevertheless graciously and generously *accept* a "draft" for an unprecedented third term *if* the delegates at the 1940 Democratic Convention, in their infinite wisdom, enthusiastically "insisted" that he do so. This cunning (albeit transparently calculating) declaration essentially wiped out all other candidacies, including John Nance Garner's.

So once again, a Texan's pursuit of the Democratic presidential nomination was quickly reduced to so much sand – by *a northern liberal politician and his biased northern supporters.*

The bastards.

Yankee bastards . . .

Moreover, Cactus Jack's obstreperous opposition to FDR's policies beginning in 1937 had clearly doomed any possibility of Garner being chosen yet again for the

VP spot on the 1940 ticket. Roosevelt had had enough of the ornery Texan's frequently reiterated criticisms and objections.

In short, Cactus Jack was now *out.*

Sam Rayburn, however – theoretically – still had a chance.

Even as the Democratic convention opened on July 15th, 1940, FDR still brazenly (and falsely) claimed no desire for a third term as president. In addition, that very day he released to the media a list of Democratic *presidential* nominees supposedly acceptable to him, and Sam Rayburn's name was first on the list.[209] But two days later, when the time came for delegates to actually *vote,* the supposedly "reluctant" Roosevelt won his party's re-nomination overwhelmingly, on the very first ballot of the convention.

Thus Garner would certainly not be elected president in 1940 – and *neither would the Baron of Bonham.*

Texas had been shafted.

But a glimmer of hope still survived.

Rayburn was described by FDR aide Jim Farley as "a red-hot candidate for *Vice* President" on that year's Democratic ticket.[210] Rayburn made efforts to generate support for his last-minute VP candidacy at the 1940 convention, but he failed. (Politically, Rayburn had hurt himself badly with FDR by initially supporting Cactus Jack for President that year.)

So in 1940, the devious FDR *refused* to run with either Cactus Jack *or* Garner's political protégé, Sam Rayburn[211] – choosing instead to face the electorate (and win resoundingly) with running mate Henry Wallace, a progressive Northern bureaucrat then serving as the Secretary of Agriculture.

Yankee bastards . . .

In a final humiliating twist of the political knife, northerner Roosevelt phoned southerner Rayburn personally at the Democratic convention and asked him to make a public speech seconding Wallace's nomination.[212]

Texans had been shafted yet again.

Garner, his political career now utterly finished, retreated to his vast property in the town of Uvalde, Texas, where he lived quietly for another quarter century until finally dying in 1967 at the age of 98.

---

[209] Alfred Steinberg, *Sam Rayburn,* p. 162.

[210] Alfred Steinberg, *Sam Rayburn,* p. 162.

[211] Rayburn bitterly complained later, with legitimate justification, "*I* might have been president if [Franklin] Roosevelt hadn't wanted to stay in the White House forever." (Anthony Champagne, *Congressman Sam Rayburn,* p. 142.)

[212] Rayburn, crushed and weak, obediently did so. (Alfred Steinberg, *Sam Rayburn,* p. 163.)

Vice President John Nance Garner – known as "Cactus Jack" – urgently told Sam Rayburn, "You've got to get your knuckles bloody."

Frustrated and embittered, Rayburn took that sinister advice to heart decades later and successfully plotted the murder of JFK.

Author's exclusive original discovery.

John Nance "Cactus Jack" Garner faded into the abyss of obscurity after his long fall from the precipitous political heights. Had he remained overtly loyal to the Roosevelt program, Garner might have been retained as vice president long enough to have become president upon FDR's sudden death in April 1945. But Cactus Jack made the politically fatal mistake of decrying Roosevelt's policies far too openly, far too repeatedly and far too *early,* while FDR was still alive and still more than healthy enough to retaliate by *picking another running mate* – and thus Garner, the prickly Texan, would never occupy the Oval Office.

Cactus Jack had been *just a heartbeat away from the presidency* – but his big mouth and his unbridled, indiscreet conservatism had irremediably and permanently spoiled his chances to reach the White House.

After 1940, Garner lived an astoundingly long time – but his name receded dramatically from public consciousness. He was remembered, if and when he was remembered at all, mostly for his contemptuous statement that the vice presidency was "not worth a quart of warm piss" – a phrase which was routinely restated and altered by later writers to "a pitcher [or 'bucket'] of warm spit" in order to avoid offending prudish readers.[213]

Thus even Garner's greatest claim to fame – the earthy, blunt aphorism which is forever associated with his name – was shamefully bowdlerized. It was a sad spectacle, from a Texas viewpoint.

But Cactus Jack did not disappear *completely* from history, nor was he absent from the JFK assassination plot.[214] Even in obscurity and advanced old age, he had one more task he could perform in service to his longtime protégé Rayburn – and to his beloved Texas.[215]

Cactus Jack provided a fictitious "alibi" of sorts – a very clumsy, false alibi – to the two sinister Texans who personally created and headed the nascent JFK assassination plot.[216]

If that powerful duo's ugly criminal machinations of 1960 had become known, then the entire JFK case could have been promptly blown wide open – with devastating

---

[213] Variants of the blunt *original* phrase from 1932 appeared over the years. Patrick Cox tracked the development and transformation of Cactus Jack's actual words in a useful article entitled "John Nance Garner on the Vice Presidency — In Search of the Proverbial Bucket," available online.

[214] Author's exclusive original discovery.

[215] Author's exclusive original discovery.

[216] Author's exclusive original discovery.

consequences. Old John Nance Garner, still feisty and calculating even in his dotage, helped head off that disturbing possibility at the proverbial pass with a lie.[217]

It was a very thin lie – laughably thin, transparently false.

Pathetic.

Embarrassing, really.

But in the world of political assassination, *every little lie helps the guilty.*[218] And in America, the patent unreality of official accounts is clearly not seen as a hindrance by those who perpetrate those crimes – nor by their odious, loathsome friends and accomplices.[219]

* * *

Sam Rayburn and *his* political protégé, Lyndon Johnson, both benefited directly from Garner's preposterous lie about events in 1960.

Rayburn also benefited from the fawning, obsequious, adulatory paeans which were peddled by his own political allies, aides, friends and office staff for several decades *before* – and several years *after* – his own 1961 death.

What emerges from their plentiful platitudinous prattle about Rayburn is a cartoon figure: a glorified little country bumpkin with a heart of gold; a selfless, bipartisan, diminutive patriot; a wise everyman always ready with a folksy, corny expression for every occasion.

Mr. Magoo in a suit, as it were.

But the reality is very different.

The truth about Sam Rayburn is only found through exhaustive and critical *reading* (burrowing through hefty hagiographic homages and finding revealing disclosures tucked away in seldom-consulted endnotes and other very dark corners) – plus exceptional (and fearless) critical *analysis.*

Anything less is grossly insufficient.

"I am not certain that *anyone* ever fully understood him," opined Congressman Carl Albert, who knew Rayburn for decades.[220]

But I did.

---

[217] Author's exclusive original discovery.

[218] Author's exclusive original discovery.

[219] Nor by gutless corporate media hacks masquerading as "journalists" [*sic*]. Nor by the pathetic, evasive, gutless wimps who masquerade as "historians" [*sic*].

[220] Carl Albert's foreword to Anthony Champagne, *Congressman Sam Rayburn,* p. x.

None of Rayburn's many hagiographers and aides and friends and admirers (let alone any conventional "professors" or "reporters") ever uncovered the most important story of his long life.[221]

But I did.

It appears in this book, exclusively, for the very first time *anywhere*.[222]

* * *

Sam Rayburn, the ambitious Baron of Bonham, wanted desperately to be remembered – to link his name indelibly with the history of his country.

He succeeded.

But from now on, thanks to my exclusive original findings, Samuel Taliaferro Rayburn will be remembered chiefly – and correctly – for his conscious and knowing and deliberate participation in criminal conspiracy, blackmail, sedition, and murder.[223]

For *in mid-August 1956,*[224] Samuel Taliaferro Rayburn personally came up with the insidiously brilliant plan to slaughter the next Democratic president of the United States, and to thereby finally make a "real" Texan president.[225]

And in the early morning hours of July 14th, 1960, **under cover of night,** Samuel Taliaferro Rayburn – a scheming man who was always "alert to his opponent's weaknesses"[226] – knowingly and deliberately and personally committed the dark felony which *officially* launched the violent and successful assassination plot against John Fitzgerald Kennedy.[227]

* * *

Rayburn did it with information gleaned from his own intimate knowledge of Capitol Hill; from his protégé Lyndon Johnson's own intimate knowledge of Capitol Hill; and from items supplied through the eager cooperation of FBI Director J. Edgar

---

[221] "I felt somehow that he had not told the whole story," admitted Rayburn biographer C. Dwight Dorough.

[222] Author's exclusive original discovery.

[223] Author's exclusive original discovery.

[224] Author's exclusive original discovery.

[225] Author's exclusive original discovery.

[226] C. Dwight Dorough, *Mr. Sam,* p. 307.

[227] Author's exclusive original discovery.

Hoover, whose source of power over several decades was a nearly limitless supply of blackmail material known as his "Official and Confidential" files.[228]

Thanks to his deep venality, Hoover gets most people's attention – but Rayburn and Johnson were hardly amateurs themselves when it came to acquiring and using useful data. The two Texans possessed "the two best intelligence systems that have ever been devised by the human mind," in the awestruck words of Congressman Fred Ikard, a Rayburn ally.[229]

But damaging information and blackmail were only the *initial* tools needed in the covert operation to seize the White House for a Texan.

From the beginning, it all ultimately came down to *premeditated murder.*

Bloody assassination.

Because as Sam Rayburn himself understood very well, *sudden death* was always the key to political ascendancy in America.[230]

* * *

John Nance "Cactus Jack" Garner's successor as Speaker of the House, Henry Thomas Rainey, died suddenly of a heart attack in August 1934.

Rainey was succeeded by new Speaker Joseph Wellington Byrns, Sr.

Speaker Byrns in turn *also* died – also of a heart attack – in June 1936.

He was succeeded by new Speaker William B. Bankhead.

During this string of fatalities – and *because of* those fatalities – Sam Rayburn moved up in the House, becoming Majority Leader.

And then it happened *yet again.*

Sam Rayburn finally became Speaker of the House after the abrupt, unexpected death in mid-September 1940 of then-Speaker William Bankhead – from a devastating abdominal hemorrhage.

The Baron of Bonham had benefited handsomely – *again* – from *the sudden demise of a higher-ranking official.*[231]

---

[228] Rayburn once said that he survived his tenure in the Texas state legislature "by God, by desperation and by ignorance." (Alfred Steinberg, *Sam Rayburn,* p. 23.) But by 1960, the cunning killer had long eschewed such amateur carelessness. When he went to Los Angeles to blackmail JFK at the Democratic National Convention, Sam Rayburn was clearly *very* well-armed – and he was loaded with *knowledge,* not ignorance.

[229] Quoted in Anthony Champagne, *Congressman Sam Rayburn,* p. 155.

[230] Author's exclusive original discovery.

[231] Author's exclusive original discovery.

Rayburn relished the top role and wielded substantial power as Speaker of the House, but he still wished to reach the ultimate pinnacle of American power – so in 1944 he tried once again to obtain a spot on the national Democratic ticket.

He came tantalizingly close.

But when push came to shove, Rayburn refused to gamble everything.

He *declined* to absent himself from the very tight race down in his own Fourth Congressional District in Texas in order to actively fight for the VP slot at the 1944 Democratic National Convention up in Chicago. Rayburn simply couldn't bear to risk the threatening possibility of losing his House seat – and with it, his cherished Speaker's gavel.

An obscure senator from Missouri named Harry Truman got the VP nod instead; was elected Vice President in November 1944; and then became president himself just five months later when FDR died suddenly in April 1945.

Another elevation to high office via sudden death.

Had Rayburn fought successfully for the number-two spot on the 1944 Democratic ticket, then *he* – not Truman – would have become president upon Franklin Roosevelt's death.

The lesson was harsh and unforgiving:

*Rayburn had **not** been willing to play for keeps.*

He had lost his nerve just when he was on the verge of winning it all.

It was an astounding and depressing turn of events.

To add insult to injury, Democrats then lost control of the House of Representatives in the 1946 congressional elections, so therefore Rayburn lost the Speakership *anyway* for the next two years (1947-1949) – and thereby fell completely out of the then-current presidential line of succession, as well.

He settled very reluctantly for being Minority Leader during that time.

Rayburn's admirers then did something which ultimately revealed the *true* cause of the JFK assassination[232] – a foul crime which was still years in the future.

* * *

In 1947, House Democrats pooled substantial amounts of cash to purchase a large new Cadillac limousine for Sam Rayburn as a consolation prize. They also arranged for a special engraved plaque to be affixed inside the vehicle: a plaque which read, "To Our Beloved Sam Rayburn – Who would have been President if he had come from any place but the South."[233]

The phrase was a political epitaph.

---

[232] Author's exclusive original discovery.

[233] Alfred Steinberg, *Sam Rayburn,* p. 236.

If he had come from any place but the South . . .

Rayburn loved the car, but the plaque was so painfully true that it had to hurt.

If he had come from any place but the South . . .

The curse of being a Texan.

If he had come from any place but the South . . .

The damnable power of northern bosses, northern politicians, northern hacks.

If he had come from any place but the South . . .

Yankee bastards.

If he had come from any place but the South . . .

Rayburn would continue to try for higher office again and again, but his patience was not inexhaustible – and his anger was building internally.

If he had come from any place but the South . . .

Sam Rayburn was denied his ultimate prize because he represented Texas.

The injustice of it infuriated him and galvanized his energies. Rayburn was determined to place *a Texan* in the White House, come hell or high water. The Baron of Bonham was already 65 years old in 1947 – but either he would somehow achieve that singular and elusive and daunting goal of putting a Texan into the Oval Office, or he would die trying.[234]

Or, as it happened, *both.*

* * *

After earlier failures (in 1932, 1940 and 1944) to obtain a coveted spot on the Democrats' national ticket, Sam Rayburn decided to play it coy and attempt a bit of "reverse psychology."[235] In the autumn of 1947, he proclaimed loudly that he was definitely *not* a candidate for the vice presidency the following year.[236]

At the Democratic national convention in July 1948, a cagey politico named Les Biffle stunned both Truman *and* Rayburn by quietly assembling enough delegate votes to make seventy-year-old Senator Alben W. Barkley of Kentucky the VP nominee. The sudden, subtle *fait accompli* was another embarrassing political fiasco for the Baron of Bonham.

The tiny titan of Texas had been hornswoggled *yet again.*

* * *

---

[234] Author's exclusive original discovery.

[235] Author's exclusive original discovery.

[236] C. Dwight Dorough, *Mr. Sam,* p. 398.

President Truman's famous 1948 whistle-stop campaign included a late-September stop in northeast Texas, and a visit to Sam Rayburn's home in Bonham. The Secret Service agent in charge of the White House Detail on that day was an individual named *James Rowley.*

The very same Jim Rowley would become chief of the SS during the final months of Rayburn's life in 1961 – and Rowley would still hold that post on the very day of John Kennedy's bloody assassination, two years after that.

Rowley was not the only key 1963 figure whom Sam Rayburn had known long before creating and initiating the JFK assassination plot. Another Rayburn associate was U. S. Army officer Lucius D. Clay, who supervised construction of a major construction project in Rayburn's district (the Denison Dam) beginning in 1937. A decade later, now-General Clay became military governor of Germany; while in that post he initiated the Berlin Airlift, which was largely run by a certain USAF general named Curtis Emerson LeMay.

These extraordinary connections would serve Sam Rayburn and Lyndon Johnson extremely well as the two Texans' murderous 1956 plot to seize the presidency came to full fruition during the era that later came to be called Camelot.[237]

* * *

Meanwhile, in order to keep Lyndon Johnson in the Senate – and in order to keep Lyndon Johnson *out of jail* – Rayburn and LBJ had to work together in another, much *earlier* criminal conspiracy to obliterate a serious threat to Johnson's freedom, reputation and political future.

And conspire they did – successfully.

In the 1950s, Rayburn and Johnson teamed up and *personally* engaged in *a successful, multi-year conspiracy* to benefit LBJ and preserve his political viability.

The plot first began in the spring of 1950, when Collector of Internal Revenue Frank L. Scofield – whose professional domain included Austin and Houston – was probing fraudulent donations to Lyndon Johnson's political campaigns. Cunning and devious as always, Rayburn and Johnson identified the critical figure (Scofield), then jointly maneuvered and bullied and pressured the man into *doing something he didn't want to do.*

Together, Rayburn and Johnson personally called Scofield on the telephone and demanded that he and his IRS office employees purchase tickets to a May 1950 Democratic political dinner.

---

[237] Author's exclusive original discovery.

Then the two Texas criminals waited patiently to spring their trap.[238]

In January 1953, Rayburn and Johnson successfully used the "dinner tickets" issue against Scofield (as an alleged violation of the Hatch Act, which *they themselves had initiated and pressured him into!*) in order to oust him from office and thereby destroy the investigation of LBJ.[239]

Scofield soon resigned; his compliant successor moved protected files that were deeply incriminating to LBJ to a vulnerable warehouse where they suddenly and mysteriously burned, *in toto,* in June 1953; and the problem was thus "solved."

It didn't matter that Frank Scofield was *fully acquitted of all charges* a year later in June 1954; the damage had already been done.

The honest investigator was out; the key incriminating evidence was totally destroyed; LBJ was in the clear.

A successful, multi-year criminal conspiracy.

Rayburn and Johnson had done it once.

Years later, they would do it again.[240]

* * *

The two Texans' inspiration for killing John Fitzgerald Kennedy was simple outrage – not at JFK *personally*, but at American presidential politics overall.

Sam Rayburn and Lyndon Johnson had ample reason to bitterly resent their own ostensibly "un-electable" status as white Southern politicians – and particularly, as white Southern politicians *from Texas.*

They were certainly not helped inside Washington itself by what was widely perceived as already excessive Texas dominance of most senior *congressional* committee posts.

But it was their repeated rejection on the *national* political stage that most frustrated, wounded and angered Rayburn and Johnson. The list of Texas figures' failures in the national arena was long, ugly and painful:

1. John Nance Garner, Rayburn's mentor, first saw his own presidential ambitions frustrated in 1932. Congressman Rayburn had personally managed "Cactus Jack" Garner's campaign for the top spot on the Democratic ticket that year, but both Texans bowed to the inevitable northern push for FDR. They agreed to release Garner's

---

[238] Joseph Rauh once accurately described Rayburn and Johnson as employing "'cloakroom-and-dagger' tactics." (Quoted in J. Evetts Haley, *A Texan Looks at Lyndon,* p. 192.)

[239] The ugly plot against Scofield is described in vivid detail in the J. Evetts Haley book called *A Texan Looks at Lyndon,* pp. 89-93.

[240] Author's exclusive original discovery.

support to Roosevelt, and Garner consented to taking the second spot on the ticket. It was not a happy political marriage, particularly during FDR's second term.

2. Garner sought the top spot on the Democratic ticket in the 1940 presidential campaign as well, believing that FDR would not (and should not) run, but Roosevelt cleverly permitted himself to be "drafted" by the party for an unprecedented third term, swamping Garner's presidential bid. Worse, Garner's strong and open opposition to key aspects of FDR's second-term program led to his replacement on the national Democratic ticket.

3. Rayburn himself lost out as a possible VP nominee in 1940 to northern progressive politician Henry Wallace.

4. Rayburn came within a hair's breadth of the presidency himself when he narrowly lost the 1944 VP nomination to Harry Truman. However, hampered and seriously distracted by a frighteningly close electoral campaign to preserve his own House seat down in his own Texas congressional district, Rayburn failed to attend the Democratic convention in Chicago that year – thus sealing his national fate. It was the closest Rayburn ever came to taking the White House. Everyone knew that the clearly ailing FDR would not survive his entire fourth term, and indeed Vice President Truman ascended to the Oval Office upon Roosevelt's death, *less than six months after the election,* in April 1945. To add insult to injury, Truman was literally *in Rayburn's physical presence at the Capitol itself* when he was summoned telephonically to the White House to take the oath of office.

5. Political operative Les Biffle surprised Rayburn and Truman in 1948 by quietly lining up support for Alben Barkley of Kentucky as the VP candidate.

6. In early 1952 a small "boomlet" in support of a Rayburn bid for the Democratic presidential nomination occurred as President Truman declined to run again – but it ended before gaining any significant strength. Rayburn did himself no favors by again playing the role of humble, reluctant candidate; in January of that year he turned 70, and he claimed to be "one man in public life who does not aspire to be president."[241] By springtime 1952 Rayburn was more candid, admitting in writing that he would indeed accept a draft by the Democratic National Convention[242] – but Illinois governor Adlai Stevenson, a northern liberal, ultimately came away with the party's nomination instead. Stevenson's choice for running mate was Alabama Senator John Sparkman; that dubious duo was crushed in November by former general Dwight Eisenhower and former human Richard Nixon.

7. At the 1956 Democratic convention, Rayburn actually offered himself as a vice presidential candidate – sending emissary Hale Boggs (a Rayburn congressional protégé and later a member of the "Warren" Commission) to make the pitch to nominee

[241] C. Dwight Dorough, *Mr. Sam,* p. 438.

[242] C. Dwight Dorough, *Mr. Sam,* p. 440.

Adlai Stevenson. But the Democratic standard-bearer rejected Rayburn's offer, threw open the VP nomination decision to a convention-wide vote, and ended up with running mate Estes Kefauver of Tennessee (who narrowly prevailed over Senator John Kennedy of Massachusetts).

8. Lyndon Johnson's own doomed effort to seek the 1956 presidential nomination was a dismal and humiliating failure, garnering just 90 first-ballot votes at the convention to Adlai Stevenson's overwhelming 900 first-ballot votes.

9. Johnson's pursuit of the *vice-presidential* nomination at the very same 1956 convention likewise failed; Johnson then transferred his support to JFK, hoping to derail the attractive Massachusetts senator's political future by getting him onto the losing Stevenson ticket. Instead, in a remarkable bit of political jujitsu, Kennedy turned his own losing but graceful fight for the VP nomination into a platform for national media exposure and political goodwill.

Thus by the time the 1956 Democratic convention concluded, Texans as a whole had been rejected *nine times* in the previous quarter-century; moreover, Rayburn and Johnson *themselves* had been *personally* rejected for high-level spots on their party's ticket a total of *seven times*. Even when Sam Rayburn had gamely offered himself to Adlai Stevenson as a widely acceptable "compromise" VP candidate in 1956, he was turned down.

Texas had been shafted again.

It was infuriating.

Texas Democrats were wrongly shut out of national office.

It was absolutely intolerable.

Rayburn and Johnson had actively campaigned for national roles; had promoted themselves; had offered themselves, both openly and secretly; and yet *neither* of the two Texas legislative titans had achieved *any access whatsoever* to spots on national Democratic tickets.

None at all.

"I *hate* to take a licking," Rayburn said on numerous occasions.[243]

He meant it – and the endless rejection, *by his own party,* was consuming him.

For Rayburn, even being the Chairman of the Democratic National Convention three times – in 1948, 1952 and 1956[244] – had been of no help.

He and LBJ got nowhere.

They had been stymied, stiffed and rejected – again and again and again.

And time was running out.

In late 1956 Sam Rayburn was 74 years old, and was going blind.

---

[243] C. Dwight Dorough, *Mr. Sam,* p. 496.

[244] C. Dwight Dorough, *Mr. Sam,* p. 493.

In late 1956 Lyndon Johnson was 48 years old, and was recovering from a pair of massive heart attacks the previous year.[245]

It was now clear that as far as White House ambitions were concerned, at best the aging Rayburn would have to live vicariously through his ambitious protégé, Lyndon Baines Johnson.

Of the two of them, only LBJ now had any realistic prospects of a potential future top-level role in government – but multiple serious obstacles still loomed.

Johnson was still a *white southern politician* in an era of ongoing and dramatically increasing racial strife and tension in America. Despite his unchallenged mastery of the Senate itself, he lacked any genuine *national* political base. Moreover, a presidential victory by the GOP in 1960 – or a presidential term won and filled by *another* Democrat in 1960, like JFK – would promptly put any potential Johnsonian White House aspirations on the back burner.

The White House would then be utterly out of reach until *at least* 1964 and quite likely until the 1968 election, when LBJ would be 60 years old.

Men in Johnson's family had a history of dying relatively young, a fact of which Johnson was already keenly aware. An actuarial study later commissioned by LBJ revealed that his own expected lifespan would only be 64 years.[246] Thus if Johnson were unsuccessful in gaining the Oval Office until January 1969 (following JFK's presumptive two terms in office and the 1968 election), it was a near-certainty that LBJ would *die in office – during his first term.*[247]

Actuarial statistics (the original application of "big data") rarely lie.

And *one-term presidents* rarely have the time or opportunity to achieve great deeds and receive acclaim along the lines of FDR, whose domestic achievements Lyndon Johnson both idolized and wished to outperform.

The bottom line was this:

In order to have a lengthy, meaningful and complete presidency, Lyndon Baines Johnson would have to commence that presidency *much sooner than* January 20th, 1969.

And as LBJ himself knew and acknowledged, *"You don't become president without going through Sam Rayburn."*

That was no mere flattery, either.

---

[245] Most "historians" [*sic*] erroneously claim that Lyndon Johnson suffered "a" heart attack in 1955. The reality is that he actually suffered *two* (2) serious coronary events – one in June, then another two weeks later in July. (Alfred Steinberg, *Sam Rayburn,* p. 298.)

[246] Jack Valenti noted this in his book *A Very Human President.*

[247] Author's exclusive original discovery.

Rayburn was intimately acquainted with the route.[248]

* * *

As I dug into the evidence and exclusively uncovered the true story, I realized an important fact: *Sam Rayburn's entire political career* was based on, and aided enormously by, *the sudden deaths of higher-ranking individuals.*[249]

That series of astonishingly fortuitous deaths literally paved the way for the success which Rayburn himself enjoyed in the U. S. House of Representatives – and moreover, those deaths made several other men President.[250]

The morbid but undeniable lesson was not lost on the Baron of Bonham.

In the House of Representatives, various deaths led directly to opportunities for Congressman Rayburn to become House Majority Leader and then House Speaker.

And staring down Pennsylvania Avenue toward the White House, Rayburn saw a separate series of deaths elevate three men to the Oval Office instantaneously.

The assassination of William McKinley in 1901 made Vice President Theodore Roosevelt the president.

The sudden death of Warren Harding in 1923 made Vice President Calvin Coolidge the president.

The sudden death of Franklin Roosevelt in 1945 made Vice President Harry Truman the president. Sam Rayburn *personally* attended Truman's swearing-in at the White House that evening, less than three hours after FDR died.[251]

Moreover, the attempted assassination of Harry Truman by Zionist Jewish terrorists via letter-bombs in 1947 [252] – and the failed effort by two Puerto Rican nationalist gunmen to shoot Truman to death at Blair House in 1950 – would have elevated men *other than Rayburn* to the Oval Office.

---

[248] Author's exclusive original discovery.

[249] Author's exclusive original discovery.

[250] Author's exclusive original discovery.

[251] C. Dwight Dorough, *Mr. Sam,* p. 365.

[252] A White House staffer named Ira Robert Taylor Smith first disclosed the murderous 1947 Jewish terrorist attempt against President Truman's life in the book *Dear Mr. President ... The Story of Fifty Years in the White House Mail Room.* None other than the former head of the United States Secret Service, Urbanus Edmund Baughman, then corroborated and confirmed that Zionist assassination plot in his own 1962 book, *Secret Service Chief.* President Truman's daughter, Margaret, further confirmed it in a 1973 volume called *Harry S. Truman.*

Moreover, a separate Puerto Rican nationalist shooting attack against the House of Representatives in 1954 could have drastically altered the membership of the small group who were legally and constitutionally in the presidential line of succession.

* * *

The truth was staggering in both its scale and in its remorseless nature:

An entire bloody tapestry of murder, mayhem and sudden death charted the course of American history beginning at the very dawn of the 20th century – *Rayburn's* century. The Baron of Bonham had a front-row seat to many of the most stunning political developments that ever occurred in the USA.

The scorecard was a lengthy litany of death.

There were three (3) three elevations of a Majority Leader to Speaker of the House via the death of the incumbent during Sam Rayburn's lifetime prior to 1956:
- The elevation of Joseph Byrns following the death of Henry Rainey;
- The elevation of William Bankhead following the death of Joseph Byrns;
- The elevation of Rayburn himself following the death of William Bankhead.

There were six (6) major attempts on a president, president-elect or presidential candidate during Sam Rayburn's lifetime prior to 1956:
- The assassination of President McKinley in 1901;
- The attempted assassination of Theodore Roosevelt in 1912;
- The shooting attempt on FDR in 1933 (which killed Anton Cermak);
- The domestic coup attempt against FDR in 1933;
- The attempted assassination of Truman in 1947 by Zionist Jewish terrorists;
- The attempted assassination of Truman in 1950 by Puerto Rican nationalists.

There were three (3) three elevations of a vice president to the Oval Office via the death of the incumbent during Sam Rayburn's lifetime prior to 1956:
- The elevation of Theodore Roosevelt following McKinley's assassination;
- The elevation of Calvin Coolidge following the death of Warren Harding;
- The elevation of Harry Truman following the death of Franklin Roosevelt.

A full *dozen* opportunities for significant political advancement had occurred. The lesson was clear to anyone paying attention:

Death – *not* skill or talent or dedication or devotion or loyalty – was in fact the primary mechanism by which ambitious men rose to the heights of power in America.

Death made careers.
Death elevated the worthy to their rightful place.
Death was the answer.
No one could deny it.
Least of all Sam Rayburn.

* * *

Moreover, during the 1940s and 1950s both President Truman and President Eisenhower proposed, attempted, discussed and in one case successfully implemented *major changes in the line of presidential succession.* All of this presidential scheming and line-of-succession shuffling occurred during the ten years *immediately prior to* the creation of the Rayburn-Johnson JFK assassination plot in 1956.

Harry Truman's recommended change to the presidential line of succession (a change he promoted in 1945 and which was finally passed into law as the Presidential Succession Act of 1947) benefited Sam Rayburn *personally* and *directly* – but not immediately. As of January 1949, when he once again became Speaker of the House, Rayburn was now in that vital sequence *himself.*

He was not the only one who recognized the fact, either.

Introducing Rayburn at a political luncheon in the autumn of 1949, former Texas governor William Pettus Hobby made the point quite explicitly. "It's only a hair's breadth," said Governor Hobby, "from Speaker to President . . ."[253]

Thus, *the line of succession* was very much on Rayburn's mind – personally as well as professionally. He had to deal with it as *part of his job,* which was – in his own words – his *life.*

Dwight Eisenhower's major health issues in the late 1950s (including a serious heart attack in 1955; bowel surgery for ileitis in 1956; and a stroke in 1957) could have made Vice President Richard Nixon the president on a number of occasions. Therefore, the line of presidential succession was very much on Sam Rayburn's mind just as the JFK assassination plot – *Rayburn's and Johnson's plot* – was first created by the Texas duo in 1956.[254] Indeed, the power of elevation-through-death was *the specific enabling mechanism* of the sinister-but-brilliant Rayburn-Johnson plot.

Sam Rayburn deliberately left very few meaningful working papers to history, and he wrote very few things down – for good reason, especially as he descended into

---

[253] C. Dwight Dorough, *Mr. Sam,* p. 422.

[254] Author's exclusive original discovery.

the very worst criminal act of his extraordinarily long career: the murderous plot which eventually took the life of John Fitzgerald Kennedy.[255]

* * *

Sam Rayburn, as I first discovered exclusively in 2010, was *the true intellectual author of the Kennedy assassination.*[256]

It was Rayburn.

No other author, historian, journalist, researcher or investigator had *ever* figured this out.

I alone did.

It was Rayburn.

And I have discovered a true wealth of *additional* data points which overwhelmingly corroborate, confirm and conclusively prove my exclusive original discovery.

It was Rayburn, America – and these are the reasons why:

1. Rayburn's lifelong ambition and deepest, most fervent desire was to see a Texan – a "real" Texan, not a haughty dismissive denialist like Dwight Eisenhower – in the White House as President of the United States.

2. Rayburn was a white southern politician at a time of increasing racial strife and turmoil in America. Major recent events including the Brown v. Board of Education Supreme Court decision (in 1954), the Montgomery Bus Boycott (in 1955) and the Little Rock school integration struggle (in 1957) ensured that race relations remained painfully at the forefront of national consciousness. There was much more to come, of course. And all that conflict graphically emphasized to the country as a whole the brutally inhuman nature of southern segregation – from nauseating Jim Crow laws to open violence against black citizens. Neither major political party – but in particular, the Democratic Party – was inclined to nominate someone for President whose very presence would automatically inflame existing racial tensions and quite possibly cost the party victory in the election.

3. Rayburn had no national political base to speak of and no proven vote-getting abilities in the North.

4. Rayburn's vanishingly few opportunities to compete directly for, or even be considered for, the presidential nomination of his party (notably a brief "boomlet" in 1952) fizzled miserably and evaporated quickly.

---

[255] Author's exclusive original discovery.

[256] Author's exclusive original discovery.

5. Rayburn's best opportunity to occupy the White House himself would have been to win the 1944 VP nomination, since the ailing FDR was clearly moribund at that point – but Rayburn failed to attend the Democratic convention that year because of an extremely tight race in his home district, and he lost out to Harry Truman for the #2 spot on the ticket. Truman thus became president just five months after the election, upon FDR's death in April 1945.

6. By 1956, Sam Rayburn was already 74 years old. He was widely perceived as being "too old" to be President.

7. Moreover, by 1956 *Sam Rayburn was going blind.* He could no longer function independently as a viable, credible candidate for such a high national office – let alone actually serve effectively as President – himself.

8. In 1956, even Rayburn's last-ditch offer to serve as the VP nominee along with Adlai Stevenson (instead of opening the selection process to a chaotic convention scramble, as Stevenson so unwisely decided to do) was briskly rebuffed.

9. By the conclusion of the 1956 Democratic convention, Rayburn's political protégé and surrogate son, Lyndon Baines Johnson, had *also* been coldly rejected for both the Presidential *and* Vice-Presidential nominations by his own party. Adlai Stevenson easily obliterated LBJ on the very first ballot by a massive, humiliating, totally overwhelming margin: 900 votes to 90.

10. Rayburn's political protégé and surrogate son, fellow Texan Lyndon Baines Johnson, had suffered two (2) major heart attacks in the previous summer of 1955 – requiring months of strict rest, rendering LBJ politically vulnerable, and making time itself a very precious commodity for the Texans. The two men obviously had a severely limited window of opportunity to take the White House while a recuperating LBJ was still relatively healthy enough for the task, and while the aging Rayburn would still be alive to witness it, enjoy it and lend his vital assistance to the effort.

11. Due to President Eisenhower's own strong personal and political popularity among the American electorate, the results of the 1956 presidential election were essentially a foregone conclusion: the Democratic ticket, again headed by 1952 loser Adlai Stevenson, would almost certainly lose again to Ike. Former president Harry Truman presciently predicted that Stevenson would not even win nine states in 1956; indeed, Stevenson ended up winning *precisely* nine states (and nine states *only*) in another crushing defeat by the GOP's Eisenhower. Sam Rayburn, a veteran lawmaker and masterful politician, could read the political tea leaves every bit as capably as Harry Truman did, and despite some expressions of optimism, Rayburn clearly realized that the odds were extremely poor for a Democratic national electoral victory in 1956.

12. Ever since 1956, Democratic Party Chairman Paul Butler, a northerner, had been engaged in a vocal, active, intense, ongoing campaign of strident criticism directed against both House Speaker Sam Rayburn and Rayburn's political protégé,

Senate Majority Leader Lyndon Johnson, because of what Butler regarded as the two congressional titans' far-too-cozy and far-too-accommodating relationship with the Republican president, Dwight D. Eisenhower. Butler's repeated comments about the two men's lack of leadership buffeted, damaged and weakened the status of both Rayburn and Johnson inside the Democratic Party, and constituted a significant *additional* factor which mitigated *against* the possibility of either Texan winning the party's presidential nomination in 1960.

Since Rayburn was now viewed as "too old" – and, in practical terms, was fast becoming too *blind* – to become president in that era, it was patently obvious that he would have to settle for experiencing that ultimate Texas triumph vicariously (if at all) through the future elevation of his much younger protégé, LBJ.

But extremely stern measures were called for if Rayburn was to achieve his lifelong goal – *seeing a Texan occupy the White House* – before dying himself.

Clearly, *the 1960 election would be the last hurrah for Rayburn and Johnson* in their dogged efforts to somehow put a Texan in the Oval Office.[257] Given the worsening racial and political climate of the country at the time, both men knew (and both men openly *believed*) that the odds against achieving their mission through any normal, *legitimate* means were as daunting and prohibitive as ever.

No southern white man would *ever* receive the top spot on a Democratic national ticket in such an atmosphere.

Certainly no *Texan* would.

Period.

So under those circumstances, *What were they supposed to do?*

Some other approach was needed. Some other mechanism was required. Some solid method of guaranteeing success *had* to be developed and implemented.

And therefore, nothing – absolutely *nothing* – could be left to chance.

Once the sure-to-lose ticket of Adlai Stevenson and Estes Kefauver was finalized and foolishly approved at the Democratic National Convention in Chicago in August of that year, the 1956 presidential campaign was already over – because *no one* was going to beat the popular "Ike" in the November 1956 election.

No one.

Thus in August 1956, all the Democratic political pros – including of course Sam Rayburn and Lyndon Johnson – knew with absolute certainty that the *real* prize now lay in the future.

---

[257] Author's exclusive original discovery. The irony was that President Dwight D. Eisenhower was in fact born in Texas, in the very Fourth Congressional District which Rayburn now represented – and both Rayburn and Johnson knew this fact.

But Ike was a Republican – and moreover, he strenuously disavowed the very place of his birth. As Eisenhower once contemptuously sneered, "Just because a cat gives birth in a stove, that doesn't make the kittens *biscuits*." (Alfred Steinberg, *Sam Rayburn,* p. 290.)

Three months before the actual November election, the 1956 presidential campaign was already *over.*

And the *1960* presidential race was already *on.*

But nothing could be left to chance this time.

Absolutely *nothing.*

The time for "fair play" and "honest competition" and mere "political maneuvering" was past.

Done and over.

Finished.

Rayburn and Johnson – proud, talented, driven, deeply ambitious men – had already had a bellyful of losing and of outrageous rejection. Conventional efforts by both men (publicity; promotion; politicking; cullying favor) had failed repeatedly. The two felt unjustly penalized for their Texas roots; indeed, they felt that the country itself was being penalized by being unfairly deprived of their proven leadership. Bold, tough, brutal new tactics were called for to remedy the intolerable situation. Conventional "politicking" alone was plainly insufficient to obtain the prize that they felt they absolutely deserved.[258]

Therefore, the upcoming Rayburn-Johnson pursuit of a spot for a Texan on the 1960 national Democratic ticket (a pursuit beginning *immediately,* in late 1956)[259] would not be a real "campaign" at all – rather, it would necessarily have to take the form of *a criminal covert operation.*[260]

It required a series of rough, vicious, patently illegal steps – but for Rayburn and Johnson, there was simply no other way.

It started with an abuse of the political process, moved on to an abuse of the constitutional process, and culminated in an abuse of the legal process.

No quarter would be given; no holds barred.

"We must be tough if need be," Rayburn had once declared.[261]

Now was the time.

No more waiting, or hoping, or whimsical wishing.

We must be tough if need be.

Beginning in the late summer of 1956, long-denied Texas titans Samuel Taliaferro Rayburn and Lyndon Baines Johnson were – *finally* – playing for keeps.[262]

---

[258] Author's exclusive original discovery.

[259] Author's exclusive original discovery.

[260] Author's exclusive original discovery.

[261] C. Dwight Dorough, *Mr. Sam,* p. 379.

[262] Author's exclusive original discovery.

* * *

They had to begin early and move quickly, for in 1956, Samuel Taliaferro Rayburn – the Baron of Bonham – *was going blind.*[263]

The 1956 Democratic convention was the last that he would ever chair.

Rayburn was now visually incapable of running a major national political convention ever again – let alone running for high national office in a demanding nationwide campaign, or actively serving as president (given the heavy daily workload of reading involved in the chief executive's role). Rayburn was rapidly growing very old, and he was rapidly going very blind – and above all, he was now plainly incapable of ever becoming President.[264]

His burning lifelong goal – *succeeding in having a "real" Texan occupy the White House* – would therefore have to occur in the very next election cycle (1960), or not at all.[265]

And it would have to be LBJ in the Oval Office – not Rayburn himself.[266]

Yet all the same insurmountable impediments which had long kept Texans out of meaningful spots on the national ticket still remained. Rayburn's protégé and surrogate son, Lyndon Johnson, was – like Rayburn himself – *a white southern politician,* without any true national political base, in an era of significant and worsening racial turmoil in America. For those and other reasons, the powerful northern party bosses of the Democratic Party, who wielded extensive power and who often decided the party's nominee in infamous "smoke-filled rooms," were certainly not going to accept – much less promote – the candidacy of a *Texan* for the top spot on the Democratic ticket.

It simply wasn't going to happen.

It would have been political suicide for the party.

The political reality of the era was cold and brutal and stark and unquestioned, and it was neatly summed up in three discouraging, presumably accurate and seemingly unassailable statements:

(A) "No white southerner can win his party's *nomination* for President"

---

[263] As his biographers note, Rayburn strove to mask his infirmity, but those closest to him – political aides and friends – knew the truth, and did what they could to "cover" for his increasing blindness.

[264] This is not to say that a blind person could not effectively serve in the Oval Office *today*; but the proud and extremely stubborn Rayburn was not literate in the Braille system, and no other technologies of the era provided any substantial options to adequately assist a blind or severely visually impaired president.

[265] Author's exclusive original discovery.

[266] Author's exclusive original discovery.

and its equally depressing corollary,

(B) "No white southerner, *even if nominated,* can be ***elected*** president."

Combining (A) and (B) inevitably resulted in the gloom-inducing conclusion that, therefore,

(C) "No white southerner can *become* president."

The reasoning seemed perfectly clear. It was entirely logical, and well-nigh impossible to contradict.

Rayburn believed it; Lyndon Johnson believed it; their friends and supporters believed it; everyone believed it!

JFK believed it, too.[267]

The political calculus was clear:

- *No white southerner can win his party's <u>nomination</u> for President.*
- *Even if that were somehow possible, no white southerner can be <u>elected</u> president.*
- *Therefore, no white southerner can <u>become</u> president. Period.*

The perception was the reality:

No white southerner can become president.

Thus, the stately mansion at 1600 Pennsylvania Avenue was basically barred to all those politicians who were unfortunate enough to have been born in, or to later represent, districts and states located south of the Mason-Dixon Line.

No white southerner can become president.

But Samuel Rayburn – who as Speaker of the House was in the line of succession himself, and who had personally come within a mere *whisker* of attaining the presidency had he won the Democratic VP nomination in 1944 – plainly realized

---

[267] LBJ declared in a 1955 letter that it was still too close to Appomattox, chronologically, for a southerner to be elected president. JFK used a similar reference in a conversation with Walt Rostow prior to the 1960 convention.

Oddly, at one point Lifton contacted an expert JFK assassination analyst named Pete Rupay to ask him what "uh-PALM-uh-tox" [*sic*] was.

Lifton, who claimed to be a graduate of Cornell University, *plainly did not know what Appomattox **was** – let alone how to **pronounce** it* (Peter Rupay to the author, 2017).

That baffling episode was yet another sad and appalling example of how bizarrely *disconnected* Lifton was – even decades *after* his massive mental collapse and his involuntary confinement for severe mental illness in the mid-1960s – from regular American life, common knowledge, and everyday reality.

(as his own later actions proved, beyond the shadow of any doubt)[268] that there *was,* in fact, a tantalizing *exception* to the devastating political calculus specified above.

Despite the cynical naysayers' harsh and universally accepted declarations, there *was* a way.

A white southerner *could* become president.

It could be done!

The goal could actually be accomplished.

Rayburn himself was of course – by definition – intimately, personally and very painfully aware of every single aspect of presidential succession. Indeed, he had *personally* analyzed and argued vociferously against the somewhat bizarre and clearly extra-constitutional Eisenhower plan, unveiled in March 1957,[269] to name a "temporary president" in the event of presidential disability[270] – and Rayburn had succeeded in killing the proposal. Clearly, the subject was very much on his mind.

As Rayburn himself put it, the qualities that a Speaker of the House needed were "determined ambition plus shrewdness."[271]

Determined ambition plus shrewdness.

Sam Rayburn personally spent a lot of time thinking about practical, viable solutions to the vexing conundrum – the damnable political curse – of being a Texan.[272]

Thanks to his own deep intelligence, cleverness, proven analytical abilities and pertinent personal experience, the crafty septuagenarian Sam Rayburn figured out that – contrary to all the conventional political wisdom – there *was* a way.[273]

There was a way.

The widely held notion that *No white southerner can become president* was indeed true, *as far as it went* – but upon long and careful analysis, Sam Rayburn came to understand that that universally accepted, utterly poisonous political prohibition was woefully incomplete.

*It didn't cover **all** the possibilities.*

---

[268] Author's exclusive original discovery.

[269] C. Dwight Dorough, *Mr. Sam,* pp. 514-515.

[270] Eisenhower – like Rayburn – could not stomach the thought of Richard Nixon ever becoming president, and therefore he was actively seeking a legal way to avoid that nightmarish possibility. The effort failed, and so Ike ended up trading secret letters with Nixon regarding the assumption of powers in the event of infirmity or catastrophe.

N.B.: Ike ultimately suffered at least three serious health issues (a coronary thrombosis; ileitis; and a stroke) during his two-term presidency (*New York Times,* March 29th, 1969.)

[271] C. Dwight Dorough, *Mr. Sam,* p. 297.

[272] Author's exclusive original discovery.

[273] Author's exclusive original discovery.

It overlooked a vital pathway.

It was incorrect.

No one believed that a white southerner could become president – but Rayburn, the master politician and expert parliamentarian, knew better.

And this is what Sam Rayburn figured out:

No white southerner could ever be *elected* president of the United States . . . unless he already **was** the president of the United States.[274]

And to *become* the president, that white southerner would clearly have to ascend to the office *via **the death** of his predecessor.*[275]

In that era, under those political circumstances, no other route to the Oval Office was likely, plausible or possible – period.

Death *was the route to 1600 Pennsylvania Avenue.*

*The **only** route.*

That stunning realization meant three things:

First, *whoever* won the Democratic Party's presidential nomination in 1960 would somehow have to be *forced* to take Lyndon Baines Johnson as his vice-presidential running mate.[276] This vital step could not be left to chance, or luck, or hope, or good fortune, or general "ticket-balancing" considerations, or to the vagaries of political friendship.[277]

Second, *whoever* won the Democratic presidential nomination in the summer of 1960 would have to *win the November election that year* (at all costs, without fail, no matter what). Otherwise, the entire effort would be for naught.[278]

And finally, having won the actual election – and thereby having brought Lyndon Johnson along with him, to within a heartbeat of the Oval Office – the new President inaugurated in January 1961 – *whoever he was* – would have to **die**.[279]

It was as simple and fiendishly brilliant as that.

The next Democratic President, *whoever he was,* would have to die.

Thus the JFK assassination in reality was **not** actually designed or intended to be "the assassination of John F. Kennedy," *per se*; rather, it was simply and generically *the assassination of the next Democratic President of the United States.*

Be very clear on this point:

---

[274] Author's exclusive original discovery.

[275] Author's exclusive original discovery.

[276] Author's exclusive original discovery.

[277] Author's exclusive original discovery.

[278] Author's exclusive original discovery.

[279] Author's exclusive original discovery.

Had JFK **not** won his party's nomination in the summer of 1960, then Sam Rayburn and Lyndon Johnson would have targeted, blackmailed and murdered **whoever** the ultimate Democratic nominee was that year – and today, we would be discussing the *Symington* assassination, or the *Humphrey* assassination, or the *Stevenson* assassination, instead of the JFK assassination.

John Kennedy was **not** murdered *because he was John Kennedy,* nor because of anything that JFK believed or said or did (or failed to do); rather, he was murdered because *he was the Democratic nominee of 1960* and the victoriously elected *President of the United States.*[280]

That is the stark truth:

JFK was assassinated in order to make a Texan president.[281]

That is the true reason for the Dallas slaying, America:

JFK was assassinated in order to make a Texan president.[282]

* * *

During Sam Rayburn's lifetime, two presidents (Warren Harding and Franklin Delano Roosevelt) had died in office, *officially* of natural causes;

Two presidents (FDR and Harry Truman) had *nearly* been assassinated by gunfire and letter bombs;

And two other presidents (Woodrow Wilson and Dwight Eisenhower) had suffered extremely serious, debilitating, life-threatening health crises.

In addition, in 1881, the year *prior to* Rayburn's birth, President James Garfield was assassinated by gunfire.

And in 1901, *during* Sam Rayburn's lifetime, President William McKinley was assassinated by gunfire.

Finally, in 1912, *during* Sam Rayburn's lifetime, presidential candidate and *former* president Theodore Roosevelt narrowly escaped death from a would-be assassin's bullet.

The lesson was crystal clear: presidents *sometimes* fall seriously ill, and they *sometimes* die of natural causes. But in order to truly **guarantee** a president's death in office, *you have to kill him.*[283]

You have to kill him.

---

[280] Author's exclusive original discovery.

[281] Author's exclusive original discovery.

[282] Author's exclusive original discovery. (Contrary to popular myth, JFK was **not** slain because of his policies, his attitudes or his political positions.)

[283] Author's exclusive original discovery.

You have to kill him.
You have to kill him.
Sam Rayburn had never forgotten Cactus Jack's blunt admonition from 1931:
You've got to get your knuckles bloody . . .
Those seven words changed history.
By 1956, after *decades* of disappointment and outrage and endless bitter frustration, Sam Rayburn was finally, *definitely* ready to get his knuckles bloody.
His protégé Lyndon Johnson was ready, too.

* * *

Advancement through death was the lesson – and Sam Rayburn had seen it play out repeatedly.
So what did that mean in terms of 1960?
JFK was the likeliest Democratic nominee in 1960, despite his Catholicism (which had led to electoral ruin for candidate Al Smith back in 1928).
JFK indeed had a serious illness called Addison's Disease – and both Rayburn and Johnson knew it – but the ailment was carefully and skillfully controlled through modern medications.[284]
Kennedy was a multi-millionaire. He already had – and could always afford – the very best medical care in the world.
Additionally, as president, Kennedy would also have all the medical resources of the federal government at his disposal if he wanted, needed or required them.
JFK was not going to die in office.
Not of natural causes, at any rate.
JFK would have to be murdered – and he would have to be murdered *during his first term in office.*

* * *

Nor could anyone ensure that John Kennedy would not ultimately *drop* Johnson as a running mate during a second run for the White House in favor of someone else. After all, FDR himself – LBJ's political idol – had had *three* different running mates in his four presidential campaigns: Cactus Jack (1932), Cactus Jack again (1936), then Henry Wallace (1940), and finally Harry Truman (1944).
Being Vice President is no guarantee of *remaining* Vice President – and therefore it is no guarantee of being retained on the ticket for the next election.

---

[284] Indeed, *after* the Democratic convention, Sam Rayburn himself admitted in an August 4th, 1960, letter that John Kennedy was "vigorous in health." (C. Dwight Dorough, *Mr. Sam,* pp. 574-575.)

Rayburn and Johnson knew all this, of course. Rayburn had personally witnessed it, from very close range. He and LBJ were both masterful, talented, experienced political animals of the highest ability. Shrewd observers, they could read the tea leaves, the atmosphere *and* the electorate. They harbored no illusions about what they were up against.

In 1956, Sam Rayburn was 74 years old. His own father had perished at the age of 76. Several of Rayburn's many siblings had also already died. Despite doctors' cheery assessments of his overall health to date, Rayburn possessed no special dispensation from the inexorable laws of time and aging and encroaching weakness. The Speaker of the House did not have endless time to wait around, hoping fruitlessly *ad infinitum* for an unlikely bolt from the blue that would fortuitously lead to the sudden fulfillment of his lifelong dream.

As the old saying goes, *you have to make your own luck.*

And as Cactus Jack had personally advised Sam Rayburn more than a quarter-century before, *"You've got to get your knuckles bloody . . ."*

There was no other way.

There was just no other way.

There was simply no other way.

And specific, concrete statements and documented actions taken by these two powerful men – Samuel Rayburn and Lyndon Johnson – enabled me to uncover their motives, identify their decisions, and establish for all time their *direct criminal culpability* in the JFK assassination.[285]

* * *

In 1944, his very best chance at the Presidency, Rayburn simply quailed when the hour of decision came. Unwilling to risk possibly losing his House seat (and the powerful Speakership with it), he declined to leave his Texas district during a tight local election race in order to attend the Democratic National Convention in Chicago that year. Rayburn's failure to show up in Illinois and actively pursue the #2 slot in person guaranteed that he would *not* secure the vice-presidential nomination, and thus Senator Harry Truman of Missouri became the vice-presidential nominee (and then president, upon FDR's death a few months after the election) in his stead.

Rayburn's final quadrennial efforts on his *own* behalf — in 1952 and 1956 – were pallid, weak gestures that predictably flamed out and went nowhere.

When the chips were down, Samuel Rayburn simply lacked the killer instinct *for himself*[286] – but as he demonstrated incontrovertibly in 1960 and in 1961, he had

---

[285] Author's exclusive original discovery.

[286] Author's exclusive original discovery.

no such qualms when it came to formulating, facilitating, aiding and actively abetting a murderous criminal conspiracy on behalf of *someone else.*[287]

* * *

On the night of Wednesday, July 13th, 1960, John Fitzgerald Kennedy won the Democratic Party's nomination to be its presidential standard-bearer in the upcoming November election.

JFK won on the very first ballot; LBJ finished a distant second.

This was *entirely expected* and *entirely anticipated* by Rayburn and Johnson; Kennedy's nomination victory was *not* a surprise to the two veteran Texas politicians.

But JFK's unexpected personal appearance *at the convention* that very night certainly *was.*[288]

John Kennedy dropped by in person once the balloting was over to publicly thank the convention delegates for making him the nominee – and this sudden personal appearance certainly *did* disturb and panic Rayburn and Johnson, for Kennedy's brief remarks to the assembled delegates might well have included an immediate announcement of the name of his desired running mate, *Senator Stu Symington!*[289]

Fortunately for the Texas titans, JFK did *not* voice his choice for VP right then and there. That announcement would wait until tomorrow.

And *that* meant that Rayburn and Johnson's long-simmering plan – first created in August 1956 [290] – could indeed be executed, *as planned,* that very night:

The night of July 13th-14th, 1960, in Los Angeles.

Force the nominee to make LBJ his running mate.

It was an ugly and criminal but very straightforward transaction:

Simple blackmail, committed *under cover of night.*

* * *

---

[287] Author's exclusive original discovery.

[288] Author's exclusive original discovery.

[289] "It was always going to be Symington," said JFK campaign aide (and attorney) Hyman Raskin. (Seymour Hersh, *The Dark Side of Camelot,* p. 124.)

[290] Author's exclusive original discovery.

SEAN FETTER

First, Lyndon Johnson braced Robert Kennedy individually[291] while Sam Rayburn met separately with John Kennedy in a hotel room in the *presence* of (but not within earshot of) a Rayburn aide named John Holton.[292]

Then Rayburn and Johnson *jointly* corralled JFK in private and obviously presented him with an overwhelming collection of photographic and other proof of his many infidelities – proof happily provided to the duo by LBJ's longtime ally, the crocodilian FBI Director J. Edgar Hoover.[293]

The deed was done.

The plot worked.

At a luncheon held several hours later on July 14th, in daylight, JFK pulled attorney and campaign aide Hyman Raskin aside and confessed explicitly what had happened. "I was left with no choice," Kennedy said to Raskin. "[LBJ] and Sam Rayburn made it damn clear to me that Lyndon had to be the candidate. Those bastards were trying to frame me. They threatened me with problems . . ."[294]

Kennedy could not have been more blunt or more explicit.

Rayburn and Johnson blackmailed him into making LBJ his running mate.

As I personally determined from careful analysis of witness accounts and chronological data, the Rayburn-Johnson blackmail perpetrated against of John Fitzgerald Kennedy took place between 1:00 a.m. and 5:00 a.m. on the morning of Thursday, July 14th, 1960.[295]

Everything after that was just theater and lies and conscious cover-up.[296]

By both sides.[297]

---

[291] John Knight's story in the *Miami Herald* from Friday, July 15th, 1960 (cited in Seymour Hersh, *The Dark Side of Camelot*, p. 127).

[292] Author's exclusive original discovery;

[293] JFK's loyal secretary, Evelyn Kennedy, made it *abundantly* and *explicitly* clear in later interviews with Anthony Summers that FBI Director Hoover was the major source for the compromising sexual materials employed in the successful Rayburn-Johnson blackmail of John F. Kennedy at the 1960 Democratic Convention.

[294] Quoted in Seymour Hersh, *The Dark Side of Camelot*, p. 126.

[295] Author's exclusive original discovery.

[296] Author's exclusive original discovery.

[297] To save face, the Kennedy team aggressively put out a false and fraudulent narrative about a mere "token offer" [*sic*] whose unexpected "acceptance" [*sic*] by LBJ had *(gosh golly gee, Ma!)* really "surprised" them [*sic*].

To protect themselves from serious criminal charges *then or later* (meaning, after the JFK assassination), Rayburn and Johnson aggressively put out false and fraudulent denials of the fact that *their deliberate blackmail* had *forced* Kennedy to (unwillingly) pick LBJ as his running mate.

Kennedy's plans were completely undone by 5:00 a.m., before the sun rose.

JFK was "sort of stunned" on July 14th, said his longtime friend (and journalist) Charlie Bartlett.[298]

But the Texas duo of Rayburn and Johnson were *elated.*

Rayburn's sinister and sordid scheme to put a "real" Texan into the White House was now *on.*

Definitely ***on.***

* * *

And what about crusty old Cactus Jack?

How did he figure into the dark drama of 1960?

At the advanced age of 91, former Vice President John Nance "Cactus Jack" Garner himself helped *aid* Rayburn & Johnson by falsely claiming that he had verbally advised a friend named Lawrence "Chip" Roberts to tell LBJ to "accept" the second spot on the Democratic ticket.

Cactus Jack claimed that he successfully *shouted* a very lengthy and complex message about all this to Chip Roberts, at the top of his own (extremely aged) lungs, *from a car,* as Roberts (and his wife) *just happened* to be passing by – *on a moving train.* The Roberts couple then supposedly reduced Garner's frantic shouting to elegant written form in a lengthy (but secret) memo for the record.[299]

The story was obviously ludicrous on its face.

But the supposed memo about it was the type of document deliberately created to help give a veneer of verisimilitude to the false claim that JFK had "invited" LBJ to join him on the 1960 Democratic ticket.

That wasn't true at all – but Rayburn & Johnson employed the former Vice President's ludicrous story about *yelling highly articulate dictation to a man on a passing railroad train* as material for a possible future legal defense.[300]

The document was held secretly by Garner, Robert and LBJ.[301]

No one else saw it – but it lay in wait, ready to be sprung as a supposedly "exculpatory" courtroom surprise in the event that Rayburn & Johnson's plot ever fell

---

Pathetically, America's weak national media and cowardly conventional "historians" [*sic*] have dutifully swallowed the false 1960 pablum whole.

[298] Seymour Hersh, *The Dark Side of Camelot,* p. 122.

[299] Evelyn Lincoln, *Kennedy and Johnson,* pp. 99-100.

[300] Author's exclusive original discovery.

[301] Evelyn Lincoln, *Kennedy and Johnson,* pp. 99-100.

apart,[302] or some brilliant and intrepid investigator[303] ever began to ask questions about the ugly blackmail of JFK in July 1960, and its central importance to the bloody assassination of President Kennedy in November 1963.

* * *

Rayburn's stately columned Texas home in Bonham was just off Highway 82, and when he was there during congressional recesses, loyal constituents of the Fourth Congressional District could and did troop directly through the structure's long central hallway to make brief petitions and requests personally to the Baron of Bonham, who sat in the living room – conspicuously spitting tobacco juice into the fireplace as he conferred with them in order to demonstrate that their exalted congressman, the Speaker of the House, was just a "plain old humble farmer" and a regular "good ol' boy" like them.[304]

While in the nation's capital, the Speaker sported carefully tailored suits; enjoyed the comforts of a chauffeured Cadillac limousine; lived in a variety of Washington hotels before settling in an apartment near DuPont Circle; ate at fine restaurants; enjoyed bourbon and whiskey with congressional cronies each afternoon at the Capitol; and squired various Washington women around town.

But when *back in Texas* during congressional recesses of varying durations, Rayburn carefully and ostentatiously demonstrated his populist *bona fides*.

He consistently donned ill-fitting denim and a battered old hat; dispensed folksy bromides known as "Rayburnisms"; eschewed liquor; dated no one locally; and ostentatiously drove not just an "old" pickup truck, but an *old and extremely dented* pickup truck. It was a virtuoso performance of humility by a master politician – and a stunning Jekyll-and-Hyde display that would have impressed any chameleon.[305]

But when Sam Rayburn *really* wanted to get away from it all, he retreated from his home in Bonham to a 972-acre cattle ranch which he owned, about thirteen miles away near the small community of Ivanhoe. By Rayburn's *specific intention and*

---

[302] Author's exclusive original discovery.

[303] Like me.

[304] Anthony Champagne, *Congressman Sam Rayburn*, p. 28.

[305] Rayburn also fondly extolled the virtues of favorite foods from his youth like "crummin" (cornbread crumbled in milk) and "Hopkins County Stew" (a hearty lard-based concoction featuring lard, pork, lard, fatback, lard, chicken, lard, potatoes, lard, corn, lard, bacon, lard, turnips, lard, onions, lard, tomatoes, lard, spices and . . . lard).

Like many of his rural north Texas constituents, Sam Rayburn had indeed known terrible poverty as a child, but as Congressman and Speaker of the House he was no longer even *remotely* poor. In essence, the well-to-do Rayburn donned a *costume* every time he returned to Fannin County.

deliberate design, the large comfortable cabin built there (measuring twenty feet by forty feet) had no telephone or radio[306] – and therefore it *could not be wiretapped.*[307] Rayburn indisputably met there, at that secluded cabin, with his protégé: Lyndon Baines Johnson.[308]

Surrounded and defended by barbed-wire fences, and infested by hundreds of venomous copperhead snakes,[309] Sam Rayburn's Ivanhoe ranch was isolated, protected, remote and quiet – and on starlit Texas nights, the silent ranch cabin was an excellent place for an elderly man to sit by the fire, drink his liquor, smoke his unfiltered cigarettes, and think intently about the intricate details of pulling off a colossal crime.[310]

* * *

What was it that Cactus Jack Garner had said, way back in 1931?
You've got to get your knuckles bloody . . .
With a deliberate act, you control events.
You've got to get your knuckles bloody . . .
In order to take advantage of the killing, *your protégé would have to be in the vice presidency already,* poised to ascend to the Oval Office.
You've got to get your knuckles bloody . . .
And what would such a murder involve, precisely?
Killing a president inside the White House itself was out of the question, of course. Any murder *there* would virtually *prove* the existence of a palace plot – an inside job – and that would lead, promptly and inexorably, to probing investigations.
So methods like poisoned oatmeal – or strangulation – or drowning – or violent assault – or simply pushing the chief executive down the stairs – were clearly out.
But killing a president *in public,* out in the hinterlands, among the great "unwashed masses," was a much more practical and eminently more doable matter.
You've got to get your knuckles bloody . . .
Guns, a crowd, and a great deal of concomitant fear would help.
It would have to be fast, of course, and therefore confusing to witnesses.
You've got to get your knuckles bloody . . .

---

[306] Alfred Steinberg, *Sam Rayburn,* p. 206.

[307] Author's exclusive original discovery.

[308] Anthony Champagne, *Congressman Sam Rayburn,* pp. 44, 46.

[309] Alfred Steinberg, *Sam Rayburn,* p. 205.

[310] Author's exclusive original discovery.

Disguises or camouflage would help hide the assassins from prying eyes and stray photographs.

Quick, clean and effective.

You've got to get your knuckles bloody . . .

You would naturally have to control the autopsy, the subsequent legal process, and any resulting trial(s) which might occur. So the physical setting chosen for the actual commission of the deadly deed was paramount.

You've got to get your knuckles bloody . . .

Best to set someone up as the putative "assassin" and quickly kill him before any actual investigation or public trial could take place.

You've got to get your knuckles bloody . . .

Just idly pondering these things was not a criminal act, of course. "Thought experiments" are just that – thought experiments. No harm, no foul. In America, a bitter old man can sit in a room on a quiet, isolated ranch in northeast Texas and have a drink or two or three or four and let his clever, ruthless mind wander – all without breaking (or even bending) the law.

Rumination, by itself, is not a crime.[311]

It only *becomes* a crime when you share those thoughts with someone else and begin to jointly plan to carry out a criminal act. Then it becomes what prosecutors call a *criminal conspiracy* – which is a **crime,** not a "theory."[312]

And thanks to Sam Rayburn and Lyndon Johnson, in the summer of 1956 the deliberate murder of the next Democratic President of the United States – *whomever he might be* – became an operational criminal plot.[313]

* * *

Solving the JFK assassination requires intensive and honest *analysis,* not just the mere assemblage of data points. Without sophisticated analysis, the data do not yield complete or accurate answers.

The most spectacular evidence of Sam Rayburn's direct, central role in the Kennedy assassination is his undeniable and deliberate act of *personally* blackmailing JFK during the wee hours of Thursday, July 14th, 1960 – thereby forcing Kennedy to put *Lyndon Johnson* (not Stuart Symington, JFK's actual choice) on the Democratic ticket as his running mate.

---

[311] Yet.

[312] See Title 18 of the U. S. federal code. That's 18 USC 371, to be precise.

(Go ahead – look it up. I'll wait.)

[313] Author's exclusive original discovery.

But the very fact that this despicable criminal act took place *in* 1960 means – *by definition* – that the JFK plot's *origin* actually occurred well *before* 1960.[314] The blackmail was *not* a spontaneous, spur-of-the-moment act! Rather, it was a vital element of a well-thought-out, brilliantly conceived plan whose existence *pre-dated* 1960.[315]

Sam Rayburn did *not* just wake up in Los Angeles on the sweltering morning of July 13th, 1960, and say, "Gee – I think I'll blackmail that little bastard Kennedy before dawn tomorrow. What a swell idea!"

To the contrary – Rayburn was clearly very well prepared, ***in advance,*** with *all the material he needed* in order to successfully frighten John Kennedy into meekly and immediately succumbing to the loathsome blackmail demand.[316] As Texas Congressman Frank Ikard put it, "[Sam Rayburn] and Lyndon Johnson had the two best intelligence systems that have ever been devised by the human mind."[317]

The fatal product of the Rayburn and Johnson intelligence systems – augmented *dramatically* with devastating material supplied by their mutual ally J. Edgar Hoover[318] – was what one keen observer quite correctly labeled a "political shotgun wedding."[319]

The 1960 blackmail was the foundation stone of the JFK assassination plot[320] – and it was designed to permit the actual *implementation* of that plot as soon as practicable (as early as 1961, if possible). This means that *the entire JFK assassination plot sequence —* including the convention blackmail itself *and* Kennedy's subsequent post-inauguration murder – had all been carefully sketched out previously, in some detail, by *a man who was intimately familiar with the presidential line of succession.*[321]

One man fit that description better than anyone else on the planet.

Just one man.

Only one.

---

[314] Author's exclusive original discovery.

[315] Author's exclusive original discovery. (Lifton, strangely and erroneously, insisted that the plot began in 1959 with JFK's acquisition of a campaign airplane. As usual, Lifton's "reasoning" was faulty and badly incorrect.)

[316] Author's exclusive original discovery.

[317] Anthony Champagne, *Congressman Sam Rayburn,* p. 155.

[318] JFK's longtime secretary, Evelyn Lincoln, made this explicitly clear in an interview televised by PBS in 1993.

[319] J. Evetts Haley, *A Texan Looks at Lyndon,* p. 73.

[320] Author's exclusive original discovery.

[321] Author's exclusive original discovery.

And that man was none other than *Sam Rayburn himself*.[322]

* * *

By 1956, the presidential line of succession had been on Sam Rayburn's mind – repeatedly – for almost *twenty-five years*.

By 1960, the presidential line of succession had been on Sam Rayburn's mind – repeatedly – for almost *thirty years*.

No one else in American government was more attuned to the awesome power inherent in the line of succession – ***no one.***

It was Rayburn.

1956 had been the very last opportunity for Rayburn or Johnson to *legitimately and legally* obtain a place on the party's national ticket – but that year's Democratic convention constituted a dismal, painful, humiliating failure for both men, and was yet *another* stunning party rejection of Texans seeking high national office.

For Rayburn and Johnson, *the time had clearly come for harsher tactics.*[323]

Once the Democrats had officially nominated Adlai Stevenson and Estes Kefauver in mid-August, the 1956 election was essentially over. Thanks to President Eisenhower's strong personal popularity, the results were pre-ordained. Therefore, in the late summer of 1956, the *1960* presidential race had already begun.[324]

Thus a plot which finally began secretly manifesting itself *under cover of night* in July 1960 (with Rayburn's brutal blackmail of JFK in Los Angeles) actually began a full *four years earlier,* in Chicago, in mid-August 1956.[325]

That was when the die was cast.

That was when the JFK assassination plot truly began.[326]

* * *

The bottom line is this:

Sam Rayburn and Lyndon Johnson were the originators and intellectual authors of the JFK assassination.[327]

---

[322] Author's exclusive original discovery.

[323] Author's exclusive original discovery.

[324] Author's exclusive original discovery.

[325] Author's exclusive original discovery.

[326] Author's exclusive original discovery.

[327] Author's exclusive original discovery.

JFK's murder was ***not*** the work of a lone warehouse employee named Lee, or a clique of violent New Orleans homosexuals, or a Louisiana corporation, or racist right-wing amateurs from the National States' Rights Party.

The assassination of John Kennedy was ***not*** the work of the Bilderberg Group, or the Council on Foreign Relations, or the Rockefeller Foundation, or the Shickshinny Knights of Malta – among many other dubious groups which have been erroneously specified by (equally dubious and unsophisticated) researchers.

Nor was it the brainchild of the odious Central Intelligence Agency, despite that agency's undeniable involvement in certain minor *aspects* of the 1963 crime.[328]

It wasn't CIA Director Allen Dulles who peremptorily summoned John Kennedy in mid-July 1960 and, *under cover of night,* personally blackmailed him into putting LBJ on the Democratic ticket.

Nor was it Fidel Castro or Nikita Khrushchev.

And it certainly wasn't Clay Shaw, Guy Bannister, David Ferrie, Lee Oswald, Ted Shackley, David Sanchez Morales, George Bush, George Joannides, "Reuben Efron," George Lincoln Rockwell, Joseph Milteer, Bernard Barker, Felix Rodriguez, Jimmy Hoffa, Richard Cain, Carlos Marcello, "Milwaukee Phil," Harry Weatherford, or Sam Giancana.

It was Samuel Taliaferro Rayburn.[329]

Determined ambition plus shrewdness.

Sam Rayburn had both traits, in spades.

Determined ambition plus shrewdness.

Rayburn was also, as one biographer candidly admitted, "Filled with the venom of a diamondback rattler."[330]

But he was capable of *grinning* when his vicious criminal schemes worked.

After successfully blackmailing John Kennedy in Los Angeles, *under cover of night,* to place Lyndon Johnson on the 1960 Democratic ticket – thereby kicking the assassination plot (originally hatched back in August 1956[331]) into high gear – Sam Rayburn contentedly returned to his home in Bonham, Texas for a summertime visit before the national presidential election campaign ramped up.

---

[328] Author's exclusive original discovery. As I prove conclusively in this book and in my subsequent books, the CIA was certainly ***not*** "running the show" when it came to killing John Kennedy.

The Agency was happy to manipulate the patsy, and happy to fabricate and suppress documents (all very easy and decidedly *minor* tasks), but the CIA was certainly ***not*** in charge of the JFK assassination.

[329] Author's exclusive original discovery.

[330] C. Dwight Dorough, *Mr. Sam,* p. 457.

[331] Author's exclusive original discovery.

Surprised observers of the normally dour Rayburn noted that, in contrast to his *usual* gruff demeanor, "He was all smiles."[332]

* * *

The moment that John Kennedy weakly capitulated to Rayburn and Johnson's ugly blackmail during the wee hours of July 14th, 1960, the Rayburn/Johnson JFK assassination plot instantaneously became a viable, working operation – a "going concern," to use business parlance.

But the question looms:

Why take such a tremendous risk themselves?

Why did Sam Rayburn and Lyndon Johnson themselves *personally* blackmail Kennedy in the dead of night? Why not use a plausibly deniable *intermediary*? Why openly expose themselves as brazen criminals to their victim, JFK?

The answer is as simple as it is startling:

Because they literally had no one else![333]

In July 1960, the Kennedy assassination plot was still, of necessity, relatively small.[334] It was not yet a "given" or a definite "go" (operationally), because *unless and until* Rayburn and Johnson actually succeeded in forcing the party nominee (JFK) to *actually put LBJ onto the Democratic ticket,* the entire plan was an absolute bust.

And of course, until the 1960 nominee was actually *chosen* by the Democratic Convention, then he (*whoever* he turned out to be, per the delegates' votes) could not even be *approached.*

And no "lesser emissaries" who might have been employed to commit the deed possessed sufficient *clout* and *gravitas* to convince John Kennedy of the deadly seriousness of the blackmail.[335]

Moreover, no one else – no matter *how* supportive of the upcoming coup they were – was going to needlessly risk severe criminal penalties *until and unless* Rayburn and Johnson had successfully sprung the trap themselves and had actually forced JFK to put Johnson on the ticket as his running mate. The "Victory Twins" from Texas had to have some skin in the game.[336]

---

[332] C. Dwight Dorough, *Mr. Sam,* p. 574.

[333] Author's original discovery.

[334] Author's original discovery.

[335] Author's original discovery.

[336] Author's original discovery.

Finally, as the undisputed leaders of the House and Senate, *only* Rayburn and Johnson themselves had the unquestioned political power to totally cripple and repudiate JFK's entire future legislative program.[337]

Thus they had to make their criminal power play *directly,* face-to-face.[338]

Nothing less would suffice to crush Jack Kennedy's sky-high confidence as the newly-minted nominee of the party.

Later on – once JFK had been elected and had taken office and had repeatedly offended the most reactionary organizations within the federal government – certain allies came forward to *assist* Rayburn and Johnson.[339] "Recruitment" of such allies was extraordinarily easy – but it came at a very steep price.

Not in money, mind you; nor in gold or diamonds.

The price was another (far more precious and *liquid*) currency.[340]

* * *

Lesser JFK researchers (and many other uninformed/misinformed Americans) believe that the U. S. "national security state" killed President Kennedy for alleged "national security" or "foreign policy" reasons.

They are wrong – *completely* wrong.

The JFK assassination was *not* a CIA initiative, or an NSA initiative, or even a Pentagon initiative.

It was a Rayburn-Johnson initiative.[341]

---

[337] Author's original discovery.

[338] The diminutive Rayburn was no stranger to the personal practice of cruelty and violence; whenever any male bovine on his Ivanhoe cattle ranch did not exhibit complete physical perfection in Rayburn's eyes, he immediately castrated the helpless animal.

[339] Author's original discovery. **N.B.:** Note the true sequence! Rayburn and Johnson *created* the plot in 1956; *initiated* the plot; took *concrete steps* to further the plot. Then, *later,* following Kennedy's January 1961 inauguration, other powerful figures and organizations within the federal government merely *joined* the *existing* Rayburn/Johnson plot for reasons of their own – having been thoroughly angered by the millionaire from Massachusetts.

Most JFK researchers hold the totally erroneous view that "the CIA" [*sic*] or "the National Security State" [*sic*] initiated the plot (in 1961 or later) [*sic*] and merely "used" poor little ol' LBJ [*sic*] as a gofer and front man and "false sponsor" [*sic*] – which is pathetically absurd, embarrassingly ignorant, and completely incorrect.

Wake up. Grow up. Man up. Leave simplistic juvenile "theories" in the trash, where they belong.

[340] Author's original discovery.

[341] Author's original discovery.

If the American "national security state" killed President Kennedy for "national security" reasons, *why wait until 1963 to assassinate him?*

Why give JFK a thousand perilous days in which to put the country at needless risk of ruin?

Why wait until so late in Kennedy's first term?

If JFK was such an "existential threat," then why didn't the vaunted "national security state" eliminate him much sooner – *perhaps during his inaugural speech?*

If the "national security state" or "the CIA" killed President Kennedy for reasons of their own, why did they willingly give JFK *so much time* – so much opportunity for serious mischief and for actions which they clearly hated?

The answer is simple:

They didn't.

Moreover, if the "national security state" killed President Kennedy, why would Sam Rayburn – a *politician,* not a bureaucrat or a general – knowingly and voluntarily commit *serious felonies* on behalf of that shadowy entity, to further a plot of which he supposedly had no knowledge?

The answer is simple:

He didn't.

The "national security state" did *not* kill President Kennedy on its own initiative, or of its own volition, or by itself.

JFK's killers, led by Sam Rayburn and Lyndon Johnson themselves, waited so long not because they "wanted" to or "planned" to, but because they *had* to.

The Rayburn-Johnson plot wasn't fully ready yet.

Key assets were still not in place. Moreover, certain very specific personnel issues had not yet been resolved.

And the JFK assassination plot included a *built-in* cover-up – not the illogical, ludicrous, separate, "after-the-fact" cover-up imagined by many JFK researchers, but a *built-in, integrated cover-up* designed from the very beginning to mask the perpetrators of the deed forever.

The plotters, led by Rayburn and Johnson, had to wait because the whole point was not simply to "kill" John Kennedy, but *to kill him and get away with it* [342] – thus permitting the installation of Lyndon Baines Johnson as president *without suffering subsequent prosecution for the assassination.*[343]

---

[342] Author's exclusive original discovery.

[343] Author's exclusive original discovery.

The "national security state" did not kill President Kennedy on its own initiative or of its own volition; rather, *Sam Rayburn and Lyndon Johnson did – with the **help and assistance and willing support of** the "national security" state.*[344]

Now you understand why those two senior politicians personally committed the blackmail of Democratic nominee John Kennedy in July 1960.

You commit risky felonies yourself, *under cover of night,* because the plot in question is *your very own plot!* [345]

* * *

Sam Rayburn was an extremely laconic man. He wrote or dictated occasional letters to constituents, to his family, and on occasion to politicians – but he rarely spoke on the floor of the House of Representatives, and he rarely prepared actual written speech drafts for his public appearances elsewhere.

Frequently, he fobbed people off – both verbally and in writing – with nothing but stale Polonian bromides re-labeled by his admirers as so-called "Rayburnisms." His daily Capitol Hill "press conferences" lasted five minutes or less; they were also "off the record." He did not document or preserve much of his long life; even his fawning and superficial biographers have complained that the Sam Rayburn Library's most important holdings consist of numerous oral histories *about* the man, not primary documents created by the man himself.[346]

Strangely, most of Rayburn's congressional papers dating up to 1940 were mysteriously destroyed during an office move which occurred *inside the Capitol building itself* – and subsequently, *after* 1940, Rayburn deliberately left a very sparse paper trail. The Baron of Bonham had learned early on in his political life that "He could not be blamed for something he had not said."[347]

Rayburn – who was *far* more intelligent and restrained and circumspect than the overly voluble Lyndon Johnson – left no diary, no memoranda for the record, no summaries of key conversations, no journal, no autobiography, no written confession of his principal role in the murder of JFK.

Murderers seldom do.[348]

---

[344] Author's exclusive original discovery.

[345] Author's exclusive original discovery.

[346] A Rayburn Library staffer confirmed this in the 21st century.

[347] C. Dwight Dorough, *Mr. Sam,* p. 94. In making the remark, Rayburn was actually paraphrasing an earlier statement made by President Calvin Coolidge (Alfred Steinberg, *Sam Rayburn,* p. 75).

[348] LBJ was a glaring exception.

Moreover, Rayburn was ***not*** a compulsively *confessional* individual, like LBJ.[349] At most, the Speaker would occasionally jot terse, cryptic notes on the back of an envelope to remind himself of commitments he had made to fellow politicians on Capitol Hill in exchange for their legislative support on pending bills.

Even Lyndon Johnson, his protégé and surrogate son, noted disapprovingly that Rayburn ran the House of Representatives "from his back ass pocket" – i.e., with stunning informality.[350] The Speaker's word was his bond when it came to political horse-trading and backroom deals – but it was a word that was very rarely reduced to actual written form.

So it was Rayburn's own *concrete actions* that permitted me to clearly discern his intentions, and accurately uncover and conclusively *prove* his direct criminal culpability in the JFK assassination.[351]

Those actions – direct and verifiable – spoke much louder than words.[352]

And those actions opened a hidden doorway which revealed the thinking of a notoriously laconic man – enabling me to uncover, analyze and expose the indisputable fact of Sam Rayburn's principal role in secretly scheming to elevate his Texas protégé to the White House through a series of major felonies including criminal conspiracy, extortion, sedition, and murder.[353]

* * *

On January 6th, 1961 – exactly two weeks before John F. Kennedy was inaugurated as the 35th President of the Unite States – Samuel Taliaferro Rayburn

---

[349] Author's exclusive original discovery.

[350] Anthony Champagne, *Congressman Sam Rayburn,* p. 87.

[351] Author's exclusive original discovery.

[352] Even Rayburn's very-late-in-life decision to join the Primitive Baptist Church reflected what was really going on.

The official baptism took place on September 2nd, 1956. (C. Dwight Dorough, *Mr. Sam,* p. 502.)

Note that Rayburn did ***not*** become a so-called "Hard-Shell" Baptist until ***after*** the fateful August 1956 Democratic Convention – which is when *the Speaker began actively planning the murder* of the next Democratic President of the United States (Author's exclusive original discovery).

Rayburn's biographers have tried desperately (and in vain) to attribute this belated church membership to the deaths of three close relatives several months *earlier* that year, but I realized correctly that in truth the 74-year-old Rayburn plainly wanted some "soul insurance" as he initiated and launched the murderous and seditious plot which ultimately assassinated President John Fitzgerald Kennedy. (Author's exclusive original discovery.)

[353] Author's exclusive original discovery.

turned 79 years old. He was virtually blind now, able only to detect light and shadows – not discrete shapes or details.[354] Rayburn could no longer read text, count coins or recognize people's facial features, even at close range. But he soldiered grimly on, assisted by helpful younger aides who whispered colleagues' names to him in advance, or who greeted visitors loudly for him as they approached, so that the Speaker would be spared the profound humiliation of others recognizing his optical infirmity.[355]

Even though his eyesight had deteriorated horrendously, Rayburn was determined to carry out his role in the JFK assassination plot insofar as he was able.[356] To that end he gamely continued to perform those acts which he could, disguising the most important of them to minimize revelation or detection. Rayburn was old and severely hindered by his failing eyes, but there were at least four (4) major tasks which he could execute for his murderous protégé Lyndon Johnson during the next several months – and execute them he did.[357]

The first took place on January 20th, 1961. Shortly before JFK was inaugurated by Chief Justice Earl Warren, *Samuel Taliaferro Rayburn himself personally swore in Lyndon Baines Johnson as Vice President of the United States* in the chilly winter air outside the Capitol.

Rayburn himself had put Johnson on the Democratic ticket through blackmail just six months earlier, in Los Angeles.

Rayburn himself now swore in the man whom he knew would become president of the United States via murder.

Rayburn himself had now quite literally placed Lyndon Johnson within a bullet of the American presidency.[358]

Americans watching on television that day had no idea what they were witnessing. But in retrospect it is genuinely chilling to observe. Rayburn's awkward inauguration of Lyndon Johnson that cold day in Washington[359] was not a sacred traditional ceremony or a "celebration of the miracle of democracy" [*sic*]; it was,

---

[354] Anthony Champagne, *Congressman Sam Rayburn,* p. 60.

[355] Anthony Champagne, *Congressman Sam Rayburn,* p. 61.

[356] The criminal actions which I have documented in this chapter prove that fact beyond **any** possibility of denial.

[357] Author's exclusive original discovery.

[358] Author's exclusive original discovery.

[359] Both Rayburn and Johnson were extremely nervous that day; multiple observers noted that the verbal articulation wording of the vice-presidential oath was bobbled by the two Texans.

rather, the opening *public* act of a murderous political plot that would culminate in Texas just over one thousand days in the future.[360]

Determined ambition plus shrewdness.

As of midday on January 20th, 1961, Lyndon Johnson of Texas was now *finally* in position – first in the line of presidential succession, ready for instant elevation to the Oval Office once the JFK assassination plan was fully ready to be implemented.

Number one with a bullet.

And John Kennedy, without realizing it, was already a dead man.

Now it was time for Rayburn and Johnson to concentrate on *other* vital elements of their deadly plot.

* * *

Throughout his career on Capitol Hill, Rayburn was a vocal and ardent partisan of the Democratic Party, consistently trumpeting its role in passing significant legislation that improved the lot of (white, rural) America. He functioned in a bipartisan way when he felt he could, and he frequently assisted Republican presidents when he thought that a particular program or policy genuinely benefited the country – but he was definitely a Democrat, through and through.

Yet simple "party loyalty" did not explain Rayburn's willingness in early 1961 to help JFK break the legislative stranglehold which the powerful Rules Committee held over bills in the House.

Something *else* was going on.

And only I discovered the answer.

Rayburn did not enlarge the Rules Committee in order to "rescue" the legislative program and the political agenda of a new President whom he in fact despised and was plotting to kill; rather, he enlarged it in order to ensure that a special piece of legislation – *a law which was vital to the operational success of the upcoming JFK assassination plot* – was not bottled up endlessly in the committee by stubborn and obstructionist legislators who were not even privy to its meaning.[361]

In other words, the committee-packing maneuver was **not** designed or intended to "save" John F. Kennedy's legislative program.[362]

Rather, it was to enable the *murder* of John F. Kennedy.[363]

---

[360] Author's exclusive original discovery.

[361] Author's exclusive original discovery.

[362] Author's exclusive original discovery.

[363] Author's exclusive original discovery.

No one realized it at the time, of course.

No one.

As a result of the Rules Committee victory (and the eventual passage of a law in October 1962), Lyndon Johnson got his own full-time Secret Service detail – *his own personal, fully armed Praetorian Guard.* His very own cadre – an armed group that would prove vital to LBJ's success on November 22nd, 1963.[364]

The successful Rules Committee maneuver in early 1961 earned Rayburn gratitude and relief from the Kennedy White House and from ignorant liberals everywhere. But the few genuine loyalists of the New Frontier had *no idea* that this seeming "victory" was in reality a lethal Trojan horse that would facilitate the vicious slaying of their leader.[365]

* * *

Killing a president is a matter of mere seconds – but smart men know that *things can always go wrong.* And in such situations, the principal leader of a plot must not remain alone, vulnerable, unprotected, subject to the whims of irony and the vagaries of fate. Once the shooting subsided, Lyndon Johnson alone – unless he had *his own personal phalanx of dedicated hatchet men* – would be just an unarmed man, his proverbial "nether regions" dangling in the proverbial breeze.

That simply wouldn't do, of course.

Not at all.

LBJ needed a praetorian guard.[366] He needed his own team of armed men – his own personal cadre, reporting directly to him, loyal to him, familiar to him, obedient and resourceful and motivated and authorized to take extreme actions in extreme situations.[367]

But therein lay a huge problem.

For in January 1961, no such entity existed within the federal government of the United States.

Not for the Vice President . . .

The problem could not be remedied by mere fiat, either. A new law was required. And naturally that new law would, by definition, have to pass through the United States House of Representatives.

Sam Rayburn's domain.

---

[364] Author's exclusive original discovery.

[365] Author's exclusive original discovery.

[366] Author's exclusive original discovery.

[367] Author's exclusive original discovery.

So Rayburn set out to remedy this vital and dangerous gap in the assassination arrangements. And as a result of the Speaker's work, Lyndon Baines Johnson would not face the tension, the confusion and the stunning plot failures in Dallas all alone.

Clearly initiated by the wheedling of Lyndon Johnson, a letter over President Kennedy's signature was sent to Speaker Rayburn in the spring of 1961, "requesting" statutory authorization and funding for the creation of a formal, *full-time* vice-presidential Secret Service detail which had never previously existed.

Having rejected Johnson's brazen power play *earlier* in 1961, soon after the January 20th inauguration – in which the Vice President audaciously sought unwarranted control over American military and security affairs[368] – President Kennedy was clearly persuaded that the subsequent issue (of "merely" creating an armed SS detail for LBJ) was a relatively minor matter of far less importance, which would serve as a convenient sop to Johnson's titanic ego.

JFK did not know how grievously wrong he was.

The events of November 22nd would prove that, in spades.

* * *

"Sam stays hitched," old Cactus Jack Garner once remarked approvingly about his longtime political protégé from Bonham.[369]

Sam stays hitched.

Rayburn was deadly earnest about making a Texan – a *real* Texan, not a diffident GOP impostor like Dwight Eisenhower – president of the United States.

Since it couldn't be Rayburn himself, it would have to be Lyndon Johnson.

And Rayburn stayed hitched to LBJ from the initial commencement of the assassination plot back in August 1956 until the very end.

All the way with LBJ.

Rayburn himself didn't make it all the way to 1963, however.

He wanted to, of course; but he simply couldn't.

In 1961 Speaker Rayburn began experiencing severe back pain. At first, he wrote it off as being merely a bad case of lumbago – but in reality, it was (like his own true personality) much darker and far more malevolent. This ultimately meant that in 1961, Sam Rayburn's key personal role in the JFK assassination plot – and his very own life – were about to end.

---

[368] Robert Dallek noted this LBJ power play but failed (or refused) to understand what it meant.

[369] Alfred Steinberg, *Sam Rayburn,* p. 178.

The pain intensified and became so bad by spring and summer that it made rising from a chair or sofa an agony. It made Rayburn weep and cry out in private.[370] It made him feel dizzy and faint in public. It led him to become disoriented and lost during brief daily walks near the Capitol.[371] It finally forced him to step out of the Speaker's chair at the end of August in 1961 and return to Texas for medical exams and treatment.[372]

Rayburn was a very shrewd and calculating man, but *he had waited too long.*

When he was finally examined and diagnosed properly in the latter half of 1961, it was immediately apparent that Speaker Rayburn was suffering from deadly pancreatic cancer which had already metastasized throughout his 79-year-old body. The cancer was now totally inoperable, the pain barely manageable. Nevertheless, Rayburn held on for almost six weeks. Near the very end of his life, he drifted in and out of a coma.

As the severity and extent of Rayburn's condition became known that summer and fall, politicians and newspapers fawned over the aged and diminutive Baron of Bonham, most being utterly unaware of his sickening true colors and his hidden criminal actions. Top leaders went to visit him in Texas before the end.

Even President Kennedy himself flew down in October 1961 to see the sharp-tongued, poisonous little felon who had forced him to put Lyndon Johnson on the 1960 ticket, because it was simply politically impossible for Kennedy *not* to visit him – Rayburn was a Democrat and was the Speaker of the House, after all, and the American public would not learn of Rayburn's shameful 1960 blackmail of JFK for several more decades. So JFK flew to Texas in October and made an obligatory personal visit to Rayburn (in the presence of a hospital nurse, thus limiting the candor of their conversation), then went back again to Texas the following month to attend Rayburn's funeral on November 18th, 1961.[373]

Lyndon Johnson came too, of course.

---

[370] Anthony Champagne, *Congressman Sam Rayburn,* p. 62.

[371] Anthony Champagne, *Congressman Sam Rayburn,* p. 62.

[372] C. Dwight Dorough, *Mr. Sam,* p. 34.

[373] Stark and humiliating *political* considerations also forced President Kennedy to publicly compliment the dead Rayburn; to accede to the issuance of a federal medal in Rayburn's honor; to lend his name to a fundraising effort for the Rayburn Library in Texas; to name a new nuclear submarine after Rayburn; and to appear at a public ceremony for the laying of a cornerstone for the new Rayburn House Office Building near the Capitol.

Obviously, JFK could not publicly disclose and decry the vicious 1960 ***blackmail*** perpetrated against him by Sam Rayburn and Lyndon Johnson without exposing the very peccadilloes which had given the two Texans such nasty and overwhelming leverage over him in the first place, thus severely damaging his *own* public image in the process.

In the first week of October, a few days *before* President Kennedy traveled to see the Speaker, LBJ himself arrived for a personal farewell. Samuel Rayburn had been his mentor, his father figure, his friend and – finally and most importantly – *his chief co-conspirator* in the JFK assassination.[374] During LBJ's visit, Rayburn was unconscious and unresponsive – but Lyndon Johnson silently made a secret pledge to his dying co-conspirator.[375] Later photographs prove that fact, as I discovered and as I explain in a later chapter.[376]

As both Texas titans now recognized, the moribund Speaker would clearly not live long enough to see their vicious dream actually come to fruition, because in late 1961 the JFK murder plot was – to their enormous mutual frustration – *still* not fully ready to be implemented. For one thing, designated patsy Lee Oswald (a former Marine and aspiring writer[377]) was still stubbornly residing inside the Soviet Union and had not yet been brought back to the United States; for another, certain major preparations in Dallas itself were not yet complete.

Thus Rayburn would die at 6:20 in the morning on Thursday, November 16th, 1961[378] without ever seeing the culmination of his brilliantly conceived assassination plot. He perished *before* Dallas, without witnessing his ultimate triumph. The Speaker was buried in the Texas soil a full *two years* before the gunshots finally rang out in Dealey Plaza and permanently spattered American democracy with blood.

But Sam Rayburn's murderous *plot* continued apace – and his chief co-conspirator, LBJ, never forgot the intellectual author of the JFK assassination.

Never.

The very night of President Kennedy's assassination, Lyndon Johnson raised a glass toward Rayburn's portrait in Johnson's Washington D. C. home, The Elms, and verbally saluted his dead co-conspirator. *"I wish to God you were here,"* said LBJ.[379]

And two weeks after JFK was slaughtered in Dallas, as Lyndon Johnson and his wife formally moved into the White House in early December 1963, Lady Bird

---

[374] Author's exclusive original discovery.

[375] Author's exclusive original discovery.

[376] Author's exclusive original discovery.

[377] Oswald's literary aspirations were *explicitly* mentioned in a Dallas newspaper in the immediate aftermath of the JFK assassination – one of the very few points that any local or national media outlet *ever* got right, either at that time or in all the decades since. (My thanks to Melanie for her generosity in letting me examine an authentic original 1963 edition containing that article.) The truth is that Lee Oswald was a *writer,* not a sniper. His tool of choice was a *pen* or a *typewriter* – not a rifle.

[378] C. Dwight Dorough, *Mr. Sam,* p. 40.

[379] Jim Bishop, *The Day Kennedy Was Shot,* p. 418.

herself *personally* hand-carried Sam Rayburn's framed portrait into the Executive Mansion at LBJ's behest. Official White House photos captured the act.[380]

Johnson thus kept his final promise to his dead friend. By bringing Rayburn's portrait into the White House itself, LBJ posthumously "shared" their murderous victory – the ultimate Texas triumph – with its true intellectual author, the venal and corrupt and murderous politician known as "Mr. Sam."[381]

* * *

Samuel Taliaferro Rayburn, longtime Speaker of the United States House of Representatives, committed no fewer than seven (7) overt acts in furtherance of the murderous plot to assassinate John Fitzgerald Kennedy.[382]

Knowingly, deliberately, and with malice aforethought:

1. Rayburn originated the conceptual architecture of the JFK plot, focusing on the murderous abuse of the legal line of presidential succession.[383]

2. Rayburn conspired with Lyndon Baines Johnson, beginning in 1956, to kill JFK – the presumptive 1960 Democratic nominee, and likely the next President of the United States.[384]

3. Rayburn arranged an early discharge from the Marine Corps in mid-1959 for a young Texas resident named Lee Harvey Oswald, the pre-designated *patsy* in the upcoming assassination.[385] Freed from his USMC obligations, Oswald would promptly thereafter be sent to the USSR on a covert mission for the CIA, in the autumn of 1959, posing as a supposed "defector" – and thus be successfully *branded,* well in advance of the upcoming assassination, as a supposedly "pro-Communist" individual.

4. Rayburn *personally* blackmailed JFK at the Democratic National Convention in Los Angeles in July 1960 in order to force Kennedy to put Johnson on the 1960 Democratic ticket as his running mate, thereby putting LBJ in position to vault instantly into the presidency upon JFK's upcoming murder.

---

[380]Author's exclusive original discovery. Official White House photos from December 1963 prove this point indisputably.

[381] Author's exclusive original discovery.

[382] Author's exclusive original discovery.

[383] Author's exclusive original discovery.

[384] Author's exclusive original discovery.

[385] FBI agent Vincent Drain, who was personally involved in the post-assassination investigation, revealed something extraordinary in a 1988 interview: ". . . as a matter of fact, *Sam Rayburn is the one who got [Lee Harvey Oswald] a hardship discharge out of the Marine Corps."* (Larry Sneed, *No More Silence,* p. 254.)

5. Rayburn actively obstructed justice by *covering up* the 1960 blackmail with false accounts of what had actually happened at the Los Angeles convention.

6. Rayburn knowingly swore in Lyndon Johnson as Vice President of the United States in order to enable LBJ's elevation to the Oval Office through murder.

7. Rayburn drove successful passage of a federal law (finally passed in 1962, after his death) creating an armed Secret Service cadre for now-Vice President Johnson – a cadre which would be indispensable to, and integrally involved in, the execution of the JFK assassination plot in Dallas in 1963.

Seven concrete actions.

Seven absolutely vital steps which were essential to the Kennedy assassination plot were taken by Sam Rayburn *himself,* in person.

It was Rayburn.

It was Rayburn.

It was Rayburn.[386]

* * *

Samuel Rayburn died of pancreatic cancer at the age of 79 in mid-November 1961, before all the elements of the JFK assassination plot were ready to be implemented. He did not live to see his murderous plan come to fruition in Dallas in 1963. Nor did he leave behind a convenient written confession of his deeds (very few murderers do). But his guilt is now established for all the world to see through the actions which I have thoroughly documented and analyzed here.[387]

Rayburn's longtime protégé, surrogate son and assassination co-conspirator Lyndon Baines Johnson gamely soldiered on without him – calling on support from other governmental and ex-governmental sources of power, as you will see. But upon returning to his Washington residence ("The Elms") on the night of November 22nd, 1963, *one of the very first things that Johnson did* was sit down, raise a glass toward a picture of Sam Rayburn on his wall, and say aloud in front of several witnesses, "I wish to God you were here."[388]

---

[386] Author's exclusive original discovery.

[387] Author's exclusive original discovery.

[388] Jim Bishop, *The Day Kennedy Was Shot,* p. 418.

The following night, November 23rd, LBJ *repeated* this personal invocation of Rayburn in front of additional witnesses, including journalist Nancy Hanschman Dickerson.[389]

There is an old saying which goes, *Ya dance with who brung ya.*

And that is precisely what Lyndon Johnson did.

LBJ was now the (totally illegitimate) chief executive – and by his gesture to his dead friend and mentor *on the very night of the JFK assassination,* he was clearly remembering and saluting the diminutive, frustrated man who had brought him to the ultimate pinnacle of power.

As Lyndon Johnson had remarked as early as the 1940s, *"You don't become president without going through Sam Rayburn."*

LBJ was living proof of the truth of that remark.

* * *

When the new Rayburn Congressional Office Building was completed in Washington D.C. in 1965, Lyndon Johnson was there. A black-and-white image taken by a photographer captures LBJ in profile, standing beneath a statue of his dead co-conspirator.[390]

That single photograph says it all.

It was Rayburn.

Sam Rayburn & Lyndon Johnson.

Together.

Sam Rayburn & Lyndon Johnson: *the actual creators, the actual intellectual authors, and the actual leaders* of the bloody JFK assassination plot.[391]

---

[389] Nancy Hanschman Dickerson typed up notes of her November 23rd visit to The Elms, and her son John later wrote an article based on them. (John Dickerson, "Inside LBJ's Home the Night After JFK Died," *Slate,* November 22nd, 2013.)

[390] Author's exclusive original discovery.

[391] Author's exclusive original discovery.

Congressman Albert Thomas (left) and
USAAF veteran Jack Valenti (right)
were Texans tapped by Lyndon Johnson
to assist him following the death
of LBJ's chief co-conspirator,
House Speaker Sam Rayburn, in late 1961.

Thomas was a powerful and experienced politician;
Valenti was an experienced mass murderer.

Author's exclusive original discovery.

Chapter Twenty-Eight:
The Henchmen of Houston

"Nobody is indispensable."
– Lyndon Baines Johnson

*"The president is dead . . .
No one is indispensable . . ."*
– Jack Joseph Valenti

*"These things do not just 'happen.'
They are **made** to happen."*
– John Fitzgerald Kennedy

Sam Rayburn's death from cancer in November 1961 – which was followed just a month later by General Curtis LeMay's *near-death* from serious cardiac trouble – constituted a serious blow to Lyndon Johnson's long quest to murder JFK and take the White House for himself.

Rayburn had been a father figure and mentor to LBJ; he had also been a brilliant operator and masterful politician of truly reptilian skill and cold-bloodedness.

And above all, Sam Rayburn was *the intellectual architect of,* and *the chief co-conspirator in,* the plot to kill JFK.[392]

Despite Rayburn's demise, Johnson would certainly not abandon their long-planned, murderous joint quest to have a Texan occupy the Oval Office – but the Vice President now definitely needed some new *support.*

Allies.

Companions.

Men he could trust.

Friends, in a word.

Fellow *Texans.*

Fellow *operators.*

And so LBJ cast about for men who could step up – not "replace" Rayburn, but *succeed* Rayburn – as his close allies in the extremely dangerous and criminal pursuit of the top prize in America.

---

[392] Author's exclusive original discovery.

Lyndon Baines Johnson needed men who could be as cold and calculating and grim as Sam Rayburn had been.

He needed some *men*.

Two men.

An inside man, and an outside man.[393]

They would never actually replace "Mr. Sam," of course.

No one could possibly do that.

But LBJ certainly needed them, and they would be there for him – starting well *before* Dallas.

One was a cagey veteran politician.

The other was a cagey veteran *murderer*.[394]

* * *

The deadly duo hailed – professionally – from Houston, Texas.

The "inside" man was none other than Congressman Albert Langston "Al" Thomas, who represented the Eighth District. Al Thomas ultimately became an ally of a fellow Texan named Lyndon Baines Johnson.

The "outside" man was a USAAF veteran named Jack Joseph Valenti, a Texas advertising agency owner who had done extensive "work" over the years for Congressman Albert Thomas.[395]

LBJ would leverage their proven skills to brutally and successfully maneuver President Kennedy into making the fatal November 1963 trip to the Lone Star State.[396]

* * *

---

[393] Author's exclusive original discovery.

[394] Author's exclusive original discovery.

[395] Author's exclusive original discovery. When I first discovered and raised the possibility of Jack Valenti being involved in the JFK assassination, *decades ago*, Lifton (in typical fashion) quickly and wrongly dismissed and ridiculed the idea.

Pro tip: haste and stubbornness are lousy qualities in anyone supposedly seeking the truth.

[396] For decades, the ignorant and the timorous have spewed utterly specious poppycock about the supposed "reason" for JFK's fatal trip to Texas in November 1963. The standard claim is ludicrous nonsense about "the need to try to calm and reconcile warring conservative and liberal factions within the Texas Democratic Party."

That childish notion is nothing less than a bucket of malodorous bovine excrement.

In this chapter you will learn the cold hard reality behind John Kenney's last journey as president.

When Speaker of the House Sam Rayburn died in 1961, his successor as Speaker was the longtime House Majority Leader, Congressman John William McCormack. Despite being from Massachusetts and being a fellow Catholic, McCormack was no close friend of President Kennedy; after all, JFK's brother Edward had beaten McCormack's nephew Edward in the 1962 Massachusetts senate race, and had thereby damaged McCormack's own political power in the Bay State.

Such crimes are unforgivable in politics, of course.

So McCormack would *not* be a reliable rubber-stamp ally for Kennedy, but he *was* nevertheless still a damned Yankee – a northerner with whom LBJ would never be entirely comfortable.

McCormack was certainly no "replacement" for Sam Rayburn.

Johnson needed a fellow Texan with serious clout – and Al Thomas fit the bill. *Perfectly.*

Congressman Thomas was head of the House appropriations subcommittee with control of budgets for independent federal agencies including NASA, the showy centerpiece of JFK's domestic political agenda. Without Al Thomas's approval, money for the Mercury and Gemini and Apollo space programs would be delayed or denied – putting Kennedy's ambitious and very public goal of achieving a moon landing prior to decade's end at serious risk.

Thomas was therefore *perfectly* positioned to apply severe political pain at the precise point where JFK was most vulnerable to such pressure.

And apply it he did.

It all began gradually and positively, with smiles and handshakes between John Kennedy and Al Thomas while Lyndon Johnson quietly lifted key pieces into place to ensure that all was set before carrying out the bloody noontime assassination of the nation's chief executive.

* * *

In May 1961, following the catastrophic April failure of the criminal American "Bay of Pigs" invasion against Cuba, President Kennedy gave what was, in essence, a second inaugural address – a "do-over." As Sam Rayburn and Lyndon Johnson watched with undisguised hatred from their seats behind him on the rostrum,[397] JFK boldly called for America to accomplish the herculean goal of "landing a man on the Moon and returning him safely to the Earth" before 1970.

While the actual crewed rocket *launch* facilities would remain in Florida, NASA headquarters would not be located there. Lyndon Johnson (head of the Space

---

[397] A photographer from NASA was on hand to document Kennedy's speech to Congress, and thereby captured for all time the seething hatred which Rayburn and Johnson had for their target, the president.

Council and nominally in charge of the U. S. space program, with JFK's agreement), Sam Rayburn (prior to his death), and Al Thomas (in charge of the space program's congressional *funding*) had all helped ensure that NASA's vital Manned Spacecraft Center ("Mission Control") facility would be headquartered in the Houston area instead.[398] Massive quantities of money soon began pouring into the Lone Star State.

In September 1962, President Kennedy visited Texas and gave a rousing outdoor speech at Rice University in Houston. "We choose to go to the moon," he thundered. "We choose to go to the Moon in this decade and do the other things, *not* because they are easy, but because they are *hard;* because that goal will serve to organize and measure the best of our energies and skills . . ." JFK told the huge crowd that space exploration would demand – and reveal – America's talents and capabilities in an unprecedented way.

At the airport on September 11th, Al Thomas gamely posed with the arriving president and guided him – literally with a hand on his back – as JFK greeted various local dignitaries.

At Rice University Stadium on September 12th, Al Thomas gamely sat near the president and applauded his lofty words about the space program.

Everything was "A-OK" [399] and "hunky-dory."

Or so it seemed.

* * *

In early 1963, as Lyndon Johnson laboriously neared completion of his extensive strategic maneuvers and detailed criminal preparations for the upcoming JFK assassination, the first jarring note of cosmic discord affecting *NASA* (and therefore, affecting JFK's political fortunes) was sounded by LBJ's smart and crocodilian ally, Congressman Al Thomas.

In a public statement which hit the White House like a thunderbolt, Al Thomas announced that he would regrettably have to *retire from Congress* – and of course, depart from his vital role on the House appropriations subcommittee! – due to cancer.

The cancer was real; the retirement was *not.*

Naturally alarmed at what might happen to his much-ballyhooed space program without the veteran Houston congressman's guidance and support, a nervous President Kennedy quickly expressed the fervent hope that Thomas's medical retirement would not actually be "necessary."

---

[398] Memo to the ignorant: This was not a "coincidence."

[399] USAF Lieutenant Colonel John Anthony ("Shorty") Powers did not invent the term, but he made it quite famous during his narration of NASA's Mercury rocket launch countdowns in the early days of the U. S. space program.

The ingenious trap had been set by LBJ and Al Thomas, working in tandem.

It would be baited by none other than *Jack Valenti.*

Soon it would be sprung, by Congressman Al Thomas himself – with fatal consequences for JFK.

* * *

The chronology of those events is a vitally important tool for understanding the reality of the JFK assassination.

Al Thomas's initial "retirement" statement came in April 1963.[400]

That very same month – April 1963, which was a key month in the JFK assassination plot[401] – Lyndon Johnson openly and knowingly and deliberately made extremely disturbing *public statements* about the *timing* of the approaching presidential assassination.[402]

Then in June 1963, Congressman Thomas suddenly announced that *after speaking with his old pal, Vice President Johnson,* he (Thomas) had begun to "reconsider" his planned medical "retirement" – thereby opening the door to possibly remaining in office and shepherding the JFK space program's budget through the congressional process.

At that point, Kennedy naturally owed Al Thomas a huge political debt.

On September 17th, 1963, Jack Valenti wrote to the president – formally asking him to attend a November 21st testimonial dinner in Houston, Texas, honoring Congressman Al Thomas.[403]

JFK could hardly say no.

Valenti's "invitation" reached the White House on September 19th.

---

[400] Thomas's purported "retirement" in 1963 echoed the earlier reports about Sam Rayburn's purported "retirement" which hit the national press in 1961. (Author's exclusive original discovery.)

In both instances, the point of such sinister maneuvers was to *force President Kennedy to make **a trip to Texas** for a "salute" to a "retiring" Texas politician – a trip during which JFK could be assassinated in a public setting **controlled by Lyndon Baines Johnson.*** (Author's exclusive original discovery.)

[401] Author's exclusive original discovery. Note carefully: As I document in this book, LBJ made *several* crucial moves in April 1963 to put the JFK assassination plot into high gear.

[402] LBJ was doing so for reasons which I discovered exclusively, and which I reveal in later chapters of this book.

[403] Al Thomas himself even visited the office of JFK's congressional liaison, Larry O'Brien, to *personally* request that the president attend the upcoming testimonial dinner in Texas. It was an extraordinary, unprecedented and totally unexpected move by a very powerful politician, and it was something which stunned O'Brien enough to mention it with awe in his 1974 memoir, *No Final Victories.* What O'Brien did ***not*** grasp was that LBJ and Al Thomas were pulling out all the stops to *ensure* that President Kennedy came to the Texas killing ground in November.

SEAN FETTER

The trap had been baited.

But then JFK stupidly committed a very noisy *faux pas* which only *deepened* his debt to Al Thomas.

On September 20th, 1963, JFK made a dramatic public speech at the United Nations in New York in which he openly advocated *a joint U.S.-USSR mission to the moon* in order to lessen Cold War tensions, minimize needless competition, and reduce unnecessary costs.[404]

The very next day, September 21st, Al Thomas quickly dispatched a letter to the White House demanding an explanation for the unexpected JFK initiative – a shocking, outrageously pacifist, patently pinko proposal which naturally threatened the river of pork-barrel spending which NASA sent flowing to Houston and to the rest of Thomas's Texas congressional district.[405]

On September 23rd, 1963, *Lyndon Johnson met privately with Al Thomas* in Washington D. C. at The Elms, LBJ's then-residence as Vice President.[406]

They did not gather to discuss twelfth-century Turkish architecture, nor the poetry of John Keats.

On the evening of September 24th, 1963, the White House caved to the pressure and acceded to the Texas trip to attend the Al Thomas testimonial dinner.

On the evening of September 25th, 1963, the White House informed the *Dallas Morning News* that JFK would indeed visit Texas in late November.

On October 11th, 1963, Kenny O'Donnell replied in writing to Jack Valenti, formally confirming that President Kennedy would indeed attend the Al Thomas testimonial dinner.

And *that very night,* October 11th, LBJ and Thomas once again dined together at The Elms, LBJ's home.[407]

They were celebrating – and planning.[408]

Congressman Thomas's visit to Larry O'Brien – and Jack Valenti's letter to JFK himself – had done the trick.

---

[404] JFK had urged such a joint mission both in his own inaugural speech and in his June 1961 summit meeting with Soviet leader Nikita Khrushchev, but the idea had gone nowhere. Kennedy's insistence on raising it *again* at the UN in September 1963 – a year *after* his rousing "moon" speech at Rice University – seemed hypocritical in the extreme.

[405] As finally approved by the House of Representatives on October 10th, 1963, the NASA budget contained *not a single penny* for any "joint" US-USSR moon ventures. Al Thomas certainly knew how to "manage" his turf.

[406] Author's exclusive original discovery, documented in the Vice-Presidential Daily Diary (LBJ Library).

[407] Author's exclusive original discovery. See the Vice-Presidential Diary for October 11th, 1963 (LBJ Library).

[408] Author's exclusive original discovery.

The fatal journey was now a reality.

It wasn't about "healing a rift among Texas Democrats."

It wasn't about "fundraising for the party."

It wasn't about "launching the 1964 presidential campaign."

It wasn't about "solidifying the national ticket's image in Texas."

It was about killing John Fitzgerald Kennedy.

*The Texas trip was an inescapable "debt" owed by JFK to Johnson's ally and assassination co-conspirator, Al Thomas – a **forced** visit, under threat of severe budgetary trouble for the much-ballyhooed American space program.*

Political blackmail once again.

In July 1960, LBJ used Kennedy's *sexual* Achilles heel to blackmail him.

In September 1963, Lyndon Johnson used Kennedy's *political* Achilles heel to blackmail him.

It worked both times.

There was no escape.

Kennedy *had* to go to Texas, and he *had* to attend the Al Thomas dinner.

*The true linchpin of the Texas trip – the politically **obligatory** Thomas testimonial dinner on the night of Thursday, November 21st, 1963 – is what enabled Lyndon Johnson and his subordinate U. S. government accomplices to aggressively finalize the scheduling and planning for the murderous ambush in Dallas on Friday, November 22nd, 1963.*

Johnson had masterfully employed his two Houston henchmen, Al Thomas and Jack Valenti, to *keelhaul* President Kennedy – and to thereby *force* him to visit the Lone Star State.

The key pieces were being artfully moved into place.

Now it was all over except for the shooting – and the subsequent slaughter.

* * *

Jack Valenti was a short, ambitious, hard-driving Houstonian who had returned from World War II and, from all appearances, "made good." He earned a master's degree in business from Harvard, and he opened a successful advertising agency[409] with a partner named Weldon Weekley.[410]

But Valenti was not merely a hard-driving Houston advertising man with a Harvard degree who had "returned from the war and made good."

Not at all.

He was much more than that.

Lyndon Johnson first noticed him in the mid-1950s when Valenti wrote a fatuous piece extolling LBJ's alleged virtues – and he had kept in contact with the diminutive but ambitious Houstonian. Johnson had a good eye for men with talents and skills that he could use in the future.

Jack Valenti had such skills – and a deeply criminal temperament, to boot.

By his own written admission, *Jack Joseph Valenti was a bag man.*[411]

He handled and transported and delivered massive cash bribes and payoffs and kickbacks to and from wealthy contributors and politicians.

In the early 1960s, Valenti was a corrupt crook in a nice suit.

But there was much more to his hideously ugly story.

Valenti was also, as he admitted to me in person, *a mass murderer.*[412]

* * *

As a USAAF lieutenant in World War II, Jack Valenti piloted a B-25 bomber in Europe – but he was certainly no hero.

He actually received *medals* for what he did there – but no one in the public knew *what Valenti actually did there* until I elicited the chilling truth from him myself, face to face.

---

[409] Valenti was **not** a public relations (PR) man; in reality, he ran an *advertising* agency. (Lifton – and many others – never understood the difference.)

That difference, in simplest terms, is this: advertising means that a company **pays** to say whatever *it* wants to say in a particular forum (e.g., "Acme Soap is the best!").

By contrast, PR generally means that a company has to convince *others* of the value of what it is saying, thereby persuading *them* to say it on the company's behalf as "news" (e.g., "Amalgamated Press reports that Acme Soap has been named the best soap in America, as documented by the Guggleschlager Foundation's annual survey of ten million doctors and twenty million formerly filthy consumers.")

An advertisement is a company doing *its own* talking; a news article or "media placement" is usually someone else talking *about* that company.

[410] Their biggest client was Humble Oil – the company which donated the land eventually used for NASA's "Mission Control" in Houston.

[411] Author's exclusive original discovery. Valenti admitted in his book *This Time, This Place.*

[412] Author's exclusive original discovery.

In the spring of 2001, I attended an appearance by Jack Valenti in Chicago *specifically in order to ask him about matters pertaining to the JFK case.* I chose a seat in the front of the room where he spoke and I observed him very closely, taking copious real-time notes during the event. Following Valenti's canned, well-rehearsed speech (his own stump speech, which had nothing to do with "Media Violence and American Culture," the actual topic of the forum) I rode an elevator downstairs with him to a reception before stepping into a lobby and questioning him there in person.[413]

Like former Secretary of Defense Robert McNamara was in *his* later years, Jack Valenti in 2001 was a pathetically shabby, threadbare, unkempt version of the extremely dapper, well-dressed man he had once been during Camelot and during the criminal, utterly illegitimate Johnson administration.[414] Valenti's yellow cloth shirt was topped by a noticeably ragged, contrasting white collar; the knot of his dark tie was noticeably askew; his ugly dark plaid jacket emphasized his shockingly white hair. He looked like a has-been huckster – a snake-oil salesman on his last ride.

I asked Valenti, face-to-face, whether it was *ever* acceptable for the U. S. government to alter or censor *vital evidence in a criminal case.*

"Like what?" Valenti asked me.

I answered cagily – with important Dealey Plaza images in mind.

"Films – or photographs," I replied.[415]

Valenti allowed as how "Every case is individual," and he further declared piously, "I'm hesitant to alter anything."

But then he got down to the nitty gritty.

Censorship or mutilation of the photographic record would be acceptable "to prevent a shooting – or a war," Valenti said to me. "The government has martial law – and *that* doesn't violate the First Amendment!"

Then he spontaneously launched into a stunning, brutal, revelatory *non sequitur* about his *actual* wartime activities in Europe during the 1940s as a USAAF B-25 pilot.

*"I killed **ten thousand** civilians,"* Jack Valenti confessed to me bluntly, without the slightest hint of guilt or remorse. *"I strafed them from one hundred feet at a depot. I never saw their faces."*[416]

---

[413] I also took copious *additional* written notes within minutes of our lobby conversation.

[414] I was immediately struck by the fact that Valenti, the wealthy and highly paid head of the MPAA, resembled nothing so much as the cheap, posturing, dishonest and contemptible fraudster once portrayed so brilliantly on screen by actor Frank Morgan (Francis Phillip Wuppermann) – namely, "Professor Marvel," the thoroughly deceitful title character of the 1939 movie *The Wizard of Oz.*

[415] I didn't add "or the wounds on presidential corpses."

[416] Valenti did **not** include this horrifying and disturbing admission in his memoirs. But he confessed it directly to me, face-to-face, in person.

The powerful head of the MPAA then put forth the literal *Nazi* defense that was articulated – and rejected – at the Nuremberg trials following World War II:

"I was *following orders*," said the USAAF veteran self-righteously. "No matter how scared you are – that's the mark of a military professional."[417]

Valenti, the mass murderer, then had the gall to label the courageous Vietnamese civilians who heroically resisted murderous American warfare against their country in the 1960s and 1970s as "killers and grenade throwers."[418]

* * *

Aside from his chilling confession to *mass murder,* the Valenti phrase that echoed in my mind long after the conversation ended was his chilling "justification" for *the United States government deliberately altering evidence in a criminal case.*

Valenti looked at me that day with utter coldness in his blue eyes and declared that "When a dagger is at the nation's belly," anything is permissible.

It was a phrase he used often in his public speeches, but it was particularly vivid and disturbing nonetheless, especially when uttered one-to-one.

When a dagger is at the nation's belly . . .

I was a total stranger asking Valenti probing questions about *criminal governmental falsification of evidence in a major crime.*

And his response was,

When a dagger is at the nation's belly . . .

That is precisely how extremists regarded John Fitzgerald Kennedy:

A dagger at the nation's belly . . .

JFK's appalling idealism; the endless women; the drugs; the peace talk; the détente; Kennedy's repeated refusal to confront and destroy communism, anywhere and everywhere across the globe . . .

A dagger at the nation's belly.

"A dagger at the nation's belly" is a threat to the security of the United States. Jack Valenti was very clear:

Anything is justifiable at that point.

Absolutely ***anything.***

* * *

On November 22nd, 1963 – *before taking off from Love Field to fly back to Washington* – Lyndon Johnson specifically requested Jack Valenti's presence on SAM

---

[417] This despicable attitude is responsible for innumerable war crimes committed all over the world.

[418] Valenti to the author, April 27th, 2001.

26000; then hired Valenti immediately at Love Field; and then made Valenti a top White House aide.

Not *despite* his past, but *because* of it![419]

Jack Valenti was a bag man and a ruthless mass killer of unarmed civilians.

And the fact is that right up until 1964 (when LBJ secretly commenced the massive bombing of Laos) and 1965 (when LBJ openly authorized insanely violent and utterly criminal American military escalation via the massive bombing of North and South Vietnam) – Jack Joseph Valenti had personally murdered *far* more people than Lyndon Baines Johnson *ever* had.[420]

---

[419] Author's exclusive original discovery.

[420] Author's exclusive original discovery.

Lyndon Baines Johnson
was obsessed with becoming president, but was certain that
his Texas background – and America's racial turmoil –
would prevent him from *ever* being nominated by his party.

His longtime friend and mentor Sam Rayburn
figured out another way to take the Oval Office.
Several major felonies were required.

Author's exclusive original discovery.

Chapter Twenty-Nine:
The Sultan of Stonewall

"The traitor moves amongst those within the gate freely,
his sly whispers rustling through all the alleys,
heard in the very halls of government itself.
For the traitor appears not a traitor;
he speaks in accents familiar to his victims,
and he wears their face and their arguments,
he appeals to the baseness that lies
deep in the hearts of all men . . .
he infects the body politic
so that it can no longer resist."

– Marcus Tullius Cicero

"At least wait until next November
before you shoot him down."

– Lyndon Baines Johnson
April 1963

"These things do not just 'happen.'
*They are **made** to happen."*

– John Fitzgerald Kennedy

The most important fact is this:
Lyndon Johnson wanted to be president of the United States.
It was he had always wanted: his highest ambition, his lifelong goal.
Ever since his youth.
Lyndon Johnson wanted to be president of the United States.
An entire country and an entire political culture stood in his way, but the man from Texas was not to be denied.
Lyndon Johnson wanted to be president of the United States.

"There is no question that he was *consumed* with the desire to be president," said North Carolina Governor Terry Sanford.[421]

Lyndon Johnson wanted to be president of the United States.

Understand that clearly, America.

Lyndon Johnson wanted to be president of the United States.

Nothing else.

Nothing less.

Lyndon Johnson wanted to be president of the United States.

And in the end, after committing *multiple felonies* by way of preparation – and with extraordinary help from his co-conspirator and longtime political mentor, Sam Rayburn – LBJ had arranged it so that only one man, a slender cocky bastard from Massachusetts, stood in the way of his triumph.

It was cold on that inaugural platform in January 1961, and the two nervous Texans muffed the actual administration of the vice-presidential oath as Speaker Rayburn personally swore in Lyndon Johnson to the second-highest office in the land – but no matter.

It was now official.

Lyndon Baines Johnson of Texas was now Vice President, and he was now first in the line of presidential succession.

Perfectly positioned.

Number one with a bullet.

Only a gunshot away.

And as soon as LBJ had every major aspect of his and Rayburn's long-simmering assassination plot – dating from August 1956! – fully squared away and *really locked down tight,* the Oval Office would finally be his.[422]

* * *

The Vice-Presidential oath, prescribed by federal law, is actually slightly **different** from the Presidential oath (which is spelled out explicitly in the U.S. Constitution itself).

The differences are intriguing and revealing.

The President takes an oath to, among other things, "preserve, protect and defend the Constitution of the United States."[423]

---

[421] Strober and Strober, *Let Us Begin Anew,* p. 26.

[422] Author's exclusive original discovery.

[423] U.S. Constitution, Article II, Section I, Clause 8.

But the *Vice* President's oath, as dictated by federal law, goes much further, and consists of the following words:

> "I do solemnly swear (or affirm) that I will support and defend the Constitution of the United States *against all **enemies**, foreign and **domestic;*** that I will bear true faith and allegiance to the same; that I take this obligation freely, without any mental reservation or purpose of evasion; and that I will well and faithfully discharge the duties of the office on which I am about to enter. So help me God."[424]

For the record, the Vice-Presidential oath is the very same oath as that taken by ***military*** officers and other high-level U.S. government officials.

The same oath which Johnson's uniformed allies at the Pentagon had taken.

The same oath which USAF General Curtis LeMay so ostentatiously referred to on the final page of his co-written 1965 autobiography.

The same oath which USAF General Power invoked in another 1965 book.

The same oath quoted by USAF Lt. Col. "Buzz" Patterson in his book.

The same oath whose words contain the seeds of – and the ostensible "justification" for – a domestic, military-backed *coup.*

Like the one which America suffered in the autumn of 1963.[425]

* * *

---

[424] US Code, Title 5, Section 3331.

[425] Plenty of pathetic posturing pundits have gnashed their teeth and wrung their hands over what they fatuously and wrongly and melodramatically labeled a "coup" [*sic*] or "coup attempt" [*sic*] in Washington D. C. on January 6th, 2021 – but the truth is that an ugly, disorganized and totally unsuccessful *mob action* by a bunch of angry, inept and ill-informed blowhards (at least one rioter was so astoundingly ignorant that he believed he was at *the White House,* not the Capitol building!) was certainly ***not*** a coup.

Not even close!

The gruesome daytime assassination of America's Chief of State in a murderous plot – a plot led personally by the Vice President of the United States – ***was*** a coup.

And that is precisely what *actually* occurred in November 1963.

Capisci?

The same cowardly and moronic media cranks and prattling politicians who opine so loudly and exaggeratedly and melodramatically about the supposed "cataclysm" of January 6th, 2021, stubbornly refuse to come to grips with the grim, brutal, bloody, catastrophic ***reality*** of November 22nd, 1963 – which tells you all you need to know about their hypocrisy, their ignorance, their sickening dishonesty and their utter lack of gonads.

It is clear and undeniable that Lyndon Baines Johnson was, *by definition,* the principal beneficiary of the JFK assassination. But he was ***not*** some absurdly lucky, ignorantly innocent fellow who just happened to be in the right position at the right time via historical "coincidence" or random "happenstance."

LBJ lived a very deliberate life based on *very deliberate decisions.*

In an instant, the bloody crime in Dallas – *his* crime – vaulted him to the very pinnacle of power.

It was a pinnacle that Johnson knew he could not have reached *on his own* in that era[426] – and he was certainly not the only one who believed that.

Sam Rayburn believed it as well.

And John Kennedy believed it, too.

It was the conventional wisdom of the time:

No southern white man can be elected president of the United States.

Johnson admitted as much in a 1955 letter to JFK's father, in which LBJ ruefully and candidly and accurately declared that, *nearly a century after the Confederacy surrendered to the Union,* it was still "too close to Appomattox" for a white southerner to conceivably win an American presidential election.[427]

Everyone believed that.

The *difference* was that Sam Rayburn and Lyndon Johnson were now fully determined to actually ***do something*** *about it* – to shatter the maddening conventional wisdom and put a Texan into the Oval Office via a hail of gunfire.

It was the only way.

You've got to get your knuckles bloody.

* * *

[426] LBJ also admitted as much on more than one occasion – including, quite explicitly, to Jack Valenti (Strober and Strober, *Let Us Begin Anew,* p. 23); and equally explicitly, during a recorded post-presidential 1969 interview with Robert Hardesty; and equally explicitly, in his own 1971 memoir, *The Vantage Point* (pp. 88-90).

[427] In yet another bizarre example of his strange disconnection from – and breathtaking ignorance of – American life and culture and history, Lifton (allegedly a graduate of an "Ivy League" school called Cornell University) contacted a longtime associate named Peter Rupay and made it mind-bogglingly clear that, more than century after the end of the Civil War, he (Lifton) *did not even know what Appomattox was* – let alone how to ***pronounce*** it! (Peter Rupay to the author, 2017.)

The Liftonian "uh-PALM-uh-talks" [*sic*] incident referred to immediately above reminded me of Lifton's equally bizarre unfamiliarity – displayed repeatedly in the 21st century, while in his *seventies* – with the extremely common surname "Campbell" and how to pronounce it properly.

In several conversations, Lifton strangely kept referring to an executive of the TSBD as "Ochus 'Camp-BELL'" [*sic*].

I thought to myself: *Had Lifton never heard of famous music star* ***Glenn Campbell****? Was Lifton actually unfamiliar with the name of a certain extremely famous American* ***soup*** *company? Seriously?*

Lyndon Johnson was the longtime protégé and surrogate son of House Speaker and fellow Texan Sam Rayburn, who indisputably ruled the House in the late 1950s and early 1960s just as LBJ indisputably ruled the Senate as Majority Leader. LBJ and Rayburn constituted two-thirds of America's national leadership triumvirate, and in fact they regarded themselves as much more than merely "equal to" the duly elected President, former U. S. Army General Dwight D. Eisenhower.

They believed that in important respects, ***they*** (not Ike!) *ran the country.*

LBJ publicly revered the much older Rayburn; "He's like a Daddy to me," Johnson frequently remarked.[428] The much taller LBJ frequently leaned down and kissed the top of Rayburn's head in public, making his affection for (and tight connection to) the Speaker of the House plain for all to see.[429]

Rayburn harbored the very same political ambition as Johnson, but like LBJ he initially felt constrained and excluded by the same cold political calculus: *no Southern white man, no matter how talented or qualified he may be, will be elected President by the American public – especially not during a time of national upheaval over civil rights for black citizens.*

It was an absolute outrage to the two Texans, of course. Together, Rayburn and Johnson in fact *ran the country,* both in their own eyes and in the eyes of many other observers. "Ike" was regarded by many as just a likeable figurehead – spending more time golfing than actively leading the nation.[430]

So ran the argument.

The two prominent Texans, true titans of politics, were being crudely and unjustly shut out of the corridors of ultimate power – corridors that were rightfully theirs, they believed – by shameful sectional prejudice and what later generations would call "reverse racism."

It was a disgrace, of course.

A damned disgrace.

An infernal injustice.

---

[428] Nancy Hanschman Dickerson, *Among Those Present* (paperback edition, 1977), p. 51.

[429] The LBJ Library photo collection has several images of Johnson unabashedly osculating Sam Rayburn's pate.

[430] Many underestimated Eisenhower's cunning, cruelty and criminality. The supposedly moral and grandfatherly "Ike" knowingly authorized several assassinations; knowingly authorized illegal coups; and stupidly "pre-delegated" nuclear war authority to military commanders who were not accountable to the American people. Although he is remembered for his famous warning about the rise of the "military-industrial complex," the truth is that *Eisenhower himself personally **ended** civilian control over the U. S. military* (Author's exclusive original discovery). The abysmally poor quality of American "journalism" and American "education" leads to mass ignorance – not to "exceptionalism."

Thus Rayburn's unmet ambition smoldered in frustration – until a spark of inspiration occurred in 1956.[431] That sinister spark would eventually put Rayburn's surrogate son, Lyndon Johnson, into the Oval Office itself.

Several major felonies were required, however.

* * *

Sam Rayburn was the Speaker of the House of Representatives. As such, he was second in the line of succession. *If President Eisenhower and Vice President Nixon had somehow **both** died suddenly, Sam Rayburn of Texas would have immediately become President of the United States in his own right.*

A Texan would occupy the Oval Office.

Political justice would finally be served.

And there was an intriguing glimmer of hope in that simple political fact.

Of course, sudden dual deaths were unlikely in the extreme. And Rayburn was not about to gun down *both* "Ike" and "Tricky Dick" in order to achieve his dreams. He was not so foolhardy.

Moreover, he could not run normally for the White House himself in 1960, for – apart from being a Southerner – by the time of the January 1961 inaugural he himself would already be 79, and in that pre-Reagan era, a chief executive of such an advanced age was politically unthinkable to most voters.

Rayburn was also rapidly going *blind.*

And yet . . .

A man *can* live vicariously through a trusted protégé – a younger man of similar outlook and beliefs but possessed of much more energy, vitality, passion, health and strength.[432]

*If **I** cannot hold the office, then **we** can hold the office . . .*

And the presidential line of succession indeed offered a way – *if* Lyndon Johnson could somehow first *be inserted **into*** that line of succession.

The upcoming 1960 election would be the enabling mechanism.

If the initial task of actually *getting LBJ onto the national ticket* could be accomplished in the summer, and the presidential election were then won by the Democrats in the autumn, then just *one* death – a carefully plotted *murder* – would put a Texan in the White House.[433]

The political logic of the era proved it.

---

[431] Author's exclusive original discovery.

[432] Cameras once captured Rayburn and Johnson grinning together in front of a sign which read, "Victory Twins."

[433] And if the plot were handled correctly and *executed flawlessly,* no one would ever suspect a thing.

They won't vote for a Southerner at the top of the ticket, of course.
*But they **will** accept a Southerner in the **second** spot.*
And that's all we need!

As I first discovered exclusively, Speaker of the House Samuel Rayburn of Texas was the true intellectual godfather of the JFK assassination[434] – and the murderous plot which slew President Kennedy in 1963 was actually hatched by Rayburn in earnest in *August 1956*,[435] just as soon as the politically doomed *second* national candidacy of Adlai Stevenson (along with Tennessee running mate Estes Kefauver) against incumbent Republican president Dwight Eisenhower was formally ratified by vote of the party faithful at the Democratic National Convention held in Chicago, Illinois.[436]

Sam Rayburn was the *intellectual author* of, and the *chief co-conspirator* in, the JFK assassination plot.[437]

Lyndon Johnson was the *leader* of, the chief *executive* of, and the principal *beneficiary* of the JFK assassination plot.[438]

All that remained were the (not inconsiderable) nuts and bolts and details – namely, *"which levers, in what manner, must be pressed . . . to bring about the occupation of the White House."*[439]

---

[434] Author's exclusive original discovery.

[435] Author's exclusive original discovery.

[436] Author's exclusive original discovery.

Also worth noting is the fact that LBJ energetically supported JFK's unsuccessful bid to be the Democrats' 1956 VP nominee. Johnson clearly did so because he knew that no matter who the second spot went to, the Stevenson campaign would certainly fail to unseat President Eisenhower and thus would help to taint Kennedy as a loser. JFK's wealthy father had tried the same trick; in 1955 Joseph P. Kennedy actually offered to fund a Johnson presidential run at the top of the ticket in 1956 against the popular "Ike" for the same reason. Johnson saw through the obvious gambit and declined (Jeff Shesol, *Mutual Contempt,* pp. 31-32).

As it turned out, Tennessee Senator Estes Kefauver got the VP nod over JFK and accompanied Adlai Stevenson to a predictable electoral defeat in November 1956. Once the losing Stevenson-Kefauver ticket was a formal reality in August 1956, the inevitable *1960* clash between JFK and LBJ became a pre-ordained fact – starting a fatal hourglass running on what was left of John Kennedy's life, and ultimately culminating in the assassination in Dallas (Author's exclusive original discovery).

[437] Author's exclusive original discovery.

[438] Author's exclusive original discovery.

[439] Theodore White, quoted in Jeff Shesol, *Mutual Contempt,* p. 26. Ironically, White was quite naively describing the 1960 *Kennedy* campaign. But unwittingly, White's words are in fact *much* more relevant to the challenges faced by Lyndon Johnson and his mentor, Sam Rayburn – men who had by far the tougher and more dangerous task.

For Lyndon Baines Johnson, those levers included criminal conspiracy, extortion, sedition, and murder.

* * *

When JFK sent his brother Bobby to Johnson's Texas ranch in the autumn of 1959 to find out whether or not LBJ would be running for president in 1960, Johnson made it quite clear that he would *not* be doing so.[440]

And, in reality, that was true.

For Lyndon Johnson, subterfuge was a fundamental method of operation. So was an astonishing level of *hands-on participation* in all manner of activities that most men of his stature would normally tend to leave to subordinates and other "cut-outs." Thus when the crucial election year of 1960 dawned, Johnson lashed out at those allies who were clumsily unaware of his true goal (and the methods he was going to employ to achieve it) and he shouted angrily, *"Just let me do it my way!"*[441]

Unbeknownst to many of his ordinary political supporters, "my way," for LBJ, involved late-night blackmail in Los Angeles – and, three years later, mid-day murder in Dallas.[442]

* * *

John Kennedy handily won his party's nomination for President on the night of Wednesday, July 13th, 1960, at the Democratic National Convention in Los Angeles. JFK unexpectedly came to the convention podium to thank the delegates (in a heart-stopping moment for Rayburn and Johnson); then celebrated at a famous restaurant; and was ready to publicly announce his chosen selection of running mate, Senator "Stu" Symington, after a good night's sleep.[443]

But the happy announcement – and the good night's sleep – never occurred.

Lyndon Johnson and Sam Rayburn had a nasty surprise up their sleeves, and the morning sun would never rise on a Kennedy-Symington ticket.

Rayburn and Johnson would *personally* see to that.

---

[440] In a 1997 book, Jeff Shesol amply documented the RFK-LBJ *blood feud* but utterly failed (or refused, or feared) to even *understand* it – let alone to properly link it to the JFK assassination. (Shesol's stunningly obtuse and gutless brand of "history" [*sic*] only goes so far.)

[441] Jeff Shesol, *Mutual Contempt,* p. 28.

[442] In a 1997 book, Seymour Hersh amply documented the 1960 blackmail but utterly failed (or refused, or feared) to properly link it to the JFK assassination. Obviously, Hersh's brand of "investigative journalism" only goes so far.

[443] Making Symington his running mate was a "done deal" for both Kennedy himself *and* for Symington.

* * *

In the 1950s, Missouri Senator William Stuart ("Stu") Symington – a former Secretary of the Air Force and former NSC official – was carefully laying the groundwork for a presidential run based largely on the creation and exploitation of unbridled (and unwarranted) *fear.*

As a committee chairman, Symington deftly orchestrated a Greek chorus of unmitigated *doom* from a variety of extremely conservative Air Force officers. Their grim declaration that the Soviet Union was about to pull ahead of the U.S. in terms of air supremacy was "a complete fantasy," as a later observer correctly perceived.[444] Nevertheless, frightening USAF tales of relentless Soviet advances in bomber superiority did the trick in 1956, and the Air Force budget soon blossomed accordingly.[445]

The handsome, urbane, extremely well-credentialed Symington indeed ran for the Democratic presidential nomination in 1960, against a field that included the equally handsome but far-less-well-credentialed Massachusetts Senator John F. Kennedy. JFK knew that, on paper at least, Symington seemed to be a formidable candidate – in particular against the likely Republican nominee, right-wing Vice President Richard Nixon, a well-known master of slurs, red-baiting innuendo, cheap shots and gutter fighting.

Kennedy, widely regarded as too young and inexperienced to sit in the Oval Office, made a strategic move that turned out to be decisive. He neatly *co-opted* Stu Symington's chilling message about a "missile gap," *adopted it as his own,* and then *used it* to literally "out-Symington Symington."[446]

To this day, most observers erroneously think that the "missile gap" scare which overlay and dominated the 1960 campaign was JFK's own cynical creation. In

---

[444] James Carroll, *House of War*, p. 225. Indeed, the ambitious and intrepid Senator Symington even goosed up the Air Force's dire prognostications by altering and intensifying the testimony of General Curtis LeMay. In other words, the crafty Symington – incredibly – *out-LeMayed LeMay.* (L. Douglas Keeney, *15 Minutes,* pp. 162-163.)

[445] The so-called "bomber gap" which Senator Symington aggressively promoted (with General LeMay's witting and unwitting assistance) was a vital prelude to the centerpiece of Symington's upcoming 1960 campaign for the White House: the equally mythical "missile gap," which soon bedeviled Ike and his VP/political heir, GOP candidate Richard Nixon.

Senator Symington claimed with great dismay that the rabid Russkies would soon possess some 3,000 ICBMs; but in early 1960, the *true* number of functioning Soviet nuclear intercontinental missiles was actually only *four.*

Not four thousand; not four hundred; just *four.* (James Carroll, *House of War*, p. 225.)

[446] Author's exclusive original discovery.

reality, it was *Senator Symington's* chosen tool of manipulation from the very beginning – but in a stunning feat of political judo, John Kennedy brazenly *appropriated* his competitor's core message, used it stridently to great effect on his *own* behalf, and thereby eked out a victory by first out-hawking Symington (for the Democratic nomination) and then out-hawking Nixon (for the presidency itself).[447]

The fundamental necessity of doing so – *in order to win the White House during the height of the Cold War* – has led to plenty of laughably erroneous latter-day caterwauling about JFK's supposedly having been nothing but "a conventional Cold War hawk." The reality is that such specious claims fail utterly to take into account the rough political realities of the 1960 campaign, in which the young Kennedy felt obligated to "prove" his "toughness against Communism" through such talk. Given the ugly tenor of the times, it is obvious that taking the worst elements of JFK's 1959 and 1960 campaign speeches *at face value* is an inherently unwise, misleading and badly mistaken approach.

JFK was a committed pragmatist who said what he said and did what he did *in order to win in 1960.* Winning was everything. Kennedy knew full well that unless he actually won both the nomination *and* the election, nothing else mattered. Thus if winning meant bending the truth, loudly and cleverly parroting certain aspects of right-wing ideology, and otherwise ensuring that his adversaries had no way to successfully position themselves well to the *right* of him on the political spectrum, JFK would do so. By consciously and deliberately *stealing Symington's thunder* and raising a hue and cry about a "missile gap" – which left the incumbent Republican Party decidedly uncomfortable and defensive – Kennedy had a chance to succeed.

But JFK did not simply want to use Symington's *message*; he wanted to use *Symington himself* as an effective shield against any potential charges of being "weak" or "inexperienced" or "soft on Communism."[448]

This is demonstrated graphically and quite conclusively by JFK's true choice of running mate in 1960 – something of which few people are aware. As of July 13th, 1960 – the night he won his party's nomination in Los Angeles as their standard-bearer in the campaign – John Kennedy's choice for Vice President on the Democratic ticket was none other than . . . *Senator Stuart Symington of Missouri.*[449]

Stu Symington, **not** Lyndon Johnson.

Symington, not LBJ.

Symington.

---

[447] Author's exclusive original discovery.

[448] Author's exclusive original discovery.

[449] Seymour Hersh, *The Dark Side of Camelot,* p. 124.

The source for this crucial fact is none other than that longtime pillar of the Establishment, attorney Clark Clifford.

A former attorney for JFK (during the scandal over the true authorship of the book *Profiles in Courage*), Clifford was now working as Senator Symington's presidential campaign manager – and on July 13th, 1960, *John Kennedy himself* personally told Clark Clifford to advise Senator Symington that he was JFK's choice for running mate.[450]

Period.

No ifs, ands or buts. This was not a possibility, but a concrete fact. Kennedy wasn't "dangling" the offer to Symington; he was ***making*** the offer to Symington.

It was a done deal.

Reporter Nancy Hanschman Dickerson obtained the information directly from Clark Clifford himself. After two *previous* "conditional" offers to Symington, predicated on obtaining the Missouri delegation's votes for his own nomination, Kennedy finally made an outright invitation.

"There were no strings attached. It was a straight offer," Clifford said. This third offer was made in Los Angeles, at the convention, ***prior to*** Kennedy's nomination – and Symington in fact *accepted* the offer.[451]

So as of the night of July 13th, 1960, the Democratic ticket was going to be a *Kennedy-Symington* ticket. No question about it.

Kennedy-Symington.

Kennedy-Symington.

Kennedy-Symington.

"We had a deal signed, sealed and delivered," Clifford told reporter Nancy Hanschman Dickerson later. There was no waffling; no ambiguity of any kind. As she correctly noted, "Clifford is one of the world's most sophisticated men, and *he does **not** make mistakes about matters like this.* "[452]

JFK also disclosed to a friend, journalist Charles Bartlett, that "he [JFK] had ***already*** picked Symington, and that Symington aides had started drafting an acceptance speech."[453]

The other man who knew full well that Stu Symington was Kennedy's actual VP choice was none other than *Lyndon Baines Johnson himself.*[454]

---

[450] Seymour Hersh, *The Dark Side of Camelot,* p. 125.

[451] Nancy Hanschman Dickerson, *Among Those Present* (paperback edition, 1977), p. 47.

[452] Nancy Dickerson, *Among Those Present* (paperback edition, 1977), pp. 47-48.

[453] Nancy Dickerson, *Among Those Present* (paperback edition, 1977), pp. 51-52.

[454] Author's exclusive original discovery.

A secretary who was present with LBJ at his suite in the Biltmore Hotel on the night of July 13th wrote, "During the first ballot when Missouri switched its votes to Kennedy, Senator Johnson said a deal had been made. *'There's your vice-president,'* he said."[455]

Johnson, a masterful politician, was absolutely correct.

Symington was John Kennedy's choice as running mate – period.

But strangely, by early the next morning (July 14th, 1960), a clearly shell-shocked John Kennedy summoned a very surprised Clark Clifford to a secret meeting at the Biltmore Hotel. There, the new nominee privately confessed to Clifford that, incredibly, he would have to *renege* on the *already-made* VP offer to Symington. JFK explicitly discussed the reasons for the inexplicable and abrupt reversal, and he was clearly humiliated at having to go back on his word to Symington.[456] Attorney Clifford dutifully went back and advised his Missouri boss, who was disappointed but hardly surprised by the shocking turn of events.

The same was true of Clifford.

After all, both men had known of Kennedy's reckless womanizing *more than a year before* the 1960 Democratic Convention.

The proof of JFK's limitless libido had come to them *through the U. S. mail.*

* * *

In 1958, while engaged in a sexual affair with his young Senate staffer Pamela Turnure, JFK was photographed late one night – departing Turnure's apartment – by her deeply offended landlords, a couple named the Katers.

In 1959, the Katers mailed photos and typed statements to Senator Stu Symington – *already* one of JFK's major rivals for the 1960 Democratic nomination. The material provided a means for Symington, *if he had wished,* to try to blackmail Kennedy and demand the second spot on the 1960 ticket if Jack succeeded in winning the top prize.[457]

---

[455] LBJ Daily Diary, July 13th, 1960, prepared by secretary Mary Margaret Wiley.

[456] Articulating the obvious with massive understatement, Clifford drily commented that JFK was "considerably embarrassed." (Nancy Dickerson, *Among Those Present* [paperback edition, 1977], p. 51.)

[457] As I proved above, JFK had myriad **legitimate** and politically useful reasons to select Stu Symington anyway, and no information has ever emerged to suggest that Symington ever actually *tried* to force (let alone succeeded in forcing) JFK to pick him as his running mate.

The Kater materials, *in and of themselves,* were ultimately insufficient leverage for anyone, compared to the damning and truly monstrous **avalanche** of material possessed by – and successfully wielded by – Sam Rayburn and Lyndon Johnson.

In typical Washington fashion, Senator Symington had his attorney and campaign manager Clark Clifford – a very smooth operator – contact JFK and arrange to "discreetly" send the Kater materials (in a private envelope) over to Kennedy's Senate office – along with a cryptic, opaque note.[458]

This "professional courtesy" [*sic*] between these "men of the world" served to let JFK know that both Symington and Clifford knew about the Turnure affair.

Thus, *a full year **before** the Democratic National Convention,* Symington and Clifford were both intimately familiar with JFK's weaknesses and vulnerabilities. It was Clark Clifford who dealt with them in 1959, and it was Clark Clifford who dealt with the inevitable *result of them* in 1960.

Therefore, Kennedy's abrupt decision to renege on making Symington his 1960 running mate was plainly related to *those very same weaknesses and vulnerabilities,* writ large.

The irony was that Rayburn and Johnson simply possessed far ***more*** (and far more *striking,* and far more *damaging*) sexual blackmail material to employ against Kennedy than Stu Symington ever did; therefore, the two Texans' *tidal wave* of pressure on JFK completely overshadowed Symington's relatively *limited* material (and thus his relatively *limited* ability to ever exploit) JFK's myriad peccadilloes and vulnerabilities.

On the grim morning of July 14th, 1960, Kennedy made it clear to Clark Clifford why he was suddenly – *literally overnight!* – dumping Stu Symington as his running mate.

Clark Clifford, of all people, understood *precisely* what had occurred.[459]

* * *

Kennedy *also* revealed the essence of the matter quite bluntly to Senator Henry "Scoop" Jackson (another prominent conservative Democrat, who had been RFK's preferred choice to be JFK's running mate). JFK himself flatly told Scoop Jackson the stark, ugly truth: *"Rayburn has intervened and insists that LBJ be on the ticket . . ."*[460]

It was that explicit!

---

[458] The Kater materials sent to Symington were subsequently auctioned – more than 50 years later.

[459] The situation was as crude and simple and vicious as this:

Lyndon Johnson wanted to be President – so in 1960, he ***committed*** blackmail.

John Kennedy also wanted to be President – so in 1960, he ***permitted*** blackmail.

That's the fundamental truth of the matter. (You're welcome.)

[460] Nancy Dickerson, *Among Those Present* (paperback edition, 1977), p. 51.

Rayburn has intervened.
Rayburn insists that LBJ be on the ticket.

That was the unvarnished reality of 1960.

Kennedy *also* personally disclosed the painful truth to one of his own top campaign aides, Chicago attorney Hyman Raskin, on the very same day it occurred – July 14th, 1960. Pulling Raskin aside, JFK put it plainly: "You know we had never considered Lyndon, but *I was left with no choice. He and Sam Rayburn made it damn clear to me that Lyndon **had** to be the candidate. Those bastards were trying to **frame** me. They **threatened me** with problems* and I don't need more problems. I'm going to have enough problems with Nixon."[461]

Just a few hours had passed since Kennedy exulted in his hard-earned, first-ballot nomination. However, something very significant – and sinister – had clearly happened during those intervening hours.

Neither Jack nor Bobby realized it *at the time,* in 1960, but the criminal event in question led *directly* to the JFK assassination in 1963.[462]

Precisely as it was intended to.

The 1960 blackmail of John Kennedy by Rayburn and Johnson, *under cover of night,* was the indispensable act which enabled everything – everything! – that occurred subsequently.[463]

* * *

Had John Kennedy been permitted to have the running mate of his choosing, it would have been Stu Symington. Only a *felonious criminal act* committed against JFK overnight – during the wee hours of the morning of July 14th, 1960 – forestalled Kennedy's original plan.

By dawn, it was all over – and thus John F. Kennedy, the freshly minted nominee of the Democratic Party, the man of the hour, *was no longer at liberty to announce Senator Symington of Missouri as his choice.*

All sorts of laughably pathetic stories were soon bandied about to explain Kennedy's sudden and *forced* choice of Lyndon Johnson instead of Symington. Claims of "shocked surprise" [*sic*] and "pro forma offers" [*sic*] and "unexpected acceptance" [*sic*] were issued and repeated by both the (humiliated) Kennedy and (exultant) Johnson camps until the ugly truth was conveniently obscured and buried.

---

[461] Seymour Hersh, *The Dark Side of Camelot,* p. 126. Hersh was happy to engage in deriding JFK; but Hersh has never had the *cojones* to investigate the JFK assassination (which is, by definition, a *far* more important issue). Strange, no? I guess we know the limits of Hersh's so-called "journalism."

[462] Author's exclusive original discovery.

[463] Without the 1960 blackmail, the JFK assassination would not have – indeed, *could not have* – occurred.

Vague "cover" stories about the supposed "electoral benefits" of picking a Texan were also promulgated – but the reality is that *Symington's* presence on the ticket would have helped guarantee California (home of many major military contractors) for the Democrats, which in itself would have been electorally critical.

Texas was actually *irrelevant* to the 1960 election.[464]

I checked the electoral college results, and I did the math.

Texas was totally irrelevant to the 1960 election.[465]

So Kennedy did not "need" Texas (or its votes) at all.[466]

Therefore, Kennedy did not "need" Lyndon Johnson as a running mate.[467]

Moreover, as a ferocious "hawk," Symington would naturally have guarded and protected Kennedy's flank from smear attacks by the vicious Richard Nixon.

A Kennedy-Symington ticket would have reassured pundits and the public that the Republic was in safe hands from the dreaded "Commies." But *under cover of night,* a pair of prominent Texans changed the political equation completely – and thereby changed history. Their secret post-midnight criminal deed on July 14th, 1960, was the principal actuating mechanism for the murderous plot to elevate Lyndon Johnson to the Oval Office – and it was the *sine qua non* for the deadly ambush carried out in Dallas's Dealey Plaza, a full three years later.

* * *

Plenty of plainly ridiculous mythology has sprung up (and calcified into a brittle, idiotic orthodoxy) about Kennedy's sudden, inexplicable betrayal of Stuart Symington – and JFK's unwilling, unhappy, unwanted shift to Johnson as VP. Much of that mythology in fact *originated with the Kennedy brothers themselves* – because as absurd and ludicrous and embarrassing as their lame "cover" story was, it was still plainly preferable to the devastating *truth* of the matter.[468]

---

[464] Author's exclusive original discovery.

[465] Author's exclusive original discovery.

[466] Indeed, as Alabama Governor John Patterson correctly pointed out, "Truman proved in 1948 that *you did not have to carry a single Southern state to be elected president.*" (Strober & Strober, *Let Us Begin Anew,* paperback edition, p. 475.)

I personally checked the final 1960 electoral math myself; JFK did not "need" LBJ – or Texas – *at all.*

[467] Author's exclusive original discovery. Claims to the contrary – insisting desperately that naming LBJ was a "brilliant electoral strategy" – are nothing but hoary myths designed to cover up *the criminal 1960 blackmail* of John Fitzgerald Kennedy by Samuel Taliaferro Rayburn and Lyndon Baines Johnson.

[468] Ironically, the Kennedy brothers' own 1960 embarrassed lies about the matter unwittingly helped – and *gave cover to* – Sam Rayburn and Lyndon Johnson, the *true* authors of JFK's 1963 assassination.

The official, *received* version of the 1960 Democratic VP nomination is that at *mid-morning* on July 14th, at about 10:30 or 11:00 a.m., John Kennedy went downstairs to Johnson's hotel suite to talk with LBJ *for the first and only time* [*sic*], made a meaningless, *pro forma* [*sic*] "offer" [*sic*] of the number two slot to Lyndon Johnson – merely as a symbolic [*sic*] gesture of "respect" [*sic*] – and was "shocked" [*sic*] and "appalled" [*sic*] when the Texan "unexpectedly" [*sic*] "accepted" [*sic*] the JFK "offer" [*sic*].

None of that is true.

None of it!

The risible story, which resembles a pathetically contrived and unusually artificial Victoria-era stage farce, has about as much credibility as the calculated exclamations of actor Claude Rains in the classic movie *Casablanca*.

Yet as usual, all *conventional* pseudo-historians and pseudo-journalists have bought that smarmy official story hook, line and sinker – and as usual, all *conventional* pseudo-historians and pseudo-journalists are completely ignorant and ***dead wrong*** about the true nature, reality, cause and effect of the events in question.[469]

The truth, as always, is far different than what the pathetic water-carriers of officialdom would have you believe.

Far uglier, and far more brutal as well.

In the early morning hours of Thursday, July 14th, 1960, Sam Rayburn and Lyndon Johnson successfully *blackmailed* the Democratic nominee into reneging on his pledge to choose Symington – and they *forced* him to select LBJ as his running mate in the 1960 election instead.

It was a stunning and totally overwhelming maneuver carried out with deadly effectiveness, *under cover of night* – and a shaken JFK had absolutely no option but to meekly comply with the blunt, ferocious and criminal demand made by Rayburn and Johnson.

As always, the *chronology* of the events is the major key to unraveling the subsequent lies – and to uncovering the truth of the matter.

JFK's midnight restaurant celebration was interrupted by an urgent summons from a Rayburn emissary, young Congressman Thomas "Tip" O'Neill, insisting that Kennedy meet personally with the Speaker *later that very same night*.

---

[469] Pathetically, famous longtime "journalists" Jack Germond and Jules Witcover wrote an idiotic 1997 piece in the *Baltimore Sun* striving to downplay the reality of the 1960 blackmail – even moronically referring to it as "a most serendipitous development." Decades later, other veteran reporters like Thomas Oliphant and Curtis Wilkie were still parroting the official story while claiming pathetically that the bottom-line truth about 1960 was simply "impossible" to reconstruct. *Balderdash.* Of such weak and lazy nonsense is American corporate "journalism" made. What those four famed "reporters" could not figure out (or dared not admit) is *right here in this chapter* – explained and properly analyzed by me. (You're welcome.)

Meanwhile that same night, LBJ personally confronted Robert Kennedy and demanded to be on the ticket.

Subsequently, JFK returned to the Biltmore Hotel; met with Sam Rayburn first, in a room where Rayburn aide John Holton was present but out of earshot; then finally was confronted by both members of the powerful duo from Texas (Rayburn *and* LBJ), at which point JFK capitulated completely – *well before dawn.*

That's what really happened.

First LBJ threatened Bobby, on his own; then Rayburn threatened JFK, on his own; and finally LBJ and Rayburn jointly teamed up to threaten and coerce JFK *together.*

As a domineering and deadly determined duo.

Their blackmail of John Kennedy worked fantastically well.

It was all perpetrated *under cover of night,* and it was achieved long before sunrise on July 14th.[470]

The sequence is proven by the timing of Kennedy's subsequent call to Symington campaign manager (and longtime Establishment heavyweight) Clark Clifford *soon after dawn broke* on Thursday, July 14th.[471] Poor Clifford, a dapper Washington insider, was summoned to the Kennedy suite *before he had even had a chance to complete his morning shave.*[472] Kennedy apologetically broke the bad news to Clifford in person, explaining that it was a situation that was absolutely *impossible* for him to get out of – and so the normally dapper lawyer then left to inform Symington (and, one hopes, to finally shave).

Without warning, Lyndon Johnson was in – and poor Stu Symington's VP candidacy was *toast.*

Clifford, an insider's insider[473] who knew a rotten situation when he smelled one, learned from John Kennedy's own lips that the Democratic nominee had been made the proverbial "offer he could not refuse."[474]

---

[470] Author's exclusive original discovery.

[471] Author's exclusive original discovery.

[472] Seymour Hersh, *The Dark Side of Camelot,* p. 126.

[473] Clifford had been JFK's own personal attorney at one point in the 1950s. Later he went on to become a very hawkish *outside* adviser on Vietnam to Lyndon Johnson, and then (in 1968) a far less bellicose Secretary of Defense to LBJ (succeeding the ousted Robert Strange McNamara). *Thanks to his devastating insider knowledge of numerous (and staggering) Democratic Party scandals and crimes,* Clifford skated away from criminal charges of conspiracy and fraud and receipt of bribes related to his involvement in the BCCI banking scandal of the 1980s and 1990s.

[474] Hyman Raskin, quoted in Seymour Hersh, *The Dark Side of Camelot,* p. 123.

Clark Clifford then informed Missouri governor James T. Blair, who personally informed Knight Newspapers publisher and journalist John S. Knight, who promptly wrote and published an accurate news story revealing the ugly and sinister truth. (Pierre Salinger, *With Kennedy,* p. 45.) Both the Kennedy and

The question is:

Who does that?

Who has the sheer effrontery to blatantly blackmail the powerful, newly-minted Democratic presidential nominee?

And who has the power and "the goods" to actually get away with it?

The answer is stark and simple:

Two senior American politicians.[475]

Sam Rayburn and Lyndon Johnson were both longtime friends of sinister FBI Director J. Edgar Hoover,[476] and all three men were naturally well acquainted with Kennedy's extensive sexual dalliances. With a mixture of envy and condescension, LBJ angrily (and correctly) referred to Senator Kennedy as "just a playboy" who was "always off with some girl."[477]

In Washington, D.C., *information* – not money! – is the coin of the realm.

Evelyn Lincoln, JFK's longtime secretary, was fully aware of the dynamics at play. As she put it, "LBJ had been using all the information Hoover could find on Kennedy – during the campaign, even before the Convention. And Hoover was in on the pressure on Kennedy at the Convention."[478]

A host of both contemporaneous and later writers from all across the political spectrum have tried in vain to put a false but acceptable face on this irredeemably ugly situation by citing fragmentary comments from grossly uninformed outsiders in a vain attempt to attribute the Johnson VP nomination to a savvy, well-thought-out, cynical, even *necessary* "electoral calculation" [*sic*] by John Kennedy and his campaign team.

But the stark reality is otherwise.

The undeniable true chronology of events which I have assembled (and the numerical reality of the 1960 electoral math, which I correctly analyzed[479]) totally destroys the false conventional story and all latter-day efforts to put any kind of "legitimate" gloss on it.

The truth is this:

Johnson camps then worked furiously to *deny* that truth, and they succeeded in lying to the (infinitely weak and stupid) American press.

[475] Author's exclusive original discovery.

[476] In fact, LBJ lived on the same street as J. Edgar Hoover for many years; Hoover himself frequently visited *chez LBJ* for dinner.

[477] Booth Mooney, *LBJ: An Irreverent Biography,* p. 48.

[478] Anthony Summers, *Official and Confidential,* p. 272.

[479] Author's exclusive original discovery.

It was all over by the time John Kennedy picked up a telephone and called Clark Clifford around dawn.[480]

It was all over by the time RFK personally briefed Kenny O'Donnell and Pierre Salinger around dawn.[481]

Therefore, the blackmail itself was perpetrated *well **before** dawn.*[482]

And by definition, that means that the deed was done between 1:00 a.m. and 5:00 a.m. on Thursday, July 14th, 1960.[483] *That's* when the Rayburn-Johnson blackmail occurred – no two ways about it.[484]

There **was no** "offer" (token or otherwise!) made to LBJ, *hours later* at 10:58 a.m.; there was no "surprise" or "confusion," *hours later* at 10:58 a.m.; *the deed had already been done, via blackmail demand, several hours earlier!* [485] It was a *fait accompli* long before John Kennedy walked downstairs and *publicly* entered Johnson's suite (in front of several waiting newsmen) late that morning.[486]

That 10:58 a.m. pantomime performed on July 14th, 1960, was nothing but a necessary **charade** [487] – simply the final act required of John Kennedy as part of what he had **already** been blackmailed into doing between 1:00 a.m. and 5:00 a.m. that very same morning.[488]

To hide the illicit and criminal nature of the secret blackmail deal which had been forcibly consummated in the pre-dawn darkness, the supposed "pro forma offer to LBJ" [*sic*] now had to be **acted out, *in public, in the light of day, in front of witnesses, as if it were* a "legitimate" thing.**[489]

---

[480] Author's exclusive original discovery.

[481] Author's exclusive original discovery.

[482] Author's exclusive original discovery.

[483] Author's exclusive original discovery.

[484] Author's exclusive original discovery.

[485] Author's exclusive original discovery.

[486] Author's exclusive original discovery. (Lifton was strangely unable and unwilling to bring himself to admit that the Rayburn-Johnson blackmail of JFK was deadly serious; during lengthy and intense debates between us on this subject in the 2010s, Lifton clung to the pathetic position that JFK was *not* blackmailed into actually **making LBJ the VP nominee**, but was "only" blackmailed (*a felony!*) into merely making Johnson an "offer" – an utterly absurd and preposterous proposition which was totally disconnected from reality. Typical Lifton.)

[487] Author's exclusive original discovery.

[488] Author's exclusive original discovery.

[489] Author's exclusive original discovery.

And that pathetic charade is precisely what was performed publicly by the victim, John Kennedy.

The defeated nominee followed the "stage directions" dictated by his two Texas blackmailers, Rayburn and Johnson: JFK dutifully went downstairs late on Thursday morning, not long before noon; dutifully spoke his lines; then dutifully trudged back upstairs to his own hotel suite.

An angry and incensed Bobby subsequently tried to undo the deed, but the task was impossible. Rayburn and Johnson simply had too much dirt on JFK to permit any real resistance. Kennedy himself shut down RFK's final efforts in that regard.

It was *over* – and it had ***been*** over since *long before dawn* that morning.[490]

The bottom line is quite simple:

In mid-July 1960, Samuel Rayburn and Lyndon Johnson brazenly and personally blackmailed John F. Kennedy, *under cover of night,* in order to force him to put LBJ in position as nominee for Vice President (just a bullet away from the Presidency, following electoral victory). They did so knowingly and deliberately and with malice aforethought, *as part of their assassination plot* to put a Texan into the White House – *and they succeeded.*[491]

Rayburn himself said it best on July 14th, 1960, during Bobby's desperate, failed efforts to somehow "undo" the ugly nighttime deed: Sam and Lyndon would show "the goddamn Kennedys" who was really in charge. *"We'll teach them how we do things,"* the Speaker spat venomously.[492]

And shortly *after* the 1960 Democratic convention ended, Lyndon Johnson himself – relaxing back at his Texas ranch – just couldn't resist making "an oblique reference" to JFK's numerous sexual indiscretions in front of reporter Nancy Hanschman Dickerson.[493]

Johnson was a deeply confessional individual.[494] It was impossible for him not to brag, not to proclaim – however subtly – his triumphs.[495]

As LBJ obliquely revealed to Dickerson, *sex* was the key to Kennedy's capitulation and Johnson's elevation to the VP slot.

Sex.

---

[490] Author's exclusive original discovery.

[491] Author's exclusive original discovery.

[492] Nancy Dickerson, *Among Those Present* (paperback edition, 1977), p. 51.

[493] Author's exclusive original discovery. At the time, in the summer of 1960, the woman who later became "Mrs. Nancy Dickerson" was still Nancy Hanschman (her maiden name). (Nancy Dickerson, *Among Those Present,* 1977 paperback edition, pp. 54-55.)

[494] Author's exclusive original discovery.

[495] Author's exclusive original discovery.

Not the supposed specter of JFK's most worrisome physical ailment, Addison's disease – a medical issue which was openly and very publicly raised by Johnson's allies at the Democratic Convention, but which was very quickly and *easily* knocked down by the deft Kennedy brothers *days **before*** the successful late-night sexual blackmail.[496]

The "Addison's disease" gambit failed completely.[497]

It didn't work.

It wasn't enough.

Contrary to what LBJ ally India Edwards said at the Democratic National Convention in 1960, John Kennedy did *not* have a "fatal" disease from which he was likely to perish while in office. Rather, JFK had a *serious* disease which – like many other illnesses – *could* prove fatal, *if it were left untreated.*

Certainly, that sort of total medical negligence was **not** going to occur in Kennedy's case – so the India Edwards statement, while technically true in part, was grossly inaccurate and highly misleading.[498]

Ironically, the very first person to conclusively identify and specifically "out" John Kennedy as a person suffering from Addison's disease was none other than *John Kennedy himself.* Speaking at an intimate dinner party, JFK casually mentioned the serious illness to his small group of guests – *a group which included journalists* – in a breathtakingly stupid act of indiscretion for an American politician seeking the highest office in the land.[499]

* * *

Rayburn and Johnson were under no *genuine* illusions that Kennedy – a vibrant, otherwise robust man of 43 – was going to suddenly "keel over" prior to the relatively young age of 51 (which would have been JFK's age at the end of two full four-year terms as President).

---

[496] Robert Kennedy promptly issued an indignant, *technically* true but highly misleading denial that JFK was an Addisonian – based on very narrow, antique definitions of the ailment – and RFK's supremely stilted statement satisfied gullible and lazy reporters. Not for nothing was Bobby later made Attorney General; when necessary, RFK could slice and dice and obscure the truth as well as grizzled veteran politicians who were literally twice his age.

[497] Author's exclusive original discovery.

[498] Indeed, *after* the Democratic convention concluded, Sam Rayburn himself explicitly admitted – in a letter dated August 4th, 1960 – that John Fitzgerald Kennedy was "vigorous in health." (C. Dwight Dorough, *Mr. Sam,* pp. 574-575.)

[499] JFK undoubtedly though it was a very clever way to utterly impress (and disarm) his influential listeners with a refreshing blast of totally unexpected candor and vulnerability. Nevertheless, it was a monumentally stupid move.

By contrast, Lyndon Johnson would have *already* been 60 years old when John Kennedy's presumptive second term as president expired on January 20th, 1969. Thus even if Johnson had suffered *no* other significant health problems in the interim (and even if LBJ had *not* been indicted for multiple crimes and ethics violations in the interim – and/or impeached and removed from office in the interim – and/or prosecuted and convicted of fraud, extortion, unjust enrichment and other offenses in the interim – and/or simply dropped from the ticket in the interim), LBJ would almost certainly have *died in office during his own first term as president* (or, at best, very early in his second term).

And why would that particular calculation matter to Lyndon Johnson?

Because LBJ would have had an extremely limited and highly circumscribed opportunity to establish a major legacy of his own, which formed a large part of his goal of becoming President in the first place. Lyndon Johnson wanted to surpass *even his powerful and revered political idol, Franklin Delano Roosevelt,* in terms of making an extraordinary and lasting domestic impact on American society. But the cold hard math of the actuarial tables – and the equally cold calculus of the political realm – were decidedly **not** in LBJ's favor.

Franklin Delano Roosevelt enjoyed the unprecedented advantage (luxury, really) of *twelve full years as president* to make his own stunning impact on the country[500] – but based on the grim, unsentimental actuarial statistics, a Lyndon Johnson who patiently waited until 1969 to *perhaps* become president in a normal, legitimate, *legal* fashion (all of which assumed that a whole host of other factors conveniently fell into place for him and that myriad existing obstacles somehow miraculously evaporated in the interim) would likely have, at best, *only four years total* in which to try to somehow equal or exceed the towering achievements of FDR.

So it was a poor bet by any standard.

A *worthless* bet, by Lyndon Johnson's exacting standards.

For an eager and ambitious man like LBJ, simply *waiting around* until 1969 to (just possibly, if all went well) *finally* take the reins of ultimate power was simply not acceptable.

No one could know or predict whether racial tensions in the U. S. would abate sufficiently by the time the 1968 election rolled around to make a winning, first-time Johnsonian presidential candidacy even *possible.*

Indeed, no one could know or predict whether *any* southerner would be able to be elected president in his own right as a candidate in 1968.

So to hell with "waiting around."

---

[500] Indeed, had FDR remained healthy following his 1944 re-election, he would have served (at least) an astounding *sixteen (16) full years* as President of the United States.

Cactus Jack's blunt advice to Sam Rayburn, decades earlier in 1931, showed the only way forward:

You've got to get your knuckles bloody.

* * *

The Texas duo's successful sexual blackmail of the Democratic nominee at the Los Angeles party convention in July 1960 was the *indispensable prerequisite* for ultimately carrying out the murder of JFK.[501] But Sam Rayburn and Lyndon Johnson weren't through jointly laying the groundwork for John Fitzgerald Kennedy's upcoming assassination.

The year 1960 still held a major *opportunity,* plus a fundamental *challenge.*

The opportunity (a truly extraordinary one) was this: *Practicing the deadly motorcade in Dallas, three years **before** the crime itself was actually committed!* [502]

The challenge was winning the presidential election in November.

Both items were completed well before the new year dawned.

* * *

In September 1960, JFK flew to Texas and joined LBJ and Rayburn in touring the state as part of the presidential campaign. Previous books about the three men have focused on Kennedy's courageous stance against religious bigotry in the face of a hostile Protestant ministerial audience in Houston.

But that isn't the important story.

Not at all.

The important story is the fact that, unbeknownst to John Kennedy, *the 1960 Texas trip actually served as a **reconnaissance exercise** and a **practice run** for the fatal 1963 Texas trip.*[503]

In September 1960, Kennedy and Rayburn and Johnson went from Fort Worth in the morning over to Dallas – where they then participated in *an open-car motorcade* through the city, and even *traversed Dealey Plaza itself.*

And afterward, Kennedy departed the city by aircraft from *Love Field.*

The timing and the route of the September 1960 Dallas visit *almost precisely* presaged the November 1963 Dallas visit.

---

[501] Author's exclusive original discovery.

[502] Author's exclusive original discovery.

[503] Author's exclusive original discovery.

The only significant difference was that in 1960, the candidate's motorcade drove *eastbound* through Dealey Plaza, on *Main* Street, at a decent rate of speed.

In November 1963, the presidential motorcade drove *westbound* through Dealey Plaza, on *Elm* Street, at an extremely *slow* rate of speed.

The 1960 campaign motorcade event in Dallas gave Lyndon Johnson and Sam Rayburn – through their own personal observations, as well as through the work of their assistants and supporters – the excellent opportunity to *see, photograph, time, analyze* and *carefully evaluate* the true potential of that triangular green park called Dealey Plaza as the ultimate kill zone for their planned murder of JFK.

Texas attorney Harold Barefoot Sanders Jr., who worked at a Dallas law firm, was a campaign coordinator for the Democratic candidates. Sanders actually spent Monday, September 12th, 1960, standing outside *personally* scrutinizing GOP presidential candidate Richard Nixon's identical parade through Dallas.[504]

The following day – Tuesday, September 13th, 1960 – Barefoot Sanders *personally* rode in the Kennedy-Johnson motorcade over *that very same route* – this time getting a passenger-level view of the scene, as did Sam Rayburn and Lyndon Johnson themselves.[505]

Ultimately, the evaluation conducted by the killers of JFK clearly mandated that the fatal caravan's speed be *dramatically reduced,* and the direction of travel *reversed,* when the actual day arrived to slaughter the president.

An *eastbound* motorcade on Main Street, moving properly at a *brisk* pace through the very center of Dealey Plaza as it did in September 1960, posed far too many unnecessary problems for JFK's killers.

So fix it they would – and *fix it they **did.***

The September 1960 Dallas visit was an astounding *trial run,* conducted in public and in real time – and it therefore constituted a priceless chance to literally set the stage for the midday assassination of John Kennedy when he returned to that city, for *another* motorcade, as president of the United States.[506]

* * *

[504] Alan Peppard, "JFK's Forgotten Dallas Motorcade: The Unseen Film and Photos," a *Dallas Morning News* interactive feature, October 2013.

[505] After becoming president, JFK made Barefoot Sanders a U. S. Attorney in northern Texas, a predictable part of typical post-election political patronage – but ***LBJ*** gave Sanders much more: two (2) high-level jobs in the Justice Department in Washington D. C., plus an actual White House appointment as legislative counsel. Moreover, Johnson later nominated Sanders to a federal appeals court judgeship.

In America, *crime pays.* It pays exceedingly well.

[506] Author's exclusive original discovery.

Flashing forward in time for a moment to late 1963, much has been made by some assassination investigators of the fact that President Kennedy intended to dump Lyndon Johnson from the 1964 Democratic ticket.

That was absolutely true, despite JFK's public and private denials, but ironically it is also ***totally irrelevant*** to *the JFK assassination itself*[507] – which, as I exclusively discovered and have conclusively demonstrated, had actually been in the works *since the late summer of 1956*.[508]

The plot preceded the JFK *administration*.

The plot preceded JFK's *inauguration*.

The plot preceded JFK's *election*.

The plot preceded JFK's *nomination*.

The plot was ***not*** – I repeat, ***not*** – a "response" to the Kennedy brothers' belated, autumn 1963 "dump Johnson" campaign![509]

The assassination of JFK was ***not*** a last-minute act of "political self-defense" [*sic*] or "desperate self-preservation" [*sic*] by LBJ.[510]

Rather, the plot was a very calculated, long-planned act of ruthless political *ambition* by LBJ and his political mentor, Sam Rayburn.

Be very clear:

The plot preceded the JFK *administration*.

The plot preceded JFK's January 1961 *inauguration*.

The plot preceded JFK's November 1960 *election*.

The plot preceded JFK's July 1960 *nomination*.

* * *

The plot actually began in August 1956.[511]

And that immutable fact governs the proper analysis of all that followed.

Yes, John Kennedy *was* indeed going to dump Lyndon Johnson as his vice-presidential running mate in 1964.

But – as interesting as that is – the president's decision to choose a new running mate was nevertheless totally *irrelevant* to the JFK assassination![512]

---

[507] Author's exclusive original discovery.

[508] Author's exclusive original discovery.

[509] Author's exclusive original discovery.

[510] Author's exclusive original discovery.

[511] Author's exclusive original discovery.

[512] Author's exclusive original discovery.

No less a personage than JFK's bitter enemy, USAF Chief of Staff Curtis LeMay, knew and believed that Johnson's upcoming "dumping" by Kennedy was a fact – as the general revealed in an oral history conducted for the LBJ Library in the summer of 1971:

> *"For several months before the President was assassinated they were [sic] rumors, and then they got to be a little **more** than rumors, [that] Vice President Johnson was going to be dropped for the coming [1964] election."*[513]

In a manuscript published posthumously, key LBJ aide Horace Busby recorded the fact that LBJ himself was personally aware in early November 1963, weeks *before* Dallas, that the rightfully vengeful Kennedy brothers – who had never forgotten nor forgiven the 1960Rayburn-Johnson blackmail in Los Angeles – had managed to orchestrate the dispatch of an armada of journalists down to Texas to probe Johnson's life, finances, relationships and crimes.[514]

Moreover, *TIME-LIFE* executive James Wagenvoord acknowledged several decades later that Robert Kennedy had indeed been feeding information to *LIFE* for a devastating exposé on Lyndon Johnson which was originally scheduled for publication soon *after* the lethal Texas trip.[515]

And President Kennedy's devoted longtime secretary, Mrs. Evelyn Lincoln, made it explicitly clear in her 1968 book, *Kennedy and Johnson,* that JFK himself

---

[513] Curtis LeMay oral history, June 1971, LBJ Library.

[514] LBJ was in Europe at the time, dispatched by JFK on a largely meaningless early-November trip in order to get the VP "out of the way" as the journalists dispatched to Texas actively probed Johnson's life and finances. During the European journey, LBJ kept in touch with another top aide back in Washington (Walter Jenkins) via daily transatlantic telephone calls. See *The 31ˢᵗ of March,* by Horace Busby. (My appreciation to Robert P. Morrow for wisely calling this to my attention.)

But I learned separately that there was much more. Johnson also took advantage of this European trip to personally "stroke" a key JFK assassination accomplice, as I discovered exclusively. (See the following chapter of this book.)

[515] The pace of scandals and controversies in the 1960s was *far* slower than the *instantaneous* outrage and *immediate* consequences generated today in the world of rabid social media and 24-hour "news." The fact is that even if *LIFE* had indeed run its planned LBJ exposé in late November or early December 1963, Lyndon Baines Johnson was **not** going to be quickly and magically ousted from his vice-presidential perch "overnight" in that more leisurely era.

That's precisely why the Kennedy brothers actively launched their get-Lyndon campaign in late 1963: in order to be able to *finally* rid themselves of LBJ *by Labor Day, 1964,* which was the traditional start of the presidential campaign season in that era.

confided to her during the final week of his life – just days before Dallas – that he was *definitely* going to dump Johnson.[516]

On November 19th, 1963, in a private White House conversation with Mrs. Lincoln just outside the Oval Office, President Kennedy addressed the issue head-on.

"It will not be Lyndon," said the president unequivocally.[517]

It will not be Lyndon.

Kennedy could not possibly have been clearer or more explicit.

It will not be Lyndon.

Johnson was "out" in 1964.

Moreover, JFK *even specifically identified his choice for Johnson's replacement as running mate and vice president.* Kennedy stated to Mrs. Lincoln that he was leaning toward choosing North Carolina Governor Terry Sanford, a progressive Southern moderate, as his vice-presidential running mate for the 1964 campaign.[518] Sanford embodied the type of modern, relatively enlightened individual who could help lead the South out of the vicious, violent, frightful Jim Crow era – and he lacked Lyndon Johnson's risky and extensive criminal baggage.[519]

*Yet the planned ouster of LBJ is **not** pertinent to the JFK assassination.*[520]

It is vital for the reader to understand the true overall chronology – from the assassination plot's *original inception in August 1956,*[521] to the successful blackmail in July 1960, to the actual shooting in November 1963 – and what that means in evaluating the 1963 "dump Johnson" data.

While the evidence cited above makes it quite plain to any rational, honest observer that by 1963 President Kennedy and his brother, the Attorney General, *were indeed* actively engaged in a deliberate campaign to eliminate Johnson from the 1964 Democratic *ticket* (and perhaps even from the Vice Presidency *itself, prior to* the next

---

[516] A number of asinine and patronizingly sexist observers (including some former Kennedy aides) have tried to wrongly dismiss Evelyn Lincoln as a flighty and unreliable individual, but such slanderous slurs are false. A writer checked her original, handwritten, *real-time shorthand notes* of that conversation, which are held at the JFK Library, and confirmed that Mrs. Lincoln recorded Kennedy's remarks that day with absolute precision and fidelity, *precisely* as she later quoted them in her 1968 book. (Thurston Clarke, "'It Will Not Be Lyndon': Why JFK Wanted to Drop LBJ for Reelection," *The Daily Beast,* 18 November 2013.)

[517] Evelyn Lincoln documented the incident *in real time* and wrote about it in her book *Kennedy and Johnson.*

[518] Evelyn Lincoln documented the incident *in real time* and wrote about it in her book *Kennedy and Johnson.*

[519] Keep Terry Sanford's name in mind as you continue reading this book. As you will see, *it matters* – greatly.

[520] Author's exclusive original discovery.

[521] Author's exclusive original discovery.

election, if criminal charges ensued), it is nevertheless **completely incorrect** to conclude that LBJ "suddenly" decided in the autumn of 1963 to kill JFK *"because of"* those late 1963 Kennedy machinations, real though they were.

That superficially appealing notion – the idea that Johnson killed Kennedy *in order to "save" his own political career, and to "avoid being dumped" from the 1964 ticket* – is simply and utterly **false.**

I reiterate:

The JFK assassination plot actually began in *1956 – **not** in 1963.*[522]

Moreover, Johnson and Rayburn personally blackmailed JFK into putting LBJ on the ticket back in July 1960 – *years **before** the late-1963 "dump Johnson" effort even began.

Thus, the Kennedy brothers' moves in 1963 to dump Johnson did ***not** in any way* "provoke" the Texan to suddenly "initiate" the Dallas assassination plot, beginning at that absurdly late date; rather, the Kennedy brothers' 1963 moves only *accentuated* the need for LBJ to *execute* the existing, laboriously constructed plot (which had literally been seven full years in the making![523]) in a timely fashion – before negative publicity, presidential fiat, public censure, Congressional action or federal prosecution ultimately ended Lyndon Johnson's existing position and thereby eliminated his political power.

One obvious, overriding factor dominated every other consideration: Lyndon Johnson had to still *be* Vice President in order to constitutionally *become* President upon JFK's upcoming murder.

If LBJ were dismissed from the ticket, or impeached, or indicted and prosecuted and convicted at any time *prior* to the successful execution of the JFK assassination plot, then all of that laborious, intensive planning and effort (and blackmail) by Rayburn and Johnson – *dating all the way back to August 1956! –* would be for naught.[524]

* * *

Ironically, it was Sam Rayburn's death late in 1961 which actually freed President Kennedy – for the first time – to actually dump Lyndon Johnson from the 1964 ticket.[525]

---

[522] Author's exclusive original discovery.

[523] Author's exclusive original discovery.

[524] Author's exclusive original discovery.

[525] Author's exclusive original discovery.

While Rayburn was still alive and was still Speaker of the House, JFK dared not dump Lyndon Johnson – who was Rayburn's longtime protégé, longtime friend, surrogate son and full co-conspirator in the 1956 origin of the plot and the vicious 1960 blackmail which successfully forced Kennedy to put LBJ on the ticket instead of Senator Stu Symington.

Why not?

Because – all blackmail considerations aside – the simple fact is that President Kennedy indubitably *needed* Sam Rayburn's active cooperation in order to get *any* desired legislation through the House of Representatives.

Had JFK dumped Lyndon Johnson "early," then Speaker Rayburn would have undoubtedly retaliated by vengefully strangling the president's entire legislative program in retaliation.

But with Rayburn now dead, Kennedy was free to try to push his bills through the House with the aid of new House Speaker John W. McCormack, a fellow Massachusetts politician (and a fellow Catholic, to boot).[526]

McCormack was 72 years old when President Kennedy was assassinated, and after Dallas he was next in line to the presidency until Hubert Humphrey finally took office as the newly elected Vice President in January 1965.

Lyndon Johnson cynically and very deliberately *used* John McCormack's relatively advanced age as "assassination insurance" during the post-Dallas/pre-Humphrey period, sometimes ostentatiously gesturing publicly toward the aging Speaker during public appearances in order to indicate to the American people what a frail, elderly man would take the reins of presidential (and nuclear) power if anyone decided to kill LBJ.[527]

* * *

The numerous specific actions taken by LBJ to facilitate the JFK assassination make his leading role and his criminal culpability for Dallas both undeniable and totally inescapable.

---

[526] **N.B.:** McCormack served on the congressional committee which held cursory hearings about the chilling 1934 coup plot against Franklin Roosevelt – a very real coup plot which was revealed to Congress by former USMC general and two-time Medal of Honor winner Smedley Butler.

Predictably, the corporate press (including the *New York Times*) trivialized and dismissed General Butler's damning revelations because those damning revelations made it plain that *powerful, wealthy, right-wing forces – including many extremely famous names in American politics and business and finance – were utterly disloyal and seditious criminals with complete contempt for democracy.*

Three decades later, in 1963, the same was true.

[527] It was a grotesque display on Johnson's part.

It was Johnson, America.

Not "Big Oil"; not "the CIA"; not "the Bilderberg Group."

It was Lyndon Baines Johnson.

It was Lyndon Johnson and his mentor and chief co-conspirator, House Speaker Sam Rayburn of Texas, who in August 1956 conceived of and created and initiated the JFK assassination plot.

It was Lyndon Johnson and his mentor and chief co-conspirator, House Speaker Sam Rayburn of Texas, who in July 1960 *personally* blackmailed JFK into making Johnson his running mate.

It was Lyndon Johnson and his mentor and chief co-conspirator, House Speaker Sam Rayburn of Texas, who in 1961 agitated for the expansion of the Secret Service in order to create a new Vice-Presidential SS detail reporting directly to Lyndon Johnson.[528]

It was Lyndon Johnson who publicly described the exact itinerary of the fatal Texas tour *seven months before Dallas – and more than five months before JFK had even formally agreed to make the trip!*

It was Lyndon Johnson who said publicly and chillingly in April 1963, a full seven months before the JFK assassination, *"At least wait until next November before you shoot him down."*[529]

It was Lyndon Johnson who in early June 1963 "persuaded" Rep. Al Thomas of Texas ***not*** to retire from Congress.

It was Johnson & Thomas associate (and future top White House aide) Jack Valenti who actually authored the formal September "invitation" to President Kennedy to visit Texas in November 1963 to attend a dinner honoring Rep. Al Thomas.[530]

It was LBJ's ally and co-conspirator, powerful Texas Congressman Al Thomas, who in late September 1963 applied the final *budgetary* pressure that literally *forced* President Kennedy to make the Texas trip.[531]

---

[528] The SS bill finally became law in October 1962 – eleven months after Rayburn's death.

[529] Johnson's chilling remarks were made in Texas on April 23rd, and were dutifully printed verbatim in the next day's Dallas newspapers. As I discovered exclusively – and as I pointed out earlier in this chapter – by speaking as bluntly as he did, *what LBJ was doing in reality* was "broadcasting in the clear" to fanatical right-wing *amateurs,* telling them to "stand down" and to avoid making any premature shooting attempts against President Kennedy, since such acts would likely foul up Johnson's own very sophisticated and comprehensive plan to assassinate JFK in November 1963 (Author's exclusive original discovery).

[530] Valenti wrote to JFK on September 17th, 1963. The White House received the letter on September 19th, and *formally* replied with a "yes" to the "invitation" on October 11th, 1963 – although the trip was actually approved by late September.

[531] On September 21st, the day after Kennedy's public proposal at the UN to conduct a *joint* lunar mission *in cooperation with the Soviets,* Rep. Al Thomas fired off a letter to the White House questioning the administration's commitment to NASA and its moon landing effort. Having previously made an American lunar mission in the 1960s a key political goal of Camelot, JFK could hardly afford to irredeemably alienate the Texas congressman who oversaw NASA's budget – particularly *before* any actual agreement

It was Lyndon Johnson who dined at home ("The Elms," located at 4040 52nd Street NW in Washington D. C.) with key co-conspirator Congressman Al Thomas on September 23rd, 1963.[532]

It was Lyndon Johnson who again dined at home ("The Elms," located at 4040 52nd Street NW in Washington D. C.) with key co-conspirator Congressman Al Thomas on October 11th, 1963.[533]

It was Johnson who *refused to permit a proper local autopsy in Dallas on November 22nd, as required by Texas law.*

It was Lyndon Johnson who *refused to leave Texas without the body of JFK.*[534]

It was Lyndon Johnson who, on November 22nd, personally ordered all the window shades of *Air Force One* pulled down – thus preventing the passengers inside from seeing what was going on outside and around the aircraft at Love Field.[535]

It was Lyndon Johnson who on November 22nd called Attorney General Robert Kennedy from Air Force One at Love Field, *long before takeoff,* and obtained from the stunned RFK his silent pseudo-"acquiescence" to vague and unspecified "security" measures. Thus Johnson cleverly gained an ostensible but unwitting Bobby Kennedy *imprimatur* for various acts of obstruction of justice, conspiracy, and destruction of evidence by the assassins – both on November 22nd and subsequently.[536]

It was Lyndon Johnson who was captured in an official photograph sharing a sinister, infamous, gloating wink and smile with Congressman Al Thomas, his close ally and criminal co-conspirator, *immediately* after LBJ was sworn in aboard Air Force One at Love Field.[537]

---

with the USSR had been made confirming an agreement by the two superpowers to "share" the costs of such a joint moon landing effort.

The funding bill that was ultimately approved by the House weeks later on October 10th forbade NASA from blowing so much as *a single dime* of taxpayer money on any "joint" moon venture with the Soviets. Al Thomas was a crafty and formidable individual indeed.

[532] Author's exclusive original discovery. See the Vice-Presidential Diary, September 23rd, 1963 (LBJ Library).

[533] Author's exclusive original discovery. See the Vice-Presidential Diary, October 11th, 1963 (LBJ Library).

[534] Jim Bishop, *The Day Kennedy Was Shot,* pp. 193-194.

[535] William Manchester, *The Death of a President,* p. 239. (Air Force One Pilot James B. Swindal confirmed this to me during an extraordinarily revealing interview that I conducted with him in the 1990s.)

[536] Author's exclusive original discovery.

[537] The photo was taken by principal White House photographer Cecil Stoughton, and it is now available in digital form from both the JFK and LBJ presidential libraries.

It was Lyndon Johnson who, on November 23rd, tried to falsely convince Kennedy loyalist Ted Sorensen that *Cuba* was to blame for the JFK assassination.

It was Lyndon Johnson who, early on the morning of November 24th, personally visited the Pentagon and falsely declared that Fidel Castro was responsible for John Kennedy's assassination.[538]

It was Lyndon Johnson who, on the very weekend of the assassination, secretly declared a *reversal* of President Kennedy's policy to withdraw from Vietnam.[539]

It was Lyndon Johnson who, on the very weekend of the assassination, *personally* ordered top White House aides to lie to the press and falsely declare that LBJ's policy was one of "continuity" with President Kennedy's policies.[540]

It was Lyndon Johnson who, on November 26th, 1963, formally *reversed* Kennedy's Vietnam withdrawal policy, *in writing,* by signing National Security Action Memorandum (NSAM) 273.

It was Lyndon Johnson who, by November 29th, 1963, cajoled Chief Justice Earl Warren into heading a pseudo-probe of the JFK case in order to crush rumors of his own involvement in the crime and to supposedly stave off a nuclear war.

It was Lyndon Johnson who created, selected the members of, directed and ***paid for*** the federal commission that "investigated" [*sic*] the JFK assassination.[541]

It was Lyndon Johnson who *refused to testify* before his very own hand-picked Commission, and who refused to submit even his cagy written answers *under oath.*

It was Lyndon Johnson who repeatedly refused to be interviewed by the Kennedys' designated author, William Manchester, for a major book about the JFK assassination.[542]

It was Lyndon Johnson who, at a White House reception in December 1963, just a month after the assassination, said to the Joint Chiefs of Staff regarding the

---

[538] Alexander Haig with Charles McCarry, *Inner Circles,* p. 115.

[539] LBJ announced to his subordinates that he would ***not*** be the first American president to lose an armed conflict, and he specifically directed McGeorge Bundy to alter the original draft of NSAM 273 in order to open the door to massive Americanization of the Vietnam War.

[540] Johnson also ordered McGeorge Bundy to relay that lie to outlets like the *New York Times,* which solemnly and uncritically printed the false leak as if it were legitimate "news."

[541] Executive Order 11330.

[542] William Manchester, *The Death of a President,* p. xiii.

Significantly, LBJ gave at least two (2) interviews (in 1965 and in 1968) to his own "designated hitter," the writer Jim Bishop. Published in 1968, a year after Manchester's 1967 volume *The Death of a President,* Bishop's book – *The Day Kennedy Was Shot* – functioned as Lyndon Johnson's *riposte* to the Kennedy clan.

timing of the criminal American escalation in Vietnam, *"Just let me get elected* [in November 1964], *and then you can have your war."*[543]

It was Lyndon Johnson who very smoothly arranged for all unpublished records from the so-called "Warren" Commission to be transferred to the National Archives and thus to be sealed for 75 years, until 2039[544] – thereby putting a great deal of key data out of reach until many of the *scores* of guilty men involved in the crime[545] would be long dead.

It was Lyndon Johnson who in January 1964 angrily threatened the careers of any complaining Secret Service agents, after receiving a memorandum about low morale on the SS White House Detail. The reality was that LBJ wanted to intimidate and silence *any* agents who might still harbor *any loyalty whatsoever* to the slain President Kennedy – or to the truth about what had really happened in Dallas.[546]

It was Lyndon Johnson who personally crushed any effort inside his administration to reopen the JFK assassination investigation in the 1960s.

"He [LBJ] kept tabs on *everything* through the Secret Service or the Signal Corps [White House Communications Agency]," said LBJ aide George Christian.[547]

It was Lyndon Johnson who, in 1967, was supposedly sitting on "a political H-bomb" – a false story blaming Fidel Castro and Robert Kennedy for the JFK assassination – the very story which supposedly "could have sparked nuclear war" just four years earlier. Yet in 1967 the USSR still had all those nuclear bombers and ICBMs, *plus many more;* the nuclear danger had not diminished in the slightest; so why was such a dangerous story now no longer a risk?

---

[543] Stanley Karnow, *Vietnam: A History,* p. 326. (The cowardly Karnow and several other Establishment eunuchs spent decades frantically denying the clear meaning and chilling significance of Johnson's blunt, explicit 1963 admission to the Joint Chiefs of Staff.)

[544] **N.B.**: LBJ did *not* issue an actual presidential "executive order" specifically sealing all unpublished Commission records for 75 years; *he did not need to do so!* It was unnecessary because his hand-picked Commission deposited those documents in the National Archives. LBJ and his closest attorneys and his Commission knew that the Archives' outrageous 75-year secrecy policy would protect the information in those sealed records until *most* key participants in the JFK assassination – including LBJ himself – were dead and beyond the reach of the law.

[545] Over the course of forty years of in-depth research and analysis thus far, I have carefully determined that no fewer than *ninety (90) specific individuals* took an active part in the JFK assassination. Not all of them acted in Dealey Plaza itself, obviously, but all of them participated in essential ways – in a variety of locations. (Read on.)

[546] LBJ spoke to SS agent Rufus Youngblood about this on January 6th, 1964 – less than two months after the JFK assassination.

[547] Jeff Shesol, *Mutual Contempt,* p. 298.

It was Lyndon Johnson who, in 1968, discussed the JFK assassination secretly with Attorney General Ramsey Clark in order to keep the lid on the ghastly crime and suppress his own principal role in it.[548]

It was Lyndon Johnson who, in the late 1960s, told media figures Howard K. Smith and Walter Cronkite lies that yet again falsely implicated the government of Cuba in the JFK assassination.

It was Lyndon Johnson.

It was Lyndon Johnson.

It was Lyndon Johnson.

Even the conventional and JFK-plot-agnostic Establishment "historian" Stephen Ambrose belatedly admitted, "The brazenness of the lies told by leaders is often in direct proportion to *the degree of guilt . . .*"[549]

* * *

The assassination of John Fitzgerald Kennedy in 1963 was a bravura performance by a greedy and cynical and crude murderer named Lyndon Baines Johnson – but it was, nonetheless, a bravura performance. No other politician of that era would have *dared* to try to pull it off; moreover, no other politician of that era would have *succeeded.*

Lyndon Johnson was uniquely motivated, uniquely ambitious and uniquely ruthless, and he permitted nothing – *not even imminent disaster in Dallas following several astounding plot failures in Dealey Plaza and at Parkland Hospital* – to deter him from securing his most coveted and valuable prize: the presidency.

The personal cost to himself, however, was quite different than LBJ had ever imagined.[550]

* * *

For Lyndon Johnson, the stress unleashed by his deliberate murder of his predecessor, coupled with gnawing guilt and the ongoing need to tamp down increasing public calls for a genuine, serious investigation of the JFK assassination – plus, above all, the inevitable onrushing destruction of his own administration by the

---

[548] LBJ recorded several conversations with Ramsey Clark on this topic.

[549] Ambrose essay in the *New York Times,* February 2nd, 1992.

[550] Author's exclusive original discovery.

looming escalation of the Vietnam War – initiated a precipitous decline into ill-concealed madness.[551]

Author Fletcher Knebel, who along with Charles W. Bailey II co-wrote the chilling and prescient 1962 thriller *Seven Days in May,* later penned a less-well-known but equally chilling 1965 book – a novel called *Night of Camp David* – concerning a U.S. President who exhibits disturbing signs of insanity. It was clearly based on Lyndon Baines Johnson.[552]

Two of LBJ's closest White House aides – the ambitious young sycophant and press secretary Bill Moyers (later of hypocritically moralistic fame on PBS television) and speechwriter Richard Goodwin (the supposed "liberal") both recognized this fact as they witnessed Johnson's bouts of insanity become more and more frequent.[553]

At first independently, and later jointly, Moyers and Goodwin began to quietly research the subject of mental illness, and to quietly share their fears of what it meant to have a madman in the Oval Office. Even Moyers, the longtime Johnson protégé and doggedly silent loyalist,[554] was truly shocked by what he saw and heard from LBJ.

Though he himself was an ordained Baptist minister and a fellow Texan, Bill Moyers felt that at times it seemed that the Johnson was "*something other than a human being.*"[555] Another White House aide bluntly referred to Johnson as a "vampire."[556] These are *not* terms commonly used to describe normal, healthy, sane, rational, sitting Presidents of the United States.[557]

---

[551] Author's exclusive original discovery. Ironically, the onset of Lyndon Johnson's most open and severe mental illness in the mid-1960s coincided with the onset of Lifton's most open and severe mental illness in the mid-1960s.

[552] Author's exclusive original discovery.

[553] Arthur Schlesinger recorded their concerns in his journal in 1969; Richard Goodwin eventually wrote an article in 1988 about LBJ's insanity.

[554] Tiny little tidbits are all that Moyers has ever deigned to disclose. Moyers has refused for several decades to write a book about his inside knowledge of Lyndon Johnson (a Democrat), but he is more than happy to spout off about the crimes of *Republican* presidents.

In this sickening hypocrisy, Moyers is much like another disgusting coincidence theorist, the late (and repulsive) Vincent "Vinny the Bug" Bugliosi. Bugliosi wrote a (largely plagiarized) 2007 volume regurgitating and re-arguing the lies of the "Warren" Commission, then produced a 2008 book quite properly excoriating GOP president George W. Bush for launching the criminal Iraq War – but somehow, Vinny the Bug never published a similar jeremiad about Democrat Lyndon Johnson's brutal escalation of the criminal Vietnam War. Grotesque hypocrisy is the coin of the Establishment realm.

[555] Jeff Shesol, *Mutual Contempt*, p. 324.

[556] Jeff Shesol, *Mutual Contempt*, p. 325.

[557] Assuming, of course, that there *are* (or ever *have* been) any normal, healthy, sane, rational, sitting Presidents of the United States – a notion which is certainly questionable at best.

Indeed, Bill Moyers confessed to Arthur Schlesinger Jr. that the challenge in writing the ugly truth about Lyndon Baines Johnson – "the private monster" hiding behind the façade of a "statesman" – was that *no one would believe it*.[558]

* * *

Astoundingly, another of Johnson's top aides – the USAAF veteran and casual mass murderer Jack Valenti, who became the powerful head of the Motion Picture Association of America – later penned an extremely important, semi-confessional novel called *Protect and Defend*.

Critics roundly panned the book as bad literature and bad writing.

They had *no idea* what it was **really** all about.

Published in 1992 by Doubleday, it concerned *a deeply disloyal and audaciously calculating vice president from Texas who is plotting to overthrow an American president*. At Doubleday, the editor of the book was none other than Jacqueline Kennedy Onassis herself – and she *thanked* Valenti for writing it![559]

Protect and Defend actually constitutes Jack Valenti's thinly veiled *admission* of what really happened in 1963 – that Lyndon Johnson killed President Kennedy! **That** is why JFK's widow agreed to edit the project, and **that** is why she thanked Valenti for writing it.[560] It was the *only* public acknowledgment from a member of the Establishment that she ever received about the JFK assassination, and therefore it was the *only* semi-official recognition of the truth behind the horror and anguish that she experienced in Dallas.

Coming from LBJ's uber-sycophant and perpetual defender, Jack Valenti, *Protect and Defend* was all the more extraordinary since it came from such a totally unexpected and unlikely source.

But there it was, in black and white.

Like his former boss, LBJ himself, *Jack Valenti laid it all out,* right there in the open, for everyone to see.

Valenti didn't have to worry too much, though.

In America, hardly *anyone* sees.

---

[558] Arthur Schlesinger, Jr., *Journals,* p. 306. And Bill Moyers, plainly, didn't have the balls to even *try*.

[559] Author's exclusive original discovery.

Note that in America, sadly, truth is usually permitted to be expressed **only** in works of fiction (like novels or movies) or under the guise of "comedy." Deniability is a *cultural* imperative, not just a *governmental* imperative.

[560] Author's exclusive original discovery.

* * *

As he relentlessly expanded the Vietnam War which JFK had pledged to end, Lyndon Johnson began having nightmares about Robert Kennedy. Ostensibly, they were sparked by LBJ's supposed fear of future RFK opposition in the event of Johnson's eventual failure to *win* the war. (The reality was 180 degrees opposite.)

But in telling this to his embarrassingly shallow Establishment biographer Doris Kearns,[561] LBJ twisted his complaint in order to assert that RFK would be angry over Johnson's *loss,* his *failure to carry through* on JFK's supposed "commitment" to South Vietnam (when in reality, of course, it was Johnson's *betrayal* of President Kennedy's commitment to *withdraw* from Vietnam by 1965 that was the real issue).

And Bobby knew it.[562]

The dreams are extremely noteworthy for what they reveal about LBJ's own massive personal sense of guilt and fear, his terror of ***being held accountable*** – for Dallas *and* for Vietnam. In those dreams, a helpless Johnson was securely tied to the ground as large angry crowds advanced toward him – crowds screaming, quite accurately, *"Traitor!"*[563]

Traitor.

You do not have to be a psychiatrist in order to recognize a Freudian slip.[564]

---

[561] Doris Kearns later married Richard Goodwin, thereby becoming "Doris Kearns Goodwin." Kearns Goodwin – like Ambrose, Posner, Lifton and Bugliosi – is a plagiarist. She is also – like Beschloss, Logevall, Caro, Dallek, and many other asinine pseudo-historians – someone who refuses to face the hideous truth about 1963. As is the case with the despicable coward Bill Moyers, Doris Kearns Goodwin's lack of character (and her excessive personal closeness to Lyndon Baines Johnson) explains a great deal.

[562] RFK made it explicitly clear in a JFK Library oral history interview that JFK sought, *at best, **neutralization*** in Vietnam – just as he had pursued it already in the case of Laos. Roger Hilsman also acknowledged this in a later book, *To Move a Nation.*

[563] Quoted in Lloyd Gardner, *Pay Any Price,* p. 233.

[564] Indeed. In 2013, after more than thirty years of repeatedly claiming to be "the" [sic] "author" [sic] of the book *Best Evidence,* Lifton made a gigantic Freudian slip of his own. He explicitly admitted to me that he had ***not*** written the book which bears his alias! Lifton's precise words, which I copied down *verbatim,* were ". . . when Pat Lambert and I wrote *Best Evidence . . .*"

Lifton did not even list his own name first!

". . . when ***Pat Lambert*** *and I* wrote *Best Evidence . . ."*

Over the years, Lifton repeatedly and voluntarily stated to me that Patricia ["Pat"] Lambert was paid $25,000 for *Best Evidence.* (Her erstwhile co-author, Lifton himself, only received $10,000 in advance.)

Lambert & Lifton ***also*** co-authored a never-produced movie screenplay called *Best Evidence* (a "script" which differs significantly from the book) which Lambert ***was*** careful to put her name on. But ultimately, Lifton became suddenly and permanently estranged from his erstwhile "best friend" Pat Lambert in the 1990s, and they never worked together again. Nor did Lifton ever manage to eke out *any* subsequent completed book manuscript by himself in the *forty-two (42) years* since the co-authored book *Best*

* * *

There was another deliberate act which dramatically revealed Lyndon Johnson's direct involvement in every detailed aspect of the JFK assassination.

I made an astonishing and exclusive original discovery in the1990s: *the first written proof, from U. S. government records, of an **actual payoff** in the JFK assassination to an actual participant.*[565]

It is the very first hard evidence of a payoff to an identifiable individual for JFK assassination-related services.[566]

Evidence was turned in to the publisher – which constitutes overwhelmingly conclusive proof of Patricia Lambert's true co-author role.

More than *four decades* have now passed since *Best Evidence* first went on sale. Lifton often bragged about the fact that four different publishers put out various editions of that book (***none** of which,* I emphasize, ever included USAF Col. Joe Sofet's vital revelations).

But Lifton – a public figure – ***also*** freely and voluntarily stated to me on several occasions that four (4) *other* publishers *canceled* him for his repeated failures to deliver a completed manuscript of a subsequent book per his contractual deadlines.

Those shocking failures occurred despite ***massive*** funding (nearly $2 million of Other People's Money, by Lifton's own free and voluntary statements) as well as truly *massive* writing & editorial help from *several* different people (including Peter David Rupay and this author) over a period of several *decades.*

In typically outrageous fashion, Lifton became furiously angry with *a major benefactor* – a wealthy Jewish executive whom Lifton loudly and repeatedly and angrily referred to in my hearing as "That *putz!*" and "That *schmuck!*" even after receiving some *half a million dollars* from the man for the rights to a never-finished "book" – rather than Lifton being furiously angry *with himself,* for his own mind-boggling failure to ever complete the manuscript.

Appalled by Lifton's stunningly pathological inability to *get things done,* I personally dictated thousands of words of crisp, polished, perfectly composed text to him over the telephone more than a decade ago – from scratch, *spontaneously,* right off the top of my head, in real time, to demonstrate what is possible when a ***real*** writer actually composes and writes – while Lifton hurriedly typed away on the other end of the phone connection.

But the truth is that some people are simply beyond help (and are completely unworthy of it in the first place), and eventually I learned that it was a completely wasted effort to ever even *attempt* to aid Lifton.

I did not know who and what Lifton really was when I first met him, decades ago. But I certainly found out – in spades.

It took a while to recognize the full hideous picture of Lifton's dishonest and malignant nature – but it's absolutely clear now. Lifton was like toxic quicksand – or, more accurately, like a malevolent and destructive black hole in outer space which seeks to seize, absorb, consume and destroy anything and anyone that comes near it.

[565] Author's exclusive original discovery.

[566] Author's exclusive original discovery.

It was handled quietly, behind the scenes, never reaching public consciousness until my astounding exclusive original discovery of it in the 1990s.[567]

But the very worst payoff – which would be far more public – was yet to come.

And it had to be paid, of course.

It simply *had* to be paid.

For it was a truly massive debt, owed to a group of highly aggressive, extremely well-placed individuals who had *personally* ensured and guaranteed – *come hell or high water* – the ultimate success of LBJ's bloody 1963 coup.[568]

---

[567] Keep reading.

[568] Author's exclusive original discovery.

USAF General William F. "Bozo" McKee was
Air Force Vice Chief of Staff in November 1963,
and thus second-in-command to Curtis LeMay.

Lyndon Johnson rewarded McKee with a job at NASA,
then a major presidential appointment as head of the FAA.

The FAA tower logs from Andrews Air Force Base
for Friday, November 22nd, 1963,
are missing or have otherwise been
"rendered inaccessible."

President Kennedy's *real* assassins –
Vice President Lyndon Baines Johnson and
Speaker of the House Samuel Taliaferro Rayburn –
glare at their target with homicidal wrath
as JFK addresses Congress
in May 1961.

Author's exclusive original discovery.

President Kennedy bracketed by two of his killers:
Army Chief of Staff General Earle Wheeler (center rear)
and Vice President Lyndon Baines Johnson (far right)
at a military base in New Mexico in June 1963,
just five months before the assassination.

Wheeler supplied massive firepower to back LBJ's coup;
Johnson made Wheeler the Chairman of the JCS.

Author's exclusive original discovery.

Chapter Thirty:
The Guarantors

*"We **can** take effective action*
if proper management is provided."
– USAF Brigadier General Edward Lansdale

"The responsible people
prevail in our country
unless intolerable provocations occur."
– Interior Secretary Stewart Udall

". . . In truth, military force is a
pretty damn blunt instrument."
– USAF General David Burchinal

"A civilian always loses
when he tries to meddle with the military."
– John Fitzgerald Kennedy

"There must be military secrets."
– Lyndon Baines Johnson

"These things do not just 'happen.'
*They are **made** to happen."*
– John Fitzgerald Kennedy

In August 1956, Sam Rayburn and Lyndon Johnson came up with a brilliant and sinister plot to forcibly and violently place a "real" Texan (namely, LBJ himself) into the White House after the November 1960 presidential election.[569]

Taking advantage of the constitutionally-prescribed presidential line of succession, the two co-conspirators would first arrange to place Johnson on the 1960

---

[569] Author's exclusive original discovery.

national Democratic ticket (*by any means necessary*); next, they would exert all of their considerable political might to *win* that crucial November 1960 presidential election; and finally (sometime after the January 1961 inauguration ceremony had formally put LBJ just a heartbeat away from the Oval Office) they would coldly murder Johnson's new boss, the president of the United States – *whomever* he might turn out to be.[570]

They would do it without apology or remorse, without shame or regret, as cruelly and dispassionately as a veteran angler guts a helpless fish.

Yet plainly, the two determined Texas politicians who *conceived of* and *personally led* this fiendish assassination plot could not possibly pull off the bloody masterstroke all by themselves.

There was just too much to do.

They simply could not perform all the necessary tasks on their own.

They needed skilled allies, confederates, supporters, subordinates.

Accomplices, in a word.

Men with power and weapons and skill and a willingness to follow orders.

Men who could be relied upon to execute their assigned tasks.

Men who could be controlled – or at least *restrained* – once Johnson was (illegitimately and violently) ensconced in the White House as America's new Commander-in-Chief.

Men in uniforms.

Bold men.

Cruel men.

Effective men.

Rayburn and Johnson undeniably needed vital *military* assistance.

And when Sam Rayburn died of cancer in November 1961, Lyndon Johnson needed the help of ***"uniformed assassins"*** [571] even more than he had before.

The three biggest branches of the U. S. military *each* devoted substantial personnel and resources and expertise to Johnson's 1963 coup – not only in Dallas itself, but *nationwide.*[572]

Knowingly and willfully and deliberately.

These military conspirators had no particular love for LBJ himself, of course.

---

[570] **N.B.**: John Kennedy was ***not*** singled out and marked for assassination because of his "liberal" attitudes or his "progressive" policies or his "pacifist" goals; the stark truth is that Sam Rayburn and Lyndon Johnson planned to kill *whichever* Democratic candidate won (A) the party's 1960 nomination and (B) the 1960 presidential election.

[571] The term "uniformed assassins" comes from the autobiography of Samuel Langhorne Clemens (alias "Mark Twain"), who was, sadly, *afraid to publish it during his lifetime* and who dictated that it remain secret *for an entire **century** after his death.* Here's the reality: Truth is distinctly unwelcome in America – and it always has been.

[572] Author's exclusive original discovery.

They had zero interest in "Texas pride," and they had zero overtly political ambitions of their own.

They did, however, certainly have *their own* sinister reasons for ***joining*** *the* ***existing*** *Rayburn-Johnson plot* – and for eagerly *facilitating* the bloody killing of the maddening millionaire from Massachusetts.[573]

Thus they were willing and eager to *help* LBJ, and they were laughably easy to recruit *into* the ***already-existing*** Rayburn/Johnson assassination plot.

But the grim men in uniforms and braid had a *price* in mind for their support and cooperation, and that price was no small thing.

It was, in fact, gigantic.

And devastating.

And lethal.

* * *

To put it mildly, the extremely conservative upper echelons of the American military were *deeply* displeased that John Kennedy emerged victorious from the bitter 1960 presidential election.

Red-baiting Republican Richard Nixon was their obvious choice;[574] JFK was plainly anathema.

USAF Vice Chief of Staff Curtis LeMay, no paragon of subtlety, felt that Kennedy's 1960 victory was "a goddamned *disaster*" for the country.[575]

Fortunately for chief JFK assassination plotters Sam Rayburn and Lyndon Baines Johnson, such blunt and furious feelings were not limited to General Curtis LeMay alone.[576]

* * *

In 1961, after interviewing USAF General Curtis LeMay, *Look* magazine reporter Fletcher Knebel and his equally shocked friend, writer Charles W. Bailey –

---

[573] Author's exclusive original discovery.

[574] Given the fact that Genghis Khan was unfortunately unavailable . . .

[575] General LeMay's visceral assessment was noted by journalist Ben Bradlee, who was quoted in Strober & Strober, *Let Us Begin Anew,* p. 382.

[576] The American military were clearly very well informed about John Kennedy's various peccadilloes, illnesses and medications; *on the very day of JFK's inauguration,* an officer watching JFK speak on television shouted, "He's all hopped up!" (Eisenhower's White House military physician made the remark on January 20th, 1961.)

reeling from the bizarre attitudes which they had heard expressed by the new Air Force Chief of Staff – were completely appalled.

Their response to LeMay (and to the rantings of another extremist general, the U.S. Army's Edwin Walker, who had been fired by President Kennedy) was to write a gripping novel called *Seven Days in May* – a chilling and timely warning about a military coup plot right here in the United States, *led by a stubborn Air Force general,* sparked by the Pentagon's vitriolic objection to a liberal president's push for a ban on atomic weapons testing.

Seven Days in May was hardly just a simple, random work of creative fiction.

It was published in 1962 – and soon thereafter, within a year, President Kennedy himself would be in *precisely* the same situation as the coup target in the novel: a liberal American president, pursuing a Limited Test Ban Treaty with the Soviets, facing intense, virulent opposition from both the military itself and from its many right-wing allies in Congress.

Tough, intelligent, realistic and unusually sophisticated, *Seven Days in May* eerily and presciently captured the tensions boiling beneath the placid surface of Washington political life in 1962 and 1963.[577]

By the time a movie version of the novel was underway in 1963, the Joint Chiefs of Staff had *already* urged direct U.S. intervention following the disastrous Bay of Pigs invasion; *already* pushed for American military involvement in Laos; *already* pushed repeatedly for American use of nuclear weapons in southeast Asia; *already* urged Kennedy repeatedly to launch an unprovoked American nuclear strike on the Soviet Union; *already* pushed for the commission of *American government terrorist attacks against American citizens on American soil* as part of a despicable and utterly criminal false-flag campaign to "justify" an attack on Cuba; and *already* repeatedly recommended a massive American land war in Vietnam.

John Kennedy had rejected *all* of the U. S. military's major gambits.

*What happens when ostensibly legitimate criticism of an elected President comes from the lips of illegitimate, **unelected** actors?*

What happens when those who utter words of righteous indignation are themselves far worse than the man whom they propose to oust?

What happens when a powerful group of military men decide that their leader has betrayed the nation – and their trust?

What happens when those military men are recruited into a sinister plot led by an ambitious politician who shares many of their views and who is willing to repay them handsomely for their assistance and support?

---

[577] In the United States of America, truth is widely considered a toxic and dangerous and radioactive substance. Generally, truth is permitted and tolerated and accepted *only* when it is comfortably couched in works of fiction or comedy. *This* uncompromising *nonfiction* book in your hands completely obliterates that cowardly taboo forever.

What happens when frustrated and powerful military men find an outlet into which it can channel its resources and energy in order to permanently oust their most hated enemy?

It is but a small step to a tempting solution – uttered "regretfully," of course, but uttered nevertheless and acted upon in the holy names of patriotism, and national security, and "responsibility."

Better that one man should die for the good of the people, to paraphrase a line found in an obscure ancient text from the Middle East.

One man should die for the good of the people.

The Roman Senate clearly agreed with that philosophy when scores of its members jointly conspired in 44 B.C.E. to brutally assassinate Julius Caesar – and to do so openly, *in broad daylight* no less.

But was the hatred and contempt *that* intense in 1963, two full millennia *after* Caesar's gory demise?

Did high-ranking uniformed American officers join Lyndon Johnson's brutal assassination plot?

Did the U. S. military actively participate in the murder of John F. Kennedy?

The answer – proven here for the very first time anywhere – is ***yes.***

* * *

Understand something very clearly:

The U. S. military *actively spied on* John Fitzgerald Kennedy.[578]

Part of their spying involved what America's so-called "intelligence community" calls HUMINT – human intelligence, gleaned by people. This included efforts *inside the White House and the Executive Office Building* by a small squad of uniformed men working with and for U. S. Army General Maxwell Taylor, a man whom JFK stupidly brought out of retirement to serve as a White House "military adviser" and then (incredibly) as Chairman of the Joint Chiefs of Staff (JCS).

Taylor easily seduced the naïve Kennedy brothers, John and Robert, by posing as a reasonable and calm "intellectual" – quoting the ancient Greek general and writer Thucydides, and even spouting poetry on occasion. Taylor expertly and easily wormed his way into the Kennedys' good graces and stayed there by masquerading as a relatively "enlightened" warrior, which certainly appealed to JFK's and RFK's own self-image.[579]

---

[578] Author's exclusive original discovery.

[579] In a stunning example of Kennedy blindness to reality, RFK actually named one of his own sons after General Maxwell Taylor. (The general cleverly conned Bobby by appealing to his ego and saying that RFK could have been a paratrooper.)

In reality, General Taylor was something else entirely.

Beginning in 1961, Maxwell Taylor established a cadre of military spies inside the Kennedy West Wing. The group included Colonel Laurence Legere as well as Colonel William Y. Smith, and these clever military men (joined by CIA officer Thomas A. Parrott)[580] deftly infiltrated JFK's closely held decision-making councils and secretly reported back to their brethren over at the Pentagon.

"General Taylor had a small group over there with him that he carefully had moving around through the White House to the State Department and elsewhere where they kept their fingers on the pulse of what was going on," Army General Earle Wheeler disclosed in a surprisingly candid interview less than a year after Dallas.[581] The information that General Taylor and his men obtained went directly to the JCS and to their Joint Staff at the Pentagon; moreover, Maxwell Taylor himself engaged in "frequent personal consultation" – twice weekly – with the JCS Chairman, General Lyman Lemnitzer.[582]

JFK's own Army military aide at the White House, General Ted Clifton, put it aptly when he stated that General Taylor had "a small Joint Staff" of his own – *operating right under Kennedy's nose.* General Wheeler described Taylor's highly effective spy group as a cadre of "very active, very intelligent young officers" who would "fan out," obtain information, and then "transmit it" to senior officers over at the Pentagon.[583]

* * *

But apart from the valuable HUMINT gathered by Maxwell Taylor's cadre of spies, *America's military brass also gathered electronic intelligence on JFK* [584] – what the so-called "intelligence community" calls ELINT, which is obtained through machines and *devices* (like microphones).

One of the actual recipients of this intrusive, illegal and damaging ELINT was none other than USAF General Thomas Power – Curtis LeMay's rabid successor as commander-in-chief of the mighty Strategic Air Command.[585]

---

[580] Earle Wheeler oral history interview, conducted by General Ted Clifton, JFK Library, 1964.

[581] Earle Wheeler oral history interview, conducted by General Ted Clifton, JFK Library, 1964.

[582] Earle Wheeler oral history interview, conducted by General Ted Clifton, JFK Library, 1964.

[583] Earle Wheeler oral history interview, conducted by General Ted Clifton, JFK Library, 1964.

[584] Author's exclusive original discovery.

[585] Author's exclusive original discovery.

At one point, CINCSAC Power let slip the fact that he was aware of something that President Kennedy had said *in private, to just one person, without anyone else being present.*[586]

And it was quite a statement, for the era.

Speaking to young White House staffer Marion "Mimi" Beardsley in private during the late stages of the Cuban Missile Crisis on the night of October 27th, 1962, President Kennedy – a nervous father, thinking about the lives and future of his own two very small children, Caroline and John Jr., in the face of potential *global nuclear annihilation* – said aloud in a moment of deep anguish, "I'd rather my children be 'red' than dead."[587]

This was **not** an expression of latent "communist" tendencies on the part of JFK, but simply a basic recognition that being alive is (presumably) far preferable to being dead.

Being alive (even under a horrible "red" system) means that things like *survival* and *escape* and *resistance* and *change* and *ultimate freedom* are still possible – while being dead snuffs out any such outcomes completely and permanently and irrevocably.[588]

But to uniformed officers like Thomas Power, President Kennedy's stunning remark – which General Power *actually quoted afterward,* and coyly cited as having been spoken by "another famous contemporary,"[589] meaning JFK[590] – was proof positive that the chief executive whom they hated was in fact a gutless pinko who certainly did not deserve to lead the United States of America, and who would undoubtedly sell out his country in a pinch rather than steadfastly face (and eliminate) the dreaded communist menace.

And that, of course, made JFK himself a menace to America.

General Power's *personal* awareness of what JFK had quietly said – *in total privacy, upstairs at the White House, to Mimi Beardsley alone* – was damning proof that *United States military men had successfully bugged the residence of their own commander-in-chief.*[591]

---

[586] Author's exclusive original discovery.

[587] Mimi Alford (Marion Beardsley Fahnestock Alford) recounted JFK's remark in her book *Once Upon a Secret.*

[588] As far as we know, at least on *this* planet, at least in *this* dimension – whatever your *metaphysical* beliefs may be.

[589] Thomas Power with Albert A. Arnhym, *Design for Survival,* p. 69.

[590] Author's exclusive original discovery.

[591] Or that the SS was feeding data from its own secret "bugs" to the Pentagon. (Author's exclusive original discovery.)

Thomas Power's irresistible compulsion to publish that phrase[592] revealed that *the American military had microphones (generating ELINT) inside the president's personal quarters at the Executive Mansion during the JFK administration.*[593]

And therefore, the American military had John F. Kennedy "dead to rights." Soon, they would have him literally *dead.*

* * *

Knowingly and unknowingly, John Fitzgerald Kennedy gave his enemies in the U. S. government and the U. S. military *ample* (metaphorical) ammunition to use against him.

From his interactions with the American military *before* taking office[594] to his insufficiently bellicose actions and policies *while* in office, JFK alienated the top brass thoroughly and repeatedly.

The process began quite early.

John Kennedy was personally briefed by U. S. Army General Earle Wheeler (then the Director of the Joint Staff, which serves the Joint Chiefs of Staff at the Pentagon) in a Senate office space in September 1960, months before the presidential campaign ended. In typical fashion, Senator Kennedy was *late* to the meeting – obviously a cardinal sin to highly disciplined military men. JFK also rudely *insulted* Wheeler (and Wheeler's three lower-ranking military assistants who were present that day) by permitting himself to be "continuously interrupted by phone calls coming in from all over the country" – calls of a plainly *political* nature, pertaining to *campaign* issues.[595] In fact, candidate Kennedy was so extremely distracted that *he didn't even remember General Wheeler's first name* at a later press conference.[596]

At the conclusion of this often-interrupted military briefing, JFK had the nerve to boldly ask Earle Wheeler, "General, don't you have any doubting Thomases in the Pentagon?"

General Wheeler replied briskly, "Senator Kennedy, we have *lots* of doubting Thomases."

The number of doubting Thomases in the Pentagon would increase *exponentially* once JFK was inaugurated and officially became Commander-in-Chief

---

[592] *Design for Survival* came out in early 1965.

[593] Author's exclusive original discovery.

[594] Author's exclusive original discovery.

[595] Earle Wheeler oral history interview, conducted by General Ted Clifton, JFK Library, 1964.

[596] Noted in Jay M. Shafritz (editor), *Words on War*, p. 205.

– but their doubts were of ***President Kennedy,*** not of their own destructive doctrines and dark dogmas and doomsday desires.

* * *

JFK's youth rankled the crusty uniformed men who regarded themselves as military experts and as the grim guardians of "democracy." The military's contempt for JFK began early; General Wheeler was one of many who mocked JFK's inexperience and lack of an extensive martial background. In the wake of that September 1960 briefing, Earle Wheeler regarded Kennedy as "a man who probably *didn't know too much as to the details of national defense.*"[597]

That assessment didn't change at all between September 1960 and JFK's January 1961 inauguration at the Capitol.

"When President Kennedy took office," sniffed Earle Wheeler, "*he really didn't know too much about the military* although he had served as a naval officer in World War II."[598]

Moreover, added Wheeler icily, "At the beginning of the Kennedy administration, for several months, *there was confusion within the government.*"[599]

The cold calculus of the Joint Chiefs and their subordinates on the Joint Staff took on darkly ominous tones quite early during the JFK administration. General Wheeler was remarkably blunt and explicit in an interview conducted months after JFK's assassination: "There was a strong feeling on the part of 'people in the know' around here [the Pentagon] that the disorganization or lack of organization in the government [JFK's executive branch] was *just plain **dangerous.***"[600]

How dangerous?

General Wheeler pulled no punches:

"This could," he declared, "be a real serious matter as regards *the security of the United States.*"[601]

* * *

---

[597] Earle Wheeler oral history interview, conducted by General Ted Clifton, JFK Library, 1964.

[598] Earle Wheeler oral history interview, conducted by General Ted Clifton, JFK Library, 1964.

[599] Earle Wheeler oral history interview, conducted by General Ted Clifton, JFK Library, 1964.

[600] Earle Wheeler oral history interview, conducted by General Ted Clifton, JFK Library, 1964.

[601] Earle Wheeler oral history interview, conducted by General Ted Clifton, JFK Library, 1964.

JFK soon infuriated the JCS and other senior officers by his actions (and inaction) pertaining to Laos and Cuba in 1961. These were not minor quibbles over debatable matters like jungle pursuit tactics or the acquisition of spare parts; they went to the heart of American military doctrine – and the senior American military's criminal insanity.

The catastrophic failure of the criminal and illegal Bay of Pigs invasion perpetrated against Cuba in April 1961 by CIA-backed exiles humiliated the president and virtually destroyed any remaining particle of faith that John Kennedy might have ever harbored concerning the U. S. military. According to General Wheeler, "the Bay of Pigs business" had "poisoned his [JFK's] mind against the military"[602] despite the fact that the exile invasion was primarily a CIA project and *not* the actual brainchild of the Pentagon.[603]

Post-invasion criticism leveled against the Joint Chiefs – via anonymous leaks from JFK and his executive branch personnel to the national media – absolutely enraged the Pentagon brass. Wheeler noted that the JCS "were bitter indeed" about the barbs aimed at them. "They felt that they were being very unfairly blamed publicly, and in a sense *pilloried,* for a series of events for which they were not responsible."[604]

America's top generals were not merely "miffed" or "irritated" or "slightly annoyed" by the aspersions cast their way in the wake of the failed exile invasion; they were *infuriated* – to an astounding and dangerous degree. "Don't think," said General Wheeler, just months after Dallas, "that this didn't *burn their souls to a crisp.*"[605]

"As a result," he added in massive understatement, "their opinion of certain people [meaning primarily JFK] went down to a pretty, pretty low ebb."[606]

* * *

The military's furious *anger* toward JFK was accompanied by massive *contempt* as well.

In General Wheeler's words, President Kennedy returned from his bruising Vienna summit meeting with Soviet Premier Nikita Khrushchev in June 1961 "rather

---

[602] Earle Wheeler oral history interview, conducted by General Ted Clifton, JFK Library, 1964.

[603] For his part, following the Bay of Pigs debacle, President Kennedy referred acidly to the Joint Chiefs as "the sons of bitches with all the fruit salad" (i.e., medals and ribbons and braid) on their uniforms and military caps. (Richard Reeves, *President Kennedy: Profile of Power*, p. 103.)

[604] Earle Wheeler oral history interview, conducted by General Ted Clifton, JFK Library, 1964.

[605] Earle Wheeler oral history interview, conducted by General Ted Clifton, JFK Library, 1964.

[606] Earle Wheeler oral history interview, conducted by General Ted Clifton, JFK Library, 1964.

a shaken man."[607] Obviously, no American officer worth his stars or his braid could possibly respect a "shaken" Commander-in-Chief who had plainly been badly rattled by the hated overlord of the hated communist world.[608]

President Kennedy had flinched in Cuba; he had again flinched in Vienna; as far as the brass were concerned, the millionaire from Massachusetts was plainly *a menace to the country.*

To the generals of the Pentagon, JFK was not merely a "sub-optimal" president; he was completely out of his depth and completely out of his league.

And that put America itself at *unacceptable risk.*

But be very clear on this point:

The Joint Chiefs of Staff did ***not*** create or initiate or "launch" the JFK assassination plot; *the plot was already well underway and had been underway for five years* before John Kennedy even took the oath of office![609]

Rather, the JCS promptly and predictably *joined* the ***existing*** Rayburn-Johnson plot[610] – which had actually begun back in 1956 [611] – once the Pentagon brass got a horrifyingly close look at JFK "in action" as their Commander-in-Chief.

Recruiting key military men to the Rayburn-Johnson plot wasn't difficult.

It wasn't difficult at all.

* * *

Apart from his policy decisions as Commander-in-Chief, JFK's often unethical and frequently ill-advised and sometimes criminal actions in the personal realm made him a veritable *archetype* of the dangerous, untrustworthy, self-absorbed, selfish and reckless politician who can easily be (and often is) labeled "a genuine threat to national security."

---

[607] Earle Wheeler oral history interview, conducted by General Ted Clifton, JFK Library, 1964.

[608] The senior military's anger and contempt were also accompanied by *fear.* General Wheeler noted that at the Pentagon, senior staff quickly recognized that President Kennedy was going to "slowly but surely *get rid of one or more of the Joint Chiefs of Staff* and change the composition of the body." (Earle Wheeler oral history interview, conducted by General Ted Clifton, JFK Library, 1964.)

JFK did precisely that – ultimately replacing four (4) of the JCS: General Lemnitzer (Chairman), General Decker (USA), General White (USAF), and Admiral Anderson (USN). Unfortunately for President Kennedy and for America, the replacement Joint Chiefs (the trio of Taylor, Wheeler and LeMay, in particular) were *even worse than their predecessors.* Personnel choices matter, particularly in the executive branch of government. JFK's choices were *fatal.*

[609] Author's exclusive original discovery.

[610] Author's exclusive original discovery.

[611] Author's exclusive original discovery.

Therefore, it was no large step for the U. S. military to go from using *metaphorical* ammunition against President Kennedy to using *actual* ammunition against him, as it did in Dallas in November 1963.[612]

JFK's frequently hated policy decisions, and his extravagant personal behavior, gave the U. S. military and the Secret Service ample grounds for thinking – *and actually doing* – the supposedly "unthinkable."

And in 1963, in the United States of America, the "unthinkable" came true.

* * *

The only ones who didn't see this were Americans, of course.

Foreigners understood immediately what had happened.

And one foreigner *in particular* grasped the essence of the situation right away.

On November 22nd, 1963, French President Charles de Gaulle turned 73.

Three days later, following President Kennedy's afternoon funeral at Arlington National Cemetery, de Gaulle spent a quarter of an hour speaking with the widowed Jacqueline Bouvier Kennedy upstairs at the White House.

The French leader accurately told Jackie that her husband had died "like a soldier under fire."[613]

It was not an empty compliment, nor an idle or hyperbolic remark.

De Gaulle knew all too well the risks that Kennedy had faced; de Gaulle himself had nearly been assassinated on *multiple* occasions because of *murderous attacks by disaffected members of his very own military* – most recently, just 15 months before the JFK assassination – as de Gaulle *rode in a motorcade*.

As Kennedy did in Dallas.

De Gaulle definitely knew whereof he spoke.

He knew firsthand of the rage and fury aroused in ultra-conservative military men when a political leader decides to withdraw from a foreign country – as de Gaulle had withdrawn from Algeria and as Kennedy was withdrawing from Vietnam.

De Gaulle was correct, in ways that no American "journalist" of the era (or since) ever was:

---

[612] Many lesser JFK assassination researchers *still* believe fervently that "rabid Cuban exiles" or "rogue CIA personnel" or "Mafia riflemen" (Mafia *riflemen*? Really?) gunned down JFK. They are sadly (and badly) incorrect, as my additional future works on the killing of President Kennedy will demonstrate indisputably.

I strongly urge the members of the "JFK research community" to become much more serious and sophisticated and focused than they have previously been during their long decades of lamentable failure to truly solve the case. (Just maybe, *compadres,* foolish groupthink and stale cliches and utterly superficial "theories" are not the answer.)

[613] Quoted in Sally Bedell Smith, *Grace and Power*, p. 455.

John F. Kennedy *did* die like a soldier under fire.

And soldiers, of course, are generally fired upon by . . . *other soldiers.*[614]

The difference in Dallas was that JFK – unlike regular troops in the field – was both totally unarmed and totally unprotected.[615]

* * *

In the decades since 1963, American "journalists" and "academics" have done a *miserable* job (a cowardly *non-job*, to be precise) of investigating and analyzing the assassination of John Kennedy.

And in the decades since 1963, JFK researchers in general have done a *terrible* job of probing the U. S. military's involvement in the assassination of John Kennedy – until the publication of this book.

Most researchers remain forever lost in the soggy swamps of weak and vague "theory" rather than engaging in tough analysis and finding hard proof – contenting themselves with endlessly disproving the "Warren" Report (quite needlessly, for the ten millionth trillionth time)[616] while chanting shallow claims of "CIA culpability" rather than focusing on truly central issues.

John Judge was one of the very few researchers who emphasized Pentagon responsibility for the assassination in Dallas – but even John did not look quite far enough, or quite high enough.

Judge did uncover some absolutely *vital* information, though.

And there was another truly amazing individual who uncovered the fact of American military involvement in the JFK assassination – ***before*** *the JFK assassination even occurred!*

* * *

In September 1963, a brilliant U. S. Army private named Eugene B. Dinkin, a codebreaker stationed overseas in Germany with the 599th Ordnance Group, personally uncovered the upcoming late November plot to assassinate President Kennedy – and he *also* uncovered the U. S. military's prominent role therein. Moreover, Dinkin's stunning original analysis correctly revealed that the murderous JFK plot was designed to *falsely* blame either a black person or a "communist" for the crime.

---

[614] Author's exclusive original discovery.

[615] I will have much more to reveal in additional books on the JFK assassination, already well underway.

[616] For example, as of the year 2022 Dr. Cyril Wecht was still loudly and predictably wailing about the government's ludicrous "Single Bullet Theory," as if he were still stuck in a totally obsolete debate from the year 1964.

Before entering the military, Dinkin had studied psychology at the university level, and he was extremely knowledgeable about key concepts and practices – including the persuasive psychological techniques used in commercial advertising to "sell" products, attitudes and beliefs to innocent and unwitting consumers.

Dinkin discovered that a very clever and subtle program of *psychological warfare* had been implemented in American media in the months prior to the JFK assassination. This program took the form of what he termed "psychological sets" – meaning certain materials (words, phrases and images) deliberately placed in major American newspapers aimed at civilians, as well as in the widely read U. S. military publication *Stars and Stripes*.

The purpose of these "psychological sets," Dinkin realized, was to quietly convince readers that President Kennedy was "soft on communism," and therefore *deserved* to be assassinated and replaced – in other words, the psychological sets would psychologically *prepare* the American populace for, and gain their tacit *acceptance* of, a coup.[617] (For the record, such perverse psychological manipulation was not limited to the sadistic psychotics over at the Central Intelligence Agency; the U. S. Air Force had its very *own* programs of psychological warfare. This is documented in the National Security Files of the Kennedy White House – files I found which are held at the JFK Presidential Library.[618])

By mid-October 1963, Private Dinkin had assembled sufficient written proof documenting his findings about the upcoming plot. On October 16th, 1963 – *five weeks before Dallas* – Dinkin sent a registered letter to Attorney General Robert F. Kennedy warning that the assassination of his brother, the president, would occur in late November 1963.

In late October 1963, one month *before* the JFK assassination, Private Dinkin – who had been transferred from a post in Germany to a military depot in Metz, France – courageously visited the U. S. embassy in nearby Luxembourg in an effort to expose the murderous plot. He was ignored completely by the American *Charge d'Affaires* there, who refused to even *see* Dinkin in his office.

---

[617] A series of gruesome and disturbing newspaper articles was used in order to unsettle and psychologically manipulate the population of Chile prior to the bloody right-wing coup of September 11th, 1973, and the brutal assassination that day of elected president Salvador Allende. (See *Death in Washington: The Murder of Orlando Letelier* by Donald Freed with Fred Landis).

For the record, President Allende did *not* commit suicide; he was assassinated in the presidential palace by right-wing Chilean soldiers – shot to death while courageously defending democracy against the American-backed fascist army of self-installed dictator Augusto Pinochet. (See *The Murder of Allende and the End of the Chilean Way to Socialism,* by Robinson Rojas Sandford.) Decades later, the Chilean government exhumed Allende's body but repeated the insulting and false version of his death, as promulgated by the dictatorship – an outcome which must *not* be repeated in the United States when President Kennedy's body is (and it will be!) finally exhumed and re-examined.

[618] Author's exclusive original discovery.

Word of Private Dinkin's stunning *knowledge* of the assassination plot – and word of his lonely, courageous efforts to *expose* it – was getting around.[619]

As a result, the U. S. Army now ordered Dinkin to undergo punitive and utterly unwarranted psychiatric examinations in Europe in early November 1963, in a patently obvious ploy to discredit him *prior to* the JFK assassination.

Instead, Dinkin went AWOL and wisely fled to Geneva, Switzerland. There he spoke with both a *Newsweek* reporter and a Swiss newspaper editor in order to publicly expose the JFK plot. The *Newsweek* reporter, quite predictably, refused to listen to Dinkin's urgent findings. Private Dinkin also tried valiantly but unsuccessfully to communicate with personnel of the TIME/LIFE media empire.

Stymied and defeated at every turn, PFC Dinkin ultimately traveled back to Germany, where he surrendered. While he was in military detention there, all of his evidentiary material was taken and removed by a man claiming to be a Pentagon official – and then either destroyed or otherwise "rendered inaccessible."

Back in the U. S., people inside the federal government worked overtime to intercept Dinkin's letter to Bobby Kennedy – and to simultaneously construct a false chronology hiding the federal government's knowledge of Dinkin's vital information *prior to* the assassination.[620]

In early December 1963, less than two weeks *after* the JFK assassination, Private Dinkin was wrongfully and punitively reassigned to the psychiatric ward at Walter Reed Army Hospital in Maryland. There he was illegally held against his will for four months until – desperate to escape this criminal and unjust imprisonment – he offered a supposed "recantation" of his chilling discoveries about the president's murder and the plot which had taken John Kennedy's life.

Only then was Dinkin finally released; only long *after* President Kennedy had been murdered (just as Dinkin had correctly revealed, well in advance), *with the support of the U. S. armed forces* (just as Dinkin had also correctly revealed, well in

---

[619] Some JFK researchers cling to the shallow notion that Dinkin "heard" actual radio traffic about the JFK assassination, but they are *completely wrong* about that being the source of Dinkin's discovery. As investigator Ronald Redmon has correctly pointed out, Dinkin himself wrote to the HSCA in 1977 and explicitly noted that his discovery of the plot against JFK did **not** stem from intercepting or "decoding" any radio or electronic traffic. (Ronald Redmon, "Eugene Dinkin: The Saga of an Unsung Hero," posted online on October 17th, 2017.)

The plot which killed JFK was **not** run by careless amateurs from a "Matt Helm" movie; it was a much more intelligent operation than that. Dinkin in fact analyzed *unclassified printed material* to uncover the JFK plot, and I later independently discovered key *additional unclassified printed materials* that Dinkin never saw – materials which absolutely corroborate and reinforce his 1963 finding that *unclassified printed items* were key to conditioning their targeted audiences.

[620] Assassination investigator Ronald Redmon provides a solid, detailed and very useful summary of these ugly and sinister events in "Eugene Dinkin: The Saga of an Unsung Hero," posted online on October 17th, 2017.

advance), in a bloody crime which was falsely blamed on a "communist" (just as Dinkin had also correctly revealed, well in advance).

This insidious psychological indoctrination program plainly worked. JFK's murder was accepted docilely if mournfully by most American civilians that awful November weekend in 1963.

U. S. Army Private Eugene B. Dinkin was wrongfully and criminally held in the psychiatric ward of Walter Reed Army Hospital for four terrifying months. By the beginning of April 1964, he was discharged from the Army and finally released from confinement at Walter Reed. He was interviewed by the FBI in 1964; ignored by the HSCA in 1977; and never given his due prior to his death in 2012.

But let there be no mistake:

Dinkin was right.

And he was right from the very beginning.

Dinkin was right.

What Eugene Dinkin brilliantly discovered in 1963 was true and correct, and he discovered it *in advance of* the JFK assassination.

Dinkin was right.

He did ***not*** uncover Lyndon Baines Johnson's leading involvement in the coup, but he ***did*** uncover the U. S. military's major role as a key participant in the upcoming crime which slaughtered American democracy.

Dinkin was right.

Two months before Dallas, he uncovered military aspects of the JFK assassination plot and he valiantly sounded the alarm.

Dinkin was right.

Instead of being rewarded and honored and revered for his intelligence and his integrity and his courage, Dinkin suffered singularly vile abuse and injustice at the hands of the very military whose uniform he wore, and the very government which he had loyally served.

It was a truly despicable outrage.

Dinkin was right.

Because of his unjust incarceration in late 1963 and early 1964, Private Eugene Dinkin did not have the opportunity to find *all* the published examples of the sinister "psychological sets" which he brilliantly discovered while in Europe during the summer and autumn before the JFK assassination.[621]

---

[621] Some additional powerful examples of printed "psychological sets" from major American corporate media articles were later found and highlighted by Cuban intelligence officer Fabian Escalante in his 2006 book *JFK: The Cuba Files.*

Other valuable examples published in major media outlets were located and described by Ronald Redmon, author of the excellent 2017 online article "Eugene Dinkin: The Saga of an Unsung Hero."

And Dinkin ***didn't*** find the chilling phrases and articles which targeted the men at a giant and vitally important military installation located in the state of Texas.

But I did.

I found them.[622]

Eugene Dinkin was right.

* * *

The United States Air Force played a *massive* role – indeed, *the **principal** military role* – in the 1963 assassination of the president of the United States.[623]

But nevertheless, there were certain aspects and contingencies of the JFK assassination plot which required guarantors in the form of *ground* forces.

Forces that General LeMay, as an Air Force officer, simply could not supply.

Overwhelming *land-based* forces.

Mobile, intimidating, *armored* forces.

In a word, *tanks*.

* * *

What typically characterizes a coup, anywhere in the world?

Tanks.

Tanks in the streets.

Across the globe, tanks have become the most widespread, obvious, *characteristic* visual symbols of a coup.

Tanks.

From Iran in 1953 to Iraq in 1963 to Chile in 1973 to Russia in 1991 to Turkey in 2016, coups around the world – those examples mentioned, plus many more both before and since – have featured *tanks*.

Tanks in the streets.

Lyndon Johnson needed an overwhelming *guarantor* of his well-planned but highly risky JFK assassination plot – a massive force that could absolutely *ensure* the success of the upcoming Rayburn-Johnson coup, *no matter what*.

After all, many things could go terribly wrong on November 22nd.

Lyndon Johnson needed a truly significant armed force – not simply his (also extremely vital) personal cadre of SS men on the ground with their .38 revolvers and

---

But neither Escalante nor Redmon found the printed items in an obscure publication that specifically targeted ***military*** men at a key base located in ***Texas*** – printed items which I discovered exclusively.

[622] Author's exclusive original discovery.

[623] Author's exclusive original discovery.

their shotguns and their AR-15 rifles, but truly *heavy-duty weaponry* as well – in order to generate *total intimidation* of any state, local or federal authority who might *possibly* summon the temerity to actively oppose LBJ's bloody coup.

In a word, Lyndon Johnson needed *tanks.*

Tanks.

Tanks in the streets to crush any opposition.

Tanks to ensure his bloody takeover.

Tanks to annihilate any *possible* opposition from loyal state and local police units (if any) or loyal federal agents (if any) or loyal U. S. military units (if any).

LBJ needed a *land-based* guarantor.

LBJ needed massive *armored* force.

Power. Mobility. Speed. Firepower.

LBJ needed *tanks.*

And in the spring of 1963, he *got* them.[624]

* * *

LBJ's tanks for November 1963 required a *commander,* of course.

Someone violent and uncompromising and totally willing to open fire – even against legitimate domestic authority.

Even against American civilians.

Someone vicious and cruel who actually *enjoyed* warfare, and killing, and risk.

Someone whose veins pulsed with genuine, totally authentic bloodlust.

Someone without a shred of fear or hesitation or inconvenient scruples.

Someone much like the late General George S. Patton, Jr., the ruthless officer who died in December 1945 soon after the end of World War II.

Someone *exactly* like that Patton.

Another George Patton, in fact.

Yes.

That's *precisely* what Lyndon Johnson needed to truly guarantee that his upcoming coup would succeed:

Another George Patton!

Such a man did indeed exist – and in 1963, he was definitely *available.*

In fact, he made his famous father – the well-known and tyrannical tank commander of World War II – look like a choirboy.[625]

---

[624] Author's exclusive original discovery.

[625] Patton *père* slapped and insulted two American soldiers who were suffering from shell shock in 1943.

And in the spring of 1963, LBJ *got* him.[626]

Months later, in November 1963, Lt. Col. George Smith Patton of the U. S. Army would *personally* serve as a key military guarantor of Lyndon Baines Johnson's bloody coup against the president of the United States of America.[627]

* * *

While assigned to the Pentagon in 1961, then-Major George S. Patton[628] volunteered to go to Vietnam. He first traveled there in April, 1962,[629] and that same spring he was assigned by the American commander, General Harkins, to be a liaison with the CIA.[630] In Vietnam, Patton worked with both Saigon CIA Station Chief John Richardson (ousted in late 1963 by JFK's new ambassador, Henry Cabot Lodge, Jr.) and the infamous CIA officer Lucien Conein[631] (who delivered money for the American-backed and American-financed[632] South Vietnamese military coup of November 1963, which toppled the existing dictatorial regime and assassinated the brutal Ngo brothers – Diem and Nhu – who headed it).

Major Patton "worked closely with the CIA" and admired the Agency's operatives because they were, quite plainly, "very focused on victory in Vietnam."[633]

Patton *fils* sent out Christmas holiday cards in December 1968 featuring a color photo of mangled and dismembered Vietnamese corpses, emblazoned with the sneering slogan, *"Peace on Earth."* (Brian Sobel, *The Fighting Pattons,* p. 131.)

And when Patton departed Vietnam for the final time in April 1969, his farewell *soiree* featured an unusual and grisly "gift" from his men, which he held in his arms – the skull of a Vietnamese victim, with a bullet hole through it. (Brian Sobel, *The Fighting Pattons,* p. 131.)

[626] Author's exclusive original discovery.

[627] Author's exclusive original discovery.

[628] Strangely, this son of the famous World War II general was originally named "George S. Patton IV," even though there *was no* "George S. Patton III." But eventually he legally changed his name by removing the spurious and superfluous Roman numeral at the end of it, and thereby became merely "George Smith Patton." (Helena Payne, "Son of the WWII general Patton dies at 80," Associated Press, June 30th, 2004.)

[629] Brian Sobel, *The Fighting Pattons,* pp. 101-102.

[630] Brian Sobel, *The Fighting Pattons,* p. 102.

[631] Brian Sobel, *The Fighting Pattons,* p. 102.

[632] The sickeningly cynical McGeorge Bundy, the National Security Adviser, actually *groused aloud* in a White House meeting that the U. S. government – JFK's administration – had ***overpaid*** financially for the November 1963 Saigon coup that toppled and assassinated Ngo Dinh Diem and Ngo Dinh Nhu. (See Patrick Sloyan's little-noted but valuable book *The Politics of Deception.*)

[633] Brian Sobel, *The Fighting Pattons,* p. 104.

President Kennedy was ***not*** focused on victory there; to the contrary.

By early 1962 (just months after grudgingly boosting the number of American "advisers" in Vietnam but firmly and permanently rejecting Pentagon requests for large-scale introduction of full U. S. combat units), JFK was instructing his aides to seek ways for the United States to begin *withdrawing* from Vietnam just as soon as practicable.[634]

Although Major George Patton was working for a group with the completely innocuous title "Combined Studies,"[635] he was no mere desk jockey in Vietnam. Indeed, Patton's primary responsibility during this first tour in the country was helping to bring Special Forces teams (who had originally been overseen and financed in Vietnam by the CIA) under the control of the American military.[636] Patton's work took him all over Vietnam – and, by definition, it introduced Patton to many of the toughest, coldest killers in the entire U. S. Army: the Green Berets.[637]

The American Special Forces commandos were "obviously mission-oriented," Patton recalled with open admiration (and severe understatement).[638] Many of the Green Berets who gained actual killing experience in Vietnam were soon rotated back to the United States, where some were assigned to a variety of murderous clandestine missions *inside* America's borders.[639]

---

[634] Arthur Schlesinger, Jr. and James K. Galbraith (son of Ambassador John Kenneth Galbraith) – among many other well-connected observers – have made it repeatedly and undeniably clear that JFK was actively and explicitly seeking an exit from Vietnam.

[635] A common tactic of evil governments and their worst agencies is to hide nefarious activities behind deliberately misleading, utterly banal designations. You can count on the reality that any organization, program or group with the name "planning" or "studies" or "observation" or "coordination" in its title is, in fact, ***actively*** devoted to sinister, extremely violent and brazenly illegal activities.

[636] Brian Sobel, *The Fighting Pattons*, p. 103. **N.B.**: The number of Special Forces "teams" operating in Vietnam grew from just 5 to more than 30 during Major Patton's 1962-1963 "tour."

[637] The Green Berets did ***not*** just operate overseas, in combat theaters, during wartime; in the 1960s they were operating actively *inside the United States* from bases in southern states. Special Forces personnel were not just jungle commandos who specialized in eating snakes while killing foreigners in distant lands; their ranks included expert snipers, spotters, photographers and others with deadly skills essential to the planning and execution of public assassinations *in America* of anyone regarded by them as inimical to the interests of the United States.

[638] Brian Sobel, *The Fighting Pattons*, p. 107.

[639] The truth is stark and ugly: highly trained *military death squads roamed major American cities during* the most tumultuous decade in modern history. U. S. government reports, plus revelations by several former Green Berets themselves, plus the work of Memphis journalist Wayne Chastain and independent investigator William F. Pepper, have made this abundantly and irrefutably clear. Congressional hearings held in the 1970s revealed that the Army illegally maintained files on many thousands of Americans; moreover, numerous U. S. citizens were featured – and targeted for deliberate murder – in photographic "mug books" carried around *within the continental United States* by domestic Special Forces murder teams. (And you thought you lived in a "democracy" . . .)

His year of work with the CIA and Special Forces was looked upon favorably by his superiors; while still in Vietnam, George Smith Patton was promoted from major to lieutenant colonel.[640]

In April 1963 – *which was a critically important and decisive month in the JFK assassination plot* [641] – Patton was transferred from Vietnam back to the United States in order to take on a key assignment.

In Texas.

Lieutenant Colonel Patton was given command of a vital American military unit: the 2nd Medium Tank Battalion of the 81st Armor of the mighty and formidable 1st Armored Division at Fort Hood, Texas – located less than 200 miles from Dallas.

The division's primary weapon was the M48 "Patton" battle tank – named, of course, for Lt. Col. Patton's famous father, the legendary World War II general. Weighing some fifty tons yet capable of speeds up to 20 miles per hour, the M48's armament included a 90 mm main gun along with a .50 caliber machine gun as well as a .30 caliber machine gun.[642]

Tanks.

Powerful, mobile, *overwhelming* force.

The perfect tool for supporting a violent coup.

---

[640] Brian Sobel, *The Fighting Pattons,* p. 110.

[641] Author's exclusive original discovery.

April 1963 was an absolutely critical juncture in the long-planned murder of John Kennedy.

Peter Dale Scott has noted that during that crucial month of April 1963, Lucius D. Clay, a highly experienced logistics expert and U. S. Army general (whom I learned was a longtime friend of Sam Rayburn) – now retired from the military and working for the Lehman Brothers investment firm of Wall Street – met personally in Washington, D. C. with two sinister figures: former CIA director Allen Dulles (fired by JFK after the Bay of Pigs) and Morris Liebman, a right-wing financier from Chicago who was involved with funding a violent right-wing Cuban exile group called JGCE.

Logistics, coup expertise and money – all in the same room.

Clay and Dulles and Liebman did not convene in the nation's capital in April 1963 in order to casually discuss obscure aspects of Bulgarian literature, nor to debate the finer points of competitive badminton.

Moreover, I learned that one of General Clay's sons – Lucius Clay, Jr. – was an *Air Force* general who worked for SAC (under USAF General Thomas Power) between 1958 and 1961 – and then served at the Pentagon for the Joint Chiefs of Staff (under USAF General Curtis LeMay) from 1961 until 1964 (the period encompassing the JFK assassination).

April 1963 was *also* the month when LBJ arranged for George Patton to be brought back from Vietnam to Texas – and it was, *above all,* the month when *LBJ **publicly announced*** that JFK's assassination was *set for November.*

All in all, a hell of a month.

[642] John Pike has provided useful data and technical details about the M48 tank on the FAS.org web site.

Army Lt. Col. George S. Patton
(son of the famous World War II general)
was brought back from Vietnam to Texas in April 1963 –
a key month in the JFK assassination plot.

On November 22nd, Patton was ordered to lead the
2nd Medium Tank Battalion, 81st Armor, 1st Armored Division
from Fort Hood to Dallas – *to protect Lyndon Johnson's coup.*

Right here in the United States of America.

* * *

Two months *before* Dallas, in late September 1963, a joint U. S. Air Force - U. S. Army field exercise called "Triple Threat" (originally scheduled for the last two weeks of October 1963) was abruptly canceled.[643]

Just like that.

The order *terminating* the planned maneuvers was issued by the head of United States STRIKE Command (STRICOM), U. S. Army General Paul DeWitt Adams, whose special unit was based at MacDill Air Force Base in Tampa, Florida.

Here's the chilling reality: the planned "Triple Threat" joint exercise was to have involved the 1st Armored Division based at Fort Hood, Texas, plus the USAF's Tactical Air Command.[644]

The 1st Armored Division.

The massive unit which included Lt. Col. Patton's 2nd Medium Tank Battalion of the 81st Armor.

STRICOM headquarters in Florida proffered only a vague and clumsy excuse for the plainly unexpected *cancellation* of the planned military maneuvers, claiming unconvincingly that the exercise had been suddenly called off because of "a change of maneuver schedules" affecting several unidentified STRICOM components.[645]

The designated Joint Task Force commander for the canceled "Triple Threat" exercise was none other than U. S. Army General Harvey Jablonsky, who was (in September 1963) the commander of the 1st Armored Division at Fort Hood.

Lt. Col. Patton's commanding officer.

Patton's boss.

Someone clearly realized that a massive field exercise in late October might well involve unfortunate accidents, injuries or other unintended casualties as well as mechanical issues and other adverse outcomes *which could negatively affect the 1st Armored Division's ability to respond effectively with its tanks* after President Kennedy's upcoming assassination in Dallas.[646]

---

[643] The (Temple, Texas) *Armored Sentinel,* September 20th, 1963.

[644] Author's exclusive original discovery.

[645] The (Temple, Texas) *Armored Sentinel,* September 20th, 1963.

[646] Author's exclusive original discovery.

As I correctly discerned, the "Old Ironsides" division was being *held in readiness* for an operation *far more important* than the "Triple Threat" exercise.[647]

So was STRICOM commander Paul Adams himself.[648]

* * *

U. S. Army Lt. Col. George Patton, a violence-loving fanatic[649] who had already earned both a Silver Star and a Bronze Star, certainly needed no additional motivation or "stroking" in order to willingly and eagerly participate in the upcoming LBJ coup against JFK – but in early October 1963, at Fort Hood, Patton was awarded a second Oak Leaf Cluster (added to his Army Commendation Medal) in recognition of his past activities in Vietnam relating to the Green Berets.[650]

And in early November 1963, while on a trip to Europe just weeks before the JFK assassination, Vice President Lyndon Baines Johnson made very sure to "stroke" Lt. Col. George Patton even *further* by deliberately paying an ostentatious visit to the grave of Patton's *father,* the notorious American general and tank commander of World War II, who is buried in the American Cemetery and Memorial located in Luxembourg.[651]

LBJ, a very hands-on conspirator, left absolutely nothing to chance. *Nothing.*

* * *

On October 11th, 1963, just as President Kennedy was signing NSAM 263 at the White House in order to concretize and document his firm decision to *end* all American involvement in the Vietnam War in 1965 – *win, lose or draw* – the U. S. military was publicizing a staggeringly massive intercontinental exercise that would

---

[647] Author's exclusive original discovery.

[648] Author's exclusive original discovery.

[649] "I *enjoyed* it," said Patton of combat. "I'd have done it for ***nothing*** . . ." (p. xvi.)

Even Lt. Col. Patton's own sister once wrote to him in an unsuccessful effort to get him to modify or tone down his blatant, outspoken bloodlust. It was, of course, a thoroughly lost cause. (Her failed attempt is duly noted in Brian Sobel, *The Fighting Pattons,* p. 156.)

[650] The (Temple, Texas) *Armored Sentinel,* October 11th, 1963.

[651] Author's exclusive original discovery; see the LBJ vice-presidential diary for Tuesday, November 5th, 1963.

not be canceled the way that the "Triple Threat" maneuvers had been suddenly called off just three weeks earlier.

It would be the biggest airlift and training maneuver ever conducted in peacetime *in all of American military history.*

During October and November 1963, the U. S. Air Force would rapidly ferry a *huge* contingent of U. S. Army troops from America to Europe in just a few days. After performing rigorous practice maneuvers in the field, the Army troops would board the planes again and the Air Force would fly them all back to the United States.

The extraordinarily massive exercise was called "Operation Big Lift," and it was scheduled to largely conclude by the fourth Friday in November.

The fourth Friday in November.

That particular date on the calendar was November 22nd, 1963.

The very day of John Kennedy's upcoming assassination in Texas.

* * *

Meanwhile, in late October 1963, Vice President Lyndon Baines Johnson had the perfect "cover" opportunity to meet again with certain key uniformed allies – senior American military leaders who were of central importance to LBJ's overall chance for success in the upcoming JFK assassination.[652]

The occasion was the five-day national conference of the Association of the United States Army (AUSA), which met in Washington D. C. from October 20th through October 24th that year.[653]

There was nothing covert or secret about the conference itself; it was an annual event which was publicized all over the country. No suspicion was attached to those attending or appearing at the conclave. Therefore, it was a truly *outstanding* opportunity for President Kennedy's chief killer, LBJ, to meet with vital military accomplices and co-conspirators under seemingly "innocuous" circumstances.[654]

Notable speakers who would "brief" attendees at the 1963 event included General John K. Waters, head of Continental Army Command (CONARC); General Earle "Bus" Wheeler, the U. S. Army's Chief of Staff; and Vice President Lyndon Johnson himself.[655]

As Army Chief of Staff, General Wheeler had command authority over *all* Army forces – both nationwide and worldwide (*including Lt. Col. Patton's own tank*

---

[652] Author's exclusive original discovery.

[653] The (Temple, Texas) *Armored Sentinel,* October 11th, 1963.

[654] Author's exclusive original discovery.

[655] The (Temple, Texas) *Armored Sentinel,* October 11th, 1963.

battalion in Texas). And of course, upon murdering President Kennedy, LBJ himself would soon become *all* those officers' new Commander-in-Chief.

Thus the AUSA conference in Washington in late October 1963 – *just one month before Dallas* – was a priceless opportunity for LBJ and key military supporters of his to meet and hold vital private discussions *without generating any suspicion whatsoever.*[656]

No one was the wiser.

No outsider ever put it all together at the time.[657]

Perfect.

* * *

The preferred method to disguise the U. S. military's operational involvement in major crimes is to announce and conduct "exercises" [*sic*] which provide cover and concealment for both criminal *activities* and criminal *communications*.

Operation Big Lift was just such an extraordinary project.

First officially proposed in an August 8th, 1963, memo from Defense Secretary Robert McNamara to JFK (classified SECRET), the planned "Strategic Mobility Exercise" (still unnamed at the time) was *tentatively* approved by the president on August 12th, 1963.[658]

But JFK, rightfully suspicious of the military, quickly had second thoughts.[659]

The very day after giving his tentative approval to the massive exercise, President Kennedy *hedged* – and he hedged in the same terms that he had hedged prior to giving final authorization to the disastrous Bay of Pigs invasion back in 1961.

JFK promptly had McGeorge Bundy send *another* memo to McNamara – this one emphasizing that the president **reserved the right to cancel the entire exercise** even though he had already approved the "general plan." The president specifically requested that he be apprised anew of the proposed venture "*before execution orders are given to the participating forces.*"[660]

---

[656] Author's exclusive original discovery.

[657] **N.B.**: suspiciously, the Vice Presidential "daily diary" presented online by the LBJ Presidential Library lacks any records or entries *whatsoever* for October 20th, October 22nd, and October 23rd, 1963. (Author's exclusive original discovery.)

[658] McGeorge Bundy memo to McNamara, labeled SECRET, August 12th, 1963.

[659] Life imitated art in this instance; JFK's hesitation about the massive 1963 exercise reflected the nature of the sinister military maneuver highlighted in the 1962 book *Seven Days in May* (which JFK had definitely read) – an "exercise" which was in fact a cover for **a military coup against the president.** (Author's exclusive original discovery.)

[660] McGeorge Bundy memo to McNamara, SECRET, August 13th, 1963.

John Kennedy's gut instincts were warning him again.

* * *

A SECRET memo from USCINCEUR-CINCSTRIKE dated September 10th, 1963, outlined the Big Lift exercise and explicitly illustrated the type and sequence of orders employed by the U. S. military in implementing *projects of extreme importance.*

There were three types of such military edicts*:*

Alert orders.

Warning orders.

And then, finally,

Execution orders.

* * *

There are five (5) points about BIG LIFT which merit particular emphasis:

First is the fact that Operation Big Lift, in which the U. S. Air Force ferried *huge* numbers of U. S. Army troops back and forth across the Atlantic Ocean, constituted an ideal means by which to "import" murderous snipers from Europe – be they American troops stationed there, or American expatriates, or even foreign nationals – *all under American military cover.*[661]

The sheer scope and titanic scale of the operation – involving, as it did, the massive airlift of *tens of thousands of U. S. soldiers* on large USAF transport planes – made it laughably easy to put several individuals (for example, frontline U. S. troops or even fanatical members of Operation Gladio, a covert European anti-communist network) into American uniforms and helmets and simply have them stand in line and board one of the numerous crowded military flights back to the United States, able to remain essentially anonymous among the many thousands of innocent American troops flying home.

Second, Fort Hood itself – although it was an *Army* base, not a USAF facility – *actually possessed two (2) major airfields,* one with a lengthy two-mile runway

---

[661] Author's exclusive original discovery.

Both the 1989 theatrical film *The Package* and John Calvin Batchelor's 1994 novel *Father's Day* specifically envisioned the American military transport of American military killers back into the United States in order to have them commit major political assassinations (including the assassination of the president) on American soil.

My original discovery, however, stems from the nature of an *actual* 1963 military maneuver – namely, Operation Big Lift – not any fictional scenario.

sufficient for landing the largest military aircraft in use.[662] Some of the Operation Big Lift planes flew back from Europe *directly to Fort Hood,* and disgorged their military passengers there at the big Texas base between November 14th, 1963, and November 22nd, 1963.[663]

Third is *another* vital aspect of Operation Big Lift.

Decades ago, longtime assassination researcher and political analyst John Judge said and wrote that on the day of JFK's assassination, *American combat troops were in the air above the United States,* ready to fly to any city where unrest might break out in the wake of the president's murder if the U. S. population sensed or realized that what had taken place down in Dallas was, in reality, a bloody *military-backed coup.*[664]

It was a chilling notion, but John did not seem to have any data to back it up.

Judge never specifically mentioned Operation Big Lift (and he may not have ever *known* about that operation), and therefore I myself did not understand, decades ago, exactly what he was referring to – nor how (or where) John got his intriguing but totally undocumented information on that particular topic.

I didn't know what to make of it, or how much credence to accord it.

But many years later, completely on my own, I learned about Operation Big Lift and I studied it in some detail – and then I realized that John Judge's earlier claim (despite his lack of any documentation on the subject) had been absolutely correct:

There were indeed American combat troops in the air above the United States at the time of the JFK assassination.[665]

Those combat troops included members of the 2nd Armored Division at Fort Hood, Texas, who were being flown back to America from Europe *that very day* by the United States Air Force, and who were *already flying over U. S. territory* when JFK was shot down in Dealey Plaza.[666]

Fourth is an extremely chilling insight that occurred to me as I reviewed original documents from Operation Big Lift: classified U. S. military cables sent to *numerous* operational commands over the course of *months* (August through November) in the summer and autumn of 1963 constituted the ***perfect*** cover for ***coded***

---

[662] Author's exclusive original discovery. See the (Temple, Texas) *Armored Sentinel,* October 11th, 1963.

[663] Author's exclusive original discovery. See the (Temple, Texas) *Armored Sentinel,* November 15th, 1963; the base newspaper actually referred to November 22nd as "the ***scheduled termination*** date" – words which obviously applied to JFK himself as much as they did to Operation Big Lift.

[664] See, for example, the John Judge anthology called *Judge for Yourself.*

[665] Original insight by John Judge; absolute proof uncovered by me.

[666] Author's exclusive original discovery. See the (Temple, Texas) *Armored Sentinel,* November 15th, 1963.

internal military communication by the JCS to a wide variety of senior officers worldwide *regarding the upcoming JFK assassination in November.*[667]

Big Lift cables went to an astonishingly vast array of generals and key units of the American military, particularly between September and November 1963. Vitally important addressees – including many *not even remotely involved* in actually executing Operation Big Lift itself![668] – included:

USCINCEUR

CINCSTRIKE [head by U. S. Army General Paul Adams, who *did not participate in Big Lift!*]

SACEUR PARIS

CINCAL

CINCLANT

USCINCSO

CINCONAD

CINCPAC

CINCNELM

CINCSAC [USAF General Thomas Power, *the bloodthirsty head of America's nuclear strike force*]

CINCUSAREUR

CINCUSNAVEUR

Fifth and finally, President Kennedy was actually going to *mention* Operation Big Lift in the text of a public speech that was scheduled for delivery on Friday, November 22nd, 1963, in Texas.

But JFK never got a chance to give that address; instead, he was shot down by multiple gunmen *firing from in front of him* in a small triangular plaza just west of downtown Dallas.

Many men in the American military actually *cheered* Kennedy's violent demise that day.

High-ranking officers actually *celebrated.*

* * *

---

[667] Author's exclusive original discovery.

[668] Author's exclusive original discovery.

Operation Big Lift was a massive U. S. military exercise
in the autumn of 1963. It involved USAF transport of
a major Army tank division to Europe, then back to Texas –
an exercise scheduled to largely conclude by November 22nd,
the very day of the JFK assassination.

It provided an exceptional method to support the murderous plot.

Author's exclusive original discovery.

Operation Big Lift was plainly a very big deal.

Strangely, though, the 1st Armored Division at Ft. Hood – *Lt. Col. George Patton's division,* known as "Old Ironsides" – was ***not*** a part of Operation Big Lift.

Not at all.

"Old Ironsides" was *left behind* at Ft. Hood in Texas while its sister unit, the 2nd Armored Division (known as "the Iron Deuce" and "Hell on Wheels"), commanded by Army General Edwin H. Burba, was flown to Germany to duel there in military exercises with the 3rd Armored Division.

The Iron Deuce flew to Europe from Fort Hood.

*The 1st Armored Division stayed home **in Texas.***

Its own upcoming joint exercise with USAF's Tactical Air Command, "Triple Threat," was canceled; moreover, as I discovered in my own investigation, *no other major field activities or maneuvers by the 1st Armored Division took place during the crucial run-up to the JFK assassination.*[669]

Instead, the 1st Armored Division did what an important tank unit would intelligently do prior to a major engagement: it focused on *preparing itself.*[670]

From late October through mid-November 1963 – until *a week before the president's assassination in Dallas* – the 1st Armored Division of the U. S. Army at Fort Hood conducted a special, highly intensive *maintenance and repair regimen* on the unit's "vast reservoir of military hardware," a task involving "an inestimable number of man hours of labor."[671]

Preparation, after all, is essential to the success of any military operation.

When JFK was finally slain on Elm Street in Dallas on November 22nd, the newly oiled tanks (and certain knowledgeable officers) of the 1st Armored Division ("Old Ironsides") would be primed and fully ready to ensure the triumph of Lyndon Johnson's brutal coup.[672]

Tanks in the streets.

Success guaranteed.

* * *

---

[669] Author's exclusive original discovery.

[670] Author's exclusive original discovery.

[671] Author's exclusive original discovery. See the (Temple, Texas) *Armored Sentinel,* November 15th, 1963.

[672] Author's exclusive original discovery.

Something very strange occurred at the actual kickoff of the massive Operation Big Lift, too.

U. S. Army General Paul D. Adams, the head of United States STRIKE Command (STRICOM) based in Tampa, *canceled his own participation* in Operation Big Lift![673]

General Adams traveled from Florida to Texas to *personally* address the men of the 2nd Armored Division as they prepared to embark on their flights from Fort Hood to Germany. He warned them of possible *real* war in Europe (with the Soviets) at some future date – and then Adams said something incredibly bizarre and extremely peculiar to the assembled troops and their officers.

He would ***not,*** General Adams declared, be going with them to personally oversee and observe and evaluate Operation Big Lift – which was *the biggest peacetime military transport mission in American history* – because he had "even more important matters" to attend to.[674]

What?

Even more important matters?!

More important than an operation of vital importance to the U. S. military in general, and to STRIKE Command (STRICOM) in particular?

More important than *the biggest peacetime military airlift in all of American history?*

Really?

Even more important matters?

What could ***possibly*** qualify as "even more important matters"?

Few of General Adams's listeners knew what he was alluding to.

Even more important matters?

Sure. Absolutely, boys. You betcha.

A daylight assassination and a coup.[675]

*　*　*

---

[673] Author's exclusive original discovery. See the (Temple, Texas) *Armored Sentinel,* October 25th, 1963.

[674] Author's exclusive original discovery. See the (Temple, Texas) *Armored Sentinel,* October 25th, 1963.

[675] Author's exclusive original discovery.

U. S. Army General Paul DeWitt Adams was the head of
STRIKE Command (STRICOM) in November 1963.

Adams *canceled* a major military exercise set for October,
then absented himself from Operation Big Lift in November,
because he had "even more important matters" to prepare for.

Author's exclusive original discovery.

There was more, of course.

I always discovered more.

In late October 1963 the commander of "Old Ironsides," Army Major General Harvey Jablonsky, curiously announced that he was designating *November 1963* as "Religious Emphasis Month" for the 1st Armored Division at Fort Hood.[676]

A base chaplain serving under Jablonsky's command, Army Lt. Col. Alexander J. Turner, explained that the odd *religious* focus in November that year would help a soldier to "reconcile his faith [with] the vital issues and problems posed by the space age."[677]

Normal concepts of "faith" would ostensibly dictate that *thou shalt not kill.*

But John Fitzgerald Kennedy himself, in the eyes of many senior American military officers, clearly constituted *a vital problem in the space age.*

A problem. A danger. A Communist. A traitor.

And "reconciliation" is hardly the military's *forte.*

So according to the U. S. military, the choice came down to . . . JFK or faith.

One of them had to *go* – and it damned sure wasn't going to be "faith."[678]

* * *

To the vicious senior military officers (both active duty *and* retired) who hated John Fitzgerald Kennedy with a white-hot passion, his violent slaughter in Dallas was a welcome event – and a much-deserved punishment for the helpless victim.

On the afternoon of November 22nd itself, as the news of the JFK assassination reached Washington, D. C., a retired Marine Corps general who was relaxing inside the exclusive Cosmos Club in the nation's capital declared aloud to his colleagues, with unmasked satisfaction, *"It was the hand of God that pulled the trigger that killed Kennedy."*[679]

---

[676] Author's exclusive original discovery. See the (Temple, Texas) *Armored Sentinel,* October 25th, 1963.

[677] Author's exclusive original discovery. See the (Temple, Texas) *Armored Sentinel,* October 25th, 1963.

[678] Author's exclusive original discovery. (**N.B.**: This sinister *religious* priming, which I discovered exclusively, was clearly analogous to the sinister *secular* "psychological sets" which U. S. Army Private Eugene Dinkin discovered in various printed media outlets prior to Dallas. Both campaigns were designed, intended and deliberately used to "prep" and "condition" people to consciously or subconsciously *accept* the upcoming JFK assassination.)

[679] William Manchester, *The Death of a President,* p. 250.

U. S. Army General Harvey Jablonsky
commanded the 1st Armored Division
on November 22nd, 1963.

He was also the acting commander of
III Corps and Fort Hood, from which
Army tanks were ordered to go to Dallas
to protect LBJ's coup.

Author's exclusive original discovery.

But the final act of the ugly *religious* indoctrination operation which preceded and facilitated the JFK assassination[680] was delivered by the coup leader himself.

The very day after the assassination, at 4:45 p.m. Eastern time on Saturday, November 23rd, Lyndon Baines Johnson – the leader and chief beneficiary of the coup – went on national television and radio from the White House to brazenly tell the stunned and grieving members of the American public (including some innocent and loyal members of the U. S. military) that they should "bow down in submission to *the will of almighty God"* – thereby obscenely and deliberately planting in their consciousness the disgusting notion that the vicious, gruesome murder of his predecessor was not LBJ's own bloody, criminal handiwork in order to seize the presidency (which it was), but rather some sort of "divine act" – which it was not.[681]

The assassination of John Kennedy was ***not*** the will of an invisible deity.

It was the will of two very visible and mortal men: Samuel Taliaferro Rayburn and Lyndon Baines Johnson.[682]

And their iron will – forged by lifetimes of disappointment and bitterness and perennially frustrated political ambitions – drove the creation, development, planning and execution of the JFK assassination.[683]

In carrying out the crime, the traitorous duo from Texas were knowingly aided and abetted by key members of the United States Air Force; the United States Army; the United States Navy; and the United States Secret Service.[684]

John Fitzgerald Kennedy survived the guns of August (1961) and the missiles of October (1962) – but he would *not* survive the triggers of November (1963).

* * *

A story published in the *de facto* Fort Hood base newspaper ***exactly a week prior to the JFK assassination*** provides a stunning real-life example of the disturbing material that Army Private Eugene Dinkin saw *repeatedly* published in various other major media outlets during the months before President Kennedy's vicious murder in Dallas, Texas.

---

[680] Author's exclusive original discovery.

[681] Proclamation 3561, November 23rd, 1963.

[682] Author's exclusive original discovery.

[683] Author's exclusive original discovery.

[684] Contrary to the simplistic, ignorant, decidedly juvenile "scenarios" which some lesser minds still cling to, their favorite bogeyman – the odious and thoroughly despicable Central Intelligence Agency – was ***not*** the prime mover behind President Kennedy's slaying. To pretend that it was is to willfully ignore ***the*** central truth of the entire JFK assassination: *It was a Sam Rayburn & Lyndon Johnson production.* (Author's exclusive original discovery.)

I found things which Pvt. Dinkin, already in U. S. military custody, *never saw.*

In an article printed on November 15th, 1963 – a piece which ostensibly concerned only the prosaic conclusion of Operation Big Lift – the *Armored Sentinel* declared baldly that *"The **final accounting** should come Nov. 22 . . . . "*[685]

That gob-smacking statement wasn't the final shocking item in the piece, either. *"**Many things** could happen **before** the last plane lands,"* the story announced with stunning prescience.[686]

Many things could happen.

Many things, fellas.

Many things could happen.

You know?

Like a presidential murder and a coup.

For the record, the "last plane to land" in Operation Big Lift was scheduled to touch down in Texas on November 22nd, 1963 – *at 1:20 p.m. CST, less than an hour after* President Kennedy's bloody assassination.[687]

Private Eugene Dinkin of the U. S. Army was *already* being wrongfully held in military custody *well prior to* that particular story's publication in Texas on November 15th, 1963, so he never saw that particular article – but he would have *instantly* recognized the eerie "psychological conditioning" language contained in that strange and unsettling account.[688]

Dinkin was right.

* * *

The men of the 1st Armored Division had plenty of time to rest up as well as to re-fit, maintain and repair their tanks and other vital equipment in the two months prior to the JFK assassination.

The joint USAF & Army exercise called "Triple Threat" had been canceled.

Operation "Big Lift" had pointedly *excluded* the 1st Armored Division.[689]

---

[685] Author's exclusive original discovery; see the (Temple, Texas) *Armored Sentinel,* November 15th, 1963.

[686] Author's exclusive original discovery; see the (Temple, Texas) *Armored Sentinel,* November 15th, 1963.

[687] Author's exclusive original discovery; see the (Temple, Texas) *Armored Sentinel,* November 15th, 1963.

[688] Author's exclusive original discovery; see the (Temple, Texas) *Armored Sentinel,* November 15th, 1963.

[689] Author's exclusive original discovery.

No distractions were permitted to interfere with or derail this premier tank unit's operational readiness prior to President Kennedy's trip to Texas.[690]

All that remained for the troops of the 1st Armored Division now was to diligently execute their mission on November 22nd, when called upon by their Army superiors or by their new Commander-in-Chief himself.

Most of the men in the 1st Armored Division were completely innocent and totally unwitting of what about to occur.

Those like Lt. Col. George Smith Patton were *not*.

His *confession* came several decades later.

Patton discussed the events of November 22nd with a later biographer, and he ultimately revealed everything when he bragged, *"It takes a special type of person to do the things we have to do, and luckily there are not too many of us, if you know what I mean."*[691]

* * *

On Friday afternoon, November 22nd, soon after John Kennedy was shot to death inside the presidential limousine in Dealey Plaza at 12:30 p.m. CST, a soldier at Fort Hood brought initial news of the Dallas shooting to the military chaplain who was conducting a "National Day of Prayer" service at the massive army base. Lieutenant Colonel Patton and most of the members of his own tank unit were very conveniently gathered, *already,* at this religious service.[692]

A few minutes later, *another* soldier burst into the gathering, scanned the crowd, spotted Patton himself and hurried over with an urgent, revealing message:

"Sir," he said to Lieutenant Colonel Patton, "your battalion has been put on alert to go to Dallas."[693]

Your battalion.

The 2nd Medium Tank Battalion of the 81st Armor of the 1st Armored Division.

Your battalion.

Fort Hood, a vast military base, was home to the entire 1st Armored Division ("Old Ironsides") – and it was *also* the home of the entire 2nd Armored Division ("the Iron Deuce," also known as "Hell on Wheels").

Both were huge units.

Tens of thousands of men; hundreds of tanks.

---

[690] Author's exclusive original discovery.

[691] Patton's stark confession appears in Brian Sobel's book *The Fighting Pattons*.

[692] Brian Sobel, *The Fighting Pattons*, p. 111.

[693] Brian Sobel, *The Fighting Pattons*, p. 111.

But *George Patton's tank battalion* was the one selected to go to Dallas.

Lieutenant Colonel George Patton – who had been transferred back from Vietnam and assigned to Fort Hood in April 1963, seven months *before* the JFK assassination.[694]

And the reason that *George Patton's tank battalion* was selected to go to Dallas on November 22nd was the perceived need to "protect" Lyndon Johnson and his disastrously executed, badly faltering coup.[695]

Lt. Col. Patton promptly set about urgently preparing his battalion to move its M48 tanks to Dallas via railcar, for maximum speed. Hours later, however – *after* LBJ had (barely) stabilized his floundering murderous plot and narrowly avoided the catastrophic exposure of his crimes – the 2nd Medium Tank Battalion of the 81st Armor of the mighty and formidable 1st Armored Division of the U. S. Army was told that it could stand down.[696]

Why?

Through his own brilliant, insidious and herculean efforts, Lyndon Baines Johnson had (just barely) salvaged his own failing plot.[697] LBJ had successfully bluffed and conned the Attorney General.[698] Johnson had also completed a hasty but illegitimate "inauguration" at Love Field, aboard Air Force One. *He had thereby assumed the full powers of the presidency.* Furthermore, LBJ had given control of the JFK autopsy proceedings to his subordinate criminal accomplices in the U. S. Navy. Johnson had left Dallas and flown back to Washington, D.C. He was now safely ensconced inside his Vice-Presidential residence, The Elms.

Above all, LBJ had *not been arrested for the murder of JFK.*

So, barring any further disasters by Johnson's Secret Service accomplices, Lt. Col. Patton's tanks would no longer be needed – certainly not *in Dallas.*

---

[694] Author's exclusive original discovery.

[695] Brian Sobel, *The Fighting Pattons,* p. 111. George Patton admitted that his command's role that day was to provide "protective services" – which of course was completely absurd and inexplicable and oxymoronic if the JFK assassination had actually been the work of a supposed "lone gunman" who was quickly taken into Dallas police custody.

[696] Brian Sobel, *The Fighting Pattons,* pp. 111. Speaking about the day's events many years later – *after burning all his papers and notes* in a home fire supposedly caused by his own bafflingly careless disposal of a cigar – Patton misspoke and told an interviewer that the tank battalion's mission was called off on the evening of the *following* day (which was Saturday, November 23rd, 1963). That was a clear error on Patton's part, since LBJ had long since departed Dallas for the nation's capital on Friday afternoon, November 22nd.

1963 coup guarantor George Smith Patton eventually succumbed to Parkinson's disease in 2004.

[697] Author's exclusive original discovery.

[698] Author's exclusive original discovery.

But Lt. Col. Patton had been called upon, and Lt. Col. Patton had been *ready.*
And he had *responded,* all according to plan.

He had done his job.

He had answered the call.

His tank battalion was ready, willing and able.

Have armor, will travel.

The Constitution be damned.

Tanks in the streets of an American city.

American tanks.

American tanks to support an American coup.

As an officer in the U. S. military, Lieutenant Colonel Patton had not only the right but the duty and the obligation to **refuse** to execute unlawful orders.

He did not do so.

And tellingly, such orders could *only* have come from Lyndon Johnson; the Joint Chiefs of Staff; or top echelons of the U. S. Army itself.[699]

Apart from LBJ himself – the illegitimate, brand-new Commander-in-Chief of all U. S. armed forces – the number of senior American army officers who actually had the *authority* (not the "legal" right, but the *command authority*) to issue or relay such orders was miniscule, and it included the following four (4) men:[700]

U. S. Army General Maxwell Taylor, Chairman of the Joint Chiefs;

U. S. Army General Earle "Bus" Wheeler, Army Chief of Staff;[701]

U. S. Army General Paul DeWitt Adams, head of U. S. Strike Command (STRICOM); and

U. S. Army Major General Harvey J. Jablonsky, Commander of the 1st Armored Division (and *acting* head of III Corps and Fort Hood).[702]

Four high-ranking officers had the authority to send Lt. Col. George Patton to Dallas with a battalion of powerful M48 tanks.

Superior firepower.

Tanks in the streets.

Note carefully:

There was **no** rioting or civil disorder in Dallas following President Kennedy's brutal 1963 assassination. There was **no** breakdown of civilian authority; **nothing whatsoever** in the "official" version of events (or in the actual streets of Dallas itself,

---

[699] Author's exclusive original discovery.

[700] Author's exclusive original discovery.

[701] General Earle Wheeler certainly knew tanks; he had once commanded *the 2nd Armored Division at Fort Hood, Texas.*

[702] Author's exclusive original discovery.

post-assassination) to justify or excuse *domestic military intervention* of any kind – let alone with *tanks*.

Yet the U. S. Army issued *precisely* such orders.

And it actively prepared to fulfill them.

M48 Patton tanks much like this one
were ordered by the U. S. Army to go to Dallas
on November 22nd, 1963,
to protect Lyndon Johnson's coup
because of its many colossal failures
both in Dealey Plaza and at Parkland Hospital.

And the existence of those orders, *issued specifically to guarantee the success of LBJ's coup plot,* was something that the U. S. Army would ***never*** permit Lyndon Johnson to forget.[703]

Twenty months later, in July 1965, U. S. Army General Earle Wheeler – a former commander of the 2nd Armored Division, who was now the Chairman of the Joint Chiefs of Staff himself, having been promoted by LBJ to succeed Maxwell Taylor – would stand over Lyndon Johnson menacingly in the Cabinet Room of the White House while LBJ sat at the long table *pretending* (in front of his civilian advisers) to "waffle" on escalating and expanding the Vietnam War.[704]

An angry Wheeler stood and leaned over, pointed directly at his new commander-in-chief, and made clear his burning displeasure.[705]

LBJ dropped his empty charade and fell in line promptly; he knew what General Wheeler had done for him back on November 22nd, 1963, and there was simply no way that Lyndon Johnson could possibly renege on *that* enormous debt without being publicly exposed as a traitor and a murderer.[706]

Army tanks had been ordered to Dallas to protect LBJ's bloody coup.

That was the bottom line.

Lieutenant Colonel Patton himself admitted it, on the record.[707]

The U. S. Army's willing support of the murderous JFK assassination paid enormous and continuing dividends – *for the U. S. Army.*

By the summer of 1965, General Wheeler – *still* Chairman of the JCS – had succeeded in commencing a massive, murderous ground war in Vietnam, *featuring the*

---

[703] Author's exclusive original discovery.

[704] Author's exclusive original discovery and analysis. Official White House photos taken in late July 1965 captured these extraordinary moments for history; *even when seated again,* General Wheeler leaned intensely into LBJ's personal space, pressuring the commander in chief, plainly angered by Johnson's pretense of "reluctance" to escalate war. *No one* acts that way around an American president unless they have something *dreadful* on him. General Wheeler clearly did – and it was Dallas (author's exclusive original discovery).

[705] Author's exclusive original discovery.

[706] Author's exclusive original discovery.

[707] Brian Sobel, *The Fighting Pattons,* p. 111. Thanks to his traitorous actions on November 22nd, tank commander Patton predictably enjoyed a meteoric rise following the JFK assassination. He received a prestigious appointment to the Army War College within a few months of Dallas; enjoyed combat commands in Vietnam; received medals; and ultimately became a senior officer.

Between 1962 (when he was first sent to Vietnam and groomed for his role in the upcoming JFK assassination) and 1975, George Smith Patton went from being a *major* to being a *major general.*

In America, ladies and gentlemen, crime – civilian or military! – clearly pays.

use of the very same M48 Patton battle tanks which had been ordered to Dallas in 1963 to back the JFK assassination plot and the LBJ coup.[708]

And by late 1967, one of LBJ's own top White House aides had stated *in writing* that the U. S. military was *blackmailing* Lyndon Johnson regarding Vietnam War policy.[709]

And by early 1968, Wheeler was actively exploring – *at LBJ's personal direction* – the use of nuclear weapons in Vietnam (despite Johnson's previously articulated fear of inciting the Russians and the Chinese and thereby setting off a global thermonuclear war).

Yes, you read that correctly.

Lyndon Johnson didn't want to lose the American base at Khe Sanh. So in January and February 1968, LBJ himself was *actively considering the use of tactical nuclear weapons in Vietnam* in order to avoid a humiliating military defeat along the lines of the devastating 1954 French loss at Dien Bien Phu.[710]

Because of his inescapable debt to the American military for its major assistance with the JFK assassination, Lyndon Johnson *had* to consider tactical nukes.

He had no choice.

As I have now clearly established beyond any chance of refutation, *the major branches of the U. S. military were the armed* **guarantors** *of the Rayburn-Johnson Coup of 1963, which was carried out through the violent assassination of John Fitzgerald Kennedy.*[711]

---

[708] Author's exclusive original discovery.

[709] White House aide Harry McPherson wrote a chilling memo to LBJ on October 27th, 1967, explicitly mentioning the military blackmail. Lloyd Gardner mentioned and quoted that vitally important McPherson memo in his book *Pay Any Price* (page 396) – yet bizarrely, Gardner exhibited *zero* awareness of the true meaning and significance of McPherson's explicit words to LBJ.

By contrast, I understood their massive and devastating import *instantaneously.*

[710] An embarrassingly shallow and pathetically conventional "historian" [*sic*], Michael "See-No-Evil" Beschloss, wrote a grossly erroneous account of the chilling 1968 nuclear episode in a later book; incredibly, Beschloss wrongly praised LBJ for supposed heroism in supposedly quashing the use of nuclear weapons in Vietnam – and that ludicrously false version of events was foisted on the public in an embarrassingly fawning and equally erroneous *New York Times* story written by David Sanger in the autumn of 2018.

Happily for the cause of truth, Beschloss's flimsy and fatuous folly (and Sanger's silly secretarial synopsis thereof) were promptly eviscerated, totally obliterated and conclusively disproven by journalist and author Gregg Jones in a superb article published in the *Dallas Morning News* (October 24th, 2018).

The pathetic but typical episode proved once again, for all to see, just how shockingly weak, moronic, ignorant, gutless and foolish those Establishment "historians" [*sic*] and Establishment "newspapers" [*sic*] really are.

[711] Author's exclusive original discovery.

That – and *only* that – is why the U. S. military was able to successfully **blackmail** the president of the United States in 1967 and in 1968.[712]

* * *

Key officers and elements of the U. S. military – from the Air Force, Army and Navy – knowingly served as armed *guarantors* of the Rayburn-Johnson coup.[713]

Lyndon Johnson himself paid only a trivial price for their 1963 services.

But *nine million people worldwide*[714] *paid the ultimate price* – and many millions *more* were savagely wounded, burned, dismembered, blinded, amputated, scarred, tortured, and driven to insanity by horrific trauma.

Further millions grieve them to this very day.

* * *

The U. S. military knowingly, deliberately and actively ensured and *guaranteed* that Lyndon Johnson's murderous 1963 coup would succeed and would be protected.[715] Their powerful support of the long-simmering Rayburn-Johnson plot (which was originally conceived in 1956 [716]) gave LBJ the physical, logistical and psychological backing he needed to carry out the JFK assassination and thereby take the White House.[717]

---

[712] Author's exclusive original discovery.

[713] Author's exclusive original discovery.

In briefest terms: The U.S. Air Force restrained SAC; covered LBJ at Love Field; transported falsified evidence to Washington, D. C.; played a key role in censoring both the Zapruder film and Dallas media reports; and both outlined and wrote the "Warren" Report. The U. S. Army ordered tanks to go to Dallas. The U. S. Navy hosted the bizarre autopsy at Bethesda on President Kennedy's mutilated remains, and then deliberately falsified the final autopsy report in order to obscure JFK's true wounds – and to hide the murder plot's massive failings in Texas.

[714] Innocents in Vietnam, Laos, Cambodia, Indonesia, Palestine and elsewhere were slaughtered as a result of the JFK assassination.

[715] Author's exclusive original discovery.

[716] Author's exclusive original discovery.

[717] Author's exclusive original discovery. To reiterate: as I discovered exclusively, the JFK assassination plot originated with Sam Rayburn and Lyndon Johnson *in August 1956,* long before JFK was even elected to the White House and *long before* key figures in the American military were brought on board as armed *guarantors* of the coup's success.

The very moment that the fatal bullet struck John Kennedy's skull in Dealey Plaza at 12:30 p.m. CST on Friday, November 22nd, Lyndon Johnson achieved his greatest ambition and instantly secured for himself a major place in history.

By Friday night his principal target was dead and mutilated; JFK's butchered remains – flown out of Dallas by the U. S. Air Force – were in the hands of the Secret Service and the U. S. Navy, all of which reported to LBJ himself.

So the assassination itself – the *shooting* – was now accomplished.

But the plot hardly ended there.

Much more remained to be done.

Yes, John Fitzgerald Kennedy was now dead.

But as LBJ knew, there remained one tenacious, living target – a wounded, anguished, coiled rattlesnake of a man – who had to be neutralized promptly and successfully if Lyndon Johnson's newly-acquired *presidency* was to remain Lyndon Johnson's cherished *prize.*

However, *recruiting* the military *during* the Kennedy presidency (1961-1963) was laughably easy; JFK alienated the Pentagon brass early and often, and in return they deeply despised the multi-millionaire from Massachusetts.

"A man on horseback" is the traditional phrase
to describe a coup leader.

Dallas newspaper publisher Ted Dealey told JFK to his face
that *that* was what America needed:

A man on horseback.

Lyndon Baines Johnson fully agreed.

The absolute leader of the JFK assassination plot
on horseback at his Texas ranch – December 27th, 1963.

PART THREE:

The Reckoning

Robert Francis Kennedy was the Attorney General in 1963.

Within *days* of the JFK assassination, RFK knew that
Lyndon Baines Johnson had murdered President Kennedy.

Author's exclusive original discovery.

Chapter Thirty-One:
Freezing Bobby

"Bad men need nothing more to compass their ends,
than that good men should look on and do nothing."
– John Stuart Mill

"Prompted to my revenge by heaven and hell,
Must like a whore unpack my heart with words . . ."
– Thomas North / William Shakespeare

"But break, my heart, for I must hold my tongue!"
– Thomas North / William Shakespeare

"Bobby knew everything."
– JFK Junior

"These things do not just 'happen.'
*They are **made** to happen."*
– John Fitzgerald Kennedy

As I have pointed out repeatedly in this book, an assassination plot always has *two* targets: the body of the *victim,* and the body *politic.*

But in the particular case of the JFK assassination, there was also – of dire necessity – a *third* target: the Attorney General of the United States.

John Fitzgerald Kennedy was Lyndon Johnson's *immediate target* on November 22nd; but Robert Francis Kennedy was Lyndon Johnson's *ongoing nightmare.*[718] Killing the president ***and getting away with it*** – which was the *actual* goal of the JFK assassination[719] – is a much more challenging venture when the

---

[718] This was true both literally and figuratively. RFK haunted Johnson's dreams for years, as LBJ confessed to aide, companion and Establishment scribe Doris Kearns (later Doris Kearns Goodwin).

[719] Author's exclusive original insight.

murdered chief executive's own intelligent and highly capable brother is the top lawman in the country.

Since the true objective of the JFK assassination was **not** simply to "kill" President Kennedy, but rather *to kill JFK **and get away with it**,*[720] significant planning and effort had to be devoted *in advance* to the singular and crucial problem of how to "freeze" Bobby Kennedy effectively in the immediate aftermath of the president's bloody murder.

Somehow, some way, Lyndon Johnson and his murderous confederates had to fool, confuse, stun, bamboozle, muffle, distract, embarrass, frighten, intimidate, cow, blackmail, threaten, silence or otherwise *neutralize* the Attorney General of the United States – an extremely tough, ruthless individual who loved, and was fiercely loyal to, his slain brother.

Thus on November 22nd, 1963, the plotters led by LBJ actually had three (3) key targets:

> ➢ President Kennedy himself, riding in his limousine through Dallas;
> ➢ Robert Kennedy, head of the U.S. Justice Department; and, ultimately,
> ➢ The American public.

In other words, ***you.***

Any failure to kill or mortally wound the President in Dealey Plaza would be disastrous. If JFK somehow *survived* the planned outdoor ambush, then SS security measures thereafter would have to be (at least "officially") tightened to such an extent that *another public, outdoor, open-air assassination attempt might never again be practical or possible.* This would of course eliminate the possibility of setting up another patsy to take the fall for a public, outdoor murder. And naturally, any attempt to kill JFK subsequently *inside* the White House or in any other nominally "secure" environment would be, by definition, "an inside job" – drawing instant attention to, and prompt exposure of, the perpetrators.

A successful kill, *out in the open,* was imperative; President Kennedy could not be permitted to leave Dealey Plaza alive.[721] All else flowed from that central, non-negotiable imperative. For the president's assassins, the ironclad rule was that *JFK must be dead before the presidential motorcade reached the Triple Underpass – no matter what it took.*[722]

---

[720] Author's exclusive original insight.

[721] Author's exclusive original insight.

[722] Author's exclusive original insight.

Handling RFK was another matter, potentially requiring much more skill, sophistication, maneuvering and finesse. Robert Kennedy was tough and smart and relentless – not easy to fob off with unlikely "explanations." He also possessed genuine legal authority to arrest and indict anyone who invited his suspicion.[723]

Yet Bobby had his own significant vulnerabilities as well. Most obvious was the fact that although he was the titular head of the Justice Department, real power resided principally with his nominal subordinate – the venal and corrupt longtime FBI Director, John Edgar Hoover. The Director was extremely hostile to both Kennedys, and had managed to amplify his own substantial existing power by "helping" them to dispose of several messy and embarrassing problems – as recently as the summer and autumn of 1963.[724] Although Bobby could technically give Hoover orders, the reality was that Hoover's men recognized only one genuine authority – and that was Hoover himself. Hoover's jaw-dropping arrogance was so unbridled that he and his men referred to the FBI headquarters as "SOG" – Seat of Government. (Since Hoover possessed derogatory and incriminating material on many members of the executive and legislative branches of the federal government, the arrogant phrase was actually not far off the mark.)

Thus in any post-assassination crisis pitting Robert Kennedy against Lyndon Johnson, it was clear that Bobby would *not* be able to count on the agents of the FBI to do their jobs thoroughly or efficiently or professionally – let alone demonstrate any loyalty either to him or to his slain brother. Such loyalty would be anathema to the

---

Various researchers have speculated about additional possibilities beyond the physical confines of the plaza. Larry Hancock has posited the notion of a bomb being used against the presidential limousine on Elm Street *after* Dealey Plaza, if necessary; and the individual who used the *alias* "David S. Lifton" [*sic*] speculated about a possible subsequent shooting attempt elsewhere in Texas later on the same trip.

But none of those weak notions takes into account the cold and obvious reality that any *failed* shooting in Dealey Plaza itself would have indubitably led to *an immediate presidential departure from Dallas and a return to Washington;* moreover, such hypothetical "post-plaza" attempts would have been impossible to blame on the designated patsy working at the TSBD, Lee Oswald. Therefore, those theories are – by definition – *non-starters.*

Remember: the point wasn't simply to "kill" JFK; it was to kill JFK *and get away with it.*

[723] While killing the president was, incredibly, *not* itself a specific federal crime in 1963, RFK could certainly pursue the perpetrators on *other* federal charges such as conspiracy, sedition, misprision of a felony, civil rights violations, etc.

[724] Among other "favors," Hoover had kindly "informed" President Kennedy that the FBI knew of his brief dalliance with Marilyn Monroe; had interceded with Congress to squash an investigation of Kennedy's reckless dalliance with an attractive German woman (Ellen Rometsch) who was soon deported; and had otherwise "saved" JFK from exposure on occasions when the desperate Kennedy brothers had nowhere else to turn. As I noted earlier: in Washington D.C., *information* and *access* are the coins of the realm – and when it came to the passionate Kennedy brothers, FBI Director J. Edgar Hoover had a breathtaking collection of (*ahem*) "coins."

venomous Hoover, and virtually no agent was willing to go up against the crocodilian head of the FBI.

Thus the ostensibly powerful Attorney General was actually *an unwelcome guest in his own department,* and could in reality count on the integrity of only a few men – principally the small but extremely dedicated and devoted group of U.S. Marshals who had proven their mettle and repeatedly put their bodies on the line to uphold the law in Mississippi and Alabama and elsewhere while Hoover's FBI agents stood by, doing nothing, in the face of brutal, outrageous, racist mob violence. The U.S. Marshals were a strong, courageous and noble group – among the very best men in the federal government[725] – but they were drastically outnumbered by the Bureau's vast army of agents. Therefore any genuine, independent, meaningful investigation of the JFK assassination by Bobby Kennedy would be severely hamstrung from the start.

For President Kennedy's killers, *led personally by Lyndon Johnson himself,* this state of affairs was good – but it was not considered truly good *enough.* The assassination of an American President is a huge undertaking,[726] and the stakes for the plotters were literally life and death. Methods had to be found not merely to "frustrate" RFK, or "hamper" him, or "impede" him slightly, or "discourage" him from carrying out a serious, full-on criminal investigation of his brother's murder, but rather to *ensure* that he would not even dare to *begin* such a dangerous and wide-ranging probe.

For their own safety, the LBJ-led plotters had to try to *freeze* Bobby Kennedy – and the evidence is clear that they managed to do so, *barely,* for a brief but critical period of time soon after the JFK assassination.

In so doing, they immobilized the Attorney General just long enough to permit them to savagely alter and erase the most important evidence available to subsequent investigators: (A) the authentic original 12:30 p.m. CST wounds on the body of the slain President, and (B) the original images captured on the uncensored, *true* camera

---

[725] In a moving display of loyalty, integrity and courage, *every single one of the ninety U. S. marshals available locally* volunteered to stand guard and protect Robert Kennedy and his family after the JFK assassination was announced on November 22nd, 1963. ***Every single one of them.*** (William Manchester, *The Death of a President,* p. 259.)

[726] Contrary to the absurdly minimalist fantasies of some armchair researchers, the JFK assassination plot was ***not*** – I repeat, ***not*** – a "minor" operation consisting of only "a tiny handful" of men (supposedly as few as just four or six people, in some theorists' badly deluded view).

My own lengthy investigation over the course of 40 years (thus far) has uncovered no fewer than *ninety-one* (91) *specific individuals* who knowingly participated in the 1963 assassination of President Kennedy. (Author's exclusive original discovery.) And be advised that 91 is a very "conservative" number, which will certainly *increase* as additional information – and confessions – become available. (Author's exclusive original discovery.)

original Zapruder film and related still and motion photographic materials shot in Dallas on November 22nd.[727]

Bobby Kennedy was totally unaware of these vital subterfuges until it was too late.[728] By the time he regained his mental and emotional equilibrium, and shook off the fog of pain and personal grief that had clouded his normal prosecutorial vision during the first three days after Dallas, the dispositive evidence which would have served as the primary basis for a successful prosecution of the *actual* guilty parties (namely, Lyndon Johnson and scores of additional individuals *other than* the hapless and innocent Lee Oswald) had been *literally* cut and slashed away.[729]

Some of that evidence stained the belly of an advanced jet aircraft; other pieces were literally lying on the cutting-room floor of two (2) state-of the-art photographic facilities owned and operated by the U.S. government.[730]

Thus the horrid truth which Bobby Kennedy soon *realized* [731] – namely, that Lyndon Johnson led the plot to assassinate President Kennedy – was a horrid truth that Bobby Kennedy would be unable (initially) to *prove.*[732]

Reality itself had been permanently altered on November 22nd and in the subsequent 48 hours – principally with a crash axe, a hammer, a razor, an enlarger, an "aerial imaging" special effects photography set-up, an optical printer, and an ultra-fine paintbrush.

By the time his brother was buried on Monday afternoon, November 25th, 1963, the Attorney General of the United States had been outfoxed, outmaneuvered and outgunned. Instead of being *the central, leading figure* in a comprehensive,

---

[727] The felonious evidence tampering was, in both cases, part of a coordinated, ***pre-planned*** effort to "sanitize" the record of what actually happened in Dealey Plaza – ***not,*** as some deluded half-wits would have you believe, a bizarre "after-the-fact" move by people inexplicably "covering up for" the mysterious and anonymous "real" assassins.

[728] Author's exclusive original discovery.

[729] Both the president's corpse and the true camera-original Zapruder film (plus other movies and still pictures taken by motorcade witnesses) underwent analogous sequences of destruction and alteration: first, the *removal* of ***authentic*** data; then the *addition* of ***artificial*** data designed to obscure the truth and mislead all viewers.

[730] These were the U. S. Air Force's Lookout Mountain facility located in California and the CIA's "Hawkeye Plant" photographic laboratory located in Rochester, New York.

[731] Within days of the president's murder, White House photographer Cecil Stoughton showed RFK the damning and revelatory photograph taken on November 22nd which captured Lyndon Johnson and Congressman Al Thomas exchanging a gloating and celebratory wink just seconds after the swearing-in of JFK's assassin aboard Air Force One at Love Field.

Stoughton himself recognized the image as sinister; so did Attorney General Robert Francis Kennedy.

[732] Author's exclusive original discovery.

aggressive and utterly fearless federal investigation of his brother's brutal assassination, Robert F. Kennedy was suddenly the odd man out.[733]

* * *

Bobby Kennedy had been a player at the highest levels of government – he often functioned as his brother's personal James Bond,[734] and RFK was certainly no stranger to conducting "off-the-books" operations of varying degrees of importance.

But in the first 72 hours after Dallas, *he* was the one who was "played" – by the very men who had murdered his brother. Stunned and saddened, trying to contain his grief and hardly operating at full capacity, RFK was unable to summon the fire, ferocious focus and penetrating insight that normally would have guided his actions.

Among his first instincts on the very afternoon of November 22nd was fear of unsavory revelations about JFK – and thus instead of concentrating on aggressively investigating *the crime of his brother's assassination,* RFK began with the physical protection of some of his slain brother's various secrets. For example, the locks on various White House safes were to be changed promptly, so that Lyndon Johnson would not obtain access to them.[735]

---

[733] Author's exclusive original discovery.

A number of JFK researchers (including Lifton) darkly postulated or foolishly adopted the absurdly illogical idea that Robert Kennedy himself *knowingly* and *willingly* and *actively* participated in the cover-up of his own brother's murder (!), allegedly in order to somehow "preserve" the "viability" of his (RFK's) *own* possible future candidacy for the presidency.

Apart from the infinite incoherence and illogic of that noxious notion, there is one other consideration:

That bizarre concept requires its adherents* to subscribe to the false idea that Bobby was just a homicidal, narcissistic psychopath for whom JFK's ghastly assassination was merely an annoying *speed bump* on his [RFK's] own road to the White House – an obscenely ambitious career goal which supposedly took priority over the truth about Dallas.

[*If this is you, seek professional help immediately.]

At one point, Lifton actually suggested to me that *Robert Kennedy personally ordered, authorized or approved the murder of Lee Harvey Oswald.* "It may be *that bad,"* said Lifton dramatically. When I subsequently reminded Lifton of his absurd remark, Lifton vociferously *denied his own words.* (Truth and reality and integrity were *not* Lifton's friends . . .)

[734] Author's exclusive original insight.

[735] Why Bobby thought that JFK was foolishly hiding damning *personal* secrets in White House safes has never been satisfactorily explained; the immensely wealthy Kennedy family had innumerable *other* options in terms of places in which to securely sequester (or bury) their worst secrets.

Obviously, if RFK knew or believed that *official* papers and memoranda contained substantial evidence of crimes committed by JFK himself (e.g., personal discussion of assassination, coups, murder, invasion,

RFK also cast about vainly, attempting through his grief to form a coherent image of who was likely responsible for the assassination. The correct answer was right in front of him (and indeed, *was on the telephone with him, within 90 minutes of the shooting*), but RFK's mind could not consciously recognize or identify or articulate that chilling possibility just yet.

* * *

Ordinarily, foreknowledge of the commission of a crime means personal guilt for, personal participation in, and direct personal culpability for that crime.

Ordinarily.

But the JFK assassination – led by master manipulator Lyndon Baines Johnson himself – was no ordinary crime.

For those who have been confused for decades about the *real* meaning of the Chicago plot, and of other similarly designed and similarly aborted November plots (in Tampa, Florida, for example), the reality is this:

They weren't the real deal.[736]

*They were **never** the real deal.*[737]

The reckless amateurs involved in all of *those* failed ventures were *precisely* the people whom Lyndon Baines Johnson personally "called off" and ordered to "stand down" back in April 1963 [738] – when he said publicly in Texas, *"At least wait until next November before you shoot him [JFK] down."*

Most of LBJ's intended audience listened.

Most of them understood.

Most of them received Johnson's message "loud and clear."

Most of the laughably loudmouthed, staggeringly indiscreet, poorly equipped, poorly trained, fanatical but idiotic private citizens (American fascists and Cuban exile fascists) who actually "received and understood" LBJ's blunt April admonition quickly relaxed, and promptly abandoned their own amateurish and doomed efforts to kill JFK.

They stopped their crazed covert maneuvering – *which was the purpose and the goal and the desired outcome of Johnson's utterance.*[739]

---

war, etc.), then the rush to seal JFK's presidential files was itself a very incriminating admission by the Attorney General.

[736] Author's exclusive original discovery.

[737] Author's exclusive original discovery.

[738] Author's exclusive original discovery.

[739] Author's exclusive original discovery.

The amateurs happily contented themselves not with grimly preparing the assassination of a president, but merely with smug *awareness* – gleeful foreknowledge which in their case meant **not** hands-on guilt in carrying out the actual JFK assassination, but the simple pleasurable satisfaction of being "insiders" – of knowing "approximately" when the vile deed would be done by forces larger, stronger and far better equipped than they themselves could ever hope to be.[740]

They were satisfied with being "off the hook" for carrying out a dangerous and deadly mission. Others would do it for them. *The Vice President himself had told them so.* Things were well in hand. It would all be taken care of by the "serious" people.

These pathetic amateurs included such ugly figures as John Martino and Clay Shaw and Joseph Milteer and other utterly peripheral characters, all of whom did indeed talk in advance about President Kennedy's assassination but who **did not know** *the nature of the **real** plot* [741] and were *far removed from any meaningful participation in the actual crime*[742] (a crime which they themselves were totally unqualified to execute and would likely have botched badly).[743]

People like Shaw and Martino and Milteer and Marcello knew that President Kennedy was going to be killed, and they knew that the assassination would occur in Dallas – but the key fact is that that's **all** they knew.[744]

And these fifth-rate, peripheral figures knew of President Kennedy's upcoming assassination only because Lyndon Baines Johnson himself had *told* them so, quite *publicly* and deliberately, by *broadcasting the news in the clear* via his sinister comments back in April 1963.[745]

Johnson wanted these clumsy and incompetent amateurs to *hold their fire and stand down* until (after) November 1963, when he himself would execute *his* plot – a

---

[740] Author's exclusive original discovery.

[741] Author's exclusive original discovery. National States' Rights Party (NSRP) figure Joseph Milteer was among those fringe elements who were deliberately fed the entirely **false** notion – which Milteer subsequently regurgitated, on tape, to a law enforcement informant – that President Kennedy would supposedly be shot *from a tall building* [sic] by someone armed with a high-powered rifle [sic].

That was **not** what actually happened in Dallas, however. Sadly, many Americans (ironically including most JFK researchers) stupidly and uncritically swallowed that completely false "somebody-fired-a-rifle-from-a-tall-building" scenario – hook, line and sinker. They will learn otherwise – to their great discomfiture – in my next major book on the subject.

[742] Author's exclusive original discovery.

[743] Author's exclusive original discovery.

[744] Author's exclusive original discovery.

[745] Author's exclusive original discovery.

powerful, sophisticated and very well-planned plot backed by the full might and massive resources of the United States government and its massive military.[746]

LBJ wanted to prevent the antsy addled amateurs from "spooking" JFK by taking woefully unsuccessful premature potshots at him and thereby causing the catastrophic cancellation of future public trips by the president – like the upcoming one to Dallas.[747]

Johnson also cleverly wanted to make these fanatical fifth-rate characters *stupidly **incriminate themselves** by talking in advance about the JFK assassination.*[748] Such remarks could be – and ***were*** – recorded by government informants, and were noted by a variety of other people, thereby "documenting" the careless speakers' supposed "complicity," and thereby created the very convincing but *completely false* impression that they *(Shaw! Ferrie! Martino! Milteer! Marcello!)* were actually involved in killing JFK.[749]

Thus, should LBJ's high-powered plot somehow fail – or should Oswald somehow survive and talk indiscreetly, and the existence of "a" plot inevitably became known – then Lyndon Johnson and his subordinates could easily arrange to feed these *pathetic peripheral figures* to prosecuting authorities as the so-called "plotters" of the president's violent assassination.[750]

Some of those assorted freaks and fanatics and ne'er-do-wells were clearly more "convenient" candidates for framing than others.

* * *

In 1963, the only people in American society more universally loathed and hated than Communists were homosexuals. By specifically directing Lee Oswald to meet and interact with a clique of extremely right-wing *homosexuals* in New Orleans during the summer of 1963 – which is in fact *precisely* what occurred – Lyndon Johnson and his subordinate accomplices were knowingly and deliberately and very cleverly creating a group of "extra" patsies, *should they be required eventually.*[751]

Clay Shaw, David Ferrie and others in their fanatically right-wing New Orleans homosexual clique were ***not*** the cunning "masterminds" of the Dallas crime;

---

[746] Author's exclusive original discovery.

[747] Author's exclusive original discovery.

[748] Author's exclusive original discovery.

[749] Author's exclusive original discovery.

[750] Author's exclusive original discovery.

[751] Author's exclusive original discovery.

rather, they were *secondary patsies*[752] to be quickly inculpated and convicted in the event that the criminal framing of Lee Oswald somehow failed.[753]

If the "lone-nut theory" did not gain public traction and acceptance in the immediate aftermath of John Kennedy's brutal assassination, then this *second tier of suspects* – a relatively "small" conspiracy consisting of a few deeply unsympathetic, universally reviled "degenerates" based in New Orleans – would constitute the federal government's "fallback position" (i.e., revised official story) on the JFK assassination.[754] Their prompt arrests and conviction for the murder of the president of the United States would follow predictably, just as night follows day.[755]

* * *

While many lesser JFK assassination researchers have repeatedly clutched at the names of utterly *peripheral* figures (*Shaw! Ferrie! Martino! Milteer!*) like high society matrons nervously clutching their pearls, the cold fact is that such ugly characters are, in truth, *irrelevant* to the JFK assassination.[756]

Their "foreknowledge" of the upcoming presidential murder *did not* – and *does not* – indicate that they had high stature in, or meaningful roles in, or any genuine understanding of the details of, the *true* Dallas plot; to the contrary!

Rather, their "foreknowledge" marks those overhyped figures as two things:

First, it marks them as *the trivial buffoons that they were:* weak superficial clods who could be easily fobbed off with nothing more than a bit of coded language from the true plot's true leader, Lyndon Baines Johnson.[757]

It also marks them as what else they were: *convenient, utterly disposable, second-level patsies* should the false initial "lone gunman" myth end up not surviving public scrutiny.[758]

I reiterate that in American society in 1963, the only group more hated than Communists were homosexuals. The fanatical right-wing clique around Clay Shaw in New Orleans – homosexual males who actually met and talked with Lee Oswald during

---

[752] Author's exclusive original discovery.

[753] Author's exclusive original discovery.

[754] Author's exclusive original discovery.

[755] Author's exclusive original discovery.

[756] Author's exclusive original discovery.

[757] Author's exclusive original discovery.

[758] Author's exclusive original discovery.

the summer of 1963 – were perfect targets should a fallback strategy be required later by the LBJ regime.[759]

Again, the resulting "official" storyline is not difficult to write:

Local authorities initially believed that President Kennedy's assassination was the work of one disgruntled Dallas loner with Communist tendencies. However, diligent investigation by J. Edgar Hoover's Federal Bureau of Investigation has since revealed that a clique of utter degenerates based in the Crescent City were conspiring jointly with Lee Oswald to carry out the deed. Members of that deviant criminal group met in New Orleans repeatedly, several months in advance, in order to discuss and plan the terrible crime.

Perfect, easy, simple.

So to reiterate:

Clay Shaw was certainly no "mastermind" of anything.

He was – like David Ferrie and others in that New Orleans homosexual circle – easy to manipulate and to blackmail and to paint irredeemably through damning personal acquaintance with the alleged "shooter" [*sic*] – and damning "foreknowledge" [*sic*] of the crime.[760]

Lyndon Baines Johnson left nothing to chance.

As I have made clear throughout this book, LBJ always set up *multiple options* in case things went wrong.[761]

So if the fictitious "lone gunman" story ultimately failed, then the fallback option was ***not*** (as many JFK researchers fervently but incorrectly believe) "blaming Fidel Castro and invading Cuba" [*sic*], but instead serving up a small group of *the most despised people in the country* for the nation to convict.[762]

---

[759] Author's exclusive original discovery.

[760] Author's exclusive original discovery.

[761] Author's exclusive original discovery.

[762] Author's exclusive original discovery.

For decades, many JFK researchers have also wrongly assumed that a major goal of the JFK assassination was to use it as an excuse to launch a full American military invasion of Cuba (an action which was definitely ***not*** on LBJ's agenda!) and that the official story of a "lone gunman" was merely a "fallback" position, adopted when the Cuba invasion never materialized.

As is often the case, their inaccurate theorizing is *the complete **opposite** of reality*.

Yes, some fanatics in the U. S. military certainly wanted (and even tried!) to "piggyback" a Cuba strike on top of the JFK assassination, but that was ***not*** Lyndon Johnson's desire *at all*. Moreover, it was certainly ***not*** part of the deal which LBJ had made with the heads of USAF and SAC to *restrain* their forces on November 22nd.

It was a very clever move, by a very clever killer.

* * *

Lyndon Johnson was consciously clearing the decks[763] so that his **real** accomplices could operate successfully without tripping over laughably idiotic *amateurs* (Shaw, Ferrie, *et. al.*) who were merely posturing and posing and *playing* at being "assassins."[764]

However, what LBJ had intended in April 1963 as a clever and necessary order – *broadcast in the clear,*[765] in order to successfully halt and prevent all the clumsy reckless bastards who could easily screw up his own brilliant assassination plot by engaging in premature gunfire at JFK in random locations *prior to the Dallas trip*[766] – turned out to be *not clear enough* to actually prevent certain impatient, murderous, right-wing-Cuban-exile enemies of President Kennedy from going ahead with *their own* independent plans to kill JFK the very moment the calendar page turned from October to November.[767]

In short, LBJ was a "victim" of his own linguistic finesse, or lack thereof.

"Until next November" *wasn't specific or accurate enough.*[768]

Unfortunately for LBJ, the reckless and impatient amateurs in the ugly world of right-wing Cuban exile fury took him precisely at his word.

Literally.

Johnson said to await "November."

To those exiles, quite understandably, "November" meant "November."

As in, *"Beginning no later than 12:01 a.m. on November 1ˢᵗ, 1963."*

LBJ's message was quite literally "lost in translation" to some listeners; but it was *deliberately* misinterpreted and *willfully* "misunderstood" by others.[769]

Dallas was a *Lyndon Baines Johnson* production – and LBJ had **zero** interest in invading Cuba in November 1963.

[763] Author's exclusive original discovery.

[764] Author's exclusive original discovery.

[765] Author's exclusive original discovery.

[766] Author's exclusive original discovery.

[767] Author's exclusive original discovery.

[768] Author's exclusive original discovery.

[769] Author's exclusive original discovery.

To Alpha-66 and similar terrorist groups, the message received from Lyndon Johnson's April 1963 declaration was this: "Okay, boys; beginning November 1ˢᵗ, *feel free to go at it with guns blazing!*"

As the aborted Chicago plot in early November 1963 amply demonstrated, the traitorous Texan LBJ had been too clever by half in his April remarks.

President Kennedy ultimately canceled his Chicago trip at the very last minute after being belatedly and reluctantly advised by the Secret Service that "a" plot existed there. This was not an act of kindness or solicitude or professionalism by the SS; their concern was only that *the particular plot in question* (a renegade, unsanctioned Cuban exile plot) was not *their* plot – meaning, *LBJ's* plot – and therefore, there was no guarantee that the Cuban exiles' plot would succeed *at all*.

Remember:

As I first recognized and pointed out several decades ago and have repeated throughout this book, the purpose of the JFK assassination was ***not*** simply to "kill" President Kennedy, but to kill him *and get away with it.*[770] The fact is that *none* of the participants in the *actual* JFK assassination plot – LBJ's plot – wanted or desired to go to jail or face the electric chair following the murder of the president.[771]

It wasn't a suicide mission, folks.

Therefore, it was no place for foolish, loudmouthed, incompetent amateurs like Martino and Ferrie and Shaw and Milteer and Marcello and Alpha-66 and their ilk – loose-lipped, contemptible men who could easily gum up the works and, through their rampant idiocy and indiscretion and ineptitude and lack of planning, *destroy LBJ's entire JFK assassination plot.*[772]

* * *

Agonized, devastated and bewildered, Bobby was obviously not at his best that awful afternoon of November 22nd. He simply could not "put it all together" quickly enough to forestall or prevent – let alone promptly expose – the pertinent actions of the true authors of the plot.

Worst of all – *unlike many wise American military men at all levels, in all branches, both at home and abroad* – RFK did not instantly and instinctively grasp the fundamental fact that *Lyndon Baines Johnson was leading the coup* and that top

---

[770] Author's exclusive original insight.

[771] Author's exclusive original discovery.

[772] Author's exclusive original discovery.

echelons of *the U. S. military* were fully and very actively on board with LBJ's seditious, murderous operation.[773]

Robert Kennedy also failed to publicly assert *any* control over the investigation of the murder;[774] failed to protect the innocent Lee Oswald, now locked up in a Dallas jail;[775] and failed to publicly call for a pause in the rapid tempo of official events.

Those failures by RFK were devastating and catastrophic.

Later on the afternoon of November 22nd, after personally confronting John McCone and talking to Enrique Ruiz Williams by phone, Robert Kennedy went to the Pentagon and there met with Defense Secretary Robert McNamara (whom both Kennedy brothers had foolishly and mistakenly regarded as an intelligent individual and a genuine ally).[776] The two men were joined by JCS Chief Maxwell Taylor (whom both Kennedy brothers had *also* foolishly and mistakenly regarded as an intelligent individual and a genuine ally). The trio then traveled over to Andrews Air Force Base in Maryland to await the arrival of Air Force One when it returned from Dallas.

* * *

The efforts of LBJ to "freeze" Bobby Kennedy continued for much of the weekend of the JFK assassination. But those efforts began long *before* Air Force One ever touched down in the Andrews darkness that evening.

It began with a telephone call *from Lyndon Johnson himself* at 1:56 p.m. Central time – which was 2:56 p.m. Eastern time – during which Johnson told the

---

[773] Author's exclusive original discovery. **N.B.**: The JFK assassination was *not* a *military* coup (which is designed to openly install either a single uniformed officer or a uniformed military *junta* as the overt head of state); rather, it was a *military-backed* coup which was run and led by a civilian (Lyndon Johnson) and designed to illegally and murderously install a *civilian* (Lyndon Johnson) as head of state.

[774] Technically, JFK's murder itself was a state-level crime, subject to Texas law, but that certainly didn't stop LBJ from ordering J. Edgar Hoover to move in and take over much of the so-called "investigation," using the FBI. Bobby Kennedy had no less authority than Hoover, so RFK could have asserted Justice Department jurisdiction by invoking existing federal laws against conspiracy, sedition and violation of civil rights (namely, JFK's own civil rights).

[775] By promptly and publicly declaring that *any harm coming to Lee Oswald would* **prove** *the existence of a major domestic coup and lead to an aggressive Justice department investigation,* RFK could have literally saved Oswald's life and helped quickly unravel the actual JFK assassination plot.

[776] Author's exclusive original discovery. Most writers in the past half-century have parroted the slimy (and unexamined) fiction that Robert McNamara was some sort of well-combed, bespectacled Sir Galahad – a friendly and loyal "ally" to JFK and Bobby.

In reality, McNamara was loyal to *himself,* and therefore he gravitated to anyone with power who could maintain *his* power. Once JFK was murdered, the despicable McNamara *instantly* toadied up to Lyndon Johnson (beginning the night of November 22nd!) and ardently pushed for expansion of the deadly war in Vietnam which – as McNamara himself well knew – JFK was absolutely determined to end.

stunned RFK that due to "problems of special urgency," *secret security measures were required* at Love Field in Dallas.[777]

By obtaining a grunt of unwitting "approval" or even just silent acquiescence, LBJ thus secured a "get out of jail free" card, straight from the Attorney General's own uncomprehending lips – because Johnson could thereafter use such unwitting "assent" [*sic*] to "justify" everything that came next.

Indeed, LBJ made a point of specifically mentioning this telephone conversation, and the pregnant term *"the practical problems at hand – problems of special urgency"* in his criminally cagey July 1964 written responses (***not*** given under oath)[778] to questions from the so-called "Warren" Commission.[779] Robert Kennedy actually remained silent on the telephone on November 22nd when Lyndon Johnson called from Love Field and made his extremely risky verbal gambit;[780] therefore LBJ was *forced* to take the risk of including the strange, pregnant phrase in his own (written, unsworn) statement to the Commission in July 1964.[781]

* * *

---

[777] Author's exclusive original discovery. I was the first and only person to find, properly analyze and accurately understand this damning piece of data.

[778] Author's exclusive original discovery. (William Manchester quotes from LBJ's statement in *The Death of a President,* p. 269.) Tellingly, Lyndon Johnson *refused* to testify in person, or even answer in writing *under oath,* to the very commission that *he himself had established* to "investigate" the assassination of his predecessor – even though he had also personally hand-picked all of its members!

As LBJ knew perfectly well, testifying under oath would have put him at grave risk for subsequent charges of perjury, obstruction of justice, conspiracy and murder. Robert Kennedy would have examined any sworn testimony by LBJ with a high-power microscope, looking for any evidence of LBJ's role in the plot. A single unexpected question – or a single slip of the tongue by Johnson – could have spelled absolute disaster for the Texan.

LBJ's reticence extended well beyond sworn testimony. LBJ obstinately refused to speak with the Kennedys' authorized writer, William Manchester, because the risks of an inadvertent admission were far too great.

Four decades later, *another* President from Texas (George W. Bush) would *also* refuse to testify under oath about *another* violent criminal event that deeply traumatized America – the attacks of September 11th, 2001.

[779] Author's exclusive original discovery.

LBJ's *refusal to testify to his own commission* cannot be "innocently" attributed to a healthy respect for "the separation of powers," nor to an "executive privilege" issue; after all, as a creature of LBJ himself, the so-called "Warren" Commission was a creation of *the executive branch,* not of Congress. (Author's exclusive original insight.)

[780] William Manchester, *The Death of a President,* p. 269.

[781] Author's exclusive original discovery.

In the early evening of November 22ⁿᵈ, a group of LBJ's subordinate accomplices (consisting of U. S. Navy officers and a cadre of SS agents) needed to complete the very tricky task of reuniting President Kennedy's battered body (which had *already* been inside the morgue at the *rear* of Bethesda Naval Hospital for a full 20 minutes) with the deluxe bronze "official" coffin from Dallas (which JFK's widow and brother had just now arrived with at 6:55 p.m. EST, inside a gray Navy ambulance, at the *front* of the Bethesda hospital building beneath its looming tower).

Upon arriving at the *front* entrance of the facility (completely oblivious to what was already occurring in the *back*), Robert Kennedy and his blood-spattered sister-in-law Jacqueline walked inside through the tiny main entrance doors of the hospital and stepped across the small ground-floor rotunda. They then took an elevator to the upper-floor VIP suite in the tall Bethesda tower.

There Bobby made his *second* huge mistake (from an investigative and prosecutorial standpoint) when he failed to descend to the morgue and observe the extraordinary (and deeply criminal) things that were happening there.

Yes, it might have been too much to expect of any man.

Yes, it might have been too much to ask of *any* brother of *any* murder victim, *anywhere* – for an autopsy is admittedly a very gruesome and unpleasant process even under "normal" circumstances.

But these were anything **but** normal circumstances, and – despite the fact that horrendous and massive changes had *already* been wrought upon the president's helpless body in the five ugly hours *well prior to* 6:35 p.m. Eastern time – Robert Kennedy's presence and observations and questions in the Bethesda morgue that night could have changed the course of history, significantly hindered the criminal conspiracy, and prevented it from succeeding and going unpunished.

And, as it turned out, *there was really no one else to do it.*

No one but Bobby.[782]

---

[782] Kennedy's loyal USAF aide, Brigadier General Godfrey McHugh, who rode with Jackie and Bobby from Andrews, bravely entered the Bethesda morgue *after* 8:00 p.m. EST and stayed there throughout most of the night, occasionally holding his dead Commander-in-Chief's hand in a touching gesture of love and fidelity and respect. But despite his own personal toughness and integrity, General McHugh was understandably very distraught emotionally, and thus he was (quite understandably) in no real condition to understand or critically question the actions and statements and procedures going on in front of him on that grim, stainless steel morgue table.

Admiral George Burkley, President Kennedy's White House physician, also entered the morgue and purported to be representing "the wishes of the Kennedy family" – but Burkley, *at a minimum,* knew about the assassination plot; behaved suspiciously; and failed to ever report the postmortem damage that he knew had been inflicted upon JFK's corpse. In 1977, a very nervous Burkley – through his attorney – alerted the HSCA that *more than one person was involved in the JFK assassination,* and that *"others besides Oswald must have participated,"* but his attorney's overture – practically *begging* for the admiral to be subpoenaed in order to reveal all, under oath, in a staggering sworn confession – was ignored by the

No one else in the American military or the Secret Service (let alone among conventional American "journalists" or "academics," later), was going to stand up for the truth about the murder of the man whose nude, bloody, cruelly battered body now lay on a cold metal table, surrounded by his killers and their accomplices and a small group of mute, sorrowing, innocent witnesses.[783]

* * *

Robert Kennedy was not a pathologist or a medical expert of any kind, of course – but he *was* a lawyer, and he *was* the Attorney General of the United States, and he damn well understood *the primacy of a victim's **body** as the core evidence in **any** homicide investigation.*

RFK's failure to attend the autopsy (or, failing that, to at least assign one or more extremely hard-nosed members of the Justice Department's veteran prosecutorial staff as his designated *representatives* inside the Bethesda morgue that night) left some of JFK's killers (in the Secret Service) and their high-ranking accomplices (in the Navy) free to pressure, cajole, harass and intimidate the three military autopsy pathologists (Navy Commander James J. Humes, Navy Lt. Commander J. Thornton Boswell and Army Lt. Col. Pierre Finck) as they puzzled their way through a bizarre procedure that ultimately lasted for an astounding nine-and-a-half hours.[784]

President Kennedy's battered body was only *partially* dissected that evening by the three pathologists; proper examination of the massively mutilated wound in his

---

cowardly congressional committee. When Admiral Burkley realized that the HSCA would just be another whitewash, he relaxed and even signed a false affidavit for the committee.

[783] Several young U.S. Navy medical technicians present that awful night – including the brilliant and thoughtful James Curtis Jenkins and the refreshingly blunt, candid, courageous Paul Kelly O'Connor – recognized that something was seriously wrong with the condition of President Kennedy's body upon its arrival. They and their Navy colleagues were promptly and deliberately silenced by a threatening written "gag order" from their Navy superiors, issued that same weekend. Only in 1978 did the HSCA obtain a letter from a Department of Defense attorney reluctantly rescinding the prohibition on revealing what they had seen. The HSCA, led by the despicable Robert Blakey (who had once worked for Robert Kennedy), then trivialized and misrepresented and suppressed their vital observations. Later, in the 1990s, Blakey fathered the JFK Records Act which created the ARRB – and Blakey ensured that under the provisions of that odious federal law, the ARRB would be comprised of denialist Establishment shills; would be *forbidden* to actually *reinvestigate* the JFK assassination; and would therefore be completely castrated before it was even formed.

[784] President Kennedy's body *first* arrived at the Bethesda morgue (inside a cheap gray shipping casket) at 6:35 p.m. Eastern time on Friday night, November 22nd.

It was brought into the morgue *again* (inside the deluxe bronze coffin) at 8:00 p.m. EST on Friday night, November 22nd.

It finally departed Bethesda (in an African mahogany coffin) at 3:56 a.m. EST on Saturday, November 23rd, 1963, and ultimately returned to the White House at 4:23 a.m. EST.

neck was specifically prohibited by a senior military officer present in the morgue.[785] The U. S. government's entire – and entirely false – "official" theory of the case ultimately hinged on the fatuous assertion that a "single bullet" [*sic*] passed through JFK's neck [*sic*] from back to front [*sic*] before striking John Connally [*sic*], ultimately causing [*sic*] seven wounds [*sic*] in two men [*sic*] but somehow [*sic*] conveniently emerging [*sic*] virtually intact [*sic*].[786]

Robert Kennedy himself, or *a designated Justice Department representative acting on RFK's behalf in the morgue,* would also certainly have picked up on the obvious tensions, hostilities and verbal outbursts which Navy technician James Curtis Jenkins noted that night – and would have properly and aggressively pursued them.

The sad reality is that Robert Kennedy and his Justice Department performed *no* serious investigation of his brother's assassination *at all* – certainly not promptly enough to stop the treasonous criminal conspiracy in its tracks. Bobby did ask certain trusted individuals to "look into" the case informally, but these private requests were pitifully weak and pitifully absurd – as were the so-called "results" thereof.

Many subsequent observers have asked why Robert Kennedy did not openly launch a major investigation himself at the time of the JFK assassination in 1963. The real answer was hidden for decades, but it finally emerged when I began to take a very hard look at what exactly was involved in "freezing Bobby."

I am the person who exclusively discovered that Lyndon Johnson's afternoon call to RFK from Love Field, regarding unspecified "problems of special urgency," was *a deliberate act on Johnson's part* to gain "cover" for criminal deeds.[787]

It was the *first* of several actions taken by LBJ to "freeze" Bobby Kennedy.[788]

And as I conducted lengthy additional research and investigation, I also discovered that Lyndon Johnson's afternoon call to RFK from Love Field, regarding unspecified "problems of special urgency," was only the tip of a very bloody iceberg.[789]

* * *

Robert Kennedy failed to issue *any public statement of any kind* in the critical first hours after the shooting in Dealey Plaza. Such a statement would have established

---

[785] Autopsy doctor Lt. Col. Pierre Finck disclosed this, *under oath,* at the Clay Shaw trial in New Orleans in 1969.

[786] If all that "[*sic*]" makes you sick, it should. The official story is both intellectually insulting and demonstrably untrue. *Quelle surprise.*

[787] Author's exclusive original discovery.

[788] Author's exclusive original discovery.

[789] Author's exclusive original discovery.

strict parameters for the probe; asserted Justice Department (*not* FBI!) primacy in any investigation of the assassination; highlighted the possibility of U.S. government involvement in the crime; *saved Lee Oswald's life;* and prevented a host of subsequent problems.[790]

But Bobby said nothing, publicly.

RFK *also* failed to immediately mobilize his legitimate deputies at the Department of Justice, who could have acted promptly and effectively *in his stead,* and who could have seized proper control of the nascent federal "investigation" of the crime. Instead, the probe was soon totally dominated by FBI agents who reported fearfully and obediently to the untrustworthy, venomous and grotesquely disloyal J. Edgar Hoover – a longtime ally of the JFK plot leader, Lyndon Baines Johnson.

Further, Bobby inexcusably failed to institute a secure cordon of federal protection around the alleged "suspect," Lee Oswald, in order to ensure that Oswald had counsel and could be properly and immediately interviewed by professional Justice Department investigators in fully recorded, thoroughly documented interrogation sessions. The tough, dedicated, proven and fearless U.S. Marshals would have been superb choices to protect Lee Oswald.

Though the assassination itself – *as a murder* – was only a state-level crime in 1963 (not a federal offense, incredibly enough), almost no one could have prevented RFK from asserting jurisdiction, on a pretext if nothing else. And, as I discovered during my research for this book, there were actually numerous pertinent federal laws already on the books which gave Robert Kennedy legitimate legal oversight.[791]

A relaxed Lee Oswald, speaking freely while held in protective federal custody by *innocent* federal agents, would have wittingly or unwittingly exposed and destroyed the JFK assassination plot (and any false notion of his own supposed "guilt") within hours. As it was, Oswald was surrounded by Dallas police and Secret Service agents – *men who worked for organizations which had actively participated in the assassination of the president.*

Worst of all, Robert Kennedy also failed to obtain *possession of his brother's body in a timely fashion* in order to ensure that a painstakingly thorough, absolutely detailed and truly professional forensic autopsy was conducted by experienced experts with a view to uncovering (not suppressing) key evidence.

A strong and early declaration to this effect (for example, *"No autopsy or other medical or forensic examination of any kind shall be undertaken by anyone until I, the Attorney General, personally arrive in Dallas with Justice Department personnel who will oversee and carefully document the postmortem procedure . . ."*) would have severely hamstrung Lyndon Johnson and the Secret Service and would have

---

[790] Author's exclusive original discovery.

[791] I researched and examined many pertinent federal laws; they are presented in Appendix 1 of this book.

immediately put the onus on them to explain the macabre, illicit damage which had clearly been inflicted upon the body of the president well prior to the Bethesda "autopsy" that night.

In sum, in the immediate wake of his brother's murder an understandably shocked and deeply wounded RFK *completely abdicated his legal and professional responsibilities as Attorney General of the United States* – and as a result the basest criminals in the country were left at liberty to secretly destroy evidence, brazenly obstruct justice, and plainly get away with murder in the short term.

Robert Kennedy's emotional paralysis on November 22nd is eminently understandable – but what about the next few days?

Shock *alone* cannot explain Bobby's failure.

Grief *alone* cannot explain his total absence from the investigation.

Alleged "conflict of interest" or "recusal from the case" does not explain his distance from the aftermath of the killing.

So how did Lyndon Johnson and his criminal allies inside the federal government manage to freeze Bobby?

As I discovered, the process consisted of a series of several very specific, very deliberate, separate *incremental* steps of increasing severity – each one orchestrated *personally* by the totally illegitimate new "president" of the United States, Lyndon Baines Johnson of Texas.[792]

Within three days of Dallas, the toughest man in Camelot – Robert Francis Kennedy himself – was essentially crippled and hogtied by LBJ's machinations.[793]

* * *

Bobby's *first* grave mistake had been arguably "assenting," *even by his silence,* to Johnson's sinister insistence on (carefully unspecified) *security measures* to deal with "problems of special urgency" in that first telephone conversation at 1:56 p.m. Central time on Friday, November 22nd, as LBJ sat in John F. Kennedy's gleaming presidential jet at Love Field.[794]

RFK's *second* major mistake was the failure to *immediately* issue some kind of public statement declaring that the Justice Department was in complete charge of the assassination investigation.

---

[792] Author's exclusive original discovery.

[793] Author's exclusive original discovery.

[794] Author's exclusive original discovery. I was the **first** and **only** person to correctly identify the purpose and meaning of the call – and Johnson's phrasing – as the sinister mechanism to secure (A) unwitting "approval" or (B) silent "acquiescence" from RFK for actions that RFK did not realize were, in reality, *criminal measures perpetrated by the governmental assassins of his brother.*

But ironically, Bobby's strange silence – and Jackie's, as well – ended up triggering the next step in Lyndon Johnson's sinister escalation of the pressure.

* * *

To their credit, neither JFK's widow nor JFK's brother said *anything* publicly that weekend to "recognize" the illegitimate new *coup regime* of Lyndon Johnson.

Yes, the dazed and bloodstained Jacqueline Kennedy had very unwisely and obligingly stood next to LBJ as he took the oath of office in the presidential stateroom of Air Force One prior to takeoff from Love Field (a grave error on her part that played into Johnson's hands by permitting him to stage a widely disseminated photo projecting supposed "unity") – but after that, she had stayed firmly ensconced in the rear of the aircraft during the flight back to Washington, refusing all of LBJ's entreaties to come forward and join the Johnson party amidships.

After publicly boarding the presidential aircraft now parked near the Andrews Air Terminal building, RFK quickly ran past Lyndon Johnson without the slightest acknowledgment of his presence, let alone his new status as Bobby's boss.

Neither Jackie nor Bobby addressed the waiting media upon arrival at Andrews, either.

Neither Jackie nor Bobby disembarked *with* Lyndon Johnson, nor stood with him during his brief remarks to the media at Andrews Air Force Base that evening.

Neither Jackie nor Bobby issued any statement during the night-long autopsy at Bethesda.

Neither Jackie nor Bobby issued any statement the *following* day, either.

The point is that the Kennedy family's two most important and visible members *did not utter a single word recognizing Lyndon Johnson's "legitimacy" as "president."*[795]

At no time that awful November weekend did either Robert or Jacqueline issue any "call to unity" statement – such as, "We humbly request that all Americans unite behind President Johnson and pray for him as he assumes the terrible burdens and responsibilities of the presidency."

Nothing of the sort.

Their silence was, politically and legally, *deafening.*

So by Saturday, November 23rd, 1963, Lyndon Johnson himself began to *personally* ratchet up the pressure.[796]

* * *

---

[795] Author's exclusive original discovery.

[796] Author's exclusive original discovery.

On November 23rd, CIA officer Tennent H. ("Pete") Bagley[797] sent a memorandum to the agency's Assistant Deputy Director for Plans, alleging darkly that the falsely-accused suspect, Lee Oswald, had recently met in Mexico City with a supposed Soviet KGB assassination-meister, a man named Valeriy Kostikov.

The Bagley memo laid the groundwork for Lyndon Johnson's next step in the effort to freeze Bobby Kennedy.

LBJ's **second** tactic was to brazenly summon Ted Sorensen – JFK's special counsel, principal speechwriter, friend and "alter ego" – to LBJ's multi-room Suite 274 in the Executive Office Building, just across the street from the West Wing of the White House. There, on Saturday evening, November 23rd, LBJ presented the Kennedys' unofficial emissary with a secret document darkly and falsely alleging that a "foreign nation" was supposedly involved in the assassination of JFK.[798]

Sorensen, deeply stricken and emotionally wounded by President Kennedy's murder but no political naïf, glanced at the paper; dismissed it brusquely and correctly as insubstantial; and eventually departed completely unimpressed and totally unconvinced.[799]

Johnson's naked gambit had failed miserably.

Had Ted Sorensen taken the document seriously, and had he reported it to Bobby as a serious matter, then RFK might have been successfully cowed into thinking that his own energetic efforts – to spur the CIA to topple or kill Fidel Castro – had resulted in an awful example of preventive self-defense known as "blow-back."[800] This would naturally paralyze Bobby from both a legal and political standpoint, and Johnson would thus escape any unwanted investigation by the murdered President's fierce younger brother (who could normally be expected to be nothing if not an avenging angel with a savage wrath).

*But that's **not** what happened – at all.*[801]

Ted Sorensen intelligently saw through the transparent ruse of the document, and quickly dismissed it. Thus Sorensen would *not* serve (wittingly or unwittingly) as

---

[797] Bagley was a brutal and paranoid individual who shared James Jesus Angleton's fear that Soviet defector Yuri Nosenko was a disinformation agent. Ironically, Bagley himself was later investigated as a possible Soviet "mole."

[798] Neither LBJ nor Sorensen ever confirmed whether the item in question was the Bagley memo itself or another document, similar in nature, falsely "linking" a foreign government to the murder of JFK.

[799] Sorensen recounted the episode in his book *Counselor.*

[800] A number of incredibly stupid Establishment writers have fallen for and actively promoted that false theory for years – *just as Lyndon Johnson wanted them to do.*

[801] Author's exclusive original discovery.

an errand boy for Johnson in convincing Robert Kennedy that he, RFK, was somehow "at fault" [*sic*] in Jack's death.

LBJ's *second* tactic to "freeze Bobby" had clearly failed to do the trick.

Stronger coercive measures were clearly called for, and stronger coercive measures were *taken* by Lyndon Johnson – within less than twenty-four hours.[802]

* * *

LBJ's ***third*** tactic was a secret, early-morning visit *to the Pentagon* on Sunday, November 24th, 1963.

There LBJ met behind closed doors with Defense Secretary Robert McNamara and top aide Cyrus Vance,[803] who were well-known to JFK and RFK, and who were (mistakenly) regarded by the Kennedys themselves as Kennedy "allies."

At this secret meeting, LBJ *knowingly* and *falsely* declared that Cuban leader Fidel Castro was behind the JFK assassination – and further averred that Castro had supposedly acted in *preemptive self-defense* as a response to the Kennedy brothers' numerous and violent criminal plots against his own person and against his revolutionary government.[804]

Since Robert Kennedy headed the violent anti-Castro committees known as the SGA and the ICCCA inside the federal government's executive branch, and since Robert Kennedy and Robert McNamara had **each** foolishly (and casually) *spoken aloud* about eliminating Fidel Castro (RFK spoke of "knocking off" Castro – and McNamara spoke explicitly of "eliminating" and "liquidating" Fidel),[805] and since they had *each* stupidly done so in front of *unimpeachable U. S. government witnesses*, LBJ's

---

[802] Author's exclusive original discovery.

[803] Alexander Haig with Charles McCarry, *Inner Circles,* p. 115. U. S. Army officer Al Haig worked for McNamara, Vance and Joe Califano at the time, but as a relatively junior officer he did not rate personal inclusion in the secret LBJ confab that morning. Nevertheless, Haig was informed of the content of LBJ's remarks promptly afterward by *a firsthand participant in the meeting.*

Significantly, LBJ's sinister Pentagon excursion is ***not*** included in the LBJ "Daily Diary" for November 24th, 1963; in fact, I discovered that the original handwritten version of that LBJ calendar is full of major, *hours-long gaps* in the record. Al Haig was absolutely crystal clear that it occurred early in the morning of Sunday, November 24th, 1963.

[804] Alexander Haig with Charles McCarry, *Inner Circles,* p. 115.

[805] McNamara's homicidal comments are quoted in Patrick Sloyan, *The Politics of Deception,* p. 41.

chilling remarks that Sunday morning immediately "resonated" with his high-level listeners at the Pentagon.[806]

Moreover, Lyndon Johnson piously opined, this terribly sordid state of affairs posed an extremely grave threat to *the future viability of the Democratic Party itself* [meaning, Robert Kennedy's future viability, and the viability of the careers of key appointees in a future Democratic administration] because the Kennedy brothers' own ill-advised and criminal anti-Fidel fanaticism had (supposedly) "caused" the JFK assassination.[807]

It sure would be awful, LBJ made clear, if any word of this terrible "truth" [*sic*] about the president's murder were to ever get out publicly.

Just *awful,* fellas.

Goodness gracious me.

*Really **awful.***

Since LBJ knew full well that McNamara and Vance were considered very close to the Kennedys, he was certain that his false but masterfully delivered message to the Pentagon's civilian leadership would get through to RFK quickly, clearly and unmistakably.

And Johnson was correct.

The secret and deeply discomfiting early-morning "conversation" at the Pentagon would be promptly reported to Robert Kennedy, and it would serve as an extremely intimidating "shot across the bow" of the grieving Attorney General.

But Lyndon Baines Johnson didn't stop there.

* * *

Lyndon Johnson's ***fourth*** coercive tactic was much more violent.

On Sunday, November 24th, Jacquelyn and Robert paid their respects to the fallen President at Kennedy's flag-draped bier in the Rotunda of the U.S. Capitol. Senator Mike Mansfield and others gave tributes to the slain Commander-in-Chief. Lyndon Johnson made sure to be there as well, ostentatiously placing a wreath near the coffin of his victim.

---

[806] People take written notes of such things. Strangely, this obvious fact seems not to have occurred to either RFK or to McNamara – or, in their arrogance, they simply ignored it. (Richard Goodwin was one of those who documented McNamara's murderous remarks in the book *Remembering America*, p. 189.)

[807] Alexander Haig with Charles McCarry, *Inner Circles,* p. 115.

At 11:21 a.m. Central time that day (which was 12:21 p.m. Eastern time in Washington),[808] *upon receiving the obvious signal of a car horn honking loudly,*[809] a USAAF veteran named Jacob Rubenstein emerged from a crowd in the basement parking area of the Dallas jail and fired a single shot at point-blank range into the abdomen of the helpless Lee Oswald, who was walking handcuffed between two local law enforcement officers.

The stunning scene was broadcast live on national television.

Lee crumpled to the ground, shaking his head mutely when a police detective leaned over him and asked whether there was anything he wanted to say. Oswald was seriously (but *not* fatally) wounded, and the repulsive Jacob Rubenstein – better known by his new name "Jack Ruby" to the many Dallas police officers whom he had bribed and befriended – was quickly disarmed and taken into custody.

Jacob Rubenstein shot, *but did not kill,* Lee Oswald. And thus even at this critical juncture, Oswald – who constituted one of Bobby Kennedy's most valuable potential sources of information – was still alive, and was still capable of recovering from his severe abdominal bullet wound.[810]

Oswald was transported to Parkland Hospital, and there he was initially treated in Trauma Room 2 – just across the hall from where President Kennedy had been treated, 47 hours earlier. Then Oswald was hurried upstairs to an actual surgical operating room, where *some* of the doctors present sincerely labored to save him – and *had in fact succeeded in stabilizing him satisfactorily* despite the extremely serious nature of the bullet wound that Lee had suffered.[811]

But not every physician there was dedicated to Oswald's survival.

Nor did Lee die, as some of the innocent doctors naively believed, simply from a sudden "cardiac arrest."

---

[808] **N.B.**: Lyndon Johnson's unannounced Sunday morning visit to the Pentagon occurred several hours *before* the shooting of Lee Oswald down in Dallas, which occurred at 11:21 a.m. CST (which is 12:21 p.m. EST).

[809] The horn is clearly and unmistakably audible on recorded news coverage of the crime.

[810] Some of the Parkland Hospital surgeons later stated that they had actually succeeded in *stabilizing* Lee Oswald before his sudden and mysterious demise on the table.

N.B.: There are many ways to kill a man in an operating room.

[811] Dr. Charles Crenshaw was one of those present who noted that the massive internal bleeding suffered by Lee Oswald from the gunshot wound had in fact been successfully stanched by the doctors – and that some 45 minutes into the emergency surgery at Parkland Hospital, Oswald was in *stable* condition! (Charles A. Crenshaw with Jens Hansen and J. Gary Shaw, *JFK: Conspiracy of Silence,* paperback edition, p. 186.)

The truth is that while Lee Oswald was indeed *shot* in the basement parking area of the Dallas Jail, he was actually *murdered* on the operating table at Parkland Memorial Hospital.

* * *

Killing Lee Oswald on the operating table at Parkland accomplished two things. First, it silenced the innocent patsy forever, permanently preventing him from proving his own innocence – and thereby laying waste to the government's utterly fictitious version of the JFK assassination – at an upcoming public trial.

Secondly, and equally importantly, it brutally emphasized the central fact that Lyndon Johnson would literally stop at *nothing* to preserve his hard-won (and totally illegitimate) "presidency."

But ironically and disturbingly, the news of Lee Oswald's death barely registered on the emotionally ravaged, grief-stricken Kennedys that awful Sunday.[812]

Lyndon Johnson, however, was delighted.

Yet even *the assassination of Lee Harvey Oswald* – a staggering blow to Robert Kennedy's early efforts to learn the truth about Dallas – did not cause the Attorney General of the United States to surrender completely.

Not yet.

Bobby Kennedy was bowed and stunned, but not yet beaten.

And RFK still had issued no statement of any kind recognizing Lyndon Johnson as the "legitimate" president of the United States.[813]

* * *

LBJ now had to resort to his *fifth* coercive tactic, employing the biggest weapon of all – something that would rock RFK to the core, shatter his equilibrium and finally bring JFK's dizzied brother to his knees.[814]

This *fifth* coercive tactic was implemented courtesy of some of Johnson's accomplices and confederates – not his senior uniformed military allies inside the Pentagon, but cynical civilians inside a sinister three-letter government agency headquartered in a place called Langley, Virginia.

---

[812] William Manchester, *The Death of a President,* pp. 525-527 and p. 543.

[813] Author's exclusive original insight.

[814] Bobby's effective collapse would be short-lived, but it was sufficient for LBJ's needs. By the day of John Kennedy's funeral and interment at Arlington National Cemetery – Monday, November 25th, 1963 – Robert Kennedy was *temporarily* immobilized, from a political and prosecutorial standpoint.

That Sunday, November 24th, the Central Intelligence Agency – now reporting to LBJ – was busy generating the insidious tool that would temporarily cripple RFK and briefly immobilize his ability to resist Lyndon Johnson's *fait accompli.*

And as usual, the most lethal weapon in Washington D.C. was made of *paper,* not of lead.[815]

* * *

As noted above, on Saturday, November 23rd, CIA officer "Pete" Bagley had written a memo claiming that Lee Oswald had met with a Soviet attaché, a man named Valeriy Kostikov, who was then posted to the Mexican capital of Mexico City.

At the time, the "official" U.S. government claim was that Kostikov was a KGB agent supposedly working as part of "Department 13," which purportedly handled all USSR sabotage and assassination operations in the Western Hemisphere – and thus Kostikov was officially regarded as a particularly nefarious and malevolent character.[816]

Yet Bagley's sinister Saturday memo about Oswald and Kostikov, *in and of itself,* was plainly just *not enough to achieve the desired effect.*[817]

So LBJ's eager subordinates at CIA headquarters in Langley, Virginia sent a *pair* of cables to the CIA's Mexico City station on Saturday, November 23rd, requesting a list of *all* people who had recently been in contact with Comrade Kostikov *and* with an associate of his.

All of them.

The CIA's Mexico City station – which, along with CIA headquarters itself, has a long record of lies, distortions and bare-faced obstructionism when it comes to the JFK assassination and many other major crimes – dutifully sent a pair of cables concerning those supposed "contacts" back to Agency headquarters in Langley on Sunday, November 24th, 1963.

The point is this:

---

[815] In America's capital, the deadliest and most feared weapon is usually a *memo,* not a bullet.

[816] Later analysis by Professor Peter Dale Scott indicated that poor Comrade Kostikov had *no* such assassination role in reality – but as a temporary and frightening claim, it was plausible enough to cow many people in Washington *at the time,* in 1963. And that, as they say in America, was plainly "good enough for government work."

In May 1982, a CIA official identifying himself as "David H. Blee" (CIA pseudonyms are almost always bizarre and grossly artificial-sounding monikers) admitted *in writing* that the Agency had *no proof* that Valeriy Kostikov was ever part of the fearsome "Department 13." Moreover, Blee abjectly confessed that as far as the CIA was aware, the Soviets had *not* engaged in such "executive action" (meaning, *assassination*) since 1959 – a full four years *before* the JFK assassination.

[817] Author's exclusive original discovery.

It was a deadly bureaucratic game of "pitch and catch"[818] between two cooperating CIA locations – both working for LBJ.

The CIA cables neatly buttressed Johnson's false early-morning claims to McNamara and Vance and Califano over at the Pentagon.[819]

Note carefully: In the context of the moment, it didn't really matter whether the lists themselves (or the descriptions of the people on it) were actually *true* or *accurate* or *real;* their mere *existence* represented a grave threat to both domestic tranquility and to superpower relations.

And to Robert Francis Kennedy.

Two names that arose in the CIA's "probe" of the assassination were significant. The most obvious (and all-too-pat) name was Kostikov – a supposedly malevolent mastermind – who had (supposedly) met with Lee Oswald, who had (supposedly) visited Mexico City (supposedly) two months earlier and had (officially) stopped by a Cuban facility and a Soviet facility, in person, at least once.[820]

The notion that Lee Oswald had met personally with Mr. Valeriy Kostikov, a supposed "top KGB assassin," just sixty days before allegedly killing the President of the United States would have made a weaker, less sophisticated man than Robert Kennedy immediately conclude that if the JFK plot *were* indeed a conspiracy, it *must* have been a *Soviet* conspiracy, and that this dangerous "fact" more than justified the prompt suppression of any and all evidence indicating that more than one man was involved in the crime – lest a nuclear war against the USSR be demanded by an outraged American public.[821]

This was, in fact, *precisely* the type of argument that Lyndon Johnson himself made within a week of the JFK assassination in order to wheedle and cajole the reluctant Chief Justice of the Supreme Court, Earl Warren, into heading the commission that would ultimately turn Warren's name into an ignominious synonym for failure and weakness and dishonesty and cover-up.

But as I discovered exclusively, it was not Valeriy Kostikov's name that temporarily paralyzed Robert Kennedy in late November 1963.

---

[818] Author's exclusive original discovery.

[819] Author's exclusive original discovery.

[820] However, it must be emphasized and reiterated that Dr. John Newman and other investigators have proven conclusively that Lee Oswald was also deliberately and clumsily *impersonated* in Mexico City in several telephone calls made to the Soviets there. Moreover, the CIA also distributed photos of a portly man who was clearly a full decade older than the real Oswald – yet the Agency claimed, with a straight face, that the hefty 35-year-old pictured in them was indeed the slim 24-year-old Lee Oswald.

[821] CIA officer John Whitten (*alias* "John Scelso") wrote a report stating that it was clear that there had been neither Soviet nor Cuban involvement in JFK's assassination. For this dangerous and utterly impermissible heresy, Whitten was quickly forced out of the JFK "investigation" by fellow CIA officers James Angleton and Richard Helms.

Nor was it even Lee Oswald's name.

It was the name of *someone else* who was mentioned in connection with the CIA's November 23rd cable query.[822]

And it was enough to shake the toughest man in Camelot.

* * *

By the time that the JFK assassination occurred, Robert Kennedy had been giving the work of the Justice Department – his official role in the U. S. government – far less than his full and undivided attention. In fact, Bobby had been spending much of each 1963 workday *at an office inside CIA headquarters,* overseeing the government's illegal anti-Castro operations against Cuba – criminal actions which undeniably constituted American state-sponsored terrorism. Only *after* putting in several hours at the CIA building did Bobby get into a car and travel downtown to the Justice Department, where he then often worked late into the night.

So in 1963, Bobby was, in effect, working *two full-time jobs* simultaneously.[823] There were even reports circulating that after being re-elected in 1964, President Kennedy planned to officially make RFK the new head of the CIA – thereby finally bringing the rebellious and insubordinate agency to heel, under full Kennedy White House control at last.[824]

Despite his own risky and covert 1963 efforts toward *rapprochement* with Castro, President Kennedy also continued to personally authorize illegal terrorist raids by right-wing Cuban exiles against the island nation. Innocent Cuban citizens suffered and died because of those criminal, violent, pointless raids;[825] there is no legitimate excuse or rationale whatsoever for their authorization. And Robert Kennedy, his brother's personal representative, was heading up the murderous ICCCA and SGA

---

[822] Author's exclusive original discovery.

[823] Hugh Sidey, *John F. Kennedy, President,* p. 121.

[824] After the 1961 Bay of Pigs disaster, a furious JFK famously threatened to shatter the CIA into myriad fragments. His understandable rage eventually subsided, but his severe distrust of the Central Intelligence Agency never fully did. Formally putting Bobby in charge of the Agency would have given JFK greater peace of mind (but *not* an absolute guarantee of safety) during his presumptive second term in the White House.

[825] See Fabian Escalante's extremely useful book *JFK: The Cuba Files* (available in both English and Spanish versions), which identifies *by name* some of the many innocent Cuban victims of the murderous and criminal exile raids which the Kennedy brothers knowingly and illegally unleashed against the island nation.

committees, which continued generating a variety of illegal plots to undermine and overthrow Castro.[826]

The Kennedy brothers themselves – along with their anti-Castro accomplices within the U.S. government – made a number of contradictory statements about their goals, *and* about their chances of success. Undeniably, top administration officials including JFK and RFK themselves were all engaged in major crimes, including *criminal conspiracy* and *state-sponsored terrorism*.

One figure who seemed to offer a glimmer of possibility in terms of arranging or even personally carrying out the assassination of Cuban leader Fidel Castro was Rolando Cubela Secades – a Cuban doctor and official, once close to Castro, who had supposedly become disillusioned with the revolutionary government. Robert Kennedy saw the Cubela option (code name AM/LASH) as a potentially viable way to oust or assassinate Fidel.

There is (not surprisingly) profoundly conflicting testimony about Bobby's precise 1963 role from a variety of CIA sources – some of whom later declared under oath that RFK was never even *consulted* about the AM/LASH operation, while others suggested that Bobby was in fact aggressively *running* the AM/LASH operation. But it is clear that in 1963 *both Kennedy brothers literally had direct telephone lines to key CIA officers like Desmond Fitzgerald of the agency's SAS division, which was focused on ousting Castro.*[827] Fitzgerald met directly with Rolando Cubela in person in Paris in 1963, and spoke with him there about the assassination of Fidel Castro.[828]

And it is also undeniable that – all CIA machinations aside – the Attorney General was also the principal force behind the innocuous-sounding but sinister Interdepartmental Coordinating Committee on Cuban Affairs (ICCCA).[829]

---

[826] Joe Califano was Cyrus Vance's alternate representative on the ICCCA, and therefore attended a number of those meetings in person. Califano later wrote about the two brothers' furious determination to eliminate Castro. (Joseph Califano, *Inside,* pp. 115-116.)

[827] Desmond Fitzgerald, no angel himself, complained later that he often received urgent phone calls *directly from JFK and RFK themselves,* expressing their impatience with unproductive Agency efforts to depose or otherwise eliminate the bearded Cuban leader.

And over at the Pentagon, Joe Califano was tasked with various related efforts, all stemming from RFK's relentless demands that Castro be eliminated. Califano felt that he was laboring for RFK and JFK themselves to *take out the Cuban leader.* (Joseph Califano, *Inside,* p. 119.)

[828] Desmond Fitzgerald's sinister CIA superior told him that it was *unnecessary* to actually seek Bobby's direct approval in order to chat candidly with Cubela about committing homicide, but it is worth noting that powerful Pentagon (and later LBJ White House) aide Joseph Califano – no stranger to criminal USG plots and illegal machinations against Cuba in the 1960s – regarded it as totally impossible that Fitzgerald would dare do such a thing without the express agreement of one or both of the Kennedy brothers. (Joseph Califano, *Inside,* p. 125.)

[829] The author hastens to take this opportunity to pointedly remind the reader that the most horrifyingly evil units of government are generally the ones deliberately camouflaged with intentionally boring,

Though the ICCCA[830] was nominally an entity of the State Department, and although it was run on a daily basis by an individual named Sterling Cottrell, RFK himself was the true "officer in charge" of the group. And at various 1963 meetings of the ICCCA and other government bodies, *Bobby himself* personally made stupid, careless, repeated and explicit verbal references to "knocking off" Castro. Robert Kennedy's casual, indiscreet, sensationally reckless, and (at best) *profoundly ill-advised* spoken remarks naturally made a substantial impression on fellow attendees – and quite predictably, those deeply incriminating remarks soon found their way into notes and journals and diaries and memoranda which were immensely helpful to those planning to both eliminate JFK himself and to effectively neutralize his brother, the fiery Attorney General.

Some CIA officials argued bitterly in 1963, *prior to* the JFK assassination, that Rolando Cubela was actually a double agent who was secretly working for Fidel Castro – and that by dealing with him, the CIA and the Kennedy administration were making a major (even *dangerous*) mistake. Joseph Langosch was one of those making this argument; Ted Shackley, later of Vietnam and Iran/Contra infamy, was another.[831]

On Saturday, November 23rd, CIA headquarters in Langley, Virginia sent a cable (DIR 84837) to the CIA's Mexico City station "urgently" requesting information about Valeriy Kostikov's travels; his activities in November 1963; and his location on November 22nd. The response on November 24th (cable MEXI 7051) contained nothing particularly interesting.

Just over an hour after sending its first request, CIA headquarters sent *another* cable (DIR 84885) to the CIA's Mexico City station seeking the very same information on an *associate* of Kostikov's – a *Pravda* journalist named Ivan Gavrilovich Alferyev.

This *second* request yielded old – but desirable – "results."

---

misleading, totally hum-drum names – usually involving one or more of such words as "planning," "study," "coordinating," "observation," "review," or similar opaque terms.

N.B.: These units are frequently the ones plotting kidnapping, rape, torture, assassination, mass murder, war crimes, coups, invasions, aggressive wars and other acts of state-sponsored terrorism.

[830] Oddly, even the U. S. government itself could never quite decide on the precise name of the group. Various official records and even group participants' statements described it variously as "the Interdepartmental Coordinating Committee *on* Cuban Affairs"; "the Interdepartmental Coordinating Committee *for* Cuban Affairs"; and "the Interdepartmental Coordinating Committee *of* Cuban Affairs."

As first created via NSAM 213 on January 8th, 1963, the USG terrorist group was called three different things on a single page! First it was the "Interdepartmental Organization for Cuban Affairs"; then the "Interdepartmental Committee on Cuba"; and finally, the "Interdepartmental Coordinating Committee." (So much for the alleged "brilliance" of the sinister McGeorge Bundy, American war criminal *extraordinaire,* who wrote the document.)

[831] Their concerns are noted in *The Very Best Men,* by Evan Thomas – another empty Establishment suit who is *completely unreliable* about serious questions like the truth behind the assassinations of John and Robert Kennedy.

And when it developed on November 24th, 1963, that – according to the MEXI 7045 cable sent from the CIA's Mexico City station back to CIA headquarters in response to DIR 84885 – *Rolando Cubela's* name was mentioned, Bobby Kennedy had to feel the ground spinning beneath his feet.[832]

Rolando Cubela Secades, who had been part of the Castro government, was someone whom RFK and his Agency minions had been counting on as one possible avenue to help foment a successful killing of Fidel Castro and overthrow of the Cuban government; but now it *appeared* from the CIA's exchange of cables that Rolando Cubela was (however vaguely and tenuously and faintly) "connected" to the supposed Russian "assassin" [*sic*], Valeriy Kostikov – who had *also* reputedly met with JFK's (falsely accused) supposed American "assassin" [*sic*], Lee Oswald.

It wasn't just a question of a supposed random "loner" (Oswald) meeting with the putative KGB "assassin"; it was now a question of *one of the Attorney General's own Cuban assets (Rolando Cubela) being "connected"* [*sic*] *to Kostikov,* too.

The ostensible implications of this very thin information were astounding:

First, the Mexico City cable obviously implied to "intelligence" types that by virtue of a remote, third-party "connection" with Valeriy Kostikov, Rolando Cubela was indeed a double agent whose *true* loyalty actually lay with Fidel Castro – *not* with the Kennedy brothers and the CIA. Why else would Cubela be associated in *any* way, however distant, with an alleged KGB "assassin"?

Second, if Cubela were indeed a double agent working for Castro, then Robert Kennedy had inexcusably and amateurishly failed to properly *vet* this dangerous man, and had thereby put American lives – *including his own brother's life* – at risk. This was a particularly egregious failure given that, prior to Dallas, certain CIA operatives like Ted Shackley had ostentatiously and vociferously warned about the ugly possibility that Cubela was a double agent.

Third, if Cubela were indeed a double agent, then he had presumably been feeding *all* of the CIA's Castro assassination plans – and, by extension, *Bobby Kennedy's* Castro assassination plans – to Fidel, which might explain the frequent pre-emption and dismal failure of so many *previous* murderous American-backed plots to kill Castro.

---

[832] The so-called "contact" occurred in late December 1960, and it merely involved liaison by *Pravda* journalist Ivan Gavrilovich Alferyev with Cuban official Teresa Proenza to set up a press conference for Rolando Cubela.

That's right: it was a tale of two third parties coordinating a news conference – *not* an indication that Cubela had ever actually met in person with Kostikov, let alone that he did so in 1963 – yet the flimsy, paper-thin "connection" [*sic*] was nevertheless staggering to official Washington.

This ugly tale of CIA hype proves that even the shoddiest nonsense *can* be used – and actually *has* been used – to knowingly prop up false official narratives and thereby to blackmail public officials. Welcome to America, folks.

Fourth, Fidel Castro had already publicly (and rightfully) denounced the murderous American attempts on his life.

Finally, and worst of all, a Cuban official who was "linked" to Robert Kennedy himself (Cubela had demanded to meet an actual representative of the Kennedys, and the CIA's Desmond Fitzgerald – Bobby's point man on Cuba – had passed himself off as just such a representative) was now also "linked" (via the CIA cable) to a supposed "top KGB assassin" – Valeriy Kostikov, a man who had also reportedly met with alleged killer Lee Oswald.

Thus the ostensibly innocuous but thoroughly toxic response generated on November 24th by the CIA's Mexico City station, *in response to a specific additional request from CIA headquarters,* created a dark and insidious triangle of false – but mutually reinforcing and superficially quite damning – possibilities.[833]

A man of Robert Kennedy's intelligence and political experience could certainly envision how this could be effectively "spun" by those who had killed his brother, through incriminating governmental memoranda or via incriminating leaks to cooperative members of the press, who would then predictably ask the following predictable questions:

Did Rolando Cubela pass along evidence of RFK's personal involvement in overthrow/assassination plans to his own boss, Fidel Castro – and did this news "incite" Castro to launch an assassination attempt against JFK as a matter of understandable, predictable and pre-emptive self-defense?

Did Kostikov then "coordinate" a Castro-backed "hit" by funneling information or payments via Rolando Cubela to Lee Oswald?

Alternatively, did Cubela somehow "coordinate" a Soviet-backed "hit" by funneling information or payments from Kostikov to Lee Oswald?

Worst of all, were all three men – Kostikov, Cubela and Oswald – consciously working together, in concert, to carry out the assassination of JFK?

It was *Cubela's* name – **not Oswald's!** – which was the final factor in temporarily freezing Robert Kennedy's resistance to the Johnson coup.[834]

---

[833] Author's exclusive original insight.

[834] Author's exclusive original discovery.

Some JFK assassination researchers believe that Lee Oswald himself was personally known to RFK in advance of JFK's murder – and that Oswald may have even been working in an "undercover" (role-playing) capacity for RFK prior to Dallas. Also, in late October 2021, the *Miami Herald* reported that the son of a dead Cuban exile claimed that the deceased man had once confessed to supposedly "training" Lee Oswald as a "sniper" in Florida.

But none of those decidedly hazy notions can equal the clear and irrefutable trail from Robert Kennedy to Desmond Fitzgerald to Rolando Cubela – and therefore, my own discovery (that the *Cubela* angle was ultimately the linchpin of the effort to successfully "freeze" Bobby) stands unrebutted.

The truth is that CIA headquarters and the CIA Mexico City station were plainly playing a pre-rehearsed game of "pitch and catch" with each other[835] – featuring HQ dutifully "asking for" and the station dutifully "responding with" information that would obviously *hang* Robert Kennedy, politically.[836]

It was a seemingly inescapable trap, and on November 24th, 1963, Robert Francis Kennedy – for all his own cunning and intelligence – simply could not see any way out of it.[837]

* * *

And that was the entire point of the exercise.[838]

Robert Kennedy was effectively "frozen" for a critical period of time shortly after the JFK assassination by the supposed "Oswald-Kostikov-Cubela" connection – particularly the *Cubela* node, which ostensibly linked RFK himself to the supposedly deadly triangle.[839]

This was the actual reason for the (supposed) Oswald trip to Mexico City[840] – a journey which was created and arranged by Lee Oswald's U. S. government handlers *as part of the JFK assassination plot,* and whose *real* meaning and *true* purpose has stumped and flummoxed everyone for decades.[841]

---

[835] Author's exclusive original discovery.

[836] Author's exclusive original discovery.

[837] Author's exclusive original discovery.

[838] Author's exclusive original discovery.

[839] Author's exclusive original discovery.

[840] Author's exclusive original discovery.

[841] In the 1960s, the "Warren" Commission treated the "Mexico City trip" as a genuine journey by Lee Oswald; in the 1970s, HSCA investigators wrote a very lengthy but inconclusive (and long-censored) report about the trip; and independent JFK researchers have studied and debated the subject for many years without any success whatsoever.

Here's the thing:

Those who take "the Mexico City trip" seriously, on its own merits, as a "real" and intrinsically "meaningful" event in its own right, are damned fools. In reality, "Mexico City" was never *about* Mexico City, nor about Lee Oswald, nor the CIA, nor the FPCC, nor Cubela, nor Kostikov – nor about any other "still-undisclosed covert operations" [*sic*]!

Rather, it was all about setting up a series of events (and generating a paper trail "documenting" those events) in order to successfully *freeze Robert Kennedy immediately after JFK's upcoming assassination in Dallas. (*Author's exclusive original discovery.)

This was the true motivation behind Oswald's alleged Mexican sojourn:[842]
Freezing Bobby.
Freezing Bobby.
Freezing Bobby.[843]
Not to "set up" Lee Oswald himself for the upcoming JFK assassination;
Not to embarrass or destroy the Fair Play for Cuba Committee;
Not to send Lee to Cuba in order to subsequently incriminate Fidel Castro;
Not to get Lee to Cuba in order to assassinate Fidel Castro;
Not to lay the groundwork for an American invasion of Cuba;
Not to create a justification for a nuclear war with the Soviets;
None of the above.
The Mexico City "trip" wasn't even about Lee Harvey Oswald – at all![844]
*It was all about freezing Bobby Kennedy **after** the JFK assassination.*[845]

There is further intriguing evidence of *additional* efforts by the plotters to tie Robert Kennedy directly to Lee Oswald himself – efforts which began no later than 1962 and which continued well into the 1960s, even after as the Johnson Commission's superficial "investigation" ended. But on November 24th, 1963, *Rolando Cubela* (***not*** Lee Oswald!) was the supposed "link" [*sic*] which demonstrated to Bobby Kennedy that, *for the moment,* he was facing an overwhelming – indeed, likely insurmountable – task in aggressively seeking the truth about Dallas.[846]

The following day, November 25th, Robert Kennedy's subordinate Nicholas Katzenbach sent an infamous memorandum to LBJ's subordinate, Bill Moyers. Sickeningly, the memo declared that it was imperative that the American public be convinced that Lee Oswald killed JFK and did so alone.

It is a disgusting, cynical and appalling document.

Some researchers have leapt prematurely to the conclusion that the Katzenbach memo was actually RFK addressing LBJ through subordinates.

But the reality is that Robert Kennedy plainly was *not functioning normally* on the weekend of the JFK assassination. And to date, there is no available evidence that Robert Kennedy himself initiated, suggested, dictated, drafted or otherwise authored the Katzenbach memo.

---

[842] Author's exclusive original discovery.

[843] Author's exclusive original discovery.

[844] Author's exclusive original discovery.

[845] Author's exclusive original discovery.

[846] Author's exclusive original discovery.

Nor is there any proof thus far that Nicholas Katzenbach created and sent that odious November 25th memo at Robert Kennedy's personal direction, command, order, suggestion or "request."

In fact, the Katzenbach memo actually echoes comments made on the *previous* day, November 24th, by none other than two of Bobby's longtime *nemeses* – the thoroughly criminal Lyndon Johnson and the thoroughly corrupt and reptilian FBI Director, J. Edgar Hoover – plus LBJ aide Bill Moyers and Nicholas Katzenbach himself.[847]

But had RFK either proposed *or* even reluctantly "approved" that criminally cynical memo from Katzenbach to Moyers, then it represented Bobby's ill-advised, *temporary* (and terribly *premature*) white flag of surrender.

Lyndon Johnson's sinister trap had been sprung.

* * *

Yet within three days of his murdered brother's solemn state funeral on November 25th, a shattered Robert Kennedy had finally regained his emotional footing.

It is true that, *unbeknownst to the attorney general,* the two most important pieces of evidence in the entire case – the authentic original wounds on President Kennedy's body (inflicted in Dealey Plaza at 12:30 p.m. CST on Friday, November 22nd), and the true "camera original" Zapruder film of the assassination (created at the same time) – had already been promptly and irretrievably *disfigured* and *altered irredeemably* in order to eliminate and suppress the shocking proof of criminal conspiracy which they contained.

Yet by Thanksgiving Day (Thursday, November 28th, 1963), Bobby possessed *another* powerful piece of incriminating and revelatory evidence from November 22nd.

It was fully intact evidence – and it was extremely damning.

Army Captain Cecil Stoughton, the principal (but *not* the *only*) White House photographer during the Kennedy administration,[848] was unquestionably back in the nation's capital no later than November 25th, the day of President Kennedy's funeral,[849] and he had personally shown Robert Kennedy the disturbing and incriminating picture

---

[847] Gerald McKnight makes this particular point clear in his book *Breach of Trust,* which contains some useful tidbits but is otherwise *very* far off-base on most JFK assassination issues.

[848] Others included Robert Knudsen of the U. S. Navy; Harold Sellers; and Dan Lewis. In addition, their U. S. government colleague, Abbie Rowe of the National Park Service, also took many extremely valuable photos of JFK and his administration which are available through the JFK Library and the National Archives.

[849] Cecil Stoughton was definitely back in Washington in time for JFK's funeral on Monday, November 25th, 1963; indeed, Stoughton collapsed on the steps of St. Matthew's Cathedral that day. (William Manchester, *The Death of a President,* p. 584.)

of LBJ receiving a sinister congratulatory wink from his co-conspirator, Texas Congressman Al Thomas, right there aboard Air Force One in Dallas – mere *seconds* after Johnson was sworn in as JFK's illegitimate successor.

That shocking photo said it all.

It was Johnson.

It was clear as day.

It was Johnson.

So Bobby knew.

It was Johnson.

Bobby knew![850]

The frightening CIA cable of November 24th (MEXI 7045) which had served to help "freeze" Bobby temporarily was just deliberately misleading disinformation. The "Cubela-Kostikov" nonsense was just so much garbage. There **was no** Cuban plot, or Soviet plot, or "Italian-Sicilian-American-Mafia" plot to kill JFK. And Lee Oswald was *indeed* just a patsy, as he himself had truthfully proclaimed to the press in Dallas prior to being shot viciously on nationwide television.

It was Johnson.

Jesus, Mary and Joseph –

It was Johnson.

The knowledge quickened Bobby's pace and strengthened his resolve.

It was Johnson.

So that very same week, just days after JFK's funeral, RFK held a Thanksgiving meeting in Florida with Treasury Secretary C. Douglas "Doug" Dillon. (In 1963, the Treasury Department included – and oversaw – the U.S. Secret Service.) In confronting Dillon personally, Bobby Kennedy was finally back on the right track.

Moreover, soon after the RFK-Dillon meeting, Bobby's private emissary and friend William Walton[851] arrived in Moscow with a chilling secret message from the

---

[850] Author's exclusive original discovery. Previous writers have inexplicably missed the central fact that *Robert Kennedy **knew** and recognized and understood, just **days** after the assassination, that Lyndon Johnson had murdered JFK.*

Earlier authors fell for pseudo-psychological claptrap about Bobby Kennedy's supposed belief in his own alleged culpability for Dallas; or his supposed belief that "the Mafia" did it, etc. In reality, **Bobby quickly knew that LBJ was guilty** – and Bobby succeeded in keeping that stunning vital awareness *largely to himself* lest it slip out, make its way to LBJ, and *alert Johnson prematurely to Bobby's vengeful intentions toward him.* (Author's exclusive original discovery.)

[851] William Walton was an artist and a friend of President Kennedy. While ignorant people tend to stereotype artists as wan, effete individuals, Walton was a true tough guy. Prior to becoming an artist, he had been a writer and journalist – and in June 1944, he personally parachuted into Normandy along with the 82nd Airborne Division of the U. S. Army during Operation Overlord, the Allied invasion of Europe.

Attorney General himself to the Soviet government: *The JFK assassination was a large-scale **domestic American conspiracy** involving **right-wing elements.**[852]*

It was Johnson – *and Bobby knew.*[853]

But by then an alarmed Lyndon Johnson had himself *also* met with Treasury Secretary Dillon (on Friday, November 29th, the day after Bobby did),[854] and LBJ had also established the "President's Commission on the Assassination of President Kennedy" (the Johnson Commission,[855] which was stupidly and misleadingly dubbed the "Warren" Commission by America's endlessly incompetent, weak and inept corporate media hacks) via executive order on Friday, November 29th.

Thus every move that Bobby made toward the truth was quickly and deftly *countered by* Lyndon Johnson himself.[856] Unbeknownst to the American public, the two men – LBJ and RFK – were engaged in a secret and very intense game of chess, playing for the highest stakes imaginable.[857]

After Dallas, the Attorney General spent most of the following year in a marked depression. Shallow observers erroneously blamed this simply on profound grief over the loss of his beloved brother; errant writers have suggested that Robert Kennedy actually believed himself to be "morally guilty" of his brother's death (because of Bobby's relentless pursuit of a Castro assassination, which supposedly had resulted in an act of lethal "preemptive" retaliation by Fidel).

Both arguments are completely wrong.

Both arguments miss the real point.

Both arguments are oblivious to the real story.

RFK's profound, brooding melancholy was ***not*** a simple expression of deep sadness alone (although he certainly did mourn and miss JFK), ***nor*** was it the result of

---

[852] Aleksandr Fursenko and Timothy Naftali revealed William Walton's vital 1963 mission in their book *One Hell of a Gamble.*

[853] Author's exclusive original discovery.

[854] Author's exclusive original discovery. LBJ met with Treasury Secretary Douglas Dillon (who had authority over the Secret Service) in the Oval Office for 37 minutes – from 2:37 p.m. EST to 3:14 p.m. EST.

(See the LBJ Daily Diary, November 29th, 1963.)

[855] The author's correct original description.

[856] Author's exclusive original discovery.

[857] Author's exclusive original discovery. (Establishment scribe Jeff Shesol completely missed this absolutely central fact in his absurdly obtuse and laughably virginal book about the two men's lethal blood feud.)

carrying around a painful burden of presumed "personal guilt" on his own part for President Kennedy's demise.[858]

Rather, Bobby's severe and lengthy depression was the result of the acid realization that his beloved brother Jack, who had held the Oval Office for a thousand precious days, had been murdered by none other than *the man who now occupied it – Lyndon Baines Johnson.*[859]

RFK was now the literal embodiment of Hamlet on the Potomac.

As he grieved like a deeply wounded animal in those long months after the assassination, the raw and lacerated Robert Kennedy had a great deal of time to *think.*

He had plenty of time to analyze and consider many things, among them Johnson's (and Rayburn's) ugly and aggressive blackmail of JFK and Bobby at the 1960 convention, thus forcing the nominee to give LBJ a spot on the Democratic ticket. RFK also had time to ponder Johnson's behavior as Vice President, which Bobby had been in the process of exposing publicly both in Congress and in *LIFE* magazine in 1963 – information which would have resulted in Johnson's utter and permanent political ruination.

Bobby had *also* had ample time to parse and dissect and ponder Johnson's strange telephone call about secret, unspecified measures to deal with "problems of special urgency" on November 22nd.[860]

And RFK had *also* been shown the infamous photo of Congressman Al Thomas winking at a grinning LBJ, a picture taken just *seconds* after Johnson was sworn in aboard Air Force One at Love Field on November 22nd. Even Cecil Stoughton, the White House photographer who captured the chilling moment and showed Bobby a print of it, recognized it as a sinister and revealing act.

---

[858] At one point after Dallas, RFK remarked ruefully in a major understatement that he and his brother had perhaps been a wee bit too enthusiastic about certain things, particularly in the Caribbean region – a clear reference to the brothers' overwhelming (and criminal) obsession with toppling the government of Cuba. However, the ironic comment was **hardly** a declaration of RFK's belief in his own supposed culpability for the JFK assassination.

Rather, it was a tardy recognition that the world-threatening Cuban Missile Crisis was in fact precipitated by the Kennedy brothers' illegal war on Cuba. Moreover, it was a belated acknowledgment that although Fidel Castro was still in power, the world had clearly not ended as a result; shockingly, the sun somehow continued to rise each morning as if nothing were amiss. Bobby was simply admitting that his ferocious and excessive passion to oust the Cuban leader during the Kennedy administration had been woefully exaggerated and grotesquely misplaced – and more than a little absurd.

Sadly, RFK failed to mention that it was, above all, *morally wrong* and *indisputably criminal* and *utterly reprehensible.* He also failed to note that his own obsession with eliminating Castro had been cleverly used against him by LBJ.

[859] Author's exclusive original discovery.

[860] Author's exclusive original discovery. I was the first and **only** person to recognize and correctly interpret the true meaning and gargantuan importance of that call.

Thus Bobby's profound depression in 1963 and 1964 was in reality the product of his stunned realization that *Lyndon Baines Johnson* – who now held almost unlimited power and authority as "president" of the United States – *was the true author of the deed.*[861]

The awful awareness of that horror – coupled with RFK's own frustration and his maddening indecision about precisely *how* to seek and obtain justice under these extremely daunting circumstances – is what *actually* accounts for the Attorney General's profound gloom.[862]

Frankly, after Dallas, Robert Kennedy was the living embodiment of Shakespeare's *Hamlet* – a wounded man deeply torn over how to go about the daunting task of achieving justice for a beloved close relative, the victim of a heinous crime whose vicious perpetrator now held absolute power in the land.[863]

Johnson did it – and Bobby knew it.[864]

And Bobby knew it in November 1963.[865]

RFK *also* knew that in practical terms, *he would actually have to be president himself* in order to successfully go after Lyndon Johnson "hammer and tongs" for the murder of JFK. Reflecting that awareness, Bobby told William Walton in late November 1963 to inform the Soviets that he would resign as Attorney General in 1964; seek some elective office in 1964; then seek the American presidency itself subsequently.[866]

And Bobby indeed did each one of those things – *not*, as some would have you believe, out of mere self-aggrandizement or family pressure or pompous posturing or overweening personal ego, but rather *as specific elements of his own private, long-term plan to acquire the power and resources necessary to make Lyndon Baines Johnson pay for his monumental crime.*[867]

---

[861] Author's exclusive original discovery.

[862] Author's exclusive original discovery. RFK dressed almost exclusively in black suits and ties for several months after the assassination, always accompanied with a PT-109 tie clip as a tangible badge of his fierce allegiance to his murdered brother. Official White House photographs capture RFK sitting, absolutely livid, in Cabinet meetings – visibly *radiating* deep rage, completely unable to contain his smoldering fury.

[863] Author's exclusive original discovery.

[864] Author's exclusive original discovery.

[865] Author's exclusive original discovery.

[866] In the book *One Hell of a Gamble,* Aleksandr Fursenko and Timothy Naftali mentioned RFK's secret message to the Soviets (delivered via William Walton) without *any understanding whatsoever* of what that message revealed about Robert Kennedy's *personal* awareness of LBJ's direct personal culpability for the JFK assassination.

[867] Author's exclusive original discovery.

The proof came from Bobby's own lips, in person.

* * *

On the night of July 25th, 1966, Robert Kennedy spoke personally in New York with speechwriter Richard Goodwin, who raised questions about the unresolved issues of the JFK assassination. At first Bobby tried to avoid the subject, making it clear to Goodwin that the subject was *still* too painful, *still* too fresh, *still* too personally difficult for him to confront.[868]

But before going to bed for the night, RFK turned to Goodwin and said the words which would ultimately *cost him his own life* in 1968.[869]

Bobby – still emotionally unable to even *utter* the words "Dallas" or "assassination" to anyone outside his own family – began in vague terms.

Then, after making a quick and deliberately ***diversionary*** remark[870] about "organized crime" (an *absurd* red herring),[871] RFK declared that he had no power to deal with his brother's killing yet.[872]

Bobby meant, of course, not ***yet*** – that is, not as a mere *senator*.

A *junior* senator, to boot.

Just one of a hundred legislators in that body.

But as *president* . . . that would be a very different matter.

A different matter *entirely*.

---

[868] Richard Goodwin, cited in David Talbot, *Brothers,* p. 305.

[869] Author's exclusive original discovery.

Incredibly, Lifton was absolutely *stunned* when I pointed this out to him in the 2000s; Lifton confessed to me that (strangely) he had never before even *considered* the possibility that the JFK and RFK assassinations were connected! For my part, I was frankly shocked by Lifton's utterly bizarre and inexplicable *obtuseness* on the issue.

[870] Author's exclusive original discovery.

[871] Bobby Kennedy held his knowledge of LBJ's leading role in the JFK assassination – and his (Bobby's) own intentions regarding LBJ – *extremely close to the vest*. RFK fobbed off many close friends and political associates and top aides with a variety of alternate "suspects," rightly fearing that if he revealed his personal awareness of the actual truth, it would soon "leak" to Lyndon Johnson and thereby enable Johnson to prepare adequately and effectively for RFK's eventual onslaught.

Had RFK *actually* believed that "the Mafia" murdered his brother [*sic*], then he (Bobby) would have remained in office as Attorney General and personally prosecuted the mob for the assassination. Instead, *knowing that he was up against the most powerful person in the country (LBJ),* Bobby resigned his post in 1964 and ran for the Senate in order to establish an independent political base – because he knew that *Lyndon Johnson* was the actual killer of JFK. (Author's exclusive original discovery.)

[872] Richard Goodwin, cited in David Talbot, *Brothers,* p. 305.

* * *

The very worst factor that froze RFK in 1963, however – the crushing, *overwhelming* factor – was **not** the Cubela "connection," or Manuel Rodriguez Oscarberro, or the documented misdeeds of the Kennedy brothers while in office.

Those things paled into insignificance compared to the biggest factor of all.

Within days of his brother's murder, Robert Kennedy personally realized that the *actual* assassin and leader of the plot was not a lone warehouse clerk; or a band of renegade right-wing Cuban exiles; or a few disgruntled CIA officers; or a batch of violent Mafia brutes.

Bobby knew *prior to Thanksgiving 1963* that the true killer of John Fitzgerald Kennedy was none other than a Texan named Lyndon Baines Johnson.[873]

That devastating awareness – reflected in RFK's words, posture, and open fury beginning in the first days after Dallas – was what froze Bobby into inaction about JFK's bloody assassination.[874]

Stunned, grieving and woefully outgunned, Robert Kennedy lacked the evidence, the courage, the ability and the willingness to successfully go after the most powerful man on the planet in late 1963.

To try and *fail* would leave LBJ immune from any further federal prosecution for the horrible crime.

And the State of Texas plainly wasn't going to prosecute one if its own.

That meant that Bobby had two and *only* two genuine options: to somehow maneuver his way onto the 1964 Democratic ticket as Johnson's running mate, then *kill* (or otherwise oust) LBJ soon after the 1964 election; or, alternatively, to conserve his own energies, keep silent, bide his time, seek the White House himself in 1968 and then go after the brutal Texan "hammer and tongs" – armed with the massive powers of the American presidency.

LBJ cleverly forestalled the first of those options by refusing to name RFK as his 1964 running mate.

That left only the second possibility open to Bobby.

To effectively and successfully prosecute and convict Lyndon Baines Johnson for the assassination of President Kennedy, RFK would have to go "all the way."

All the way to the Oval Office.

Nothing less would suffice if justice were to ever be obtained.

*Bobby would have to actually **be** president in order to **avenge** the murder of the president.*

---

[873] Author's exclusive original discovery.

[874] Author's exclusive original discovery.

That was the real reason RFK ran in 1968 – not Vietnam, not civil rights, not societal ills or any of the other false, idiotic, superficial reasons bandied about by ignorant observers for decades.

Bobby ran in 1968 **in order to prosecute LBJ** *and achieve justice for JFK.*[875]

Meanwhile, in 1964, Robert Kennedy would have to watch and endure the nauseating charade of an "investigation" [*sic*] by a federal "commission" which was nothing but the bureaucratic creature of the killer himself.

---

[875] Author's exclusive original discovery.

Earl Warren was the Chief Justice of the Supreme Court in 1963.

Weak and gullible, Warren was buffaloed into heading
Lyndon Johnson's "Commission" on the JFK assassination.
There was *no* genuine governmental investigation of the crime.

Chapter Thirty-Two:
The Johnson Commission

"The beginning of wisdom
is to call things
by their proper name."

– Modern paraphrase of Confucius

"I want you to do
whatever is needed
to clean this up."

– Lyndon Baines Johnson
November 22nd, 1963

"This is a very explosive thing
and it could be a very dangerous thing
for the country . . ."

– Lyndon Baines Johnson
November 28th, 1963

"These things do not just 'happen.'
*They are **made** to happen."*

– John Fitzgerald Kennedy

An assassination plot always has **two** targets: the body of the *victim,* and the body *politic.*[876]

That means that one of the targets of the JFK assassination was **you.**[877]

And you have been targeted over and over and over again, *for several decades,* with a ***provably** false* version of the event – a lie authored by your own government.

---

[876] Author's exclusive original insight.

[877] Author's exclusive original insight.

That fraudulent version was produced by, and publicized through, a panel literally created by *the very same man who personally led the plot* to murder John Fitzgerald Kennedy.

It's about damned time you understood that.

* * *

Criminal conspiracy?

In America?

But . . . but . . . but what about the Warren Commission?

So goes the plaintive wail of credulous coincidence theorists.

What about the Warren Commission, huh?

First of all, this needs to be clearly understood:

*There **was no** Warren Commission.*

Ever.

No such body ever existed.

No such body was ever formed or established or created.

Ever.

The organization which came to be known – *colloquially and erroneously* – as "The Warren Commission" [*sic*] was no such thing at all.

It was, in point of fact, *the Johnson Commission* – the Lyndon Baines Johnson Commission – and no amount of awkward, evasive contortion or verbal gymnastics or ludicrous denialism can ever change that ugly fundamental fact.[878]

The official name of the small group that was created by LBJ on November 29th, 1963 – ostensibly to "investigate" JFK's murder – was in fact "The President's Commission on the Assassination of President Kennedy."

The *President's* Commission.

Not the "Warren" Commission; the *President's* Commission.

Lyndon Baines Johnson's Commission.

The Johnson Commission.[879]

The fact that the group *came to be referred to* (glibly and erroneously) as the "Warren" Commission by the lazy and totally inept corporate media of the United States only served to mask and obscure the genuinely vital and central fact that in

---

[878] Author's exclusive original discovery. Certain lesser JFK assassination researchers who are blindly obsessed with the CIA (and who mistakenly believe that the notorious Agency was the driving force behind the murder of JFK) have tried to label the commission "The Dulles Commission," because of the former CIA director's active role thereon. But Allen Welsh Dulles did not create, select, fund, pay or oversee the commission – nor did Dulles initiate, direct or execute the JFK assassination. A man named *Lyndon Baines Johnson* did.

[879] Author's exclusive original discovery.

reality it was a panel formed by, selected by, paid for by, and reporting directly to *Lyndon Baines Johnson himself.*

Not to the United States; not to Congress; not to the press; not to the American people and the world, but to one man:

Lyndon Baines Johnson.

The fact that the corporate media and the American public quickly and falsely dubbed The President's Commission on the Assassination of President Kennedy "the 'Warren' Commission" [*sic*] was a monumental failure – an atrocious linguistic shortcut that served to conveniently distance Lyndon Johnson from suspicion in his predecessor's murder; to conveniently distance Lyndon Johnson from his deliberate creation and control and funding of the Commission; and to fundamentally mislead the public by drastically clouding its perceptions about both the nature of the crime itself and the nature (and actual purpose) of the so-called "investigation."[880]

* * *

Anyone who thinks that U. S. governmental commissions are honest groups of brilliant, dedicated, selfless investigators deeply devoted to ferreting out the truth is . . . well . . . *several sandwiches short of a picnic,* intellectually speaking.

If you believe the conclusions and findings of governmental commissions, then you know *very little about government* – and *very little about commissions.*

For the naïve, the uninitiated, and the just plain stupid, here's a pro tip:

Government commissions are empaneled in order to *hide, obscure* and *minimize* the truth – **not** to uncover it.

The President's Commission on the Assassination of President Kennedy was no exception to that rule; indeed, it is the absolute *epitome* of that rule.

One of the most damning facts about the President's Commission is this:

Lyndon Johnson refused to testify in person to his own commission!

LBJ also refused to answer *any* questions from the commission – even *written* questions – *under oath.*

In 1964, Lyndon Baines Johnson was a very careful man when it came to saying or writing *anything* that might incriminate him in the worst political murder in American history.[881]

Indeed, when the Kennedy family (in the persons of Jackie and Bobby) chose author William Manchester to write a book about the assassination, LBJ refused to cooperate in the slightest. White House memos are covered with Lyndon Johnson's

---

[880] It was as misleading and destructive as many of Lifton's horrid, grossly inaccurate phrases and nicknames and decidedly odd "code words" for various aspects of the JFK assassination.

[881] That changed by 1971, as I myself discovered exclusively and as I reveal later in this book.

angry scrawl – furiously and very nervously rejecting any possibility of an interview with Manchester.[882]

"I'm not under any obligation to Manchester," wrote Johnson icily across a memo from top aide Jack Valenti.[883]

Johnson had very good reason to fear an interview – any *real* interview – on the subject.

Manchester was working for the Kennedys.

And Robert Kennedy was a very intelligent man.

RFK was in a position to provide William Manchester, *in advance,* with specific questions that might cleverly elicit a damaging admission (or an inadvertent revelation, or an unintended, psychologically revealing response) from LBJ.[884]

RFK was in a position to provide *others* with specific questions as well.

* * *

Despite the fact that they were devastated and still in shock, the sophisticated members of the Kennedy camp would not be persuaded easily by LBJ's false cover story concerning the JFK assassination ("Castro did it, so therefore we must do everything possible to cover up that fact in order to avoid inexorable public pressure for a military strike on Cuba that could lead to general nuclear war with Russia and millions of American casualties").

But the craven and pliable Chief Justice of the Supreme Court, Earl Warren, was another matter entirely. Johnson knew that he could bend the weak-spirited Warren to his will – and within a mere *week* of the JFK assassination, LBJ had successfully done so. Shamelessly conjuring up the specter of a devastating nuclear holocaust that supposedly moved the aging judge to tears, Johnson convinced the Chief Justice to head a "blue-ribbon presidential commission" – and to suppress what had really happened to this country.

Earl Warren actually admitted as much, and he did so quite explicitly – first secretly, then publicly.

On January 20th, 1964, at the initial Commission staff meeting, Earl Warren addressed those present and described his late November 1963 conversations with LBJ. The Chief Justice described those talks in startling detail, then declared that "The

---

[882] Johnson, the Texan who was criminally occupying the Oval Office, twice refused to talk to the Kennedys' authorized scribe. Moreover, LBJ refused to release Air Force radio transcripts or recordings to Manchester, either. (William Manchester, *The Death of a President,* pp. xiii and 3; see also Jack Valenti's memorandum of August 31st, 1965.)

[883] LBJ response to a Jack Valenti memorandum of August 31st, 1965.

[884] Author's exclusive original discovery.

President convinced him that *"this was an occasion on which **actual conditions** had to override **general principles**."*[885]

LBJ's chilling (and deeply deceitful) words to Warren in November 1963 are yet another graphic and authoritative piece of proof that a deliberate criminal conspiracy – a *plot,* not a "lone nut" – actually took the life of John F. Kennedy.

The true leader of that murderous plot, of course, was none other than *Lyndon Baines Johnson himself.*

As LBJ personally told Earl Warren, what he (LBJ) wanted Warren to quash most of all were various "rumors" – particularly, the most damning one *"attributing the assassination to a faction within the government wishing to see the Presidency assumed by President Johnson."*[886]

There ***was*** in fact such a group – but contrary to the laughably puerile myth clung to by the least intelligent researchers out there, it was ***not*** some anonymous generic cabal giving orders to a hapless little pawn and gofer named LBJ.

Rather, the traitorous faction within the U. S. government was itself led and directed by none other than the powerful and aggressive Lyndon Baines Johnson, who was the indisputable head of the JFK assassination plot.[887]

In simplest terms:

Lyndon Johnson *wanted to make Lyndon Johnson president.*

And he did.

So LBJ's little "talk" with Earl Warren boiled down to this:

The author of the crime told the Chief Justice of the United States to head a "commission" that would exculpate *the author of the crime.*[888]

* * *

The false claim has been repeated for decades that the Johnson Commission was an intellectually "virginal" group which was completely "unaware" of the numerous U. S. government murder plots against Fidel Castro, and thus also unaware of any potential "motive" for Castro to have ordered, directed, influenced or been in any way involved with the assassination of John Kennedy.

Yet plainly the Johnson Commission *did* know (or suspect) something, because the Commission actually dispatched a lawyer on a secret cloak-and-dagger mission to meet personally with *El Líder Máximo* on a boat in the waters off Cuba and

[885] Memo by Johnson Commission Assistant Counsel Melvin A. Eisenberg, February 17th, 1964.

[886] Memo by Johnson Commission Assistant Counsel Melvin A. Eisenberg, February 17th, 1964.

[887] Author's exclusive original discovery.

[888] Author's exclusive original discovery.

confront Castro face-to-face with the baseless suspicion that he (Castro) might have been behind the death of his American counterpart, JFK.[889]

The irony is pathetic and disgusting:

The Johnson Commission confronted the man who ***didn't*** do it – Fidel Castro.

But much more importantly, the Commission *never* truly confronted the most important, dangerous and obvious suspect of all: the brutal man who illegitimately became "president" upon John Kennedy's brutal murder, *Lyndon Baines Johnson.*

* * *

The craven champions of willful ignorance in the Establishment corporate press immediately lauded and repeated the fraudulent "findings" of the Johnson Commission as if they constituted a sacrosanct new political gospel. Even several decades later, a variety of despicable gutless wonders[890] debased themselves completely as they submissively regurgitated and amplified the grotesque perversion of history which is the Johnson Report.

Be very clear:

The Johnson Report is a work of *fiction* – and not "honestly mistaken" fiction, or "accidentally erroneous" fiction, but *tendentious* fiction.

Conscious fiction.

Deliberate fiction.[891]

---

[889] The attorney, Assistant Counsel William Thaddeus ("Bill") Coleman Jr., somehow "neglected" to mention this momentous meeting *even in his own memoir.* (So much for "truth" and "history.")

Coleman's efforts – and his long silence – did not go unrewarded; the utterly slimy Gerald Ford, who as a Johnson Commission member spied for the FBI and made deliberate alterations to the record of JFK's wounds in order to boost the false Single Bullet Theory, later (as President of the United States in the 1970s) made good ol' *Bill Coleman* the Secretary of Transportation. Yes, ***that*** Bill Coleman. In America, crime ***always*** pays.

[890] Unsurprisingly, these witless latter-day scribes include former *New York Times* reporter Phil Shenon, who reported the Bill Coleman-Fidel Castro meeting in *A Cruel and Shocking Act,* but failed to understand or explain its true meaning and context. Like the Johnson Report itself, Shenon's misleadingly subtitled, weak and slipshod book is notable principally for the gargantuan quantity of what it ***leaves out,*** not for what it reveals.

Pro tip: If you have a choice between (A) *watching paint dry* or (B) examining the endlessly evasive and execrable ennui-inducing emanations of Establishment eunuchs, choose the paint.

[891] The Johnson Commission was ***not*** a swell group of innocent fellows who were simply "deceived" by (perpetually unnamed and unidentified) "plotters," as Lambert & Lifton foolishly argued; rather, it was a ***government*** panel doing a ***government*** job ***for the government.*** And the Commission's members knew damn well what was expected of them – from Earl Warren on down to the lowliest staffer. Eisenberg's 1964 memo makes that painfully, undeniably clear. *Crystal* clear.

The Johnson Commission was *not* a serious, vigorous, independent investigation of the murder of the head of state; rather, it was simply *a work-for-hire project* which was created for, and delivered to, the very client who had *commissioned* it and *paid for it* in the first place: one Lyndon Baines Johnson, from a ranch near the appropriately named town of *Stonewall,* Texas.[892]

The Johnson Commission was not naively "fooled" or innocently "deceived" by the killers' violent abuse of President Kennedy's corpse, as Patricia Lambert & Samuel Lifton bizarrely argued several decades ago in the 1981 book *Best Evidence.*

Rather, the Johnson Commission carried out its true mandate of effectively *protecting Lyndon Johnson and his key allies in the U. S. federal government from ever facing responsibility* for the dastardly crime which they had committed.

That was the goal from the outset; and that was the inevitable result.

The ugly, despicable behavior of commission attorney Arlen Specter *alone* makes it undeniably clear that the entire Johnson Commission staff knew *exactly* what their marching orders were.

The members of the Commission and their staff constructed an insulting *caricature* of the truth which bears about as much resemblance to reality as a sawhorse does to an actual horse.

If Earl Warren had truly cared about John Kennedy, he would have found out – and publicly revealed – who actually killed the president.

Instead, Warren merely presided over a fraudulent exercise.

The Johnson Commission spoke to Lee Oswald's mother – but it did *not* investigate the top echelons of the U. S. Air Force.

The Johnson Commission spoke to former Marine Corps colleagues of Lee Oswald – but it did *not* investigate the direct involvement and complicity of many of President Kennedy's SS bodyguards.

The Johnson Commission spoke to *postal service* officials – but it did *not* investigate the U. S. Army's 1st Armored Division.

The Johnson Commission obtained a photo of Marina Oswald's *bracelet* – but it did *not* investigate senior officers of the U. S. Navy.

The Johnson Commission even collected and published photos of Lee Oswald's *pubic hair* – but it did *not* investigate what Lyndon Baines Johnson had been doing and saying in July 1960.

Or in April 1963.

Or in November 1963.

The Johnson Commission's members and staff attorneys made a show of interviewing many witnesses, but the government's craven crew asked bizarre and

---

[892] As should be crystal clear to you by now, the "Warren" Commission was, in reality, the Whorin' Commission.

grossly misleading questions; *refused* to ask penetrating questions; deliberately *suppressed* important lines of inquiry; and actively *intimidated* a number of witnesses.

Most importantly of all, the dishonest frauds on the Johnson Commission did **not** interview all of the truly *pertinent* witnesses.

The Commission did not speak to scores of **key** witnesses – including the Air Force crews of the presidential jet and various other vital USAF aircraft, as *I* did during my own lengthy, independent, extraordinarily productive and successful investigation.

I, Sean Fetter – *just one man, without a staff or a budget or even a secretary!* – found and revealed vital central truths that the Johnson Commission in the 1960s (and the HSCA in the 1970s, and the ARRB in the 1990s) didn't even *look for,* let alone *discover.*

And I uncovered what bloated national corporate media behemoths never even dared to seek.

The old adage is quite correct:

If you want the job done right, you have to do it yourself.

And so I did.

* * *

One of the most interesting and ironic aspects of the JFK case is the stunning fact that the Johnson Commission's accumulated *evidence* (some of it presented in 26 volumes of "Hearings and Exhibits," but in other cases buried and ignored by the government) disproves the Johnson Commission's own *Report!*

Many people are, incredibly, still unaware that the official conclusions in the formal Johnson Report itself (published as one single volume) *are not supported by* the evidence in the 26 *additional* volumes of data that supposedly "back up" that report.

That's right: to put it bluntly, *the* **work** *of the Commission disproves the* **conclusions** *of the Commission.*

It's worth repeating:

The **work** of the Johnson Commission disproves the **conclusions** of the Johnson Commission.[893]

The stark truth is this:

The Johnson Report has more holes in it than the average kitchen colander.

While a great deal of additional, independent evidence has since been discovered to further disprove the official "lone gunman" fairy tale to which pathetic coincidence theorists still cling, the fact is that the Johnson Commission received from a few courageous witnesses, and had in its possession, *abundant* evidence

---

[893] You will learn much more of this in a subsequent book of mine; the intellectual effect upon you will metaphorically approximate the intensity of a shotgun blast to the face. (Fair warning.)

demonstrating a large criminal conspiracy in the JFK assassination – but the Commission deliberately chose not to address it.

At least the Commission didn't burn it all, fortunately.

Yet even the *published* portion of the "record" (available in the 26 volumes of Hearings and Exhibits) actually *contradicts the government's formal conclusions.*

How is that possible?

What you don't know is that the Johnson Commission gathered a great deal of highly important and very illuminating *proof of criminal conspiracy* during its brief existence – but in its final Report, it selectively quoted only certain innocuous pieces of the overall record in order to fabricate a deliberately false narrative that carefully avoided *reality* (meaning, *criminal conspiracy*) like the plague.[894]

Early on, commission chairman Earl Warren sanctimoniously told his staff that "Truth is your only client," but both Warren himself – and the arrogant lawyers who actually conducted the Commission's "investigation" – all knew better.

Actual conditions have to override general principles, boys.

Push a false narrative, but make it look good.

The fate of the nation is at stake.

Suppress, ignore or trivialize all contradictory data.

Don't let the disturbing truth see the light of day.

Kill dangerous narratives.

Avoid trouble at all costs.

Truth is trouble.

The Commission's *real* client was Lyndon Baines Johnson, who reluctantly created the commission *only* in order to head off growing pressure for independent, in-depth *Congressional* investigations which might (even accidentally) turn up disturbing evidence of the plot which in fact murdered JFK.

The creation of the Johnson Commission was announced by LBJ on November 29th, 1963 – just a week after the JFK assassination. Its seven official members included longtime friends of Johnson. Incredibly, LBJ even appointed veteran conspirator Allen Dulles, the former OSS operative and CIA Director *whom JFK had fired after the failed 1961 Bay of Pigs invasion.*[895]

---

[894] The same cowardly technique has been used by pathetic, longtime Establishment errand boys like Gerald "Poseur" Posner, Vincent "Vinny the Bug" Bugliosi and Phil "The Shill" Shenon, all of whom avoided dealing honestly with central JFK assassination issues and evidence in their weak, boring, sophomoric, laughably demented tomes.

[895] LBJ himself (in a 1969 interview) falsely claimed that it was Bobby Kennedy who urged him to appoint Allen Dulles to the Warren Commission. But since Allen Dulles himself was the architect of JFK's greatest humiliation in office (the Bay of Pigs) – and since Dulles spent considerable time overtly and clumsily attempting to convince fellow commissioners that the president's killing was *not* a plot – the suggestion that RFK "pushed" LBJ to add Dulles to the Warren Commission is ludicrous. Indeed, Bobby

So let's review:

The Commission was *created* by Lyndon Johnson.

The Commission's members were *chosen* by Lyndon Johnson.

The Commission owed its very *existence* to Lyndon Johnson.

The Commission was *funded* by Lyndon Johnson.[896]

The Commission would deliver its *Report* to Lyndon Johnson.

So . . . who exactly was the Commission's real client?

Surely you can figure that out.

Tellingly, Lyndon Johnson gave the President's Commission – *his own commission* – a curiously strange and truncated lifespan of just a few months.[897]

A few months to investigate the murder of a President.

Months.

Why not a full year?

Why not *twelve* months?

Why any fewer?

Why pick such an arbitrary and obviously insufficient limit?

Indeed, why impose *any* limit at all?

Why not let the commission continue its work, unimpeded, *until it discovered the truth* – whether that ended up taking three weeks, three months, three years or three decades?

Why the rush?

Was that "just a coincidence"?

No.

Hardly.

But the answer isn't revealed by any "secret government file"; it's revealed by a simple glance at *the calendar.*

In November 1963, Lyndon Johnson pushed Earl Warren for a rapid conclusion to the Commission's work *because he, LBJ, was going to run for a full term as President in the 1964 U.S. presidential election.*

And of course, that election would be held in November 1964.

---

even arranged to have Allen Dulles's *sister* fired from a federal job, so angry was RFK at the damage that Dulles's failed Bay of Pigs invasion plot had done to JFK's reputation at the very outset of Camelot.

[896] LBJ's Executive Order 11130, which established the Johnson Commission, explicitly specified – *in writing* – that "Necessary expenses of the Commission may be paid from the 'Emergency Fund for the President.'" Lyndon Johnson was the new (albeit totally illegitimate) "president"; therefore, by definition, Lyndon Johnson controlled the fund. The so-called "Warren" Commission [*sic*] was, in every possible sense, *a Lyndon Baines Johnson production.*

[897] At LBJ's urging, Earl Warren explicitly stated that he wanted the Commission's work wrapped up by June 1964 – well before *the traditional Labor Day start of the national presidential election campaign.*

Johnson demanded that the final Report be completed and delivered to him as soon as possible *because he wanted an "official certification" from a "blue-ribbon" panel declaring (falsely) that he had **not** been involved in the assassination of his predecessor.*[898]

And he wanted that certification in his hands *well before* the campaign kicked off, and *well before* American voters actually went to the polls in November 1964.

In other words, LBJ didn't want the bloody specter of guilt and treason and utter illegitimacy hanging over him during the 1964 presidential election itself.

He wanted to be publicly "exonerated," in advance of the election, of knowingly committing the very crime which had made him President.

Plainly, the Commission's *actual* client was not "the truth," or even "the American people."

The Commission's client was *Lyndon Baines Johnson himself.*

Hence the rush.[899]

* * *

As William O'Neill deftly noted in a 1971 book, the actual *investigative* phase of the Commission's brief ten-month lifespan only lasted *ten weeks.*[900]

Moreover, few of the seven titular "commissioners" participated regularly; fewer still actually attended witness interviews! The entire President's Commission rarely met as a body. The actual work of the Commission was handed off to a relatively small staff of young, ambitious, *breathtakingly* unscrupulous attorneys[901] who were certainly not interested in bucking the Establishment, making waves, or pursuing any dangerous, inconvenient truths. They clearly understood their *actual* role, and they fulfilled it.

---

[898] Author's exclusive original discovery.

[899] Commission member (and future president of the United States) Gerald Ford was an FBI informant, and he secretly told the Bureau in December 1963 that Earl Warren was pushing to have the panel's work concluded "prior to July, 1964, when the Presidential campaigns will begin to get hot." (Joe Stephens, "Ford Told FBI of Skeptics on Warren Commission," *Washington Post,* August 8, 2008.)

N.B.: The Chief Justice was not a politician under suspicion; LBJ *was.* The pre-presidential campaign "deadline" was ***Lyndon Johnson's*** urgent imperative – not Earl Warren's.

[900] William O'Neill's book *Coming Apart* did not address the JFK assassination itself, but the book did devote a brief and pointed section to effective exposure of the massive and undeniable *failings* of the Commission.

[901] I duly recognize that the term "unscrupulous attorneys" is plainly (and quite unnecessarily) redundant.

Thus the Johnson Commission's staff attorneys deliberately suppressed certain reports and other data; refused to publish key evidence;[902] verbally insulted and intimidated several witnesses;[903] repeatedly altered and misreported witness testimony;[904] and refused to call a number of vital witnesses.

Moreover, a number of the original stenographic tapes documenting what people actually said to the Commission have been destroyed.[905]

Commission attorneys argued with witnesses who had dangerous information; constantly *interrupted* and *changed the subject* when evidence of conspiracy came up in witness testimony; went "off-the-record" repeatedly during depositions to ensure that certain key evidence of criminal conspiracy was never mentioned or included in the "official" record; illegally coached and rehearsed witnesses; engaged in twisted, tortuous and leading questioning based on false and unproven hypothetical assumptions; and otherwise engaged in a host of criminal activities which should have resulted in (A) their immediate disbarment and (B) their immediate arrest for *obstruction of justice.*

That, ladies and gentlemen, is the "basis" of the formal Report findings.

Behold, America: *your tax dollars at work.*[906]

---

[902] The Sibert & O'Neill FBI report on the JFK autopsy – the first true smoking gun to emerge in the JFK case – was not even *mentioned* in the 888-page Warren Report itself, and it was not published in the Commission's 26 "supporting" volumes of "Hearings and Exhibits," either.

Lordy – that must be just a goldang *coincidence* or somethin' . . .

[903] See, for example, Barry Ernest's book *The Girl on the Stairs,* which tells the true story of TSBD employee (and important Dealey Plaza witness) Victoria Adams.

[904] Numerous witnesses were shocked to see the false *printed* versions of what they had supposedly said.

[905] Barry Ernest, *The Girl on the Stairs,* p. 329.

[906] Commission depositions of Parkland Hospital doctors were a prime example of this outrageous behavior; instead of simply asking those doctors *what had happened* and *what they had observed,* Commission attorneys would routinely say bizarre and misleading things like the following absurdity (USAF veteran and staff attorney Arlen Specter, speaking to Dr. Carrico):

*"Permit me to add some facts [sic] which I shall ask you to **assume as being true [sic]** for purposes of having you express an opinion.*

*First of all, **assume** that the President was struck by a 6.5 mm copper-jacketed bullet [sic] from a rifle having a muzzle velocity of **approximately** 2,000 feet per second at a time when the President was **approximately** 160 to 250 feet from the weapon [sic], with the President being struck from the rear [sic] at a downward angle [sic] of **approximately** 45 degrees [sic], being struck on the upper right posterior thorax [sic] just above the upper border of the scapula [sic] 14 centimeters [sic] from the tip of the right acromion process [sic] and 14 centimeters below the tip of the right mastoid process [sic].*

***Assume further** that the missile passed through the body of the President [sic] striking no bones [sic], traversing the neck [sic] and sliding between the large muscles in the posterior aspect of the President's body [sic] through a fascia channel [sic] without violating the pleural cavity [sic], but bruising only the apex of the right pleural cavity and bruising the most apical portion of the right lung [sic], then causing*

* * *

One of the most extraordinary and ugly things about the Johnson Commission is that its infamous Report – literally, the federal government's false and illegitimate "official story" concerning the JFK assassination – was in fact *constructed and written by the United States Air Force.*[907]

Yes, you read that correctly:

The U. S. Air Force wrote the official story of the JFK assassination.[908]

Not the Commission; the Air Force!

The Johnson Report was **not** written by Earl Warren – nor by any other member of the principal seven-man panel.

A few Commission staff attorneys did "participate" in creating it.

But the fundamental truth is shocking and deeply offensive:

The majority of the Johnson Report – and indeed, the very early outline which guided its construction and sequence – was in fact the work of *a longtime USAF historian named Alfred Goldberg,* who was a USAAF veteran and was still a member of the U. S. Air Force Reserve.[909]

Earl Warren obtained Goldberg's "services" on loan from the United States Air Force's Historical Services Division, where Goldberg was a senior "historian."[910]

---

a hematoma to the right of the larynx which you have described, and creating a jagged wound in the trachea [sic], then exiting [sic] precisely at the point where you observe the puncture wound to exist.

Now based on those facts [sic] was the appearance of the wound consistent with being an exit wound [sic]?"

[907] Author's exclusive original discovery.

[908] Author's exclusive original discovery.

[909] Goldberg did not formally leave the Air Force until 1978, when he retired as a colonel – fifteen years *after* the JFK assassination.

[910] Alfred Goldberg was explicitly, vehemently opposed to ever acknowledging the **existence** of a criminal conspiracy. After finishing his work on the intellectually insulting rubbish known as the "Warren" [sic] Report, Goldberg moved on to work at the odious RAND Corporation and then joined the Office of the Secretary of Defense for literally *decades* – a full 34 years – and there, he ultimately had a hand in writing the "official" report about the September 11th (2001) attack at the Pentagon.

How incredibly *convenient* for the U. S. government. Quite a "career" of "service." Strikingly odd "bookends."

As late as October 2019, the centenarian Goldberg was *still* stubbornly pushing the official 1964 government line about the JFK assassination in a public appearance with other Commission alumni. The program was presented by the United States Capitol Historical Society (!) and was "supported by" by a drug store lobbying organization.

According to the Department of Defense itself, Dr. Alfred Goldberg, USAF Reserve, functioned "as a historical advisor and as **co-author** and **co-editor** of the Warren [*sic*] Commission Report."[911]

Be very clear on this point:

The American military – in the person of *a USAF historian* – largely created the grotesque "official story" about the assassination of America's chief of state.[912]

The so-called "Warren" Report (which was and is, in reality, the *Johnson Report*) was not just fictitious propaganda from the American government; it was (and is) fictitious propaganda *from the American **military**.*[913]

And in a so-called "republic" like the United States, which is supposedly run by elected civilians, that is horrendously disturbing and completely unacceptable.

Be very clear on this point:

Lyndon Johnson's USAF military allies wrote the official report "exonerating" him.[914]

Moreover, Alfred Goldberg submitted his proposed outline of the Report *in advance of* the Commission's so-called "investigation"!

There are other direct and disturbing Commission links to the U. S. Air Force, as well:

LBJ *nearly* appointed USAF General Lauris Norstad – Curtis LeMay's and Thomas Power's former WWII boss – to the Johnson Commission.[915] As Supreme Allied Commander in Europe (SACEUR), General Norstad had drawn President Kennedy's ire and suspicion for his dangerous attitudes relating to the control (or lack thereof) of American nuclear weapons in Europe. JFK *replaced* General Norstad as SACEUR in January 1963, and Norstad retired at the very end of the same year – a month after JFK's violent assassination.[916]

The odious and disgusting Arlen Specter – a slimy, criminally dishonest, deeply corrupt and sickeningly sinister lawyer who was one of the most notorious staff

---

Goldberg's latter-day intellectual cousin, Phil Shenon, went from writing a book about the 9/11 Commission to writing an asinine tome praising the staff of the Johnson Commission. (Nauseating stuff, but lucrative work if you can get it – and if you can stomach doing it.)

[911] Goldberg profile piece by the Historical Office, Office of the Secretary of Defense, online.

[912] Author's exclusive original discovery.

[913] Author's exclusive original discovery. For the record, *Under Cover of Night* proves beyond cavil or question the utter falsity of the "official story."

[914] Author's exclusive original discovery.

[915] LBJ's old mentor, Senator Richard Russell, suggested General Norstad for this role.

[916] Edward Lansdale, a USAF general and CIA operative, retired from the Air Force shortly *before* the JFK assassination.

attorneys on the Johnson Commission – was another vital U. S. Air Force link to the LBJ panel.

Specter was a USAF veteran and had actually been an agent of AFOSI – the Air Force Office of Special Investigations. Specter went out of his way to ask grotesquely leading questions of Parkland Hospital medical personnel; strenuously avoided all discussion of pertinent points proving conspiracy; deliberately intimidated important witnesses; actively obstructed justice; suborned perjury; and actively, deliberately dissuaded Dr. Ronald Jones (among others) from voicing the dangerous truth about the *frontal* source of shots which *actually* struck President Kennedy.[917]

Moreover, USAF veteran Arlen Specter was the most vocal proponent of the false "Single Bullet Theory," and he *personally* blackmailed the Commission into accepting that lie.

Richard M. Mosk, the youngest staffer on the Commission, actually joined the panel *directly from the U. S. Air Force!* Mosk "volunteered" to join the Commission; leveraged his father's acquaintance with Earl Warren; and, decades later, wrote bizarre articles mindlessly and pompously praising the Johnson Commission's foul "work."[918]

* * *

The Johnson Report tells a story – not the ***true*** story, but "a" story.

In fact, the Report tells a *fictitious* story – and in doing so it brazenly libels a dead Marine Corps veteran who was shot down on live national television.

As one brilliant wit put it in a pithy, decades-later "review" of the despicable Johnson Report:

"The story you are about to read is false. The names have been left unchanged to slander the innocent."[919]

No finer assessment of the Johnson Commission's Report has ever been written by anyone, anywhere.

Commission members did what was expected of them: they exculpated a guilty man (Lyndon Johnson), and they demonized an innocent man (Lee Oswald).

Truth was not their client; *truth was not even the object of the exercise.*[920]

---

[917] Arlen Specter's ugly (and criminal) comments to Dr. Jones – made in a hallway, after deposing Jones in March 1964 – are related in Allen Childs, MD (editor), *We Were There,* p. 157.

[918] See, for example, the ludicrous piece called "Truth Was Our Only Client" [*sic*], in *Stanford Magazine,* November/December 2013.

[919] The words were penned by someone calling himself "Baron Wrangle," writing on Amazon.com on August 5th, 2016.

[920] Author's exclusive original discovery.

In reality, *providing legal cover for Lyndon Baines Johnson* was the purpose of the exercise.[921]

And it worked, for a while. Certainly long enough to help Johnson get *elected* in 1964 – *which was the whole point.*

When published in late September 1964 – just six weeks before the presidential election – the Johnson Report instantly became a bestseller. That reliable Establishment whore and self-appointed guardian of the status quo, the *New York Times,* gushed fawningly over the Commission's hollow product to help ensure that the U.S. government's propaganda got into the hands of – and infected the minds of – as many American citizens as possible.[922]

Copies of the cheap AP version of the Johnson Report even appeared in racks located at the checkout aisles of supermarkets nationwide; that autumn of 1964, Americans could conveniently purchase the *false* version of what had supposedly happened in Dallas along with their toilet paper and their scouring pads and their itch cream and their hair gel.[923]

It was a marketing triumph of vast proportions.

There's only one little problem:

You cannot find the truth by reading the Johnson Report.

It isn't in there.

It never was.

And it was never *supposed* to be.

You **can** find tiny *pieces* of the truth scattered throughout its 26 *back-up volumes* of "Hearings and Exhibits" – and you can encounter fragments of truth scattered in a few works by a few previous independent researchers.

But the Report *itself* is devoid of truth. It is simply a sanitized snack for the credulous – an odious, toxic, empty vanilla cupcake for the gullible. Its 888 pages of dense, ugly, government print essentially represent Lyndon Johnson's raised middle finger, vertically extended in a gesture of utter contempt for the American people.

---

[921] Author's exclusive original discovery.

[922] Under the communist system, governmental lies are generally given to you for free; under the capitalist system, governmental lies are **sold** to you at a profit. This clearly proves the superior morality and economic efficiency of the capitalist West; at least *we* typically have some disposable income with which to purchase official propaganda. *Swell.*

[923] And by December 1964, you could purchase the *New York Times's* own sanitized paperback book on the JFK assassination, called *The Witnesses.* The newspaper's unintentionally revealing slogan is "All the news that's fit to print"; obviously, the dark and bloody truth about the very public, daylight slaughter of the Chief of State in 1963 was not deemed "fit to print."

I hate to break it to you all, but the *New York Times* – the "newspaper" [*sic*] unwarrantedly revered by American *ignorati* as the "Gray Lady" of "journalism" [*sic*] – is nothing but an incurably diseased government whore.

Chief Justice Earl Warren himself admitted as much when he candidly responded to a media question about whether the Commission's evidentiary materials would ever be made public. "Yes," said Warren, "there will come a time. But it might not be in your lifetime."[924]

Huh?

The chairman of the Johnson Commission was *publicly admitting that his vaunted Report was a lie* – and was doing so *in advance of the Report's publication!*

Why would he say such a thing?

Why would the truth *not* emerge during the lifetime of his listeners?

The answer was both simple and obscene:

Because *Lyndon Johnson himself wanted it sealed and suppressed for seventy-five years* – until 2039, presumably long after LBJ himself and all the other guilty men who assisted him and participated in the brutal JFK assassination would be dead, and therefore *safely beyond reach of prosecution.*[925]

Obviously if Lee Oswald had actually killed JFK, and had done so *alone,* then no such action by Johnson would have been *taken* – because it wouldn't have been *necessary.*

But in this case, it clearly *was* deemed necessary – by none other than Lyndon Johnson himself.

It was a very revealing overt act in furtherance of a crime.[926]

* * *

Ordinarily, people protest when someone – *anyone* – dares to act as judge, jury and executioner.

But strangely, *no one* raised a peep when Lyndon Johnson slammed the doors on the truth in 1964.

Judge, jury and executioner.

By murdering President Kennedy, then creating the Johnson Commission to ostensibly "ratify" his own "legitimacy" as President, and then brazenly *sealing key evidence for a lifetime* by having it transferred to the National Archives,[927] Lyndon

---

[924] Earl Warren, quoted in the *New York Times* on February 5th, 1964.

[925] This did *not* require a brazen, overt and self-incriminating presidential executive order; it was achieved much more subtly by depositing Commission records in the National Archives, where they would be sequestered for several decades according to oh-so-convenient Archives "policy."

[926] Warren offered up the pathetically weak excuse that "There may be some things that would involve security." (*New York Times*, February 5th, 1964.) Indeed: **Lyndon Johnson's** security, not the nation's.

[927] Contrary to myth, LBJ did *not* need to personally issue a presidential "executive order" sealing the Commission's records for 75 years; such a deeply self-incriminating action was (fortunately for him) completely unnecessary. Instead, thanks to the extremely clever lawyers advising him, Lyndon Johnson

Johnson simply performed all those roles in reverse order: he was first executioner, then jury, then judge.[928]

It was not the last time that Lyndon Johnson would cover up the assassination of a Kennedy, either.[929]

* * *

Ultimately, the Johnson Commission – officially announced on November 29th, 1963, one week after Dallas – was the vehicle used to try to wipe the blood and gore and the stench of criminality off Lyndon Johnson's public reputation.

It was not always thus, however.

On the very day of the crime, LBJ deputized his sinister friend and longtime ally, FBI Director J. Edgar Hoover, to monopolize the "investigation" [*sic*] of the JFK assassination. Both LBJ and Hoover desired that the tightly controlled and rigidly hierarchical Bureau function as the exclusive *federal* arbiter of what had happened to President Kennedy; both LBJ and Hoover hoped that the FBI's own lengthy but superficial report on the JFK assassination would suffice to serve as the lone "official" record of events.

Yet despite Hoover's massive power and influence (and the terror he widely inspired thanks to his extensive blackmail efforts), loud voices in both media and government soon declared that such an arrangement was inadequate.

Soon after the JFK assassination (which, as a homicide, was a state-level offense and not a specific federal crime as such in 1963) a Texas Court of Inquiry was formed – but it too was regarded as grossly insufficient and inherently devoid of the requisite "impartiality" to assess the crime honestly and satisfactorily.

Rumblings even emerged from Capitol Hill of potential *congressional* probes.

---

knew that as long as his subservient *Commission* placed the materials *into the National Archives,* then Archives "policy" would seal those records *for* him.

[928] Author's exclusive original discovery.

[929] Before reading my own upcoming book addressing that subject with jaw-dropping new evidence, the intelligent reader can obtain very useful information about key evidentiary issues in the RFK case by consulting *The Assassination of Robert F. Kennedy,* a book by William Turner and Jonn G. Christian.

N. B.: In the late 1970s, when the members of Congress finally decided to officially look into major assassinations of the 1960s, they appropriated funds to investigate the JFK and MLK murders – but bizarrely declared that there "just wasn't enough money" to probe the assassination of RFK, too.

Apparently, cutting obscene Pentagon waste – or simply holding a Congressional bake sale to help raise the funds needed for an RFK assassination investigation – was out of the question.

Tough break for Bobby. Tough break for America.

And it is undeniable that Lyndon Johnson ultimately created the Johnson Commission, *in part,* specifically in order *to head off* the formation of nominally "independent" Congressional committees designed to look into into the JFK assassination – committees whose formation was a very real possibility in those first grim days after Dallas. There is unassailable proof that this factored into LBJ's thinking; he discussed and opposed it on the telephone with members of Congress and others, and he actively and personally moved to head off any such potentially risky developments in the House *or* the Senate.[930]

But there is more.

Expert JFK assassination analyst Peter Rupay provided an even more chilling and provocative original insight about the true origins of LBJ's cover-up panel.

Pete did not believe that the group was a *post hoc* creation at all.

"The Commission [concept] was hatched long *before* the assassination," Rupay told me during one of our many highly productive discussions of the case. "Now don't tell me that's an *afterthought,* a week *after* the assassination!"[931]

He continued articulating one of the better insights to ever emerge from advanced independent analysis of this crime.

"Johnson *used* the Commission [concept]," said Rupay, "*to recruit people* [for the JFK assassination, well in advance] . . . *To assure them that they wouldn't be prosecuted* . . . That there'd be a *presidential* commission [created after the deed was done] . . . That *he'd take care of it.*"[932]

It was a typically brilliant insight from Pete.

* * *

Long before he was a poorly regarded vice president and a poorly regarded president, Gerald "Jerry" Ford was a Johnson Commission *spy.*

That's right; the Republican congressman and future POTUS was a spy for the Federal Bureau of Investigation.

"Ford indicated he would keep me thoroughly advised as to the activities of the Commission," wrote high-level FBI official Cartha "Deke" DeLoach in a contemporaneous 1963 Bureau memorandum.

---

[930] Perpetually fraudulent federal "investigations" (whether conducted by the executive branch or by Congress) are always tightly controlled and are rigidly designed *to conceal and suppress the truth* – but the guilty parties know that there is always the disconcerting possibility that a staffer will ask an unexpected question, or a witness will give an unexpected answer, or someone will unexpectedly volunteer damning information, thereby gumming up the works and exposing the true perpetrators of monstrous crimes.

[931] Expert JFK assassination analyst Peter Rupay to the author, 2019.

[932] Expert JFK assassination analyst Peter Rupay to the author, 2019.

Gerald Ford's covert role as an FBI mole – a role allegedly occasioned via *blackmail*, due to the FBI's reported possession of an audio tape of the Michigan congressman happily receiving sub-umbilical osculation from a woman other than his wife[933] – was not the most disturbing aspect of his work on the Johnson Commission.

Gerald Ford personally, knowingly and deliberately fought to *alter* the written description of a (false) "wound" (only seen on JFK's corpse at autopsy in Maryland that night, hours *after* the noontime assassination in Texas) in order to "raise" the apparent location of that postmortem injury from President Kennedy's *back* to the back of President Kennedy's *neck,* and thus make it appear anatomically "higher."[934] That way it would superficially appear more logical and more compatible with the supposed trajectory of a supposed "Magic Bullet" supposedly fired from behind and above – namely, the false "window perch" of the false TSBD "sniper."[935]

Ford's criminal act constituted obstruction of justice.

Yet even the corrupt and devious Jerry Ford admitted a portion of the truth years later while speaking privately to another head of state.

When questioned frankly in May 1976 by visiting French President Valery Giscard d'Estaing about what had *really* happened to President Kennedy,[936] Gerald Ford *admitted* that a criminal conspiracy took the life of America's 35th president, but claimed that the identity of the organizers and perpetrators of the assassination had supposedly been "impossible" [*sic*] to ascertain.[937]

* * *

Yet there was even uglier, even more dispositive ***proof*** of the Johnson Commission's willful, knowing, deliberate suppression of the truth about the assassination of JFK – and it came straight from the horses' (plural) mouths.

---

[933] United States Senate oral history interview of Bobby Baker, 2009. Baker – LBJ's longtime protégé and aide and accomplice – said that the woman happily providing oral delight to Ford on the audio tape was a sociable German known as Ellen Rometsch, whom the Kennedy brothers promptly deported in 1963 out of pure political panic. After all, according to Bobby Baker, JFK himself had enjoyed the very same services from Rometsch.

[934] George Lardner, "Ford's Editing Backed 'Single Bullet' Theory," *Washington Post,* July 3rd, 1997.

[935] In reality, ***no*** shots struck JFK from behind. *None.* **Zero.** Get used to dealing with that fundamental truth, which I will document and prove in an upcoming book.

[936] The conversation, ironically enough, took place inside *a government limousine* – en route to a dinner at Mount Vernon on May 19th, 1976.

[937] Valery Giscard d'Estaing related Gerald Ford's admission in later interviews with French radio network RTL and with French magazine *Le Parisien.* The HSCA later echoed Ford's plaintive wail, stating in its final report that JFK was "probably" [*sic*] killed by a criminal conspiracy whose sinister members (gosh darn it to heck!) just could not be determined or identified.

On June 27th, 1964, months prior to the Report's release, the Kennedys' designated writer William Manchester was present at a meeting of Johnson Commission staff attorneys.[938] What they admitted aloud, in his hearing, was supremely damning and extremely revelatory: *"If we write what we really think,"* said the Commission lawyers, *"nobody will believe anything else we say . . . The whole report will be discredited as controversial."*[939]

* * *

As I have stated repeatedly in this book:

An assassination plot always has **two** targets: the body of the *victim,* and the body *politic.*

The bullets in Dealey Plaza in 1963 were aimed at President Kennedy.

The Johnson Report in 1964 was aimed directly at the American *public.*

But even before the Johnson Commission was created, and long before its false Report was *outlined,* and long before that false Report was *written,* and long before that false Report was *released* (weeks before the 1964 presidential election), a number of people inside the federal government and inside the U. S. military *already* knew the sinister truth about the gruesome murder of President Kennedy – and they *already* knew exactly who was *actually* responsible for it!

They knew it because they were deeply, knowingly, actively *involved* in it.

And many of those who knew the sinister truth – *because they were involved in the JFK assassination themselves* – wore the muted blue uniform of a decidedly martial organization called the United States Air Force.[940]

---

[938] Earl Warren had extended Commission access privileges to Manchester as a courtesy to the Kennedy clan.

[939] William Manchester, *The Death of a President,* p. 426. Cowardice is the most plentiful commodity in Washington.

[940] Author's exclusive original discovery.

Sinister USAF "historian" [*sic*] Alfred Goldberg
personally outlined and wrote much of the fictitious
"Warren" Report (which was actually the **Johnson** Report).

The result was promoted by governmental and media whores
in the most obscene propaganda effort in American history.

*The United States Air Force literally wrote
the false "official" version of the JFK assassination.*

Fortunately, the stunning truths which I discovered
destroy the official story forever.

The U. S. government thought that it could
permanently bury the truth about
the assassination of President Kennedy.

I *personally* ensured that that didn't happen.

USAF General Joseph Cappucci worked in
counterintelligence, security and special investigations.

In 1969, Cappucci bluntly told an Air Force subordinate that
Lyndon Johnson had had John F. Kennedy killed.

Chapter Thirty-Three:
Roman Holiday

"These things do not just 'happen.'
*They are **made** to happen."*

– John Fitzgerald Kennedy

In late November 2013, on the day *before* the fiftieth anniversary of the JFK assassination, an elderly American woman – a Texan, born in Dallas – stood in Dealey Plaza with a protest sign.

She was ignored by virtually everyone standing there and passing by – except for one man.

Assassination researcher and analyst Robert P. Morrow was in the plaza that day, saw her sign, and had the intelligence and the presence of mind to approach her and talk.[941] Politely he asked whether she knew who killed John F. Kennedy.

Absolutely, the elderly woman replied.

She truly *did,* too.

She had gotten the word from an unimpeachable source, in a land far away, on a strikingly memorable evening long ago.

But like every other vital new witness cited in this book, she was never contacted or interviewed by any government commission, congressional committee, newspaper, TV network, national magazine, academic, or lazy shallow corporate "journalist."

So much for "official investigations" in America.

* * *

The elderly woman's name was Jan Amos – and she was the former wife of a USAF officer, Lieutenant Colonel William Henry "Bill" Amos.

---

[941] Robert **P.** Morrow of Austin, Texas (***not*** to be confused with Robert **D.** Morrow, a different and much older individual who was reputedly involved in contract work for the CIA in the early 1960s) first discovered this witness and he first interviewed her, in great depth. He deserves enormous credit for this vital original find and major contribution to history.

In the late 1960s, Jan and her then-husband Bill and their children were stationed abroad in Rome, Italy. Lt. Col. Amos worked for and reported to another USAF officer, Brigadier General Joseph J. Cappucci.[942]

Back in 1963, at the time of the JFK assassination, Cappucci was Director of Special Investigations for the Office of the USAF Inspector General.

By the following year, 1964, Cappucci was the head of AFOSI – the Air Force Office of Special Investigations. He held that post until 1972, and his rank and his role gave him extensive access to high-level figures in the U. S. government.

Cappucci's rank and his role *also* gave him extensive access to high-level *secrets* of the U. S. government – including the very biggest secret of them all.

Cappucci had a good friend in the executive branch of the federal government.

That good friend's name was John Edgar Hoover – Director of the FBI, master of blackmail, and the longtime Washington neighbor and ally of a certain criminal Texas politician named Lyndon Baines Johnson.

Cappucci and Hoover were fellow conservatives.

" 'Cappoose' didn't like the Kennedys either," said Jan Amos.[943]

Cappucci and J. Edgar Hoover became very close.

* * *

In the latter part of 1969, Jan Amos accompanied her then-husband, Bill, to an "unbelievable" formal-dress diplomatic event held at an upscale hotel in Rome. Naturally, the couple joined Lt. Col. Amos's boss, USAF Brigadier General Cappucci, who was in the Eternal City for the occasion.

Many people attended the event, but the trio sat together.

It was just the three of them, seated together at one small table.[944]

Jan Amos never forgot that night – nor did she ever forget what General Cappucci *disclosed* that night.

After dinner, Cappucci began to denigrate the Kennedy clan – a line of conversation sparked initially by mention of the recent horror at Chappaquiddick, Massachusetts, involving the death of a young woman named Mary Jo Kopechne inside Senator Edward Kennedy's car.

General Cappucci began deriding the immorality and callousness of the Kennedy men, and he made it clear that he had discussed these issues quite extensively with his very powerful friend, FBI Director J. Edgar Hoover.

---

[942] The general told intimates to refer to him as "Cappoose" (pronounced "kah-*poos*") – the shortened phonetic moniker that he preferred. Jan Amos consistently referred to him this way.

[943] Author interview with Jan Amos, 2014.

[944] Author interview with Jan Amos, 2014.

JFK's own bad acts were very well known to Lyndon Johnson, Hoover had informed Cappucci.[945]

Moreover, the fearsome FBI Director had given Cappucci a particularly damning version of Senator Edward M. Kennedy's actions and inaction in July 1969. As General Cappucci spoke to the Amoses at length about Teddy's reported behavior – before, during and *after* the death of Mary Jo Kopechne at Chappaquiddick – he became angrier, more agitated and more disgusted with the entire Kennedy clan.

"That's the Kennedys for you," Cappucci said contemptuously.[946]

Then he added a simple short declarative sentence:

"That's why LBJ had JFK killed," he said.[947]

* * *

That's why LBJ had JFK killed.

USAF Brigadier General Joseph J. Cappucci – the head of AFOSI in 1969 – had just openly declared that *Lyndon Baines Johnson murdered his predecessor, President John Fitzgerald Kennedy.*

Jan Amos was stunned by what she heard.

She was also shocked by the matter-of-fact way that Cappucci made his statement. "*One sentence* is exactly what came from his mouth," she told me. "It came out just like 'That's why the sun went down.' You know what I mean? It was such a simple statement."

Yet another aspect of General Cappucci's devastating declaration was particularly worth noting. "He didn't [even] say *'assassinated'*," Mrs. Amos pointed out to me. Instead, Cappucci merely used the term *"killed."*[948]

"And evidently he [General Cappucci] approved," said Jan. "He *approved* of it [LBJ killing JFK] – which I think is awful, but I never pushed him . . ."

* * *

Lyndon Johnson was out of office, but still very much alive, in 1969.

---

[945] Hoover himself was the source of much of LBJ's information – including the data that was *personally* employed by Lyndon Johnson and Sam Rayburn, *under cover of night,* to successfully blackmail John Kennedy into putting Johnson on the Democratic national ticket in July 1960, thereby making the JFK assassination a fully operational plot.

[946] Author interview with Jan Amos, 2014.

[947] Author interview with Jan Amos, 2014.

[948] Author interview with Jan Amos, 2014.

The fact that General Cappucci had indiscreetly revealed such a devastating bombshell in a moment of angry anti-Kennedy candor – in front of a *civilian,* no less – plainly alarmed his military subordinate, USAF Lt. Col. Bill Amos.

The lieutenant colonel himself was certainly no fan of LBJ. "That is the most uncouth sonofabitch I've ever known," Amos told Jan privately. "My husband could not stand Johnson," she informed me. "He absolutely despised him."[949]

But Lt. Col. Amos also knew how dangerous Cappucci's disclosure was.

So after the dazzling soiree and the chilling conversation concluded, and the couple began driving back to their Rome apartment, Lt. Col. Amos turned to his wife with an urgent dictum. "On our way home, Bill said to me, 'Jan, don't *ever* repeat that,'" she recalled. "He said 'never, never' – I mean he was really – 'Never never never *ever* repeat that.'"[950]

* * *

That's why LBJ had JFK killed.

Cappucci and Hoover were wrong about the actual *reason* that LBJ had had JFK killed – obviously no moralist himself, Lyndon Johnson was every bit as hedonistic and every bit as dedicated a womanizer as John Kennedy, and far more personally venal and abusive and corrupt – but the Air Force general and the FBI director were absolutely correct about the central fact:

Lyndon Johnson had John F. Kennedy killed.

General Cappucci knew it.

Director Hoover knew it, too.

J. Edgar Hoover knew what LBJ had done – and Hoover easily extracted from Johnson an exemption from the mandatory retirement-at-age-70 rule.[951]

LBJ promptly and compliantly and publicly waived that rule in May 1964 (shortly before the FBI Director gave false and "safe" testimony to the Johnson Commission), and thereby enabled Hoover to continue running the FBI (and blackmailing much of the federal government) with an iron fist until Hoover's own eventual death in May 1972.

J. Edgar Hoover knew what LBJ had done.

Indeed, Director Hoover made sure to "remind" LBJ that he knew – lest the illegitimate new president should ever change his mind

---

[949] Author interview with Jan Amos, 2014.

[950] Author interview with Jan Amos, 2014.

[951] Following his own presumptive reelection in 1964, JFK was going to ensure J. Edgar Hoover's mandatory retirement in early 1965.

Hoover did this – in *writing,* no less! – by forwarding to a Johnson aide in December 1966 an FBI memorandum concerning certain very accurate *Soviet* analyses of the JFK assassination, which correctly and explicitly put the blame for the vicious crime on the Texan.[952]

Hoover's point was received "loud and clear" by Lyndon Johnson.

Hoover knew.

LBJ had JFK killed.

Hoover knew.

He didn't care, but he knew.

Johnson did it.

Hoover himself *knew* that Lyndon Johnson was the principal culprit in the JFK assassination; Hoover *assisted* Johnson in escaping justice for the deed;[953] Hoover consciously *capitalized* on that knowledge for his own benefit; and Hoover was powerful enough and comfortable enough and secure enough in his own political invincibility to confidently *share* the stunning fact of Johnson's murderous guilt with a fellow archconservative, USAF General Joseph Cappucci of AFOSI, in a private conversation.[954]

Plainly, Cappucci himself felt comfortable enough with the politics of Lt. Col. Amos (who was a Republican)[955] to willingly share the shocking revelation with his subordinate at that dinner in Rome in 1969.

Amos adamantly demanded that his wife Jan never divulge the information. At a time when American women were rarely taken seriously – and were even *barred*

---

[952] The fact that a brutal foreign government like the USSR rapidly and accurately ascertained the ugly truth about the JFK assassination within *just twelve days* – correctly calling it a coup – while the supposedly enlightened American government (and its whorish media accomplices) actively *suppressed* it for several decades remains one of the most deeply ironic – and pathetically disgusting – aspects of the entire JFK case. (See J. Edgar Hoover's TOP SECRET memo to LBJ White House aide Marvin Watson, December 1st, 1966 – with a cover page dated December 2nd, 1966.) Hoover made sure to note that the explosive and correct Soviet information about Lyndon Johnson's involvement in the JFK assassination had *not* been provided to the then-acting U. S. Attorney General, Ramsey Clark.

[953] In the 1980s one (vanishingly rare) *honest* analyst bluntly pointed out that the FBI's much-touted, five-volume, late -1963 "report" on the JFK assassination was primarily garbage – and consisted of lies, bias and a collection of utterly irrelevant statements. (See Charles G. Wilber, Ph.D., "The Assassination of the Late President John F. Kennedy," *American Journal of Forensic Medicine and Pathology,* Volume 7, Number 1, 1986.)

[954] As mentioned in a previous chapter, the utterly despicable and venal Johnson Commission assistant counsel, Arlen Specter – a key player in committing obstruction of justice and witness tampering in the JFK case – was himself a USAF veteran who had worked for AFOSI in the 1950s.

[955] Author interview with Jan Amos, 2014.

from the ranks of reportorial jobs at major American news magazines[956] – Jan Amos did not have many options, and she didn't know whom to turn to with the information. "I just had nobody," she told me.[957]

But when Robert P. Morrow spoke to her at length – and when I and others did subsequently – she willingly brought the truth to light.

*   *   *

That's why LBJ had JFK killed.

I interviewed Jan Amos in great detail for nearly two hours in November 2014.

Knowing full well the dishonest and asinine efforts that would be made by the lone-nut-theorist, see-no-evil, coincidence-mongering cultists of cowardly corporate media to try to downplay, deny or attack Jan Amos's vital revelations, I openly and deliberately asked her a lengthy series of questions from the perspective of a typical Establishment jackass intent on "knocking down the story" (which is always the primary goal of the pathetic eunuchs in corporate pseudo-journalism) rather than finding the truth.

Are you certain that General Cappucci's statement occurred in Italy?

"I was sitting at the table with him!" she replied.

Was General Cappucci drunk?

"No, no – no no no. No. Nobody was drunk," Jan replied.

Was General Cappucci serious?

"Absolutely!" Mrs. Amos replied. "It wasn't a joke at all!"

Was General Cappucci just joking?

"No. No . . . This wasn't a joke," Jan told me. "He wasn't drunk, and we weren't laughing; we were carrying on a pretty serious conversation . . . He was very serious."

Was General Cappucci just being sarcastic?

"No."

Was General Cappucci on drugs?

"Oh my God; no," said Jan.

Was General Cappucci intoxicated or otherwise impaired?

"No, no, and neither was Bill, and neither was I," Mrs. Amos replied.

Was General Cappucci just joking around?

"No. No . . . If he was anything, he was angry," said Jan.

---

[956] Former LBJ aide and longtime Establishment attorney Joseph Califano eventually negotiated a deal in mid-1973 to finally permit women at *Newsweek* to actually work as news reporters and bureau chiefs, rather than be relegated to behind-the-scenes jobs as mere "researchers." (Joseph Califano, *Inside,* p. 237.)

[957] Author interview with Jan Amos, 2014.

Was General Cappucci in the habit of making wild or erroneous claims?

"Oh, no – he was very serious . . . This was no joke . . . This was a serious conversation," she replied.

*Did General Cappucci state that Johnson killed President Kennedy as a **fact**?*

"Absolutely," said Jan.

*Did General Cappucci appear to **approve** of Lyndon Johnson having had Kennedy killed?*

"Well, of course!" said Jan matter-of-factly.

Did your husband take General Cappucci's statement seriously?

"Are you kidding me? On the way home, he said 'Jan . . .' He was upset – he said, 'Don't ever repeat this.' "

*Was Lt. Col. Amos serious in his warning to **you**?*

"Absolutely . . . He was dead serious."

Was this the only occasion when General Cappucci said LBJ killed JFK?

"Absolutely," said Jan. "Bill was his fair-haired boy . . . I don't think he [Cappucci] would have made that statement in front of anyone else."

Jan Amos was very clear and firm and direct about the experience. "Everything in that conversation with Bill and 'Cappoose' and myself . . . It was not a joking thing," she said to me. "And Bill was very serious when he said, 'Don't *ever* repeat that.' "

Jan herself – who was a fan of both John and Robert Kennedy – was stunned by General Cappucci's blunt revelation about LBJ. But interestingly, her husband Bill did *not* seem shocked by the general's bald statement that night in Rome; Jan believes that Lt. Col. William Henry Amos of the U. S. Air Force *already knew* that Lyndon Johnson was responsible for killing JFK.[958]

* * *

"You get that book *out* there, young man," Jan Amos said to me in the autumn of 2014. "You *write* that book, and you're doing something for this country – because after all, *these military people you interviewed have offered their lives for this country.*"

She was correct, and I fully understood the gravity of that.

"We've been fed so many lies for so many years," Jan continued. She recognized and lauded the major battle being waged by me and a few others to, in her words, "bring truth forward."[959]

I heard similar sentiments frequently during my long years of research on the JFK assassination – coming mostly from *veterans of the U. S. Air Force.*

---

[958] Author interview with Jan Amos, 2014.

[959] Author interview with Jan Amos, 2014.

Sgt. Charles Ruberg of the 1254th Air Police Squadron, who flew on Air Force One on November 22nd, 1963, and who wept openly over President Kennedy's death, encouraged me as well: "Stay with it!" he said urgently.

Ruberg added, *"If there's anything 'underground' I hope to hell you dig it up – because **it's not right,** you know."*[960]

Sgt. Thomas Michl of the 1000th ACCS said to me, "I do hope that it comes out – the truth about Kennedy's assassination comes out – *because it was a total cover-up and **everyone up there at Andrews knew it**...*"[961]

Like the civilian Jan Amos, these American military men were painfully aware that the official story of the dark events of November 1963 was terribly, horribly wrong – and they wanted me to uncover the truth.

I've spent decades fulfilling that quest and earning their trust.

* * *

LBJ had JFK killed.

Hoover knew.

Cappucci knew.[962]

LeMay knew.

Power knew.

Patton knew.

Wheeler knew.

Taylor knew.

It was a massive undertaking, of course. Killing an American president – *and getting away with it* – is no easy task, let alone a task which can be adequately handled by just a small group.[963]

---

[960] Author interview with USAF veteran Charles Ruberg, 2013.

[961] Author interview with USAF veteran Thomas Michl, 2013. "I enjoy speaking with someone with intelligence," Michl said to me. He added, "I enjoyed conversing with you because you're the *only* person that I've spoken with that has *ever* asked me any questions about anything." In fact, he declared, "You're so much more informed . . . than anyone I've ever spoken with – you know so many different subjects! . . . I just love talking to someone that has *knowledge* of things that I knew and have known for years . . . I'm glad there are still people like you that are interested in history and the truth."

[962] Interestingly, USAF General Cappucci – like USAF General Charles Cabell, USAF General Edward Lansdale, and USAF Colonel Howard Burris (who was a military aide Vice President Johnson *and* his secret backchannel to the Joint Chiefs of Staff) – also worked with the Central intelligence Agency, in addition to laboring for his own uniformed service.

[963] Anyone claiming, in the 21st century, that the JFK assassination was committed by "a lone gunman," or "a tiny clique," or "a mere handful" of men, or "just a few rogue agents," is (to put it as politely as possible) an ignorant twit with all the brainpower of a rotting pomegranate.

The assassination of John Kennedy required *many* concrete decisions, *scores* of specific steps, and *numerous* personnel with a variety of skills, clearances, and undisputed access to both the victim and the evidence.[964]

Following the November 1961 death of the JFK assassination plot's intellectual author and chief co-conspirator, House Speaker Sam Rayburn,[965] the ultimate responsibility for *all* of those many vital decisions about staffing, backup plans, emergency contingencies and the timing of the murder fell *exclusively* upon the shoulders of Lyndon Baines Johnson – the JFK assassination plot's remaining leader, chief conspirator, and principal beneficiary.

In making those key decisions and in taking the requisite steps to ensure their execution, LBJ knowingly and deliberately committed numerous *highly specific and concrete crimes* in furtherance of the criminal conspiracy to assassinate President John Fitzgerald Kennedy.[966]

There is a special term in the American legal system for such crimes.

Prosecutors and judges call them "overt acts."

---

[964] As I have carefully determined based on documented actions by real people in connection with the crime, the true number of specific individuals who were *actively and knowingly involved in the JFK assassination* was *at least* **91**. (Author's exclusive original discovery and analysis.)

Yes, Virginia, such a "large" number of people *can* and *could* and *did* keep such a major secret; after all, they literally faced *the death penalty* had they *failed* to keep it. That's what's known in the trade as "a really powerful incentive."

Proponents of a "very small" JFK plot (or of a "lone" gunman [*sic*]) are breathtakingly ignorant, deeply deluded fantasists.

[965] Author's exclusive original discovery.

[966] Author's exclusive original discovery.

Lyndon Baines Johnson
personally committed more than **160** overt acts
in furtherance of the seditious criminal conspiracy
which he *personally* led and supervised
to assassinate President John Fitzgerald Kennedy.

Author's exclusive original discovery.

Chapter Thirty-Four:
Overt Acts

"Now you help us and protect my flanks there."
– Lyndon Baines Johnson

"And you'll protect my flank on it."
– Lyndon Baines Johnson

"You've got to protect my flank . . ."
– Lyndon Baines Johnson

"Just keep them from investigating!"
– Lyndon Baines Johnson

"These things do not just 'happen.'
*They are **made** to happen."*

– John Fitzgerald Kennedy

In the year 1517, a relatively obscure German professor and priest compiled and distributed ninety-five arguments regarding his disagreements with certain practices of the Catholic Church. Those devastating charges caused widespread consternation, ignited discussion and revolts, led to the creation of new faiths and sects, changed the world, and profoundly altered the history of the next 500 years.

Yet poor Martin Luther was, relatively speaking, an *amateur*.

He only managed to eke out a paltry 95 theses.[967]

But when it comes to actually proving the direct guilt and personal criminal culpability of Lyndon Baines Johnson in the JFK assassination, I have rigorously

---

[967] Luther was actually preceded by a full *year* by fellow German theologian Andreas Karlstadt, who produced a whopping **151** theses of his own in 1516, roundly criticizing church corruption.

identified and compiled a stunning and insurmountable number – ***more than 160*** overt criminal acts.[968]

Despite *abundant, specific* and *incontrovertible* evidence which has been available for *decades* (not to mention the brand-new information which I have personally and exclusively uncovered and documented in this book), there are a number of whorish pseudo-historians and conventional shills who mindlessly ***deny*** that Lyndon Baines Johnson was involved in – and was in fact *principally responsible for* – the 1963 assassination of President Kennedy. In the process they have made asinine fools of themselves; they have abandoned all pretense of honesty, professionalism, intelligence or integrity; and they have slavishly devoted themselves to vile Establishment fiction.

Pathetic, but hardly a surprise.

Concurrently, despite *abundant, specific* and *incontrovertible* evidence which has been available for *decades* (not to mention the brand-new information which I have personally and exclusively uncovered and documented in this book), there are a number of shrill intellectual lightweights who correctly recognize criminal conspiracy in the JFK assassination, but who nevertheless insist (wrongly) that the crime was committed by a massive multitude of nefarious suspects ranging from "rogue CIA agents" to "the Schlumberger Company" to "the Federal Reserve" to "the Freeport Sulphur Company" to "the Shickshinny Knights of Malta" – and these shrill lightweights laughably claim that Lyndon Johnson, the single most powerful politician in American history other than Franklin Delano Roosevelt himself, was merely a lowly "water boy" [*sic*] for the nameless members of the numerous exotic groups whom they say supposedly slew John Kennedy.

Meanwhile, despite abundant, specific and incontrovertible evidence which has been available for decades (not to mention the brand-new information which I have personally and exclusively uncovered and documented in this book), a few authors who *have* previously and correctly asserted that Lyndon Baines Johnson was involved in – and in fact principally responsible for – the JFK assassination have ultimately (and inexplicably) ***failed*** to make a cogent, compelling, solid case.

Their intentions were noble and good; but their results were sadly insufficient.

Instead of focusing on *actual JFK assassination-related data,* they instead tended to wander off into the noxious, barren weeds of utter irrelevancy – indulging in tortuous, banal, fruitless excursions into LBJ's ugly psychology; or his nasty and cruel and abusive personality; or his repulsive table manners; or his hideous scatological acts; or his alleged mental illness; or his pathetic exhibitionism; or his past history of

---

[968] Author's original work thus far, from 1983 through 2023. No other JFK assassination investigator, anywhere, has *ever* put together such a devastating list of accurate, pertinent, hard data which clearly and irrefutably and concretely ***documents*** the criminal guilt of the *actual leader* of the JFK assassination plot: Lyndon Baines Johnson of Texas.

financial corruption; or his endless philandering; or the slew of *other* individual murders of lesser figures (as many as eight people, by some accounts) which LBJ may have ordered – all *prior* to 1963.

But from a practical and legal and historical point of view, those other matters – even if they are all absolutely true in every awful, nauseating detail (and at a bare minimum, most of them *are* true) – are fundamentally *irrelevant* to the JFK assassination.[969]

That's right, America; ***irrelevant.***

They are entirely unsatisfactory and unconvincing in *this* case.

They're simply not enough.

Those facts may tell us a great deal about Johnson's *character* (or lack thereof); they may tell us a great deal about his *capabilities* as a human (or inhuman) being; they may illuminate his ugly *personality;* but such things don't tell us *anything at all* about whether or not he was actually involved in the deliberate murder of his White House predecessor, John Kennedy.

They're simply not enough.

In order to demonstrate any actual personal involvement by Lyndon Johnson in *the JFK assassination itself*, it is imperative to document *specific overt acts* which are directly related thereto.

Not hunches or suppositions or beliefs or "hypotheses" or "scenarios" or "theories" or assumptions, but *evidence.*

As it turns out, there is a massive trove of precisely such evidence. It simply has never before been discovered, correctly identified, properly assembled, accurately analyzed and diligently gathered in one place, by anyone, *ever.*

The time has come to do so.

Here.

Now.

For the very first time, anywhere.

Knowingly, willfully and with malice aforethought, Lyndon Baines Johnson *personally* engaged in the following criminal acts – acts *directly* related to the planning, commission and cover-up of the assassination of John Fitzgerald Kennedy:

- Conspiracy to commit extortion
- Conspiracy to solicit murder
- Conspiracy to commit murder
- Extortion
- Misprision of a felony
- Capital murder

---

[969] You read that correctly; *irrelevant.*

- Murder under color of law
- Obstruction of justice
- Criminal facilitation
- Aiding and abetting
- Witness tampering
- Evidence tampering
- Obstruction of justice
- Corruption of justice
- Perversion of justice
- Desecration of a corpse
- Violation of the vice-presidential oath of office
- Seditious conspiracy
- Sedition
- Violent overthrow of the government of the United States

As the old saying goes in American jurisprudence, the average prosecutor (with *minimum* effort) can easily arrange the indictment of *a ham sandwich* – on virtually *no* evidence!

Armed with the ***more than 160 overt acts*** which I have assembled and documented here, *any* competent district attorney or state's attorney or U. S. attorney anywhere in America could successfully indict and convict *anyone*.

Even a president.

Even a president.

Even a president.

These are very specific, deadly serious charges – and they are *not* based on hazy speculation; or on vague, generic allusions to hoary television courtroom clichés like "means, motive and opportunity"; or on supposed "connections" between LBJ and the fourth cousin of the third wife of the nephew of the uncle of the guy who cleans the windows at the Council on Foreign Relations (or other such useless tripe).[970]

---

[970] Some of the most weak-minded, embarrassingly ignorant yet grotesquely abusive and shockingly immature denizens of certain pathetic little online JFK "forums" argue vociferously that LBJ was nothing but a "false sponsor" [*sic*] of the assassination, and not ***the principal player*** (which he was, in reality). These foul, intellectually-stunted *wunderkinds,* who spew their shallow venom in dark stale digital caves, assert that instead a veritable *galaxy* of sinister national and international groups (apparently including every nefarious organization on the planet at the time) was responsible for killing JFK.

Frankly, the notion that *Lyndon Baines Johnson* – a cunning, vicious, experienced and masterful manipulator of astounding skill, who was at the height of his intellectual powers and who was completely committed to the brutal and relentless pursuit of his lifelong goal, the presidency – was nothing but a mere "puppet" or "water boy" for amorphous (and ultimately *generic)* bogeymen like "the CIA" or "the Bilderberg Group" or "the Shickshinny Knights of Malta" is beyond laughable.

Rather, these charges are based on *LBJ's own documented statements and actions* – concrete activities that were specifically related to the JFK assassination. *His own overt acts,* numbering more than **160** separate, identifiable instances of criminal involvement by LBJ, make it painfully clear that Lyndon Johnson *himself* was personally and directly involved in the creation, organization, leadership, management and hands-on *execution* of the JFK plot.

Lyndon Johnson was the *leader,* not a puppet.

He was certainly not a mere "figure-head"; not a "sponsor"; not a "facilitator"; not a mere "ignorant beneficiary" of Dallas; not a mere "accessory after the fact" who simply "helped" with a post-event "cover-up" of a plot supposedly conceived by others; but rather, *the driving force behind the JFK assassination – and its principal ringleader.*[971]

Lyndon Baines Johnson was no mere bystander at his own parade; *he was the grand marshal.*[972]

His own conscious, deliberate, specific actions – performed *before, during and after* the JFK assassination – make that crystal clear and completely irrefutable.

And any honest, competent, *professional* prosecutor (at the state or federal level) will agree wholeheartedly.

LBJ himself – along with key USAF officers, SS agents, allies and staff, all reporting to him and acting under his direct and immediate personal control – personally committed multiple overt acts in furtherance of the JFK murder plot.

As documented in this book, LBJ committed – at a bare minimum![973] – the following overt acts in the commission and furtherance of the assassination of John Fitzgerald Kennedy.[974] These criminal actions are presented here in generally chronological order:

In the *real* world, **real** people with real names planned and directed and committed the JFK assassination. The very first name, at the very top of the list, is *Lyndon Baines Johnson.*

[971] Author's exclusive original insight.

[972] Author's exclusive original insight and phrasing.

[973] My list is extraordinarily comprehensive. There are certainly *additional* pertinent acts by LBJ which have not yet come to light that can be *added to* the devastating case which I have assembled; but the massive list which I have compiled is **more** than completely sufficient to overwhelm and permanently drown any possible "objections" to the indisputable fact of Lyndon Baines Johnson's undeniable guilt as **the hands-on leader** of the JFK assassination plot.

[974] The statute numbers and text of many of the pertinent *federal* laws knowingly violated by Lyndon Baines Johnson in connection with the JFK assassination plot are presented in Appendix 1 of this book.

1. Lyndon Johnson, along with chief co-conspirator Sam Rayburn, *personally* planned and initiated the JFK assassination plot beginning in mid-August, 1956.[975]

2. Lyndon Johnson *personally* contacted, met with and recruited key figures in the United States military and in the executive branch of the federal government between 1956 and 1963.[976] Senior military officers of the United States Air Force; senior officials and agents of the Secret Service; a Texas congressman; senior military officers of the United States Army; officers of the United States Navy; and (to a *much lesser* extent) a few senior officials of the Central Intelligence Agency were LBJ's principal accomplices in the lengthy run-up to Dallas.

3. Lyndon Johnson *personally* met with Speaker of the House Sam Rayburn at Rayburn's remote, isolated 972-acre ranch in north Texas (near the community of Ivanhoe, in Fannin County) to plan and discuss the JFK assassination.[977]

4. Lyndon Johnson *personally* accosted Bobby Kennedy on the night of July 13th-14th, 1960, and demanded that he (LBJ) be named JFK's running mate.

5. Lyndon Johnson, along with chief co-conspirator Sam Rayburn, *personally* blackmailed John Kennedy in the early morning hours of July 14th, 1960.[978]

6. Lyndon Johnson *personally* admitted his blackmail of JFK to reporter Nancy Hanschman Dickerson in late July 1960.[979]

7. Lyndon Johnson *personally* met with CIA director Allen Dulles in July 1960, days after successfully blackmailing JFK and thereby making the upcoming assassination plot fully "operational."

8. Lyndon Johnson *personally* attempted to set up an illicit "parallel government" in early 1961 upon taking office as Vice President.[980]

9. Lyndon Johnson *personally* attempted to take operational control and review of all national security components of the U. S. government in early 1961.[981]

10. Lyndon Johnson *personally* established a secret backchannel to the Joint Chiefs of Staff in 1961 in the person of his own aide, USAF Colonel Howard L. Burris.[982]

---

[975] Author's exclusive original discovery.

[976] Author's exclusive original discovery.

[977] Author's exclusive original discovery.

[978] JFK admitted this fact to a number of people contemporaneously, within just hours; see, for example, Seymour Hersh's book *The Dark Side of Camelot.*

[979] Author's exclusive original discovery.

[980] Harry McPherson, *A Political Education,* pp. 184-85.

[981] Harry McPherson, *A Political Education,* pp. 184-85.

[982] See John Newman's book *JFK and Vietnam.*

11. Lyndon Johnson *personally* sought a Secret Service cadre in 1961, and successfully acquired it through final passage of federal legislation in late 1962.

12. Lyndon Johnson knowingly and deliberately infiltrated President Kennedy's own presidential SS White House Detail between 1961 and 1963, as evidenced by their *instantaneous* defections to him on November 22nd, 1963.[983]

13. Lyndon Johnson *personally* forecast and outlined the fatal Texas trip in April 1963, a full *seven months in advance.*

14. Lyndon Johnson *personally* – and publicly, and repeatedly – *threatened JFK's life* seven months in advance, in April 1963.

15. Lyndon Johnson *personally* broadcast a message "in the clear" to third parties (the NSRP, right-wing Cuban exiles, and other "amateurs" interested in killing Kennedy) in April 1963 to demand that they cease their crude, independent JFK assassination plots and related activities *so as not to interfere with his own formal, serious, high-level, governmental JFK assassination plot* scheduled for execution in November 1963.[984]

16. Lyndon Johnson *personally* "persuaded" Congressman Al Thomas not to retire in the summer of 1963 as part of the criminal maneuvering necessary to compel JFK to visit Texas in the fall.

17. Lyndon Johnson *personally* met with a key member of the Fourth Estate in August 1963 in furtherance of the JFK assassination plot.[985]

18. Lyndon Johnson *personally* met with powerful Congressman Albert "Al" Thomas of Texas on September 23rd, 1963, in furtherance of the JFK assassination plot.[986]

19. LBJ had his ally Al Thomas *force* President Kennedy to make the Texas trip in September 1963 by feigning Thomas's "imminent" demise from cancer *and* by threatening Kennedy's NASA funding in Congress.

20. LBJ *personally* met with a key military co-conspirator, U. S. Army Chief of Staff General Earle "Bus" Wheeler, in October 1963 in furtherance of the JFK assassination.[987]

---

[983] William Manchester, *The Death of a President,* p. 170; Jim Bishop, *The Day Kennedy Was Shot,* p. 151. Neither Manchester nor Bishop exhibited any idea of what that brazen defection actually signified, in reality.

[984] Author's exclusive original discovery.

[985] Author's exclusive original discovery.

[986] Author's exclusive original discovery.

[987] Author's exclusive original discovery.

21. LBJ *personally* met with U. S. Army General Paul Adams – the head of STRIKE Command – in October 1963 in furtherance of the JFK assassination.[988]

22. Lyndon Johnson *personally* met yet again with powerful Congressman Albert "Al" Thomas of Texas on October 11th, 1963, in furtherance of the JFK assassination plot.[989]

23. Lyndon Johnson arranged for longtime ally and supporter Jack Valenti (a Texas advertising executive and USAAF veteran who also worked as a bag man for various corrupt politicians) to author the actual letter "inviting" President Kennedy to Texas, *ostensibly* to honor Al Thomas at an "appreciation dinner" for the supposedly "dying" Texas congressman.

24. Lyndon Johnson and his allies controlled the fatal Dallas motorcade route, which *reversed* and *dramatically slowed* the route taken back in September 1960.

25. Lyndon Johnson's aides falsely claimed that the Bottlers' Convention in Dallas "prevented" political organizers from choosing another luncheon speech site (and thus, a different motorcade route) for November 22nd, 1963.[990]

26. Lyndon Johnson *personally* met with former CIA director Allen Dulles just weeks before the JFK assassination; as head of the Agency, Dulles was responsible for Lee Oswald's superficially "incriminating" 1959 trip to the USSR.

27. Lyndon Johnson *personally* dispatched aide Bill Moyers to see Texas Governor John Connally, *just one week before the assassination in Dallas*, to calm Connally down and allay the governor's legitimate and very serious security concerns about the president's upcoming visit to Texas.[991]

28. On Thursday night, November 21st, 1963, Lyndon Johnson *personally* argued with President Kennedy over motorcade seating the following day in Dallas; LBJ *personally* tried to have Mrs. Kennedy ride with him in a separate car in order to minimize the presence of dangerous independent witnesses to JFK's assassination inside the presidential limousine.[992]

29. Lyndon Johnson *personally* brought Texas advertising executive and longtime "bag man" Jack Valenti from Houston to Fort Worth with him on the vice-presidential jet on the night of Thursday, November 21[st,] in anticipation of *needing*

---

[988] Author's exclusive original discovery.

[989] Author's exclusive original discovery.

[990] Author's exclusive original discovery.

[991] Obstruction by Intimidation, Threats, Persuasion, or Deception, 18 USC 1512 (b).

[992] Author's exclusive original discovery.

*cash and **fleeing the country*** if the risky JFK assassination plot in Dallas failed on Friday, November 22nd.[993]

30. Lyndon Johnson *personally* met with USAF Brigadier General Edward Lansdale at the Hotel Texas in Fort Worth in the early morning hours of November 22nd.[994] (Lansdale was photographed in Dealey Plaza the next day just minutes after the JFK assassination, and was subsequently identified in those photos by two former military colleagues who had worked with him at the Pentagon.)

31. On the morning of November 22nd, 1963, moments before Air Force One landed in Dallas, *SS agents working for Lyndon Johnson* instructed JFK loyalist and potential witness USAF General Godfrey McHugh ***not*** to ride in the front seat of the presidential limousine – as he normally did – during the Dallas motorcade. This crucial and deliberate act kept General McHugh from preventing the JFK assassination.[995]

32. At Love Field on November 22nd, 1963, *prior to the JFK assassination,* Lyndon Johnson's own SS cadre told Dallas Police motorcycle cops slated to accompany JFK's limousine to stay back *regardless of what occurred* during the fatal Dallas motorcade.[996]

33. On November 22nd, 1963, Lyndon Johnson *personally* monitored the JFK assassination *in real time* over the SS radio in his car.[997]

34. On November 22nd, 1963, *SS agents reporting to LBJ* covertly removed the dead body of John Kennedy from Parkland Hospital on a stretcher, under a purple cover, in a secret criminal diversion for illicit purposes in furtherance of the assassination plot.[998]

35. *SS agents reporting to LBJ and acting at his behest* arranged to raise (via forklift) *a second coffin* – not the heavy deluxe bronze "official" Dallas coffin – up and into Air Force One on November 22nd, 1963.

36. *SS agents reporting to LBJ and acting at his behest* violently mutilated President Kennedy's corpse on November 22nd, 1963.[999]

37. Lyndon Johnson himself *personally* instructed his wife, Claudia Alta Taylor Johnson, to *write down everything that everyone did and said* on November

---

[993] Author's exclusive original discovery.

[994] Author's exclusive original discovery.

[995] Author's exclusive original discovery.

[996] Two Dallas police officers disclosed this chilling admonition from the SS prior to the motorcade.

[997] Author's exclusive original discovery.

[998] Author's exclusive original discovery; see Nathan Pool's sworn testimony to the HSCA.

[999] Obstruction by Intimidation, Threats, Persuasion, or Deception, 18 USC 1512 (b).

22nd, 1963. In doing so, LBJ was knowingly attempting to lay the groundwork for a future legal defense by enabling and constructing a false "narrative" of events.[1000]

38. Lyndon Johnson himself *personally* ordered SS agent Jerry Kivett to tell the crew of Air Force One *not to file a flight plan* on November 22nd, 1963.[1001]

39. Lyndon Johnson prepared to *flee the country* on November 22nd, 1963, in order to avoid criminal prosecution and punishment for the JFK assassination.[1002]

40. Lyndon Johnson *personally* raised the specter of "Communist conspiracy" on November 22nd in order to facilitate his getaway from Parkland Hospital and to enable his escape from the United States.[1003]

41. Lyndon Johnson departed Parkland Hospital without informing the press, the country, the Kennedy White House staff or even the U. S. Air Force itself as to *where he was actually headed,* thereby facilitating his own *flight from prosecution* for his crime and advancing his goal of keeping Attorney General Robert Kennedy completely in the dark as to LBJ's actual location, itinerary and intentions and preventing duly constituted federal authorities from tracking, pursuing, intercepting and capturing LBJ and his men.[1004]

42. Lyndon Johnson *personally* ordered his commandeered vehicle to stop as it left Parkland Hospital in order to pick up and transport a key assassination co-conspirator, Congressman Al Thomas, out to Love Field with him.

43. Lyndon Johnson *personally* ordered shades on Air Force One pulled down at Love Field on November 22nd in order to shield his criminal post-assassination machinations from as many witnesses as possible.[1005]

44. Lyndon Johnson *personally* telephoned the office of tax attorney and trustee J. "Waddy" Bullion on the afternoon of November 22nd and sought a prompt stock sale *in order to raise cash to finance an exile abroad.*[1006]

45. Lyndon Johnson *personally* ordered his clothing, his possessions, and *SS machine guns* brought over from Air Force Two to Air Force One at Love Field on

---

[1000] Nurse Diana Bowron, cited in Harrison Livingstone, *Killing the Truth,* p. 184.

[1001] Author's exclusive original discovery. Obstruction by Intimidation, Threats, Persuasion, or Deception, 18 USC 1512 (b).

[1002] Author's exclusive original discovery.

[1003] Obstruction by Intimidation, Threats, Persuasion, or Deception, 18 USC 1512 (b).

[1004] Author's exclusive original discovery.

[1005] Author's exclusive original discovery.

[1006] Author's exclusive original discovery.

November 22nd, 1963, in anticipation of a flight out of the country; long-term *foreign exile*; and a possible serious gun battle with legitimate authorities.[1007]

46. Lyndon Johnson himself *personally* ordered USAF Sgt. Paul Glynn to guard a pile of LBJ's luggage (which concealed the *second* Dallas coffin, located in the forward cabin of Air Force One) on November 22nd, 1963.[1008]

47. Lyndon Johnson deliberately waited until designated patsy Lee Oswald had finally been arrested by Dallas police (at 12:50 p.m. CST) before finally dialing Bobby Kennedy (at 12:56 p.m. CST).[1009]

48. Lyndon Johnson *personally* called RFK on November 22nd, 1963, and deliberately invoked the opaque term "problems of special urgency" in order to gain a measure of "legal cover" for the criminal commission of violent crimes against the dead body of JFK (under the guise of "security measures" [*sic*]) in furtherance of the JFK assassination plot.[1010]

49. Lyndon Johnson *personally* ordered that Jack Valenti – a self-confessed bagman (extremely close to JFK assassination co-conspirator Congressman Albert Thomas of Texas) be brought *forthwith* from Parkland Hospital to Love Field to join and accompany Lyndon Johnson on Air Force One. as a White House aide when the illegitimate new "president" finally ventured back to Washington, D. C. on the afternoon of the assassination after stabilizing the foundering assassination plot.

50. *The SS cadre reporting to LBJ* removed the expensive bronze "official" Dallas coffin (which did **not** contain President Kennedy's body)[1011] from Parkland Hospital at gunpoint on November 22nd, 1963.[1012]

51. Lyndon Johnson himself *personally* delayed departure from Dallas until *after* he had possession of John Kennedy's body on November 22nd, 1963. LBJ wanted a valuable hostage – the president's corpse.[1013]

52. Lyndon Johnson himself *personally* delayed departure from Dallas until *after* he had physical custody of John Kennedy's *widow* on November 22nd, 1963. LBJ wanted a priceless *living* hostage – Jacqueline Kennedy – as well.[1014]

[1007] Author's exclusive original discovery.

[1008] Obstruction by Intimidation, Threats, Persuasion, or Deception, 18 USC 1512 (b).

[1009] Author's exclusive original discovery.

[1010] Author's exclusive original discovery.

[1011] Author's exclusive original discovery.

[1012] Obstruction by Intimidation, Threats, Persuasion, or Deception, 18 USC 1512 (b).

[1013] Author's exclusive original discovery.

[1014] Author's exclusive original discovery.

53. Lyndon Johnson *personally* lied to Jackie Kennedy at Love Field about when departure would occur and deliberately *stalled for additional time for his SS agents to mutilate JFK's original wounds and retrieve authentic bullets from JFK's corpse* on November 22nd, 1963.[1015]

54. Lyndon Johnson literally authored a false and materially misleading version of events by *personally* ordering his secretary and subordinate Marie Fehmer to "write this down as what has happened" when she boarded Air Force One at Love Field after the assassination on November 22nd, 1963.[1016]

55. Lyndon Johnson himself *personally* instructed SS agents aboard Air Force One to make a written record of their movements on November 22nd.[1017] In doing so, LBJ was knowingly attempting to lay the groundwork for a possible legal defense by creating and producing a false "narrative" of events.[1018]

56. Lyndon Johnson refused to return to Washington, D.C. on November 22nd, 1963, without being formally sworn in first and thereby *indisputably* acquiring and possessing the full powers of the presidency, *including* the pardon power for those *federal* crimes committed by himself and by his confederates in the violent JFK assassination plot.[1019]

57. Lyndon Johnson *personally* hired co-conspirator Jack Valenti as a White House aide on the very afternoon of the JFK assassination.

58. Lyndon Johnson *personally* gave a White House job to operative Bill Moyers in late November 1963.

59. Lyndon Johnson *personally* arranged and deliberately *used* Jackie Kennedy's presence to try to "legitimize" his oath-of-office ceremony photo aboard Air Force One at Love Field on November 22nd, 1963.[1020]

60. Immediately after being sworn in as president via murder on November 22nd, 1963, Lyndon Johnson *personally* shared an incriminating wink and smile with a top co-conspirator, Congressman Al Thomas, who had *forced* President Kennedy to come to Texas. This was captured in an official photograph by White House photographer Cecil Stoughton, who described it as "sinister" and showed it to Robert Kennedy within days of the JFK assassination.

[1015] Author's exclusive original discovery. Obstruction by Intimidation, Threats, Persuasion, or Deception, 18 USC 1512 (b).

[1016] Obstruction by Intimidation, Threats, Persuasion, or Deception, 18 USC 1512 (b).

[1017] William Manchester, *The Death of a President,* p. 266.

[1018] Author's exclusive original discovery.

[1019] Author's exclusive original discovery.

[1020] Obstruction by Intimidation, Threats, Persuasion, or Deception, 18 USC 1512 (b).

61. Moments later, Lyndon Johnson *personally* shared a knowing look with SS agent Jerry Kivett aboard Air Force One on November 22nd, 1963. This too was captured in an official photograph by White House photographer Cecil Stoughton.

62. Lyndon Johnson *personally* called FBI Director J. Edgar Hoover on the evening of November 22nd and instructed Hoover to do "whatever is needed to *clean this up*."[1021]

63. Back home in Washington D. C. after the flight from Dallas, Lyndon Johnson *personally saluted and specifically invoked his chief co-conspirator – the late Sam Rayburn, the true intellectual author of the JFK assassination plot* [1022] – on the night of November 22nd, 1963.[1023]

64. Lyndon Johnson *personally* urged Americans to *accept* the JFK assassination as a *fait d'accompli* and "bow down in submission to the will of Almighty God" [*sic*] on November 23rd, 1963 – the very day after the murder.[1024]

65. Lyndon Johnson *personally* tried to obstruct justice by peddling a false claim of Cuban responsibility for the JFK assassination to Ted Sorensen on the evening of Saturday, November 23rd, 1963.[1025]

66. Lyndon Johnson *personally* interfered with Dallas law enforcement, the very weekend of the JFK assassination, by contacting Dallas officials.[1026]

67. Lyndon Johnson *personally* attempted to cover up his illegal intrusion on the work of various Dallas authorities by specifically demanding that they not identify him as having made calls to them on the weekend of the assassination.

68. On orders from Lyndon Johnson himself, his aide Cliff Carter *personally* interfered with Texas authorities by making telephone calls that same weekend.[1027]

69. Lyndon Johnson *personally* interfered with Dallas medical personnel – and with the health of an innocent shooting victim – in a disruptive call to Parkland Hospital medical personnel regarding Lee Oswald on Sunday, November 24th, 1963.[1028]

[1021] *TIME Magazine,* "The Transfer of Power," November 29th, 1963.

[1022] Author's exclusive original discovery.

[1023] *TIME Magazine,* "The Transfer of Power," November 29th, 1963.

[1024] Presidential Proclamation 3561, delivered on television and radio to the entire nation by Johnson himself at 4:45 p.m. EST on Saturday, November 23rd, 1963.

[1025] Obstruction by Intimidation, Threats, Persuasion, or Deception, 18 USC 1512(b).

[1026] Obstruction by Intimidation, Threats, Persuasion, or Deception, 18 USC 1512(b).

[1027] Obstruction by Intimidation, Threats, Persuasion, or Deception, 18 USC 1512(b).

[1028] Obstruction by Intimidation, Threats, Persuasion, or Deception, 18 USC 1512(b).

70. Lyndon Johnson *personally* told key figures at the Pentagon that the government of Cuba was to blame for the JFK assassination, on Sunday morning, November 24th, 1963.[1029]

71. Lyndon Johnson *personally* reversed President Kennedy's policy on Vietnam withdrawal on the very weekend of the JFK assassination.

72. Lyndon Johnson *personally* ordered senior White House staff to lie to the *New York Times* regarding his supposed "continuity" with JFK's policies on the very weekend of the assassination in November 1963.[1030]

73. Lyndon Johnson *personally* met with chief JFK autopsy prosector James J. Humes, presented him with presidential trinkets, and *promoted* Humes in order to help buy Humes's silence on the central JFK assassination issue of the *criminal postmortem mutilation* of the President Kennedy's wounds.[1031]

74. Lyndon Johnson *personally* engineered an award for SS agent Rufus Youngblood in November 1963 for fictitious, non-existent "heroic action" supposedly performed during the JFK assassination in Dealey Plaza.

75. Lyndon Johnson *personally* shared a knowing look with a key SS agent on November 25th, 1963 – the very day of John Kennedy's funeral and burial.[1032]

76. Lyndon Johnson repeatedly *looked away* from President Kennedy's coffin during the burial service at Arlington National Cemetery on November 25th, 1963 – a telltale sign of his own guilt.[1033]

77. Lyndon Johnson *personally* urged America "not to turn about and linger over this evil moment" in a speech to Congress on November 27th, 1963.[1034]

78. Lyndon Johnson *personally* had the presidential limousine (which was an active *crime scene* containing vital physical evidence) shipped to two commercial companies, stripped and rebuilt during the final week of November 1963.[1035]

[1029] Al Haig with Charles McCarry, *Inner Circles,* p. 115. Obstruction by Intimidation, Threats, Persuasion, or Deception, 18 USC 1512 (b).

[1030] Obstruction by Intimidation, Threats, Persuasion, or Deception, 18 USC 1512 (b).

[1031] Obstruction by Intimidation, Threats, Persuasion, or Deception, 18 USC 1512 (b).

[1032] Author's exclusive original discovery.

[1033] Author's exclusive original discovery through my examination of numerous White House and NPS photos from that day; also documented in the *New York Herald Tribune* article by Jimmy Breslin, "Digging JFK Grave was his Honor" (November 26th, 1963), in which Breslin correctly noted that "In front of the grave, Lyndon Johnson kept his head turned to his right."

[1034] Author's exclusive original discovery.

[1035] Obstruction by Intimidation, Threats, Persuasion, or Deception, 18 USC 1512 (b).

79. Lyndon Johnson arranged the acquisition and censorship of the Air Force One radio communications tapes from November 22nd during the final week of November 1963.[1036]

80. Lyndon Johnson arranged to specifically eliminate Curtis LeMay's name from the Air Force One tapes during the final week of November 1963.

81. During the final week of November 1963, Lyndon Johnson *personally* and *deliberately* prevented the formation of risky and potentially dangerous independent congressional inquiries into the JFK assassination.[1037]

82. Lyndon Johnson *personally* told FBI director J. Edgar Hoover by telephone on November 23rd that "I may – have a lot more complications – *you know about them* so – *it may lead deeper.*"

83. Lyndon Johnson *personally* told FBI director J. Edgar Hoover by telephone on November 25th, 1963, that establishing a presidential commission on the JFK assassination "would be very bad and ***put it right in the White House.***"

84. Lyndon Johnson *personally* told his old friend FBI director J. Edgar Hoover by telephone at 10:30 a.m. on November 25th, 1963, that "we can't be checking up on every shooting scrape in the country . . ."

85. Lyndon Johnson *personally* urged FBI director J. Edgar Hoover by telephone at 10:30 a.m. on November 25th, 1963, to try to influence the *Washington Post **not*** to call for an investigation of the JFK assassination.

86. Lyndon Johnson *personally* told FBI director J. Edgar Hoover by telephone in November 1963 that "*the only way we can **stop** them*" [i.e., prevent a series of independent congressional investigations] was to appoint a high-level review commission concerning the crime.

87. Lyndon Johnson *personally* spoke to FBI director J. Edgar Hoover by telephone at 10:30 a.m. on November 25th, 1963, and explicitly expressed his desire for a cover-up by stating that "sometimes a Commission *that's not **trained*** hurts more than it helps."

88. Lyndon Johnson *personally* urged Congress and the nation "not to turn about and linger over this evil moment" on November 27th, 1963 – meaning, not to probe too deeply into the crime lest they discover his leadership of it.

89. Lyndon Johnson *personally* spoke to Senator James Eastland by telephone at 3:21 p.m. on November 28th about what LBJ disparagingly referred to as "this Dallas thing" in a criminal effort to ***discourage*** a Senate investigation of the JFK assassination. LBJ – as subtle as a dump truck – said "I've had some hesitancy to have a bunch of congressional inquiries." Senator Eastland, instantly realizing what Johnson desired, said to LBJ, "Now if you want it dropped . . . we'll drop it."

[1036] Obstruction by Intimidation, Threats, Persuasion, or Deception, 18 USC 1512 (b).

[1037] Obstruction by Intimidation, Threats, Persuasion, or Deception, 18 USC 1512 (b).

90. Lyndon Johnson *personally* spoke to Senator James Eastland by telephone at 3:21 p.m. on November 28th and admitted that the JFK assassination was "a very explosive thing" and added that "it could be a very dangerous thing for the country." LBJ *meant,* of course, that a serious probe would be a very dangerous thing *for himself.*

91. Lyndon Johnson *personally* spoke to Senator Mike Mansfield by telephone at 11:10 a.m. on November 29th in a criminal effort to persuade the Majority Leader not to permit a Senate probe of the assassination.

92. Lyndon Johnson *personally* spoke to Congressman Hale Boggs by telephone at 11:30 a.m. on November 29th in a criminal effort to *discourage* a House investigation of the JFK assassination. LBJ said to Boggs, "We are having some serious things present themselves in connection with *all these investigations going on*" regarding what LBJ coldly and haughtily dismissed as "the Dallas thing."

93. Lyndon Johnson *personally* spoke to Senator Everett Dirksen by telephone at 11:40 a.m. on November 29th in a criminal effort to *discourage* any congressional investigation of the JFK assassination. LBJ complained to Dirksen about "these investigations from the House and the Senate" regarding what LBJ rudely and patronizingly dismissed as "this Dallas affair."

94. Lyndon Johnson *personally* spoke to Congressman Charles A. Halleck by telephone on November 29th in a criminal effort to *discourage* a House of Representatives investigation of the JFK assassination. LBJ told Halleck, "Now you *help us* and *protect my flanks* there [in Congress] because *I don't want a bunch of television cameras running on this thing."*

95. Lyndon Johnson *personally* spoke to Congressman Charles A. Halleck by telephone on November 29th and admitted his real fear: "There might *somebody say a Texan did it . . . you know . . . you see what I mean."*

96. Lyndon Johnson *personally* spoke to Speaker of the House John McCormack by telephone on November 29th to discourage *any* congressional probes of the JFK assassination. McCormack replied, "Well, as far as the House is concerned, I'll do anything I can to stop investigations."

97. Lyndon Johnson *personally* stated flatly to Senator Richard Russell, during a telephone call beginning at 4:05 p.m. on November 29th, that "He [Soviet Premier Khrushchev] didn't have a damned thing to do with this." How could Johnson *possibly* "know" such a thing, at that early date, after only a week of "investigation" of the crime? The only way Johnson could *possibly* know for a fact that Khrushchev did not commit the JFK assassination was that *he himself (LBJ) committed the JFK assassination.* Johnson's vehement, categorical declaration unintentionally revealed much too much certainty, much too soon – and LBJ thereby incriminated himself in John Kennedy's murder.[1038]

[1038] Author's exclusive original discovery.

98. Lyndon Johnson *personally* spoke to Senator Richard Russell on November 29th and stated that the JFK assassination "is a question that has a good many more ramifications than on the surface . . ." In a question betraying his own obvious consciousness of guilt, LBJ explicitly pleaded with Russell, "How do I *stop* it [an independent congressional investigation of the JFK assassination]? How do I *stop* it, Dick?"

99. Lyndon Johnson *personally* spoke to Senator Richard Russell on November 29th and voiced his deep concern that – in addition to various nascent congressional investigations of the JFK assassination – an even more frightening (and legally threatening) possibility loomed, saying: ". . . and Bobby Kennedy has got *his* ideas . . ."

100. Lyndon Johnson *personally* spoke to Senator Everett Dirksen by telephone again at 5:03 p.m. on November 29th and declared, "I've got the House to agree *not to do anything* [about investigating the JFK assassination] . . ."

101. Lyndon Johnson *personally* spoke to Senator Everett Dirksen by telephone at 5:03 p.m. on November 29th and asked, "Well . . . [will] *you protect my flanks in the Senate,* Everett?" Dirksen replied, "OK. I will."

102. Lyndon Johnson *personally* spoke to a co-conspirator, former CIA director Allen Dulles, at 5:41 p.m. on November 29th and named him to the Johnson Commission on what LBJ mockingly called "the assassination of our beloved friend."

103. Lyndon Johnson *personally* spoke to the powerful House Majority Leader, Congressman Carl Albert, by telephone at 6:37 p.m. on November 29th in a criminal effort to *prevent* any congressional investigation of the JFK assassination. LBJ said, *"We don't want **anything** going in the House and Senate . . . bunch of television cameras or **a lot of loose testimony around . . ."** Carl Albert responded drily, "You've got it all under control all right."

104. Lyndon Johnson *personally* spoke to the powerful House Majority Leader, Congressman Carl Albert, by telephone on November 29th in a criminal effort to *prevent any* congressional investigation of the JFK assassination. Using the same criminal phrasing that he had used with other congressional figures, LBJ said to Congressman Albert, *"And **you'll protect my flank** on it."*

105. Lyndon Johnson *personally* spoke to Senator James Eastland *again* by telephone at 7:03 p.m. on November 29th. Regarding the presidential commission which he was forming [which would totally supplant any and all independent congressional investigations of the JFK assassination], LBJ informed Eastland that "He [J. Edgar Hoover] said he'd *protect* this Commission – I mean *the flanks* . . ."

106. Lyndon Johnson *personally* spoke to Senator James Eastland by telephone at 7:03 p.m. on November 29th and *explicitly demanded protection from*

investigation and prosecution. "And you've got to ***protect my flank*** over in the Senate now," LBJ said to Eastland.[1039]

107. Lyndon Johnson *personally* created the Johnson Commission (formally titled "The President's Commission on the Assassination of President Kennedy") in November 1963.[1040]

108. Lyndon Johnson *personally* staffed the Johnson Commission (formally titled "The President's Commission on the Assassination of President Kennedy") in November 1963.[1041]

109. Lyndon Johnson *personally* paid for the Johnson Commission ("The President's Commission on the Assassination of President Kennedy") out of presidential emergency funds in November 1963.[1042]

110. Lyndon Johnson *personally* harangued, terrorized and fraudulently manipulated Supreme Court Chief Justice Earl Warren into heading the Johnson Commission in November 1963 by raising the devastating specter of global nuclear war – despite LBJ's own direct *personal* knowledge that there was in fact no "Soviet" or "Cuban" involvement in the JFK assassination.[1043]

111. Lyndon Johnson *personally* put co-conspirator Allen Dulles (with whom he had personally met and conspired between 1956 and 1963, including just weeks before the assassination in Dallas) on the Johnson Commission in November 1963.[1044]

112. Lyndon Johnson *personally* ordered top White House aides to arrange and secure a pardon for an individual involved in the JFK assassination in late 1963.[1045]

113. Lyndon Johnson *personally* instructed his wife to bring Sam Rayburn's framed portrait into the White House on December 7th, 1963, thereby paying specific posthumous tribute to LBJ's chief assassination co-conspirator.[1046]

114. Lyndon Johnson *personally* welcomed key assassination co-conspirator Al Thomas of Texas into the White House living quarters on December 7th, 1963.

[1039] Contemptible courtier and Establishment shill Michael Beschloss denies *the plain English meaning* of LBJ's frenzied pleas and desperate demands that Congress ***not*** investigate the JFK assassination.

[1040] Obstruction by Intimidation, Threats, Persuasion, or Deception, 18 USC 1512 (b).

[1041] Obstruction by Intimidation, Threats, Persuasion, or Deception, 18 USC 1512 (b).

[1042] Obstruction by Intimidation, Threats, Persuasion, or Deception, 18 USC 1512 (b).

[1043] Obstruction by Intimidation, Threats, Persuasion, or Deception, 18 USC 1512 (b).

[1044] Obstruction by Intimidation, Threats, Persuasion, or Deception, 18 USC 1512 (b).

[1045] Author's exclusive original discovery.

[1046] Author's exclusive original discovery.

115. Lyndon Johnson *personally* lied to White House staffer Pierre Salinger in late1963, saying that President Kennedy was killed in retaliation for the American-backed coup against the Diem dictatorship in South Vietnam.[1047]

116. Lyndon Johnson *personally* admitted his own sinister "trade" of the escalated Vietnam War for *U. S. military support of the JFK assassination and LBJ's coup* in remarks made to the Joint Chiefs of Staff at the White House itself in late December 1963. "Just let me get elected, and you can have your war," said LBJ to his uniformed senior accomplices.[1048]

117. Lyndon Johnson *personally* ordered the initiation of USAF U-2 mapping and reconnaissance flights over Vietnam in late December 1963, as an initial "down payment" on the massive expansion of the Vietnam war which he had promised to the American military in exchange for its support of his murderous coup in Dallas.[1049]

118. Lyndon Johnson and the SS *personally* threatened and intimidated Governor John Connally into **not** seriously challenging the false official story of the JFK assassination.[1050]

119. Lyndon Johnson *personally* promoted and rewarded USAF Sgt. Paul Glynn, who covered and guarded the second coffin in Air Force One's main cabin on November 22nd, 1963.[1051]

120. Lyndon Johnson *personally* promoted and rewarded USAF Sgt. Ken Gaddis, who ultimately maintained a desk outside LBJ's White House bedroom.[1052]

121. Lyndon Johnson *personally* threatened any SS agents who might have harbored or retained any lingering loyalty to President Kennedy in January 1964.[1053]

122. Lyndon Johnson *personally* harassed the Johnson Commission to finish faster in 1964.[1054]

[1047] Obstruction by Intimidation, Threats, Persuasion, or Deception, 18 USC 1512 (b).

[1048] The sickeningly pathetic Stanley Karnow reported the incident but gutlessly refused to acknowledge the obvious meaning of LBJ's thoroughly self-incriminating statement. The source was U. S. Army Chief of Staff General Harold K. Johnson, who was personally present at the White House reception and was a firsthand earwitness to LBJ's blatant *quid pro quo.*

[1049] Author's exclusive original discovery.

[1050] Obstruction by Intimidation, Threats, Persuasion, or Deception, 18 USC 1512 (b).

[1051] Author interviews with USAF veteran Joe Chappell, 2012 and 2013.

[1052] LBJ aide Horace Busby noted this in his posthumously published book, *The 31st of March.*

[1053] Obstruction by Intimidation, Threats, Persuasion, or Deception, 18 USC 1512 (b).

[1054] Obstruction by Intimidation, Threats, Persuasion, or Deception, 18 USC 1512 (b).

123. Lyndon Johnson *personally* refused to testify under oath to his own Commission regarding the JFK assassination in 1964.[1055]

124. Lyndon Johnson *personally* put information about "problems of special urgency" into his 1964 written statement to the Johnson Commission as a "get-out-of-jail-free" card.[1056]

125. In 1964, Lyndon Johnson deliberately *lied* regarding RFK's statements about taking the presidential oath in Dallas on November 22nd, 1963.[1057]

126. Lyndon Johnson *personally* refused to make Robert F. Kennedy his vice-presidential running mate in 1964 – an act done *specifically in order to prevent a retaliatory assassination* [1058] or any other form of political ouster (and prosecution for Dallas) by RFK.

127. Lyndon Johnson *personally* prevented RFK from being nominated for president at the August 1964 Democratic National Convention in Atlantic City by *personally* changing the sequence of events and delaying RFK's scheduled speech until after LBJ's own nomination was absolutely secured – *specifically to prevent Bobby from being in a position to do to LBJ what LBJ did to JFK*.[1059]

128. Lyndon Johnson *personally* ensured that the Commission records would be transferred to the National Archives, and thereby sealed for 75 years (beyond the expected lifetimes of all JFK assassination participants).

129. Lyndon Johnson campaigned openly in public in the autumn of 1964 (including long, slow, open-car motorcades and lengthy stops for public speeches), betraying the fact that *LBJ himself had run and led the JFK assassination* and that therefore he knew with absolute certainty that there was no genuine "danger" lurking in public exposure during campaign events.[1060]

130. Lyndon Johnson exhibited multiple signs of severe mental illness in mid-1965[1061] because his huge debt to the U. S. military was coming due – and as LBJ fully understood, the gargantuan cost of escalating the Vietnam War to repay the JCS for its

---

[1055] Obstruction by Intimidation, Threats, Persuasion, or Deception, 18 USC 1512 (b).

[1056] Obstruction by Intimidation, Threats, Persuasion, or Deception, 18 USC 1512(b).

[1057] Obstruction by Intimidation, Threats, Persuasion, or Deception, 18 USC 1512 (b).

[1058] Author's exclusive original discovery.

[1059] Author's exclusive original discovery.

[1060] Author's exclusive original discovery.

[1061] Richard Goodwin, "President Lyndon Johnson: The War Within," *New York Times Magazine,* August 21st, 1988.

support in assassinating JFK would ultimately *destroy* Johnson's own ill-gotten presidency.[1062]

131. Lyndon Johnson *personally* and *vehemently* refused to speak to the Kennedy family's designated author, William Manchester, regarding the JFK assassination – lest he (LBJ) slip up and inadvertently make damning, self-incriminating statements.[1063]

132. Lyndon Johnson *personally* and *vehemently* refused to release full versions of Air Force One radio transcripts from the day of the JFK assassination to author William Manchester in August 1965[1064] – lest Manchester and the Kennedys discover incriminating comments by LBJ and the obviously massive censorship of numerous damning statements by guilty personnel on that day.[1065]

133. Lyndon Johnson *personally* gave a White House job to SS agent and Dallas shift leader Emory Roberts.

134. Lyndon Johnson *personally* gave a key White House job to USAF pilot Jim Cross in 1965.[1066]

135. Lyndon Johnson *personally* put USAF pilot Jim Cross in charge of a major White House slush fund in 1965.

136. Lyndon Johnson *personally* made USAF pilot Jim Cross the new pilot of Air Force One in 1965.

137. Lyndon Johnson *personally* promoted SS agent Rufus Youngblood to SAIC-WHD, then to the role of Assistant Director of the Secret Service.

138. Lyndon Johnson *personally* made SS agent Lem Johns the SAIC-WHD.

139. Lyndon Johnson *personally* made SS agent Clint Hill the SAIC-WHD.

140. Lyndon Johnson *personally* gave land in Texas to USAF Sgt. Paul Glynn, his valet.[1067]

141. Lyndon Johnson *personally* made SS agent Jerry D. Kivett a member of the White House detail.

142. Lyndon Johnson *personally* tried to give a parole board job to SS agent Emory Roberts.

[1062] Author's exclusive original discovery.

[1063] Author's exclusive original discovery.

[1064] William Manchester, *The Death of a President,* p. 371.

[1065] White House aide Jack Valenti's typewritten August 31st, 1965, memo to LBJ on the subject – with LBJ's repeated handwritten refusal – was highlighted on Bill Kelly's *Countercoup* blog in June 2014.

[1066] The role of White House Military Aide was *in addition to* Cross's role as chief pilot for Air Force One under LBJ.

[1067] Author interview with USAF veteran Joe Chappell, 2013.

143. Lyndon Johnson *personally* escalated the Vietnam War in 1965 as an explicit *quid pro quo* payment for massive U. S. military backing of his bloody November 1963 coup.[1068]

144. Lyndon Johnson *personally* made the former USAF Vice Chief of Staff, General William "Bozo" McKee, the new head of the FAA in 1965. Significantly, the original November 22nd, 1963, FAA tower log from Andrews Air Force Base has disappeared, been destroyed or otherwise been rendered "inaccessible."

145. Lyndon Johnson *personally* nominated Abe Fortas to the Supreme Court in 1965. This was not simply a reward to an old crony and past co-conspirator in other illegal schemes; by putting Fortas on the Court, LBJ was literally placing a loyalist on the bench who could legally issue a *stay of execution* in the event that Johnson were ever arrested, indicted, prosecuted and sentenced to death for his leading role in the JFK assassination.[1069]

146. Lyndon Johnson *personally* promoted Richard Helms to be Director of the CIA in 1966.

147. Lyndon Johnson *personally* made his own lawyer, Austin attorney Ed Clark, the American Ambassador to Australia (!) and literally *sent him to the other side of the planet* in 1966 when questions about the JFK assassination mounted even in the normally whorish corporate American media. Sending Ed Clark literally half a world away meant that Clark could not easily be arrested or subpoenaed by any potential new American investigative body, and thus be forced to testify against LBJ in the JFK assassination.[1070] (While embassies themselves are legally considered American soil, Clark could simply go for a short walk and thereby place himself on Australian turf.)

148. Lyndon Johnson *personally* brought Johnson Commissioners to his Texas ranch after the Wesley Liebeler memorandum about postmortem JFK wound alteration was sent to government officials in November 1966.[1071]

149. Lyndon Johnson *personally* prevented any re-opening of the federal government's JFK assassination investigation during the 1960s.[1072]

150. Lyndon Johnson *personally* knew of and *personally* discussed "missing" JFK autopsy evidence with U. S. Attorney General Ramsey Clark in 1967.

151. Lyndon Johnson *personally* assisted friendly author Jim Bishop with interviews and vital access to key people and places for the research and writing of

---

[1068] Author's exclusive original discovery.

[1069] Author's exclusive original discovery.

[1070] Author's exclusive original discovery.

[1071] Obstruction by Intimidation, Threats, Persuasion, or Deception, 18 USC 1512 (b).

[1072] Obstruction by Intimidation, Threats, Persuasion, or Deception, 18 USC 1512 (b).

Bishop's 1968 book, *The Day Kennedy Was Shot* – which constituted an LBJ retort to the Kennedy family's "authorized" account, William Manchester's 1967 book *Death of a President*.[1073]

152. Lyndon Johnson *personally* lied to key White House aide Joseph Califano later in the 1960s, years after Dallas, by falsely telling Califano that Fidel Castro had killed JFK.[1074]

153. Lyndon Johnson *personally* lied to White House staffer Marvin Watson in 1967, saying that "the CIA" [*sic*] killed President Kennedy – as if the Agency were not in fact participating in the crime (albeit at a very minor level) at the behest of the true plot leader: LBJ himself.[1075]

154. Lyndon Johnson *personally* lied to journalist Howard K. Smith, falsely telling him that Castro killed JFK.

155. Lyndon Johnson personally succumbed to deliberate blackmail by the Joint Chiefs of Staff regarding *the removal of Robert McNamara as Secretary of Defense* as well as *serious consideration of the potential use of nuclear weapons* in the Vietnam War (both of which occurred in early 1968) because of his inescapable debt to the American military for its assistance and armed guarantee of the success of the JFK assassination in 1963.[1076]

156. Lyndon Johnson *personally* and *repeatedly* threatened RFK's life before assassinating him in 1968 to *prevent future prosecution and punishment* of LBJ for the JFK assassination.[1077]

157. Lyndon Johnson *personally* had Robert Kennedy assassinated in 1968 *specifically to prevent* any serious investigation of the JFK assassination while Johnson was still alive.[1078]

158. Lyndon Johnson *personally* harangued White House staff in early June 1968 and inquired repeatedly and explicitly as to whether or not Robert Kennedy was *"dead yet."*[1079] Those remarks are proof positive that LBJ himself was behind the bloody 1968 assassination of RFK[1080] – a murder whose *only* motive was to prevent

---

[1073] Author's exclusive original discovery.

[1074] Joseph Califano, *Inside,* p. 126.

[1075] Obstruction by Intimidation, Threats, Persuasion, or Deception, 18 USC 1512 (b).

[1076] Author's exclusive original discovery.

[1077] Author's exclusive original discovery.

[1078] Author's exclusive original discovery.

[1079] Jeff Shesol noted this in his book *Mutual Contempt,* yet was utterly oblivious to the obvious meaning of LBJ's chilling query.

[1080] Author's exclusive original discovery.

Robert Kennedy from winning the White House and (armed with the nearly unlimited power of the presidency – successfully prosecuting LBJ for the 1963 assassination of President Kennedy.[1081]

159. Lyndon Johnson *personally* canceled a U. S. government plane intended to take a top doctor to help RFK in 1968 following the Los Angeles shooting, thereby totally eliminating any remote chance of saving Bobby's life. This was part of LBJ's deliberate criminal effort to *absolutely ensure* that the gravely wounded senator would certainly die.

160. Lyndon Johnson *personally* promoted USAF Major Jim Cross rapidly and dramatically, advancing Cross all the way to Brigadier General by 1969.

161. Lyndon Johnson *personally* made USAF General Jim Cross the commander of Bergstrom Air Force Base in Texas in 1969 *as part of a conscious scheme to avoid having to actually serve **prison time*** in the event of any prosecution for the JFK assassination.[1082]

162. Lyndon Johnson *personally* arranged spacious and comfortable quarters for possible long-term *house arrest* for himself at the Bergstrom Air Force Base hospital in 1969 through USAF General Jim Cross (where LBJ would feign cardiac problems and thus *avoid* actual trial and incarceration for his crimes).[1083]

163. Lyndon Johnson *personally* tried to reward longtime crony and fellow criminal conspirator Abe Fortas even further by nominating him to be the Chief Justice of the Supreme Court in 1968.

164. Lyndon Johnson *personally* told close aides in 1969 that he feared *prosecution* by new president Richard Nixon – which could ***only*** mean prosecution for *the JFK assassination*.[1084]

165. Lyndon Johnson *personally* misled CBS (and thus, the nation) in 1969 interviews with Walter Cronkite interview (released in censored form in 1972), by falsely hinting that Cuba had killed JFK.[1085]

166. Lyndon Johnson *personally* made a key admission (known in the legal world as an utterly damning "statement against penal interest") about his own criminal

---

[1081] Author's exclusive original discovery.

[1082] Author's exclusive original discovery.

[1083] Author's exclusive original discovery. (See James Cross with Denise Gamino and Gary Rice, *Around the World with LBJ*, pp. 171-172.)

[1084] Author's exclusive original discovery. Robert Dallek mentioned LBJ's fear without understanding (or admitting) what it *actually* (and obviously) referred to.

[1085] Obstruction by Intimidation, Threats, Persuasion, or Deception, 18 USC 1512 (b).

activity in a post-presidential interview with Leo Janos. LBJ bragged, "They never once found out about the things I ***did*** do."[1086]

167. Lyndon Johnson *personally* made false statements – again blaming the JFK assassination on Cuba – while speaking in Texas with a British publisher in March 1971.[1087]

168. Finally, Lyndon Johnson *personally* made several *other* key admissions (known in the legal world as utterly damning "statements against penal interest") *specifically regarding the JFK assassination* in his own 1971 memoir.[1088]

* * *

The last item listed above is the subject of the following chapter.

Incredibly but predictably, for all his assiduous and far-reaching efforts to *avoid prosecution* for JFK's assassination during his blood-soaked and completely illegitimate tenure in the Oval Office, Lyndon Johnson did ***not*** want to simply ride off into the sunset and disappear into history without *somehow* finding a way to beat his chest and boast openly of his bloody, seditious, hard-won criminal "victory" in Dallas in November 1963.

Ultimately, he found a way to do so – and it was vintage Johnson.

In fact, America, it was *vantage* Johnson.[1089]

[1086] Author's exclusive original discovery. (See Leo Janos, "The Last Days of the President," *The Atlantic,* July 1973.)

[1087] George Weidenfeld, *Remembering My Good Friends,* pp. 350-351. Robert P. Morrow found this information.

[1088] Author's exclusive original discovery.

[1089] Author's exclusive original discovery.

Lyndon Baines Johnson actually *confessed*
his leadership of – and his central involvement in –
the assassination of President Kennedy.

Author's exclusive original discovery.

Chapter Thirty-Five:
The Confessions of Lyndon Baines Johnson

*"There might somebody say
a Texan did it."*

– Lyndon Baines Johnson

*"They never once found out about
the things I **did** do."*

– Lyndon Baines Johnson

*"These things do not just 'happen.'
They are **made** to happen."*

– John Fitzgerald Kennedy

It's far too much to hope for, of course.

Isn't it?

The idea that the coarse, brutal killer who had authored a crime of staggering dimensions and gargantuan destructive impact would actually *lay bare his actions and announce his bloody deeds to the world* seems . . . totally "impossible."

Much less that he would do so *while he was still alive.*

Tough to accept, for naïve and stupid and weak-minded individuals.

*I just can't **believe** that he would **do** that, Martha. Hell – I just can't **believe** it!*

Well, for better or worse, the time has come to believe it.

You frankly have no choice in the matter, America – because it's *true.*[1090]

* * *

[1090] Author's exclusive original discovery.

From an astonishingly early date, a number of books have indicated, hinted, suggested, implied, alleged, theorized and even openly asserted that Lyndon Johnson was guilty of the JFK assassination.

Some of those books are *marginally* better than others (which, in all candor, isn't saying very much); but frankly, **none** of them have ever been truly good enough.

Not one.

Yes, America, Lyndon Johnson **was** indeed guilty of the JFK assassination.

But the plain truth is this:

None of those earlier books ever **proved** it.

Unfortunately, previous authors have often wallowed in decidedly *peripheral* issues – contenting themselves by merely painting a portrait of LBJ's truly vicious personality, his abusive personal interactions, his ugly bullying of others, his nasty personal habits, his warped psychology, and his ruthless lust for power.

All those things are true, by the way – *but they do **not** prove Lyndon Johnson's criminal culpability for Dallas!*

They simply prove LBJ's lack of any boundaries whatsoever.

Prim, prudish, pathetically naive Americans don't like to *think* that a President could really behave in the grotesque fashion that LBJ did, but Lyndon Johnson actually did do so. Had LBJ not been the president – had we the people seen those sickening, often criminal behaviors *publicly,* at the time – had corporate "journalists" and Senate colleagues and cowardly bureaucrats not willingly and deliberately covered them up – then, as one government observer later remarked, LBJ would have been confined to a mental hospital.[1091]

But no one said a word publicly, and LBJ (for whom norms and ethics and morals and laws were mere trifling obstacles to be ignored or violated at will) remained free to go on to commit a series of stunning crimes – crimes of ever-greater proportions.

A very important principle is at work here – a principle which *I* first discovered and articulated in the early 1990s:

Whatever you cannot (or will not) imagine to be possible *is **absolutely** possible* – precisely **because** you cannot imagine it.[1092]

Criminals *count on* normal people's civilized (and quite pathetic) *inability* to think like them, to anticipate their worst acts, and to respond effectively (or at all).[1093]

To paraphrase Marshall McLuhan, the only secrets that actually require protection are *tiny* secrets. Huge secrets are fully protected by the populace's sheer *inability* to believe them.

[1091] Secret Service agent Richard Roth made the observation to writer Ronald Kessler.

[1092] Author's exclusive original insight.

[1093] Author's exclusive original insight.

Major *crimes* are likewise carried out successfully thanks largely to public incredulity – and major criminals (including presidents) are subsequently protected largely by public incredulity.[1094]

The public's cowardly "discomfort" *literally grants impunity to killers.*

The crimes occurred.

But *proving* those crimes conclusively and identifying those criminals through *specific, pertinent data* – as I have done thoroughly and definitively and decisively in this book, for the very first time anywhere – is another matter entirely.

And incredibly, *LBJ himself* assisted me in proving his guilt for all time.

* * *

Lyndon Johnson was guilty of homicide – the murder of his predecessor.

He was also guilty of conspiracy and sedition, among other things.[1095]

Not only have I proven that conclusively in this book, but *LBJ himself made it clear* with *his very own* words and actions – before, during and after November 22nd.[1096]

But . . . *is there **more?***

Is there something more graphic, something more overt, something more specific in this vein than all the other overwhelming mountain of probative and dispositive evidence previously revealed in this book?

The answer is ***yes.***

I realized it only after *decades* of studying the case, becoming highly attuned to the import and relevance of data and statements which, strangely, pass right over the heads of myopic and cowardly conventional hacks (the pseudo-"historians" and pseudo-"biographers" who strive to *suppress* the truth, not to reveal it).

I made a truly startling discovery one springtime day:

The domineering killer from Texas who reveled in public adulation declared his guilt not only in notes to himself and in quiet moments and in small gatherings of underlings, but also in the place he most wanted to proclaim it: *right out in the open, under everyone's very noses.*[1097]

[1094] Those who ignorantly guffaw at the notion of serious crimes being committed by famous Americans always end up subsisting on a steady diet of ***crow.*** If you are one of those supremely foolish individuals, then plan on stocking your pantry *immediately* with copious quantities of Worcestershire sauce. You're going to *need* it, bucko.

[1095] See Appendix 1 of this book for a revealing list which I assembled listing the *numerous* federal criminal statutes violated by Lyndon Baines Johnson in the planning, commission and furtherance of the JFK assassination.

[1096] Author's exclusive original discovery.

[1097] Author's exclusive original discovery.

Finally, I understood.

Finally, I recognized the meaning of his words.

Lyndon Johnson made his ultimate confession not as a contrite, sincere *mea culpa,* but as an arrogant declaration of his power.

And he made it *in writing.*

As an *announcement,* not an apology.

LBJ spelled it out, right there in front of all of us.

He did so *not* as a somber admission of guilt, but a gleeful expression of *pride.*

He actually *bragged* about what he had done.

I did this.

I made it happen.

I pulled the burning chestnuts out of the fire.

Only I could have salvaged the imploding JFK assassination plot.

For Lyndon Baines Johnson, confession of crimes was not an act of contrition but rather an act of braggadocio. And it was hardly a rare act. It was in fact an integral part of Johnson's usual, customary pattern and practice.[1098]

* * *

It began early on.

LBJ had always been a braggart, but confessing to *crimes* was a step beyond.

In July 1960, short days after successfully blackmailing John F. Kennedy into putting him on the Democratic ticket, Lyndon Johnson returned to his Texas ranch and there held forth to journalist Nancy Hanschman (later Nancy Hanschman Dickerson).

LBJ alluded very clearly that day to JFK's sexual peccadilloes – but as Nancy dutifully listened, either (A) she was not intelligent enough to fully grasp the fact that Johnson had just successfully *blackmailed* his way onto the Democratic ticket with that sexual information, or (B) she simply was not bold or honest enough to specify the true meaning of Johnson's words in her later book mentioning the conversation.[1099]

* * *

[1098] Candor compels me to note that the only individual I have ever known personally who exhibited the same hideous mix of bullying, abuse, manipulation, connivance, deep dishonesty, evasion, cowardice, grotesque narcissism, kleptoparasitic and predatory behavior, and *braggadocio about criminal acts* as Lyndon Baines Johnson was the self-acknowledged public figure and self-acknowledged former mental patient and self-acknowledged *burglar and thief* named Samuel D. Lifton – the extraordinarily nasty fellow who for decades used the *alias* "David S. Lifton."

[1099] See Nancy Hanschman Dickerson's book *Among Those Present.*

In a revealing 1967 episode, Johnson hosted Texas journalist and longtime LBJ critic Ronnie Dugger at the White House. Having reached the ultimate pinnacle of power, Johnson no longer feared the Texas newsman and longtime gadfly.

In fact, the Confessional Lyndon Johnson was on full display that night.

LBJ disappeared into Lady Bird's room and returned to brazenly display a picture documenting and proving one of his own biggest earlier crimes: a photograph of the infamous Box 13, a container of votes which was criminally employed by Johnson's forces to fraudulently swing the 1948 Senate race in Texas to LBJ and thereby enable him to become a senator and thus a "national" politician.[1100]

Deliberately and brazenly showing that deeply incriminating photo to Ronnie Dugger was a staggeringly arrogant act by a staggeringly arrogant individual.

But even *that* stunning disclosure paled next to LBJ's other confessions.

The most damning and serious *JFK-assassination-related* admissions also came directly *from Lyndon Johnson himself.*

Over and over and over again.

* * *

Lyndon Baines Johnson was an experienced confessor. He enjoyed it. He did it on multiple occasions. He reveled in the power that he held and the total impunity that he felt – the sheer guilty joy of having *gotten away with something monumental.*[1101]

In short, Lyndon Johnson was a confessional man.[1102]

Extremely confessional.

And LBJ actually confessed to the JFK assassination *multiple times, in multiple ways.*[1103]

* * *

On November 22nd itself, Lyndon Johnson's astounding *direct* order to SS agent Jerry Kivett – the order *not* to tell the trusted USAF crew of SAM 26000 what LBJ's *actual destination was* going to be – was a stunning confession of Johnson's

---

[1100] Dugger recounted the stunning incident in his book *The Politician* (in an unpaginated photo caption).

[1101] In this regard too, the striking and ugly parallel between LBJ and Lifton (one of many) is very pronounced. My considered view – based on *decades* of personal experience and direct observation; literally *thousands* of interactions; and Lifton's own numerous, voluntary, extremely disturbing revelations about himself – is that Lifton's primary motivation in life was *not* "the pursuit of truth," but rather the perverse desire to see *just how much he could get away with.*

[1102] Author's exclusive original discovery.

[1103] Author's exclusive original discovery.

guilt because it revealed *LBJ's intention to flee the country to avoid prosecution for JFK's murder.*[1104]

* * *

Johnson also confessed to the JFK assassination via his ugly and repeated *trivialization of the crime* within days of the slaying.[1105] Speaking to senior politicians and a high government official and a major journalist during the first week after Dallas, LBJ uttered disgusting and dismissive comments about the very crime which he had engineered and personally led.

"The President . . . must not inject himself into *local* killings," he declared piously to widely read columnist Joseph Alsop.

"Now we can't be checking up on every *shooting scrape* in the country," he said to FBI Director J. Edgar Hoover.

Johnson even referred to the bloody daylight murder of President Kennedy as "this Dallas thing" and "the Dallas thing" and "this Dallas affair" (!) in conversations with top members of Congress – as if he were merely mentioning a mildly unpleasant incident involving a brief fistfight at a Shriners' convention rather than *the deliberate slaughter of the president and the destruction of American democracy.*

LBJ's deliberate efforts over several days to *actively minimize* the sheer enormity of the crime which he had perpetrated is further evidence of his guilt.

* * *

Johnson's *numerous* pleas to key members of Congress in November 1963 during the week after the JFK assassination were additional confessions.[1106] LBJ *explicitly* begged top leaders of the House and Senate ***not*** to conduct ***any*** investigation of what had actually happened to President Kennedy!

No innocent man would have *dared* to make (or even been *inclined* to make) such outrageously inappropriate and patently illegal requests; moreover, no innocent man would have feared the results of any proper independent investigation.

But Lyndon Baines Johnson was no innocent man.

He was the leader of the coup.

* * *

[1104] Author's exclusive original discovery.

[1105] Author's exclusive original discovery.

[1106] Those pleas were itemized in the preceding chapter.

On November 29th, 1963 – one week to the day after the JFK assassination – Lyndon Johnson summoned Chief Justice Earl Warren to the Oval Office and openly noted that talk was circulating that the assassination of John Fitzgerald Kennedy was in fact the work of *a group within the U. S. government that wished to see LBJ occupy the presidency.*

There was indeed such a group. It really existed, and it was headed by none other than Lyndon Baines Johnson himself.

LBJ actually *unveiled the ugly truth* – falsely veiling it as a "rumor" – to help buffalo Earl Warren into conducting only a pitiful sham of an "investigation" [*sic*] into JFK's slaying.

In his jaw-dropping private admission to the chief justice, LBJ was once again brazenly "broadcasting in the clear,"[1107] as he had done back in April 1963 when he *publicly* warned various right-wing American figures and Cuban exile renegades to cease their own amateur assassination plotting because he, Lyndon Johnson, was heading a *serious* plot – a high-powered, *U. S. government* plot – that would come to bloody fruition in November 1963.[1108]

* * *

In December 1963, LBJ spoke to the Joint Chiefs of Staff at a White House reception and *explicitly articulated* the brutal bargain he had struck with them for their role as guarantors of Johnson's coup against JFK.[1109]

Lyndon Johnson traded Dallas for Vietnam.[1110]

He actually said it aloud.

"You just let me get elected [in 1964]," Johnson assured the Pentagon brass in December 1963, "and then you can have your war."

LBJ was explicitly *acknowledging* his debt to the U. S. military for their vital assistance in making the JFK assassination happen (and for *restraining* themselves from following their instincts and desires by launching an aggressive war or an illegal invasion in its immediate aftermath).[1111]

It was not a chance remark, or a random comment, or a "coincidence."

[1107] Author's exclusive original discovery.

[1108] Author's exclusive original discovery.

[1109] Author's exclusive original discovery.

[1110] Author's exclusive original discovery.

[1111] Author's exclusive original discovery.

It was an explicit verbal admission of their bloody *quid pro quo*.[1112]

* * *

Lyndon Johnson also confessed his role in killing JFK through his 1964 political machinations. An innocent man would have had no problem *whatsoever* with making Robert Kennedy his running mate that year; indeed, an innocent man would have *craved* the votes that RFK would certainly have brought to the Democratic ticket in the autumn presidential election.

But strangely, Johnson obstinately refused.[1113]

Why?

Why deliberately toss *millions of guaranteed votes* in the garbage?

The reason is stark and simple:

He didn't want to put Bobby Kennedy in a position to do to LBJ what LBJ had done to JFK![1114]

The Kennedy family had ample wealth, and thus possessed all the funds necessary to put together a successful *revenge killing* of its own against the man who assassinated John Kennedy.

And *that* is why Lyndon Johnson refused to make Robert Kennedy his running mate in 1964.[1115]

In fact, LBJ actually expressed open and explicit *dread* about justifiable revenge from RFK!

Regarding his choice for running mate in the 1964 presidential campaign, Lyndon Baines Johnson rejected Robert Kennedy – very explicitly and completely – because, as LBJ himself declared vehemently, "I'm not going to let them [i.e., the Democratic Party] put somebody in bed with me [i.e., on the ticket with me] that'll *murder* me."[1116]

Read that again, America:

[1112] Author's exclusive original discovery.

[1113] Author's exclusive original discovery.

[1114] Author's exclusive original discovery.

[1115] Author's exclusive original discovery.

[1116] Lawrence Leamer, *Sons of Camelot: The Fate of an American Dynasty,* p. 465.

Robert P. Morrow kindly brought that extremely damning quote by Lyndon Johnson to my attention in 2021 – several years after I had already made my own exclusive, original intellectual discovery that *LBJ feared a revenge killing by Robert Kennedy,* and for *that* reason had refused to put Bobby on the Democratic ticket in 1964. The chilling quote which Morrow alerted me to provides *absolute corroboration* of my earlier original insight.

I'm not going to let them put somebody in bed with me that'll murder me.

The Texan meant it, too.

Johnson was *that explicit* about his fear that as Vice Presidential running mate, Bobby Kennedy would arrange to have LBJ killed during – or just after – the 1964 presidential election campaign.

Robert Kennedy would obviously then replace Lyndon Johnson as Chief Executive.

The fact is that LBJ would not have ever *imagined* such a thing unless he, Johnson, *had **in fact** murdered John Kennedy,* and therefore felt both the consciousness of guilt *and* a very real and grave concern about the risk of violent retribution by the fallen victim's fierce, avenging brother.

* * *

During his bloody reign in the White House, LBJ bellowed angrily that every six months or so the press would (supposedly) report *that he had killed Kennedy.* Johnson's claim about the laughably deferential and cowardly American corporate media wasn't true (after all, there aren't enough balls in all of corporate American "journalism" to even play a game of pool), but LBJ's frustrated and highly self-incriminating outburst *accurately reflected and expressed Johnson's own guilty knowledge and his direct personal culpability* in the murder of President Kennedy.[1117]

* * *

On a scrap of blank paper which he used for note-taking during a White House meeting in March 1968, LBJ himself personally inscribed the word *"murderer."*[1118]

It doesn't get any more explicit than that, America.

An aide recovered and preserved the piece of paper, but apparently did not stop to wonder whether Johnson, who was *literally and correctly labeling himself a murderer,*[1119] was doing so due to the massive ongoing slaughter which he was currently presiding over in Vietnam, or because of the 1963 assassination he had overseen in Dallas – and the rapidly approaching assassinations that he was *already*

[1117] Author's exclusive original discovery.

[1118] Lloyd Gardner, *Pay Any Price,* p. 457. Gardner mentioned the note but was evidently ***oblivious*** to its true significance.

[1119] Author's exclusive original discovery.

engineering[1120] of both Martin Luther King in Memphis *and* Robert Francis Kennedy out in Los Angeles.[1121]

Be very clear:

*Lyndon Baines Johnson committed **all three** of the most significant American political assassinations of the 1960s.*[1122]

JFK's 1963 murder in Dallas gave Lyndon Johnson *the White House, his lifelong goal.*

MLK's 1968 murder in Memphis prevented disruption of the capital and the concomitant disruption of *the Vietnam War,* which LBJ owed to his U. S. military backers in exchange for their support of his Dallas coup.[1123]

RFK's 1968 murder in Los Angeles protected Lyndon Johnson from future federal prosecution by *President* Robert F. Kennedy for JFK's assassination.[1124]

All three murders were *absolutely necessary,* from LBJ's standpoint.[1125]

All of them were *essential.*

And all of them were ultimately carried out, at his command.[1126]

Lyndon Baines Johnson would not be denied.

* * *

But as I have correctly pointed out several times in this book, LBJ always made *contingency* plans.

[1120] Author's exclusive original discovery.

[1121] Author's exclusive original discovery. Lyndon Baines Johnson *personally* ordered the assassination of **all three** men, as I will thoroughly document and conclusively prove in a future book which is already in progress.

[1122] Author's exclusive original discovery.

[1123] Author's exclusive original discovery.

[1124] Author's exclusive original discovery. I possess extraordinary information documenting LBJ's *direct personal role* in **all three** of those key 1960s assassinations, which I will unveil in a future book.

Sadly, as of 2023, many lesser JFK assassination researchers are still wallowing in the primitive and shallow and laughably erroneous "CIA did it!" [*sic*] puddle, embarrassingly oblivious to the reality of who *actually* killed the three foremost American figures of the 1960s – and *why.*

[1125] Author's exclusive original discovery.

[1126] Author's exclusive original discovery.

Once again, just as he had done in leading and perpetrating the assassination of President Kennedy, *Lyndon Johnson would call upon – and rely upon – the assets and the personnel of the United States Air Force.*[1127]

As usual, LBJ had planned his maneuvers **well in advance** – and he had made several *very specific, documented moves* in order to position loyal subordinates in places where they could do him the most good.[1128]

Key to Johnson's plans was none other than USAF officer James U. Cross.[1129]

Johnson arranged for his longtime personal pilot (on both the C-140 JetStar and the 707 Air Force One), Jim Cross, to receive training in reconnaissance aircraft at Bergstrom Air Force Base in Austin, Texas in July 1968. Bergstrom was just a short "hop" from Johnson's ranch near Stonewall, Texas.

Next, LBJ ensured that Jim Cross received a *very* abbreviated "tour of duty" in Vietnam (less than *three months,* not a full year like most military personnel).[1130] Johnson promoted Cross to Brigadier General; and Johnson ensured that Cross was safely transferred *back* to Bergstrom Air Force Base in a comfortable role as commanding officer of the 75th Tactical Reconnaissance Wing by February 1969 – the very month after LBJ left office and returned to his Texas ranch nearby.[1131]

As early as April 1968, after falsely telling a national television audience that he would not run in the upcoming November presidential election, Johnson was *personally* wheedling and cajoling and pleading with Jim Cross[1132] to fall in line with a very detailed, carefully-thought-out LBJ plan for post-presidential – *or more precisely, post-**arrest** –* life.[1133]

The Sultan of Stonewall had it all figured out.

Lyndon Johnson was arranging to live out his final days in – at worst – a very comfortable "house arrest," just like many other murderous "leaders" elsewhere.[1134]

[1127] Author's exclusive original discovery.

[1128] Author's exclusive original discovery.

[1129] Author's exclusive original discovery.

[1130] James U. Cross, *Angel is Airborne,* p. 282.

[1131] James U. Cross, *Angel is Airborne,* p. 276; additional USAF data on Cross from the online military site *af.mil.*

[1132] Author's exclusive original discovery. (Cross recounts the conversation in *Angel is Airborne,* pp. 271-272.)

[1133] Author's exclusive original discovery.

[1134] Author's exclusive original discovery.

SEAN FETTER

That was the ***actual purpose*** of his long campaign to protect and promote and carefully position USAF officer James Underwood Cross.[1135]

By arranging with Cross, *in advance,* to establish a presidential medical suite at Bergstrom AFB, *LBJ wouldn't actually have to go to prison (or even jail!)* despite his upcoming published confessions regarding the JFK assassination.[1136] Instead, thanks to his long and convenient history of cardiac problems, Johnson would enjoy a luxurious, air-conditioned, well-protected abode on the Air Force base – with television and stewards and comfortable furniture and personal service and preferred foods and telephone privileges![1137]

By giving USAF officer Jim Cross extremely favorable treatment, LBJ was greasing all the right wheels. Lyndon Johnson was actually willing to risk *publicly disclosing his leadership of the JFK assassination plot* as long as his eventual "punishment" for it amounted to little more than a very mild form of "house arrest" – namely, restriction to *a large, comfortable hospital suite located on a secure military base run by a friendly USAF officer who was a long-time subordinate, companion, and personal beneficiary of LBJ's largesse.*[1138]

Such an arrangement wouldn't carry the shame and disgrace of actually being tried, convicted and sent to a ***real*** prison; in fact, as long as he was ostensibly just a "cardiac patient" [sic] *at an Air Force hospital,* Lyndon Johnson could easily delay and ***avoid*** an actual *criminal* trial and live out his remaining days in relative luxury.[1139]

In fact, LBJ would be able to indulge in eating and drinking and smoking with total abandon while protected and supported by his friend, General Cross;[1140] his resulting (and quite predictable) death from cardiac failure would certainly be less ignominious than – and far *preferable* to – the everlasting shame of actual criminal conviction and subsequent execution (or lifetime imprisonment) for criminal conspiracy, capital murder and sedition.[1141]

It was a typically ingenious LBJ solution to a very difficult problem: how to *confess publicly to conspiracy and murder and sedition* without ever actually suffering

---

[1135] Author's exclusive original discovery.

[1136] Author's exclusive original discovery.

[1137] Author's exclusive original discovery.

[1138] Author's exclusive original discovery.

[1139] Author's exclusive original discovery.

[1140] Johnson actually outlined this explicitly to Jim Cross in a conversation conducted in LBJ's bedroom at the White House in early April 1968. (James U. Cross, *Angel is Airborne,* pp. 271-272.)

[1141] Author's exclusive original discovery.

any real *punishment* for the monumental crime of assassinating President John Fitzgerald Kennedy.[1142]

* * *

Lyndon Johnson confessed his leading role in the JFK assassination in a variety of ways, and in a variety of settings.

And – as I discovered exclusively, not long before this book went to press – LBJ even did so in chilling nighttime remarks made to American military officers in late 1968.[1143]

Johnson always remembered the men who had made his bloody seizure of the Oval Office possible.

* * *

Five years later – *to the minute!* – after he descended over Washington in SAM 26000 on final approach toward the Andrews Air Force Base runway on the early evening of November 22nd, 1963, *Lyndon Baines Johnson explicitly acknowledged his massive debt to the United States Air Force.*[1144]

The scene was surreal.

In the early evening of November 22nd, 1968 – at 5:55 p.m. EST – LBJ strolled into the military aide's office in the White House and spoke to a few assembled uniformed staffers.[1145]

Addressing the military men, *Lyndon Johnson explicitly made reference to the fact that it was the anniversary of the JFK assassination.*

He then deliberately belittled President Kennedy; specifically praised the Joint Chiefs of Staff – *twice*; and made a startlingly open statement:

"I am pretty strong for the Air Force," said Johnson.

I am pretty strong for the Air Force.

I am pretty strong for the Air Force.

And Johnson certainly had good reason to be "strong for the Air Force."

After all, the U. S. Air Force enabled his bloody coup.[1146]

[1142] Author's exclusive original discovery.

[1143] Author's exclusive original discovery.

[1144] Author's exclusive original discovery.

[1145] LBJ remarks to the Military Aides to the President, 22 Nov 1968. (The American Presidency Project, UCSB.edu.)

[1146] Author's exclusive original discovery.

The Air Force held its (nuclear) fire on November 22nd, 1963.[1147]

The Air Force altered the original Zapruder film – and others.

The Air Force flew falsified evidence from Dallas to Washington *on the very night of the assassination.*

The Air Force examined contemporaneous media transmissions to help find and censor damning information.

The Air Force *outlined* and actually *wrote* much of the 1964 Johnson ("Warren") Report.

No surprise, then, that LBJ was "pretty strong for the Air Force."

The United States Air Force enabled his coup.

After his brief and sinister remarks at the White House on the evening of November 22nd, 1968, LBJ turned and walked away – but he had deliberately and specifically chosen *the very minute of the very hour of his triumphant arrival back in Washington D. C. on the day of the JFK assassination five years earlier* to effusively thank the JCS and the U. S. Air Force.[1148]

That was no accident; no "random coincidence."

The message could not have been clearer if it had been carved in stone:

Thank you, boys.

Ya dance with who brung ya.

The ugly and obscene little episode in November 1968 was an explicit window into what actually happened in November 1963.[1149]

Lyndon Baines Johnson, President Kennedy's killer, said it himself:

I am pretty strong for the Air Force.

I am pretty strong for the Air Force.

I am pretty strong for the Air Force.

* * *

Between 1969 and 1973, LBJ confessed his frightening, guilt-riddled nightmares during a number of post-presidential conversations with confidante and Establishment anesthetist Doris Kearns – nightmares involving Robert Kennedy, and nightmares of being called a *traitor* by a crowd of outraged Americans.[1150]

[1147] John Judge discovered this vital fact by interviewing SAC personnel in Ohio, decades ago.

[1148] Author's exclusive original discovery.

[1149] Author's exclusive original discovery.

[1150] Kearns mentioned LBJ's nightmares in a shallow, obtuse, sophomoric and absurdly titled tome called *Lyndon Johnson and the American Dream.* Like all her fellow Establishment shills (including such contemptible clones as Beschloss, Bugliosi, Caro, Dallek, Graff, Posner, Sabato and Shenon, among

Johnson also uttered revealing statements about his own leadership of the JFK assassination plot.

In the wake of the president's murder, Johnson acknowledged, "... I was still *illegitimate* ... A pretender to the throne, *an illegal usurper*."[1151]

LBJ bragged explicitly about how he salvaged the floundering JFK assassination plot following the nearly disastrous failures in Dealey Plaza: "*I knew what had to be done* ... The man on the horse [had] to take the lead, to assume command, to provide direction. In the period of confusion after the assassination, *I was that man.*"[1152]

Johnson was indeed the "man on horseback" who "took the lead" and (just barely) snatched bloody triumph from the jaws of catastrophic failure, certain prosecution, and ignominious jail or execution.[1153]

LBJ not only *led* the plot on November 22nd; he had to *salvage* it as well.[1154]

Hence his bragging about his acts.

* * *

Speaking to speechwriter Leo Janos after leaving the White House, Johnson made three revealing statements that clearly reflected the haunting guilt of his leading role in the JFK assassination.

LBJ moaned bitterly about the media, whom he characterized as consisting of reporters who would act "like a district attorney" (!) bent on finding out "where I was on the night of the twenty-third" (!) – a statement evincing no small amount of obvious guilt and paranoia stemming from what he had done in 1963.[1155]

Lyndon Johnson complained further that "I'm always guilty unless I can prove otherwise."

---

others), Doris Kearns (now Doris Kearns Goodwin) knows that in America, the price of fame and fortune is (A) never asking dangerous questions and (B) never telling hard truths about important matters.

Obey those dismal dictates and ye shall prosper. After all, lightweight garbage always floats to the top.

[1151] Doris Kearns, *Lyndon Johnson and the American Dream* (paperback edition), p. 177.

[1152] Doris Kearns, *Lyndon Johnson and the American Dream* (paperback edition), p. 179.

[1153] Like her pathetic peers, Kearns was either (A) too stupid and naïve to realize or (B) too cynical and cowardly and dishonest to articulate what LBJ's statements actually meant.

[1154] Author's exclusive original discovery.

[1155] And what he had done in 1968 – *twice.*

Finally, LBJ – the confessional criminal – declared with evident pride and satisfaction that "The damn press always accused me of things I didn't do. *They never once found out about the things I **did** do.*"[1156]

The things he *did* do, America:

Like Dallas in November 1963.

And Memphis in April 1968.

And Los Angeles in June 1968.

* * *

In 1969, even after having assassinated Robert Francis Kennedy the year before, Lyndon Johnson was *still* nervous about the possibility of being prosecuted by his White House successor, Republican Richard Nixon.

LBJ actually said as much, explicitly, to his own aides.[1157]

As LBJ well knew, the only thing that Nixon would have *ever* gone after Johnson for was the JFK assassination – a crime in which Nixon was not involved.[1158] (The two ultimately settled for engaging in successful *mutual blackmail:* Nixon kept quiet about LBJ's lead role in killing JFK in exchange for Johnson keeping quiet about Nixon's literally *treasonous* conduct in deliberately delaying Vietnam peace talks during the 1968 presidential election campaign.)

But by 1971, when his memoir *The Vantage Point* was published, Lyndon Johnson – who had resumed smoking and eating to excess, and who had already suffered additional and quite significant post-presidential heart problems – clearly felt close enough to death to get away with disclosing the truth *without* suffering *unbearable* repercussions.[1159]

With major help from the U. S. Air Force (in the person of USAF officer James Cross), LBJ had already *carefully laid the groundwork* to make published revelations.[1160]

* * *

[1156] Leo Janos, "The Last Days of the President," *The Atlantic,* July 1973.

[1157] Robert Dallek, a dedicated denialist, noted LBJ's 1969 fear of prosecution by Nixon but failed (or pusillanimously refused) to uncover and identify *the real reason* for Johnson's fear. Plainly, poor little old "Robby D" is not in the business of dealing with serious truths. (Color me shocked.)

[1158] Author's exclusive original discovery.

[1159] Author's exclusive original discovery.

[1160] Author's exclusive original discovery.

Lyndon Baines Johnson made his biggest major confession – a *series* of declarations, no less – in the most appropriate place that a power-mad, egomaniacal killer could: in his own 1971 memoir, *The Vantage Point.*[1161]

He wasted no time in getting to it, either.

As early as *page twelve* of his self-justifying tome, LBJ begins bragging about his actions on November 22nd, 1963 – and in doing so, he is certainly *not* referring to activities as mundane as simply checking in with the White House Situation Room, or dialing up Rose Kennedy from Air Force One in order to offer his false, cynical, unctuous "condolences" to the grieving mother of the man whom he had just murdered.

Rather, Johnson is talking about *the detailed mechanics of the JFK assassination plot that in November 1963 made him the most powerful man on the entire planet*[1162] – and proudly describing his own personal, hands-on role in making his daring, lethal gamble succeed after it had nearly collapsed in utter disaster in the triangular park called Dealey Plaza.[1163]

LBJ couldn't resist including it, stating it, *proclaiming* it.

Look at his own language, in the context of the bloody covert operation which he personally directed (and barely salvaged!) on November 22nd, 1963:

"The consequences of all my actions were too great for me to be immobilized now with emotion."[1164]

"I had *many decisions to make.*"[1165]

"There were tasks to perform that only *I* had the authority to perform."[1166]

"I knew *it was* **imperative** *that I* **grasp the reins of power** and do so **without delay**."[1167]

"Doing **the impossible** was frequently necessary to **get the job done.**"[1168]

[1161] Author's exclusive original discovery. (Johnson delegated certain research-heavy portions of the manuscript to several aides for drafting, but he himself personally reviewed and aggressively edited the text. Moreover, the introduction and the key passages of *The Vantage Point* cited here are unquestionably in LBJ's own voice.)

[1162] Author's exclusive original discovery.

[1163] Author's exclusive original discovery.

[1164] Lyndon Baines Johnson, *The Vantage Point,* p. 12.

[1165] Lyndon Baines Johnson, *The Vantage Point,* p. 12.

[1166] Lyndon Baines Johnson, *The Vantage Point,* p. 12.

[1167] Lyndon Baines Johnson, *The Vantage Point,* p. 18.

[1168] Lyndon Baines Johnson, *The Vantage Point,* p. 27.

Lyndon Johnson was describing the harrowing minutes and hours following his plot's staggering collapse in Dealey Plaza at 12:30 p.m. CST.[1169]

LBJ was describing all of the dark maneuvers that he had to *immediately* and *covertly* conceive of and arrange and order his subordinate governmental accomplices to carry out in order to hide the existence of the other fatal victim of the shooting; divert the president's corpse for secret pre-autopsy mutilation by the SS; mislead both the attorney general back in Washington and the presidential party there in Dallas; obtain physical custody and control of both JFK's body and JFK's widow[1170]; determine whether he would abandon the daunting effort entirely and *flee the country* to permanent exile in Mexico;[1171] assess whether USAF General LeMay had successfully kept the lid on SAC's hair-trigger nuclear strike force;[1172] and all of the related details necessary to *implement* those major criminal acts.[1173]

Lyndon Baines Johnson was desperately juggling numerous options and priorities after his long-planned assassination plot went haywire in Dealey Plaza. But Johnson was at his most cynically calculating and his most grimly *efficient* under extreme pressure, and so within *two hours* of murdering John Fitzgerald Kennedy, LBJ had handled all the most pressing and dangerous eventualities.

By 2:30 p.m. CST – just *two hours* after the fusillade of gunfire in Dealey Plaza had died away – LBJ and his vicious accomplices had spirited the two dead victims out of Parkland Hospital; obtained physical custody and control of both the dead president and his widow; arranged for a rapid "inauguration" aboard SAM 26000; obtained plenty of high-powered weaponry; and rescued the sinister assassination plot from complete failure.[1174]

It had been an *extremely* close call for Johnson and his confederates.

Unfathomably close.

But the Sultan of Stonewall had quickly exercised every ounce of his cold cunning, his brutal iron will, and his malevolently murderous instincts to salvage the JFK assassination plot.

He was *proud* of his gruesome achievements.

So he simply *had* to brag about them.

For Lyndon Baines Johnson, ***not*** doing so was *inconceivable*.

[1169] Author's exclusive original discovery.

[1170] Author's exclusive original discovery.

[1171] Author's exclusive original discovery.

[1172] Author's exclusive original discovery.

[1173] Author's exclusive original discovery.

[1174] Author's exclusive original discovery.

* * *

For LBJ, the truth about Dallas – the stunning enormity of the achievement, and the sheer gutsiness required to salvage the JFK assassination plot when it initially failed – were impossible to keep completely under wraps.

Incredibly, *all* moronic conventional "historians" [*sic*] simply gloss over these extraordinarily revealing statements, utterly *oblivious* to (or deathly afraid of *admitting*) their true meaning and significance.[1175] But rest assured that the arrogant politician who had by far *the largest ego in American history* was not merely "rambling" or spewing "vague generalities." In the devastatingly damning phrases cited above, Lyndon Johnson was crowing about *his personal prowess* in snatching victory from the jaws of defeat on November 22nd, 1963.[1176]

No other words in his entire career gave him such satisfaction.

* * *

So consider those chilling words once again:

The consequences of all my actions were too great for me to be immobilized now.

*I had **many decisions to make**.*

*There were tasks to perform that only **I** had the authority to perform.*

*I knew it was **imperative** that I **grasp the reins of power** and do so **without delay**.*

*Doing **the impossible** was frequently necessary to **get the job done**.*
I knew what had to be done.

The man on the horse [had] to take the lead.

The man on the horse [had] to assume command,

The man on the horse [had] to provide direction.

*In the period of confusion after the assassination, **I was that man**.*

The "man on the horse" meant . . . a man on horseback.

A man on horseback.

A man on horseback.

That is *explicit **coup*** language, America – the language of a *fascist*.[1177]

[1175] Kearns, Beschloss, Caro and Dallek are among those who have exhibited willful ignorance (or sheer cowardice, or breathtaking stupidity) in this regard.

[1176] Author's exclusive original discovery.

[1177] Author's exclusive original discovery.

Certain fellow American fascists wearing blue Air Force uniforms agreed whole-heartedly with LBJ – and they personally ensured that the staggering 1956 Rayburn-Johnson plot to put a "real" Texan into the Oval Office finally came to bloody fruition on a bright Friday afternoon in late November 1963.[1178]

* * *

President Kennedy's killers – both military and civilian – had to lie endlessly, for *decades* after perpetrating the deed, in order to poison and infect the minds of millions of Americans and thereby blind them to the truth.

But here's the thing:

Lies unravel.

Blindness ends.

Murder is uncovered.

Truth prevails.

The man they killed actually helped to solve his own assassination.[1179]

Their hated target in 1963 was a human being slightly over six feet tall.

John Kennedy had copper-colored hair and a very bad back.

He was forty-six.

[1178] Author's exclusive original discovery.

[1179] Author's exclusive original discovery.

In 1968, during a White House meeting,
Lyndon Baines Johnson wrote a note
expressing his guilt (*not* remorse) for the
1963 assassination of President Kennedy.

Author's exclusive original discovery.

President Kennedy feared a U. S. military coup.

He also feared a Rayburn-Johnson coup.

JFK had ample *reasons* for those fears –
and he expressed those fears *explicitly*.

Author's exclusive original discovery.

Chapter Thirty-Six:
The Victim

"These things do not just 'happen.'
*They are **made** to happen."*

– John Fitzgerald Kennedy

I've proven – for the first time anywhere – the true *origin,* the true *chronology,* and the true *reasons* for the JFK assassination plot.

I've proven – for the first time anywhere – the true *identity* of the intellectual authors of the JFK assassination plot, and I uncovered their true *motivations.*

I've proven who actually *led* that assassination plot in 1963.[1180]

I've also proven the identities of several senior American military officers who actively *participated in* that murderous plot.

I've revealed the knowing, deliberate, criminal involvement of – and the concrete, criminal support rendered by – senior American military officers in that murderous plot.

I've quoted President Kennedy's principal assassins repeatedly and at length.

I've proven the truth beyond *any* reasonable doubt.

Now it's time to hear from the *victim* of that murderous plot.

Now it's time to hear from the man who rode anxiously in the right rear seat of that long, midnight-blue limousine as it awkwardly turned left onto Elm Street in Dealey Plaza.

Did John Fitzgerald Kennedy ever suspect or know who his real killers were?

Did he ever reveal his profound concerns to anyone prior to his murder?

Did JFK correctly pinpoint the actual sources of his own assassination?

Did President Kennedy himself ever evince any knowledge or awareness of the danger to him?

The answer, incredibly, is **yes.**

Again and again and again.

Yes. *Yes.* **Yes.**

* * *

[1180] Author's exclusive original discovery.

John Fitzgerald Kennedy rightly feared assassination.

He spoke of it often – to his wife; to his friends; and even – just a month before his violent death – to an outsider, a writer.[1181]

JFK spoke of it again, in Texas, *on the very morning of his murder*.[1182]

He sometimes hid his fear with jokes and false bravado, but his fear was real.

President Kennedy feared being murdered *even in church*.[1183]

JFK witnessed firsthand the contempt and insubordination and lunacy of his top military officers.

He knew the cruelty and criminality of his own vice president.

His fears were concrete and surprisingly accurate.

JFK sensed – and *knew* – where the real threat lay.[1184]

But he moved against it *far too late* to prevent it from taking his life.[1185]

* * *

John Kennedy told at least *six* (6) different "political" people – and told most of them *directly and explicitly* – about the criminal extortion used by Samuel Taliaferro Rayburn and Lyndon Baines Johnson, *under cover of night,* to force JFK to put LBJ onto the 1960 Democratic ticket as his vice-presidential candidate.

Those six *political* figures were Robert Francis Kennedy;[1186] attorney Clark Clifford; Chicago-based attorney and 1960 Kennedy campaign official Hyman

---

[1181] Jim Bishop, *The Day Kennedy Was Shot*, p. x.

[1182] Jim Bishop, *The Day Kennedy Was Shot*, p. 23.

[1183] JFK said this to his secretary, Mrs. Evelyn Lincoln, just three days before his assassination in Dallas. (Quoted in Thurston Clarke, *JFK's Last Hundred Days,* p. 324.)

[1184] Author's exclusive original discovery.

[1185] President Kennedy's aggressive but fatally belated effort to oust LBJ through an orchestrated campaign of damaging leaks to the press, starting in late 1963, was *much too little and much too late.* Johnson and Rayburn had been plotting to take the White House violently **since 1956,** as I discovered exclusively and have proven in this book.

[1186] RFK also knew firsthand from one of the perpetrators themselves, of course; Lyndon Johnson *personally* threatened Bobby on the night of July 13th-14th, 1960, **before** Rayburn and Johnson teamed up to jointly confront and overwhelm JFK in the early morning hours. (Journalist John S. Knight reported the story contemporaneously in the *Miami Herald,* July 15th, 1960; Seymour Hersh quoted that article in *The Dark Side of Camelot,* p. 127.)

Raskin;[1187] Senator Henry "Scoop" Jackson; Wisconsin Governor Gaylord Nelson;[1188] and Pierre Salinger.

But there was a *seventh* person, too.

There was one more key witness to whom John Kennedy confessed the truth.

I can reveal exclusively that *JFK personally told his wife Jaqueline about the 1960 blackmail by Sam Rayburn and Lyndon Johnson,* and that he did so contemporaneously.[1189]

It is true – and it is absolutely undeniable and irrefutable.

The proof is in her own hand.[1190]

* * *

Jacqueline Kennedy was, among other things, an amateur painter – and she also enjoyed making primitive drawings and sketches. Long after Dallas, some of her works were sold at auction.

When I saw the catalogue of works being offered, I was shocked – because a single item stood out like a bright glaring beacon.

Just one.

One of her hand-drawn images was in fact stunning and profoundly revelatory.

No one else ever understood what it meant.

During the long 1960 campaign, Jackie Kennedy made a number of sketches – and *one of them tells the story of the vicious Rayburn/Johnson extortion of JFK,* in graphic visual form.[1191]

On a piece of paper, Jacqueline Kennedy personally sketched three clearly recognizable figures.

On the right, a skinny and frail JFK stands meekly.

Kennedy is confronted by two strong, muscular figures.

At the far left of the picture is short, bald, stocky Sam Rayburn.

In the center of the picture is tall, domineering Lyndon Baines Johnson.

The two Texans are "all duded up" in western, cowboy-style outfits.

[1187] Seymour Hersh, *The Dark Side of Camelot,* pp. 123-126.

[1188] JFK told Gaylord Nelson, "I have no choice" but to name LBJ as his running mate, and *Kennedy specifically mentioned Sam Rayburn's pressure.* (Strober & Strober, *Let Us Begin Anew,* paperback edition, p. 19.)

[1189] Author's exclusive original discovery.

[1190] Author's exclusive original discovery.

[1191] Author's exclusive original discovery.

LBJ is ostensibly "shaking" JFK's hand – but in the drawing, Johnson is clearly not just "shaking" but *crushing* Kennedy's helpless hand in painful fashion.

Crushing it deliberately – *while he and Rayburn grin in ugly triumph.*

That single drawing by Jackie captures the very essence of the transaction.

Rayburn and Johnson forced JFK to put Lyndon on the 1960 ticket.

Kennedy then told his wife subsequently, and she drew the scene.[1192]

A picture truly is worth a thousand words – and Jacqueline Kennedy's personal drawing of the criminal July 1960 blackmail that successfully positioned LBJ to murder John F. Kennedy is no exception.

Jackie knew!

And she knew in 1960.

Jackie knew.

And she knew *only* because *John Kennedy plainly told her.*[1193]

* * *

Thus the candidate told *at least* seven (7) people in all – explicitly or obliquely – about the vicious ugly blackmail that was employed by the venomous Sam Rayburn and the cruel Lyndon Johnson, *under cover of night,* in mid-July 1960:

Robert Kennedy.

Clark Clifford.

Hyman Raskin.

Senator Henry "Scoop" Jackson.

Governor Gaylord Nelson.

Pierre Salinger.

Jacqueline Kennedy.

* * *

JFK, in his own reserved and fatalistic way, was actually leaving an evidence trail for history.[1194]

He clearly came to an eventual awareness of Rayburn and Johnson's *actual* motive for blackmailing him at the Democratic National Convention in July 1960. Kennedy sensed that the Texas duo sought ultimate power; and that awareness ultimately motivated JFK to (finally) seek Johnson's ouster or imprisonment,

---

[1192] Author's exclusive original discovery.

[1193] Author's exclusive original discovery.

[1194] Author's exclusive original discovery.

beginning in late 1963 (via Bobby Kennedy, the Delaware Senator John Williams, congressional Republicans, and leaks to *LIFE* Magazine, among others).

But President Kennedy waited much far too late to act. He left Lyndon Johnson in the vice presidency – and thus in position to strike a mortal blow – for far too long.

And JFK paid the ultimate price for that fatal mistake.

* * *

LBJ could not have acted *alone* to kill JFK, however.

The big Texan knew he needed *help* to carry out Sam Rayburn's brilliant 1956 assassination plan.

And "the help" – consisting principally of the United States military and the SS – were openly hostile to President Kennedy *for reasons of their own.*

The sinister fact is that JFK was the Commander-in-Chief of a largely *disloyal* American military. Many officers of flag rank utterly despised the wealthy, one-time Navy lieutenant who now outranked them all. Many men at all levels hated the devil-may-care civilian playboy who controlled their policies and their careers and the nation's security all while flagrantly and recklessly violating many of the tenets and precepts and basic standards of conduct which they held dear.

Their contempt for, and disgust at, the occupant of the Oval Office – contempt and disgust often expressed openly, *even while they met in person with the president* in the Oval Office and in the Cabinet Room – were no secret.

The U. S. Air Force in particular was a hotbed of fierce anti-Kennedy sentiment. As Pentagon official and LBJ White House aide Joseph Califano later put it, the Air Force was "a cauldron of Goldwater supporters."[1195]

In late September 1963, *The New Republic* published an article – "Rebellion in the Air Force?" – whose opening lines were chilling:

*"The Air Force's ruling hierarchy is in open defiance of its Constitutional Commander-in-Chief, and in some ways the situation bears a growing resemblance to the fictional story-line of last year's [1962] best-seller **Seven Days in May,** the account of a nearly successful military coup by an Air Force general in protest against a nuclear arms treaty just concluded with the Russians."*[1196]

Both President Kennedy and Attorney General Kennedy worried seriously about an overt military coup in America.

John Kennedy personally read the book *Seven Days in May* and was so impressed by the chilling novel that when Hollywood's John Frankenheimer decided

---

[1195] Joseph Califano, *Inside,* p. 140.

[1196] Raymond D. Senter, "Rebellion in the Air Force?", *The New Republic,* September 28th, 1963.

to make a movie based on it, JFK offered the director access to the exterior of the White House for filming, in order to lend utter realism to the resulting product.

President Kennedy was *that* concerned about the situation.

And he was *right* to be.

* * *

John Fitzgerald Kennedy feared assassination and an American military coup.

In July 1961, JFK confessed bluntly to important Soviet figures Alexei Adzhubei (*Izvestia* editor, and son-in-law of Nikita Khrushchev) and Mikhail Kharlamov (spokesman for Premier Khrushchev), "*You don't understand this country* [the USA]. If I move too fast on U.S.-Soviet relations, I'll either be thrown into an insane asylum *or killed.*"[1197]

On August 31st, 1962, after JFK himself spoke to journalist (and Soviet agent) Georgi Bolshakov in the Oval Office and said that he would order an immediate *cessation* of American close-inspection flights passing low over USSR vessels sailing toward Cuba (an extraordinarily bad idea), Robert Kennedy shouted at Bolshakov in the hallway outside and urged him to tell Premier Khrushchev to empathize with President Kennedy's own extremely vulnerable position: "In a gust of blind hate," Bobby warned fiercely, "his enemies [i.e., the U. S. military] may go to *any* length, including *killing* him."[1198]

And during the tensest moment of the Cuban Missile Crisis – the night of October 27th, 1962 – RFK personally told a Soviet Ambassador Anatoly Dobrynin that if an immediate solution to the crisis were not reached forthwith, the American military might perpetrate a coup against President Kennedy. "Even though the President himself is very much against starting a war over Cuba," Bobby told Dobrynin, "an irreversible chain of events could occur *against his will.* That is why the President is appealing directly to Chairman Khrushchev for his help in liquidating this conflict. *If the situation continues much longer, the President is not sure that the military will not overthrow him and seize power. The American army could get out of control.* "[1199]

What none of those six men (JFK, RFK, Khrushchev, Dobrynin, Adzhubei and Kharlamov) realized was that it was *already* too late.

The U. S. Army (and the U. S. Air Force) were *already* out of control.

[1197] Pierre Salinger, *PS,* p. 253.

[1198] Pierre Salinger, *PS,* p. 254.

[1199] Nikita Khrushchev relayed Dobrynin's account of the vital October 27th meeting (and the American military coup threat facing JFK) in a memoir, *Khrushchev Remembers* (paperback edition), pp. 551-552.

They were simply awaiting instructions from coup leader Lyndon Baines Johnson – but in October 1962, LBJ wasn't quite ready to launch his bloody plot yet.[1200]

* * *

John and Robert Kennedy, indisputably, feared an American military coup.

What the highly intelligent Kennedy brothers did ***not*** correctly anticipate was *a military-**backed** coup* – which is a subtler, more camouflaged enterprise.

There is a difference.

A *uniformed* American military officer did ***not*** openly take over the country as Supreme Leader in 1963 (as the dictator Franco did in Spain in the 1930s, and as the dictator Pinochet did in Chile in the 1970s).

Instead, uniformed senior officers in the Air Force, Army and Navy knowingly worked ***with*** *and **for*** the ambitious and seditious Vice President, Lyndon Johnson, to criminally overthrow the legitimate civilian president and thereby *illegitimately elevate a criminal civilian to the American presidency* in his place.[1201]

Had all of the criminal conspirators (both military and civilian) who were involved in the 1963 LBJ coup managed to execute their roles perfectly, then no evidence of any kind would have survived to provide *any clues whatsoever* as to what really happened.

But as I wrote in a much earlier chapter of this book, a flurry of *astounding* mistakes made by the killers that day in Dallas caused the well-planned murder of President Kennedy to devolve into what is called, in American football terminology, "a busted play."[1202]

The JFK assassination, *as it was actually executed in real time on November 22nd,* was in fact an operational ***disaster*** which transformed the carefully planned coup plot into an utter shambles requiring the direct and repeated *personal intervention* of plot leader Lyndon Baines Johnson himself in a multitude of *specific overt acts* in order to (barely) salvage the plot and (barely) snatch bloody victory from the vise-like jaws of otherwise certain, absolutely catastrophic defeat.[1203]

* * *

[1200] And Johnson certainly wasn't about to kill JFK during a global nuclear crisis that could incinerate everything and everyone, including Johnson himself.

[1201] Author's exclusive original discovery.

[1202] Author's original analogy.

[1203] Author's exclusive original discovery.

Busy though he was as president of the United States, John Kennedy always made plenty of time for sailing, and swimming, and golf, and dinner parties, and sex.

He also made plenty of time for reading, and thinking, and writing.

Not only was JFK planning to author (or co-author, or edit, or at least "supervise") an eventual memoir about his presidency; he also had *another*, quite *different* book in mind as well.

Constantly in mind.

JFK even told close friend Chuck Spalding about it – *several times* – as a sort of running update on the story line of his special, never-completed volume.[1204]

President Kennedy actually devoted a lot of thought to it during his thousand doomed days in the White House.

The subject of JFK's planned book was serious and chilling – and prescient.

While attempting to navigate the treacherous political waters of domestic policy and foreign policy, civil rights and civil wrongs, nuclear weapons and nuclear proliferation, war and peace, *John Fitzgerald Kennedy was working personally – and continually – on an original book about* **the takeover of the government of the United States by Lyndon Baines Johnson**.[1205]

* * *

And, as always in this mournful and deeply shocking case, *there is more.*

John Kennedy's unconscious mind and his keen instinct and his staggering intuition certainly did not wait until late 1963 to come to the fore.

Within *three months* of taking office, JFK discussed assassination with his wife, Jacqueline.[1206]

But again, the best and last word belongs to the actual victim of that murderous plot, John Fitzgerald Kennedy himself.

* * *

Truth emerges in fragments at times, but emerge it does – and it is devastating.

During a weekend up at Hyannis Port, Massachusetts in 1961, President Kennedy and the First Lady sat talking with friend and writer Gore Vidal.

Jackie animatedly urged JFK to describe to Vidal a movie idea which the President had recently come up with and had shared with her. In it, Kennedy takes the

---

[1204] Thurston Clarke, *JFK's Last Hundred Days,* pp. 184-185.

[1205] Thurston Clarke, *JFK's Last Hundred Days,* pp. 184-185.

[1206] William Manchester, *The Death of a President,* p. 348.

White House elevator downstairs from the second floor of the mansion one morning as usual, on his way to work over in the West Wing. But the scene immediately shifts to the Oval Office, "*'and there is **Lyndon.** Where is the president? No one knows.'*"

The grimly fatalistic Kennedy then managed a grin to cover up the ugly truth beneath his next words:

"*It's just Lyndon and Sam then,*" JFK told Vidal.[1207]

It's just Lyndon and Sam then . . .

Lyndon and Sam.

Lyndon and Sam.

Lyndon and Sam.[1208]

Precisely.

* * *

Kennedy said to Gore Vidal in 1961 that he didn't yet have the ending to his proposed movie; thus far he had only come up with the idea for the chilling *initial* portion of the film.

But eventually JFK *did* have an idea for an ending.

President Kennedy would ultimately conceive of, direct, and participate in a very eerie, disturbing, amateur film *presaging his own death.*

Two years *after* speaking to Gore Vidal – in September 1963 – JFK had Navy photographer Robert Knudsen film a grisly scene in Newport, Rhode Island, as the president feigned being shot and collapsing on a pier, "blood" spurting from his mouth.

Kennedy's own family members and friends, as previously instructed by the president, then disembarked from a boat and strolled casually onto the pier, deliberately stepping over Kennedy's prostrate form as they walked to the shore.[1209]

[1207] Gore Vidal related the episode in his book *Palimpsest,* p. 364. I am most appreciative to JFK assassination researcher David Andrews for providentially mentioning this profoundly revealing incident in a valuable online post on February 8th, 2011. Andrews did not, however, exhibit any understanding of what the incident actually meant. Having already exclusively discovered Sam Rayburn's leading role in the JFK assassination, I myself *instantly* understood the significance of President Kennedy's remarks to Gore Vidal.

[1208] In a very real sense, JFK himself endorsed my own investigative findings (as documented in this book) – and he did so ***well in advance of*** his own 1963 assassination. No one else listened carefully enough to John Kennedy; sadly, no one else understood the true import of his words. And for the record, it is vital to note that this extraordinarily revealing 1961 conversation with Gore Vidal was *not* the *only* time that President Kennedy left a trail of substantive evidentiary clues for people to follow in the event of his violent demise.

[1209] The chilling episode was described in the Ralph M. Goldberg (*alias* "Ralph G. Martin") book *Seeds of Destruction: Joe Kennedy and His Sons* (pp. 449-450).

Consciously or subconsciously, John Kennedy was foretelling his own murder.

It was a macabre and grotesque scene – but not nearly as macabre and grotesque as JFK's actual assassination, two months in the future.

John Fitzgerald Kennedy did not know that his presidency would end in a sunny plaza with several bystanders actually taking photos and films of the crime – and he did not know that due to prompt and sinister criminal intervention by the U. S. government perpetrators of the crime, *even the visual record of his own murder* would be deliberately altered, censored, and butchered beyond recognition.[1210]

* * *

As I noted earlier in this book, John Kennedy himself managed to accuse his real killers *even **after** his own death*.[1211] USAF Colonel James Swindal executed a steep right turn shortly after taking off from Love Field that afternoon,[1212] and therefore President Kennedy's left arm slid down from the narrow shelf on which his body lay, face-down, to the floor of *the forward cargo compartment of the presidential jet*.[1213]

JFK's arm naturally stiffened in that "fallen" position as the president's corpse lay face down in the forward cargo hold during the two-hour-plus flight back to Andrews Air Force Base, and as a result was ultimately perceived as a "raised" arm by U. S. Army Lieutenant Richard Lipsey later that night at the official "autopsy" conducted in the Bethesda Naval Hospital morgue.

John Fitzgerald Kennedy thus managed to raise an accusatory arm, pointing toward his actual murderers, *even after his own violent assassination.*

* * *

John Kennedy was literally surrounded by enemies during his presidency.

The plot to assassinate him – *led by Lyndon Johnson* – was large and energetic.

Predictably, both the military *and* civilian accomplices of LBJ demanded something *in return* for their valuable assistance in carrying out the JFK assassination.

Robert Knudsen himself described the JFK "death" film in detail in an interview for an Associated Press article ("Kennedy Played His 'Death' For Home Movie") which was carried by the *New York Times* (August 14th, 1983).

[1210] You literally have *no idea* how much was deleted from the ***extant*** "Zapruder film" and other visual records of the JFK assassination. But you'll learn (from me). And I'll remind you again that *I don't bluff.*

[1211] Author's exclusive original discovery.

[1212] Author's exclusive original discovery.

[1213] Author's exclusive original discovery.

They insisted on being *rewarded* for their criminal labors on Johnson's behalf. They wanted payment for their skills and talents and actions and availability. *They required substantial recompense.*
Lyndon Johnson paid them, of course.
He had to.
It was "the price of doing business."
He paid them, America.
LBJ paid them.
And as I discovered exclusively, some of those payments left a *trail.*

Governor Terry Sanford of North Carolina
(seen here with President Kennedy in 1961)
was to be JFK's vice-presidential running mate in 1964.

Instead, Lyndon Baines Johnson slew JFK
and secretly enmeshed Sanford (unwittingly)
in LBJ's scheme to pay off
a JFK assassination plot participant.

Author's exclusive original discovery.

Chapter Thirty-Seven:
The Payoff

"These things do not just 'happen.'
*They are **made** to happen."*

– John Fitzgerald Kennedy

The lazy asinine scum who engage in light labor as nauseatingly dishonest whores for the Establishment have all chanted a false mantra for *decades.*

They have dumped their pitiful, denialist, pseudo-intellectual dung into the nation's intellectual punch bowl and poisoned the mind of the body politic with toxic *E. coli* excretions until some people are unwilling even to *approach* the issue of the JFK assassination.

But those cowardly conniving conventional courtesans who keep falsely claiming that "no evidence of a plot has ever emerged" [*sic*] are lying through their rotten teeth.

They never once *looked* for the truth; they never once sought out key witnesses; and of course they never once even intended or desired to do so.

Ever.

But *I* did.

To put it just as delicately as I can:

I did the work those cowards didn't do.

And I proved that all of those pitifully self-castrated Establishment eunuchs were dead wrong. They were wrong over and over and over again, for *decades.*

And I proved them wrong over and over and over again, for *decades.*

On many occasions, I proved this in a single day.

And one *particular* day was particularly extraordinary.

* * *

All I did was check my mail.

One springtime day in the 1990s, *I checked my U. S. postal mail.*

There I found a large yellow envelope stuffed full of documents.

Inside, I personally discovered, recognized and documented the *first written proof* of a payoff – *an actual payoff* – in the assassination of John Fitzgerald Kennedy, the 35th President of the United States.[1214]

* * *

It wasn't supposed to be there.
It wasn't supposed to have been included in the packet.
It was never supposed to see the light of day.
Ever.
Ever.
But as happens so often – particularly in the JFK case – *someone fouled up.*
Someone didn't think.
Someone didn't know.
Someone didn't realize.
Someone didn't understand the import.
So the item in question was included, nestled quietly amid the scores of other pages in the thick bulging envelope sent to me from a particular place in Texas.

It was clear and explicit and glaring, and *no one else* had ever found it or seen it or recognized its chilling importance.
But I did.
Immediately.
Instantaneously.
I possess an uncommonly acute "radar" for pertinent evidence in the assassination of President Kennedy.

And this material – this *single piece of paper*, amidst many – came from an undeniable, unimpeachable, irrefutable source.

Not even the greasy, gutless Establishment whores can gainsay or deny it.

The irony of that is overwhelming – and absolutely delicious.

* * *

You see, that thick yellow envelope bulging with paper came from a little place called *the Lyndon Baines Johnson Presidential Library in Austin, Texas.*[1215]

[1214] Author's exclusive original discovery.

[1215] In a very strange document that he cobbled together years after I made my exclusive original discovery, Lifton **wrongly** indicated that I had found this vital evidence thanks to files from *Rice University* – which is completely, totally and utterly incorrect. (One more example of why Lifton was a **very unreliable source,** even on relatively mundane issues.)

It was a response to my request to see papers pertaining to the fatal Texas trip of November 1963.

And what was inside, among the trivial items and the ephemera and all the boring irrelevancies, was an evidentiary bombshell: the equivalent of the Hope Diamond, or something even more valuable – a perfect flawless sapphire, *the size of a basketball.*

* * *

I frankly wasn't expecting much from the massive pile of documents in this large yellow envelope from the LBJ Library; I knew that the thick sheaf of routine, perfunctory papers relating to the planning of the president's Texas trip in November 1963 was extremely unlikely to contain *anything* truly meaningful to the actual solution of the JFK case.

Nevertheless, in dogged good faith, I opened the fat bulging envelope and began dutifully poring over the numerous documents inside. Many of them consisted of yawn-inducing trivia.

But the one that didn't even ostensibly *belong* in this particular large batch of items was *extraordinarily* significant – and, indeed, central to the case.

I instantly recognized its import and its gravity.

* * *

The item wasn't even from the trip!

It certainly didn't **belong,** chronologically speaking, in a stack of papers connected to the planning of President Kennedy's trip to Texas in late November 1963.

It really shouldn't have been there at all.

It didn't belong.

But it *was* there – and I instantaneously understood what it was, and what it signified about the assassination.

I also understood why it was somehow mixed in with the Texas trip planning papers sent to me.

It *wasn't* related *chronologically* to the rest; but it **was** related to ***the topic.***

The Texas trip.

The assassination of President Kennedy.

It is also a perfect example of why Lifton's often bizarre, often *insanely distorted,* often fictitious "versions" of events – ranging from the JFK case itself, to the true story of his (Lifton's) own hideously ugly and abusive interactions with other people – are not to be trusted or relied upon *in the slightest.*

Certainly not if you care about accuracy or the truth . . .

The plot which took his life.
*And the identity of a specific **member** of that plot.*[1216]

* * *

That's what I found one springtime day in the 1990s when I opened up and perused a thick pile of otherwise dull and boring papers from the LBJ Library.

Proof of the plot which took JFK's life.

*Proof of the **identity** of a member of that plot.*

*Proof of a **payoff** to a member of that plot.*

*Proof as absolutely **official** as any proof can possibly be.*

It was, in fact, generated by the White House itself – **Lyndon Baines Johnson's** White House, no less – and it was one thousand percent authentic.

* * *

Remember:

It wasn't supposed to be there.

It wasn't supposed to have been included in the packet.

It was never supposed to see the light of day.

Ever.

But there it was.

And it **absolutely** related to the fatal 1963 trip to Texas, and to the murderous plot which took President Kennedy's life in Dallas.

It *absolutely* was related – because it was *a documented payoff for **services** rendered* in the assassination of JFK.[1217]

* * *

The piece of paper that I found was a *pardon.*

That's right; a pardon.

A legal document.

An official pardon for criminal offenses.

Issued in late December 1963 by (innocent and unwitting) North Carolina Governor Terry Sanford, it wasn't a private "pet project" or some longstanding

---

[1216] Author's exclusive original discovery.

[1217] Author's exclusive original discovery.

charitable cause championed by that state's chief executive for obscure or sentimental reasons of his own.

Not at all.

Rather, it was an official pardon which had been specifically **requested of** Governor Sanford in late 1963 by top White House aides *working for Lyndon Baines Johnson himself.* [1218]

And it was a pardon for an individual named . . . Carrico.

Charles Carrico.

* * *

I was chilled and absolutely stunned the instant I saw it – because *Charles Carrico* was the name of the very first physician to actually "attend" President Kennedy in Trauma Room 1 at Parkland Hospital in Dallas on November 22nd, 1963.

Charles Carrico.

Charles Carrico.

Charles Carrico.

And here, in official files sent directly to me by the LBJ Library itself, was *written proof* that a formal pardon was suddenly issued to one *Charles Carrico – at the specific request of LBJ's top aides, acting on presidential instructions –* within just weeks of the JFK assassination![1219]

This was no "accident" or "happenstance" or "coincidence" or "serendipity."

This was a naked *quid pro quo.*[1220]

No indication has ever emerged that Governor Sanford of North Carolina had *any idea* of why the LBJ White House – so soon after taking the reins of power – was suddenly pressing him for a pardon for someone named Charles Carrico.

But Lyndon Baines Johnson himself certainly knew.

LBJ was a totally illegitimate "president" by virtue of having obtained the Oval Office through criminal conspiracy, extortion, violent sedition and felony murder. Yet in the realm of ordinary and "legitimate" presidential duties, LBJ and his aides had many other *far* more pressing tasks and major burdens and onerous responsibilities to contend with at the time.

[1218] Author's exclusive original discovery.

[1219] Author's exclusive original discovery.

[1220] Author's exclusive original discovery.

But mysteriously, *just days after the JFK assassination,* Johnson plainly pushed his top aides to extract a pardon from Governor Sanford for a man named *Charles Carrico.*[1221]

It was a bizarre and strange distraction from the regular significant duties of top White House officials. Yet *do it they did,* in the very early days of the Johnson administration, and they actually made it happen – very promptly.[1222]

Which means that in fact, it wasn't trivial in the slightest.

It obviously wasn't a "distraction" for LBJ; it was a *necessity.*

Johnson **had** to do it.

Quickly.

Right away.

Lyndon Johnson had to pay off Charles Carrico promptly, and he **did.**

A pardon – a full pardon – for crimes committed in the state of North Carolina, three years before.

A full pardon for one *Charles Carrico.*

Arranged for and initiated by *LBJ himself.* [1223]

To understand why this occurred, you have to know certain salient facts.

* * *

President John Fitzgerald Kennedy was shot to death in Dealey Plaza at 12:30 p.m. Central Standard Time on Friday, November 22nd, 1963.

JFK died instantly – right there in the presidential limousine, on Elm Street.

Read that again, carefully:

He died instantly – right there in the presidential limousine, on Elm Street.

The president died instantly.

JFK was not merely "mortally wounded" in Dealey Plaza; he was *killed instantly* by his assassins.

The president died *in Dealey Plaza –* **not** at Parkland Hospital![1224]

[1221] Author's exclusive original discovery.

[1222] Author's exclusive original discovery.

[1223] Author's exclusive original discovery.

Governor Sanford was none the wiser in terms of the *actual* (sinister and criminal) reason that LBJ requested the pardon for Charles Carrico.

[1224] Contrary to the "official" story, which falsely depicted "heroic" doctors laboring to "save" JFK.

And when the midnight-blue presidential limousine first roared to a stop outside the emergency area of the hospital, President Kennedy was most certainly **DOA** – "dead on arrival."[1225]

Unquestionably.

Multiple *honest* medical personnel at Parkland recognized and attested to that fundamental medical fact.

JFK was not "alive, though gravely wounded"; he was *dead*.

He was not "moribund"; he was *dead*.

He was not "making agonal respirations"; he was *dead*.

Be very clear on this crucially important point:

*JFK died **instantly** – in Dealey Plaza.*

*Therefore, JFK was **DOA** at Parkland Hospital.*

Honest medical personnel at Parkland stated as much.

Doctors who claimed otherwise – ***including Charles Carrico*** – were lying.

And *doctors who were lying* were part of the JFK assassination plot.

* * *

Dr. Charles Carrico testified falsely that President Kennedy was still alive when first rushed into Parkland Hospital. The president was in fact dead, but Dr. Carrico busily *placed an endotracheal tube into JFK's bloody corpse* as it lay on a gurney in Trauma Room 1.

And Carrico was not the only medical professional at Parkland who knowingly engaged in *faux* "treatment" [*sic*] on the body of the dead president.

Other, more senior doctors soon arrived to evaluate the victim's condition; the small room filled up quickly. But because the JFK assassination plot had gone haywire earlier that day – and because *more people had been shot in Dealey Plaza at 12:30 p.m. CST than was ever officially acknowledged* [1226] – some of the Parkland Hospital personnel who entered Trauma Room 1 and observed President Kennedy's actual wounds were **not** part of the select cadre of medical criminals previously enlisted to participate in the assassination of the president.

Some Parkland personnel were totally *innocent* – and therefore totally *unwitting* of what their sinister colleagues had pledged to do when JFK's body arrived.

Some Parkland personnel weren't "in on it."

So they weren't part of the vicious plot to murder the president.

[1225] A *raft* of data from firsthand eyewitnesses (including medical professionals) makes this indisputably clear.

[1226] As mentioned earlier, I have carefully documented **six** (6) total casualties in Dealey Plaza – 2 dead, 4 wounded. (Author's exclusive original discovery.)

* * *

There was more, of course.

There's always more.

While present in Trauma Room 1, Dr. Charles Carrico received from a dazed and devastated Jacqueline Kennedy a bloody handful of material consisting of skull and brain matter from the president's fatally damaged head.

Carrico put the bloody material into the pocket of his coat.

He did *not* turn it over to the Dallas police or the Secret Service or the FBI.

He did *not* examine it or photograph it or x-ray it or analyze it.

He did *not* submit it to the Johnson Commission.

Instead, Charles Carrico did something very strange: the doctor went home the day *after* the assassination,[1227] tried to rinse JFK's blood out of his dress shirt in the bathtub of his house,[1228] and *personally buried a portion of President Kennedy's head in a hole in the yard of his own Dallas-area home.*

Unless that piece of skull bone was surreptitiously dug up at some point subsequently by JFK's killers (or by a curious animal), it lies there still.[1229]

* * *

Charles Carrico was not the eldest nor the most experienced member of the sinister cadre of criminal right-wing Dallas doctors who agreed to participate in the JFK assassination plot.

Yet Carrico had a key role; and *someone by that name clearly demanded payment soon after the JFK assassination.*

And Lyndon Johnson, the killer in the Oval Office, promptly complied.[1230]

LBJ ordered his aides to arrange a pardon from Governor Terry Sanford of North Carolina – and Gov. Sanford (not understanding the sinister and criminal nature of the White House request) acceded to that request.[1231]

[1227] Jessica DeLeón, "Living History," *UNT North Texan*, September 30th, 2013.

[1228] Jessica DeLeón, "Living History," *UNT North Texan*, September 30th, 2013.

[1229] Dr. Carrico's gruesome and criminal act is not simply appalling and illegal. It also has certain major ramifications which are completely unknown to **all** other JFK researchers – matters which I discovered exclusively and which I will discuss at length in a second major book of mine which is already well underway and already scheduled for publication.

[1230] Author's exclusive original discovery.

[1231] Author's exclusive original discovery.

And thus, *Charles Carrico got his pardon.*

Be very clear:

The Carrico pardon is *written proof positive of a **deal*** [1232] – a deal between the illegitimate new occupant of the White House and someone with the name of the cagey young doctor who had been first to supposedly "treat" the corpse of President Kennedy in Trauma Room 1 at Parkland Hospital.

Carrico was involved.

There was a deal.

Johnson complied.

LBJ plainly **had to** pay off Charles Carrico – and the sudden issuance of an official North Carolina pardon for crimes committed in that state in 1960 was the *price* of that particular payoff. [1233] It was obviously extremely important to Charles Carrico – and LBJ obligingly arranged it very quickly, beginning just *days* after the bloody JFK assassination (and the odious medical charade) perpetrated in Dallas.

* * *

In late 1963 – following a request from his JFK assassination co-conspirator, Congressman Al Thomas – Lyndon Johnson instructed top White House aides Larry O'Brien and Henry Hall Wilson to contact the Democratic governor of North Carolina, Terry Sanford, in order to seek a pardon for a criminal who had been arrested and convicted *years earlier* in that state.

Sanford was the relatively enlightened Southern governor who supported JFK in 1960, [1234] and whom President Kennedy was planning to nominate as VP in 1964 *to replace LBJ as his running mate* [1235] – and thus, Lyndon Johnson derived *additional* satisfaction out of this particular post-assassination maneuver.

The Johnson White House effort was successful.

The pardon was granted.

Governor Sanford clearly did not realize its sinister purpose.

* * *

[1232] Author's exclusive original discovery.

[1233] Author's exclusive original discovery.

[1234] "I'd been one of the few Southerners to be *for* Kennedy initially [in the 1960 presidential campaign]," said the former governor to me. (Author interview with Terry Sanford, 1995.)

[1235] JFK said as much explicitly to his White House secretary, Evelyn Lincoln, just three days before the assassination.

Understandably, decades later Terry Sanford did not recall the Carrico pardon specifically – "We had *hundreds* of those things," he said candidly to me[1236] – but the former governor certainly *did* instantly recall the name of key White House congressional liaison Henry Hall Wilson, who was unwittingly roped into the sinister Carrico pardon effort as well.

"Henry was our contact in the White House," said Sanford. "He was a very good friend of mine!"[1237] In fact, Sanford added, "Henry [Wilson] and Larry [O'Brien] were our contact with the Kennedy administration."[1238]

Sanford explained that while Larry O'Brien was the *overall* congressional liaison for President Kennedy (ultimately responsible for both the House *and* the Senate), the duo of Larry O'Brien and Robert Kennedy had hired Henry Hall Wilson to serve specifically as the White House liaison for *the House of Representatives* – where longtime Representative Al Thomas of Houston was a very powerful figure.[1239]

As was his usual pattern and practice, Lyndon Baines Johnson pulled *just the right strings* and tapped *just the right people* to arrange for them to carry out his Machiavellian maneuvering.[1240]

Since the request involved an issue pertaining to North Carolina, Larry O'Brien naturally gave the task to North Carolinian Henry Wilson; and Wilson naturally and predictably contacted his old boss and personal friend, North Carolina Governor Terry Sanford.

But that wasn't all.

Lyndon Johnson left nothing to chance; he always had backup plans *on top of* backup plans.

Thus his JFK assassination accomplice, Congressman Al Thomas of Texas, *personally* wrote to Governor Sanford on December 5th, 1963, specifically requesting a pardon for one Charles Carrico;[1241] and Sanford quickly and obligingly and innocently issued that pardon.

Note carefully:

[1236] Author interview with Terry Sanford, 1995.

[1237] Wilson had worked on Sanford's gubernatorial campaign, as well. (Author interview with Terry Sanford, 1995.)

[1238] Author interview with Terry Sanford, 1995.

[1239] Author interview with Terry Sanford, 1995.

[1240] Author's exclusive original discovery.

[1241] Author's exclusive original discovery.

Al Thomas wrote to Governor Sanford seeking a pardon for Charles Carrico *days before LBJ even formally moved into the White House* on Saturday, December 7th, 1963! [1242]

That's how urgent this pardon was.

*LBJ and Al Thomas **used** all three men – Larry O'Brien, Henry Wilson and Terry Sanford – without them even realizing it.* [1243]

It was a classic – and criminal – LBJ maneuver.

The Carrico pardon was plainly *essential* to the JFK plot. [1244]

And its supreme urgency is proven by the fact that the Lyndon Johnson/Al Thomas push for the Carrico pardon began just *days* after the JFK assassination – and days *before* LBJ even formally took occupancy of the White House!

Lyndon Johnson needed to keep his accomplices and confederates satisfied, content, quiet and in line. [1245]

The Carrico pardon, America, was payment for "services rendered." [1246]

* * *

And yet . . .

There was a small but nagging and intriguing mystery attached to the stunning pardon document that I discovered.

A *single initial* appearing on the pardon struck a jarringly discordant note.

The full name of the Parkland Hospital doctor was – reputedly – Charles James Carrico.

But the *pardon* that I discovered reads "Charles **A.** Carrico," rather than "Charles **J.** Carrico." [1247]

And Congressman Albert Thomas's letter to Governor Sanford actually specified "Charles **A.** Carrico," as well. [1248]

So what exactly did that mean?

Did Dr. Carrico have two or more middle names?

Did Dr. Carrico purchase, carry and use a fake ID in the past?

[1242] Author's exclusive original discovery.

[1243] Author's exclusive original discovery.

[1244] Author's exclusive original discovery.

[1245] Author's exclusive original discovery.

[1246] Author's exclusive original discovery.

[1247] Author's exclusive original discovery.

[1248] Author's exclusive original discovery.

*Did Dr. Carrico deliberately and cleverly give a **false middle initial** (verbally) when arrested years earlier, to partially **disguise his identity** and thereby avoid future legal and professional problems?*[1249]

Or . . . had some official in North Carolina – at the time of the original case, or later – been aurally mistaken (or significantly hearing-challenged), thereby confusing the pronunciation of the letter "J" for the letter "A"?

*After all, those two initials **do** rhyme perfectly . . .*

*Or . . . was it a simple **typographical** error by a hurried (and harried) police station clerk or an overworked state bureaucrat?*

*Or . . . was the pardon actually obtained for **a relative of** Parkland Hospital's Dr. Carrico?*

*Or . . . was the pardon for **someone else entirely?***

The answer obviously mattered, but it did not change the fundamental **meaning** of the Carrico pardon.

The fact was this: in the immediate aftermath of the JFK assassination, while facing much larger and graver issues of national and international concern, the LBJ White House had strangely reached out less than two weeks after the slaying and *hastily requested a pardon* – which was promptly issued, just 28 days after Dallas! – for a nominally obscure individual convicted for crimes committed in another state *three years previously.*

Why?

It was not a typical act, particularly not for *senior presidential aides* in a busy, hectic White House that was still reeling from the bloody assassination of the previous Chief Executive. Yet LBJ personally ensured that the unwitting Larry O'Brien and Henry Wilson got it done, *less than a month after the murder of President John Fitzgerald Kennedy.*[1250]

And LBJ's powerful Texas accomplice, Congressman Al Thomas, played a leading role in *personally* lobbying Governor Sanford for that pardon.[1251]

The effort was successfully completed *just four weeks after the Dallas slaying.*

That's *lightning* speed, by federal government standards!

[1249] In an interesting parallel, Lifton – a public figure who bragged to me in the 1990s that he (Lifton) had engaged in *criminal conspiracy and burglary* during the 1960s plus *criminal conspiracy and grand theft* in the 1970s – used the *alias* "David S. Lifton" [*sic*] instead of his *real* name, which was Samuel D. Lifton.

N.B.: For what it's worth, switching or changing *your middle initial* (as Lifton did) makes it much more difficult for anyone to later track you down and properly connect you to your crimes. (As the endlessly devious and deliberately deceitful Lifton liked to say, "Food for thought.")

[1250] Author's exclusive original discovery.

[1251] Author's exclusive original discovery. In essence, LBJ and Al Thomas "tag-teamed" Governor Sanford, using a "hammer-and-anvil" approach.

Absolutely lightning speed.

Why?

The truth is blunt and simple:

Lyndon Johnson *owed* certain people for their availability and their participation in the JFK assassination itself *and* for their assistance and silence in its immediate aftermath.[1252]

*One of them – **at least** one of them – was named Charles Carrico.*

And the additionally chilling thing was this:

*Perhaps **two** of them were named Charles Carrico.*[1253]

Dr. Carrico of Parkland Hospital was still a "resident" at the time of the assassination – just 28 years old, a relatively young professional. In order to move up in the medical profession and secure his future – and in order to effectively "erase" or "bury" the reputational damage that would be caused by the belated discovery of a deeply embarrassing and potentially disqualifying criminal conviction, whether it occurred in his *own* past or in, say, *a relative's* past – he needed and wanted a pardon.

Lyndon Johnson promptly made that happen.

The pardon which I discovered is ***the very first written proof*** *from U. S. government records* of an actual payoff to an identifiable individual for JFK assassination-related services.[1254]

It was handled quietly, subtly, quickly and extremely efficiently behind the scenes – never reaching *anyone's* awareness until my astounding exclusive original discovery.

* * *

One of Johnson's key assassination plot "assets" was named Charles Carrico.

*But . . . were there **two**?*

Over the years I never stopped looking for *another* possible recipient of that 1963 pardon.

Was there really someone else?

Was there really someone actually named Charles "A." Carrico?

Eventually I located a record of a man with that name and that middle initial.[1255]

At least one Charles "A." Carrico definitely existed!

[1252] Author's exclusive original discovery.

[1253] Author's exclusive original discovery.

[1254] Author's exclusive original discovery.

[1255] Author's exclusive original discovery.

In 1963, he was an adult man who was several years *younger* than the Parkland Hospital doctor – and thus far, the Charles "A." Carrico whose information I found had no *known* connection to the JFK assassination.[1256]

A person named Charles *Anthony* Carrico was born in August 1941, making him just 22 years old on the day of the JFK assassination in November 1963.

Significantly, **this** Carrico – Charles *Anthony* Carrico – was a military man. His obituary noted that he was a *U. S. Army* veteran, who ultimately retired with the rank of major.[1257]

Those facts did not exclude him from suspicion or relevance, however.

Not hardly.

Here's why:

Congressman Al Thomas's letter to Governor Sanford seeking a pardon for "Charles A. Carrico" specifically mentioned the individual's reputed ***Army*** background; explicitly noted that he had received a ***dishonorable discharge*** from the U. S. Army due to his (May 1960) criminal conviction in North Carolina; and emphasized that the man reportedly wished to ***re-enlist*** *in the Army* if he could first obtain a pardon.[1258]

And according to Al Thomas's letter, in late 1963 (the time period of President Kennedy's fatal Texas trip), Charles "A." Carrico was residing in the Houston area – the location of the Al Thomas testimonial dinner held the night before the JFK assassination, which was the linchpin of the entire Texas trip!

Moreover, Congressman Thomas blithely noted – in writing – that Charles "**A**." Carrico's family were *old friends of his.*[1259]

Naturally a number of questions arose:

Was Charles "A." Carrico of the U. S. Army an excellent shot?

Was he selected for a potential sniper role (or some other function) in the JFK assassination plot?

Was he somehow actively involved in the president's killing?

Was he a shooter, or a spotter, or a radio man, or a transportation coordinator?

Or . . . was Charles "A." Carrico yet one more vulnerable young man based in Texas in late 1963 who had ***a military background and a black mark on his record*** –

[1256] In the 1990s I spoke with a woman in Colorado who answered a telephone number associated with a "Charles A. Carrico," but she expressed no *personal* knowledge or awareness of any family or medical or professional connection to the Dr. Charles Carrico who worked at Parkland Hospital in Dallas in 1963.

[1257] The Colorado Springs *Gazette,* September 9th, 2020.

[1258] Author's exclusive original discovery; see the Al Thomas letter to Terry Sanford, December 5th, 1963.

[1259] Author's exclusive original discovery; see the Al Thomas letter to Terry Sanford, December 5th, 1963.

just like USAF veteran Billy Nolan Lovelady, and just like USAF Airman Lloyd John Wilson[1260] – whom JFK's assassins were planning to *manipulate* and *use* (and then promptly *kill*) as the unwitting patsy in President Kennedy's slaying, in the event that their *primary* designated "culprit," the doomed Lee Harvey Oswald (who also had *a military background and a bad discharge on his record*) was somehow unavailable?

The undeniable fact is this:

No one rams through a sudden pardon in the immediate aftermath of a ghastly presidential assassination unless it means something crucially important.

Remember:

The JFK plot's intellectual author, *House Speaker Sam Rayburn himself,*[1261] personally wrote the letter that facilitated Lee Oswald's sudden "hardship discharge" from the Marine Corps in 1959, so that Oswald could travel to the USSR at U. S. government behest and thereby conveniently be tarred forever as a supposed "communist"![1262]

And JFK plot accomplice *Congressman Al Thomas himself* personally wrote the urgent missive (on congressional letterhead, no less!) to Gov. Sanford requesting a pardon for "Charles A. Carrico" less than two weeks after President Kennedy's bloody slaying in 1963.[1263]

So I repeat:

No one rams through a sudden pardon in the immediate aftermath of a ghastly presidential assassination unless it means something crucially important.

Idiots and wimps and cowards cling desperately to "coincidence theory."

Strong people, as Ralph Waldo Emerson observed, believe in *cause and effect.*

A newspaper reported that Charles *Anthony* Carrico died in September 2020 in the city of Colorado Springs, Colorado – ironically enough, the home of the United States Air Force Academy.[1264]

* * *

[1260] Author's exclusive original discovery.

[1261] Author's exclusive original discovery.

[1262] FBI agent Vincent Drain, who was personally involved in the post-assassination investigation, revealed something extraordinary in 1988: ". . . as a matter of fact, *Sam Rayburn is the one who got [Lee Harvey Oswald] a hardship discharge out of the Marine Corps."* (Larry Sneed, *No More Silence,* p. 254.)

[1263] Author's exclusive original discovery.

[1264] The Colorado Springs *Gazette,* September 9th, 2020.

The Carrico pardon, issued in December 1963.

Author's exclusive original discovery.

Dr. Charles J. Carrico in Dallas falsely indicated to his own medical colleagues that President Kennedy was *still alive* upon arrival at Parkland Hospital.[1265]

Dr. Carrico lied to the Johnson Commission as well – knowingly *perjuring himself* both by testifying falsely under oath about the events of November 22nd, and by deliberately and knowingly omitting *all* of the *salient* information, *in furtherance of the crime.*[1266]

Dr. Carrico played his part in the assassination plot on the day of JFK's murder and again on March 25th, 1964, in his false Johnson Commission testimony. In fact, he continued the ongoing commission of the crime *for the entire duration of his adult life* by lying repeatedly in public appearances and media interviews, and by failing to ever report the devastating truth.

Dr. Charles James Carrico – the man who *secretly buried a portion of President Kennedy's head on his own property in Texas* – died in 2002.

* * *

As I have proven exclusively and conclusively, Lyndon Baines Johnson promptly paid off a man linked to LBJ's murderous 1963 coup plot by arranging a full legal pardon for an individual convicted of crimes committed in North Carolina *three years before Dallas.*

It was an ugly, illicit, thoroughly criminal deal – a slick, brazen payoff in exchange for *services rendered in connection with the assassination of John Fitzgerald Kennedy – on the day of the crime, and after the fact as well.*[1267]

There was another significant payoff, too:

Lyndon Johnson made U. S. Army General Earle Wheeler the successor to Maxwell Taylor as Chairman of the Joint Chiefs of Staff in 1964, thanks to certain vital

---

[1265] In reality, President Kennedy died *in Dealey Plaza* at 12:30 p.m. CST.

Unlike the 1968 case of Senator Robert Kennedy, who lingered for some 26 hours after being shot in the head *from behind* in Los Angeles, President John F. Kennedy was shot in the head *from the front* and died in Dallas *immediately.*

The two brothers were shot from opposite directions, with dramatically different types of ammunition – and unlike Bobby, the president expired instantly. JFK was indisputably "dead on arrival" (DOA) at Parkland Hospital.

[1266] In this, Dr. Carrico was much like certain Secret Service agents who offered only sanitized pablum under oath.

[1267] Author's exclusive original discovery.

"services rendered" to LBJ by the U. S. Army (the tanks ordered to Dallas) on November 22nd, 1963.[1268]

But the very worst payoff of all for the JFK assassination – a payoff which would be *far* more public than the quiet, previously unnoticed Carrico pardon[1269] or even the 1964 promotion of General Wheeler – was yet to come.

And this gargantuan obligation *had* to be paid, of course.

It simply **had** to be paid.

For it was a truly massive debt, owed to a group of highly aggressive, extremely well-placed individuals in uniform who had personally ensured and guaranteed – *come hell or high water* – the ultimate success of Lyndon Johnson's bloody 1963 coup.[1270]

By creating the Johnson Commission – and by pressuring it to hastily deliver a false conclusion regarding his culpability in the JFK assassination – LBJ cleared the way for himself to run for *two full terms* as president, beginning with the 1964 election.

The presidency was Johnson's lifelong goal – and having literally *killed* for it, he planned to make the most of it.

But in achieving his *own* desires, Johnson also initiated the countdown to a massively expanded, shatteringly violent war, half a world away.

The exponential escalation of the Vietnam War was **not** Johnson's goal; nor was it the "reason" for the JFK assassination – contrary to the shallow reasoning of many well-intentioned but hopelessly naïve researchers.

The Vietnam War was, instead, an onerous and inconvenient *obligation* – an inescapable *debt* owed by LBJ to the hard-eyed uniformed men who had reluctantly forestalled Armageddon at his behest and who had *guaranteed* the triumph of his bloody 1963 coup, *despite* its myriad operational failures.

He *owed* them, damn it.

He **owed** them!

So, because of Dallas, the sparks of war began to burst into full flame – and in the end, they would help to sear and scorch and char and vaporize and consume *millions* of innocent people, as well as the very presidency for which Lyndon Baines Johnson had knowingly and willingly *murdered* John Fitzgerald Kennedy.

[1268] Author's exclusive original discovery.

[1269] Author's exclusive original discovery.

[1270] Author's exclusive original discovery.

Vital evidence is buried beneath that stone.

MISSION ACCOMPLISHED:

Members of the Joint Chiefs of Staff
(in the foreground, Curtis LeMay at center)
walk in President Kennedy's
November 25th funeral procession
after having ensured the slaughter
of their commander-in-chief
and guaranteed the success of LBJ's bloody coup.

Author's exclusive original discovery.

Chapter Thirty-Eight:
The Price

*"The United States, as the world knows, will never start a war.
We do not want a war. We do not now expect a war."*

– John Fitzgerald Kennedy
(To the world)
June 1963

*"Just let me get elected,
and then you can have your war."*

– Lyndon Baines Johnson
(To the Joint Chiefs of Staff)
December 1963

*"There is and will be, as long as I am president,
peace for all Americans."*

– Lyndon Baines Johnson
(To the American public)
October 1964

*"There is not, and there will not be,
a mindless escalation."*

– Lyndon Baines Johnson
(To the American public)
March 1966

"Strong men believe in cause and effect."
– Ralph Waldo Emerson

*"These things do not just 'happen.'
They are **made** to happen."*

– John Fitzgerald Kennedy

They guaranteed Lyndon Johnson the presidency.
He guaranteed them the Vietnam War.
That is the reality.
That is the truth.
That is the price.[1271]

* * *

It is an extraordinarily damning indictment of the posturing, asinine, intellectually impotent creampuffs of American "journalism" and American "academe" that no one has ever figured this out previously.

Long before initial publication of excerpts from the Pentagon Papers back in 1971, and *long before* the much later "official" release by the U. S. government of a multitude of *other* formerly classified military and political papers concerning the Vietnam War (releases made in the 1990s and the 2010s), the naked truth about President Kennedy's plans to get out of Vietnam and end that evil conflict was already known and was in fact widely available to the entire American public.

It was present in a bestselling book in the 1960s.

Jim Bishop was an experienced author who wrote *The Day Kennedy Was Shot,* an imperfect but extremely useful recounting of the JFK assassination which was published in 1968. Bishop had interviewed President Kennedy in the White House, and had taken very good notes of their conversations. As Bishop admitted in the text of his 1968 bestseller, **John Kennedy wanted out of Vietnam** – and as Bishop also explicitly noted, the president had *already* demanded from the Pentagon brass **a timetable for that withdrawal.**[1272]

No one in the contemptible national media or in the hollow (not hallowed) halls of academe could (or *would*) put two and two together and generate meaningful results. Not then, and not thereafter. Real thinking and accurate analysis are far beyond their ken.

JFK researchers couldn't grasp reality either. Most quickly became infatuated with, and endlessly distracted by, idiots and idiocies like Clay Shaw, David Ferrie, "triangulated crossfire," New Orleans, Miami and the like. Easily misdirected by ludicrously irrelevant non-entities and non-issues, scads of sincere but silly sleuths focused intently on worthless red herrings as if they (the benighted researchers) were hopelessly addicted to smoked fish.

[1271] Author's exclusive original discovery.

[1272] Jim Bishop, *The Day Kennedy Was Shot,* pp. 106-107.

It didn't *have* to be that way, of course, but this is America – where the *appearance* of reality, carefully censored and "curated" prior to release so as not to offend the powerful, is much more prized than honest revelation of the truth about important events.

* * *

JFK had made it clear within the U. S. government, *since early 1962,* that he had decided to withdraw the U. S. military from Vietnam following his own presumptive reelection in the 1964 presidential campaign.

In 1962, Kennedy ordered the Pentagon to begin *planning* the withdrawal (just *months* after he had foolishly boosted the number of American military "advisers" there in November 1961) – and in 1963, JFK ordered the Pentagon to begin *implementing* the total American withdrawal.

Moreover, in addition to issuing National Security Action Memorandum 263 in October 1963, Kennedy *solidified* and *concretized* his Vietnam withdrawal decision (and thereby avoided any potential backsliding on the part of himself or anyone else)[1273] by deliberately and repeatedly informing multiple sources including senators, White House advisers, ambassadors, writers and others – *in explicit and unequivocating language* – that he was getting America out of the ugly conflict completely by the end of 1965.

Win, lose or draw.

Regardless *of the outcome militarily, on the ground.*[1274]

Publicly, in news conferences and interviews, Kennedy repeated various Cold War cliches that masked his real intent. But inside the U. S. government and inside the U. S. military, there was absolutely no mistaking JFK's real message:

We're getting out of Vietnam.

Win, lose or draw.

Regardless of the outcome on the ground.

Uniformed men at all levels knew this; the widely read military newspaper *Stars & Stripes* carried the following blaring headline in bold type on its front page in the autumn of 1963: **"U.S. TROOPS SEEN OUT OF VIET BY '65."**[1275]

Contrary to the dishonest denialist drivel still spewed by pathetic, pusillanimous Establishment lickspittles to this day, there is in reality ***no doubt***

[1273] Author's exclusive original discovery.

[1274] In the early 1990s, John Newman made this clear in his book *JFK and Vietnam* – and was promptly pilloried and censored for challenging Establishment lies.

[1275] *(Pacific) Stars & Stripes,* Friday, October 4th, 1963.

whatsoever about JFK's Vietnam withdrawal policy – nor about his decision to actually codify and *implement* it.

Robert Kennedy disclosed this in 1964 – *years before* the escalation of the war brutalized Vietnam, tore America apart politically, and became the principal public controversy in this country. In an oral history interview conducted the year after the JFK assassination, Bobby disclosed *precisely* what method JFK planned to use to close out America's misbegotten involvement in Vietnam: *neutralization.* Employing the exact same model used in neighboring Laos in 1962, President Kennedy would arrange for a "neutral" government in Vietnam, and then exit permanently – regardless of the consequences.[1276]

This was not a secret to key officials.

And there is further absolute proof of this fact – proof which I discovered and recognized exclusively in 2020.

* * *

The following point is not raised in the dubious "debates" and specious "arguments" over JFK's concrete withdrawal decision, but one of the single most powerful pieces of *proof* that President Kennedy's decision to withdraw from Vietnam was in fact *firm and irrevocable and real* came from the one person who knew better than anyone.

None other than the American ambassador to the odious South Vietnamese dictatorship – Henry Cabot Lodge Jr., appointed by JFK himself in the summer of 1963 – was fully aware of President Kennedy's absolute determination to leave Vietnam, come hell or high water.

We're getting out of Vietnam.

Win, lose or draw.

Regardless *of the outcome on the ground.*

Lodge made a blunt admission on the morning of Sunday, November 24th, 1963, which conclusively settles the matter, once and for all.[1277]

Speaking by telephone to State Department official Roger Hilsman (the Assistant Secretary of State for Far Eastern Affairs), Ambassador Lodge blurted out a complaint which proved and confirmed the unvarnished truth about JFK's *actual* Vietnam policy. "We should exact some *quid pro quo* for withdrawing American

---

[1276] Robert Kennedy 1964 oral history, JFK Library.

[1277] Author's exclusive original discovery.

forces," said Lodge with annoyance, "rather than ***handing it to them [the Communists] on a silver platter, as our present [JFK-ordered] plans for withdrawal would do.***"[1278]

Lodge's explicit statement, candidly and spontaneously uttered in a private call to a fellow senior government official just two days after the JFK assassination, is absolutely dispositive on the issue.[1279]

We should exact some quid pro quo for **withdrawing American forces** *rather than handing it to them [the Communists] on a silver platter, as our present plans for withdrawal would do.*

There is no valid "debate" or "question" or "controversy" about President Kennedy's orders.[1280]

None whatsoever.

We should exact some quid pro quo for withdrawing American forces rather than handing it to them [the Communists] on a silver platter, as our present plans for withdrawal would do.

Henry Cabot Lodge Jr. could not have been clearer.

We should exact some quid pro quo for withdrawing American forces rather than **handing it to them [the Communists] on a silver platter, as our present plans for withdrawal would do.**

End of any specious "arguments."

Forever.

Period.

President Kennedy was getting out of Vietnam – even though that meant, as JFK well knew and completely understood, that the vicious, rotten, brutal and corrupt South Vietnamese regime would inevitably collapse, and that nationalist and communist forces dedicated to Vietnamese independence from foreign domination would unquestionably take control of the entire country.

[1278] Author's exclusive original discovery. Lodge's comment was recorded in a Hilsman memo on November 24th, 1963. (See JFK Library, Hilsman Papers, Country Series-Vietnam. *Secret; Eyes Only.* Drafted and initialed by Hilsman. The text is also reproduced in *Foreign Relations of the United States, 1961–1963*, Volume IV, Vietnam, August–December 1963, Document 328.)

[1279] Author's exclusive original discovery.

[1280] Except among the gutless contemptible scum who wish to (A) frantically deny the significance of the JFK assassination itself and (B) falsely and fraudulently pretend that the massive, deliberate reversal of Kennedy's Vietnam withdrawal policy either "did not occur" [*sic*], or is somehow "debatable" [*sic*], or is somehow "unknowable" [*sic*].

Pro tip: Ignore such cowardly charlatans lest your brain turn into rancid tapioca.

JFK acknowledged as much on the very morning of his own murder. In Fort Worth, Texas, JFK stated the obvious out loud, in public: "Without the United States, South Vietnam would collapse overnight."[1281]

JFK was withdrawing from Vietnam – even though doing so would certainly and inevitably "hand the country to the communists on a silver platter."

We're getting out of Vietnam.

Win, lose or draw.

Regardless *of the outcome on the ground.*

JFK himself made this clear to writer Jim Bishop, at the White House, in October 1963.[1282]

And as a later observer correctly noted, that policy – meaning *full American withdrawal from Vietnam* – "was the actual policy of the United States on the day Kennedy died."[1283]

* * *

But that would change almost instantaneously – and quite *deliberately* – in the immediate wake of JFK's bloody assassination.

The ambassador's crystal-clear awareness of the actual nature and meaning of JFK's Vietnam withdrawal policy was not limited to Ambassador Henry Cabot Lodge.

All the key players in the U. S. government were fully cognizant of the truth.

All of them.

Including John Kennedy's murderer, Lyndon Johnson.

On November 23rd and November 24th, 1963 – immediately after assassinating President Kennedy in Dallas – Lyndon Baines Johnson met with top American officials in the Executive Office Building near the White House to discuss the Vietnam War.

LBJ himself made it very clear, on the very weekend of the assassination, that he was going to *reverse* Kennedy's withdrawal order – and *escalate* the war.

Johnson *personally* ordered top U. S. government officials to lie to the ever-gullible American press about supposed "continuity" with Kennedy's policies. Meanwhile, LBJ privately declared that *victory* (not withdrawal) was the new American goal, and he *personally* demanded a re-drafted version of a new NSAM, featuring subtle but calculated changes which profoundly altered, totally reversed and completely *destroyed* JFK's decision to end American involvement in Vietnam.

[1281] Presidential remarks to the Fort Worth Chamber of Commerce, November 22nd, 1963.

[1282] Jim Bishop, *The Day Kennedy Was Shot,* pp. 106-107.

[1283] James K. Galbraith, "JFK's Plans to Withdraw," *New York Review of Books,* December 6th, 2007.

Johnson knew full well what he was doing, and he knew full well that he was deliberately reversing Kennedy's withdrawal policy. LBJ *admitted this explicitly* in early 1964 during a conversation with Defense Secretary Robert McNamara, in which Johnson declared that "I always thought it was foolish for you to make any statements about withdrawing. I thought it was bad psychologically. But you and *the President [JFK] thought **otherwise**,* and I just sat silent."[1284]

John Kennedy certainly did not sit silently; he planned and actually *ordered the implementation of* full American withdrawal from Vietnam.

Lyndon Johnson secretly, knowingly and deliberately **canceled** and **reversed** that American withdrawal.

Kennedy was saddened and disgusted by the deaths of U. S. soldiers in Vietnam; during November 1963 the president had to personally sign at least half a dozen letters to the families of American military men whose lives had been ended in Southeast Asia: Donald C. Johansen; Walter K. Morris; Charles B. Lankford; Woodrow M. Fitzgerald; Gordon R. Brown; and William J. Everheart.[1285]

JFK agonized over the loss of six men in a single *month.*

Under LBJ, the loss of six men in Vietnam in a single *day* would have been considered *a very good day* and *an extraordinarily low number of casualties.*

A disgusted President Kennedy realized – and said aloud, shortly before his death – that further defense of the murderous dictatorship in South Vietnam was *not worth the loss of a single additional American life.*

Johnson and his uniformed accomplices in the Pentagon had no such compunction whatsoever.

* * *

Get this through your head:

Wars do not begin by accident. Wars are caused by *decisions.*[1286]

Conscious, *deliberate* decisions.

And America's criminal war against Vietnam was no exception.

The Vietnam War was **not** an inevitability. It certainly was **not** the lamentable but unstoppable "outcome" of massive, nebulous "geo-political forces" or "Cold War atmospherics" or "historic currents" or "settled national policy."

Contrary to the vapid, endlessly regurgitated declarations of generations of shallow political pundits and whorish "historians" and dishonest, demented, deceptive

---

[1284] LBJ to McNamara, telcon, February 25th, 1964.

[1285] The letters are available online in the collections of the JFK Library.

[1286] Author's original insight.

"documentarians," the Vietnam War was not merely a "quagmire," or a "morass," or a "tragedy," or an "accident," or an "error," or an innocent "mistake."

It was a ***decision*** – a conscious, deliberate, very *specific* decision.[1287]

That decision was made by *one* specific individual – Lyndon Baines Johnson himself – and there was a single, conscious, deliberate, very specific *reason* for his decision.[1288] The colossal Vietnam War in its massively escalated form – beginning openly in 1965 under Lyndon Baines Johnson – was ***not*** a "morass" into which America was somehow inexplicably "drawn."

It was a *decision* – a conscious, knowing, very *deliberate* decision.[1289]

It was, in fact, *the actual price of the JFK assassination.*[1290]

Not the ***reason*** for the assassination, mind you – but the ***price.***[1291]

Be very clear:

The *reason* for JFK's murder was *to make LBJ president.*[1292]

The Vietnam War was the awful and horrifying *price.*[1293]

The proof of this came from Lyndon Johnson's own lips, at a White House event just a month after the murder in Dallas.[1294]

The *war* was the *price* – and LBJ said so himself, *explicitly,* in December 1963.

[1287] Author's exclusive original discovery.

[1288] Author's exclusive original discovery.

[1289] Both life and history consist of a series of *decisions* – ***not*** a series of "coincidences."

[1290] Author's exclusive original discovery. Strangely, this is an absolutely fundamental fact which no one else has ever had the brains – or the *balls* – to figure out and to state publicly.

[1291] Author's exclusive original discovery.

[1292] Author's exclusive original discovery. That and ***only*** that was the true reason for the murder of John Kennedy, which was conceived of, plotted by, and led by Samuel Taliaferro Rayburn and Lyndon Baines Johnson – the two politically frustrated southern politicians who vehemently resented their ongoing penalization and humiliation and exclusion from the top echelon of power for the "crime" of having Texas roots.

Other elements of the U. S. government obviously ***joined*** and ***supported*** the existing Rayburn/Johnson plot for reasons and motives and agendas of their own. But the motives of the "joiners" (namely, the military, the SS and – in a very *small* role – the CIA) were ***not*** the true motives of the plot's two actual initiators and leaders: Sam Rayburn and LBJ.

Recognize and understand the difference!

[1293] Author's exclusive original discovery.

[1294] The gutless Stanley Karnow reported the chilling episode but frantically and repeatedly denied the true meaning and significance of LBJ's statement to the Joint Chiefs. (Self-castration is the first step in joining the Establishment.)

"Just let me get elected," said Johnson to the Joint Chiefs of Staff and other senior military officers gathered at a White House reception in December 1963, "and then you can have your war."[1295]

It was not a casual remark.

Johnson was openly acknowledging his sinister deal with the American military[1296] – a deal clearly made long *before* the JFK assassination[1297] – and in declaring that he would unleash U. S. forces *after* the upcoming 1964 election, LBJ was simply "managing the expectations" of the JCS as to the actual *timing* of his fulfillment of *his* side of the brutal bloody bargain which they had all agreed to well before November 22nd, 1963.[1298]

USAF Sergeant Robert "Mac" Macmillan, a steward on the presidential jet, disclosed to me that he *personally* heard Lyndon Johnson talking privately about the escalation of the Vietnam War, aboard Air Force One, *long before* the formal launching of that violent escalation occurred in 1965.[1299]

The preservation, escalation, expansion and continuation of the Vietnam War was the Joint Chiefs' unalterable demand – made *in exchange for* the Pentagon's secret pledge to support and *guarantee* Johnson's bloody November 1963 coup with their tanks and their planes and their resources and the open domestic use of military force in America, if necessary.[1300]

That is the long-sought answer to the bizarre enigma of why Lyndon Baines Johnson – without question the toughest, strongest, most talented, most ambitious and most effective politician in American history – mysteriously refused to rid himself of the politically poisonous *albatross* of a foreign war which was needlessly destroying his own political party, destroying his own administration, and destroying his own personal and political legacy.[1301]

The war was the price.

[1295] Stanley Karnow, *Vietnam: A History,* p. 326. (Karnow's source was none other than U. S. Army General Harold K. Johnson, who was personally present when LBJ said it – and who was soon promoted to Army Chief of Staff by LBJ.)

[1296] Author's exclusive original discovery.

[1297] Author's exclusive original discovery.

[1298] Author's exclusive original discovery.

[1299] Author interview with USAF veteran Robert MacMillan, 1994.

[1300] Author's exclusive original discovery.

[1301] Author's exclusive original discovery.

An angry General Earle Wheeler,
Chairman of the Joint Chiefs of Staff,
stands over Lyndon Johnson on July 26th, 1965,
during a Cabinet Room meeting at the White House.

Wheeler's fury exploded as
LBJ pretended to waffle about
the massive escalation of the Vietnam War
which he had *already promised* to the U. S. military
in exchange for its active support of the JFK assassination.

Author's exclusive original discovery.

The expanded, escalated Vietnam War which LBJ launched in 1965 was in reality ***the principal payoff*** made in connection with the JFK assassination of 1963.[1302]

But that payoff – *the war itself*, which President Kennedy had decided to end – also provoked a lengthy and somewhat contentious struggle between Lyndon Johnson (who was a pragmatic and deeply self-interested individual) and the Joint Chiefs of Staff (who were in fact "true believers" of the most dangerous sort).[1303]

The war itself, and its massive escalation, were nonnegotiable.

But the ultimate *conduct* of the escalated Vietnam War represented a strange, endless, bitter sumo wrestling match between the president and the JCS.

Lyndon Johnson's "hard limit" was anything that he felt might actually spark World War III – for example, the employment of *large* nuclear weapons; the bombing of China; or the *total* destruction of Hanoi.[1304] *Short* of that, and despite the American military's many whining complaints about his "restrictions," LBJ gave the Pentagon plenty of leeway to openly commit massive, unprecedented destruction – and daily mass murder – in Southeast Asia.

The Joint Chiefs' "hard limit," plainly, was *any complete abandonment* by the Commander-in-Chief of their inherently doomed, inherently murderous, inherently criminal war effort in Vietnam.[1305] *Peace* was absolutely *anathema* to them. Serious negotiations were *verboten*. Hence Johnson's endless, brazen rejection of *all* peace efforts during his presidency, regardless of their source – plus his nauseatingly dishonest characterizations of both America's true policies and those of the Vietnamese.

* * *

The Vietnam War was the price of the JFK assassination.
The war was the price.
The war was the price.[1306]

And because of that fact – because of the grim reality that *the escalated Vietnam War was the price of U. S. military support for the JFK assassination* – the

---

[1302] Author's exclusive original discovery. (It dwarfed even the ugly criminal pardon arranged for Charles Carrico *by LBJ himself,* which I discovered exclusively and which I described in detail in the previous chapter of this book.)

[1303] On June 10th, 1965, Defense Secretary Robert McNamara informed LBJ that he (McNamara) was "sure" that the Joint Chiefs of Staff did not envision *any* limitation on U. S. military involvement in Southeast Asia.

[1304] Author's exclusive original discovery.

[1305] Author's exclusive original discovery.

[1306] Author's exclusive original discovery.

Joint Chiefs of Staff therefore were ***indeed*** able to blackmail Lyndon Baines Johnson in 1967 and 1968, as White House aide Harry McPherson's stunning 1967 memo to LBJ revealed.[1307]

* * *

At a secret White House meeting in late October 1967, Lynden Johnson openly admitted the obvious fact that *"It doesn't seem we can win the war militarily."* Yet despite this explicit awareness on his part, LBJ nevertheless immediately argued that the U.S. should bomb "all the military targets [of the very few targets still remaining on the lengthy JCS hit list in North Vietnam] short of provoking Russia and China."[1308]

It made no sense whatsoever, in logical or moral terms.

The war cannot be won, but let's bomb some more ***anyway?***

But LBJ wasn't acting based on logic or morality; he was acting based on *his own gigantic and inescapable debt to the U. S. military from November 1963.*[1309]

That ugly debt – the hideous central truth about the Dallas assassination – was unbeknownst to all observers until my discovery of it and its publication in this book.

In response to Johnson's bizarre "additional bombing" proposal, White House aide Harry McPherson sent LBJ a stunning memorandum a few days later which candidly laid bare the shocking root of the matter. Conveniently citing "some people" as a mask for his own views, McPherson wrote to Johnson that "It appears . . . that *the military are* ***blackmailing you*** *into following their policy toward North Vietnam."*

There it is, in stark black and white, in an internal White House document![1310]

The military are ***blackmailing you*** *into following their policy toward North Vietnam.*

Predictably, coincidence theorist Lloyd Gardner did not understand – or could not admit the truth behind – Harry McPherson's ominous 1967 statement. Even McPherson himself didn't know *why* the blackmail of LBJ was occurring; McPherson simply documented that it ***was*** occurring.

And it was.

[1307] Author's exclusive original discovery. McPherson's memo of October 27th, 1967, is quoted in Lloyd Gardner's book *Pay Any Price* (p. 396) – with ***zero*** understanding (by Gardner) of what it truly meant, or why, or its central connection to the JFK assassination.

[1308] Meeting minutes, 10/23/1967, quoted in Lloyd Gardner, *Pay Any Price,* p. 395.

[1309] Author's exclusive original discovery.

[1310] McPherson memo to LBJ, 10/27/1967, quoted in Lloyd Gardner, *Pay Any Price,* p. 396. Poor Lloyd Gardner was quite obviously *completely oblivious* to the true meaning and import of this crucial memo.

The generals were blackmailing LBJ – and they could *only* do so because they had helped LBJ to kill President Kennedy in 1963 and thereby take the Oval Office.[1311]

That is the harsh cold reality.

The military are **blackmailing you** *into following their policy toward North Vietnam.*

Frankly, nothing short of that explains LBJ's endless, bizarre refusal to dismount from what was clearly a losing horse. *Politics is about winning,* after all, and Lyndon Baines Johnson was both an expert politician and a very experienced winner.

Yet LBJ clung stubbornly to the most destructive, pointless, losing war in American history. He clung to it like a man clings to a life preserver after a shipwreck. He clung to it as if it were life itself. He clung to it as if he *had* to.

Because he *did* have to.

Harry McPherson was absolutely right:

The military are **blackmailing you** *into following their policy toward North Vietnam.*

A month later, on November 30th, 1967, even the weak Establishment reporter Tom Wicker[1312] wrote in the *New York Times* that many serious Washington observers believed that Johnson's recent and precipitous removal of Robert McNamara as Defense Secretary signified "capitulation [by Johnson] . . . to the warlike aims of nameless generals."[1313]

The military are **blackmailing you** *into following their policy toward North Vietnam.*

Tom Wicker didn't ask why, let alone uncover or publish the answer.

* * *

The United States military blackmailed LBJ.
Be crystal clear on that fact:
The United States military blackmailed LBJ.

[1311] Author's exclusive original discovery.

[1312] Tom Wicker wrote for the *New York Times*, which is the Establishment's house rag and its most dependable, slavish, shameless media whore.

And note this: Wicker's 1963 page-one story about the JFK assassination contained ***dozens of factual errors*** (author's exclusive original discovery), yet Wicker – who didn't even spell a key assassination eyewitness's *name* correctly! – was given a Pulitzer Prize for "reporting" [*sic*].

The Establishment always rewards those who never actually uncover the real story – or who, if they ***do*** manage to uncover it, never actually *reveal* the truth publicly.

[1313] Wicker, quoted in Jeff Shesol, *Mutual Contempt,* p. 395.

White House aide Harry McPherson (at left)
wrote a 1967 memo to Lyndon Johnson
explicitly pointing out that
the U. S. military was blackmailing LBJ
regarding Vietnam policy.

Only one thing
could have given the JCS
such chilling, massive leverage
over the powerful occupant of the Oval Office:

LBJ's leading role in the JFK assassination.

Author's exclusive original discovery.

And the only *reason* that the Joint Chiefs of Staff were actually *able* to successfully blackmail Lyndon Johnson was that *the JCS had something on him* – something overwhelming, inescapable, and utterly devastating.[1314]

And only one thing – *just one!* – meets those criteria:

Dallas.

The Joint Chiefs of Staff knew full well that Lyndon Johnson had assassinated his predecessor, President Kennedy.

They knew it, of course, because *they themselves* – the JCS and other key officers in the American military – had *known* in advance about, actively *participated* in, and personally *guaranteed* the success of Johnson's bloody 1963 coup by contributing aircraft and tanks and personnel and intelligence reports and transport and other vital support to that bloody criminal operation.[1315]

This fact alone completely destroys the idiotic and specious argument made by some lesser assassination researchers that "LBJ was a mere 'water boy' for others."

Had the JFK assassination been a *purely* Pentagon plot, with Lyndon Johnson as a pathetic, low-level "go-fer" [*sic*] who was "just taking orders" [*sic*] from his supposed "masters" in uniform [*sic*], then there would have been no need whatsoever to "blackmail" LBJ. He would have simply been *given an order by the military,* and that would have been that.

But blackmail is normally used against people *with* power and resources, not against people *without* power and resources.

The fact that the weakened and frustrated Joint Chiefs of Staff – whom Lyndon Johnson loudly bullied, buffaloed and cowed for several years between 1963 and 1967 – finally had to resort to *blackmail* against LBJ in late 1967 and early 1968 is dispositive evidence that it was *Johnson,* not they, who actually held superior power.

And since LBJ held superior power, he was – by definition – no one's "water boy" at all.

Yet since LBJ had indeed murdered his predecessor, and was therefore *indeed* vulnerable to blackmail by the military, he could therefore *never abandon* the losing, pointless and astronomically expensive war in Vietnam – no matter *how* bad things got politically for himself – without tempting or provoking the Joint Chiefs (who obviously knew his deadly secret) into either open mutiny or a series of devastating covert leaks clearly implicating Johnson in the JFK assassination. (You do not rise to the level of the JCS without knowing how to play hardball political games in Washington, D. C.)

That is why Lyndon Johnson submitted to the otherwise totally inexplicable, politically suicidal, utterly self-destructive, idiotic, insanely expensive, ongoing

---

[1314] Author's exclusive original discovery.

[1315] Author's exclusive original discovery.

prosecution of the utterly unwinnable war in Vietnam[1316] – **not** because he was a "true believer" in fanatical anti-Communism, nor because he *genuinely* feared a Republican backlash in 1968, nor because he was *sincerely* afraid of being labeled "the first American president to lose a war," nor any of the other pathetic and superficial excuses which have been offered to the public by weak, dishonest and incompetent pseudo-historians; by pathetic LBJ cronies and apologists; and by Johnson himself.

LBJ was committed to the escalation and continuation of the Vietnam War **not** because he thought it was important or useful or necessary or morally right or essential to national security; rather, he was committed to the war – the Vietnam War as we know it – because that escalated war was **the price** of U. S. military backing for, participation in, and *guarantee of* the success of the murderous 1963 coup which had made Lyndon Johnson president in the first place.[1317]

The escalation, expansion and continuation of the Vietnam War was not the *reason* for the JFK assassination – but it was (and it is) the *price*.[1318]

The price.

Quid pro quo.

We ensure that you become president; in return, you give us the war that John Kennedy was determined to end.

Quid pro quo.

Nothing else explains why LBJ – the strongest, most talented, most aggressive and productive American politician in history – would permit himself to be shamefully *saddled* with (and fatally *hamstrung* by) the most destructive, politically toxic war in American history.[1319]

An "innocent" Lyndon Johnson, operating with masterful political efficiency, would have dispensed with the ugly, expensive and totally unwinnable Vietnam War at the very first opportunity – promptly "liquidating" it just like Dwight Eisenhower promptly "liquidated" the Korean War in 1953, soon after taking office.[1320] LBJ would then have focused on major *domestic* achievements and rapidly become the most popular U. S. president since Franklin Delano Roosevelt – his longtime political idol, whom Johnson wished to surpass in domestic accomplishments and in public esteem.

Yet instead, Johnson – the master politician – was forced to hastily cram as many domestic achievements through Congress during his first eighteen months in

---

[1316] Author's exclusive original discovery.

[1317] Author's exclusive original discovery.

[1318] Author's exclusive original discovery.

[1319] Author's exclusive original discovery.

[1320] William O'Neill used that exquisitely appropriate expression in his book *Coming Apart* (page 5).

office as he possibly could in that brief period, and then simply watch as his ultimate prize, *the presidency which he had literally killed for,* became merely an ugly, withered, hollow husk of what it could have been. For LBJ, the steep and bloody *price* of obtaining the Oval Office – namely, giving the U. S. military the vastly expanded and vicious war that it wanted in Vietnam – proved to be *higher than the value of the office itself.*[1321]

The reason that LBJ couldn't (and *didn't*) ever let go of the war (not even in 1968, when he cynically *pretended* to do so) – and the reason he studiously ignored even the numerous peace openings and doors toward a policy change conveniently offered to him by fellow American conservatives and right-wing American religious ministers, who thereby provided him with excellent political cover for changing course and withdrawing from Vietnam – was as stark as it was simple: Lyndon Johnson *owed* the American military the expanded war in *Vietnam* in exchange for their resolute backing in *Dallas.*[1322]

Nothing else mattered.

Nothing else – *nothing whatsoever* – could possibly outweigh that particular bloody and enormous debt.

Nothing.

Reason, sanity, practicality, morality, rationality, humanity, ethics, logic, the sheer staggering cost in money and misery and blood – all such considerations paled into insignificance compared to the stark reality of the *guarantee* which those American planes and tanks had given to Lyndon Johnson as his murderous plot came crashing down (and came perilously close to failing entirely) on November 22nd, 1963.

The American military (particularly the United States Air Force) had *been there for him* when it really counted in 1963, and the Air Force had literally *outlined and written* the false Report falsely "exonerating" him in 1964 – and they would therefore accept nothing less than the expanded and escalated Vietnam War *which he had promised them,* ***in advance,*** *as payment* for the truly priceless services which they had rendered on that bloody Friday in November.[1323]

With their planes and their tanks and their weapons and their uniforms and their laboratories and their morgue and their outlines and their Report they had guaranteed for Lyndon Johnson the biggest prize that he had ever sought in life – the American presidency itself – and by God they would now be *paid,* come hell or high water *politically* for the now-frustrated occupant of the Oval Office.

They would be ***paid,*** damn it, and their price was *Vietnam.*

[1321] Author's exclusive original discovery.

[1322] Author's exclusive original discovery.

[1323] Author's exclusive original discovery.

The war was the price, America.

The war was the price of the JFK assassination.[1324]

Opinion polls and convention delegate counts and other esoteric political considerations were not the military's goddamned concern. Lyndon Johnson *owed* them for their crucial support in November 1963. Thus he couldn't leave Vietnam even if he wanted to – even though it was utterly ravaging his presidency and rapidly destroying his own reputation.

As Johnson confessed pathetically but truthfully to Senator Eugene McCarthy in early 1966, "I can't be the architect of a surrender."[1325]

He meant it.

He meant it *literally.*[1326]

LBJ *owed* the military for Dallas.

Period.

That is why more than 58,000 of America's sons and husbands and brothers and nephews and fathers and uncles and cousins and lovers and friends died in Vietnam – well over 99% of them perishing *after* President Kennedy's violent assassination in November 1963.[1327]

That is why they never came home, except in body bags and shipping caskets – precisely the way JFK's murdered body was first secretly delivered to the Bethesda Naval Hospital morgue, *under cover of night,* early on the evening of his November 1963 assassination.

Body bags and shipping caskets.

Remains not viewable.

Body bags and shipping caskets.

Remains not viewable.

Damaged, mutilated, torn, amputated, burned, shredded, missing, *gone.*

Lyndon Johnson *owed* the American military for backing his bloody coup.

That is why they died, America.[1328]

Not for freedom, or democracy, or honor, or duty, or pride.

Nor for "national security," or "complex geopolitical strategy considerations," or supposedly "mandatory" treaty obligations.

[1324] Author's exclusive original discovery.

[1325] LBJ to Senator Eugene McCarthy, in a telephone call recorded on February 1st, 1966.

[1326] Author's exclusive original discovery.

[1327] Author's exclusive original discovery. (When President Kennedy was assassinated in November 1963, fewer than **200** American soldiers had been killed in Vietnam. Under Lyndon Johnson and Richard Nixon, the total number of American soldiers killed there surpassed **58,000.** *Do the bloody math, America.*)

[1328] Author's exclusive original discovery.

Americans died in Vietnam in massive numbers beginning in 1965 because *Lyndon Baines Johnson personally* **owed** *the U. S. military a massive debt for* **guaranteeing** *the success of his murderous 1963 coup in Dallas.*[1329]

He had promised the JCS, explicitly – both in advance of the JFK assassination[1330] and again, *in person,* at the White House itself in December 1963 – that he would give them their fucking war.[1331]

And he did so.

Lyndon Johnson owed the military.

And he paid that debt with the lives of your sons, America.

And that, obviously, is a gargantuan part of the reason why the JFK assassination *matters.*

Then, and now, and forevermore.

Most people in America know someone – a friend, a relative, a co-worker, a family member, a neighbor – who was sent to Vietnam to fight and kill; or who suffered in jail for courageously refusing to go; or who lived in lonely principled exile in Canada or Sweden.

Most people know someone who mourns.

Most people in America know someone who grieves for the marriages cut short, the families destroyed, the years truncated, the children left fatherless, the bodies destroyed, the minds shattered, the guilt and the shame and the horror and the overwhelming agony that will never go away.

Now, at long last, you finally know ***why.***

Lyndon Baines Johnson personally owed the U. S. military a massive debt because they guaranteed the success of his murderous 1963 coup in Dallas.[1332]

He repaid them with a war.

The Vietnam War.

Ya dance with who brung ya.

It was an utterly Faustian deal, paid for first in John Kennedy's blood – and then in everyone else's.

President John Fitzgerald Kennedy himself was in fact *the very first casualty* of the massively *escalated* Vietnam War.[1333]

And therefore, JFK's name should be inscribed on the Vietnam Memorial wall.

[1329] Author's exclusive original discovery.

[1330] Author's exclusive original discovery.

[1331] If you are the type of prim and proper prude who is more offended by a *word* than by a *war,* then your moral compass is grotesquely out of whack. ***Fix it.***

[1332] Author's exclusive original discovery.

[1333] Author's exclusive original insight.

The insanely vicious, murderous and illegal Vietnam War –
massively escalated in 1965 by Lyndon Baines Johnson –
was the devastating price of the JFK assassination.

Not the *reason* for it;
but the *price*.

Author's exclusive original discovery.

* * *

But the awful price of Dallas was not only the hellish destruction and murderous chaos which America rained down upon Southeast Asia in staggering quantities beginning in 1965.

It was not only the terror visited upon Palestine and Indonesia and other countries around the world by the U. S. and its vile, endlessly murderous "allies."

There was *another* cost, too – a poignant and equally priceless cost.

The price of Dallas was *the war*; but the price of Dallas was also *the peace*.[1334]

And by that I mean *not only* the end of the Cold War, which John Kennedy and Nikita Khrushchev were certainly working toward; I mean something *else*.

Something *bigger*.

Something *more*.

Something I discovered while examining files of the JFK Library.

Something extraordinary.

JFK didn't simply "want" world peace.

He didn't simply "long for" world peace.

He didn't simply "talk about" world peace.

He actually had a concrete plan for it in his files.[1335]

* * *

The document bears no date, nor any overt mention of its author.

It is not labeled as the work of an outside consultant, or an activist group.

It is not on White House letterhead; nor is it on the stationery of any U. S. government department, or Congressional office, or commercial company, or independent volunteer venture.

It is not of foreign origin, either.

It reads like a typed version of . . . verbal dictation.

Thoughts, spoken aloud, recorded on plain paper by an unknown scribe for their unidentified author.

I found it in JFK's White House papers – where it had lain silently for decades, ignored and undiscovered.

Unremembered and forgotten.

In JFK's office files.

The document I discovered does have a title, though.

It has a very specific penciled title:

[1334] Author's exclusive original insight.

[1335] Author's exclusive original discovery.

It's called *A World Fifty Year Plan.*[1336]

(And, also in pencil, someone added an ambitious phrase: *"or 25."*)

It is a serious and practical document (reflecting JFK's own repeated personal calls for *concrete, practical* steps toward peace), commencing with a proposal for a global inventory of the world's resources – not for the purposes of pillage or control, but for eliminating want and thereby reducing (and ending) conflict.

A *world **fifty-year** plan for peace* – not some cheap and empty campaign slogan; not a sop to a particular segment of voters in one particular election in one particular nation; not a vain bit of puffery; not a nice-but-doomed project for a single presidential administration's duration of four or possibly eight years; but an actual *world fifty-year plan for peace.*

A serious plan.

A plan that would certainly outlive the man who introduced it.

A plan that would require *generations* of serious commitment.

A plan that looked at the planet *in toto.*

A world fifty-year plan for peace.

Was it JFK's?

Yes.[1337]

The autumn 1963 speaking tour that President Kennedy took in the western United States proved beyond doubt that peace was wildly popular among Americans of all political stripes.

Peace – ***real*** *peace* – was going to be JFK's political "platform" in 1964.

The world fifty-year plan would have served as its foundation.

And that, too, was slaughtered in Dallas on that bloody Friday afternoon in November 1963.[1338]

So when you confront the staggering true price of the JFK assassination – the cruel butchery of one man; the vile murder of democracy itself; the deliberate and monstrous massacre of millions of innocent people half a world away – that *world fifty-year plan for peace* in Kennedy's own files, quietly waiting to be born, was one of the saddest casualties of the vicious mid-day murder of the president of the United States.

Mourn all the evil that ***was*** perpetrated as a result of JFK's assassination.

But mourn, too, all the good which therefore was ***never*** achieved.

A world fifty-year plan for peace died in Dealey Plaza, America.

A world fifty-year plan for peace.

[1336] Author's exclusive original discovery.

[1337] The JFK Library expressly acknowledges that the plan is in fact President Kennedy's work.

[1338] Author's exclusive original discovery.

A plan that would have *already been implemented* by now, had JFK lived to initiate and implement it.

* * *

None of this means that JFK was some sort of saint; *he wasn't.*
Not even close.

John Kennedy *the president* was both a war criminal (by authorizing the forced removal of a civilian population in Vietnam to "strategic hamlets") *and* a knowing sponsor of state terrorism (by authorizing numerous violent criminal actions against both Cuba and Vietnam).

John Kennedy *the man* was, undeniably, a womanizing hedonist at heart.

He took pleasure in sailing, and women, and drinks, and good cigars.

He prized winning, and appearances, and celebration, and fame.

He loved salt air, and airplanes, and music, and gossip, and secrets.

He was no saint, America – *not even close.*

But he also cherished reading and books and knowledge and poetry.

Above all, the deeply imperfect man named John Kennedy valued *courage.*

He did not always *possess* it; he did not always *demonstrate* it; he certainly did not always *exemplify* it.

But he admired and valued it highly.

Yet nothing exemplifies America's *cowardice* like its frenzied refusal to address the truth about the assassination of its own leader in 1963.

* * *

America truly *is* exceptional – exceptionally violent, exceptionally sinister, exceptionally cruel, exceptionally vicious, exceptionally vainglorious, and (above all) exceptionally dishonest and ignorant about its past.

But that ends *here* – and it ends now and forevermore.

In 1956 two senior American politicians decided to use the law against itself.

In 1960 their dark plan became an active, functioning, fully operational, viable assassination plot through blackmail.

In 1961 they successfully positioned one man just a bullet away from their goal: the Oval Office.

In 1963 their violent seditious criminal conspiracy finally came to bloody fruition in a tiny triangular plaza in a place called Dallas, Texas.

Now you know.

And there are some things, my fellow Americans, which you can never erase from your memory or "unlearn."

There are some tears which never dry.
There is some pain which never abates.
There are some truths which never erode or vanish.
Never.
Never.
Never.

* * *

Cowards reject reality, spew bland bromides, regurgitate contemptible lies, and wrap themselves in paper-thin, soporific myths of "innocence" and "happenstance" and "coincidence."

Those who *truly* love their country are willing to face the truth unflinchingly, and to boldly face the ugly reality perpetrated by scores of uniformed men and civilians who soaked the national flag in a torrent of blood which can never be cleansed or bleached or erased.

John Fitzgerald Kennedy was a deeply imperfect man – but like Abraham Lincoln (another deeply imperfect man), JFK was also one of the most valuable presidents whom the United States has ever had.[1339] What died with John Kennedy in the back seat of that dark blue limousine which swerved and stopped in sunlit Dealey Plaza was not only the end of the Vietnam War and the end of the entire Cold War, but even more importantly, *a world fifty-year plan for peace* – a plan that would have *already* been implemented and completed had JFK lived to commence it.[1340]

The pathetic failures of pathetic Democratic presidents who timidly trod in JFK's wake subsequently – supposed "liberals" [*sic*] like Carter, Clinton, Obama and Biden – can be traced in part to their own embarrassingly weak and disgustingly flawed personal characters, but *also* to their personal fear of assassination.[1341]

Thus the murder of JFK not only *elevated Lyndon Johnson to the presidency* (which was its original purpose), but has also served to threaten and limit and crush all meaningful political discourse in America – and to strangle and fatally constrict the scope of what is (conventionally) viewed as "possible."

The truth is that because of the bloody 1963 assassination of John Kennedy, America is a full *century* behind where it could and should and *ought* to be already.

But the man from Massachusetts who cherished poetry so fiercely knew that in poetry and truth lay the hope for the future.

[1339] What does it say about this country that even its best "leaders" have been criminals?

[1340] Author's exclusive original discovery.

[1341] Whether they admit it or not.

For in the passion of poetry and the power of truth exist the hope of creating ethical, inspired people – people of integrity and courage who possess the energy, determination and commitment to bring a measure of genuine justice and progress to the land that JFK once led for such a precious, priceless time.

* * *

JFK, a deeply imperfect and criminal man, was *far* less admirable than his liberal admirers and idolaters fervently believe him to have been.

He was also far less destructive and threatening – to *America* – than his most corrupt and cynical right-wing detractors fervently insisted that he was.

The painful paradox is this:

Ultimately (and ironically), President Kennedy is much less important for what he *really **was*** than for what he, at his very best, knowingly and unknowingly *inspired* so many others to be.

Similarly, JFK's violent public *death* is to a great degree much more important than his *life* – for the devastating truth about his 1963 assassination *at the hands of his own government* reveals to all of us what our country ***really is,*** rather than what we fervently *wish* that it were (and what we often desperately *pretend* it to be).

The glittering "promise of America" remains a seductive mirage.

Those who mourn John Fitzgerald Kennedy are, in fact, mourning not simply one deeply flawed individual, but *the never-realized, mythic "ideal" of America itself.*

That grief is real, and genuine, and deep, and inescapably painful.

And the razor-sharp truth – the eternal challenge – is this:

As long as that ideal survives – as long as *a single stubborn spark* of passion and hope and ennobling principle still exists in the heart of *one person* – then the ultimate *achievement* of such a mythic ideal remains (however tenuously, however remotely) an actual possibility.

It remains a tantalizing objective even though it exists, for the moment, shrouded in long crippling agony – obscured in brutal darkness, *under cover of night.*

Epilogue:
The Body on the Hill

"These things do not just 'happen.'
*They are **made** to happen."*

– John Fitzgerald Kennedy

On a placid, sloping hillside above Washington, D.C. lies a body in a grave.

It was first buried there on a sunny afternoon in late November 1963; then moved and buried again in December 1963; and finally moved a short distance and re-buried yet again, *under cover of night,* in March 1967.

Inside an African mahogany coffin beneath Virginia soil lie the mortal remains of a man who was once President of the United States.

Betrayed and murdered by his second-in-command – and by literally *scores* of the Vice President's criminal accomplices in the U. S. military and the executive branch of the federal government – John Fitzgerald Kennedy was a target *even after death*. His nude corpse was brutally mutilated in Dallas within *two hours* of his murder.

This hideous criminal act was perpetrated in order to erase physical evidence of the authentic *wounds* on his body from the gunshots which struck him (all fired from the front); to remove the actual *bullets* which struck him (all fired from the front); to inflict false "wounds" falsely indicating gunfire from the *opposite* direction (where *no* shots actually originated); and to falsely implicate an innocent young man named Lee – who would *also* be shot down in public at point-blank range, just two days later.

Left face down on a shelf in a cargo hold of Air Force One[1342] for the two hour, eleven-minute flight back to Washington D. C., John Kennedy's shattered, bloody, now-rigid body was then quickly and secretly and unceremoniously removed in the darkness[1343] at the southern end of the westernmost runway at Andrews Air Force Base in Maryland.[1344]

[1342] Author's exclusive original discovery.

[1343] Author's exclusive original discovery.

[1344] Author's exclusive original discovery.

939

It was immediately transported to Malcolm Grow USAF Medical Center[1345] on the base for hasty covert photography and additional exploratory work.[1346]

The president's corpse was then placed into a zippered military body bag, roughly wedged into a military shipping casket, and surreptitiously transferred to a military helicopter.

A short, secret chopper flight carried JFK's body, *under cover of night,* over Washington D. C. one final time. The helicopter flew from Andrews Air Force Base (southeast of the capital city) to Bethesda Naval Hospital (northwest of the capital city). There the chopper landed in back near the Officers' Club, *behind* the hospital, *away* from the huge crowd gathered out in front of the naval facility that evening.

The shipping casket containing President Kennedy's body was quickly hauled from the military helicopter and placed into the back of a black civilian hearse already waiting there in a parking lot behind Bethesda Naval Hospital. Then the battered corpse was driven the short distance through the parking lot and secretly delivered to the morgue at the rear of Bethesda Naval Hospital, *under cover of night,* at 6:35 p.m. EST.

Sailors carried the military shipping casket inside the building as at least two dozen witnesses – Marines and SS agents and Navy medical personnel – watched.

The president's battered body was taken into the morgue *a full twenty minutes before* the ornate, heavy, expensive, deluxe bronze "official" coffin (which *supposedly* containing JFK's remains) even arrived at the front entrance of that very same hospital, in a gray U. S. Navy ambulance, at 6:55 p.m. EST.

* * *

President Kennedy's body arrived *at 6:35 p.m.,* not 6:55 p.m.

President Kennedy's body arrived in *a black hearse,* not a gray ambulance.

President Kennedy's body arrived in *a cheap gray shipping casket* – not a deluxe bronze coffin.

President Kennedy's body arrived *inside a dark zippered military body bag,* not loosely covered by a cloth sheet.

President Kennedy's body arrived at 6:35 p.m. EST *already severely and deliberately mutilated,* not in its "original" condition as of 12:30 p.m. CST in Dallas.

* * *

President Kennedy's **body** is the actual "Rosetta Stone" of his assassination.

[1345] Author's exclusive original discovery.

[1346] Author's exclusive original discovery.

If exhumed today and carefully, properly, minutely and thoroughly examined for the very first time ever by serious, intelligent, perceptive, honest people – not by cowardly defenders of officialdom, but by *genuine investigators, people of courage and integrity and full awareness of the vital medico-legal issues pertinent to the case* – then that mute body would still tell us *volumes* about the brutal nature of the murder that took its owner's life.

A non-invasive "digital autopsy" would be the essential first step, followed by a painstaking physical, chemical and DNA examination of the skeletal structure, all bone fragments, and all remaining tissues.

President Kennedy's ravaged corpse still has much to tell us.

And that is not all.

The majestic airplane where President Kennedy's body was viciously slashed and violently battered that long-ago November afternoon was – *and remains* – a *crime scene.* The silent 707 at Wright-Patterson Air Force Base in Ohio should be treated as such, and the jet should be thoroughly examined with the very latest forensic tools, equipment, processes and techniques. No attempted removal of blood is ever perfect, and the sinister cleaning efforts reported to me by courageous USAF Sergeant John Wetherell – criminal acts performed *under cover of night* – did ***not*** succeed in eliminating every trace of the president's blood and DNA from the cargo hold of SAM 26000, John Kennedy's beloved Air Force One.

Serious investigation reveals serious truths.

All it takes is courage and integrity and determined effort.

Nothing more – and nothing less.

Truth demands this.

John Kennedy's *country* should demand it as well.

Postscript:
Wheels Up

"These things do not just 'happen.'
*They are **made** to happen."*

– John Fitzgerald Kennedy

I pursued a single airplane, through time and space, *until I found it.*

And in the process, I found the truth about JFK's brutal assassination.

On my final day at Andrews Air Force Base in the autumn of 1994, as the SAM FOX veterans' reunion concluded, I paused in a parking lot at the base before heading to Washington National Airport for the flight home.

I really didn't want to leave just yet.

Turning, I saw several oak trees shimmering in the cool October sunshine.

I strolled over onto a strip of lawn at this incredible place where so much hidden history had occurred, *under cover of night,* on an awful November evening more than three decades earlier.

Lingering, I picked up a trio of acorns that had fallen from the surrounding trees onto the still-green autumn grass of Maryland.

Somewhere in the back of my mind, I heard the old refrain:

From little acorns, mighty oaks doth grow.

I smiled to myself and put the acorns in the pocket of my jacket, then headed for the exit.

I still had much to do – so very much more – and, to paraphrase the timeless words of the poet Robert Frost, such an incredibly long distance to travel before I could possibly think of resting.

But I had begun.

And I swore the world would one day know what I had found here.

General Curtis LeMay, U. S. Air Force Chief of Staff,
confers with Lyndon Johnson in December 1963
down at the LBJ ranch in Texas.

Just a month after Dallas,
cunning plot leader Lyndon Johnson had already decided
to renege on his secret deal with the USAF general,
despite the extraordinary services rendered by LeMay
to LBJ in connection with the JFK assassination.

Author's exclusive original discovery.

Coda:
Brass Tacks

"Experto crede."

– Motto of the 1254th Air Transport Wing
United States Air Force

*"Any lessening
of civil power over military power
must inevitably lead away from democracy."*

– Harold Russell
U. S. Army veteran

*"No internal revolution has ever succeeded
in overthrowing a government by violence
unless the government had already lost
the allegiance and effective control
of its armed forces."*

– Martin Luther King, Jr.

*"These things do not just 'happen.'
They are **made** to happen."*

– John Fitzgerald Kennedy

The United States Air Force had its long blue tentacles in *every single key aspect* of the murderous, seditious JFK assassination plot – from planning & logistics to providing two (2) alternate patsies; from motorcade security to patsy disposal; from communications censorship to evidence tampering; from suppressing witness testimony to *outlining* and actually *writing* the false, fictitious, fatuous "official" version of the crime.

In short, the United States Air Force played a truly central role in – and was absolutely indispensable to – the 1963 assassination of John Fitzgerald Kennedy.[1347]

[1347] Author's exclusive original discovery.

Without the active, direct, *knowing participation* of deeply disloyal USAF personnel (and deeply disloyal former USAAF personnel), the bloody crime would have been *exponentially* more difficult to pull off successfully – even for the determined and ruthless Lyndon Baines Johnson.

* * *

Did *other* elements of the U. S. federal government participate and assist? Certainly.

Both the United States Army (a top general in Washington and a battalion of tanks in Texas) and the United States Navy (a fraudulent "autopsy" at Bethesda Naval Hospital overseen by high-ranking officers) obviously played key roles in the JFK assassination plot.

A few senior United States Marine Corps officers (like USMC General Victor "Brute" Krulak) clearly also knew in advance about the plot – and clearly *welcomed* the JFK assassination.

Members of the United States Secret Service were *deeply* and *directly* involved in slaughtering and butchering the man whom they were sworn to protect.

But for the record, the odious and despicable Central Intelligence Agency – a deeply criminal organization often erroneously regarded by foolish lesser minds as the "principal" [*sic*] force behind the JFK assassination – actually played a much more *peripheral* role in President Kennedy's slaying.[1348]

Yes, CIA officials sent the designated patsy, Lee Oswald, to the Soviet Union in 1959, thereby painting him as a "communist" – and the CIA also falsified, manipulated and suppressed Agency files plus its own photographic and audio records pertaining to Oswald both before and after Dallas. Yes, the CIA's former director – fired by President Kennedy – consulted and met with LBJ and other leading conspirators, and later energetically participated in the criminal work of the Johnson Commission.

But those were safe, minor and *peripheral* tasks.

The reality is that the sheer depth and breadth and scope of **USAF** involvement in President Kennedy's assassination truly dwarfs that of *every other* American governmental organization (*except* the SS!) which LBJ called upon to aid him in executing his murderous ascent to the White House.

The full panorama of the JFK case, which I discovered and have revealed here in this book for the first time anywhere, destroys *every* previous narrative – official and unofficial – of President Kennedy's assassination.

[1348] I say that as *no fan whatsoever* of the thoroughly criminal CIA – but stamping one's foot and stubbornly pretending that the rightfully despised Agency (which is many people's generic, go-to bogeyman) either initiated or led the murder of JFK is simply false.

The brutal murder of JFK in November 1963 was a major criminal operation *conceived of, initiated by and led by two senior American politicians,*[1349] supported and enabled by key segments of the American military establishment and the president's own bodyguards.

It was ***not*** the work of one warehouse clerk.

It was ***not*** a cartoonish plot consisting of a comically small band of misfits.

It was ***not*** a tiny, insular plot conceived of by a mere handful of hysterically fanatical right-wing homosexuals based in Louisiana.

It was ***not*** the work of "just a few bad apples" at the CIA'S "JM/WAVE" station in southern Florida.

It was ***not*** the work of a few disgruntled and fanatical right-wing Cuban exiles.

It was ***not*** the work of Italian, Sicilian or Italian-American mobsters.

It was ***not*** the work of Corsican mercenaries.

It was ***not*** a plan originated by, conceived by, managed by, or run solely – or even "primarily" by – the despicable Central Intelligence Agency.

Such erroneous models of the crime *do not account for the evidence.*

Those shallow, simplistic, juvenile scenarios are simply false.

The staggering truth is this:

The United States Air Force was in fact the principal provider of key personnel spanning *the entire range* of roles and responsibilities pertaining to the JFK assassination.[1350]

Thanks to my original research, original analysis and original discoveries, you can now – *finally* – view President Kennedy's 1963 assassination in its full and accurate context, and you can now – *finally* – understand the true origin, timing, nature and extent of the plot.

And you can now finally understand the true ***price*** of that plot:

The massive Vietnam War in its cataclysmically escalated, exponentially expanded form (1965-1975).[1351]

* * *

As I have revealed and proven in this book:

Several key members of *the senior staff of the United States Air Force* clearly had criminal foreknowledge that the 1963 assassination of President Kennedy was going to occur.

[1349] Author's exclusive original discovery.

[1350] Author's exclusive original discovery.

[1351] Author's exclusive original discovery. I emphasize emphatically that the Vietnam War was not the *reason* for the JFK assassination; rather, it was (and it is) the ***price*** of the JFK assassination.

Those senior USAF officers did *nothing* to sound the alarm, publicize the threat or prevent the assassination. To the contrary – they knowingly, actively and deliberately *facilitated* it.

Moreover, key senior USAF officers took specific covert steps, *in advance of the assassination,* to hamper their own SAC B-52 pilots – but only on November 22nd, 1963, *and on no other day.*[1352]

These same senior Air Force officers had personally, repeatedly and directly urged President Kennedy – *to his face* – to launch an unprovoked, unjustified, catastrophic (and criminal) *total nuclear assault* on the Soviet Union and the rest of the communist world.

The highest-ranking officer in the entire U.S. Air Force *absented himself from the country* on the day of the JFK assassination; lied to his military subordinates about his whereabouts; defied civilian authority; avoided the nation's top law enforcement official; and deliberately put out a false cover story to protect himself in the event that the Dallas assassination plot collapsed entirely. He subsequently received a one-million-dollar payment (about $10,000,000 in 2023 dollars) for his services (both action and *inaction*) pertaining to the 1963 coup.

The second highest-ranking officer in the U. S. Air Force, who exercised day-to-day control of USAF in 1963, was awarded a Distinguished Service Medal; was given a comfortable job at NASA following his retirement from the Air Force; and was subsequently appointed head of the FAA by Lyndon Baines Johnson himself.[1353] Vital FAA records which are extremely pertinent to the JFK assassination are missing.

A military aide to the Vice President of the United States in 1963 was an Air Force colonel who *personally* served as a secret back channel of covert communication between Lyndon Johnson and his supporters in the Joint Chiefs of Staff.[1354] Upon the successful completion of the violent 1963 coup, the USAF colonel soon retired from the military and suddenly became a multi-millionaire.

A USAF general (and senior CIA official) whom JFK fired after the Bay of Pigs invasion fiasco was none other than the *brother* of Dallas mayor Earle Cabell, who was a CIA asset himself.

Another USAF general (also a CIA official and a veteran of covert operations) was rejected by JFK for one key post in 1961, then fired from another in late 1962. This USAF general was *personally* aware of JFK's plans to oust South Vietnamese dictator Ngo Dinh Diem in 1963. This USAF general was present in Fort Worth, Texas at President Kennedy's hotel the night before the assassination – and, on the very day

---

[1352] Longtime JFK assassination analyst John Judge discovered this vital fact.

[1353] Author's exclusive original discovery.

[1354] John Newman discovered this; see his book *JFK and Vietnam.*

of the assassination, he was photographed in Dealey Plaza itself just minutes after the shooting. This USAF general was positively identified in that photo by two experienced, high-ranking Pentagon officers (USMC and USAF) who both knew him personally. Supposedly "retired" at the moment JFK was assassinated, this USAF general was given a job in the Executive Office Building (just steps from the White House) mere weeks after Dallas – and later, Lyndon Johnson himself *personally* applauded this USAF general's exploits.[1355]

* * *

An Air Force officer ordered a top-secret USAF unit to fly to Dallas to retrieve President Kennedy's corpse on November 22nd, 1963.[1356]

An Air Force sergeant *personally* facilitated the covert transport of President Kennedy's battered, mutilated body from Dallas back to Washington, D. C. inside the cargo hold of a jet.[1357]

A USAF aircraft rapidly transported *falsified evidence* from Dallas to Washington, D. C. on the very weekend of the assassination – items employed by JFK's killers to obstruct justice and to pollute the evidence stream with fraudulent and misleading data.

A top-secret USAF facility in the western United States possessed the personnel and the advanced capabilities to drastically censor and alter the original Zapruder film of the assassination (along with other photographic material) *before* its official release to the executive branch of government, to the corporate media, and to LBJ's puppet organization, the Johnson Commission.

A United States Air Force base in Oklahoma actually received – and its USAF military personnel definitely duplicated and "processed" – Dallas media tapes from November 22nd in order to help identify and censor any incriminating information that had been inadvertently broadcast by the media regarding the true facts of the JFK assassination.

Up to *six hours* of key Air Force radio transmissions from November 22nd have been censored, destroyed, suppressed or otherwise rendered inaccessible. The head of the company which relayed those transmissions was a personal friend – and major commercial beneficiary of – the Chief of Staff of the United States Air Force.

Lyndon Johnson's personal Air Force pilot – a mere major at the time of the JFK assassination – *personally* rejected the release of November 22nd audio tapes;

[1355] Author's exclusive original discovery.

[1356] Author's exclusive original discovery.

[1357] Author's exclusive original discovery.

received unusual special treatment from LBJ; received rapid promotion to the rank of *brigadier general;* received control of a $2 million presidential slush fund (worth some $14 million today, in 2022); received a key White House post in addition to his ordinary piloting duties; was given a conveniently *brief* combat stint in Vietnam; received a prize bull from the herd at the Johnson ranch; and was made commander of a key Air Force base in Texas by LBJ himself.

The original FAA tower log from Andrews Air Force Base for November 22nd, 1963, has been destroyed, suppressed or otherwise rendered inaccessible.

A longtime USAF "historian" [*sic*] actually wrote the *outline* for – and also wrote much of the *final text* of – the false 1964 Johnson Report about the JFK assassination.

The head of the Air Force Office of Special Investigations (AFOSI) stated privately in 1969 that Lyndon Baines Johnson had had President Kennedy assassinated.

Clearly, in 1963 a clique of important U. S. Air Force officers had extensive foreknowledge of the JFK assassination; took no measures to stop it; played a direct role in carrying out and supervising the Dealey Plaza shooting; reluctantly but actively *prevented nuclear war* on November 22nd for Lyndon Johnson's personal benefit; transported, controlled, altered and suppressed numerous vital pieces of assassination evidence subsequently; and produced a false report about the assassination in order to help ensure that the truth about what had *really* happened in Dallas would not become public knowledge.

The treasonous activities and direct criminal culpability of those USAF men in the JFK assassination can never be justified, excused, explained away, minimized, trivialized, or erased.

* * *

Former U. S. Air Force (USAF) and U. S. Army Air Forces (USAAF) personnel played equally essential roles in connection with the JFK assassination:

A USAAF veteran was Lyndon Johnson's top lawyer and active accomplice.

A USAAF veteran wrote the letter "inviting" Kennedy to come to Texas.

A USAAF veteran was the city manager of Dallas – and the actual *key authority in Dallas* – at the time of President Kennedy's assassination.[1358]

A disgraced former member of the U. S. Air Force[1359] was employed at the Texas School Book Depository on November 22nd, 1963 – available for use as a substitute patsy in the event that designated patsy Lee Oswald was unexpectedly hit by

[1358] Author's exclusive original discovery.

[1359] Barry Ernest's book *The Girl on the Stairs* (p. 301) contains very useful information about the man's legal travails.

a bus, or came down with the flu, or fled in advance, or simply failed to show up for work that day.

A *second* substitute patsy – a young active-duty USAF airman who had previously threatened the president – was stationed in San Antonio, Texas to be available for the killers' use if circumstances required it.[1360]

A USAAF veteran shot the designated patsy on live national television.

A former USAF intelligence officer on the staff of the Johnson Commission actively obstructed justice; suborned perjury; threatened and intimidated honest witnesses; suppressed key evidence; altered witness testimony; fabricated and promulgated a false narrative; and committed additional crimes in furtherance of the LBJ coup.

A USAAF *and* USAF veteran was a major driving force behind the federal government's aggressive (and criminal) efforts to falsely blame President Kennedy's assassination on an innocent warehouse clerk named Lee Oswald.

* * *

On the positive side of the USAF ledger are a number of honest, extremely well-placed Air Force personnel of decency and integrity. *Never called to testify* by the Johnson Commission in the 1960s, nor by the HSCA in the 1970s, nor by the ARRB in the 1990s, these men had personally witnessed key pieces of the truth on Friday, November 22nd, 1963 – and many of them revealed that truth exclusively to this author.

A loyal Air Force general was suddenly barred from his usual spot in the front seat of the presidential limousine just prior to the fatal motorcade because he would have interfered with – and *prevented* – the assassination of President Kennedy.

An experienced Air Force pilot saw a forklift at Love Field raising a second coffin – *not JFK's "official" deluxe bronze coffin* – up to a jet at Love Field in Dallas, well *prior to* the arrival of that deluxe bronze coffin at the airport.

A crew member in the presidential entourage confirmed to the author that a forklift raised *a second coffin* up to a jet at Love Fieldon November 22nd.[1361]

An Air Force crew member with a high-level security clearance explicitly conceded to the author that President Kennedy's body was **not** inside the heavy, expensive, "official" deluxe bronze Dallas coffin which was brought from Parkland Hospital to Love Field and then transported back to Washington on November 22nd.[1362] This is the very *first* acknowledgment – *ever* – from *any* government or

---

[1360] Author's exclusive original discovery.

[1361] Author's exclusive original discovery.

[1362] Author's exclusive original discovery.

military official who was *actually present in Dallas* on November 22nd, 1963, that JFK's body was in fact secretly ***diverted*** (not "stolen" or "intercepted" as previous writers have erroneously stated; but rather, *diverted*) prior to the Bethesda autopsy.

An experienced USAF pilot revealed exclusively to this author that he performed a special aerial maneuver on November 22nd – a maneuver which directly resulted in President Kennedy being able to physically accuse his actual murderers from beyond the grave.[1363]

An Air Force crewman revealed to me that he *personally heard an SS agent making statements which do not comport with extant physical and visual evidence in the case* while aboard a jet from Dallas back to Washington on November 22nd.[1364]

A USAF officer revealed to me that he saw a senior Secret Service agent *drenched with blood from the neck down* in the cockpit of a jet on November 22nd during its flight back to Washington, D.C.[1365]

An Air Force non-com stationed at Andrews Air Force Base personally recognized and disclosed to me the strange, secret, all-night activity pertaining to *the surreptitious cleaning of a jet's cargo hold* on the long night of the JFK assassination. No official explanation has ever been offered for that covert activity, which was carried out *under cover of night* while America slept, unaware.[1366]

Another Air Force sergeant who served in a top-secret unit at Andrews Air Force Base revealed to me that he soon learned the true number of the different types of ammunition which were *actually* used to assassinate JFK in Dealey Plaza.[1367]

These *loyal* USAF men – primarily non-commissioned officers and enlisted personnel – helped me to rescue the truth about the JFK assassination from near-certain oblivion. In the process, they provided a vital window into the devastating *true* nature, scope, mechanics and identities of the *actual* perpetrators of the murderous JFK assassination plot.

That truth has *never* been revealed, ***anywhere,*** until now.

[1363] Author's exclusive original discovery.

[1364] Author's exclusive original discovery.

[1365] Author's exclusive original discovery.

[1366] Author's exclusive original discovery.

[1367] Author's exclusive original discovery.

A number of loyal, patriotic and honest USAF sergeants
provided me with key information
that was absolutely vital to
solving the JFK assassination.

Some of President Kennedy's killers
managed to escape this mortal coil
with impunity.

Others are still here.

Afterword:
Wild Blue Yonder

*"These things do not just "happen.'
They are **made** to happen."*

– John Fitzgerald Kennedy

Lyndon Baines Johnson slaughtered some *nine million people* worldwide from the comfort of the White House after assassinating John F. Kennedy. Innocents in Vietnam, Cambodia, Laos, Thailand, Brazil, Indonesia, Greece and Palestine suffered horribly and died because of LBJ's criminal actions and criminal policies.

After literally *shooting his way into the presidency* in November 1963, LBJ was elected to the White House in November 1964 by an unwitting American public which was (thanks to the abject failure and slavish incompetence of American corporate media) *entirely ignorant* of Johnson's foul crimes, his foul deeds, his foul plans, and his foul debt to the American military. LBJ dutifully repaid those armed American military guarantors of his coup by launching the vicious escalation of the Vietnam War in 1965 – and by consistently refusing to *end* that evil war.

JFK's killer left the White House in January 1969, and quickly resumed smoking. His cardiac problems predictably worsened substantially in retirement, and Lyndon Baines Johnson died in January 1973 at his Texas ranch, in the manner in which he had long feared that he would – terrified, utterly alone, and in helpless panic. The few who attended LBJ's memorial services in Washington – and the subsequent funeral rites and interment down in Texas – were ***nothing*** like the truly *massive* crowds which had turned out in heartfelt grief and genuine respect for the brutally slain JFK, a decade earlier.

* * *

Samuel Taliaferro Rayburn, the true originator of the JFK assassination plot,[1368] did not live long enough to see LBJ – his protégé and co-conspirator – lead their murderous plan to bloody success in Dallas in 1963.

[1368] Author's exclusive original discovery.

Instead, Rayburn suffered a months-long, excruciatingly painful demise as pancreatic cancer ravaged his body from the inside throughout the course of 1961. His death in November of that year came almost exactly *two years to the day* prior to the JFK assassination itself, of which the venomous Rayburn himself was the cunning intellectual author.[1369]

* * *

Congressman Albert Langston Thomas lived for three more years after his specious 1963 "retirement" announcement set the wheels in motion on the final phase of the Rayburn/Johnson coup plot to assassinate JFK. As you learned in this book, Al Thomas was there at the White House to *personally* greet and welcome LBJ and Lady Macbeth when the murderer and his wife arrived on December 7th, 1963, to formally seize and occupy the executive mansion. *No one* understood Congressman Thomas's central role in forcing President Kennedy to go to Texas until many years later.

Al Thomas finally died in February 1966.

His insidious widow, Lera Millard Thomas, was elected to cover the remainder of Al Thomas's unfinished term; she "served" in Congress from March 26th, 1966, until January 3rd, 1967.

During 1966, Lera met personally at the White House with LBJ himself. That very same year, *while in office as an active U. S. congresswoman,* Lera Thomas (along with her secretary, Rose Zamaria) quickly set about diligently *destroying a full 96% of Al Thomas's files* lest they implicate certain Texans.[1370] The two women eliminated an astounding 24 out of 25 filing cabinets full of material in order to protect the late Al Thomas and his criminal accomplices – and they knowingly trashed "everything of a controversial nature," with a particular focus on "anything involving Texans or Houstonians" still living at that time.[1371]

For the record, *those Texans still living at that time* (1966) included JFK assassination plot leader Lyndon Baines Johnson and his key White House aide, the veteran bag man and USAAF mass murderer Jack Joseph Valenti.

Having knowingly and deliberately and successfully destroyed significant quantities of important evidence, Lera Millard Thomas left her brief Congressional

---

[1369] Author's exclusive original discovery.

[1370] Author's exclusive original discovery.

[1371] Author's exclusive original discovery. (I learned this exclusively in 1995 by querying staff at Rice University in Texas, where the pitiful remnants of Al Thomas's once-extensive papers now reside. "Administrative" notes from 1966 and 1976 documented the fate of Al Thomas's once-massive trove of documents.)

Lera Millard Thomas – the widow of a top
JFK assassination co-conspirator,
Congressman Albert Langston Thomas of Texas –
meets with Lyndon Johnson at the White House
on March 30th, 1966.

That very same year,
Lera Thomas personally oversaw
the destruction of a full 96%
of Congressman Al Thomas's papers –
an astounding 24 out of 25 filing cabinets! –
because those papers might
"embarrass" prominent Texans.

No Texan was more prominent than LBJ.

Author's exclusive original discovery.

post and eventually moved back to her hometown of Nacogdoches, Texas. She died there in 1993.

* * *

USAF General Curtis Emerson LeMay was re-appointed as Air Force Chief of Staff by Lyndon Johnson in early 1964, but only for a short period of a few months – long enough to effectively muzzle the general through the upcoming November 1964 presidential election.

LeMay "retired" from the military in February 1965 and became chairman of the board of an electronics company. He was subsequently given one million dollars (some *seven million dollars* in 2023 money) by Texas oilman Nelson Bunker Hunt in 1968, five years after the JFK assassination.

Running for Vice President on the George Wallace ticket in 1968, and still eagerly pushing for the use of nuclear weapons by the U.S. in Vietnam, LeMay soon stated ruefully that he would likely be viewed by most of the American public as a fool. He and Wallace finished third in the 1968 election with 13.5 percent of the popular vote.

LeMay co-wrote three books, but he died in 1990 without ever managing to ignite the worldwide nuclear holocaust that he so keenly desired. Buried in a little-noticed grave at the U. S. Air Force Academy in Colorado Springs, LeMay's name adorns an Air Force Training and Indoctrination Center at Maxwell Air Force Base in Alabama – ironically, the place where I began my search for vital USAF witnesses who helped me unravel the ***true*** story of the JFK assassination plot!

* * *

USAF General Thomas Sarsfield Power left the Air Force in November 1964, a year and a week after the JFK assassination. He became chairman of the board for Schick, a razor company. Power co-authored the disturbing 1965 book *Design for Survival*; campaigned for GOP candidate Richard Nixon in 1968; and died in 1970.

No one ever took Power's repeated – *and completely serious!* – advice to deliberately commence Armageddon. Despite his very best efforts, CINCSAC Power died a nuclear virgin.

* * *

Strategic Air Command (SAC) itself was disbanded in 1991, replaced by "United States Strategic Command" (USSTRATCOM), whose official seal is a very close copy of SAC's old lightning-bolt-and-mailed-fist design.

Curtis LeMay (left) joined George Wallace (right)
for a bizarre *one-month* stint as
vice-presidential running mate in the fall of 1968.

The ludicrous charade
was actually a cover for LeMay's receipt
of a massive financial payment for his major role
in the 1963 assassination of President Kennedy.

Author's exclusive original discovery.

Despite ongoing major mishaps, shocking operational errors, and widespread *drug use* in the modern American military's missile force – plus dangerous nuclear proliferation involving a number of violent criminal entities including the cowardly and brutal Israeli apartheid regime, whose illicit and deceitful acquisition of nuclear weapons President Kennedy tried so valiantly to *prevent* in the early 1960s – the world has not, *thus far,* suffered another war involving the use of nuclear weapons.

* * *

Former USAF attorney Nicholas Katzenbach sent a disgusting memo to the White House on November 25th, 1963, urging the LBJ administration to convince the public that Lee Oswald had killed President Kennedy. To his everlasting discredit, Katzenbach also aggressively defended Lyndon Johnson's 1964 Gulf of Tonkin Resolution – and Katzenbach later labeled the U.S. Constitution's specific grant *to Congress alone* of the power to declare war essentially irrelevant in the modern world.

Katzenbach failed to investigate the JFK assassination; took a legalistic and coldly detached approach to civil rights enforcement; and otherwise behaved like a typical Cold War "liberal" bureaucrat of the 1960s. LBJ promoted him to Attorney General and later, to the role of Under Secretary of State. Katzenbach's 2008 memoir, *Some of It Was Fun,* is a masterpiece of massive omission, cowardly evasion and relentless moral obtuseness. He died in 2012.

* * *

Jack Joseph Valenti, the murderous USAAF pilot who casually and deliberately gunned down *ten thousand innocent civilians* in Italy from his B-25 aircraft during World War II,[1372] wrote the actual formal "invitation" to President Kennedy to make the fatal Texas trip in 1963. The very day that LBJ assassinated JFK, Lyndon Johnson also instantly made Valenti – an advertising man by trade – a top White House aide. Incredibly, Valenti attended most of the significant Johnson White House meetings on *Vietnam.*

Valenti married one of Lyndon Johnson's many mistresses. When Valenti left the White House in 1966, he became President of the Motion Picture Association of America – where he inveighed ceaselessly against any movies or documentaries on the JFK assassination that differed from the false official government line of "lone gunman – no conspiracy" [*sic*].

Valenti succeeded in censoring a documentary that had been shown on the A&E Network which openly accused Lyndon Johnson of guilt in the JFK

[1372] Author's exclusive original discovery.

assassination, and Valenti also lashed out angrily against Oliver Stone's theatrical film "JFK" (even though Stone's film failed to accurately uncover or portray the real plot).

But the once-dapper Valenti had become just a pathetic and threadbare huckster in badly frayed clothing when I met and personally questioned him in 2001; he died un-mourned by America in 2007.

* * *

The grotesque hypocrite Bill Moyers joined Jack Valenti and a sinister chorus of LBJ sycophants who succeeded in forcing the A&E Network to censor and suppress an episode of *The Men Who Killed Kennedy* which dared to accuse Lyndon Johnson of involvement in the JFK assassination.

Though he personally investigated LBJ's mental illness while in the White House, Moyers has strangely remained largely silent about Lyndon Johnson to this day, and has cravenly refused to write (or release) a book about the murderous Texan. An ostensibly pious but hopelessly compromised pseudo-liberal, Moyers (like many other contemptible "liberals") has pompously and publicly inveighed against so-called "coup" [*sic*] attempts by Republicans like George W. Bush and Donald Trump – but he has never acknowledged Democrat Lyndon Johnson's *actual* bloody coup of 1963.

* * *

USAF Colonel Howard L. Burris was Vice President Lyndon Johnson's aide – and as John Newman discovered, Burris was also LBJ's secret back-channel to the Joint Chiefs of Staff while John F. Kennedy was President. The colonel previously ran a network of CIA agents in Europe. Burris made millions of dollars in the years just after the JFK assassination, having resigned from government abruptly in 1964 and gone into business. He died in 2009.

* * *

USAF flight engineer William Joseph ("Joe") Chappell, a sergeant who knew that President Kennedy's battered body was lying in the cargo compartment of an aircraft prior to takeoff from Dallas on the day of the assassination, continued to work for years thereafter as if nothing had happened. Chappell never admitted what he had seen and done and abetted on November 22nd, 1963 – and revealingly, *he adamantly refused to ever say anything negative about Lyndon Johnson* – but he clearly knew that *I knew* the truth. Chappell died in 2015.

* * *

Billy Nolan Lovelady, the dishonorably discharged USAF veteran who worked at the Texas School Book Depository in Dallas along with another obscure young man in his twenties named Lee Oswald, was *used* by the Johnson Commission to try to discredit vital TSBD witness Victoria Adams – the woman who *knew and testified* that Lee Oswald was **not** (as the government falsely claimed) "descending the building's rear stairway" after the killing of JFK.

Lovelady died in 1979 at the age of 41 – evidently never realizing that given his USAF background, criminal record and dishonorable discharge, he was available for the JFK plotters' cynical use (and lethal disposal) as *a substitute patsy,* if needed, on the day of President Kennedy's assassination.

* * *

Air Force pilot James Underwood Cross was rapidly and repeatedly promoted thanks to LBJ's direct influence – first to Colonel, then to Brigadier General.

Johnson made Jim Cross – who was originally LBJ's *JetStar* pilot – his new *707* pilot (ousting Colonel James Swindal, JFK's favorite).

LBJ made Cross his chief Military Aide as well, thus giving Cross a White House post and extraordinary access to the President as well as unprecedented authority – plus personal control of a $2-million-dollar presidential slush fund.

LBJ eventually made Cross the commander of Bergstrom Air Force Base – located near Austin, Texas.

General Cross retired from the U. S. Air Force at the end of April, 1971.

In 1973, Cross supervised Lyndon Johnson's funeral arrangements and flew LBJ's body to and from Washington D.C. on SAM 26000 – which had once been John F. Kennedy's beloved Air Force One. Cross even received a prize bull from the Johnson ranch herd.

In lengthy interviews with me, the retired general admitted to LBJ's Mexican property connection. James Cross died in 2015.

* * *

U. S. Army General Earle Wheeler personally ensured that LBJ did not renege on his Faustian deal with the Joint Chiefs to expand the war in Vietnam as the bloody price of their support for the Dallas coup against JFK. Wheeler was named Chairman of the Joint Chiefs of Staff in 1964 by Lyndon Baines Johnson himself. The seditious general then oversaw America's massive, utterly criminal and utterly destructive war against Vietnam until July 1970, when he retired.

For his crimes, Earle Wheeler was awarded the Defense Distinguished Service Medal by fellow war criminal Richard Nixon that very same month. The general died five years later, in 1975.

* * *

U. S. Army Lieutenant Colonel George Smith Patton prepped and mobilized his tank battalion for action to support coup leader Lyndon Johnson on November 22nd, and was handsomely rewarded for his role. Patton was promoted repeatedly; went to Vietnam for a second tour; and ultimately became a major general.

Patton "accidentally" burned all his papers later in life, but he made extremely revealing and incriminating verbal statements *directly relating to the JFK assassination* before dying in 2004.

* * *

After eventually expressing doubts about the war that he had personally promoted and supported and relentlessly pursued – in *knowing reversal* of JFK's Vietnam withdrawal policy – Robert Strange McNamara was fired by LBJ in late 1967 at the instigation of the Joint Chiefs of Staff, who were blackmailing Johnson by leveraging their indisputable knowledge of his undeniable culpability for the JFK assassination.

McNamara "officially" left the Pentagon in early 1968 to become the president of the World Bank. Meanwhile the "Pentagon Papers" project which he had initiated was completed – but strangely, it featured the *complete censorship and suppression* of National Security Action Memorandum 263, Kennedy's written October 1963 decision to exit Vietnam completely by 1965.

As published in 1971 by the *New York Times,* the Pentagon Papers did not even *include* NSAM 263 or other key documents from November 1963, let alone properly highlight McNamara's own numerous memos and statements to LBJ constantly pushing for war.

McNamara's belated apologia, the 1995 book *In Retrospect,* served only to prove how little he had learned in the decades since Dallas – and the book was deeply offensive to anyone with any moral integrity; to the devastated populace of Southeast Asia; and to the many Vietnam veterans in this country.

I interviewed McNamara twice – and although the war criminal famous for a vise-like mind and total recall initially tried to absurdly feign "memory loss" in order to avoid answering important and challenging and meaningful questions from me, I got him to admit certain key facts on the record.

McNamara offered a variety of sickeningly hypocritical "tenets" in a "documentary" called *The Fog of War,* including the classic mantra of war criminals and dictators the world over: that somehow one "must" do *evil* in order to do good.

McNamara died in 2009, and if there is a hell (and one can only hope that there is), he is presumably still conducting statistical analysis while endlessly shoveling coal for the blistering ovens of Lucifer.

* * *

Robert McNamara, Dean Rusk, McGeorge Bundy, William Bundy, John McNaughton, Maxwell Taylor, Earle Wheeler, Paul Harkins, Victor Krulak, William Westmoreland, Walt Rostow and the rest of Lyndon Johnson's despicable inner circle of closest advisers never faced prosecution and punishment for their numerous war crimes, although they knowingly and deliberately planned and implemented Johnson's illegal, unconstitutional, brutal and aggressive war in support of the evil dictatorship based in Saigon.

* * *

While JFK plot **leaders** Lyndon Johnson and Samuel Rayburn – as well as some top plot *participants* like USAF Generals Curtis LeMay and Thomas Power, plus Army General Earle Wheeler and several other key figures in the deliberate criminal conspiracy behind the Coup of 1963 – are now dead and beyond *earthly* justice, there is some "good" and unexpected news:

Quite a number of key members of the bloody JFK assassination plot – about a dozen of the 91-plus men[1373] who actually participated in or have guilty knowledge of President Kennedy's murder[1374] – *are still alive,* **today,** *in 2023.*

Yes, you read that correctly.

This band of murderous conspirators – *all* of whom are drawing federal government pensions *paid for with your tax dollars* – are alive and living inside the continental United States.

Their last years are likely to be extremely miserable – for they are the subject of my next major book.

[1373] Author's exclusive original discovery.

[1374] Author's exclusive original discovery.

Army General Maxwell Taylor was Chairman of the JCS in 1963.

He seduced the naïve Kennedy brothers by quoting Thucydides;
ran a military spy ring against President Kennedy;
undercut JFK's Vietnam withdrawal policy;
and betrayed him.

Camelot's end:

Th three remaining members
of John F. Kennedy's family
depart the White House on
December 6th, 1963.

They would never return
as long as Lyndon Baines Johnson
illegally occupied the mansion at
1600 Pennsylvania Avenue.

Codicil:
Exile and Seizure

"These things do not just 'happen.'
*They are **made** to happen."*

– John Fitzgerald Kennedy

On Friday evening, November 22nd, 1963, after flying back from Dallas to Washington on SAM 26000, Lyndon Johnson rode a helicopter from Andrews Air Force Base to the White House grounds. He then held court for a few hours that night just across the street from the West Wing in Suite 274 of the Executive Office Building.

Press aide George Reedy realized that disturbingly, *LBJ barely spoke about Dallas or the JFK assassination* that evening.[1375]

At one point, LBJ did take a moment to quickly scrawl a couple of brief letters. They were addressed to the slain president's two young children – little Caroline Kennedy and little John F. Kennedy, Jr.

This particular tiresome chore was something of an "obligation," after all.

Having just murdered their father, it was the very least that LBJ could do.

* * *

On the afternoon of Monday, November 25th, 1963, the body of President John Fitzgerald Kennedy was interred on a sloping hillside at Arlington National Cemetery.

Lyndon Johnson studiously kept his eyes averted – *avoiding* looking at the flag-draped coffin of his victim or at the veiled, grief-stunned widow standing nearby.

An Air Force bagpipe band played.

USAF fighter jets roared overhead.

And then SAM 26000 itself flew over the grave site, Colonel James Swindal gently dipping the aircraft's wings in a final salute to the slain president from Massachusetts.

* * *

[1375] William Manchester, *The Death of a President,* p. 405.

The three surviving members of John Fitzgerald Kennedy's immediate family would leave the White House for the final time *two weeks to the day* after the president's brutal murder and grisly mutilation down in Dallas.

On Thursday, December 5th, just one day *before* the forlorn trio departed their home, USAF Brigadier General Godfrey McHugh – one of the few American military officers who was loyal to the Constitution and to JFK – gave to John Jr. a model of Air Force One,[1376] the beautiful presidential jet that the little boy and his slain father had enthusiastically adored.[1377]

The next day – Friday, December 6th, 1963 – Jacqueline Kennedy deliberately had her two small children, John Jr. and Caroline, dressed in the very same powder-blue outfits which they had worn on the day of their father's devastating state funeral eleven days earlier, back on November 25th.[1378]

Now, as they departed their home forever, the tiny family left the White House in daylight – their heads held high in the bright sunlight, demonstrating a silent dignity which even the bloody premeditated assassination of John Fitzgerald Kennedy by LBJ could not destroy.

Upon leaving, Jacqueline Bouvier Kennedy silently pledged never to return to the stately presidential mansion at 1600 Pennsylvania Avenue *as long as her husband's assassin* – the odious Lyndon Baines Johnson – occupied it.

She kept her pledge.[1379]

* * *

The shattered Kennedy family left the White House on Friday, December 6th.

The very next day, Saturday, December 7th, 1963 – which was the anniversary of the murderous attack on Pearl Harbor in 1941 – the Texas usurpers moved in to seize their bloody prize.

[1376] William Manchester, *The Death of a President,* p. 642.

[1377] John Fitzgerald Kennedy Jr. sadly did not live long enough to read this book and to learn the truth about November 22nd – and about the startling role played on the day and night of the JFK assassination by the gorgeous 707 aircraft that he and his murdered father had both loved so much.

But prior to his own death, John Jr. *had* begun to ask questions about his father's 1963 assassination. That fact alone made JFK Jr. a very dangerous fellow indeed. He was killed in 1999.

[1378] The UPI photographer who captured the heart-stopping moment when John Jr. poignantly saluted his father's flag-draped coffin on November 25th, 1963, was a USAF veteran. (Adam Bernstein, "Stan Stearns dies; captured immortal image at JFK's funeral," *Washington Post,* March 2nd, 2012.)

[1379] Jacqueline Kennedy rejected a variety of White House invitations from the Johnsons. She and her children did ***not*** go back to the executive mansion until the administration of Republican Richard Nixon was in power.

And their arrival was no subtle entrance, no solemn hushed affair.

LBJ made the day an open celebration of conspiracy, murder and sedition – and White House photos, which I found and correctly analyzed, prove that fact beyond cavil or question.[1380]

* * *

As Samuel Taliaferro Rayburn – *who was the true intellectual architect of the JFK assassination*[1381] – lay dying of pancreatic cancer in the autumn of 1961, LBJ flew to Texas to visit his mentor and chief co-conspirator one last time.

Rayburn was unconscious on the day when Johnson arrived at his hospital room in early October, so no actual conversation was possible. But I discovered that LBJ made a secret silent vow to Rayburn that day[1382] – and I also discovered precisely *what that vow was.*[1383]

* * *

On December 7th, 1963, Lyndon Johnson finally fulfilled his secret 1961 vow to Sam Rayburn.[1384]

LBJ ordered his wife, Claudia Alta Taylor ("Lady Bird") Johnson to *personally* bring the framed portrait of Sam Rayburn from The Elms (the Johnsons' vice-presidential residence at 4040 52nd Street NW in Washington) to the White House, and to *personally* carry it inside.

Official photographs capture her doing precisely that – bringing the large picture of Rayburn, the dead *intellectual author of the JFK assassination plot,*[1385] into the building which the Speaker of the House had so assiduously sought and schemed to obtain for his powerful Texas protégé, LBJ.[1386]

Waiting for them inside the White House was one of their principal *accomplices,* Congressman Albert Thomas of Houston, who beamed openly as Lady

---

[1380] Author's exclusive original discovery.

[1381] Author's exclusive original discovery.

[1382] Author's exclusive original discovery.

[1383] Author's exclusive original discovery.

[1384] Author's exclusive original discovery.

[1385] Author's exclusive original discovery.

[1386] Author's exclusive original discovery.

Bird brought Sam Rayburn's portrait into what had been the home of their victim, John Fitzgerald Kennedy.

Even LBJ himself – who verbally humiliated his spouse for years and who constantly availed himself of the sexual services of many women other than his wife – could not resist happily bussing the top of Lady Bird's head as she symbolically completed their hideous bloody triumph.

Lyndon Johnson had promised the moribund Rayburn in 1961 that *he would bring him into the White House once President Kennedy was assassinated* – and in December 1963, that is exactly what Johnson did.[1387]

It was, of necessity, a *posthumous* fulfillment of the secret 1961 promise that LBJ made to his comatose co-conspirator, Rayburn – but Johnson personally ensured that that silent vow was kept.[1388]

Honor among assassins.

Ya dance with who brung ya.

Rayburn had not lived long enough to see it come to fruition in person – but Lyndon Johnson always remembered his massive debt to his fellow chief plotter.

Rayburn had figured out how to make this happen.[1389]

Rayburn had discovered the key to taking the Oval Office.

Rayburn had heeded Cactus Jack's blunt 1931 advice – and had put John Nance Garner's sanguinary counsel to work in a brilliant feat of cold and vicious political analysis.

Rayburn found the way to successfully overcome the curse of being a white southern politician in 20th century America.

Elevation through sudden death was the one and **only** ticket to the presidency for a Texan at the time – and Sam Rayburn personally figured out the route and then laid it all out for his longtime protégé, LBJ.[1390]

*Go for the **second** spot – then kill your boss.*

You've got to get your knuckles bloody – just like Cactus Jack said.

Shoot your way into the Oval Office, Lyndon.

And if that required criminal conspiracy and blackmail and sedition along the way – and it did, indubitably – then so be it.

*Kill whoever wins the 1960 nomination – just be damned sure that he actually gets **elected** in the fall, and make damned sure that you're his VP.*

Cactus Jack had it right:

[1387] Author's exclusive original discovery.

[1388] Author's exclusive original discovery.

[1389] Author's exclusive original discovery.

[1390] Author's exclusive original discovery.

You've got to get your knuckles bloody.

Now Lyndon Johnson finally possessed the ultimate prize which he and Rayburn had plotted together to obtain ever since the sweltering month of August 1956, when the Democratic Party foolishly nominated poor Adlai Stevenson to run (*again*) and lose (*again*) against Dwight Eisenhower, the same man who had already trounced Stevenson four years earlier.

It took *seven full years* for the long-simmering Rayburn-Johnson presidential assassination plot to come to fruition.[1391]

Seven years!

But come to fruition it did – in *a hail of gunfire in an open car in a public park located in a southern city.*

For Lyndon Baines Johnson, those seven long years between 1956 and 1963 had severely tested his patience and his discipline and his strength.

But it was certainly worth the wait.

LBJ had finally – forcibly – attained his lifelong goal.

All it took was criminal conspiracy, extortion, sedition, and murder.

* * *

December 7th is the date of two horrendous disasters in American history.

One involved the slaughter of thousands of sailors in a tropical Hawaiian harbor – an act which led directly to a massive and devastatingly destructive war.

The other involved the seizure of the White House by a powerful, remorseless and ruthless assassin – an act which led directly to *another* massive and devastatingly destructive war.

Now you know, America.

Now you know.

And there are some things which can never be forgotten – or denied, or covered up, or ignored, or suppressed – ever again.

[1391] Author's exclusive original discovery.

At LBJ's behest, "Lady Bird" Johnson brings
a framed portrait of Sam Rayburn
into the White House on Saturday, December 7th, 1963,
as co-conspirator Al Thomas smiles approvingly.

This act was a brazen Johnsonian tribute to
the true intellectual author of the JFK assassination plot.

Author's exclusive original discovery.

Congressman and JFK assassination co-conspirator Albert Thomas
(seated at extreme right) joins plot leader Lyndon Johnson
in the West Sitting Room of the White House
on Saturday, December 7th, 1963, as LBJ finally takes
full physical possession of the Executive Mansion
and settles into the illegitimate "presidency"
that he killed John Kennedy to obtain.

It was Al Thomas himself who maneuvered JFK into
making the fatal Texas trip in November 1963.

It was Al Thomas who met personally with LBJ in Washington
to coordinate the upcoming assassination.

And it was Al Thomas who exchanged the infamous wink with LBJ
moments after Johnson took the oath on Air Force One in Dallas.

*There is no
statute of limitations
for murder.*

Appendix 1:
Pertinent Federal Laws

"These things do not just 'happen.'
*They are **made** to happen."*

– John Fitzgerald Kennedy

Conspiracy is a *crime,* not a "theory."[1392]

That's extremely important, so I will say it again:

Conspiracy is a *crime,* not a "theory."

Be very clear about this, America:

Conspiracy is a *crime,* not a "theory" – and that's why there are *laws* against conspiracy *in all 50 states and in federal statutes as well.*

Real laws, with real penalties, for the very real *crime* of *conspiracy.*

So once again, for the idiots and the cowards in the back:

Conspiracy is a *crime,* not a "theory."

Any criminal plotting by two or more people is, by definition, a conspiracy.

Conspiracy is the most common crime in America, in fact.

It always has been – because most serious crimes involve two or more people.

And virtually *all* truly *major* crimes involve two or more people.

Particularly in America.

It's in our national DNA, after all.

* * *

The United States itself was literally *founded* via a deliberate and utterly criminal conspiracy against the power of the British Crown.[1393]

[1392] Author's exclusive original phrasing.

[1393] The Second Continental Congress knowingly launched and funded a violent, illegal, treasonous, seditious conspiracy against British royal authority. This massive criminal conspiracy was hatched by a large group consisting of literally *scores* of prominent Americans who brazenly announced their crime to the world via a sinister written document known as the Declaration of Independence. Had their shocking and outrageous criminal plot failed to succeed, the Founding Fathers would all have been hanged by the British – for *conspiracy* and *treason.*

975

Conspiracy – genuine ***conspiracy*** – is as American as apple pie.

Anyone attempting to deny that unassailable fact is a thoroughly dishonest, cowardly and utterly contemptible individual.

The U. S. Department of Justice indicts people for criminal conspiracy every single month.

The U. S. Department of Justice secures convictions for criminal conspiracy every single month.

The U. S. Department of Justice accepts guilty pleas to criminal conspiracy every single month.

You can check it for yourself online at www.justice.gov.

* * *

Conspiracy is the most common crime committed in the United States.

Get that through your head:

Conspiracy is the most common crime committed in the United States.

And the murderous Coup of 1963 was no exception.

President John Fitzgerald Kennedy was assassinated by a *large* criminal conspiracy consisting of *scores* of men led personally by the Vice President of the United States, Lyndon Baines Johnson.[1394]

That's the reality.

* * *

Contrary to the vapid vacuous *vomitus* routinely spewed by the pathetic and impotent frauds who populate American corporate media (and government, and academe), *there is no such thing* as a "conspiracy theory."

Any given crime either *is* a conspiracy, or it is *not.*

Period.

There is no "theory."

Indeed, the idiotic term "conspiracy theory" is a complete contradiction in terms – and the people who employ that term (always in a desperate effort to ignore or suppress unsettling truths) are complete idiots.

Ideas and beliefs can be true or false, correct or erroneous; but ideas and beliefs are ***not*** "conspiracy theories."

The moronic phrase "conspiracy theory" makes as little sense as the moronic phrase "oxygen beagle."

(Oxygen is real, but it ***not*** a breed of dog. *Capisci?*)

[1394] Author's exclusive original discovery.

Here's what you didn't know:

The pathetic prostrate whores and pusillanimous pundits who promulgate such insulting and evasive rubbish are, wittingly or not, slavishly following the playbook specifically authored for them by the Central Intelligence Agency itself back in 1967.

* * *

On January 4ᵗʰ, 1967, *while LBJ was still illegally occupying the Oval Office,* the CIA issued a lengthy cable to various station chiefs and other officials containing written "guidance" intended for ultimate distribution to the Agency's eager little whores in American corporate media (described as "propaganda assets" and "friendly elite contacts").

In a 52-page document titled "Countering Criticism of the Warren Report,"[1395] the CIA – jarred by the emergence of questions about the JFK assassination – swung into emergency mode and ginned up a barrage of baseless slurs, cheap epithets and hollow arguments to use against anyone who dared to challenge the false "official" version of the president's murder in Dallas.[1396]

Significantly, this repulsive and Orwellian 1967 guidance from the Agency made particular mention of LBJ: "Moreover, there seems to be an increasing tendency to hint that President Johnson himself, as the one person who might be said to have benefited, was in some way *responsible for the assassination.*"

He certainly was.

And the CIA certainly did not want *that* dangerous notion getting around!

The CIA document ranted explicitly about "conspiracy theories" [*sic*] and "conspiracy theorists" [*sic*], and then proceeded to red-bait those intelligent people who disbelieved the ludicrous and obscene Johnson Report. According to the right-wing extremists at the CIA, "parts of the conspiracy talk appear to be deliberately generated by Communist propagandists." The 1967 CIA cable even cited *Gestapo* materials (that's right, *Nazi* documents) in order to impugn the writer Joachim Joesten (a German refugee) for being a (*gasp*) Communist.[1397]

[1395] Classified as "Secret" by the CIA, the 1967 document was ostensibly the work of one "Ned Bennett." Besides being offensive and un-American, the paper is unintentionally quite revealing about the U. S. government's concerns.

[1396] Recall that the U. S. Air Force, in the person of Alfred Goldberg, *outlined and wrote* much of the Johnson Report.

[1397] Yes, that's right: the CIA was actually citing *Nazi records from the 1930s* in order to undermine and discredit a courageous critic of the official American lie about the Coup of 1963.

The Agency went on to push various other weak and patently false arguments, including the arrogant and risible canard that "Conspiracy on the large scale often suggested would be impossible to conceal in the United States" [*sic*].[1398]

The 1967 cable also predictably and patronizingly dismissed "the recollections of individual eyewitnesses" – as if their vital and devastating observations, which destroyed the official lie, somehow didn't count.[1399]

In a particularly odious and offensive passage, the CIA cable instructs recipients and their obedient "assets" to push the false line that "No significant new evidence has emerged . . ."[1400] Lazy Establishment whores have been predictably promoting that brazen lie for years.

It wasn't true then, and it isn't true now.

Here's a pro tip for the so-called "journalists" and "historians" and "pundits" of the incompetent, inept and thoroughly corrupt American Establishment:

If you're parroting the CIA, you're just a brainless slut.

Nothing more.

And nothing less.

* * *

As should be manifestly clear to even the most dimwitted clod by now, *anyone using the false and insulting term "conspiracy theory" is **not** a serious person* – and such people should be mercilessly ridiculed and derided for their cowardly and deliberate evasion of reality.[1401]

I'll say it again:

Conspiracy is a ***crime*** – not a "theory."

A *serious* crime.

And for the record, America,

Serious people take *serious* crimes *seriously.*

[1398] *Au contraire, mon ennemi.*

[1399] Hacks who employ this tactic conveniently ignore the fact that all journalism, all history, and the entire legal system are based on (you guessed it) eyewitness testimony; even the provenance and validity of documents and photos and other so-called "concrete" evidentiary items must first be attested to through *sworn eyewitness testimony* before being accepted for consideration in court. (Nice try, fellas.)

[1400] CIA memo, January 4th, 1967, page 4 – underlining as it appears in the original cable.

[1401] The breathtaking hypocrisy of pompous but pusillanimous American pontificators was never demonstrated more blatantly than in January 2021, when Establishment figures eagerly rushed to falsely and melodramatically label an ugly and violent (but thoroughly inept and laughably unsuccessful) mob action at the Capitol a "coup" (which it certainly wasn't) – while stubbornly and perpetually ***denying*** that the *actual assassination of the president in 1963 and the dramatic reversal of his Vietnam withdrawal policy* was in fact a coup (which it certainly ***was***).

* * *

In creating and leading and executing the JFK assassination plot, Samuel Taliaferro Rayburn and Lyndon Baines Johnson *actively conspired to murder the president of the United States* – and they conspired not only with each other, but with all those men in the U. S. military and in the executive branch of the federal government whom they recruited to *join* their murderous plot.

In doing so, the two Texans (and their eager subordinate criminal confederates in the U. S. armed forces and in the Secret Service) knowingly and repeatedly violated numerous federal *and* state laws – including many laws against *conspiracy.*

The following pages present the actual text of several federal laws pertinent to the JFK assassination.

Read them carefully, America.

Then immediately banish the false, lazy, idiotic and impotent term "conspiracy theory" from your mind and from your vocabulary – forever.

18 U.S. Code § 2
Principals

(a) Whoever commits an offense against the United States or aids, abets, counsels, commands, induces or procures its commission, is punishable as a principal.

(b) Whoever willfully causes an act to be done which if directly performed by him or another would be an offense against the United States, is punishable as a principal.

---

18 U.S. Code § 3
Accessory after the fact

Whoever, knowing that an offense against the United States has been committed, receives, relieves, comforts or assists the offender in order to hinder or prevent his apprehension, trial or punishment, is an accessory after the fact.

Except as otherwise expressly provided by any Act of Congress, an accessory after the fact shall be imprisoned not more than one-half the maximum term of imprisonment or (notwithstanding section 3571) fined not more than one-half the maximum fine prescribed for the punishment of the principal, or both; or if the principal is punishable by life imprisonment or death, the accessory shall be imprisoned not more than 15 years.

---

18 U.S. Code § 4
Misprision of felony

Whoever, having knowledge of the actual commission of a felony cognizable by a court of the United States, conceals and does not as soon as possible make known the same to some judge or other person in civil or military authority under the United States, shall be fined under this title or imprisoned not more than three years, or both.

---

18 U.S. Code § 111
Assaulting, resisting, or impeding certain officers or employees

(a) In General.—Whoever—

(1) forcibly assaults, resists, opposes, impedes, intimidates, or interferes with any person designated in section 1114 of this title while engaged in or on account of the performance of official duties; or

(2) forcibly assaults or intimidates any person who formerly served as a person designated in section 1114 on account of the performance of official duties during such person's term of service, shall, where the acts in violation of this section constitute only simple assault, be fined under this title or imprisoned not more than one year, or both, and where such acts involve physical contact with the victim of that assault or the intent to commit another felony, be fined under this title or imprisoned not more than 8 years, or both.

(b) Enhanced Penalty.—
Whoever, in the commission of any acts described in subsection (a), uses a deadly or dangerous weapon (including a weapon intended to cause death or danger but that fails to do so by reason of a defective component) or inflicts bodily injury, shall be fined under this title or imprisoned not more than 20 years, or both.

18 U.S. Code § 241
Conspiracy against rights

If two or more persons conspire to injure, oppress, threaten, or intimidate any person in any State, Territory, Commonwealth, Possession, or District in the free exercise or enjoyment of any right or privilege secured to him by the Constitution or laws of the United States, or because of his having so exercised the same; or

If two or more persons go in disguise on the highway, or on the premises of another, with intent to prevent or hinder his free exercise or enjoyment of any right or privilege so secured—

They shall be fined under this title or imprisoned not more than ten years, or both; and if death results from the acts committed in violation of this section or if such acts include kidnapping or an attempt to kidnap, aggravated sexual abuse or an attempt to commit aggravated sexual abuse, or an attempt to kill, they shall be fined under this title or imprisoned for any term of years or for life, or both, or may be sentenced to death.

18 U.S. Code § 371
Conspiracy to commit offense or to defraud United States

If two or more persons conspire either to commit any offense against the United States, or to defraud the United States, or any agency thereof in any manner or for any purpose, and one or more of such persons do any act to effect the object of the conspiracy, each shall be fined under this title or imprisoned not more than five years, or both.

If, however, the offense, the commission of which is the object of the conspiracy, is a misdemeanor only, the punishment for such conspiracy shall not exceed the maximum punishment provided for such misdemeanor.

18 U.S. Code § 372
Conspiracy to impede or injure officer

If two or more persons in any State, Territory, Possession, or District conspire to prevent, by force, intimidation, or threat, any person from accepting or holding any office, trust, or place of confidence under the United States, or from discharging any duties thereof, or to induce by like means any officer of the United States to leave the place, where his duties as an officer are required to be performed, or to injure him in his person or property on account of his lawful discharge of the duties of his office, or while engaged in the lawful discharge thereof, or to injure his property so as to molest, interrupt, hinder, or impcdc him in the discharge of his official duties, each of such persons shall be fined under this title or imprisoned not more than six years, or both.

18 U.S. Code § 871

Threats against President and successors to the Presidency

(a) Whoever knowingly and willfully deposits for conveyance in the mail or for a delivery from any post office or by any letter carrier any letter, paper, writing, print, missive, or document containing any threat to take the life of, to kidnap, or to inflict bodily harm upon the President of the United States, the President-elect, the Vice President or other officer next in the order of succession to the office of President of the United States, or the Vice President-elect, or knowingly and willfully otherwise makes any such threat against the President, President-elect, Vice President or other officer next in the order of succession to the office of President, or Vice President-elect, shall be fined under this title or imprisoned not more than five years, or both.

(b) The terms "President-elect" and "Vice President-elect" as used in this section shall mean such persons as are the apparent successful candidates for the offices of President and Vice President, respectively, as ascertained from the results of the general elections held to determine the electors of President and Vice President in accordance with title 3, United States Code, sections 1 and 2. The phrase "other officer next in the order of succession to the office of President" as used in this section shall mean the person next in the order of succession to act as President in accordance with title 3, United States Code, sections 19 and 20.

---

18 U.S. Code § 872

Extortion by officers or employees of the United States

Whoever, being an officer, or employee of the United States or any department or agency thereof, or representing himself to be or assuming to act as such, under color or pretense of office or employment commits or attempts an act of extortion, shall be fined under this title or imprisoned not more than three years, or both; but if the amount so extorted or demanded does not exceed $1,000, he shall be fined under this title or imprisoned not more than one year, or both.

---

18 U.S. Code § 873

Blackmail

Whoever, under a threat of informing, or as a consideration for not informing, against any violation of any law of the United States, demands or receives any money or other valuable thing, shall be fined under this title or imprisoned not more than one year, or both.

---

18 U.S. Code § 875
Interstate communications

(a) Whoever transmits in interstate or foreign commerce any communication containing any demand or request for a ransom or reward for the release of any kidnapped person, shall be fined under this title or imprisoned not more than twenty years, or both.

(b) Whoever, with intent to extort from any person, firm, association, or corporation, any money or other thing of value, transmits in interstate or foreign commerce any communication containing any threat to kidnap any person or any threat to injure the person of another, shall be fined under this title or imprisoned not more than twenty years, or both.

(c) Whoever transmits in interstate or foreign commerce any communication containing any threat to kidnap any person or any threat to injure the person of another, shall be fined under this title or imprisoned not more than five years, or both.

(d) Whoever, with intent to extort from any person, firm, association, or corporation, any money or other thing of value, transmits in interstate or foreign commerce any communication containing any threat to injure the property or reputation of the addressee or of another or the reputation of a deceased person or any threat to accuse the addressee or any other person of a crime, shall be fined under this title or imprisoned not more than two years, or both.

---

18 U.S. Code § 1001
Statements or entries generally

(a) Except as otherwise provided in this section, whoever, in any matter within the jurisdiction of the executive, legislative, or judicial branch of the Government of the United States, knowingly and willfully—

(1) falsifies, conceals, or covers up by any trick, scheme, or device a material fact;

(2) makes any materially false, fictitious, or fraudulent statement or representation; or

(3) makes or uses any false writing or document knowing the same to contain any materially false, fictitious, or fraudulent statement or entry;

shall be fined under this title, imprisoned not more than 5 years or, if the offense involves international or domestic terrorism (as defined in section 2331), imprisoned not more than 8 years, or both. If the matter relates to an offense under chapter 109A, 109B, 110, or 117, or section 1591, then the term of imprisonment imposed under this section shall be not more than 8 years.

(b) Subsection (a) does not apply to a party to a judicial proceeding, or that party's counsel, for statements, representations, writings or documents submitted by such party or counsel to a judge or magistrate in that proceeding.

(c) With respect to any matter within the jurisdiction of the legislative branch, subsection (a) shall apply only to—
(1) administrative matters, including a claim for payment, a matter related to the procurement of property or services, personnel or employment practices, or support services, or a document required by law, rule, or regulation to be submitted to the Congress or any office or officer within the legislative branch; or

(2) any investigation or review, conducted pursuant to the authority of any committee, subcommittee, commission or office of the Congress, consistent with applicable rules of the House or Senate.

---

18 U.S. Code § 1111

Murder

(a) Murder is the unlawful killing of a human being with malice aforethought. Every murder perpetrated by poison, lying in wait, or any other kind of willful, deliberate, malicious, and premeditated killing; or committed in the perpetration of, or attempt to perpetrate, any arson, escape, murder, kidnapping, treason, espionage, sabotage, aggravated sexual abuse or sexual abuse, child abuse, burglary, or robbery; or perpetrated as part of a pattern or practice of assault or torture against a child or children; or perpetrated from a premeditated design unlawfully and maliciously to effect the death of any human being other than him who is killed, is murder in the first degree.

Any other murder is murder in the second degree.

(b) Within the special maritime and territorial jurisdiction of the United States,

Whoever is guilty of murder in the first degree shall be punished by death or by imprisonment for life;

Whoever is guilty of murder in the second degree, shall be imprisoned for any term of years or for life.

---

18 U.S. Code § 1113

Attempt to commit murder or manslaughter

Except as provided in section 113 of this title, whoever, within the special maritime and territorial jurisdiction of the United States, attempts to commit murder or manslaughter, shall, for an attempt to commit murder be imprisoned not more than twenty years or fined under this title, or both, and for an attempt to commit manslaughter be imprisoned not more than seven years or fined under this title, or both.

---

18 U.S. Code § 1114

Protection of officers and employees of the United States

Whoever kills or attempts to kill any officer or employee of the United States or of any agency in any branch of the United States Government (including any member of the uniformed services) while such officer or employee is engaged in or on account of the performance of official duties, or any person assisting such an officer or employee in the performance of such duties or on account of that assistance, shall be punished—

(1) in the case of murder, as provided under section 1111;

(2) in the case of manslaughter, as provided under section 1112; or

(3) in the case of attempted murder or manslaughter, as provided in section 1113.

———————

18 U.S. Code § 1385

Use of Army and Air Force as posse comitatus

Whoever, except in cases and under circumstances expressly authorized by the Constitution or Act of Congress, willfully uses any part of the Army or the Air Force as a *posse comitatus* or otherwise to execute the laws shall be fined under this title or imprisoned not more than two years, or both.

---

18 U.S. Code § 1505

Obstruction of proceedings before departments, agencies, and committees

Whoever, with intent to avoid, evade, prevent, or obstruct compliance, in whole or in part, with any civil investigative demand duly and properly made under the Antitrust Civil Process Act, willfully withholds, misrepresents, removes from any place, conceals, covers up, destroys, mutilates, alters, or by other means falsifies any documentary material, answers to written interrogatories, or oral testimony, which is the subject of such demand; or attempts to do so or solicits another to do so; or

Whoever corruptly, or by threats or force, or by any threatening letter or communication influences, obstructs, or impedes or endeavors to influence, obstruct, or impede the due and proper administration of the law under which any pending proceeding is being had before any department or agency of the United States, or the due and proper exercise of the power of inquiry under which any inquiry or investigation is being had by either House, or any committee of either House or any joint committee of the Congress—

Shall be fined under this title, imprisoned not more than 5 years or, if the offense involves international or domestic terrorism (as defined in section 2331), imprisoned not more than 8 years, or both.

---

18 U.S. Code § 1512 (b) (c)

Obstruction by Intimidation, Threats, Persuasion, or Deception

(b) Whoever knowingly uses intimidation, threatens, or corruptly persuades another person, or attempts to do so, or engages in misleading conduct toward another person, with intent to—

(1) influence, delay, or prevent the testimony of any person in an official proceeding;

(2) cause or induce any person to—

(A) withhold testimony, or withhold a record, document, or other object, from an official proceeding;

(B) alter, destroy, mutilate, or conceal an object with intent to impair the object's integrity or availability for use in an official proceeding . . .

shall be fined under this title or imprisoned not more than 20 years, or both.

(c) Whoever corruptly—

(1) alters, destroys, mutilates, or conceals a record, document, or other object, or attempts to do so, with the intent to impair the object's integrity or availability for use in an official proceeding; or

(2) otherwise obstructs, influences, or impedes any official proceeding, or attempts to do so,

shall be fined under this title or imprisoned not more than 20 years, or both.

———————

18 U.S. Code § 1622

Subornation of perjury

Whoever procures another to commit any perjury is guilty of subornation of perjury, and shall be fined under this title or imprisoned not more than five years, or both.

---

18 U.S. Code § 2071

Concealment, removal, or mutilation generally

(a) Whoever willfully and unlawfully conceals, removes, mutilates, obliterates, or destroys, or attempts to do so, or, with intent to do so takes and carries away any record, proceeding, map, book, paper, document, or other thing, filed or deposited with any clerk or officer of any court of the United States, or in any public office, or with any judicial or public officer of the United States, shall be fined under this title or imprisoned not more than three years, or both.

(b) Whoever, having the custody of any such record, proceeding, map, book, document, paper, or other thing, willfully and unlawfully conceals, removes, mutilates, obliterates, falsifies, or destroys the same, shall be fined under this title or imprisoned not more than three years, or both; and shall forfeit his office and be disqualified from holding any office under the United States. As used in this subsection, the term "office" does not include the office held by any person as a retired officer of the Armed Forces of the United States.

---

18 U.S. Code § 2381

Treason

Whoever, owing allegiance to the United States, levies war against them or adheres to their enemies, giving them aid and comfort within the United States or elsewhere, is guilty of treason and shall suffer death, or shall be imprisoned not less than five years and fined under this title but not less than $10,000; and shall be incapable of holding any office under the United States.

---

18 U.S. Code § 2382

Misprision of treason

Whoever, owing allegiance to the United States and having knowledge of the commission of any treason against them, conceals and does not, as soon as may be, disclose and make known the same to the President or to some judge of the United States, or to the governor or to some judge or justice of a particular State, is guilty of misprision of treason and shall be fined under this title or imprisoned not more than seven years, or both.

---

18 U.S. Code § 2383

Rebellion or insurrection

Whoever incites, sets on foot, assists, or engages in any rebellion or insurrection against the authority of the United States or the laws thereof, or gives aid or comfort thereto, shall be fined under this title or imprisoned not more than ten years, or both; and shall be incapable of holding any office under the United States.

---

18 U.S. Code § 2384

Seditious conspiracy

If two or more persons in any State or Territory, or in any place subject to the jurisdiction of the United States, conspire to overthrow, put down, or to destroy by force the Government of the United States, or to levy war against them, or to oppose by force the authority thereof, or by force to prevent, hinder, or delay the execution of any law of the United States, or by force to seize, take, or possess any property of the United States contrary to the authority thereof, they shall each be fined under this title or imprisoned not more than twenty years, or both.

---

18 U.S. Code § 2385

Advocating overthrow of Government

Whoever knowingly or willfully advocates, abets, advises, or teaches the duty, necessity, desirability, or propriety of overthrowing or destroying the government of the United States or the government of any State, Territory, District or Possession thereof, or the government of any political subdivision therein, by force or violence, or by the assassination of any officer of any such government; or

Whoever, with intent to cause the overthrow or destruction of any such government, prints, publishes, edits, issues, circulates, sells, distributes, or publicly displays any written or printed matter advocating, advising, or teaching the duty, necessity, desirability, or propriety of overthrowing or destroying any government in the United States by force or violence, or attempts to do so; or

Whoever organizes or helps or attempts to organize any society, group, or assembly of persons who teach, advocate, or encourage the overthrow or destruction of any such government by force or violence; or becomes or is a member of, or affiliates with, any such society, group, or assembly of persons, knowing the purposes thereof—

Shall be fined under this title or imprisoned not more than twenty years, or both, and shall be ineligible for employment by the United States or any department or agency thereof, for the five years next following his conviction.

If two or more persons conspire to commit any offense named in this section, each shall be fined under this title or imprisoned not more than twenty years, or both, and shall be ineligible for employment by the United States or any department or agency thereof, for the five years next following his conviction.

As used in this section, the terms "organizes" and "organize", with respect to any society, group, or assembly of persons, include the recruiting of new members, the forming of new units, and the regrouping or expansion of existing clubs, classes, and other units of such society, group, or assembly of persons.

———————

18 U.S. Code § 2387

Activities affecting armed forces generally

 (a) Whoever, with intent to interfere with, impair, or influence the loyalty, morale, or discipline of the military or naval forces of the United States:

(1) advises, counsels, urges, or in any manner causes or attempts to cause insubordination, disloyalty, mutiny, or refusal of duty by any member of the military or naval forces of the United States; or

(2) distributes or attempts to distribute any written or printed matter which advises, counsels, or urges insubordination, disloyalty, mutiny, or refusal of duty by any member of the military or naval forces of the United States—

Shall be fined under this title or imprisoned not more than ten years, or both, and shall be ineligible for employment by the United States or any department or agency thereof, for the five years next following his conviction.

(b) For the purposes of this section, the term "military or naval forces of the United States" includes the Army of the United States, the Navy, Air Force, Marine Corps, Coast Guard, Navy Reserve, Marine Corps Reserve, and Coast Guard Reserve of the United States; and, when any merchant vessel is commissioned in the Navy or is in the service of the Army or the Navy, includes the master, officers, and crew of such vessel.

18 U.S. Code § 2389

Recruiting for service against United States

Whoever recruits soldiers or sailors within the United States, or in any place subject to the jurisdiction thereof, to engage in armed hostility against the same; or

Whoever opens within the United States, or in any place subject to the jurisdiction thereof, a recruiting station for the enlistment of such soldiers or sailors to serve in any manner in armed hostility against the United States —

Shall be fined under this title or imprisoned not more than five years, or both.

---

18 U.S. Code § 2390

Enlistment to serve against United States

Whoever enlists or is engaged within the United States or in any place subject to the jurisdiction thereof, with intent to serve in armed hostility against the United States, shall be fined under this title [1] or imprisoned not more than three years, or both.

United States Constitution

Amendment XIV

Section 3.

No person shall be a Senator or Representative in Congress, or elector of President and Vice President, or hold any office, civil or military, under the United States, or under any state, who, having previously taken an oath, as a member of Congress, or as an officer of the United States, or as a member of any state legislature, or as an executive or judicial officer of any state, to support the Constitution of the United States, shall have engaged in insurrection or rebellion against the same, or given aid or comfort to the enemies thereof.

———————

USAF General Curtis LeMay considered JFK and his key staffers
to be "cockroaches" – insects worthy of extermination.

His own subsequent betrayal by LBJ infuriated the general.

Five years after the JFK assassination, in October 1968,
LeMay received a massive million-dollar payout for his role in 1963.

Appendix 2:
U. S. Air Force Roster

Key figures in the year 1963

OFFICE OF THE VICE PRESIDENT:

USAF Colonel Howard Lay Burris
    (Military aide to Vice President Lyndon Baines Johnson;
    served as LBJ's secret "back channel" to the Joint Chiefs of Staff)

Walter Jenkins
    (Top civilian aide to LBJ; member, USAF Reserve)

PENTAGON HEADQUARTERS STAFF:

USAF Chief of Staff: General Curtis Emerson Lemay

Aide to General LeMay: USAF Colonel George Stanton Dorman

USAF Vice Chief of Staff: General William F. "Bozo" McKee

USAF Deputy Chief of Staff for Plans and Operations: General David Burchinal

Organization of the Joint Chiefs of Staff: USAF General Lucius Clay, Jr.

USAF Inspector General: USAF Lt. General John Dale Ryan

Director of Special Investigations,
Office of USAF Inspector General: USAF General Joseph Cappucci

Commander, Air Force Office of Special Investigations (AFOSI):
USAF Major General John S. Samuel

STRATEGIC AIR COMMAND (SAC):

CINCSAC: General Thomas Sarsfield Power

Vice CINCSAC: Lt. General Hunter Harris, Jr.

SAC Chief of Staff: Major General Keith K. Compton

SAC Director of Intelligence: Major General Robert N. Smith

SAC Director of Operations: Major General Austin J. Russell

SAC Deputy Director of Operations: Major General Harold E. Humfeld

SAC Chief, Operations Plans Division: Major General William J. Crumm

SAC Director of Plans: Major General Seth J. McKee

SAC Deputy Director of Plans: Brigadier General Winton R. Close

SAC Chief, Control Division: Brigadier General Everett A. McDonald

SAC Deputy Inspector General for Security: Colonel Edward A. Crouchley

Commander, SAC Second Air Force: Lt. General David Wade

Commander, SAC Eighth Air Force: Lt. General Joseph J. Nazzaro

Commander, SAC Fifteenth Air Force: Lt. General Archie J. Old, Jr.

USAF / CIA OPERATIONS:

USAF General Charles Pearre Cabell
Director, Air Force Intelligence, 1948-1951
Director, Joint Staff of the Joint Chiefs of Staff, 1951-1953
Deputy Director, Central Intelligence Agency, 1953-1962
       (Sought additional air strikes at Bay of Pigs – rejected by JFK)
       (Key official involved with Bay of Pigs – fired by JFK)
       (Brother of Dallas Mayor – and CIA asset – Earle Cabell)

USAF / CIA OPERATIONS:

USAF Brigadier General Edward G. Lansdale
United States Air Force, 1947-1963
Central Intelligence Agency, circa 1949 to 1963
  (Established the South Vietnamese dictator Ngo Dinh Diem in the 1950s)
  (Rejected by JFK in 1961 for ambassadorship to South Vietnam)
  (Informed by JFK in summer 1963 of upcoming Diem ouster in South Vietnam)
  Officially "retired" from U. S. Air Force, autumn 1963
  Hotel Texas, Fort Worth, Texas – November 21st, 1963
  Dealey Plaza, Dallas, Texas – November 22nd, 1963

AIR FORCE ONE (26000):
USAF Sgt. William Joseph ("Joe") Chappell
Flight Engineer

AIR FORCE TWO (86970):
USAF Sgt. Paul Glynn
(Steward, Aide and Valet to Lyndon Baines Johnson)

USAF Sgt. Ken Gaddis
(Steward, Aide and Valet to Lyndon Baines Johnson)

JETSTAR:
USAF Major James U. Cross
  (Pilot and military aide to Lyndon Baines Johnson;
  Control of Presidential Emergency Fund)

DALLAS CITY MANAGER:
Elgin Crull (USAAF veteran)

DALLAS MOTORCADE:
SS agent Rufus Youngblood (USAAF veteran)
  (Head of Vice-Presidential Detail for Lyndon Baines Johnson)

TEXAS SCHOOL BOOK DEPOSITORY:
Employee Billy Nolan Lovelady
    (Discharged from USAF)

LACKLAND AIR FORCE BASE, SAN ANTONIO
USAF Airman Lloyd John Wilson
    (Threatened JFK in 1963)

DEALEY PLAZA:
Photographer Phillip L. Willis (USAAF, retired)

ANDREWS AIR FORCE BASE, MARYLAND:
USAF Colonel Robert T. Best
Commander, 1002nd Air Police Squadron
    ("Security" arrangements at Andrews AFB for AF-1's return on 11/22/1963)

LOOKOUT MOUNTAIN AIR FORCE STATION, CALIFORNIA:
USAF 1352nd Photo Group (produced and edited highly classified films)
    USAF Lieutenant Colonel Alterio Gallerani, Commanding Officer
    USAF Major Kenneth K. Killgore, Executive Officer
    USAF Major Robert L. MacKinnon, Operations Officer
    Mr. W. Donn Hayes – *civilian* motion picture production specialist

TRANSPORTATION OF "EVIDENCE" TO WASHINGTON:
USAF - Strategic Air Command
Carswell AFB, Fort Worth, Texas
    (Flew false "assassination evidence" to Washington, D. C. for the FBI)

SHOOTING OF INNOCENT PATSY:
Jacob Rubenstein, *aka* "Jack Ruby" (USAAF veteran)
    (Shot Lee Harvey Oswald on live national television)

DEPARTMENT OF JUSTICE:
Nicholas Katzenbach (USAAF veteran; former USAF attorney)
(Urged U. S. government to blame Lee Oswald for the JFK assassination)

TINKER AIR FORCE BASE, OKLAHOMA:
(USAF personnel at Tinker combed through Dallas media recordings in order to locate dangerous information from November 22nd)

AIR FORCE OFFICE OF SPECIAL INVESTIGATIONS (AFOSI):
USAF Major General John S. Samuel
Commander, Air Force Office of Special Investigations (AFOSI), 1963-1964

USAF General Joseph Cappucci
Commander, Air Force Office of Special Investigations (AFOSI), 1964-1972
(Disclosed LBJ's principal role in the JFK assassination)

**THE PRESIDENT'S COMMISSION ON
THE ASSASSINATION OF PRESIDENT KENNEDY**
(The Johnson Commission, alias the "Warren" Commission):

Arlen Specter, staff attorney (USAF veteran; former AFOSI agent)
(Harassed witnesses, suppressed evidence, knowingly obstructed justice and deliberately promoted the false "single bullet theory")

Alfred Goldberg – USAF "historian" [*sic*]
(Personally outlined and personally wrote much of the fictitious "Warren" Report)

General Earle Gilmore Wheeler was Army Chief of Staff in 1963.
LBJ made him Chairman of the Joint Chiefs of Staff in 1964.

Wheeler ensured that U. S. Army tanks
supported, and *guaranteed* the success of,
Lyndon Johnson's coup on November 22nd, 1963.

All that Wheeler demanded in return was a promotion – and a war.

Author's exclusive original discovery.

Appendix 3:
U. S. Army Roster

Key figures in the year 1963

Chairman, Joint Chiefs of Staff (JCS): General Maxwell D. Taylor, U. S. Army

Army Chief of Staff (member, JCS): General Earle "Bus" Wheeler
(Blackmailed LBJ regarding the criminal escalation of the Vietnam War)

Army Vice Chief of Staff: General Barksdale Hamlett

Author's exclusive original discovery:
Commander-in-Chief, Strike Command (CINCSTRIKE):
      General Paul DeWitt Adams, U. S. Army
      (Mysteriously absented himself from Operation Big Lift)

Commander-in-Chief, Continental Army Command (CINCCONARC):
      General John K. Waters, U. S. Army

Acting Commander, III Corps and Fort Hood, Texas:
      Major General Harvey J. Jablonsky, U. S. Army

Commander, 1st Armored Division:
      Major General Harvey J. Jablonsky, U. S. Army
      (Commanding officer of Lt. Col. George Patton)

Assistant Division Commander, 1st Armored Division:
      Brigadier General Edward Chrysostom David ("Pony") Scherrer

Commander, 2nd Medium Tank Battalion, 81st Armor, 1st Armored Division:
      Lieutenant Colonel George S. Patton, U. S. Army
      (Ordered to take tanks to Dallas in the wake of the JFK assassination)

White House Situation Room:
> Major Harold R. Patterson, U. S. Army
> White House Communications Agency (WHCA)

JFK autopsy – consulting pathologist:
> Lt. Colonel Pierre A. Finck, U. S. Army
> Armed Force Institute of Pathology
> Walter Reed Army Medical Center
> *(Disclosed in 1969 that JFK's spinal cord was severed **prior to** autopsy)*

Planning and logistics expert:
> General Lucius Dubignon Clay, U. S. Army (Retired)
> *(Longtime associate of Sam Rayburn)*
> *(Forwarded Curtis LeMay's World War III plan to Washington)*
> *(Met in April 1963 with Allen Dulles and Morris Liebman)*

Author's exclusive original discovery:
Charles Anthony Carrico, U. S. Army
> *(Suddenly pardoned, at LBJ's request,*
> *just 28 days after the JFK assassination!)*

The American flag flies at half-staff
on the sloping hill above JFK's grave
at Arlington National Cemetery.

The story isn't finished . . .

yet.

Warning:
What Comes Next

"These things do not just 'happen.'
*They are **made** to happen."*

– John Fitzgerald Kennedy

This book has undoubtedly enlightened and educated you – but it has also undoubtedly disturbed you greatly, too.

As well it should have.

That was absolutely intentional, absolutely unavoidable, and absolutely necessary.

But as disturbing and vital and unassailable as this material is, *on its own,* it is also a gateway to something equally – or even *more* – upsetting and shocking, coming in a subsequent book by me.

That next major book which I am writing is *already well underway,* and it will further devastate you.

* * *

This present book of mine, *Under Cover of Night,* stands alone – *on its own* – as the most significant and dramatic breakthrough in serious research and advanced analysis of the JFK assassination since 1963.

It has presented exclusively – for the first time anywhere – the *true genesis* of the plot, and the real identity of the *actual intellectual authors* of the JFK assassination.[1402]

It has finally revealed the *actual motivation* for the crime.[1403]

Further, it has clearly established the *actual timeline* and proper framework for the plot.[1404] It has also made clear, for the first time anywhere, the *specific criminal culpability of Lyndon Baines Johnson* as the undisputed leader of the murderous plot

---

[1402] Author's exclusive original discovery.

[1403] Author's exclusive original discovery.

[1404] Author's exclusive original discovery.

to assassinate his predecessor, as evidenced by *more than 160 specific, documented criminal acts by LBJ.*[1405]

But in addition, this book is also the absolutely indispensable "prerequisite" to a full understanding of my *next* major book.

Without an *accurate* intellectual framework – which is to say, without a full grasp and proper understanding of the true *cause, purpose, source, nature, timing, origin* and *context* of the JFK assassination – you will quite frankly be completely unable to deal with what I will subsequently reveal.

That chilling information *literally fills an entire additional book.*

For reasons of space, it could not be included here.

For reasons of shock, it has to *follow* this book.

* * *

On a brilliantly sunny Friday afternoon in late November 1963, a committed cadre of *scores* of men deliberately overthrew the elected leader of the United States in a violent, illegal, murderous, military-backed coup which had been plotted since mid-August 1956 by *two senior American politicians.*[1406]

That is the "macro-level" truth about the JFK assassination, which I have uncovered for the first time anywhere – and proven unassailably – in this book.

As for the "micro-level" truth about the JFK assassination, meaning *the critical moments of the shooting itself,* you are in for an extremely disturbing – indeed, utterly disorienting – surprise.

Every previous published narrative of the JFK assassination – every single prior account of the shooting in Dealey Plaza – is false or completely erroneous.

That bears repeating:

Every previously published narrative about events in Dealey Plaza is wrong.

Every "theory," every "scenario," every "hypothesis," every so-called "list of shooters" out there (*Lee Oswald! Milwaukee Phil! Jimmy Files! Mac Wallace! That chick from Cuba!*) is wrong.

All of them.

Every single one.

And therefore, those things you *think* you know – and that you fervently *believe* – about the specific Dealey Plaza details of the assassination (*Triangulated crossfire! The roof of the Dal-Tex building! Harry Weatherford! Cuban exile snipers! Mafia snipers!*) are dead wrong.

You are *wrong* – no matter who you are.

[1405] Author's exclusive original discovery.

[1406] Author's exclusive original discovery.

You are *wrong* – no matter how long you have studied the case.

You are *wrong* – no matter how knowledgeable you may be (or *think* you are) concerning various *other* aspects of the JFK assassination.

You are *wrong* – no matter *how many* books that you've read (or written, or co-written, or secretly co-authored, or published under an alias).

You are *wrong* – no matter *how* many documentaries that you have watched (or produced, or been featured in) on cable television or the Internet; no matter *how* many movies you have seen; no matter *how* many JFK research conferences you have attended; no matter *how* many messages you have posted on various online forums about the JFK case.

You are *wrong* – grievously, totally wrong.

The stunning truth is more chilling, ugly, brutal and vicious than you are capable of imagining. You have *never* successfully guessed at, nor even remotely *conceived of*, what actually transpired in that tiny triangular plaza just west of downtown Dallas.

* * *

None of JFK's assassins have ever faced justice.

Not yet.

But quite a number of them (active participants as well as key material witnesses with vital pertinent knowledge) ***are still alive;*** are still living inside the United States; and are still drawing their U. S. government pensions – *all paid for with your tax dollars.*

As of 2023, at least a dozen men with crucial knowledge are still here.

One of them lives in Ohio.

Some live in Colorado.

Several live in Texas.

Several live in California.

The federal government knows their names, knows their addresses, knows who they are, and knows *what they did* in November 1963.

The *real* story of what happened right there in Dealey Plaza itself.

The true story of that violent, public, noontime assassination.

* * *

My next major book will fearlessly *tell* that shocking true story – the story of those ***36 seconds*** (not just "six" seconds!)[1407] in the bloody Dallas kill zone – in vivid,

---

[1407] Author's exclusive original discovery.

rigorously documented, jaw-dropping detail, for the very first time anywhere. It will utterly destroy all your erroneous misconceptions and will reveal a dramatically *different* story – a story which is infinitely more accurate, infinitely more precise, infinitely more vivid and infinitely more stunning.

A story called the truth.

And when you have finished carefully reading this two-volume book *as well as* that second major book, **in that order,** you will *finally* know (for the very first time) many of the principal pertinent facts about the very worst political crime ever perpetrated in American history:

The coup that slaughtered democracy.

The coup that launched a massive war.

The coup that led to the slaughter of *nine million people.*

The coup that demonstrated and exposed this country's total vulnerability to the fearsome plans of grim, determined, evil men.

The bloody coup of November 1963.

Be advised, my fellow citizens, that the stunning truth about *what actually occurred at 12:30 p.m. Central time in Dealey Plaza itself* is ghastly, astonishing, bloody, overwhelming and completely unexpected.

Don't say I didn't warn you.

SEAN FETTER

American historian & investigative journalist
Somewhere in America
Autumn, 2023

"When a great truth
once gets abroad in the world,
no power on earth can imprison it,
or prescribe its limits,
or suppress it.

It is bound to go on 'til it becomes
the thought of the world . . .
and be supported at last
by a great cloud of witnesses,
which no man can number
and no power can withstand."

– Frederick Douglass

Sources

What follows is not a conventional, generic and stultifying "bibliography" of every single source that I have ever seen, read, studied, perused, examined or considered over the course of 40 years (thus far!) while investigating the assassination of President Kennedy.

Nor is it intended to be.

The items below are those *specifically referred to in this book.*

Sources for *Under Cover of Night* fall into the following twelve categories:

1. Author's Witness Interviews

2. Document Collections

3. Presidential, Vice Presidential and other White House Files

4. Oral Histories

5. Wire Services

6. Newspapers

7. Magazines & Journals

8. Photographs

9. Film & Video Footage

10. Audio Recordings

11. Written Correspondence

12. Books

Be advised:

Unlike all the most well-known, bloated, dishonest American corporate "media" outlets[1408] (and many other lesser writers[1409]), *I do **not** grant anonymity or pseudonymity to my interview sources.*

I do not *ever* ask any reader of mine to simply "trust" in the existence of – let alone the accuracy of – invisible "unnamed sources" who allegedly held unspecified jobs in unidentified agencies.

Instead, **all** of the quotes and the stunning new data in this book – whether from military or civilian sources – come from real people who are clearly and promptly identified by name and by organizational affiliation.

Also note:

The massive totality of what I know – and what I have *personally discovered* – about the 1963 assassination of John F. Kennedy simply cannot fit between the covers of *any* single book, no matter how large.

I have several important *additional* major works scheduled for publication – works which are *already* in progress and well underway.

When I have completed the writing of those works which include and cite information from my large *personal* collection of JFK assassination research materials, then those JFK research materials of mine – including detailed witness interview notes, letters, documents, charts, memoranda, photos and other items – will be made available for detailed study by others via a publicly accessible institution such as a university library, a presidential library, an online collection, and/or another suitable archive (possibly several, in all) selected by me.

Public announcement of the availability of those materials for research will be made at that time. And anyone examining those materials will *immediately* note the extraordinarily rigorous accuracy, care, depth and sterling precision of my work.

Sean Fetter

[1408] Including but not limited to ABC, CBS, CNN, FOX, NBC, the *New York Times,* the *Washington Post,* et. al.

Notice that I do not refer to corporate media outlets as entities which practice actual *journalism.*

[1409] Including the abysmal Robert Dallek and the very disturbing individual who used the *alias* "David S. Lifton" [*sic*].

Author's Witness Interviews

The witnesses noted and quoted herein were and are, by far, the most valuable and important sources of vital *new* information from which I have successfully extracted the truth about the assassination of President Kennedy.

Note that in the following pages I list *only* those witnesses – both military and civilian – whom I contacted *in connection with this specific book.*

(For the record, I have also conducted many *additional* interviews with many *additional* witnesses – both military and civilian – whose accounts will be featured in *additional* future works of mine on the subject of the JFK assassination.)

These witnesses are profoundly important because the undeniable truth is that *most real history never gets written down at all, by anyone,* and therefore by definition, the most significant things in human experience reside in the memories of participants and witnesses – not in truncated notes, brief memoranda, carefully sanitized "official" statements or in saccharine, consciously bowdlerized "memoirs" designed to cover up major crimes and outrages.

Most lawyers, pundits and other forms of noxious pond scum love to loudly denigrate witnesses and metaphorically defecate on their supposed "unreliability." Yet the entire American legal system continues to rest on the foundation of witness testimony – encouraged and approved and relied upon every single day by *those very same* lawyers, pundits, and other forms of noxious pond scum. Even documents and other "physical" evidentiary materials presented in legal cases must always be described and characterized and attested to by *human* witnesses.

Thus it is patently clear that the supercilious dismissal of witnesses' accounts is a disgustingly hypocritical form of cheap intellectual nihilism – always employed in the service of the state and in the protection of its most criminal personnel.

The thin treacle which passes for "justice" and conventional "history" in the United States of America is just a partisan team game played by utterly disreputable advocates – not a genuine, sincere search for *the truth.* The results are as predictable as they are horrifying: honest witnesses who dare to voice dangerous realities are vilified, scorned, marginalized, defamed and ignored; conversely, dishonest accomplices who lie and willingly commit perjury and knowingly support false official narratives are praised, rewarded, enriched and protected.

But contrary to the pompous assertions and endless whining of the noxious pond scum, witness observations and recollections are *not* inherently invalid or untrustworthy. Quite the opposite!

The fact is that *witnesses* are not unreliable; rather, *unreliable* witnesses are unreliable.

And "unreliable witnesses" include *witnesses who are themselves criminals* – particularly, guilty-but-not-yet-unindicted civilian officials, and military officers, and law enforcement personnel, and government security agents, who wear suits and ties and uniforms and ribbons and medals and badges and guns. These oh-so-"official" witnesses – who are often *deeply involved in the very crimes which they speak about so pompously and vacuously and falsely* – are indisputably the most unreliable of all, and merit the most skepticism and scrutiny.

The noxious pond scum never admit that central truth.

Witnesses are *crucial,* particularly to the resolution of a case of such monumental importance.

Yet consider this stunning fact:

None of the witnesses whom I interviewed for this book were ever called to testify by the Johnson Commission in the 1960s; or by the House Select Committee on Assassinations (HSCA) in the 1970s; or by the Assassination Records Review Board (ARRB) in the 1990s.

None of them.

Zero.

Not one!

Moreover, many of these witnesses have never been interviewed by *anyone else, either* – no writer, historian, journalist, or independent JFK investigator has ever spoken with many of these people.

Despite their professional roles and their physical proximity to President Kennedy, these vital witnesses were utterly *ignored* by the federal government (obsessed with framing Lee Oswald), by corporate media (obsessed with defaming Lee Oswald), and by JFK researchers (obsessed with blaming the CIA). It is frankly an outrage that scores of people – including uniformed U. S. military personnel, with high-level security clearances, on active duty! – were completely omitted from consideration despite their impeccable credibility and their indisputable presence in Dallas before, during and after the murder of the president they served.

Some of these vital witnesses are now dead – meaning that my exclusive, groundbreaking interviews of them are literally the *only* historical record of their observations and experiences on November 22nd, 1963.

* * *

You can ***never*** – repeat, ***never*** – get to the truth by relying solely upon documents or memoranda or "official" statements about important events. You must also probe *the lived experiences of those who were there* – always conscious that the person whom you are interviewing may in fact turn out to be a criminal conspirator himself.

1021

A further irony is the fact that much of the best, most valuable information comes from witnesses who simply *do not realize what they are revealing* when they give matter-of-fact answers to key questions. Time and again, men and women who were there on November 22nd casually revealed to me items of astounding importance *without the slightest awareness of how much they were disclosing.* Thanks to my careful research and extensive preparation, I immediately realized the significance of their words – and was therefore prepared to grasp and understand the chilling meaning of what they had said, and thereby advance my analysis of the JFK case.

* * *

Many of the most important words and actions committed by people are never reduced to fixed form.

Documents rarely capture the totality of an event.

Photos do not always depict salient details.

And that is why the boring, shallow, inherently oxymoronic fiction which masquerades as official and semi-official "history" in America never even *approaches* the actual truth. Most of the fading Establishment clowns who pose as "historians" (nausea-inducing figures, all) know virtually nothing; understand even less; and clearly lack the integrity, honesty, courage or willingness to even *consider* doing any serious, substantive, meaningful work on this vital subject.

USAF WITNESSES

Interviewed by Sean Fetter (in many cases, interviewed *repeatedly*)
in person, by phone, by postal mail, and/or via e-mail.

Note carefully:

I myself first identified, located and interviewed many of these vital military witnesses completely on my own.

In a number of cases, *no one else – **no one** – had ever questioned them* about the events of November 1963.

Many of these individuals were and are completely unknown to **ALL** previous writers, government investigators, corporate "journalists," academics, and all JFK researchers who have ever studied the 1963 Kennedy assassination.

Note further:

This is **not** a complete list of **all** persons interviewed by me in the course of my 39-plus years (thus far) of investigating the JFK assassination. Rather, it is merely a list of those USAF veterans whom I spoke with in connection with the *Air Force* aspects of the JFK case, and other closely related matters specifically covered in this book.

AIR FORCE ONE:

SAM 26000

- Pilot: James B. Swindal

- Co-Pilot: Lewis "Swede" Hanson

- Flight Engineer: William Joseph "Joe" Chappell

- Steward: Robert S. "Mac" MacMillan

- Steward: John Hames

- Steward: Joe Ayres

- Air Police: Wyatt Broom

- Air Police: Charles Ruberg

AIR FORCE TWO:
SAM 86970

- Pilot: Joe Sofet
- Flight Engineer: Deroy Cain
- Navigator: Chuck Rogers
- Steward: Earl Sloan
- Steward: Ronnie Gaskill
- Steward: Paul Glynn

(Aide and Valet to Lyndon Baines Johnson)

- Steward: Ken Gaddis

(Aide and Valet to Lyndon Baines Johnson)

JETSTAR:

- James U. Cross

    Pilot and covert operative for Lyndon Baines Johnson;
    Handled multi-million-dollar presidential slush fund;
    Rejected release of AF-1 tapes from November 22nd

- Donald Short
- Paul Thornhill

ANDREWS AIR FORCE BASE:

1001st Air Base Wing:

- John Wetherell

1002nd Air Police Squadron:

- Robert T. Best

  (Colonel in charge of "security" arrangements at Andrews AFB
  for AF-1's return on the evening of 11/22/1963)

1000th Airborne Command and Control Squadron (ACCS):

- Raymond Judy – NEACP (Nightwatch) Radio Operator
- Thomas Michl – NEACP (Nightwatch) Radio Operator

1254th Air Transport Wing:

- John Alexander
- Jim "Moose" Amos
- Jack Birkenstock
- Melvin Carlton
- Richard Claire Johnson
- Frank Elam
- Joe Geiger
- Leon McRae
- Crafton L. Monk
- Joseph T. Milloy
- Ray Pascoe
- Robert Reed
- Ken Stophel
- Billy Sullivan
- Lyle Thomas
- Tom Webb

1254th Air Police Squadron:

- Wyatt Broom
- Tom Furner
- Ernest Graves
- Richard McFadden
- Murray Orvin
- Charles Ruberg

STRATEGIC AIR COMMAND:

SAC Personnel:

- Robert C. Amos
- James Bradley
- Kenneth Brown
- Philip Eramo
- Robert Frank, Jr.
- Dave Gates
- James Hoopaw
- Wayne Pittman
- Michael Snyder
- Fred Welker
- Vince Young

(One SAC interview was canceled due to a medical emergency)

OTHER MILITARY WITNESSES

Interviewed (in some cases, *repeatedly*) by Sean Fetter

BETHESDA NAVAL HOSPITAL

National Naval Medical Center – Bethesda, Maryland

- J. Thornton Boswell, USN

- Jerrol Custer, USN

- Dennis David, USN

- James Joseph Humes, USN

- James Curtis Jenkins, USN

- Paul Kelly O'Connor, USN

- Donald Rebentisch, USN

PENTAGON

General Victor Harold Krulak, USMC

Special Assistant for Counterinsurgency and Special Activities (SACSA)

for the Joint Chiefs of Staff

WHITE HOUSE

Major Harold R. Patterson, USA

White House Communications Agency (WHCA) – Situation Room on 11/22/1963

GOVERNMENT WITNESSES

Interviewed (in some cases, *repeatedly*) by Sean Fetter.

McGeorge Bundy
Former National Security Adviser to JFK and LBJ

Robert Strange McNamara
Former Secretary of Defense
Kennedy administration and Johnson administration

Terry Sanford
Former Governor of North Carolina

James W. Sibert
Former Special Agent of the FBI

CIVILIAN WITNESSES

Interviewed (in some cases, *repeatedly*) by Sean Fetter.

Mrs. Jan Amos
Former wife of Lt. Colonel William H. Amos, USAF
(Amos was stationed in Rome in 1969)

Mr. Sid Davis
Former White House Correspondent
Westinghouse Broadcasting Corporation

Dr. Thomas Tsunetomi Noguchi
Former Chief Medical Examiner-Coroner
for the County of Los Angeles, California

Mrs. Kari-Mette Pigmans (*nee* Steiner)
Pan American Airways purser and crew member
Presidential 707 press plane – Love Field & Andrews AFB

Mrs. Ophelia Odene Pool (*nee* Crossley)
Widow of Nathan Pool
Otis Elevator Company technician at Parkland Hospital

Mr. Aubrey Lee ("Al") Rike
Oneal Funeral Home employee; Dallas ambulance driver
Dealey Plaza & Parkland Hospital

Mr. Norman Similas
Dealey Plaza eyewitness and photographer
Ontario, Canada

Mr. Richard Morehead
Journalist
Austin, Texas

Documents & Records Collections

You can *never* – repeat, *never* – get to the full truth about important events (particularly important *recent* events, which occurred *within living memory*) by relying *solely* on documents (regardless of whether they consist of memoranda, reports, letters, affidavits, or any other "official" statements).

Yet strangely, it is embarrassingly obvious that all conventional "historians" of the past fifty years rely *far* too much on documents – and in particular, on "official" documents (which often simply means *lies put on paper in written form by people with titles*).

One pathetic but glaringly obvious reason for this unprofessional and unseemly paper fetish, of course, is the fact that *documents cannot sue "historians."*

By placing overweening emphasis on documents above all else, conventional hacks masquerading as historians avoid the intensive labor of actually finding and interviewing witnesses, assiduously analyzing their statements, and coming to grips with unpleasant, disturbing, perplexing and shocking new paradigms.

Documents are regarded by lazy fools as "safe" and therefore "non-problematical."

Documents are wrongly regarded as "authoritative" if they are non-controversial, but are quietly *ignored* if they reveal dangerous truths.

Documents, according to most conventional "historians," conveniently eliminate the need for actually *thinking*.

The reality is different.

* * *

History is *life*.

Therefore, thoughts, emotions, words and actions are the basis of history.

Not documents; *thoughts, emotions, words and actions*.

Thoughts, emotions, words and actions often tellingly reveal motivations.

Documents, on the other hand, are consciously (and unconsciously) constructed by their authors, often with the benefit of time and distance and calculation; and often with nefarious agendas. Documents often *hide* the truth, truncate the truth, distort the truth, compress the truth or suppress the truth entirely – when they do not actively *lie* about what really occurred.

Rarely, documents reveal something *inadvertently* – and such items can be extremely valuable.

But documents hardly deserve the drooling lust which conventional chroniclers invariably exhibit.

The bizarre fetish for documents displayed by academic lightweights and journalistic lightweights is a pathetic trend which infects virtually all who write about past and present events.

The panting exaltation of "Documents" is both illegitimate and unwise.

There are gutter-level practical considerations supporting the fetish, as well.

Documents themselves cannot sue you.

And quoting documents – in particular, quoting "official" documents – rarely leads to the filing of defamation cases.

So cowardly writers and professors have a lot of incentive to continue (and worsen) their fetishization of documents – which are certainly not "holy writ."

You can hear the whining already, of course – "But what about when all the witnesses are already dead?"

Then your retelling of those events is, by definition, inherently incomplete and inherently inaccurate.

* * *

The truth is that documents are generally only *adjuncts* to – not a replacement for – witness experiences.

Documents possess no inherent accuracy or reliability, nor any sacred properties whatsoever.

They're just documents.

The point is that all relevant evidence, whatever its source or type, must be scrutinized and evaluated in order to assess its accuracy and validity. The mere fact that a high government official or a police officer says something (or writes something, or dictates something to a secretary or a dictabelt device) is no proof at all that it is correct, dependable or complete.

Documents are no more or less reliable than any other form of evidence.

Documents can be wholly or partly false.

Documents can be erroneous.

Documents can be misleading.

Documents (or their writers) can be mistaken.

Documents can be woefully incomplete.

Documents can be forged.

Documents can be altered.

Documents can be rewritten and replaced.

Documents can be created and substituted for dangerous original papers.

Documents can be censored, redacted, or totally suppressed.

Documents can be burned, shredded, or otherwise destroyed.

Documents can be "rendered unavailable."

Documents can promulgate biased, distorted versions of events.

But sometimes, when created by honest persons, documents can shed important additional light on witness recollections. Sometimes, documents serve to demolish erroneous scenarios created by lesser investigators. Sometimes, documents legitimately and significantly augment witness testimony, photographs and other useful evidence.

In some cases – just as innocent witnesses can inadvertently reveal major evidence – seemingly "innocuous" documents can inadvertently reveal major evidence as well.

Extraordinary evidence.

And when that occurs, it behooves everyone to take notice.

I certainly did.

Documents and records collections which I consulted during my lengthy research for *Under Cover of Night* include the following:

AIR FORCE HISTORICAL RESEARCH AGENCY (AFHRA)
Located at Maxwell Air Force Base, Montgomery, Alabama
Records of the 1254th Air Transport Wing
Records of the 1001st Air Base Wing

ASSASSINATION RECORDS REVIEW BOARD
Part of the JFK Records Collection held at Suitland, Maryland
- 1963 Autopsy document generated on November 22nd by
    Gawler's Funeral Home, Washington, D.C.
- 1963 USMC Report by Sgt. Roger Boyajian documenting
    the early arrival of JFK's body at the Bethesda morgue on November 22nd
- Transcripts of ARRB witness interviews and sworn testimony
- Drawings and diagrams created by ARRB witnesses

THE AMERICAN BOTTLERS OF CARBONATED BEVERAGES
(The "American Bottlers of Carbonated Beverages" was its original name from 1919 to 1966;
it was renamed the "National Soft Drink Association" in 1966;
it was renamed the "American Beverage Association" in 2004)
Located in Washington, D. C.
Printed and written materials pertaining to their November 1963 convention in Dallas, Texas

Dallas County Elections Department
Located in Dallas, Texas

DEPARTMENT OF DEFENSE
Located in Virginia
Military Orders, 1963
Joint Chiefs of Staff; SACSA

FEDERAL BUREAU OF INVESTIGATION
Located in Washington, D.C.
Reports of Special Agents James W. Sibert and Francis X. O'Neill

"HISTORY MATTERS" WEB SITE
(Reference collection of Johnson Commission and HSCA records)

HOUSE SELECT COMMITTEE ON ASSASSINATIONS
Part of the JFK Records Collection held at Suitland, Maryland
- Witness interviews
- Witness diagrams

MARY FERRELL FOUNDATION WEB SITE
(Reference collection of Johnson Commission and HSCA records)

NORTH CAROLINA STATE ARCHIVES
Located in Raleigh, North Carolina
Department of Cultural Resources
Division of Archives and History
Archives and Records Section
Records Services Branch

THE NATIONAL SECURITY ARCHIVE
Located in Washington, D. C.
George Washington University
https://nsarchive.gwu.edu/

SAM RAYBURN LIBRARY
Located in Bonham, Texas
Letters pertaining to U. S. military members and discharges

RICE UNIVERSITY
Located in Houston, Texas
Albert Thomas Papers

PETER RUPAY ARCHIVE
Analyses, essays, e-mails, letters, certificates, receipts and reports

TEXAS STATE LIBRARY AND ARCHIVES
Located in Austin, Texas

UNITED STATES AIR FORCE
Additional materials available online at *af.mil*

UNIVERSITY OF NORTH TEXAS
Located in Denton, Texas

WESLEYAN UNIVERSITY LIBRARY
Located in Middlebury, Connecticut
Papers of William Manchester, relating to his 1967 book *Death of a President*
(Many still subject to redaction, censorship and outright suppression until the year 2067)

Presidential, Vice Presidential and other White House Files

JFK PRESIDENTIAL LIBRARY

Located in Boston, Massachusetts

- Papers of John F. Kennedy. Pre-Presidential Papers
  - ➤ Presidential Campaign Files, 1960
- Papers of John F. Kennedy
  - ➤ Presidential Papers. President's Office Files
  - ➤ Presidential Papers. National Security Files
- Papers of USAF Brigadier General Godfrey McHugh
- Papers of Ralph Dungan
- Papers of Jacquelyn Kennedy
- Papers of Robert Kennedy
- Papers of Hyman Raskin
- White House Central file
- White House Chronological file
- White House Country file – Cuba
- White House Country file – Vietnam
- USAF files

LBJ PRESIDENTIAL LIBRARY

Located in Austin, Texas

- Lyndon Johnson Vice-Presidential Daily Diary
- Lyndon Johnson Presidential Daily Diary
- Texas Trip files
- National Security files
- Country files
- USAF files

Oral Histories

JFK PRESIDENTIAL LIBRARY

Located in Boston, Massachusetts

Oral History – Roger Hilsman

Oral History – Robert Kennedy

Oral History – Earle Wheeler

LBJ PRESIDENTIAL LIBRARY

Located in Austin, Texas

Oral History – General Curtis Emerson LeMay, USAF

UNITED STATES AIR FORCE

Oral History – General Horace M. Wade, USAF

Wire Services

- Agence France-Presse
- Associated Press
- Reuters
- United Press International

Newspapers

- *Air Force Times*
- *Stars and Stripes*
- The *Arizona Daily Star*
- The (Temple, Texas) *Armored Sentinel*
- The *Austin American-Statesman*
- The *Baltimore Sun*
- The *Buffalo News*
- The *Chicago Daily News*
- The *Chicago Sun-Times*
- The *Chicago Tribune*
- Th Colorado Springs *Gazette*
- The *Dallas Morning News*
- The *Dallas Times Herald*
- The (Meridien, Connecticut) *Morning Record*
- The *New York Herald-Tribune*
- The *New York Times*
- The *Ocala* (Florida) *Star-Banner*
- The *Omaha World-Herald*
- The *Santa Maria* (California) *Times*
- The *Stillwater* (Minnesota) *Gazette*
- The *Washington Post*

Magazines & Journals

- *Air Force*
- *Air & Space*
- *Airman*
- *American Journal of Forensic Medicine and Pathology*
- *Consortium News*
- *D Magazine*
- *Esquire*
- *Gentleman's Quarterly*
- *Harper's*
- *Leatherneck (Magazine of the Marines)*
- *LIFE*
- *LOOK*
- *Minority of One*
- *Newsweek*
- *People*
- *Politico*
- *Regardie's*
- *Salon*
- *Skeptic*
- *Slate*
- *The Atlantic*
- *The New Republic*
- *The New Yorker*
- *The Saturday Evening Post*
- *The Texas Monthly*
- *The Texas Observer*
- *The Washington Monthly*
- *The Washingtonian*
- *TIME*
- University of North Texas *North Texan*
- *U. S. News & World Report*
- *Vanity Fair*

Photographs

With one exception, the images reproduced in this book are *all* in the public domain, and the overwhelming majority of them come from a variety of U. S. government archives.

The author's portrait was taken by Beth Klaisner, and it is a copyrighted image used by permission of the photographer.

In the course of researching and writing *Under Cover of Night,* I examined and analyzed more than 45,000 pertinent images which were created by, or are held by, the following individuals, entities, commercial organizations, and governmental units:

- Author's original photographs
- James Altgeld
- Associated Press
- Assassination Records Review Board
- *Baltimore Sun*
- Robert Croft
- *Dallas Morning News*
- *Dallas Times Herald*
- Dutch National Archives
- Federal Bureau of Investigation
- Florida's State Library and Archives
- Bernard Gotfryd
- Imperial War Museum
- JFK Presidential Library
- Robert Knudsen
- LBJ Presidential Library
- Dan Lewis
- Library of Congress
- *Life* Magazine
- *Look* Magazine
- Mary Moorman

- National Aeronautics and Space Administration
- National Archives
- National Museum of the United States Air Force
- National Park Service
- Justin Newman
- Yoichi Okamoto
- Rayburn Library
- Abby Rowe
- Peter Rupay Archive
- Harold Sellers
- Cecil Stoughton
- *Texas Monthly* Magazine
- *Texas Observer* Magazine
- *Time* Magazine
- United Press International
- United States Air Force
- United States Army
- United States Coast Guard
- United States Marine Corps
- United States Navy
- United States Senate
- University of North Texas
- University of Texas
- *U. S. News & World Report* Magazine
- Wesleyan University Library
- Phil Willis

Film and Video Footage

- ABC News
- CBS News
- KRON-TV
- NBC News
- Orville Nix
- Peter Rupay Archive (analytical footage of Dealey Plaza)
- WFAA-TV
- Abraham Zapruder

Audio Recordings

- Air Force One radio tapes, November 22nd, 1963 ("LBJL" and "Clifton" versions)
- JFK Presidential Library
- LBJ Presidential Library
- National Archives
- Peter Rupay Archive (network news coverage, etc.)

Written Correspondence

Written paper mail correspondence with USAF veteran John Hames

Written paper mail and fax correspondence with USAF veteran Robert MacMillan

Written paper mail correspondence with Kari-Mette Pigmans (*nee* Steiner)

E-mail correspondence with SAC veteran Robert C. Amos

E-mail correspondence with SAC veteran James Bradley

E-mail correspondence with SAC veteran Kenneth Brown

E-mail correspondence with SAC veteran Philip Eramo

E-mail correspondence with SAC veteran Robert Frank, Jr.

E-mail correspondence with SAC veteran Dave Gates

E-mail correspondence with SAC veteran James Hoopaw

E-mail correspondence with SAC veteran Wayne Pittman

E-mail correspondence with SAC veteran Michael Snyder

E-mail correspondence with SAC veteran Fred Welker

E-mail correspondence with SAC veteran Vince Young

Memoranda and extensive e-mail correspondence with
leading JFK assassination analyst Peter David Rupay

Written memoranda and paper mail correspondence
with former FBI Special Agent James W. Sibert

Written paper mail correspondence with former Westinghouse Radio
White House correspondent Sid Davis

Books

What follows is a very limited list of books.

Nothing more.

It simply includes books *cited, or specifically referred to,* in this book.

The list of more than 160 books below is not – I repeat, *not* – a conventional and stultifying "bibliography."

It is certainly *not* a comprehensive list of every single book that I have ever read, perused, consulted, studied or considered over the course of 40 years (thus far) while investigating the assassination of President Kennedy.

Nor is it intended to be.

Indeed, the list below constitutes a mere *fraction* of what I have studied.

I have read *many* more books than those which are listed here – a vast number of additional works including, but not even remotely limited to, the Johnson Report itself, plus myriad tomes by a variety of authors ranging from Gerald Ford, David Belin, Larry Sabato, Phil Shenon (and others of their ilk) to Mark Lane, Carl Oglesby, Josiah Thompson, Jim Marrs, Gaeton Fonzi, Noel Twyman (and others of their ilk) – *none of which* are quoted or relied upon or referred to herein, and which are therefore not itemized in the following list.

* * *

Moreover, it is vital to emphasize that the following list of "books cited" is certainly ***not*** a "Recommended Reading" list, nor an "endorsement" of those books.

Not at all.

Indeed, I hasten to warn all readers that the *overwhelming* majority of what has been published *previously* regarding the JFK assassination – by the American government itself; by its moronic and ever-compliant whores in corporate media and academe; and by many well-meaning but less-than-intellectually-stellar JFK assassination researchers – is sheer unadulterated *rubbish* and (equally importantly) *a colossal waste of your precious time.*

The reason that the JFK case has not been satisfactorily solved previously is because of three major factors: (A) massive government perfidy; (B) utter malpractice and blinding incompetence by media corporations and so-called academics; and (C) the fact that generations of lesser JFK researchers foolishly embraced *grossly inferior* products (books, movies, articles, etc.) and then settled into lazy, calcified, extremely limited thought patterns regarding supposed "hypotheses" and "scenarios" and "counter-myths" which bear no resemblance whatsoever to the actual truth about President Kennedy's brutal 1963 murder.

All previous JFK assassination books contain major errors.

There is no polite way to say that; nor is there any reason not to do so.

All previous JFK assassination books contain major errors.

Thus what follows is simply a list of various books whose JFK-assassination-related narratives are often screamingly incomplete, incorrect, inadequate and/or misleading, but which (ironically) *happen to contain* a few nuggets of genuinely useful information here and there – scattered data points which previous authors mentioned or included but failed to understand accurately, failed to examine intelligently, and failed to place in their proper context in relation to what happened in Dallas in 1963.

Unlike those prior authors, I made my own major, exclusive, independent and totally original discoveries about the JFK case and also correctly recognized, analyzed and extracted pertinent evidentiary fragments of previously published data points to add to my new, accurate, correct narrative – and thus for the first time assembled and integrated those data points properly; explained their true significance; and highlighted their actual meaning and relevance to the real story of John Kennedy's brutal assassination.

I wish to emphasize that I have taken *particular* joy in finding pertinent data points that were buried within specious, superficial, soporific, intellectually insulting "lone-gunman" screeds which were created by appallingly lazy, dishonest, thoroughly conventional Establishment hacks who have foolishly, negligently and obstreperously insisted that "no criminal conspiracy was involved" in President Kennedy's brutal murder – even though their very own tomes include specific material evidence of *precisely* such a plot!

It is long past time for Americans (and everyone else) to abandon shallow, puerile, false and ludicrously inaccurate narratives about the most important political crime in American history.

* * *

Anyone familiar with looking at conventionally formatted, old-style "bibliographies" knows what a tiresome and annoying chore it is to locate a particular book *title* in a jungle of extraneous data – such as the antique, archaic and laughably elitist obsession with "city of publication" and "publisher," which were and are irrelevant to the issue of the actual *truth* (if any) and *quality* (if any) *of the contents*.

The reality is that most people know *book titles* more than any other aspect of the bibliographic data. Moreover, in examining bibliographies or other lists of sources, people are seeking *book titles* more than any other piece of information.

So, for the reader's convenience, I have taken the unusually helpful step of providing *an intelligently designed* list of books cited – a fresh, clear and welcome format featuring first the ***book title,*** then the author's name.

Year of publication is only recorded in certain instances, in order to clearly distinguish between various versions of said books. (Those who wish to pursue an absurdly obsolete, antediluvian fetish for information on those books' *publishers* and *cities of publication* can knock themselves out and pursue that information on their own. I do not care to feed into such a misguided mindset.)

Sean Fetter

Books

(Alphabetically, by book title)

1. *15 Minutes* – L. Douglas Keeney
2. *A Texan Looks at Lyndon* – J. Evetts Haley
3. *A Tribute to John Kennedy* – Pierre Salinger and Sander Vanocur, eds.
4. *A Very Human President* – Jack Valenti
5. *America is in Danger* – Curtis E. LeMay
6. *Among Those Present: A Reporter's View of 25 Years in Washington* – Nancy Hanschman Dickerson (paperback edition)
7. *An Unfinished Life* – Robert Dallek
8. *Angel is Airborne* – James U. Cross, USAF retired (Cross's original *typed* manuscript version of his book, which was later revised and edited and published commercially as *Around the World with LBJ*)
9. *Another Vietnam* – Tim Page
10. *Around the World with LBJ* – James U. Cross with Denise Gamino and Gary Rice
11. *At the Door of Memory* – Aubrey Rike with Colin McSween
12. *Been There, Done That* – Eddie Fisher with David Fisher
13. *Best Evidence* (book; 1980 hardcover first edition) – Patricia Lambert & Samuel Lifton*
14. *Best Evidence* (book; 1988 trade paperback edition) – Patricia Lambert & Samuel Lifton*
15. *Best Evidence* (typed movie screenplay; soft cover; undated) – Patricia Lambert & Samuel Lifton*[1410]
16. *Between the Signal & the Noise* (online book) – Roger Bruce Feinman, 1993
17. *Bloody Jungle: The War in Vietnam* – Chris Evans
18. *Breach of Trust* – Gerald McKnight
19. *Breaking Cover* – Warren "Bill" Gulley with Mary Ellen Reese
20. *Brothers* – David Talbot
21. *Camelot's Court* – Robert Dallek
22. *Coming Apart* – William L. O'Neill
23. *Command and Control* – Eric Schlosser
24. *Congressman Sam Rayburn* – Anthony Champagne
25. *Conspiracy of Silence* – Charles Crenshaw, MD with Gary Shaw and Jens Hansen
26. *Conversations with Kennedy* – Ben Bradlee
27. *Counselor* – Ted Sorensen

[1410] Samuel D. Lifton used the *alias* "David S. Lifton" [*sic*] for several decades, beginning no later than 1967.

28. *Crime of the Century: The Kennedy Assassination from a Historian's Perspective* – Michael L. Kurtz

29. *The JFK Assassination Debates* – Michael L. Kurtz

30. *Death in Washington: The Murder of Orlando Letelier* – Donald Freed with Fred Landis

31. *Dereliction of Duty* – H. R. McMasters

32. *Dereliction of Duty* – Robert "Buzz" Patterson

33. *Design for Survival* – Thomas S. Power and Albert A. Arnhym

34. *Destiny Betrayed* (1992 edition) – James DiEugenio

35. *Destiny Betrayed* (2012 edition) – James DiEugenio

36. *Development of Strategic Air Command 1946-1976* – J. C. Hopkins with Sheldon A. Goldberg

37. *Doomsday Delayed* – John H. Rubel

38. *Eddie Adams Vietnam* – Alyssa Adams

39. *Eddie Barker's Notebook* – Eddie Barker

40. *Family of Secrets* – Russ Baker

41. *Flawed Giant* – Robert Dallek

42. *From Love Field: Our Final Hours with President John F. Kennedy* – Nellie Connally with Mickey Herskowitz

43. *Grace and Power: The Private World of the Kennedy White House* – Sally Bedell Smith

44. *Headquarters Strategic Air Command Key Personnel: 1946-1990* – Office of the Historian, HQ SAC

45. *Hearings and Exhibits of the President's Commission on the Assassination of President Kennedy* (26 volumes) – U. S. Government

46. *House of War* – James Carroll

47. *Hindenburg* (1962) – A. A. Hoehling

48. *In History's Shadow* – John Connally with Mickey Herskowitz

49. *Inside* – Joseph Califano

50. *Inside the ARRB* (five volumes, paperback) – Douglas Horne

51. *Iron Eagle: The Turbulent Life of General Curtis LeMay* – Thomas M. Coffey

52. *Is That Something the Crew Should Know?* – Lyle Don Clawson, USAF Retired

53. *JFK and LBJ* – Tom Wicker

54. *JFK and the Unspeakable* – James Douglass

55. *JFK and Vietnam* – John Newman

56. *JFK Assassination File* – Jesse Curry

57. *JFK: Conspiracy of Silence* (paperback edition) – Charles Crenshaw, MD with Jens Hansen and J. Gary Shaw

58. *JFK Has Been Shot* (paperback edition) – Charles Crenshaw, MD with Jens Hansen and J. Gary Shaw

59. *JFK: Remembering Jack* – Christophe Loviny and Vincent Touze
60. *JFK: The Cuba Files* – Fabian Escalante
61. *JFK: The Last Dissenting Witness* – Bill Sloan with Jean Hill
62. *JFK: The Memories* – Cecil Stoughton, Chester Clifton, Hugh Sidey
63. *John F. Kennedy and the Race to the Moon* – John M. Logsdon
64. *John F. Kennedy, President* – Hugh Sidey
65. *Johnny, We Hardly Knew Ye* – Kenneth O'Donnell and Dave Powers
66. *Judge for Yourself* (paper-bound) – John Judge
67. *Kennedy* – Ted Sorensen
68. *Kennedy and Johnson* – Evelyn Lincoln
69. *Kennedy Without Tears* – Tom Wicker
70. *Killing the Truth* – Harrison Livingstone
71. *LeMay* – Barrett Tillman
72. *Lemay: The Life and Wars of General Curtis LeMay* – Warren Kozak
73. *Let Us Begin Anew* (paperback edition) – Strobel & Strobel
74. *Lone Star Leaders* – James W. Riddlesperger, Jr. and Anthony Champagne
75. *Lone Star Rising* – Robert Dallek
76. *LBJ: An Irreverent Biography* – Booth Mooney
77. *LBJ: Architect of American Ambition* – Randall Woods
78. *Lyndon: An Oral Biography* – Merle Miller
79. *Lyndon Johnson and the American Dream* (paperback edition) – Doris Kearns
80. *Mission With LeMay* – Curtis LeMay and MacKinlay Kantor
81. *Mr. Sam* – Dwight Dorough
82. *Murder From Within* (original paperbound 1974 edition) – Fred Newcomb & Perry Adams
83. *Murder From Within* (commercial paperback 2011 edition) – Fred Newcomb & Perry Adams
84. *Mutual Contempt* – Jeff Shesol
85. *Nam: A Photographic History* – Leo J. Daugherty and Gregory Louis Mattson
86. *Night of Camp David* – Fletcher Knebel (novel about LBJ)
87. *No More Silence* – Larry Sneed
88. *Official and Confidential* – Anthony Summers
89. *Once Upon a Secret* – Mimi Alford
90. *Oswald: Assassin or Fall Guy* – Joachim Joesten
91. *Palimpsest* – Gore Vidal
92. *Patriots: The Vietnam War Remembered from All Sides* – Christian G. Appy
93. *Pay Any Price: Lyndon Johnson and the Wars for Vietnam* – Lloyd C. Gardner
94. *Portrait of Camelot* – Richard Reeves
95. *Postmortem* (paperback) – Harold Weisberg

96. *Power Beyond Reason: The Mental Collapse of Lyndon Johnson* – D. Jablow Hertzman
97. *President Kennedy: Profile of Power* – Richard Reeves
98. *Protect and Defend* – Jack Valenti (thinly disguised novel about LBJ and JFK)
99. *P. S.: A Memoir* – Pierre Salinger
100. *Reasonable Doubt* – Henry Hurt
101. *Remembering America: A Voice from the Sixties* – Richard Goodwin
102. *Remembering Jack* – Jacques Lowe
103. *Requiem* – Horst Faas and Tim Page, eds.
104. *Sam Rayburn* – Alfred Steinberg
105. *Sam Rayburn: A Bio-Bibliography* – Anthony Champagne
106. *Sam Rayburn: Leading the Lawmakers* – Edward Allen
107. *Secret Service Chief* – U. E. Baughman with Leonard Wallace Robinson
108. *Seeds of Destruction* – Ralph Martin Goldberg (*alias* "Ralph G. Martin")
109. *Seven Days in May* – Fletcher Knebel and Charles W. Bailey II
110. *SOG: A Photo History of the Secret Wars* – John L. Plaster
111. *Someone Would Have Talked* – Larry Hancock
112. *Some of it Was Fun* – Nicholas Katzenbach
113. *Sons of Camelot: The Fate of an American Dynasty* – Lawrence Leamer
114. *Strategic Air Command: People, Aircraft and Missiles* (second edition) – Norman Polmar and Timothy M. Laur, eds.
115. *Strategic Air Command: Unit Mission and History Summaries* – Maj. Rita F. Clark, USAF and CMSgt. Herman F. Martin, USAF
116. *Strategic Air Command and the Alert Program: A Brief History* – Dr. Henry M. Narducci
117. *Strategic Air Warfare* – USAF; Richard H. Kohn and Joseph P. Harahan, eds.
118. *Survivor's Guilt* (2013 commercial version of his first book) – Vincent Palamara
119. *The Army and Vietnam* – Andrew F. Krepinevich, Jr.
120. *The Bitter Taste of Glory* – Jack Valenti
121. *The Camera Never Blinks* – Dan Rather with Mickey Herskowitz
122. *The Camera Never Blinks Twice* – Dan Rather with Mickey Herskowitz
123. *The Day Kennedy Was Shot* – Jim Bishop (1968)
124. *The Dark Side of Camelot* – Seymour Hersh
125. *The Death of a President* – William Manchester (1967)
126. *The Development of Strategic Air Command 1946-1986* – J. C. Hopkins and Sheldon A. Goldberg
127. *The Doomsday Machine* – Daniel Ellsberg
128. *The Fighting Pattons* – Brian M. Sobel
129. *The Girl on the Stairs* – Barry Ernest

130.   *The JFK Assassination Debates* – Michael L. Kurtz

131.   *The Kennedy Mystique* – Jon Goodman

132.   *The Kennedy Years* – The Staff of the New York Times

133.   *The Man on Horseback: The Role of the Military in Politics* (second edition) – S. E. Finer

134.   *The Making of the President 1960* – Theodore White

135.   *The Making of the President 1964* – Theodore White

136.   *The Murder of Allende (and the End of the Chilean Way to Socialism)* – Robinson Rojas Sandford

137.   *The Politician* – Ronnie Dugger

138.   *The Politics of Deception* – Patrick J. Sloyan

139.   *The Rise of American Air Power: The Creation of Armageddon* – Michael Sherry

140.   *The Road to Camelot: Inside JFK's Five-Year Campaign* – Thomas Oliphant and Curtis Wilkie

141.   *The Speaker's Agent* – Valton J. Young

142.   *The Spy Who Loved Us* – Thomas A. Bass

143.   *The Texas Connection* – Craig Zirbel

144.   *The Third Alternative* (original 1990s-era typescript, paperbound version) – Vincent Palamara

145.   *The Thirty-first of March: An Intimate Portrait of Lyndon Johnson's Final Days in Office* – Horace Busby

146.   *The Truth About the Assassination* – Charles Roberts

147.   *The Vantage Point* – Lyndon Baines Johnson

148.   *The Vietnam Photo Book* – Mark Jury

149.   *The Vietnam War: The Story and the Photographs* – Donald M. Goldstein, Katherine V. Dillon and J. Michael Wenger

150.   *The Washington Payoff: An Insider's View of Corruption in Government* – Robert N. Winter-Berger

151.   *The Wizards of Armageddon* – Fred Kaplan

152.   *The Year of the People* – Eugene McCarthy

153.   *They Call It Intelligence* – Joachim Joesten

154.   *This Time, This Place: My Life in War, the White House, and Hollywood* – Jack Valenti

155.   *Tim Page's Nam* – Tim Page

156.   *To Move a Nation* – Roger Hilsman

157.   *Turbulent Years: The '60s* – The editors of TIME/LIFE Books

158.   *Under Fire* – Catherine Leroy, editor

159.   *Under the Radar During Camelot* – Layte Bowden

160.   *Vietnam* – IFCP

161.   *Vietnam* – Larry Burrows
162.   *Vietnam: The Real War* – Associated Press
163.   *We Were There: Revelations from the Dallas Doctors Who Attended to JFK on November 22, 1963* – Allen Childs, MD (editor)
164.   *With Kennedy* – Pierre Salinger
165.   *Words on War* – Jay M. Shafritz (editor)
166.   *Yours Faithfully, Bertrand Russell* – Bertrand Russell

SEAN FETTER

Acknowledgments

As of the publication of this book in late 2023, my own intensive study, research, investigation and analysis of the JFK assassination have now (so far!) spanned 40 years – the last several of which overlapped with the actual writing of *Under Cover of Night.*

For the record, I am the sole author of this book.

Period.

No one else had a hand in writing it.

I had no co-author; no ghost writer; no secret partner; no clandestine collaborator.

No Ted Sorensen; no Patricia Lambert; *no one.*

Moreover, I had no secretary; no office manager; no administrative assistant; no interns; no army of aides; no graduate-student lackeys; no captive cadre of undergrads; no massive platoon of willing helpers; no regiment of unpaid volunteers; no wealthy backers.

I wrote this book while *simultaneously* continuing to actively *investigate* the JFK case; actively *research* the JFK case; actively locate and *interview* additional witnesses; actively obtain documents; and actively *analyze* the data of the JFK case.

* * *

The past several decades have been a fascinating process of hard work and astonishing discovery. Along the way, a number of individuals helped me simply by listening to me, raising questions, and encouraging me. Others provided vital information to me. Still others provided welcome hospitality, friendship, and support. I gratefully acknowledge the assistance of a number of people – not in *writing* this book, which was solely and exclusively *my* gargantuan task, accomplished alone – but in helping in various ways to make it possible.

Yet in the hyper-critical, hyper-partisan, hyper-fanatical, hyper-polarized world which the Internet has spawned and enabled and exacerbated, it is nevertheless necessary to make it clear to all those lesser minds among the media and the public that, in thanking various people below, I am *not* stating that I know of, agree with, or share – much less condone, endorse, concur in, support, or approve of – every single aspect of their politics, or their cultural beliefs, or their religious views, or their social media postings, or their sense of humor, or their public remarks, or their private remarks, or their affiliations, or their associations, or their actions, or anything else.

Moreover, in expressing my sincere appreciation to a number of individuals, I do not intend to express or suggest my concurrence with any (or every) particular notion that they may hold – whether it concerns the JFK case *or any other topic* – nor my agreement with every *aspect* of their particular views on this subject or on any other topic. Nor do I mean to imply that they necessarily subscribe to my own analysis.

I am simply acknowledging the assistance provided by various people during the decades of intense labor which I devoted to my own in-depth research, study, investigation and analysis of the JFK case, and to the writing of this book.

My words and my views are my own.

I will *not* be judged on the words or views or actions or affiliations of others. Period.

* * *

My late father, Dr. Richard Fetter, served in the United States Air Force before it even *was* the "United States Air Force."

He was in uniform overseas when the USAF was still the United States *Army Air Forces* (USAAF), near the end of World War II. And in fact, like most men of his generation, he always referred to his branch of the military as the United States *Army Air Corps*, which was its official designation between 1926 and 1941.

Assigned to classified engineering work on the "fire control systems" (meaning the *electrical gunnery systems*) of giant B-29 bombers, my father was stationed in Nevada before shipping out through Oregon and Hawaii for remote airfields on the islands of Tinian and Saipan as part of the 20th Air Force. He arrived in the Pacific theater of war in 1945, when the conflict was nearly over, and fortunately he saw no combat himself. It was from my father – and through his vivid recollections, both humorous and painful, of his wartime experiences in the distant Mariana Islands – that I first became acquainted with the United States Air Force.

A brilliant and successful scientist with at least *ten* U. S. patents to his credit, Richard "Doc" Fetter, Ph. D., became a consultant for both NASA and the Pentagon – and along the way he learned a number of startling things which have *never* appeared in superficial corporate media narratives or in ordinary, conventional "history" books.

Politically conservative and generally a staunch Republican, my father nevertheless voted for John F. Kennedy in the 1960 presidential election – and as a well-educated, highly intelligent American veteran, an extremely accomplished scientist and a very patriotic citizen who loved his country deeply, my father naturally maintained a lively, open-minded and absolutely *fearless* interest in the real truth about the JFK assassination.

In his gentle way, he taught me from childhood that "the authorities" [*sic*] are rarely correct – and that they are often both *completely idiotic* and *dead wrong*.

He also taught me that there is usually a way to figure out even the most seemingly "insoluble" problem.

Those are two of the most important lessons of my life, and they find vivid expression on every single page of this work.

My father also kept me happily surrounded with many books from a very early age, and he encouraged me by personal example to read widely and deeply – an absolutely *vital* lesson for parents (and children) everywhere. He fostered a burning intellectual curiosity within me which has never diminished, and we had innumerable discussions over the years on a host of complex topics, including the murder of JFK. My father recognized and understood that the "official" story of Dallas was false; like so many other highly intelligent USAAF and USAF veterans across this country, he wanted the truth about 1963.

* * *

The late Benjamin Black Elk – a proud indigenous elder of the Oglala band of the Teton division of the Lakota tribe, who lived in what American occupiers now call "South Dakota" – was the very first person outside my own family whom I *ever* interviewed on *any* historical subject. Ben Black Elk's extraordinary patience, kindness, gentleness, courtesy and generosity to me (as I peppered him with numerous questions) were absolutely inspiring and absolutely unforgettable. I counted him (and still do) as my friend and as a surrogate grandfather.

* * *

An obscure fellow named Archimedes reputedly once said, "Give me a lever and a place to stand, and I will move the world." The extraordinary Lester Schomas and his talented colleague Chuck P. literally gave me a place to stand and an arena for my voice – which has had a profoundly positive, lasting and dramatic impact on my life and on my work.

The late Dr. John L. Clark was a wise, gentle, intelligent and deeply humane individual who personified dignity, class, empathy, kindness and generosity.

The late W. E. "Rick" Linneman hired me for one of my first jobs in journalism; challenged me to totally transform a newspaper; and gave me unlimited opportunity and freedom to write about important subjects of my choosing. Rick also pushed me to explore and tackle unfamiliar topics and to excel in new areas, which was an extremely valuable lesson.

Steve K. was a wise and humorous supervisor, mentor and friend. He taught me a great deal about how the American corporate media *really* function, behind their empty façade of haughty "respectability."

Larry W. listened to me thoughtfully and intelligently – and clearly understood a number of salient points about the JFK assassination – when I discussed those matters with him many years ago at a television "news" network whose senior executives didn't care in the slightest about this central issue.

* * *

In a stunning bit of irony, I owe some disgusted "gratitude" to a truly *awful* individual (who was **not** a source for this book) who shall deservedly remain nameless. During a course ostensibly concerning the 1960s, that person's gross intellectual negligence and despicable irresponsibility were the critical factors which directly drove me to *quit the class in utter disgust,* head over to a library instead, and begin studying the JFK case – in earnest and in great depth – on my own.

* * *

Several incredibly good and truly beautiful women have been absolutely essential to my life and to my work. Their wisdom, intelligence, generosity, kindness and love have made all the difference.

P, an excellent human being, supported and encouraged my interest in the JFK case and graced me with great love and tenderness.

L, a truly wonderful individual, supported my efforts as I labored intensely on my in-depth investigation of the assassination – despite many long, tedious hours of study and my inconvenient trips to far-flung places in order to research the data and meet with many of the witnesses quoted in this book. Without her, this book simply would not exist. Her profound love, goodness, patience, understanding and infinite grace were enormous. In addition, she endured frequent and annoying interruptions by another JFK researcher.

C fortified me with her extraordinary love and affection and goodness as I continued to delve into the mysteries of President Kennedy's assassination.

The final decision to turn my exclusive and original and in-depth Air Force research into a book occurred at the determined urging of one of the most extraordinary human beings it has ever been my privilege to know.

A gave me the encouragement and the love and the energy and the impetus to tackle the gargantuan task of writing this massive book. She often said softly to me, *"Háblame de Kennedy . . ."* Brilliant, practical and focused, she also endured frequent and annoying interruptions by another JFK researcher.

B provided truly astounding help – workspace, technical resources, time, care, love, patience, humor and unreserved backing – as I worked on this manuscript. Smart and perceptive, and an excellent writer in her own right, she offered invaluable advice.

Although not a student of the JFK case herself, she put her brilliant analytical mind to work on several vital matters – and she quickly and independently came up with several truly profound and stunning insights about key aspects of the events of 1963. She also endured frequent and annoying interruptions by another JFK researcher.

* * *

The Air Force Historical Research Agency (AFHRA), located at Maxwell Air Force Base in Montgomery, Alabama, holds vital unit histories and rosters which greatly aided my quest to identify and locate various USAF veterans who knew key pieces of the truth about what really happened to President Kennedy in 1963. My thanks to the AFHRA staff who assisted me in connection with my 1993 research visit, including Marvin Fisher, Lynn Gamma, and Deanne Webb.

* * *

Master Sergeant Tom Pennington, USAF – who was stationed at Andrews Air Force Base in Maryland and was serving as Senior Enlisted Adviser and Acting Historian of the 89th Airlift Wing (successor unit to the 1254th Air Transport Wing) – first informed me of the existence of the SAM FOX Association in 1993, which led to the incredible opportunity to actually attend a triennial SAM FOX reunion in person in 1994 and thereby meet and interview key Air Force veterans who possessed extraordinary knowledge of the real events which took place on November 22nd, 1963.

Lt. Col. Everett C. DeWolfe III, USAF, personally approved my request to attend the 1994 SAM FOX event at Andrews. Hugely important historical discoveries – and major portions of this book – resulted from my 1994 research trip and from my interviews with the many Kennedy-era Air Force veterans whom I met there.

Andrews Air Force Base in Maryland (today called "Joint Base Andrews") was the scene of absolutely crucial and historic incidents on November 22nd and November 23rd, 1963. Thanks to my own initiative and to the vital assistance provided by both active-duty and retired Air Force personnel, I obtained unprecedented access to important areas of the base in 1994 – sometimes at enormous personal risk to myself.

* * *

Writer and reporter Denise Gamino of Texas kindly provided contact information for an important USAF witness, which led to several key interviews.

Barbara Halbert of the Woodson Research Center at the Fondren Library of Rice University in Houston, Texas checked that institution's records and informed me of the massive destruction of the Albert Thomas files.

Barbara Cline of the National Archives and Records Administration, working at the Lyndon Baines Johnson Presidential Library in Austin, Texas, provided prompt, efficient and excellent research service to me as I sought several specific documents of vital importance to this book.

Tina Houston of the LBJ Library provided important witness contact information to me.

Jim Eskin provided information about certain holdings of the LBJ Library, plus information about the Texas trip.

J. Kevin O'Brien of the Federal Bureau of Investigation provided high-quality FBI copies of key documents to me in response to my FOIA records request.

State officials Murray Packer and Mike Unruh scoured official North Carolina records at my request for vital evidence.

Mary Stickley of InterBev provided me with a full copy of the program from the November 1963 American Bottlers of Carbonated Beverages 45th Annual Meeting held in Dallas, Texas.

Leith Johnson of Wesleyan University's Special Collections and Archives in Connecticut was helpful in fulfilling certain document requests relating to the William Manchester papers housed there. While many Manchester documents remain outrageously unavailable *in toto* until January 2067 under terms of an unconscionable contract with the Kennedy family – and while many other items in the Manchester collection are atrociously redacted until then – a few items are currently available in uncensored form, and some of them contained key information which enabled me to radically demolish both the erroneous *conventional* "history" and the erroneous *revisionist* "history" of the JFK assassination.

The staff of the Special Collections Archive at the Colorado State University library provided me with ample access to an authentic ***original*** version of the hugely important, privately published 1974 book *Murder from Within,* which unfortunately was given extremely limited distribution (to government officials, primarily) by its two co-authors at the time of its creation. CSU's copy of *Murder from Within* was located among the papers of a former Colorado congressman.

* * *

Public libraries in Ohio, Colorado and Texas provided information and support, and were highly useful in making a wide variety of books and other materials available for secondary research.

If you are in a position to financially support the public libraries in your area, kindly do so. For the record, I enjoy watching professional sports as much as the next person – but for heaven's sake, when presented with a ballot referendum, vote to fund and prioritize *libraries* over useless absurdities like *stadiums.*

Your children – and their children's children – will thank you.

* * *

Mrs. Ophelia Odene Pool (*nee* Crossley), the gracious widow of crucial Parkland Hospital eyewitness Nathan Burgess Pool, patiently answered numerous questions about her late husband's experiences on November 22nd, 1963, and she clarified several key points for the record.

A proud daughter of Norway, eyewitness Kari-Mette Pigmans (*nee* Steiner) provided priceless insights that have helped to re-write the history of her adopted country, America. Wise, candid, honest and unstintingly generous with her time and recollections over the course of several interviews, the smart and perceptive former Pan Am crew member represents the *thousands* of people who – wittingly or unwittingly – still hold key information about the JFK case.

Dallas native Jan Amos provided extremely detailed testimony about a shocking episode involving high-level USAF knowledge about the assassination of President Kennedy. She gave generously of her time, applauded my in-depth investigative efforts, and enthusiastically urged me to continue to uncover the truth.

* * *

U. S. Navy veterans Paul O'Connor, James Curtis Jenkins, Dennis David, Donald Rebentisch, James Humes and J. Thornton Boswell, all of whom were on duty at Bethesda Naval Hospital on the evening and long night of November 22nd, 1963, were among those who granted me extremely useful and fascinating interviews – more of which will be featured in another upcoming book of mine.

USMC helicopter pilot Neil van Leeuwen ("Nighthawk One") welcomed me to his home in the 1990s and shared his original logbook entry from the night of November 22nd, 1963.

FBI agent James W. Sibert, who attended the formal Bethesda autopsy that night, spoke with me in detail on several occasions and engaged in valuable written correspondence with me as well.

Famed radio newsman Sid Davis, who was the White House correspondent for Westinghouse Radio in 1963 and who rode in the fatal Dallas motorcade, spoke to me at length on multiple occasions and (quite unwittingly!) was a very candid and quite helpful interviewee.

Norman Similas, George Reedy, Senator (and former Governor) Terry Sanford, Dr. Thomas Noguchi, Julian Read, McGeorge Bundy, Robert McNamara *and a great many others* were also interviewed by me during the extensive research that I have conducted thus far on the JFK assassination. Much of what these numerous sources revealed to me will be featured in additional upcoming books by me.

* * *

Actor and activist Ramón Antonio Gerardo Estévez (known professionally worldwide as "Martin Sheen") provided thoughtful, gentle and vital moral support and encouragement in a personal phone call to me at a crucial stage of completing this book – a boost of energy for which I will always be grateful.

Barry Krozel located a very important witness for me and provided me with a copy of an extremely significant 1970s interview, which led directly to a number of vitally important historical breakthroughs by me which dramatically revise the history of the JFK assassination.

Researcher, investigator and author Robert P. Morrow alerted me to a number of pertinent quotations, citations and background information. He also generously provided me with contact information for a vital eyewitness whom he had first discovered so that I could interview her myself subsequently.

John Nagel noted Jesse Curry's statements about the second Dallas coffin.

David Andrews brought the key JFK-Gore Vidal episode to public attention.

Ronald Redmon wrote a pair of highly useful articles about Eugene Dinkin.

John Pike put valuable information about the M48 tank on the FAS.org site.

David T. Ratcliffe has preserved important writings from a variety of independent investigators online at *https://raticle.org*, and has thereby saved many useful treasures. He deserves profound thanks for keeping numerous essays, transcripts and other thought-provoking materials from oblivion. If you have been intellectually gagging on a lousy diet of empty corporate-media sawdust (and frankly, *who hasn't been?*), then visit Dave Ratcliffe's site for a refreshing change.

* * *

Some people are remarkably helpful and generous to friends and acquaintances, both new and old.

Melanie and Donald provided friendship, welcome hospitality and support – and Melanie personally brought extremely important, original 1963 newspaper evidence to my attention.

Arthur and Vickie (and Chloe!) were extremely generous, hospitable hosts. Arthur strongly urged me to forge ahead with this book.

Sarah and Doug (and Molly!) provided vital assistance and welcome hospitality at difficult times.

* * *

Jean and Joseph Weitz gave generously of their time and spoke to me about their recollections concerning the writer William Manchester. The couple's adult son, Leonard Weitz, facilitated the interview and was extremely helpful to me.

The late Charlie Roemer expressed enthusiastic and open-minded interest in my work on the JFK case.

The late Tom Wilson of Oregon (*not* the Tom Wilson known for JFK imagery research, but a different individual) was a generous and very humorous friend whose comic e-mails brightened many difficult days.

* * *

A number of people including Sharon; Phil & Kay; Lowell; Joan; Jamie; Greg; Mark; Brant; and Beth all provided vital support of various kinds that was truly indispensable to the completion of this book. Their assistance helped secure, protect, preserve, organize and make available many irreplaceable JFK research materials.

Elena offered unflagging moral support, interest and consistent encouragement as I labored on my lengthy manuscript. She also promised to be the first in line to purchase the book.

* * *

Arlington Press LLC not only agreed to publish this groundbreaking book, but (unlike most publishers) also guaranteed me the creative freedom and latitude to make sure that it met my expectations visually.

* * *

John Judge, a dedicated historical investigator with encyclopedic knowledge of many dangerous subjects vital to recent U. S. history, was a true American original. A brilliant, bearded iconoclast with a deeply humane spirit, he passed away in early 2014. His wide-ranging and profound research – coupled with an absolutely unflinching ability to stare into the ugly abyss of government horrors, and boldly call them as he saw them – was and remains educational, inspiring and admirable.

Judge was one of the very few truly sophisticated thinkers among JFK assassination researchers, because he stoutly refused to permit fear or conventional thinking to hobble his outstanding mind. We first met in person in Dallas in 1991 – and we met again, and spoke on the telephone on several occasions, between then and 2014. John's perspicacity and boldness, his keen sense of humor and his profound awareness of the absurdity of official government pronouncements were – and remain – a source of great relief and welcome perspective.

* * *

Assassination investigator and longtime Texas educator Kevin T. did extremely important and original JFK research that will be discussed in an upcoming book by me. His valued friendship and support; his laudable energy and terrific sense of humor; and his personal discovery of – and lengthy interviews with – an important witness have been much appreciated and extraordinarily helpful. Kevin also did some very valuable research – on *extremely* short notice! – to locate a key citation.

* * *

Ohio native, U. S. Army veteran, and longtime Texas educator Peter David Rupay possessed one of the finest minds to ever tackle the vexing, complicated subject of what really happened in Dallas in 1963.

Pete was virtually without peer when it came to intelligently and critically analyzing the JFK assassination. He personally made a number of vitally significant original discoveries about the case by himself – and in the process, he made *major corrections* to the erroneous "theories," ludicrous "hypotheses" and faulty "scenarios" that have been proffered by foolish lesser minds in the JFK research community.

Moreover, Pete generously provided extremely useful insights, suggestions, leads and other vital materials to me while I labored intensively on this book. Several of Pete's own stunningly important original discoveries are prominently featured in the text of this book – always with grateful attribution and proper credit.

Pete even generously purchased several JFK-related books for me, and sent them to me – out of the blue – on his own initiative and at his own expense. When I called to thank him for the unexpected gifts, and noted that I would have been happy with less-expensive *used* copies rather than brand-new items, Pete replied simply, "I wanted you to have the best."

I wanted you to have the best.

That was Pete.

Brilliant and perceptive, blessed with plenty of common sense yet stubbornly modest about his own major intellectual achievements, Pete never sought the limelight to which he was fully entitled – but he deserves extraordinary *recognition* for his extraordinary *contributions* to the accurate resolution of the most important crime in American political history.

Moreover, Peter Rupay's sheer human courage during a brutally tough, years-long struggle against both cancer *and* serious coronary illness (simultaneously!) was simply extraordinary.

On his way to significant medical appointments, Pete stopped in Dealey Plaza more than once to film the JFK assassination site and to survey some of the actual shooting angles employed by President Kennedy's killers on November 22nd, 1963.

Just prior to *heart surgery* – quite literally as Pete lay on a hospital *operating table,* about to undergo a major procedure – he gamely engaged the anesthesiologist (a man who knew several figures from UT Southwest Medical School and Parkland Hospital in Dallas) in questions and conversation about the JFK case!

In the final months of his life, Pete generously authored and sent me the exquisite Foreword to this book, which he wrote for me on his own initiative.

And fewer than *two weeks* before his death, as he was about to enter *hospice* care, Pete gave a masterful, eloquent and articulate presentation of the pertinent issues in the JFK case to a fascinated nurse who had once worked at Parkland Hospital.

Just prior to his death, Pete generously arranged to send me his valuable personal archive of JFK-related books, recordings and other research materials, which proved *extraordinarily* useful to me as I finished writing this book – and they will also be truly invaluable to additional future works by me.

Although we lived hundreds of miles apart, and circumstances never permitted us the opportunity to meet in person, Peter David Rupay was my friend and my brother during eight highly productive years of the long, arduous struggle to reach the real truth about 1963. Pete's many excellent and vitally important original insights – expressed in his own writings, in our extensive e-mail correspondence, and in my detailed notes from our numerous, lengthy and highly enjoyable telephone conversations – add significantly to this book.

Those insights will live on and will be included in *additional* future books by me about the JFK assassination, as well.

Moreover, Pete's valuable archive of JFK assassination-related research materials will be preserved and made available for public study in the future.

* * *

Finally, my profound thanks and deep appreciation go to members of the SAM FOX Association and to veterans of several key United States Air Force units from the 1960s, including:

- The 1254th Air Transport Wing (and its component squadrons);
- The 1000th Airborne Command and Control Squadron;
- The 1001st Air Base Wing (and its component squadrons); and
- The Strategic Air Command (SAC).

Many veterans of those units were extraordinarily helpful in sharing their eyewitness testimonies about vital events surrounding the JFK assassination.

I got in touch with *scores* of well-placed USAF veterans – key men who were **never interviewed** by the Johnson (*alias* "Warren") Commission in the 1960s; nor by the HSCA in the 1970s; nor by the ARRB in the 1990s.

The overwhelming majority of those Air Force veterans whom I contacted communicated with me and shared their important recollections. One refused; a few were very curt, guarded and extremely aloof; but most were very frank and generous and forthcoming about what they saw, heard and did in November 1963.

I wish to specifically thank Air Force veterans John Alexander, Jim "Moose" Amos, Robert C. Amos, Robert T. Best, Jack Birkenstock, James Bradley, Wyatt Broom, Kenneth Brown, Deroy Cain, Melvin Carlton, William Joseph "Joe" Chappell, James Cross, Frank Elam, Philip Eramo, Robert Frank, Jr., Tom Furner, Ronnie Gaskill, Dave Gates, Joe Geiger, Paul Glynn, Ernest Graves, John Hames, Lewis "Swede" Hanson, James Hoopaw, Raymond Judy, Robert "Mac" Macmillan, Richard McFadden, Leon McRae, Thomas Michl, Joseph T. Milloy, Crafton L. Monk, Murray Orvin, Ray Pascoe, Wayne Pittman, Robert Reed, Charles Rogers, Charles Ruberg, Donald Short, Earl Sloan, Michael Snyder, Joseph J. Sofet, Ken Stophel, Billy Sullivan, James B. Swindal, Lyle Thomas, Paul Thornhill, Tom Webb, Fred Welker, John Wetherell, Doyle Whitehead and Vince Young.

Without such men, this book would not exist – and central truths about the JFK assassination would have remained shrouded in mystery *forever*.

Thanks in large measure to certain USAF veterans' courage, and to their welcome (albeit sometimes unwitting!) candor about the *actual* events of November 22nd, many of the final, most vexing questions about the JFK assassination have now been fully answered by me, in this book, for the very first time anywhere – and those questions have been answered *conclusively, definitively* and *permanently*.

Those USAF men helped me to rescue the **real** truth about 1963 from oblivion.

Ultimately, *that* has truly been their most valuable service to their country.

SEAN FETTER

American historian & investigative journalist
Somewhere in America
Autumn 2023

Author photo by Beth Klaisner.

About the Author

Sean Fetter is an American historian and investigative journalist – and the foremost analyst of the JFK assassination.

Fetter has studied the murder of President Kennedy in great depth since 1983, and – as of the publication of this book in 2023 – he has actively interviewed key witnesses and performed extensive original research for four decades.

In the course of investigating the brutal assassination of JFK, Sean has performed groundbreaking primary document research and extraordinarily advanced analysis of the crime, and he has also conducted exclusive and revealing interviews with key government and civilian personnel.

Many of Fetter's JFK-related interviewees had *never been contacted before* by *any* federal commission, Congressional body, news outlet or private panel – let alone by any other journalist, historian, author, or independent assassination investigator.

And *none* of those interviewees had ever been questioned so intelligently or carefully or thoroughly or productively by anyone else.

In addition to his groundbreaking historical research and analysis, Fetter has worked as a journalist in radio news, print news, and television news. His media experience includes award-winning reporting; award-winning commentary; editing; producing; on-air program hosting; and breaking news coverage.

As a journalist, Fetter wrote and reported and produced important news stories that were carried nationally by the Associated Press and by CNN. He also conducted in-depth interviews with a variety of public figures ranging from American civil rights activist Ralph David Abernathy to Soviet dissident Tatiana Yankelevich.

Moreover, Sean wrote nationally televised public affairs commentaries and major public speeches for longtime civil rights figure Coretta Scott King (the widow of slain civil rights leader Dr. Martin Luther King, Jr.).

An exceptional writer, tenacious investigator and extraordinary analyst, Fetter is already hard at work on his next stunning, paradigm-changing book.

Contact the Author

WITNESSES, LEADS AND TIPS:

Persons of integrity with pertinent eyewitness testimony, relevant personal recollections, authentic documents, authentic photographs, leads, tips, referrals, or any other valid evidence or information pertaining to the JFK assassination are welcome to contact me. (Anyone spewing falsehoods or peddling disinformation can take a hike.)

E-mail: Evidence@SeanFetter.com

MEDIA INTERVIEW REQUESTS:

This means serious individuals (at the college and professional level) who are interested in generating intelligent, accurate, meaningful articles and broadcast pieces about **the JFK assassination.** Pro tip: Make sure you've actually *read this entire book – both volumes, cover to cover, very carefully, all by yourself –* before attempting an interview on the subject. Superficial hacks and shallow lazy frauds need not apply. Fools, morons and wannabe "hatchet" types will be badly humiliated.

Not familiar with the contents of my work? Then sit back and let *me* do all the talking/writing.

E-mail: Media@ SeanFetter.com

READER COMMENTS:

I'm always very interested in intelligent thoughts and reactions. (Demented or abusive e-mails will generate appropriate consequences.)

E-mail: Readers@ SeanFetter.com

SPEAKING ENGAGEMENTS:

Colleges, universities, JFK assassination symposia, non-profit groups and other interested organizations seeking a dynamic, highly informative, truly memorable presentation (plus an extensive Q&A session!) are invited to send requests to:

E-mail: Speeches@ SeanFetter.com

Photo Credits

With the single exception of the author photo herein (which is a copyrighted image), all photographic images appearing in this book – and on the cover of this book – are in the public domain. No credit or attribution was or is required; indeed, the author's captions are actually far more valuable than any credit line could ever be.

The overwhelming majority of the images are U. S. government photos – works "prepared by an officer or employee of the United States Government as part of that person's official duties" – which are, *by definition,* in the public domain. A very small handful of images (of the natural world and the medical world) included herein were taken by private individuals who then consciously and willingly and voluntarily deeded their photos to the public domain and thereby made them freely available for use by anyone, anywhere, for any purpose.

It was my original desire to individually credit every single image in the book. However, largely due to the frequently incomplete records of the U. S. government and its various civilian agencies and military branches, that goal turned out to be well-nigh impossible to achieve. At best, some images are labeled (*sometimes* accurately, sometimes *not*) as the alleged work of (for example) the "U. S. Air Force" or the "Library of Congress" without any further specificity as to their individual creators, or their precise date, or their actual provenance.

Moreover, certain pertinent collections – including the JFK and LBJ Presidential Libraries, which are administered by the National Archives and Records Administration – also frequently lack specific information about which specific *photographer* (of what were usually *several* employed by any given unit or department) actually took a specific image.

To make matters worse, the JFK Library very oddly and deliberately and wrongly credits the work of *other* photographers to one Cecil Stoughton, who was indeed the main White House photographer during the Kennedy administration. Yet the JFK Library instructs the public that certain images created by Harold Sellers and Dan Lewis are to be credited to "Cecil Stoughton" [*sic*], even when – as in the case of certain images taken at Andrews Air Force Base on the evening of November 22nd, 1963 – Cecil Stoughton was not even physically present at the scene being depicted!

For the sake of fairness and consistency, I therefore elected ***not*** to do an injustice to *any* individual by wrongly or incorrectly crediting his or her "boss" or "supervisor" (or simply a "better-known colleague") for works that were in fact created by those lesser-known figures.

The "Sources" section of this book lists the archives and collections from which 97% or more of the images come. I strongly encourage *all* Americans (and all other citizens of the world) to intelligently explore the visual history of the JFK case *for themselves.*

The so-called "citadel of democracy" [*sic*]
was in fact the professional home of
the two senior American politicians
who successfully plotted
democracy's destruction.

Author's exclusive original discovery.

Lyndon Johnson poses with a statue of Sam Rayburn –
his dead mentor and chief co-conspirator in the
bloody plot to assassinate President Kennedy.

Author's exclusive original discovery.

Index
Under Cover of Night

Like it or not, there is no shortcut to the truth.

Read this book *all the way through* – from the very beginning to the very end.

Take copious notes. And read it again.

By deliberate design, the following highly selective index will ***not*** help you to quickly and casually and superficially "skim" the book, nor to shirk your intellectual obligations regarding the vitally important subject of JFK's assassination.

Read thoroughly. *Think* carefully. Then think some *more*.

NUMERIC

A

B

C

G

H

I

J

M

N

O

P

R

S

T

U

V

Valenti, Jack (USAAF; LBJ aide), *passim*
van Leeuwen, Neil (USMC), 100-102, 109-110, 114-115, 122, 161, 408, 1058
Vantage Point, The (LBJ book), 181, 201, 205, 666, 688, 855, 872-873
Vietnam War, *passim*

W

Warren, Earl (Chief Justice), *passim*
"Warren Commission" [*sic*]
    (*see* President's Commission on the Assassination of President Kennedy)
"Warren Report" [*sic*]
    (*see* Report of the President's Commission on the Assassination of President
    Kennedy)
Washington National Airport, 91, 160, 165, 173, 941
Wehle, General Philip (U. S. Army), 373-375
Wetherell, John (USAF), 75-77, 81, 89, 335, 364, 381, 384, 445-447, 450, 939
Wheeler, General Earle Gilmore "Bus" (U. S. Army), *passim*
Wiarton (Royal Canadian Air Force base, Ontario, Canada), 531, 540-541
Wicker, Tom (NYT), 923
Wilson, Lloyd John (USAF), 550-554, 905
Wright-Patterson Air Force Base (Ohio), 316, 516, 939
Wurtsmith Air Force Base (Michigan), 531

Y

Yarborough, Ralph (Texas Senator), 179, 371, 450
Youngblood, Rufus (USAAF; SS), 160, 184, 203, 450, 695, 844, 851

Z

Zapruder, Abraham, 393, 562
Zapruder film (**extant** version),
    60, 333, 393-399, 452, 575-576, 579, 583-588, 748, 757, 788, 870, 947
Zevon, Warren (musician and songwriter), 180

.

Made in the USA
Columbia, SC
26 June 2024

460ffe27-a233-4e64-a30f-068231db97e5R01